Soviet Diplomacy
and Negotiating Behavior

About the Book and Author

"The foreign affairs book of the season . . . an absorbing review of the nitty-gritty of Soviet-American diplomacy over the years."
—*Stephen S. Rosenfeld,*
The Washington Post

"Vast in its historical sweep. . . . Focusing on the period since the Bolshevik Revolution, Whelan stresses five themes: the nature of negotiating behavior, its principal characteristics, elements contributing to its formation, aspects of continuity and change during more than 60 years, and the implications of the record for U.S. foreign policy in the 1980s.

"The bulk of the book traces Soviet diplomacy under Chicherin and Litvinov, the enormously complex and detailed wartime conferences with Stalin, the descent into the cold war, the transition to peaceful coexistence with Nikita Krushchev (including fascinating details on the Cuban Missile Crisis), peaceful coexistence with Leonid Brezhnev (including extensive chronological analysis of the SALT process) and finally, judgements about how U.S. policy should be informed in future undertakings with the Soviets."
—*Nish Jamgotch, Jr.,*
The American Political Science Review

Joseph G. Whelan is a senior specialist in international affairs, Senior Specialist Division, Congressional Research Service, Library of Congress.

Soviet Diplomacy
and Negotiating Behavior

The Emerging New Context
for U.S. Diplomacy

Joseph G. Whelan

Westview Press / Boulder, Colorado

FOREWORD

The controversial style, tactics, and motivations of Soviet negotiators has long been the subject of debate and discussion. In fact, the effect of Soviet negotiating behavior on the SALT II Treaty has already figured prominently in the congressional debate on the merits of that agreement.

For these and other reasons the Committee on Foreign Affairs requested Dr. Joseph G. Whelan, senior specialist in international affairs of the Congressional Research Service of the Library of Congress, to conduct a comprehensive study of the issue.

Many previous studies have analyzed Soviet diplomacy in the context of single negotiating encounters. This study takes a broader and more exhaustive approach. From a historical perspective, which makes the Soviet period more meaningful, it systematically analyzes Russian negotiating behavior in terms of its principal characteristics, trends of continuity and change, and influences contributing to its formation—including the traditional Russian obsession with national security.

Central to the study is its analyses of the implications of the Soviet approach to diplomacy and negotiation for U.S. foreign policy. These implications are explored with hypotheses offered as to the future style and motives of the Soviets.

In commissioning the study, it was hoped that it would provide valuable insights to U.S. negotiators in their present and future negotiations as to the motivations, concerns, and reasons for the operating style of their Soviet counterparts.

In conclusion, the study emphasizes that the unique character and motivation of Soviet negotiating behavior should not be considered a deterrent to negotiations on the widest possible front of mutual concerns. While painstakingly developing the evolution of Soviet negotiating behavior and emphasizing its different characteristics, the study appropriately emphasizes the vital role negotiations with the Soviet Union will play with respect to prospects for a stable international order:

Diplomacy and negotiations have always had a special value for Americans. They have encompassed the national experience from the earliest days of the Republic, as a means of averting war and settling disputes with its English and Spanish neighbors and with other nations on the larger international stage since the turn of the century; as a mechanism for national territorial expansion as in the Louisiana Purchase, the Transcontinental Treaty, and the Alaska Cession; and for maintaining the lifeblood of the Nation by establishing harmonious commercial relationships with the nations of the world. Diplomacy and negotiations are thus firmly placed in the Nation's historical tradition.

In U.S. relations with the Soviet Union diplomacy and negotiations take on an even more special value because they provide the only device for bringing rationality into the management of a relationship that is fraught with great complexities and high risks. Consider a relationship in the 1980's without diplomacy and negotiations and the consequent risks to the Nation's security of a Soviet Russia as it was in Stalin's postwar era: a total breakdown in communications; a debasement of diplomacy; and a resort to negotiations by semaphore in the manner of that ending the Berlin blockade as the only means for resolving grave disputes.

In the nuclear age, diplomacy and negotiations take on a new meaning, and, indeed, a new imperative for both the United States and the Soviet Union. For they provide the vital mechanism for survival.

The Committee on Foreign Affairs recognizes that crucial foreign affairs issues, complex in nature and with far-reaching significance to U.S. national security, require superior scholarly understanding as a foundation on which workable solutions can be based. Accordingly, the committee has undertaken to establish a "Special Studies Series on Foreign Affairs Issues." Studies in the series will be published periodically and only on conspicuously significant subjects matched by equally distinguished work. The superior quality of Dr. Whelan's study has earned it the notable distinction of being the first in that series.

The material and findings contained herein are the work of the Congressional Research Service. While coordinated with the Committee on Foreign Affairs, the material and findings do not necessarily represent the views of the Committee on Foreign Affairs or its members.

CLEMENT J. ZABLOCKI, *Chairman*,
Committee on Foreign Affairs.

Published in 1983 in the United States of America by
  Westview Press, Inc.
  5500 Central Avenue
  Boulder, Colorado 80301
  Frederick A. Praeger, President and Publisher

Library of Congress Catalog Card Number: 82-083817
ISBN 0-86531-946-4

Printed and bound in the United States of America

10 9 8 7 6 5 4 3 2 1

CONTENTS

ACKNOWLEDGMENTS

The author of this study wishes to express his personal gratitude and that of the Congressional Research Service to:
- —Hon. Jacob D. Beam, career diplomat, and former U.S. Ambassador to Czechoslovakia, Poland, and the Soviet Union, for his kindness in granting an interview which along with his new diplomatic memoir, "Multiple Exposure," provided significant insights into Soviet behavior and the Soviet-American relationship;
- —Hon. Helmut Sonnenfeldt, former Senior Member of the National Security Council and Counselor in the State Department, for an interview on a wide range of aspects of Soviet-American relations, drawing from his personal experience and knowledge as a scholar in Soviet affairs, which, along with his most recent writings, provided penetrating and comprehensive insights into Soviet diplomacy;
- —Dr. Robert V. Allen, Acting Assistant Chief of the Library of Congress, European Division, and longtime specialist in Russian affairs as a scholar and historian, who read the entire study and made significant comments as well as providing useful bibliographic references as the study was in progress;
- —Dr. George D. Holliday, analyst in international trade and finance in the Library's Congressional Research Service's Economics Division, whose expertise extends beyond international economics and the Soviet economic area to that of foreign policy, and who also read the entire study and provided significant comments;
- —Francis T. Miko, analyst in Soviet and East European affairs, whose formal graduate training in Soviet affairs at the George Washington University's Sino-Soviet Institute has been appreciably expanded by his 5 years of fruitful labor in the Soviet field in the Foreign Affairs and National Defense Division of the Congressional Research Service, and who also kindly read the entire study and provided significant comments.

To the following colleagues in the Congressional Research Service who read the final chapter of the study and gave their constructive criticisms:
- Dr. John P. Hardt, Associate Director of the Senior Specialist Division and senior specialist in Soviet economics.
- Dr. William W. Whitson, Chief of the Foreign Affairs and National Defense Division.
- Charles R. Gellner, senior specialist in national security affairs.
- John M. Collins, senior specialist in national defense.
- Raymond J. Celeda, senior specialist in American public law.

James W. Robinson, coordinator of review and longtime specialist in international relations.

Dr. Stanley J. Heginbotham, Assistant Chief of the Foreign Affairs and National Defense Division.

Stanley R. Sloan, specialist in European affairs.

To Mr. David H. Kraus, Acting Chief of the European Division, Library of Congress, and editor of The American Bibliography of Slavic and East European Studies, who was most helpful in providing bibliographic references;

And finally to Prof. Teddy J. Uldricks of the University of California (Riverside), a specialist in the origins and development of the Soviet diplomatic corps who graciously provided a galley proof of his book about to be published entitled "Diplomacy and Ideology: The Origins of Soviet Foreign Relations 1917–1930."

CHAPTER I—PURPOSE AND DESIGN OF THE STUDY

Diplomacy is the management of international relations by negotiations; the method by which these relations are adjusted and managed by ambassadors and envoys; the business or art of the diplomatist.

—*Oxford English Dictionary, quoted by Sir Harold Nicolson, 1939.*

Negotiation may be called the process of combining divergent viewpoints to reach a common agreement.

—*I. William Zartman, 1974.*

I. RELEVANT QUESTIONS AND STRUCTURAL DESIGNS

A. BASIC QUESTIONS RAISED

Negotiation is the central function of diplomacy, and diplomacy the carrying out of foreign policy. This is a study in Russian negotiating behavior within the context of diplomacy. The principal objective is to examine the style, purposes, and effects of Russian behavior in negotiations largely from the American perspective.

Five basic questions are raised which this study seeks to address, and they are as follows:

(1) What has been the Russian negotiating behavior in the Soviet period?

(2) What are the principal characteristics of this behavior?

(3) What are the elements that have contributed to the formation of this behavior? For example, the historic Russian obsession with security.

(4) What is constant and what has changed in this behavior during 60 years of Soviet diplomacy? Are there indications of a return to the traditionalism of prerevolutionary Russia? Have the Soviets repressed their obsession with security which has at least partly accounted for the historic Russian commitment to militarism? And if not, what are the prospects for reducing these anxieties through diplomacy and negotiations? And finally,

(5) What are the implications of the Soviet approach to diplomacy and negotiations for American foreign policy in the 1980's? Are the assumptions of the past on Soviet behavior still relevant and applicable, or, do grounds now exist for establishing mutually acceptable arrangements through negotiations?

B. DESIGN OF STUDY

1. STRUCTURE

This study is placed in an historical setting in the belief that Russian behavior in diplomacy and negotiations can best be understood within the perspective of history and by the analytical possibilities that it offers. The study begins with a brief commentary on diplomatic practice with respect to negotiations as it has evolved historically, noting particularly the emergence of Russian diplomacy within the traditionalism of European diplomacy. Particular attention has been given to negotiations for the purchase of Alaska and U.S. mediation at Portsmouth to end the Russo-Japanese War. The objective is to provide a background upon which to project the Soviet experience and to establish some criteria for judging Soviet behavior.

The radical change in Soviet diplomacy from the Bolshevik Revolution through the United Front in the 1930's is then examined with a principal focus on key diplomatic figures, specific diplomatic episodes, and the formation and destruction of the Soviet diplomatic service in the Great Purge, both of which had a direct impact on the quality of Soviet diplomacy.

Negotiations under Stalin are divided into two parts: One with a focus on selected wartime negotiations through 1945; the other on cold war diplomacy from 1946 to Stalin's death in 1953, and again with emphasis on selected negotiating episodes.

Negotiations under Khrushchev are examined in two sequences with the dividing point at the aftermath of the Cuban missile crisis of 1962. The purpose of this division is to illustrate through examination of selected episodes, Khrushchev's changing style of negotiations by threat and intimidation in the earlier period, and his diplomacy of accommodation in the latter. Particular attention has been given to the modernization of the Soviet diplomatic service and to the building of the infrastructure of diplomacy under Khrushchev.

Negotiations during the Brezhnev era are focused primarily on Soviet behavior in the arms control negotiations that led to the conclusion of SALT I. Attention is also given to developments in the Soviet foreign policy establishment in the Brezhnev era and to Brezhnev's style of diplomacy. The purpose is to suggest the possible relationship between these developments and the quality of Soviet diplomacy and the evolution of Soviet-American relations.

The study concludes with an analysis of the data in the context of the basic questions raised above.

2. SOURCES

Emphasis is placed on those negotiations that are most revealing of Soviet behavior through the sources examined. Specialized books and articles on Soviet negotiations, along with memoirs and other diplomatic commentaries, all together constitute sufficient material to cover the period particularly during World War II, the immediate postwar period, and through the Khrushchev era. By comparison, little material is available for the Brezhnev era (1964–1979), but the literature is growing. President Richard M. Nixon's memoirs, specialized articles and books on arms control negotiations, and other published works on the diplomatic actors in the Nixon administration, do much to fill the gap. To flesh out the data, interviews were conducted with some American diplomats who either negotiated with the Soviets or were present as observers.

The main stress of this study is on perceptions through the eyes of American actors for the most part, those like the veteran negotiator Averell Harriman; Soviet specialists and former Ambassadors George

F. Kennan, Charles E. Bohlen, and Jacob D. Beam; and U. Alexis Johnson and Gerard Smith, both seasoned negotiators on arms control—those, among others, who either had actually participated in negotiations with the Soviets or by their unique analytical skills and profound knowledge drawn from longtime experiences and close-in relationships with the Soviet system, have something to say about Soviet negotiating behavior. Observations by leading British diplomats, such as Sir William Hayter, former British Ambassador to the Soviet Union, are also recorded. In addition, assessments on the quality of the Soviet diplomatic service today by foreign diplomats, including those from the Soviet bloc, by knowledgeable scholars among Soviet citizens and recent emigrees, and by Americans close to the Soviet diplomatic scene, are also noted.

3. LIMITATIONS OF STUDY

This subject has many limitations; the most important limitation is its scope. For this reason the study, while encompassing many decades of the Soviet experience, has, nonetheless, been narrowly focused on selected negotiating cases and on selected individual negotiators. Also, emphasis has been placed specifically on Soviet behavior, not on the substance of negotiations. Substance has been treated in only a very general way. In selecting cases, the criterion was not so much political importance as it was revelations of Soviet negotiating behavior from the sources. To a great extent, therefore, selectivity was based on availability of sources.

The second limitation is that of sources. Memoirs, such as those by Kennan, Bohlen, Beam, Harriman, and former Ambassadors to the Soviet Union, Adm. William H. Standley and Gen. Walter Bedell Smith, provide rich insights into Soviet behavior. Also, specialized studies on Soviet negotiating behavior—those, for example, compiled by Raymond Dennett and Joseph E. Johnson, and Gen. John R. Deane's account of his wartime experiences in the Soviet Union as chief U.S. military liaison officer—are exceptional in their focus on the details of specific negotiations. Only a very few negotiators have made their experiences known in this way. These accounts, like memoirs, are very subjective and in large measure reflect a view of reality from only one perspective. Except for a few selected works, therefore, the subject of Soviet negotiations as a process and the behavior of the Soviets as negotiators has attracted little attention.[1]

Accordingly, the limitations imposed on this study are considerable.

[1] I. William Zartman, a specialist on negotiating theory and behavior, described the shortcomings in this general field of specialized study in political science in a review article. He wrote: "Negotiation is one of the basic political or decision-making processes, but if processes in general have been sorely neglected in political analysis, negotiation has been neglected more than most. * * * diplomacy—and more recently, collective bargaining—has been thoroughly described, and economists and mathematicians using game and utility theories have developed some complex models of bargaining. But negotiation as a political process, specifically explained in terms of power, is an underdeveloped area of theory." (Zartman, I. William. The Political Analysis of Negotiation: How Who Gets What and When. World Politics, v. 26, April 1974; pp. 385–386.)

Press coverage of negotiations seldom goes into process and procedure. Walter Pincus, correspondent of the Washington Post, made this point on the occasion of reporting from Geneva a session of the SALT II negotiations in December 1977. "While most public attention generally focuses on statements of the national leaders," he wrote, "it is the complex but seldom-publicized work of the negotiating teams in Geneva that actually bring diplomatic efforts such as the SALT treaties into being." The correspondent proceeded to describe the procedure followed in SALT II that had been previously outlined by U. Alexis Johnson, a former SALT negotiator, in a seminar on SALT II negotiations at the Institute for Sino-Soviet Studies, George Washington University. (Pincus, Walter. Behind the Scenes at SALT; Long, Complex Sessions. The Washington Post, Dec. 6, 1977, p. A13.)

II. DEFINITIONS AND ASSUMPTIONS

A. Diplomacy and Negotiation Defined

1. FROM THE AMERICAN PERSPECTIVE

Diplomacy and negotiation are interrelated terms that describe one of the primary functions of the nation-state; namely, to carry on the business of state in international relations. In a narrower sense, negotiation is specifically the bargaining process used in adjusting differences within relations, and, accordingly, it is the most important task of diplomacy.

There are many definitions of the term negotiation, some of which tend to place on it a cynical construction. Perhaps, the extreme was that by Washington Irving, a diplomat as well as a noted American writer, who once observed:

A negotiation is a cunning endeavor to obtain by peaceful maneuver and the chicanery of cabinets those advantages which a nation would otherwise have wrested by force of arms—in the same manner as a conscientious highwayman reforms and becomes a quiet and praiseworthy citizen, contenting himself with cheating his neighbor out of that property he would have formerly seized with open violence.[1]

Less provocative but still harshly realistic was the definition by Gilbert R. Winham, a student of the negotiating process:

Negotiation is an enduring art form. Its essence is artifice, the creation of expedients through the application of human ingenuity. The synonyms of the word "art" are qualities we have long since come to admire in the ablest of negotiators: skill, cunning, and craft. We expect negotiators to be accomplished manipulators of other people, and we applaud this aspect of their art when we observe it in uncommon degree. Negotiation is considered to be the management of people through guile, and we recognize guile as the trademark of the profession.[2]

Probably, the simplest (and most benign) definition of negotiation was that quoted by the British scholar of diplomacy Sir Harold Nicolson from the Oxford English dictionary:

Diplomacy is the management of international relations by negotiation: the method by which these relations are adjusted and managed by ambassadors and envoys; the business or art of the diplomatist.[3]

Similarly uncomplicated, fairly complete, and stressing the connection with diplomacy is the definition by Ivo D. Duchacek, an American specialist on international relations:

Diplomacy is usually defined as the practice of carrying out a nation's foreign policy by negotiations with other nations. This definition correctly stresses that diplomacy is an *instrument*—not policy itself; the procedures of foreign policy and not the substance.[4]

---

[1] Quoted in, Steibel, Gerald L. How Can We Negotiate with the Communists? New York, National Strategy Information Center, Inc., 1972, p. 1.

[2] Winham, Gilbert R. Negotiation as a Management Process. World Politics, v. 30, October 1977: p. 87.

[3] Quoted in, Nicholson, Harold. Diplomacy. New York, Harcourt, Brace and Company, 1939, p. 15.

[4] Duchacek, Ivo D. Conflict and Cooperation Among Nations. New York Holt, Rinehart and Winston, 1960, p. 494.

I. William Zartman, a specialist on the political science of negotiations, stresses the idea of process in his definition: Thus, "negotiation may be called the process of combining divergent viewpoints to reach a common agreement." [5]

Fred Charles Ikle, both a scholar and practitioner of negotiations as former director of the Arms Control and Disarmament Agency, is more precise in his definition: "* * * negotiation is a process in which explicit proposals are put forward ostensibly for the purpose of reaching agreement on an exchange or on the realization of a common interest where conflicting interests are present." [6]

Charles Burton Marshall, an American authority on international politics, stresses the importance of "terms." Thus, for him "negotiation embraces * * * the process of talking about terms, the achievement of terms, and the terms." [7]

In sum, diplomacy can be defined as the management of international relations by negotiations, and negotiation, diplomacy's principal instrumentality, the bargaining process—often a continuing process—for adjusting conflicting interests in order to reach a common agreement. The purpose of both is to seek solutions, adjust differences, establish a harmony of interests among conflicting parties—in brief, to create international stability. By and large this definition embraces the American perception of negotiation. And while complex constructions and seemingly infinite variations have been placed on the term, still this definition would seem to embody the essential meaning as Americans understand it. [8]

2. FROM THE SOVIET PERSPECTIVE

The view from the Soviet perspective contrasts sharply with that of the American, and it is from this incompatibility of perceptions rooted in conflicting purposes, values, and ideologies, that have arisen many of the difficulties in Soviet-American relations.

Nicolson rejects the notion that Soviet diplomacy is diplomacy at all. Soviet diplomatic scholars give assurances that they possess one powerful weapon denied their capitalist opponents; namely, "the scientific dialectic of the Marx-Lenin formula." But Nicolson fails to see "as yet that this dialectic has improved international relationships, or that the Soviet diplomatists and commissars have evolved any system of negotiation that might be called a diplomatic system." Soviet activity in foreign countries and at international conferences, he acknowledges, is "formidable, disturbing, compulsive," the "potency" or "danger" of which he does not "for one moment underestimate." But, for Nicolson, "it is not diplomacy: it is something else." [9]

Gordon Craig, an American historian of international relations, makes a similar critical assessment of Soviet diplomacy, one that even Hitler, prior to his ascendancy to power, had shared. Craig writes:

Despite the excellence of their training in the external forms of diplomacy, and their skill in using it, Soviet negotiators have always had a fundamentally differ-

[5] Zartman, Political Analysis of Negotiation, p. 386.
[6] Ikle, Fred Charles. How Nations Negotiate. New York, Harper & Row, 1964, pp. 3–4.
[7] Marshall, Charles Burton. The Problem of Incompatible Purposes. In, Duchacek, Conflict and Cooperation Among Nations, p. 519.
[8] For a summary of variations in definitions of the term negotiation, see Druckman, Daniel. Human Factors in International Negotiations: Social-Psychological Aspects of International Conflict. Beverly Hills, Calif., Sage Publications, 1973, p. 6.
[9] Nicolson, Harold. The Evolution of Diplomatic Method. London, Constable, 1954, p. 90.

ent approach toward diplomacy from that of their western colleagues. To them diplomacy is more than an instrument for protecting and advancing national interest; it is a weapon in the unremitting war against capitalist society. Diplomatic negotiations, therefore, cannot aim at real understanding and agreement; and this has profound effects upon their nature and techniques.[10]

Dean Acheson, a longtime public servant, form~r Secretary of State, and close observer of Soviet negotiators in action, places the Soviet approach to negotiation well outside the pale of Western tradition. "In Western tradition," he told a press conference on February 8, 1950, "negotiation was bargaining to achieve a mutually desired agreement. In Communist doctrine it was war by political means to achieve an end unacceptable to the other side. In both cases it was a means to an end, but in the latter case the ends were, if understood, mutually exclusive." (The background for this statement was Acheson's public elucidation of NSC–68, an administration paper whose premise accepted the adversarial nature of Soviet-American relations as national policy.)[11]

What these learned men and practitioners of diplomacy have written is, of course, at least theoretically true; and the Soviets would be the first to acknowledge this. For they view diplomacy and negotiation from the Marxist-Leninist perspective. Diplomacy is to them a component of politics. Accordingly, the foreign policy of a state is the "direct continuation of its domestic policy," and hence a vital part of the much larger international "struggle" between opposing social systems; and negotiation, a tactical device designed to achieve the ideological and foreign policy goals of the Soviet Union.

Perhaps, the Soviet view of diplomacy was best summed up by Valerian A. Zorin when he gave the following explanation for "the scientific foundations on which all diplomatic activity of socialist states rests" and for "the basis for their successful diplomacy":

The theoretical foundation of Soviet diplomatic activity is a Marxist-Leninist understanding of the international situation, of the laws of social development, of the laws of class struggle, and of the correlation of internal and international social forces, which takes account of the specific national and historical features of each country, group of countries, and continents. It is impossible to develop diplomatic activity correctly without a Marxist-Leninist evaluation of the international situation, without an understanding of the laws of social development and concrete knowledge of the situation in a particular country, and without taking into account the historical and national characteristics of a country. And it must be added that a Marxist-Leninist evaluation of international events and the formulation of a line of diplomatic struggle on this basis is a powerful element in Soviet diplomacy. As a rule, the success of the diplomatic activity of the Soviet Union is determined above all by a correct Marxist-Leninist analysis of the situation and of the correlation of forces, and on the contrary, underestimation and imperfect knowledge of the objective laws and of all the changes which are taking place in a country or in several interrelated countries are fraught with miscalculations and mistakes in diplomacy.[12]

[10] Craig, Gordon. Totalitarian Approaches to Diplomatic Negotiation, in, A. O. Sarkissian (ed.) Studies in Diplomatic History and Historiography in Honour of G. P. Gooch. London, Longmans, Green, 1961, p. 119.
It is interesting to note that Adolph Hitler, at least before he came to power, felt a basic incompatibility between Soviet and Western diplomacy. In 1932, he wrote: "I look upon . . . Soviet diplomacy not only as being unreliable but, above all, as being incapable of being considered of the same nature as the foreign political activity of other nations, and, in consequence, as being something with which one cannot negotiate or conclude treaties." (Quoted in, Craig, Totalitarian Approaches to Diplomatic Negotiation, p. 125, ff. 78.)
[11] Acheson, Dean. Present at the Creation, New York, W. W. Norton, 1969, p. 378.
[12] Zorin, Valerian A. Role of the Ministry of Foreign Affairs of the USSR. The Bases of Diplomatic Service. Moscow, Institute of International Relations, 1964. Reproduced in, U.S. Congress. Senate. Committee on Government Operations. Subcommittee on National Security and International Operations. The Soviet Approach to Negotiations: Selected Writings, 91st Congress, 1st Session. Washington, U.S. Govt. Print. Off., 1969, p. 85. This publication contains extensive reproductions of Soviet writings on diplomacy (Hereafter the entire series will be cited as, "Senate, Committee on Government Operations, International Negotiations.")

And of negotiation in the era of peaceful coexistence, the Soviet diplomatic dictionary says:

It is used extensively by socialist states both for establishing cooperation with other states in implementing measures for insuring international peace and security as well as for the peaceful settlement of controversial issues and for the easing of international tension.[13]

Reduced to simpler terms, Soviet theory of diplomacy is rooted in the Marxist-Leninist interpretation of international relations that perceives the world divided essentially into opposing forces of communism and capitalism; holds that Soviet diplomacy, as an integral part of Marxist-Leninist theory, responds to the laws of social development, the class struggle, and the correlation of internal and international forces; claims that a powerful factor in Soviet diplomacy is the Marxist-Leninist evaluation of international development which, according to their interpretation of the laws of history, the end of socialist predominance is preordained; and finally maintains that negotiation is an instrument of Soviet diplomacy founded on Leninist tactics of exploiting the contradictions of interests among their class enemies and used to achieve the goals and purposes of the Soviet Union. That the Soviet explanation of negotiation falls within the self-serving Soviet interpretation of diplomacy and is not so benign as it seems if taken at face value, is evident by the date of publication, 1960. During that time Khrushchev was pursuing his openly aggressive "missile diplomacy" and "diplomacy by threat" against the West, the most critical test being the second Berlin crisis in 1958–60.

B. Assumptions

1. ON THE VALUE OF DIPLOMACY AND NEGOTIATION

The Soviet view of diplomacy and negotiation would appear at first glance to offer little hope for creating a meaningful relationship. If that were the case, this study would be superfluous, with neither purpose nor point. Certain assumptions, therefore, have to be made, and the first is that diplomacy and negotiation have a positive value—if for no other purpose, as Henry Allen, a Washington writer, observed, than "to reduce the vagaries of international relations to reason." [14]

As long ago as 1716, François de Callières, perhaps one of the most eminent authorities on diplomacy, commented on the positive value of negotiations. "The fate of the greatest states," he wrote, "often depends upon the good and bad conduct of negotiations and upon the degree of capacity in the negotiators employed." International relations abounded with examples to illustrate this point, he said. Thus, he concluded that "the art of negotiation, according as its conduct is good or evil, gives form to great affairs and may turn a host of lesser events into a useful influence upon the course of the greater." [15]

Negotiations may end with an agreement which, as Zartman observes, "by its very existence is a good or has a value in and of itself;

[13] Diplomatic Dictionary. Moscow, State Publishing House for Political Literature, 1960, v. 1, quoted in Senate, Committee on Government Operations, International Negotiations, Soviet Approach to Negotiation, p. 80.
[14] Allen, Henry. The Negotiator's Art. The Washington Post (Potomac Section), Sept. 21, 1975, p. 22.
[15] Quoted in, Craig, Totalitarian Approaches to Diplomatic Negotiation, p. 107.

this good or value may be merely satisfaction over the end of conflict, but it is more likely to comprise additional payoffs or side-payments," that is to say, mutual gains and advantages at an acceptable cost.[16]

Or negotiations may postpone a problem for later negotiation with a provisional understanding not to use violent means for solution. Problems may move up and down the scale of negotiability, and, as in the case of the Austrian State Treaty of 1955, years of seemingly pointless negotiation may suddenly end in agreement when changing conditions create a convergence of interests.

Both cases of instant agreement and postponement, as Duchacek wrote, "represent alternatives to fatal slipping downhill toward an armed conflict." "Among nations," he rightly concludes, "negotiations appear to be the only alternative to tension and violence." [17]

Thus, diplomacy and negotiation have a positive value, an idea that is deeply rooted in the American diplomatic tradition. They respond to and satisfy the deeper moral impulses of man and the practical necessities of nation-states. They can be instruments for adjusting conflicting interests, settling disputes, and maintaining the peace; and so it is assumed in this study.

2. ACCEPTING THE REALITIES OF CONFLICTING PERSPECTIVES

While accenting the positive on the value of diplomacy and negotiation, this study, nonetheless, accepts the realities of conflicting Soviet-American perspectives and interests for whatever that may portend. Both interests are not, however, mutually exclusive in an absolute sense, nor are they necessarily always in total contradiction; for interests can converge (as in the Grand Alliance during World War II), and it is a principle of international relations that nations are more likely to be motivated by the realities of common interests than by sentiments of hatred or affection, and that from converging interests diplomacy can flourish, negotiations take place, and agreements be reached.

The principal task of diplomacy and negotiations is to pursue the national interest. As Lester B. Pearson, the former Canadian Prime Minister, internationally renowned diplomat, and winner of the 1957 Nobel Peace Prize, observed, negotiations are undertaken between governments "to further interests of your own state, whether those interests are short term or long term, good or bad, peaceful or aggressive." [18] But under certain conditions interests of competing nations can converge, and it is the task of diplomacy and negotiations to find the elements of accommodation.

Clearly, Nicolson could not accept the Soviet brand of diplomacy as legitimate. "It is not diplomacy; it is something else," he said. For Nicolson, "the chief aim of diplomacy" was "international stability,"

---

[16] Zartman, Political Analysis of Negotiation, p. 387.
[17] Duchacek, op. cit., pp. 506–507.
[18] The complete quotation reads: "A most important if not *the* most important function of diplomacy, whoever practices it, career diplomats or foreign ministers, Communists dictators or Communist functionaries, is that of negotiation. Indeed, diplomacy is, in large part, the art of negotiation between governments, undertaken to further the interests of your own state, whether those interests are short term or long term, good or bad, peaceful or aggressive." (Pearson, Lester B, Diplomacy in the Nuclear Age. Westport, Conn., Greenwood Press, 1959, p. 33.)

9

an environment that the Soviets could hardly accept, at least theoretically, if they wished to remain true to their ideology.[19]

But in his study of totalitarian approaches to negotiation, Craig raises doubts about, what might be termed, this genteel or perhaps excessively idealistic approach.[20] Nomenclature was not the point, he said, but the Soviet approach to negotiation was; for here Craig found in his comparative study of Soviet, Nazi, and Fascist Italy's diplomacy that the Soviet approach was "less impulsive, more systematic, and more effective in its results than that of either Italian fascism or German national socialism." Hence, he concluded:

> In an age when war is no longer acceptable as a continuation of policy by other means, and when the importance of reaching settlements short of war is undeniable, the Soviet methods of negotiation would appear to deserve as much study by western diplomats as their own diplomatic tradition has received from their professional colleagues within the Soviet Union.[21]

What is important about Craig's conclusion is the idea that the Soviet approach to negotiation opens up the possibility for establishing a meaningful relationship, provided that relationship is based upon the hard realities of converging interests. In contrast to German national socialism and Italian fascism, Soviet ideology establishes a structure for an analytical approach to foreign policy: It places a high value on rationality, though within a rigidly formal structure; it recognizes the role of power, force and counterforce as essential components of international relations, and, accordingly, provides guidelines for advance, accommodation, and retreat; it designs a vast historical scheme within which to perceive and establish national goals and purposes. This is a strength, however flawed the system may be and however false its assumptions and utopian goals. It is not an infallible guide to policy, as the Soviet failures in the past will attest (e.g. the Cuban missile crisis); but it does acknowledge the principle of the balance of power as a reality in international politics and thus creates the possibility for negotiation and accommodation. Moreover, as Craig implies, the system does not nourish the heady romanticism of the Nazi or Fascist totalitarian systems that led to failure in diplomacy and in war.

The Soviet approach also reflects, perhaps inevitably, the Russian national character of excessive concern for security and excessive suspicion of the outsider, conditions which by historical experiences have induced a type of conservatism and caution, a built-in mechanism against adventurism in the Hitlerian manner. Thus, Soviet diplomacy may be "something else," as Nicolson suggests, but it need not be beyond the comprehension or the management skills of its potential adversaries in the West.

3. SUMMING UP

In sum, this study assumes that diplomacy and negotiation have a positive value in themselves, and yet, while accepting the conflicting

---

[19] Nicolson, Evolution of Diplomatic Method, pp. 90–91.
[20] Craig quotes from an article in Foreign Affairs (1950) by Lord Vansittart who wrote: 'Diplomacy could flourish only so long as there was a loose, tacit and general agreement to behave more or less like gentlemen." (Craig, Totalitarian Approaches to Diplomatic Negotiations, p. 125, ff. 78.)
[21] Ibid., p. 125.

Soviet-American perspectives on international relations as a reality of their relationship, it, nonetheless, acknowledges the possibility of converging common interests that are negotiable. Perhaps, these assumptions are best summed up in two words that have come to characterize the Soviet-American relationship in the 1970's: Competition and cooperation.

CHAPTER II—DIPLOMACY AND NEGOTIATION IN HISTORICAL PERSPECTIVE

Diplomacy is "the great engine used by civilized society for the purpose of maintaining peace."

—*Sir Robert Peel.*

I. IN THE BEGINNING

A. EMERGING FORMS OF DIPLOMATIC METHOD UNDER THE GREEKS

The diplomatic method had its formal beginning in Ancient Greece and from that beginning it has evolved through stages of history to what it is today. Prerevolutionary Russia was part of this evolutionary process. So has been the United States. To what extent Russia of the Soviet era shares this same common diplomatic heritage is to some diplomatic observers a moot question, and accordingly one of the central concerns of this study.

Diplomacy had its origins in the prehistoric age. Nicolson speculated, possibly in arrangements among early man for limiting respective hunting territories. But it was the Ancient Greeks, he said, who evolved at an early age an elaborate system of international intercourse to differentiate various stages and types of agreement. This was shown by the invention of such words as reconciliation, indicating little more than a common desire to cease hostilities; followed by an arrangement, leading to a temporary local truce; to be possibly followed by either a compact or convention. Alliance and a commercial treaty were terms in use, as was the solemn sacred "Truce" on the occasion of the Olympic games and the word signifying conclusion of peace.[1]

Diplomatic missions are described in Homeric poems, Nicolson noted; and in time the Greeks developed many methods of negotiations. Permanent missions were to come 1,400 years later, but the Greek cities dispatched and received embassies on an ad hoc basis and instituted such diplomatic forms as giving credentials to ambassadors. Rewards or punishments were given out according to the success or failure of the assigned mission; expense accounts were open to public scrutiny, making ambassadors vulnerable to attack from political enemies. Thus, as Nicolson observed, it was "no sinecure to serve as the ambassador of a Greek city state." [2]

Diplomatic negotiations were conducted orally in the era of Greek democracy and, at least in theory, with full publicity. Members of an embassy would deliver a set speech to a foreign monarch or assembly. If negotiations were concluded with a treaty, the terms were recorded on a tablet for all to see. Ratification occurred with a public exchange of solemn oaths. Accordingly, as Nicolson observed, "the Greeks

---

[1] Nicolson, Evolution of Diplomatic Method, pp. 2–3.
[2] Ibid., p. 6

(11)

adopted the system of open covenants openly arrived at," a concept to gain prominence in Wilsonian diplomacy. Secret treaties were introduced during the Macedonian ascendancy.[3]

Moreover, the Greeks had a designated status for neutrality, and for them arbitration was a customary device for settling disputes. The post of consul was established, and among his tasks were to assist merchants visiting foreign cities, to initiate diplomatic negotiations, and to assuage the animosities among the states of the Hellenic world.[4]

Thus, Nicolson concluded that by the fifth century B.C. the Greeks had undoubtedly established an "elaborate apparatus of international intercourse." They had their Amphictyonic Councils, leagues and alliances, showing, in theory at least, that they recognized the value of combinations; they evolved accepted principles on such matters as declaring war, concluding peace, ratifying treaties, in addition to having such forms as arbitration, neutrality, exchange of ambassadors, functions of a consul, and certain rules of war. And they worked out regulations, widely observed, defining the status of aliens, the grant of naturalization, the right of asylum, extradition, and maritime practices.[5]

In brief, the Ancient Greeks discovered that international relations had to be governed by certain stable principles, and they did much to establish the machinery of diplomacy and international law.[6]

B. CONTRIBUTIONS FROM ROME

The Roman imperium offered little opportunity for the exercise of genuine diplomacy and negotiation, and hence the Romans failed to develop or bequeath any exemplary body of diplomatic maxims to posterity. It is perhaps axiomatic to say that diplomacy and negotiations flourish where the principle of reciprocity between sovereign and independent states is acknowledged, but tend to languish and disappear in a relationship of inequality such as that existing under the Roman Republic where one power predominated. In the imperial relationship established by Rome, surrender and conquest, not reciprocity, was the ruling principle; the weaker was not given much choice.

Still, the Romans, possessing as they did great gifts of organization, did introduce some improvements in the diplomatic method as passed on from Ancient Greece. Forms of diplomacy were improved. Ambassadors, usually men of senatorial rank, were provided with credentials and instructions from the Senate that appointed them and to which they had to report. But rarely did they have full power to negotiate, always being subject to the Senate, and could be removed for exceeding instructions. Immunity to foreign ambassadors was extended to their staffs, but as Rome's power grew, it became more contemptuous in its treatment of foreign envoys, making them, for example, subject to the pleasure of the Senate when awaiting an audience. The Romans also set up a court of recuperatores, an innovation which amounted to a mixed commission for the adjudication of claims.[7]

[3] Ibid., p. 7.
[4] Ibid., p. 8
[5] Ibid., p. 9.
[6] Ibid., p. 22. In this chapter, Nicolson also points out the negative aspects of the Greek experience.
[7] Ibid., pp. 16–20.

Less praiseworthy was the introduction of a clause into treaties calling for the delivery of hostages as a guarantee of treaty compliance. The Romans also introduced the deadline in negotiations, clearly a prerogative of only an imperial power. Macedonian ambassadors who came to Rome in 197 B.C. were thus told on arrival that if negotiations were not completed in 60 days, diplomatic immunity would be lifted, they would be regarded as spies, and conducted under armed guard to the coast.[8]

While the Romans did behave in an imperial manner, and accordingly made only peripheral contributions to the development of the diplomatic method, they accomplished two things essential in the evolution of diplomacy. They introduced order in the international relations of the time. But more important, they established the doctrine of the sanctity of contract, undoubtedly an outgrowth of the highly civilized Roman law, which added to the juridical values of treaties. "Yet even in Republican times," Nicolson cautioned, "they were too dictatorial to appreciate diplomatic niceties and too masterful to bequeath valuable examples or lessons, such as might have helped posterity to evolve a sound method of negotiation."[9]

C. The Byzantine Heritage

The disintegration of the Roman Empire and the emergence of a number of autonomous and aggressive barbarian nations, in both the East and West, produced a new spirit of intense rivalry in the international relations of the time. The imposed unity of Pax Romana was now gone, to be replaced by a mode of relations that stressed not the sharp alternatives of obedience or revolt in the Roman imperial manner, but rather the necessity of adjusting competing ambitions or strengthening national security for the conciliation of enemies and the acquisition of allies.

"It was then," Nicolson observed, that "professional diplomacy—an art which the Greeks had been too insolent, and the Romans too haughty, to study or perfect—became one of the branches of statesmanship." Nicolson regretted that this art of diplomacy, so necessary for independent nation-states, was "neither illumined by Athenian intelligence, nor dignified by Roman seriousness, but falsified and discredited by the practices of oriental courts."[10] For it was Byzantium that taught diplomacy to Venice; and Venice that established the pattern for the Italian cities, for France and Spain, eventually for all of Europe and the rest of the civilized world.

Nicolson believed that the Byzantine heritage created "an intricate and unreasonable pattern; it was a pattern that ignored the practical purposes of true negotiation, and introduced an abominable filigree of artifice into what ought always to be a simple machine."[11]

What made the Byzantine a diplomacy of artifice was the necessity of creating the illusion of strength from what was in reality weakness. Byzantine diplomacy became an instrument of survival; with barbarian tribes along the borders of the Empire, its only hope lay in playing off one potential enemy against another.

[8] Ibid., p. 21.
[9] Ibid., pp. 22–23.
[10] Ibid., p. 24.
[11] Ibid., p. 25.

Byzantine weakness inspired many innovations in the evolution of the diplomatic method. The Empire needed information about its foreign enemies in order to conduct a skillful diplomacy. For this purpose a special department of government was organized to deal with foreign affairs, the first of its kind. Professional negotiators were trained to serve as ambassadors. To compile information on conditions abroad, ambassadors were appointed on a more-or-less permanent basis at foreign courts and instructed to report back to the foreign office in Constantinople. These reports were studied; a policy formulated; and instructions drafted and dispatched to the ambassador. This was the first time that an effort had been made to use diplomacy in a systematic, professional way.[12]

Byzantium placed extreme importance on questions of protocol and ceremony, and used extraordinary artifices to impress foreign ambassadors with the might and majesty of the Empire. Upon arrival in Constantinople ambassadors and their staff were kept in a kind of protective custody of extreme luxury in a special building where their movements, visitors, and communications were carefully scrutinized by an honor guard of secret police. Fraudulent military parades were staged with the same troops entering one gate and marching out another, only to return in a changed uniform. An aura of divine mystery was created around the Emperor. Foreign ambassadors were required to kowtow before him in solemn obeisance. When the prostrated ambassador got up, he discovered that the Emperor and his throne had been elevated into the air as if by magic. But it was not magic. A handful of slaves had lifted the throne by a system of pulleys while everyone's forehead was touching the floor. To add to the effect, carved lions flanking the steps of the Emperor's throne were made to roar and belch forth fire and smoke by some mechanical devices—not unlike the scene in the American film classic, "The Wizard of Oz," when the four weary and frightened travelers to that magical kingdom faced the "terrifying" Wizard who was in reality anything but terrifying. "It was all rather like a transformation scene in a pantomime," wrote Charles Roetter, a student of diplomacy, "but let us not forget that pulleys and sham parades helped the Byzantine Empire to survive for over 11 centuries."[13]

The Byzantine heritage of diplomacy was thus first and foremost self-serving in that it served the fundamental purpose of maintaining a weak Byzantine Empire. A diplomacy of artifice, it fostered deception and fraud, and established a pattern of diplomacy for Europe, as Nicolson observed, that "ignored the practical purposes of true negotiation." Still, the Byzantine heritage, despite its shortcomings, contributed to the evolution of the diplomatic method: it grasped the essential requirements of diplomacy in an environment of multiple competing nations; it improved on the system of representation and negotiation by making the position of ambassador more of a permanent institution; and it improved on the system of policymaking by establishing a special department of foreign affairs to receive and analyze reports from the field and to formulate and carry out foreign policy through a network of trained professional negotiators.

[12] Roetter, Charles. The Diplomatic Art: An Informal History of World Diplomacy. Philadelphia, Macrae Smith. 1963. pp. 25–26.
[13] Ibid., p. 27, and Nicolson, Evolution of Diplomatic Method, p. 26.

II. IN THE MODERN AGE

A. The Venetian-Italian System

1. CONTRIBUTIONS BY THE VENETIANS

The adventurous, seafaring Vetetians had a long and intimate connection with the Byzantine Empire, and having become indoctrinated with its theory of diplomacy, they transmitted to the Italian states, in the words of Nicolson, "the oriental defects of duplicity and suspicion." Venetians came to look upon all foreigners, especially foreign diplomats, for example, as spies, and regulations governing the conduct of Venetian diplomats forbade under pain of severe punishment ambassadors to discuss politics with any unofficial foreigner or mention them in private correspondence. This attitude lapsed during the 18th century Age of Reason, but revived in recent times, Nicolson observed, "in the less civilized sections of the world." [1]

On the positive side, however, the Venetians made important contributions to the evolving diplomatic method. In general, they were the first to establish an organized system of diplomacy which as late as the 18th century won for their diplomatic service a reputation for being the most polished and best informed.[2]

The Venetians also were the first to establish and preserve their archives in a systematic way. Nearly 22,000 dispatches have been preserved covering the years 883 to 1797, all carefully summarized and indexed in a register.[3]

The Venetians, moreover, introduced the system of newsletters or circulars as the U.S. State Department of mid-19th century termed them. They were designed to keep the ambassadors informed of developments at home, and hence in touch with domestic affairs and current views so that the value of their representation would not be diminished.[4]

2. CHARACTERISTICS OF THE ITALIAN SYSTEM

Like the Byzantine Empire, the diplomacy of the Italian city-states responded to the realities of their physical weakness and the necessity of survival in a political environment of multiple competing states. In the late 15th century, the decline of the Papacy as a mediator of disputes and the changing conception of universal sovereignty as represented in theory by the Holy Roman Emperor opened up the floodgates of power politics within the Italian city-states and produced a political environment in which the idea of "raison d'état" became the predominating principle.[5]

---

[1] Ibid., pp. 27 and 30.
[2] Ibid., p. 27.
[3] Ibid.
[4] Ibid., p. 28.
[5] Ibid., pp. 30–31.

(15)

Conditions existing among the city-states impacted upon their diplomacy and produced characteristics that were later evident in the rise of the modern nation-state. Searching for individual security, the weak Italian states established balances of power in varying diplomatic combinations that had at best a precarious, and often short-lived, existence. No effort was made to establish lasting relationships but rather to live for the present. Long-term policies and the gradual creation of confidence were unappreciated values in this system. "To them," as Nicolson wrote, "the art of negotiation became a game of hazard for high immediate stakes; it was conducted in an atmosphere of excitement, and with that combination of cunning, recklessness and ruthlessness which they lauded as 'virtu'." [6]

In his works Machiavelli sought to establish some "effective truth" out of this political disorder which was directed toward the moral goal of Italian survival. While Nicolson recognized this positive value, still he judged that "it is unfortunate nonetheless that his influence should have been both so wide and so prolonged." Successive European sovereigns, he observed, had taken his *Il Principe* as their political guidebook; and "the general theory that the safety and interests of the State take precedence over all ethical considerations was, in after years, adopted and expanded by great men such as Hegel and Treitschke, with, as we know, very unfortunate results." [7]

3. CONTRIBUTIONS OF THE ITALIAN SYSTEM

However negative the impact of the contemporaries and successors of Machiavelli may have had on the theory or ethics of the art of negotiation, they, nonetheless, did much to expand and sometimes improve the diplomatic method.

Among the ideas and practices that evolved, mainly in Italy, during the 15th and 16th centuries the most important was the establishment of permanent diplomatic missions abroad with ambassadors living in the capital of the country to which they were accredited. Earlier forms of such representation were instituted in Byzantium and the Roman Papacy, but it was not until the mid-15th century that a resident embassy was established in the modern sense when an ambassador was accredited to Cosimo dei Medici by the Duke of Milan. Within 15 years the practice was followed by nearly all Italian and European states. [8]

---

[6] Ibid., p. 31.
[7] Ibid., p. 32.
[8] Ibid., p. 33. Nicolson summarizes the qualities of a 15th and 16th Century ambassador, as extracted from manuals and memoirs:

"He must be a good linguist and above all a master of Latin, which was still the *lingua franca* of the time. He must realize that all foreigners are regarded with suspicion and must therefore conceal his astuteness and appear as a pleasant man of the world. He must be hospitable and employ an excellent cook. He must be a man of taste and erudition and cultivate the society of writers, artists and scientists. He must be a naturally patient man, willing to spin out negotiations and to emulate the exquisite art of procrastination as perfected in the Vatican. He must be imperturbable, able to receive bad news without manifesting displeasure, or to hear himself maligned and misquoted without the slightest twinge of irritation. His private life must be so ascetic as to give his enemies no opportunity to spread scandal. He must be tolerant of the ignorance and foolishness of his home government and know how to temper the vehemence of the instructions he receives. Finally, he should remember that overt diplomatic triumphs leave feelings of humiliation behind them and a desire for revenge: no good negotiator should ever threaten, bully or chide.

"Surely these are excellent precepts, which I should myself recommend to young diplomatists; although I might formulate them in rather different terms."

Nicolson went on to point out that the diplomatic method of the 16th Century Italians was, however, "less exemplary," and he noted such characteristics as resort to political intrigues, assassinations, discrediting the motives of opponents among others. (pp. 35–36.)

Procedures for negotiating treaties, though complicated by the survival of feudal traditions and the conception of papal supremacy, were expanded. Aside from regular treaties as now understood, there were, for example, "protocols of agreement," containing lists of accepted points, but often not signed by the negotiating parties. Treaties, presumably negotiated among the Italian States and Catholic sovereigns, were validated by Papal notaries, making them the most birding. Treaties were also ratified with great ceremony. Repudiation of treaties, once signed by an ambassador with full powers to negotiate, was inconceivable unless the ambassador had far exceeded his powers.[9]

Commercial treaties of various kinds were also negotiated, often in great detail, to establish mutual trade among nations. In some cases tribunals were established in the countries of the contracting parties empowered to rectify grievances that might arise.[10] Tentative attempts were made to establish maritime law in order to regulate trade between trading nations.[11]

"Summit" conferences were also held in the 15th century, though with grave doubts among professional diplomats. Such conferences took the form of personal conversations between sovereigns. To prevent seizure by forces of one side by the other, such conferences took place in the middle of a bridge and conversations were carried on through an oak lattice erected between the conferees. The advantages of such conferences were balanced against substantial disadvantages, similar to those given today; for example, the arousing of exaggerated expectations at home and deep suspicions abroad, and the imprecision of verbal agreements reached by sovereigns.[12]

Other difficulties arose from the elaborate ceremonials enshrouding diplomatic activities. Diplomacy of the Renaissance attached great importance to questions of ceremony. Negotiating details on such matters as receiving an ambassador and presenting his credentials to the sovereign often consumed much time and energy.[13]

More serious was the problem of precedence, that is, the ranking of diplomats in a foreign capital. States were once ranked by their age. In 1504, Pope Julius II established a table of precedence, but with the decline of the Papacy and rise of the nation-states, the problem of precedence magnified. Not until the Congress of Vienna in 1815 was order finally established, by ranking diplomats according to date of accreditation and level of representation, in what had become by that time a free-for-all. In one instance occurring in 1768, the Russian Ambassador was severely wounded in a duel with his French counterpart as the result of the former's claim to precedence in seating at a court ball in London and the latter's attempt to deny that claim.[14]

4. A MIXED LEGACY

The Italian system of diplomacy was thus a mixed legacy in the evolution of the diplomatic method. There were positive contributions, at least in some forms, procedures, and institutions, and they clearly

---

9 Ibid., p. 40.
10 Ibid., p. 41.
11 Ibid., p. 42.
12 Ibid., p. 42.
13 Ibid., pp. 43–44.
14 Ibid., p. 45.

have lasting value. But the inner substance of the system was wanting. Nicolson summed up its deficiencies in this way:

Their methods were unsound both in theory and practice. In teaching men that international justice must always be subordinated to national expediency, in inculcating the habits of deception, opportunism, and faithlessness, the Italians did much to bring the whole art of diplomacy into disrepute. In their desire to obtain immediate results in precarious situations, they indulged in transitory "combinazioni" [combinations] and ignored what might be called the "gradualness" of good negotiation. It was for the statesmen of the eighteenth centuries to develop a more sensible and thus a more reliable diplomatic method.[15]

B. The French System and Its Impact

1. GROTIUS, A MAN BEFORE HIS TIME

What Nicolson termed the "chaotic practices" of the Italian system were brought to an end by the influence and power of Grotius, a great international jurist, and Richelieu, a great national statesman.[16]

Briefly, Grotius advocated principles that sought to improve the quality of diplomacy and create better order in the conduct of international relations. He believed and expounded on the existence of a Law of Nature that evolved from the conscience and reason of mankind and transcended doctrinal animosities of competing religions and the dynastic and national ambitions of the nation-states and their sovereigns. Order could be brought out of international anarchy only by recognition and acceptance of this Law of Nature. A genuine equilibrium of power could only be secured when principles other than national expedience governed the policies and actions of nations. He urged that the Law of Nature be administered and enforced within some institutional form of an international deliberative assembly with powers of sanction.[17]

What Grotius, the idealist, did was to establish the principle of international organization as an alternative to the disorder of competing nation-states. But three centuries had to pass and many wars endured before attempts would be made to put this concept of international diplomacy into practice.[18]

2. RICHELIEU'S CONTRIBUTIONS TO THE DIPLOMATIC METHOD

In contrast to the delayed reaction to Grotius' ideas, the impact of Richelieu, a realist and contemporary of Grotius, was immediate and durable; for he introduced new concepts in the evolution of the diplomatic methods that were put into practice during his lifetime, were emulated by other European states, and are visible in the world of diplomacy today.

Most important of Richelieu's contributions was, perhaps, his perception of the art of negotiation as a permanent, long-term, ongoing process rather than a short-term expediency. He was the first statesman to understand this unique purpose. Diplomacy, he said, should seek to create solid and durable relations, not incidental opportunistic ar-

---

[15] Ibid., pp. 46–47.
[16] Ibid., p. 48.
[17] Ibid., pp. 49–50.
[18] Ibid., p. 50.

rangements; it was a continuing process, not simply an ad hoc operation. In brief, Richelieu sought to institutionalize the concept of negotiation in the 17th century as it is understood in the 20th.[19]

For Richelieu, an ardent nationalist and realist, the national interest was the primary consideration of the diplomatist. During the modern era of emerging nation-states this idea had great force and widespread implications for international policies. An eternal and fundamental value, the national interest was perceived as transcending all sentimental, ideological, or doctrinal prejudices; it set aside all feelings of affection, and policy was calculated strictly on the criterion of service to the interests of the state.[20]

Richelieu also understood the importance of building support for foreign policy among public opinion, and accordingly was the first to introduce a system of domestic propaganda.[21] Moreover, he inculcated French diplomats and their staff with the idea that treaties were extremely important instruments of diplomacy that had to be observed "with religious scruple," as Richelieu said. French diplomacy of the 17th century may not have always observed this principle, but as Nicolson wrote, "I am merely saying that the greatest diplomatist of the age insisted upon that principle for purposes that were not ethical only, but also practical." [22]

Furthermore, Richelieu introduced what Nicholson termed "the most essential of all the components of sound diplomacy"; namely, the element of certainty. He insisted upon precision in drafting agreements so as to avoid future evasions or misunderstandings. To give greater certainty to negotiations, Richelieu concentrated direction of policy and control of Ambassadors into a single ministry. Dispersal of responsibilities among different ministeries had been the practice until then. Richelieu felt that this proliferation of responsibilities only bewildered negotiators. Accordingly, by a decree of March 11, 1626, he centralized all foreign policy responsibilities in the Ministry of External Affairs, and he, himself, undertook the task of constant supervision.[23]

3. UNIVERSALIZING THE FRENCH DIPLOMATIC METHOD UNDER LOUIS XIV

Richelieu's greatness in foreign policy went beyond improving the machinery of diplomacy: He had successfully laid the foundations for the power of Louis XIV that was to become the basis of traditional French foreign policy. It was during Louis XIV's reign that French influence on the diplomatic method became predominant and universal. What the Italians had done in setting the tone of diplomacy for the 15th and 16th centuries, the French had done in establishing the pattern that was imitated by all other European states during the 17th and 18th.

Significant improvements took place in the French diplomatic method under Louis XIV. The Secretary of State for Foreign Affairs was made a permanent member of the cabinet, and his functions, similar to those of a foreign minister today, made him a close and trusted counselor to the King on foreign policy.[24]

[19] Ibid., p. 51.
[20] Ibid., p. 51.
[21] Ibid., p. 51.
[22] Ibid., p. 52.
[23] Ibid., p. 53.
[24] Ibid., p. 54.

The Secretary of State presided over a formidable diplomatic establishment. While the French Foreign Office was small (some 5 officials), the French Diplomatic Service was more extensive than any European power. By 1685, the French had permanent embassies in such world capitals as Rome, Venice, London, Madrid, and Constantinople, in addition to lesser ranked missions in many states of Germany and cities of Italy.[25] Special attention was given to economic matters, particularly with respect to the Levant trade where something like a Levant Consular Service was set up early in the 17th century.[26]

Under Louis XIV French diplomatic correspondence became the model of diplomatic method, and the French language the lingua franca of diplomacy for it met the test of adaptability in fusing perfectly connotations of courtesy with the hard requirements of precision. "To this day," wrote Nicolson, "the despatches and notes of French Ambassadors are superior in their lucidity and concision to those of any other diplomatist." [27] Cyphers were also used to guarantee secrecy.

Louis XIV distrusted conference diplomacy, preferring confidential discussions between specialists to the slow, expensive, and cumbersome method of negotiation by conference. "Open negotiations," he wrote, "incline negotiators to consider their own prestige and to maintain the dignity, the interests and the arguments of their sovereigns with undue obstinacy and prevent them from giving way to the frequently superior arguments of the occasion." [28]

Concessions could be made far easier in private discussion, he reasoned, than when many observers were present at the negotiating table. His "abiding principle," according to Nicolson, was that "negotiation must remain as confidential as possible." [29]

Nicolson was not suggesting that Louis XIV's foreign policy be an example for the emulation of future statesmen. He recognized its shortcomings, having been governed by principles and ambitions that won the disapproval of historians. "All I am saying," he wrote, "is that, from the advent of Richelieu to power in 1616 until the Revolution [in 1789] more than 160 years later, the diplomatic method of France became the model for all Europe; and that, given the ideas and circumstances of the time, it was an excellent method." [30]

4. DE CALLIÈRES' COUNSEL TO NEGOTIATORS AND DIPLOMATS

Perhaps, the most articulate commentator on French diplomacy was François de Callières. On the basis of his long-time experience in the system as a seasoned diplomat and negotiator, he wrote his great work, "De la Manière de Négocier avec les Souverains." First published in 1716, this book remains, in Nicolson's judgment, "the best manual of diplomatic method ever written." [31] "No other writer," he observed, "not even Cambon or Jusserand, has given so clear, so complete, or so unanswerable a definition of good diplomatic method." [32]

[25] Ibid., p. 55.
[26] Ibid., p. 59.
[27] Ibid., p. 57.
[28] Quoted in, Nicolson, Evolution of Diplomatic Method, p. 61.
[29] Ibid.
[30] Ibid., pp. 61–62.
[31] Ibid., p. 62.
[32] Ibid., p. 68.

Sound diplomacy, De Callières wrote, was based not upon deceit but rather on a spirit of confidence that was inspired by good faith. In an affirmation of the principle that honesty is the best policy in negotiation, he wrote:

A diplomatist should remember that open dealing is the basis of confidence; he should share freely with others everything except what it is his duty to conceal. * * * A good negotiator will never rely for the success of his mission either on bad faith or on promises that he cannot execute. It is a fundamental error, and one widely held, that a clever negotiator must be a master of deceit. Deceit is indeed the measure of the smallness of mind of him who uses it; it proves that he does not possess sufficient intelligence to achieve results by just and reasonable means. Honesty is here and everywhere the best policy; a lie always leaves behind it a drop of poison and even the most brilliant diplomatic success gained by trickery rests on an insecure foundation, since it awakes in the defeated party a sense of irritation, a desire for vengeance, and a hatred which must remain a menace to his foe. * * * The use of deceit in diplomacy is by its very nature limited, since there is no curse that comes quicker to roost than a lie that has been found out. Apart from the fact that a lie is unworthy of a great Ambassador, it actually does more harm than good to negotiation, since though it may confer success today, it will create an atmosphere of suspicion which tomorrow will make further success impossible. * * * The negotiator therefore must be a man of probity and one who loves truth; otherwise he will fail to inspire confidence.[33]

For De Callières, credibility was a very important qualification for a good negotiator, and the search for a harmony of real interests the secret of negotiation. No threats, no deception, no self-gratification over "diplomatic triumphs"—these were in essence his rules for sound negotiations; as he admonished:

Menaces always do harm to negotiation, since they often push a party to extremes to which they would not have resorted but for provocation. It is well known that hurt vanity often goads men to courses which a sober estimate of their own interests would lead them to eschew. * * * Success achieved by force or fraud rests on an insecure foundation; conversely, success based on reciprocal advantage gives promise of even further successes to come. An ambassador must base his success on straight-forward and honest procedure, if he tries to win by subtlety or arrogance he is deceiving himself.[34]

In addition to laying down sound principles for negotiations, De Callières had also some wisdom to pass along to the ages as to what constitutes the qualities of a good diplomat. He wrote:

The good diplomatist must have an observant mind, a gift of application which rejects being diverted by pleasures or frivolous amusements, a sound judgment which takes the measure of things as they are, and which goes straight to the goal by the shortest and most natural paths without wandering into meaningless refinements and subtleties.

The good negotiator must have the gift of penetration such as will enable him to discern the thoughts of men and to deduce from the last movement of their features which passions are stirring within.

The diplomatist must be quick, resourceful, a good listener, courteous and agreeable. He should not seek to gain a reputation as a wit, nor should he be so disputatious as to divulge secret information in order to clinch an argument. Above all the good negotiator must possess enough self-control to resist the longing to speak before he has thought out what he intends to say. He must not fall into the mistake of supposing that an air of mystery, in which secrets are made out of nothing and the merest trifle exalted into an affair of State, is anything but the symptom of a small mind. He should pay attention to women, but never lose his heart. He must be able to simulate dignity even if he does not possess it, but he must at the same time avoid all tasteless display. Courage also is an essential quality, since no timid man can hope to bring a confidential negotiation to success. The negotiator must possess the patience of a watch-maker and be devoid of

[33] Quoted in, Nicolson, Evolution of Diplomatic Method, pp. 62–63.
[34] Ibid., pp. 63–64.

personal prejudices. He must have a calm nature, be able to suffer fools gladly, and should not be given to drink, gambling, women, irritability, or any other wayward humours and fantasies. The negotiator moreover should study history and memoirs, be acquainted with foreign institutions and habits, and be able to tell where, in any foreign country, the real sovereignty lies. Everyone who enters the profession of diplomacy should know the German, Italian and Spanish languages as well as the Latin, ignorance of which would be a disgrace and shame to any public man, since it is the common language of all Christian nations. He should also have some knowledge of literature, science, mathematics, and law. Finally he should entertain handsomely. A good cook is often an excellent conciliator.[35]

Nicolson added another qualification for the diplomat not included by De Callières, the gift of rhetoric. The old conception of the Ambassador as an advocate had disappeared by the 17th and 18th centuries, to be revived in the 20th century democratic method of diplomacy wherein forensic ability, as the Soviets exemplified to the point of abuse, was added to the art of negotiation.[36]

De Callières also elaborated on the machinery of diplomacy. He established the rank and order of authority among diplomats: Ambassador, envoy, resident, and deputy. A professional, he distrusted amateurs in diplomacy and urged the creation of a professionally trained diplomatic service. He warned against the weaknesses of nepotism; excluded churchmen and soldiers from the diplomatic ranks for the prejudices that their professions inculcate; and judged the legal mind inadaptable to diplomacy—to which Nicolson added this personal criticism: "Few persons who have had experience of lawyer-diplomatists will deny the truth of this assertion." [37]

Among the tasks of the diplomat De Callières recorded the importance of faithfully executing instructions from the home government, except those that might require doing something "against the laws of God or of Justice"—such as assassination or the use of diplomatic immunity to foment or protect revolutionaries intriguing against the state to which he is accredited.[38]

5. DISCREDITING THE BALANCE OF POWER CONCEPT

De Callières' principles and precepts of diplomacy were not maintained in the succeeding decades of the 18th century; they remained

---

[35] Ibid., pp. 64–65.
[36] Ibid., p. 65.
[37] The American experience contradicts this critical evaluation of lawyers as diplomats. Some of this Nation's greatest Secretaries of State were, in fact, trained and, at one time in their careers, practicing lawyers. John Quincy Adams, Secretary of State in the Monroe administration, was trained as a lawyer. He also had diplomatic service in the Netherlands, Prussia, Russia, and Britain; and he served as Peace Commissioner at Ghent empowered to negotiate an end to the War of 1812. William Henry Seward, Secretary of State under Presidents Lincoln and Johnson, was a long-time successful practicing lawyer. Both Adams and Seward are rated in that order by American historians as this Nation's greatest Secretaries of State. Other distinguished Secretaries who were lawyers, some of whom had diplomatic service abroad, could also be included, such as, Jefferson, Madison, John Hay, Elihu Root, and Charles Evans Hughes. Among lawyer-trained Presidents who similarly distinguished themselves in foreign affairs were John Adams (notably during the Revolutionary War as a diplomat abroad), Polk, Cleveland, and Franklin Roosevelt.
In attempting to explain the contradiction, it has been suggested by legal specialists in both the Civil Code and Common Law that the answer would seem to lay partly in conflicting legal disciplines as understood and practiced particularly on the European Continent and, in the United States. Training in the civil code countries, such as De Callières' France of the 17th Century, tends to produce a narrowly constricted approach to problems of law and society; while that in the common law countries, such as the United States, tends to produce an outlook that is far broader and more pragmatic, and an approach to society, especially in the American environment, that is fundamentally problem solving. The requirements of diplomacy, it is concluded, call for a cast of mind more suitable to the latter than to the former; hence, the uncommonly successful record in the American experience.
[38] Nicolson, Evolution of Diplomatic Method, pp. 66–68.

what they essentially were, ideals. Early in De Callières life the principle of the balance of power had represented a reasonably just equilibrium in the balanced strength of the Austrian Empire and France. But with the emergence of three great new European powers, England, Russia, and Prussia, the distribution of power changed intermittently and often radically. Frederick the Great of Prussia revived the old Italian theory of transitory combination for immediate gains. Thus, in Nicolson's judgment, "he discredited the system of the Balance of Power" which until then had been, at least in theory, essentially defensive: it sought to raise the threshold of danger for any single power to try to dominate Europe or suppress the liberties of others. "Frederick the Great rendered it an aggressive system, a conspiracy of loot." Nicholson wrote, "by which the strong could obtain simultaneous accessions of territory at the expense of the weak." The partitions of Poland became the classic example. Not until the statesmen of the Congress of Vienna reestablished in 1815 the balance of power as a creditable principle of foreign policy did they find a system that preserved the world from a major war for 100 years.[39]

6. VALUE OF THE FRENCH DIPLOMATIC METHOD

The French had unquestionably made a great and perhaps lasting contribution to the evolution of the diplomatic method as it is known today. This French method was described as constituting the theory and practice of international negotiation as originated by Richelieu, analyzed by De Callières, and adopted by all European countries during the three centuries prior to World War I. Nicolson gave the following appraisal:

I regard this method as that best adapted to the conduct of relations between civilized States. It was courteous and dignified; it was continuous and gradual; it attached importance to knowledge and experience; it took account of the realities of existing power; and it defined good faith, lucidity and precision as the qualities essential to any sound negotiation.[40]

C. CHARACTERISTICS OF 19TH CENTURY DIPLOMACY

1. A PERIOD OF TRANSITION

European diplomacy had its origins in the era of the emerging nation-state during the 16th to the 18th centuries, and its forms and conventions reflected the political, social, and economic conditions of that age. The age of Richelieu, Louis XIV, and De Callières was the age of absolutism, and the style of diplomacy and methods that the French bequeathed to all of Europe were uniquely adapted to the requirements of that time. Accordingly, Ambassadors were the personal representatives of the sovereign king, and those with whom he negotiated shared common values, goals, and rules-of-the-game of an inner directed aristocratic class. For the lack of communications the

[39] Ibid., p. 69.
[40] Nicolson continued: "The mistakes, the follies and the crimes that during those 300 years accumulated to the discredit of the old diplomacy can, when examined at their sources, be traced to evil foreign policy rather than to faulty methods of negotiation. It is regrettable that the bad things they did should have dishonored the excellent manner in which they did them." (Ibid., pp. 72–73.)

diplomat enjoyed great latitude and power in negotiations, and as the trusted agent of the king his role assumed great importance.[41]

During the 19th century the rise of political democracy and the emergence of the industrial revolution created conditions that changed the form, the style and substance of what has been termed, "classical diplomacy." These forces of change were only dimly perceived during the century, and not until the end of World War I did a new diplomacy take the place of the discredited old diplomacy.[42]

2. EUROPE, THE POLITICAL CENTER OF THE WORLD

First among the five chief characteristics of 19th century diplomacy was the commonly shared belief that Europe was the political center of the world. Asia and Africa were seen as inviting fields for imperial, commercial, and missionary expansion. Japan was looked upon as an exceptional phenomenon, and the United States as secure in its own isolation. No war could become major, it was believed, unless five of the great European powers became involved, and thus it was they who would decide the issue of general peace or war.[43]

3. PRIMACY OF THE GREAT POWERS

An underlying assumption in 19th century diplomacy was the primacy of the great powers by virtue of their extended interests, responsibilities, resources, and sheer power. This characteristic was the reason for the success of the concert of Europe, for it was the great powers that laid down the terms and maintained the system that kept the general peace until 1914.[44]

Smaller powers were ranked according to their place in the evolving balance of power, and their importance was judged according to their relationship to the diplomatic problem of the moment. Seldom was any concern given to their interests, opinions, and still less to their votes.[45] The great powers called the shots, and the others fell in line. United States acquiescence in this system was apparent by giving its sanction to great power intervention in Mexico during the early 1860's in order to collect outstanding debts.

4. GREAT POWER RESPONSIBILITY FOR CONDUCT OF SMALLER POWERS

Implied in the second characteristic is the common responsibility shared among the great powers for the conduct of the small powers and the preservation of peace among them. The right of intervention was a generally accepted principle. Cases in point were the punitive actions taken against the Japanese at Shimonoseki in 1864 by a combined expedition of the British, French, Dutch, and the Americans, and against the Chinese on the occasion of the Boxer Rebellion in 1900 by the great powers of Europe, including the United States.[46]

---

[41] Craig, Gordon A. and Felix Gilbert, eds. The Diplomats, 1919–39. Princeton, N.J., Princeton University Press, 1953, pp. 3–4.
[42] Ibid., pp. 5–6.
[43] Nicolson, Evolution of Diplomatic Method, p. 73.
[44] Ibid., p. 73.
[45] Ibid.
[46] Ibid., p. 74.

5. ESTABLISHMENT OF A PROFESSIONAL DIPLOMATIC SERVICE

Establishment of a professional diplomatic service in every European country on a more or less identical model was the fourth characteristic of 19th century diplomacy. These diplomats shared common values and purposes, and possessed similar traits, standards of education, and experiences. They desired the same kind of world. And as De Callières had already observed with respect to the diplomats of his era, those of the 19th century tended to develop a corporate identity independent of their national identity.[47]

Often having known each other for years from service in prior posts, "they all believed," Nicolson noted, "whatever their governments might believe, that the purpose of diplomacy was the preservation of peace." "This professional free-masonry," Nicolson added, "proved of great value in negotiations." Thus, the Ambassadors of France, Russia, Germany, Austria, and Italy, under the chairmanship of the British statesman Sir Edward Grey, settled the Balkan crisis of 1913, even though each represented national rivalries that were dangerous and sharp. Yet, as Nicolson observed, "they possessed complete confidence in each other's probity and discretion, had a common standard of professional conduct, and desired above all else to prevent a general conflagration."[48]

6. CONTINUOUS AND CONFIDENTIAL NEGOTIATION

A final characteristic of the old diplomacy was the rule that sound negotiation had to be continuous and confidential. The ambassador accredited to a foreign capital possessed many important negotiating assets by virtue of his physical presence. He knew the opposite side with whom he was negotiating; he had a good reading beforehand, therefore, on their strengths and weaknesses, their reliability and credibility. He was informed of local interests, prejudices and ambitions, and accordingly better able to judge his negotiating strategy. A continuous relationship between him and the Foreign Minister would not attract any special attention when an important matter was to be negotiated. Private conversations encouraged rational and courteous exchanges of views, and confidentiality protected the negotiators from outside pressures as they progressed through the exchanges of concession and counterconcession. Finally, the absence of time pressures on the 19th century diplomat gave the negotiator and his government ample opportunity for reflection and to pace the negotiation so as to achieve a mutually satisfactory conclusion—as Nicolson said, with "no hasty improvisations or empty formulas, but documents considered and drafted with exact care."[49]

Nicolson cited the Anglo-Russian Convention of 1907 as a good example of the value of this system. The negotiation between the Russian Foreign Minister and the British Ambassador in St. Petersburg took place over a 15-month period. At no time, he said, was an indiscretion committed or a confidence betrayed. And, of course, this

---

[47] Ibid., pp. 74–75.
[48] Ibid., p. 75.
[49] Ibid., pp. 76–77.

negotiation established the Anglo-Russian entente, an essential building block in the alliance system of the Allies prior to World War I.[50]

7. DIPLOMACY OF "CIVILIZED SOCIETY"

The characteristics of the old diplomacy of the 19th century were, therefore, distinctive: Europe as the center of international relations, the primacy and responsibility of the great powers in a concert of Europe, existence of a trained diplomatic corps having common standards of professionalism and conduct, and the assumption of negotiation as a process rather than an event where confidentiality was the rule. Much in this system which reflected the needs of the time was praiseworthy, and some diplomatists today seem to look back upon it with a certain nostalgia. But even Nicolson, who, as he said, was "born and nurtured in the old diplomacy," acknowledged that he was "fully conscious of the many faults that the system encouraged"—faults that will be noted in the next chapter.[51] Still, the transcending reality was that the machinery of this diplomacy, notably the mechanism for negotiation, was as Sir Robert Peel said, "the great engine used by civilized society for the purpose of maintaining peace."[52]

[50] Ibid., p. 77.
[51] Ibid., p. 77.
[52] Quoted in, Craig and Gilbert, Diplomats, p. 10.

III. THE RUSSIAN EXPERIENCE

A. THE EARLY YEARS

1. FORMATIVE FORCES

Russia was a latecomer to the European scene and to the art of diplomacy and negotiation as it evolved over the centuries prior to the modern age. Except for an early exposure to Byzantium, Russia was immured from the powerful, creative, and liberating intellectual and historical forces that impacted upon Europe in the late Middle Ages, the Renaissance, Reformation and Counter-Reformation, and probably was only superficially influenced by the 18th century Enlightenment.

Russia's was a history of struggle and isolation: Of struggle against two centuries of the foreign Mongol-Tartar conquest and a search for internal order and external expansion; and of isolation from those forces that made Western civilization unique in the history of man. This historical experience had done much to nurture the Russian obsession with security, their suspicion of foreigners, and their deep sense of national inferiority, all of which left an indelible mark on their behavior toward foreigners in diplomacy and negotiations.

2. EARLY CONTACTS WITH EUROPE

Despite Russia's late arrival on the European diplomatic scene, its rulers and ministers came quickly to appreciate the importance of negotiation and mastering its techniques. In earlier times they had negotiated with the khans of Asia and the caliphs of Baghdad. During Ivan III's rule (1462–1505), diplomacy and war were resorted to equally in adjusting Russia's relations with the Golden Horde and the Tartars of the Crimea. Throughout his reign, Ivan III negotiated continuously not only with his nearest neighbors, but also with the Papacy, the Hapsburgs, the King of Bohemia, and the Danish court. Reputedly, he was a skillful negotiator with foreign ambassadors, a reputation warranted by his diplomatic successes.[1]

In the early period Russia's relations with the West were only intermittent, but, as time went on, they expanded in scope. By the mid-16th century, the Moscovy court established a primitive foreign office, the Bureau of Ambassadors, for the purpose of coordinating the activities of the many Greek and Italian agents and those of other nationalities representing its interests in the West. With expanding political and territorial ambitions, the Russians turned their attention toward peripheral areas dominated by the Turks and Swedes. To achieve their purposes in these quarters, they resorted to coalition diplomacy, sending envoys to seek alliances and other forms of aid

---

[1] Craig. Gordon. Techniques of Negotiation. In, Ivo J. Lederer, ed. Russian Foreign Policy. Essays in Historical Perspective. New Haven, Conn., Yale University Press, 1962. p. 354.

to Venice, Berlin, Vienna, Madrid, London, Paris, and the Hague.[2]

By the end of the 17th century, the Russians had clearly perceived advantages of continuous contacts with foreign courts, and accordingly established their first permanent missions abroad. The process was expanded by Peter the Great (1689–1725) and by Catherine the Great (1762–96). Under Catherine, who was greatly influenced by the French Enlightenment, Russian policy was oriented toward the West. As a result, Russia became an active, and profitable, participant in the diplomatic maneuvers that pervaded the 18th century. While Peter may have entertained some doubt about the performance of the Russian connection with the West, Catherine did not; for after her reign the Russian association with the Western diplomatic community was continuous.[3]

3. PERSONAL BEHAVIOR AND NEGOTIATING TECHNIQUES OF EARLY RUSSIAN DIPLOMATS

The behavior and negotiating techniques of early Russian diplomatists provoked contempt, amusement, or exasperation among Western statesmen. One observer of the first Russians to visit the West as special envoys described them as very little more than "baptized bears." Behaving in a manner less than human, they made Russian grossness a stereotype in the West by such conduct as destroying apartments assigned to them, breaking the furniture, and, as one historical source noted, "leaving behind them unsupportable odors and indescribable filth." [4]

On Peter the Great's visit to the West in 1697–98, his entourage virtually destroyed the house assigned to them in London. The catalog of wreckage is impressive: Grease and ink covered the floor; curtains, quilts, and bed linen were reduced to rags; 50 chairs were broken or had disappeared entirely; 29 pictures were slashed and their frames destroyed; and 300 window panes were broken. "Damage of this nature could not be attributed wholly to inadvertence or to lack of breeding," wrote Craig. "Much of it appeared to be a deliberate flouting of Western convention in order to demonstrate Russian superiority." [5] Even so, according to Craig, this demonstration was in line with other boorish traits of these first Russian embassies: "Rudeness in matters of protocol, scornful disregard for the laws of the land to which they were accredited, and studied incivilities in their relations with their opposite numbers." [6]

Negotiations with the Russians of this early period were always difficult and tedious. Envoys sent abroad were bound by the strictest instructions in the conduct of their business in such matters as behavior, substance and tone of speech, and what persons they were authorized to confer with. Full powers were never given, and nothing could be decided without consultation with higher authority. Variations in the course of negotiations led to delays for clarification and new instructions. Negotiations in Moscow were subject to similar cal-

[2] Ibid., pp. 352–353.
[3] Ibid., p. 353.
[4] Ibid., p. 353.
[5] Ibid., p. 354.
[6] Ibid.

culated delays when foreign envoys dealt with the czar through his chief ministers. Foreign envoys frequently discovered, after interminable delays, that they were expected to accept the dictate of the czar, and objections on their side were countered with pressure, threats, and expulsions that gave little evidence of Russian respect for the accepted etiquette of European diplomacy.[7]

Negotiations were further hampered by characteristics in Russian behavior that always delayed and sometimes defeated understanding. Schooled in the Byzantine tradition before establishing a firm relationship with the West, the Russians retained Eastern habits of thought and discourse that irritated Western negotiators. What has been described as the Slavic capacity for "interminable conversation" tried the patience of negotiators, while the Russian arts of mystification, along with their capacity to talk in incomprehensible circles when they chose, often enshrouded negotiations with impenetrable mists of confusion. "Even such a pronounced Westerner as Peter," observed Craig, "believed that dust should be thrown in the eyes of his Western rivals and that obfuscation should be considered an important instrument of Russian policy." And accordingly his servants followed this injunction.[8]

Presumably such negotiating characteristics, like other aspects of pre-19th century Russian diplomatic behavior, could be explained by Russia's late entry into Western diplomatic society. Like Byzantium, theirs seemed to be a diplomacy of weakness, one that was geared essentially to survival in an unfamiliar world and reflected a deeply engrained consciousness of security and suspicion of foreigners. As Craig put it, Russia was "aware of the advantages of membership but suspicious of the price that might have to be paid for it, uncertain of its ability to live by the rules, therefore insistent upon the validity of its own, fearful of commitment and therefore taking refuge in confusion." [9]

B. IN THE 19TH CENTURY

1. CHANGING MODE OF RUSSIAN DIPLOMACY

How much of the essence of these characteristics of early Russian diplomacy were retained and passed on to future generations cannot be accurately determined. Observers of the Russian scene have persistently noted the Russian obsession with security and their suspicion of foreigners. Yet, it is apparent that in the 19th century at least the mode of Russian diplomacy, as manifested in the conduct of the foreign policy establishment, had changed radically as a result of Russia's full entry into the European diplomatic community and the assumption of its role as a great power in the concert of Europe.

In his study on the evolution of the diplomatic method, Nicolson did not examine Russian diplomacy, but rather concentrated on the French and other schools. Craig suggested that the omission was

[7] Ibid., p. 354.
[8] Ibid., pp. 354–355.
[9] Ibid., pp. 355–356.

possibly caused by the belief that separate treatment was unnecessary. If so, he said, it seemed justifiable. And he explained:

> Russian diplomacy in the nineteenth century was virtually indistinguishable in methods and technique from that of the states with which it dealt; and the outstanding Russian diplomats could have been put to work in other services without causing the slightest inconvenience or disruption and with no need for re-training in the instruments and techniques of their craft. Their values, their language, their methods, in a word, their style was that of Western diplomats in general.[10]

2. NOTABLE RUSSIAN DIPLOMATS

Russia produced some first-rate diplomats in the 19th century who in style and performance fit into the traditional mold of their European counterparts. Nesselrode, the foreign minister of Alexander I and Nicholas I, was a prime actor in the international community of his time; he was distinctively European. Gorchakov succeeded Nesselrode in 1856, after serving as minister in the German courts and ambassador in Vienna. Though accenting his "Russianness" as a tactic, Gorchakov in practice increasingly absorbed the ideas, policies, and methods of his predecessor. The same tendency of a Western orientation was apparent in Russian diplomats serving abroad.[11] Aside from a relatively few Panslavists in important posts, Russia's leading diplomatic representatives were, as Craig noted, "men of cosmopolitan culture who mastered their profession and were often taken as models by younger diplomats of other states." [12]

In the latter half of the 19th century a high value was placed on Russian skills in diplomacy as negotiations became a vital instrument in a foreign policy that was essentially defensive. In the peace settlements ending the Crimean War in 1856 in Paris and the Russo-Turkish War in 1878 in Berlin, Russian diplomacy was called on to correct the miscalculations of their military. In a resort to a skillful defensive diplomacy at the Paris Conference of 1856, Orlov and Brunnow, the Russian negotiators, successfully tempered the demands of the victors and, according to Craig, "freed Russia from a diplomatic isolation that might have been dangerous in the ensuing period." In 1878, the Russian Ambassador to Britain Peter Shuvalov conducted what was termed a "masterly diplomatic campaign" in London and Berlin, successfully extracting Russia from an unsupportable position created by its Panslavist policy. Bismarck, one of the greatest 19th century negotiators, described Shuvalov at the Congress of Berlin as a model diplomatist—courteous, charming, always on watch, and, in difficult stages of negotiation much "like a stag under pursuit that shows its horns when too hard pressed." [13]

Russia's triumphs in defensive diplomacy were achieved by standard diplomatic techniques. At Paris, the Russian negotiator exploited divi-

---

[10] Ibid., p. 356.
[11] Ibid., p. 357. Craig briefly notes the careers of other leading Russian diplomats, stressing their distinctive European characteristics. For example, Brunnow, a longtime ambassador to Britain, was described as "a diplomat of the * * * old school, versed in all the fine points of the game—a good speaker, a subtle dialectician, an exquisite stylist." He was said to be an encyclopedia of diplomatic lore who enjoyed the respect of all his colleagues and the affection of younger diplomats.
[12] Ibid.
[13] Ibid., p. 360.

sions between the allies and successfully won the sympathy of the French that brought some reduction of the war costs and established the basis for a Franco-Russian entente that was to last until 1863. Prior to the Congress of Berlin, Shuvalov had effectively succeeded in persuading the Russian Foreign Ministry to moderate its extreme position and through informal preliminary talks with the participants prepared the way for agreement in Berlin.[14]

C. RUSSIAN-AMERICAN ENCOUNTERS

1. NEGOTIATING FOR ALASKA

(a) *Seward and Stoeckl confer on Treaty of Cession*

In the 19th century, Russia and the United States had two major negotiating encounters: One pertaining to the purchase of Alaska in 1867; and the other, U.S. mediation of the Russo-Japanese War at Portsmouth, N.H. in 1905. Both encounters provide useful insights into determining the extent to which 19th century Russian diplomacy conformed to Western diplomatic methods, particularly in negotiations.

Negotiations for the Alaska treaty between Secretary of State William H. Seward and Baron Edward Stoeckl, the Russian Minister to the United States, were simple, direct, friendly, intimate. Conditions were right: The Russians wanted to unload Alaska—it had become a liability; Seward as the most ardent expansionist in American history wanted to acquire Alaska; in addition, Russian-American friendship had soared in the wake of the Civil War that found Russia alone among the great powers of Europe on the side of the Union cause.[15]

There was nothing startlingly original in the negotiating procedure for the treaty to purchase Alaska; there was in the treaty's final consummation. While on a home visit in late 1866 and early 1867, Stoeckl was authorized to negotiate the cession. A courtesy call to Seward on his return to Washington provided the occasion to bring up the matter. Stoeckl was anxious that Seward take the initiative in proposing the cession, presumably to put him in the position of the anxious bargainer and thus have an advantage. In the course of their conversation the opportunity arose when Stoeckl refused to grant a franchise for the California Fur Co. and stated also that his Government would not grant fishing rights in Alaska as requested by the citizens of the Washington Territory. Seward then asked Stoeckl if Russia would sell Alaska. In reply, the Russian Minister related the past history of attempts to acquire Alaska and previous American offers. Russia, he said, would be inclined to negotiate for the cession if an offer were now made. This Seward could not do until consulting with the President.

Subsequently, the Secretary was authorized to carry on negotiations for drafting the treaty of cession. At first Seward mentioned $5,000,-000 as a purchase price; Stoeckl countered with a $10,000,000 proposal.

---

[14] Ibid., p. 360.
[15] This section is based on Whelan. Joseph G., *William Henry Seward, Expansionist.* Doctoral Dissertation, University of Rochester, Rochester, New York, 1959, pp. 101–123. (Unpublished.)

A compromise figure of $7,000,000 was finally reached—$2,000,000 more than the minimum price set by Stoeckl's superiors. By March 14, 1867, negotiations for the treaty were for all practical purposes completed.

After review by the Cabinet and approval by the President, Seward, armed with full powers, resumed conversations with Stoeckl who raised questions pertaining to the cession of the territory unencumbered by certain Russian rights and privileges. Seward reconsidered his position on this matter, and on March 23 advised the Russian Minister that he had to insist upon this provision, but he added that the President authorized the addition of $200,000 to the purchase price. Two days later Stoeckl informed Seward that he would "accede literally to this request on the conditions indicated in your note." The Secretary then urged Stoeckl to request immediately from St. Petersburg full powers to sign the treaty.

(b) Signing of the Alaskan Treaty

On March 29, 1867, Stoeckl received full powers from the Czar to conclude the agreement for $7,000,000. Inasmuch as Seward's subsequent offer of $200,000 satisfied conditions in the Czar's statement of authority, Stoeckl, apparently, felt free to conclude the treaty, and he proceeded immediately to Seward's home on Lafayette Square to inform him of the good news.

On Friday evening, March 29, 1867, the Secretary was playing his favorite card game, whist, with members of his family when the Russian Minister was announced.

"I have a dispatch, Mr. Seward, from my government, by cable," he said, "The Emperor gives his consent to the cession." Stoeckl stated that if the Secretary wished he would come to the Department the next day and there conclude the treaty proceedings.

With a smile of satisfaction on his old and scarred face, Seward pushed away the whist table and looking at the Russian Minister declared: "Why wait till tomorrow, Mr. Stoeckl? Let us make the treaty tonight!"

"But your Department is closed," the Minister responded. "You have no clerks, and my secretaries are scattered about the town."

"Never mind that," Seward replied. "If you can muster your legation together, before midnight you will find me awaiting you at the Department, which will be open and ready for business."

Within less than two hours the State Department was "ready for business." And, by 4 o'clock Saturday morning, March 30, 1867, the treaty was engrossed, signed, sealed, and ready for transmission by the President to the Senate. Present at these early morning proceedings was Senator Charles Sumner, chairman of the Senate Foreign Relations Committee, but he expressed no opinion regarding the course of action he would pursue. At 10 o'clock later the same morning, just 6 hours after the signing of the treaty, President Johnson and the Cabinet met at the Capitol and remained until adjournment of Congress at noon. Seward had hoped to win Senate approval of the treaty before adjournment, and being the "first on the ground," he set out to confide personally with four or five Senators. But, the Senate adopted the motion of Sumner to refer the treaty to his committee.

(c) Stoeckl's role in consummating treaty

Stoeckl's tasks did not end here. Before final action was taken on the treaty, he was to play a major role in lobbying the Congress, building support in public opinion, and finally paying off some Members of Congress to break a deadlock in appropriating the necessary funds. For opposition to the treaty in Congress was formidable. Senators actually went to Stoeckl and told him they would not vote for the treaty not because they opposed it as such but because it bore Seward's name. In fact, Sumner even asked Stoeckl to withdraw the treaty on grounds that it did not have the least chance of success. Seward's support for President Johnson and for a general conciliatory policy toward the defeated South had added new and formidable enemies to the list of those he had gathered over his long political career. The Russian Minister responded that it would be dishonorable to do so. The United States made the offer, he said, and the United States must see it through.

To overcome the opposition and build a favorable public opinion, Seward, assisted by Stoeckl, subsequently organized a powerful public relations campaign in the press and undertook extensive lobbying activities in the Congress. On April 9, 1867, the Senate approved the treaty; on May 10, the Russian Government gave its approval; and on June 20, ratifications were exchanged and the treaty proclaimed. But the House had to appropriate the funds to complete the transaction, and there the proceeding came to a halt over the question of a doubtful private claim against the Russian Government going back to the Crimean War. Neither Stoeckl nor Seward were, however, content to let fate alone determine the outcome. Both accelerated their lobbying activities and expanded their public relations campaign for popularizing the treaty. In December 1867, they conferred several times with Nathaniel C. Banks, chairman of the House Foreign Affairs Committee, to devise some way to get the appropriations through.

Action was slow, however, owing mainly to the Presidential impeachment proceedings, and by the end of March 1868 Stoeckl began to believe that the treaty's prospects were hopeless. Apparently disgusted with the delays, he finally suggested two possible courses of action to his Foreign Ministry; he urged that the Russian Government tell the United States that it had done its part and that if the United States was unwilling to pay for Alaska, it could have the territory without payment; as a second alternative he suggested dispatching a strong but courteous note to Washington which would pique American pride. The Russians took the second course, suggesting further that payment be made first and the claim be taken up thereafter.

During this period of tension and uncertainty Stoeckl exercised the greatest caution. Through Seward, with whom he had always been on the closest terms, he dissuaded the President from sending a special message to Congress, and even urged the Secretary to maintain a low profile on the issue.

Once the impeachment issue was resolved, Congress took action on the appropriations bill. Opposition was formidable in the House, but differences were finally composed, the measure passed, and after Senate action, was signed into law on July 27, 1868. On the following day

Seward requested $7,200,000 from the Treasury Department to be paid to Stoeckl; in August, the Russian Minister received the full amount, but only $7,000,000 was actually sent back to Russia.

A cloud of suspicion hung over the disposition of the remaining $200,000 retained by Stoeckl. Charges of corruption were made; an investigation was initiated but to no avail. Strong historical evidence exists, however, to show that Stoeckl had to pay substantial amounts of money to Members of Congress in order to get the appropriations bill through. On a carriage ride to Marlboro, Md. on September 6, 1868, Seward confided to President Johnson the amounts that were expended and to whom. Johnson recorded the conservation on a small piece of paper later found in his collection that became the basis for an article published in 1912. Seventeen days later on September 23, Seward made virtually the same revelations to his close friend John Bigelow who had just returned from his post as Minister to France. This account appeared in Bigelow's autobiography published in 1913. Finally, investigations into the Russian archives by an American historian after the Bolshevik Revolution further clarified the matter; it showed through official Russian documents that bribes were paid to Congressmen, though their names were not disclosed.

(d) Significance of Stoeckl's role as diplomat and negotiator

Stoeckl played an extraordinary role in the Alaskan cession. A skillful negotiator and knowledgeable diplomat, he understood the nuances of the American political system, the value of public opinion in American foreign policy, and the importance of that vital connection between his role as Minister and Seward's as Secretary of State. Taking full measure of his responsibilities and the goals of his government, Stoeckl went beyond the specific professional task of negotiator to that of a lobbyist and public relations campaigner—all in a close and confidential relationship with the Secretary of State. And while bribery may have unfortunately tarnished the brilliance of this diplomatic transaction, still the entire affair, setting this aside, demonstrated the positive value of negotiating procedures existing in Russian-American relations over a century ago and the fundamental traditionalism of the Russian diplomatic method in the 19th century.

2. MEDIATION AT PORTSMOUTH TO END RUSSO-JAPANESE WAR, 1905

(a) Deadlock in war; search for peace

U.S. mediation of the Russo-Japanese war at Portsmouth, N.H. in August 1905 was another significant Russian-American negotiating encounter. By the spring and summer of 1905, the war, caused by conflicting imperial interests in Manchuria and Korea, had deadlocked: The Japanese, though victorious on both land and sea, were reaching the point of exhaustion, both in men and resources; the Russians, still hopeful of victory by wearing down the Japanese by virtue of their enormous resources, were facing divided counsels in government, a loss of will to fight, growing revolution in the nation, and an emerging crisis in Franco-German relations that commanded their attention in Europe.

Both sides wanted a negotiated peace; the great powers of Europe sought a role to further their own interests; but it was the United

States that became the mediator by common agreement. Operating behind the scene and in response to a secret Japanese initiative, President Theodore Roosevelt, who encouraged peace but did not covet the role of peacemaker, set the stage for mediation. Aside from humanitarian interests, Roosevelt had larger American interests to serve; namely, to protect the open door policy in China by maintaining a balance of power in the Far East.[16]

(b) Witte's negotiating plan

The Czar chose one of Russia's most eminent statesmen as first plenipotentiary, Sergius Witte. Respected and admired by the Japanese and renowned for his economic development activities in Russia's Far East, Witte had steadily opposed and criticized the policy that brought Russia into the war.[17]

Baron Rosen, a career diplomat and newly appointed Russian Ambassador at Washington, was second plenipotentiary.[18]

While aboard ship for the 6-day voyage from Cherbourg to New York, Witte had time to collect his thoughts and, as he said, to prepare himself for the "diplomatic duel" and determine his "plan of battle." He resolved to establish his negotiating tactics on the following five principles:

(1) not to show that Russia was "in the least anxious to make peace," and "to convey the impression" that consent to negotiate was "merely" because of the "universal desire" by all countries to see the war terminated;

(2) to conduct himself "as befitted the representative of the greatest empire on earth, undismayed by the fact that that mighty empire had become involved temporarily in a slight difficulty";

(3) knowing the "tremendous influence" of the press in the United States, to "show it every attention and to be accessible to all its representatives";

(4) to behave "with democratic simplicity and without a shadow of snobbishness, so as to win the sympathy of the Americans"; and

(5) not to show "any hostility" toward the Jews, in view of their "considerable influence" on the press and "on other aspects of American life, especially in New York"—which conduct, Witte added apparently with some truth, "was entirely in keeping with my opinion on the Jewish problem." [19]

(c) Negotiating sessions at Portsmouth

There were 12 sessions of the conference and a few private conversations between the principals, Baron Komura, Foreign Minister of Japan, and Witte. Both plenipotentiaries carried the major burden of negotiations; the associate plenipotentiaries played only a minor

---

[16] This section is based largely on, Dennett, Tyler. Roosevelt and the Russo-Japanese War. Garden City, N.Y., Doubleday, Page & Co., 1925, ch. IV and V.

[17] Robert M. Slusser, a specialist on Russian foreign policy, observed that Witte, as head of the Russian Ministry of Finance (1892–1903), "came to be the most powerful Russian Government official in determining the economic relations between Russia and other nations, overshadowing the ministers of foreign affairs and rivaling in prestige and actual power the Tsar himself." (Slusser, Robert M. The Role of the Foreign Minister, in, Lederer, Russian Foreign Policy, pp. 207–208.)

[18] Dennett. op. cit., p. 237.

[19] Witte, Sergius. The Memoirs of Count Witte. Translated and edited by Abraham Yarmolinsky. Garden City, N.Y., Doubleday, Page & Co., 1921, pp. 139–140.

role. For the Russians, the official language of the conference was French, the customary diplomatic language of the 19th century; for the Japanese, it was English.

The Japanese peace terms constituted 12 demands; 8 were disposed of in the first 8 sessions, marking a definite phase in the proceedings. "The last four sessions," observed Tyler Dennett in his study on the conference, "may be described almost as a new conference in which President Roosevelt had become, though not actually present, a dictator." [20] Thus, as Baron Rosen noted, having at first dealt with the "contentious matters of minor importance" and disposed of them to "mutual satisfaction," the conference settled down to the central question that threatened to break it up: Sakhalin and war indemnity. [21]

Briefly, the Japanese, in desperate financial straits, insisted on what was believed to be an extraordinarily excessive monetary indemnity of $700 million to cover their war costs. They also demanded the island of Sakhalin. (Under Japanese-Russian condominium from 1855, Sakhalin had become entirely Russian in 1875; during the war the Japanese had occupied nearly all of it with their military forces.) The Russians stubbornly refused both Japanese demands.

At a critical point in the conference, Roosevelt appealed directly to the Czar for concessions. He argued firmly but persuasively, suggesting a division of Sakhalin with some compensation to the Japanese. He urged Kaiser Wilhelm of Germany to bring pressure to bear on his close friend, the Czar. In a spirit of impartiality, Roosevelt also warned the Japanese in a similarly stern but persuasive and friendly manner against insisting upon their unwarranted demands of indemnity and appealed in a flattering way to their sense of nobility and magnanimity. [22]

After days of exhausting debates over various formulas intended to resolve the indemnity-Sakhalin question, the conference reached a clearly critical point on August 29. Roosevelt was to save the day by his successful behind-the-scene persuasion of the Japanese to accept a settlement along the lines he had already suggested. [23] Witte had been ordered to break off negotiations on the 28th if the Japanese continued to demand indemnity. But he felt it would be a great mistake if he did not listen to the last Japanese proposal. In this session Witte assumed the offensive. He handed the Japanese a note in which Russia categorically refused to pay the demanded indemnity, but he softened this with an offer to cede southern Sakhalin on condition that the northern half remain in Russian possession without compensation. He warned, furthermore, that this was the final Russian concession. [24] Witte was certain that Komura would yield. [25]

Though Witte had told Komura before the session that this was "the last one and that the only thing left to them is either to accept or reject the final and irrevocable decision," the Japanese, nonetheless, seemed to be stunned, but in control. Ivan I. Korostovetz, Secretary to

[20] Dennett, op. cit., p. 243.
[21] Rosen, Baron. Forty Years of Diplomacy. London, George Allen & Unwin, 1922, v. 1, p. 269.
[22] For details, see Dennett, op cit., pp. 255–260.
[23] Bishop, Joseph Bucklin. Theodore Roosevelt and His Time. New York, Charles Scribner's, 1920. v. 1, pp. 411–412.
[24] Ibid., p. 260.
[25] Witte, op. cit., p. 159.

Witte and later Minister to China and Persia, described this very tense scene in his diary of the conference:

Absolute silence reigned for a few seconds. Witte, as usual, kept tearing up the paper that was lying beside him. Rosen smoked his cigarette. The Japanese continued to be enigmatic. At last Komura, in a well-controlled voice, said that the Japanese Government, having for its aim the restoration of peace and the bringing of the negotiations to a successful conclusion, expressed its consent to Russia's proposal to divide Sakhalin in two, without indemnity being paid. Witte calmly replied that the Japanese proposal was accepted and that the line of demarcation on Sakhalin would be reckoned the fiftieth degree.[26]

On this basis the Treaty of Portsmouth was signed by Witte and Komura on September 5, 1905, at 3:50 p.m. in the Conference Room at the Portsmouth Navy Yard. The Russo-Japanese war came to an end.[27]

(d) Witte's performance as Russia's negotiator

Witte's success as a diplomat and negotiator can best be measured against the obstacles he faced and how well he overcame them. The obstacles were formidable: Russia had lost the war; and public opinion in the United States, sponsor of the mediation, strongly favored the Japanese. American opinion of the Russisans had taken a radically downward turn in the decades following the Civil War. At Portsmouth, therefore, Witte had to negotiate from a position of weakness. For the Russians, Portsmouth was another exercise in defensive diplomacy. But Witte made the most of a bad situation and succeeded in turning a military defeat into a diplomatic victory. For this achievement he was awarded the title "Count" by a grateful Czar, and apparently given the plenipotentiary's emolument of 15,000 rubles.

In many respects, Witte's plan for negotiation was brilliantly conceived and executed. "I believe I owe my diplomatic success partly to that program," he later wrote, and with much truth.[28] He understood, first of all, the importance of winning over the press as the principal way of changing opinion of Russia; and he understood also the relationship of this strategy to a successful negotiation. Witte went to great lengths, therefore, in achieving this purpose, even to the point of engaging Dr. E. J. Dillon, a prominent English correspondent posted in St. Petersburg, as a publicity agent, and in seeking the presence of the press at the negotiating sessions. The Japanese, who had little public relations sense, objected, as Witte felt they would, and thus gave him an advantage; a system of press releases was subsequently devised. The press was unhappy.[29] Ironically, Witte had apparently never been to America before, and much to his embarrassment he could

---

[26] Korostovetz, Ivan I. Pre-War Diplomacy: The Russo-Japanese Problem. Diary of Korostovetz. London, British Periodicals Ltd., 1920, p. 108.

Witte was not quite so cool and composed as Korostovetz suggested. An Associated Press dispatch of the event described the reception given Witte on the occasion of the news that agreement was reached and then went on to describe his state of fatigue from the prolonged negotiations:

"The Associated Press correspondent accompanied Mr. Witte to his room. The ambassador had been quite overcome by the great ovation he had received and the intense strain he had been under. He threw himself into his armchair and after a few minutes to pull himself together he began to speak slowly and deliberately, almost as if he were talking to himself.

" 'It seems incredible,' he said. 'I do not believe that any other man in my place would have dared to hope for the possibility of peace on the conditions to which we have just agreed. From all sides, from President Roosevelt down to my own friends in Russia, I received up to the last moment, even this morning, urgent representations that something should be paid to Japan.' At this point Mr. Witte, who was still labouring under excitement, again almost lost control of himself."

(Quoted in, Dennett, Roosevelt and Russo-Japanese War, p. 262.)

[27] Rosen, op. cit., pp. 271–272.
[28] Witte, op. cit., p. 140.
[29] Ibid, pp. 141 and 146.

not speak English; while Komura was Harvard-educated, proficient in English, and a long-time resident with first-hand knowledge of this country. But, as Dennett noted, Japanese public relations "suffered an inglorious defeat at Portsmouth." [30]

Witte also sought to influence public opinion through direct contact with the American people. His memoirs record the fact that he went out of his way to assuage the Jewish community in New York which at that time had deep grievances against the Russian Government in the wake of the pogroms. Moreover, he made seemingly endless goodwill gestures, at any opportunity, in his contacts with the public (autographs, posing for pictures, kissing children, et cetera, much in the style of the American politician.[31]

Again, his purpose was mainly to influence opinion. Before returning to Russia, Witte significantly made it a point to visit Mount Vernon where he paid his respects at Washington's grave and planted a tree on the grounds, as was the practice then with visiting statesmen; he visited the Capitol, both Houses of Congress, the White House, the Library of Congress, toured New York City and also reviewed the cadets at West Point in a dress parade.[32]

In his personal behavior Witte did not suddenly become a "born again" democrat, though he later evinced some reformist tendencies. Rather, his memoirs reflect the spirit of a hypercritical, pompous, arrogant European aristocrat who looked down upon the American masses with great distain. Dennett noted that, "Witte had that supercilious contempt for America which was so common in the courts of the Continent and was especially marked in Russia." [33] Furthermore, much of his benign and appealing behavior was calculated posturing; as he himself admitted: "This behavior was a heavy strain on me as all acting is to the unaccustomed, but it surely was worth the trouble." [34] But, as a diplomat, Witte understood the requirements of his task and the diversity of his role; he conducted himself accordingly. Most surely De Callières would have approved.

In general, therefore, Witte appears to have made a great impact upon the press, and no doubt he had done much to alter public opinion, though perhaps not to the extent that he claimed.[35]

---

[30] Dennett, op. cit. p. 239.

[31] While at Mount Vernon, Korostovetz recorded this incident : "On passing a family party sitting on a bench Witte stopped and kissed one of the children—this is the second time to-day that he has done it. He is evidently fishing for popularity." (Korostovetz, op. cit., pp. 140–141.)

[32] While at Mount Vernon, Witte was told in response to his inquiry that descendants of Washington were still living but that they were "people of no importance." Witte remarked : "The name of Washington is so famous that it requires nothing else to distinguish it." (Ibid., p. 140.)

[33] Ibid., p. 238.

[34] Witte, op. cit., p. 142.)

[35] Witte wrote: "* * * American public opinion, upon the whole, was on our enemy's side. Such was the situation which I found on my arrival in the United States. Anticipating upon the current of events. I may say that I succeeded in swerving American public opinion over to us." (Ibid., p. 140.) Thomas A. Bailey, an American diplomatic historian qualified this judgment : "There was undoubtedly some swing, but to the very end of the conference a substantial majority of the American newspapers were still pro-Japanese.' (Bailey Thomas A., America Faces Russia : Russian-American Relations From Early Times to Our Day. Ithica, N.Y., Cornell University Press, 1950, p. 202.)

Craig appears to have struck a balance when he observed : "The conduct of the negotiations by Witte and Rosen was marked by the same attention to public opinion that had guided Orlov's conduct in 1856 ; and, thanks to adroit management of the press, an initially pro-Japanese public sentiment in the United States had shifted so far by the end of the conference that the announcement by the Russian delegates that they had been absolved from payment of any indemnity was greeted with satisfaction by the crowd assembled outside the conference hall. In the negotiations proper, the Russians made the most of the Japanese mistake of posing excessive demands and succeeded in making them appear greedy even to themselves, with results beneficial to Russia." (Craig, Techniques of Negotiation, pp. 360–361.)

So impressed was Witte with his performance that he seriously considered a cross-country, good will tour, encouraged by Washington, to expand the gains made at Portsmouth; but an equivocal reaction from the Czar and concern for court intrigues during his absence that might be damaging to his career changed his mind.[36]

In the conference itself Witte displayed many of the high qualities associated with the old diplomacy of Eurpoe. While he was not a professional diplomat, he did reflect many of the profession's positive values and much of the 19th century diplomatic style. Still, before the negotiations began, he professed not to pay "a meticulous regard" to "antiquated diplomatic precedents and customs" but was resolved to be guided by "prevailing circumstances" and the "dictates of common sense" in furthering Russia's interests.[37]

In many respects Witte was a transition-type diplomat, one who adhered to the form and style of the old diplomacy, but introduced elements of the new: He set aside some of the excessive conventionalities and burdensome traditions of the old diplomacy in negotiations, while seeking to link public opinion with the purposes of negotiations. This was evident in his appeal to "American good sense and public opinion," as Korostovetz observed, an approach that Count Cassini, former Russian Ambassador to the United States, found exceptional, even reprehensible, to a professional diplomat.[38]

Armed with full power and authority from his government to conclude a treaty, Witte demonstrated remarkable independence as demanded by the needs and tactics of the moment; yet he kept in close touch by cable with his superiors in St. Petersburg and carefully stayed within the negotiating framework set down by them. He defended his country's interests with skill and resolution. Yet, he was sufficiently flexible to realize that a concession had to be made on Sakhalin. He was attentive to matters of precedence, to procedures in negotiation, and to planning a negotiating strategy well in advance. He maintained an outward spirit of confidence in Russian power and capabilities, while being careful not to betray the true weakness of his negotiating position. Courtesy and consideration marked his relation with the Japanese delegation, and so congenial had the negotiating environment become at one point that Witte, hoping for an outcome in the conference favorable to the Russians, intimated the possibility of an alliance.[39]

---

[36] Witte, op. cit., pp. 164–165.

[37] Korostovetz made this further observation on Witte's skill as a negotiator: "We, his assistants, were astonished to observe how easily he, who had no professional training in diplomacy, managed to assume the role of a diplomat, bringing to the fulfillment of his high office presence of mind, proficiency and adaptability to conditions which were more or less foreign to him." (Korostovetz, op. cit., p. 8.)

[38] Korostovetz described his meeting with Cassini in Paris after the Conference: "He is a man of great intelligence and full of wit, though perhaps a little too cynical in his appreciation of human nature. When at Washington he was unable to appraise the democratic spirit of the Americans and adapt himself to their psychology, associating chiefly with the chosen 'four hundred' of society. That is perhaps why he never enjoyed much popularity. Cassini was interested to know the tactics of Witte during the Conference and seemed astonished when I told him that Witte simply appealed to American good sense and public opinion. Cassini himself ascribed Witte's success to his knowledge of the questions set before him and to his not being hampered by diplomatic conventionalities and traditions, and above all, by the interference of the Foreign Office and of Petersburg red tape. A professional diplomat, he thought, would never have permitted publicity of negotiations, and especially in the face of Japanese opposition." (Ibid., pp. 153–154).

[39] Dennett, op. cit., pp. 246–247. Korostovetz made this observation on Witte's relationship with the Japanese delegation: "Owing to his tactfulness and sincerity, the cold distrust of the Japanese Delegates soon disappeared, and our opponents began to manifest that spirit of obliging courtesy which is customary with the Japanese. This certainly made the negotiations easier." (Korostovetz, op. cit., p. 9.)

A clue to Witte's attitude toward the Japanese was his comment to Korostovetz prior to their departure for America: "We must reestablish good relations with Japan, and try to regain the confidence of the world by a sound policy." [40] For Witte seemed to approach problems of international relations from the perspective of economic development rather than from that of sanctions by the sword; he seemed to perceive the need for establishing friendly relations with Japan as a means for protecting and building Russia's economic as well as political position in the Far East.

Witte was not, however, without his shortcomings at the conference. He did not establish a good rapport with Roosevelt, but Roosevelt's uncongenial attitude toward the Russians did little to encourage it. Witte, himself, described their relationship as "not particularly harmonious or cordial," noting that Roosevelt found him "intractable." [41]

In reality, Roosevelt found him a good deal more than that. In a confidential appraisal, Roosevelt gave high praise to Witte for his positive and humane attitude toward reform in Russia and emphasized that he was probably "the best man that Russia could have at the head of her affairs at present, and probably too good a man for the grand dukes to be willing to stand him." But in a more sharply critical and acerbic vein, the President continued:

He interested me. I cannot say that I liked him, for I thought his bragging and bluster not only foolish but shockingly vulgar when compared with the gentlemanly self-respecting self-restraint of the Japanese. Moreover, he struck me as a very selfish man, totally without high ideals.[42]

Also, Korostovetz revealed that Witte was not always cool and detached, as befits a good negotiator, and accordingly through body language must have communicated negative signals to the Japanese. "When Witte is nervous," wrote Korostovetz, "he begins to fidget on his chair, crosses his legs and twists his foot about." On the other hand, Komura was "cooler" and would communicate his displeasure "by the force with which he knocks the ash off his cigarette, hitting the table and speaking more shortly and abruptly." [43]

Moreover, Witte could often lose points in exchanges because his method of argument was "more emotional and based on inspiration," while that of Komura's was a "more studied manner, backed by solid arguments." [44]

Still, Witte's overall performance as a diplomat and negotiator was impressive, and the judgment of Korostovetz seems reasonable and probably correct. "Summing up Witte's activities in America,"

[40] Ibid., p. 12.
[41] Witte, op. cit., p. 66. This was not, perhaps, entirely Witte's fault. Roosevelt was "vastly annoyed" at the Russians for not conceding to the Japanese, wrote Bailey, and "growled that the Russians were unable to make war and incompetent to make peace. With characteristic intemperance he called them 'hopeless creatures' who acted with 'Chinese or Byzantine folly,' and who lied so much that they 'got into the dangerous position of lying to themselves.' They were 'quibblers,' 'stupid,' 'unrealistic,' 'sly,' 'evasive,' 'insecure,' 'treacherous,' 'double dealing,' 'shuffling,' and 'corrupt.' Even Czar Nicholas II, to whom Roosevelt appealed directly, was 'a preposterous little creature.'" (Bailey, America Faces Russia, pp. 202–203.)
[42] A letter from Roosevelt to Sir George Otto Trevelyan, Sept. 12, 1905. Quoted in Bishop, op. cit., p. 418–419. Roosevelt s contempt for the Russians was expressed elsewhere in the letter when he compared the Japanese and Russian. He commended the Japanese for their truthfulness, their independence of mind, and ability to "act together." Whereas, in contrast, "the Russians all pulled against one another, rarely knew their own minds, lied so to others that they finally got into the dangerous position of lying to themselves, and showed a most unhealthy and widespread corruption and selfishness."
[43] Korostovetz, op. cit., p. 82.
[44] Ibid., p. 78.

he wrote, "one may say that he not only showed himself an excellent diplomat, but also a Russian patriot in the highest sense of the word, and, notwithstanding the more or less unfavorable conditions in which Russia was then placed, he succeeded in obtaining the best possible results." [45]

On the whole, the negotiations at Portsmouth displayed the virtues of the old diplomacy at its best, particularly the attention given to its larger purposes and goals, its form and style. But Witte introduced new elements in his negotiating strategy that were to become virtually common practice in the new diplomacy. Hence, the judgment of Portsmouth as an example of 19th century diplomacy in transition.

What seems to emerge from the negotiations at Portsmouth is a sense of civility, delicacy, humanity, yet a sternness in defense of vital interests on both sides, but most of all, a respect for diplomatic forms and a commitment to the ultimate purpose of diplomacy; namely, to achieve and maintain peace. Baron Rosen saw all the participants and government leaders involved in this conference as being "guided solely by the dictates of reason and of statesmanship." [46] Perhaps, he best expressed its ultimate achievement when, writing 3 years after the Versailles Conference ending World War I, he gave this evaluation of Portsmouth:

Little did the signatories of the Treaty of Portsmouth dream at the time that they had affixed their names to an instrument which, in all probability, will go down in history as an act marking the close of an era when it was still possible to terminate a great war between leading nations by a peace leaving the door wide open for a reestablishment of friendly relations between them.[47]

D. TRADITIONALISM AFFIRMED

By the eve of world war and revolution, the Russian experience in diplomacy had gone through many stages, from the primitivism of the early years to the traditionalism of modern 19th century European diplomacy, and even to suggesting elements of the new 20th century diplomacy. If the 19th century experience shows anything, it is the affirmation of traditionalism in Russian diplomacy. For Russian diplomats had shown themselves to be very much a part of the European community of diplomats, bound by common values, a common international political culture, and a unifying European cosmopolitanism.

The conduct of Russian diplomacy in the 19th century had much to be commended. As Craig concluded, "all in all," it was marked "by competence and occasionally by brilliance, and, especially in conference negotiation." Russian diplomatists, he said, had shown "a special talent for making the most of bad cases." Still, there was "nothing particularly original or distinctive about Russian practice." "It was reserved for the Soviet regime," Craig concluded, "to devise new techniques of negotiation, while at the same time challenging the patience and ingenuity of the West by the way in which it adapted the traditional techniques to its own purposes." [48]

[45] Ibid., p. 10.
[46] Rosen, op. cit., p. 273.
[47] Ibid., p. 278.
[48] Craig, Techniques of Negotiation, p. 361.

CHAPTER III—FROM REVOLUTION TO "UNITED FRONT" WITH CHICHERIN AND LITVINOV IN THE 1920'S AND 1930'S

I will issue a few revolutionary proclamations to the peoples of the world and then shut up shop.
> —*Trotsky, first Commissar of Foreign Affairs, 1917–18.*

* * * G. V. Chicherin and his assistants built a large and efficient commissariat which closely paralleled the British Foreign Office or the Quai d'Orsay in form and function. The construction of a dedicated and able foreign service, whose representatives could hold their own in negotiations with the most experienced European diplomats, must be ranked as one of the greatest accomplishments of the revolutionary regime.
> —*Teddy J. Uldricks, June 1977.*

* * * the late Foreign Commissar [Litvinov] does have claim to two things of lasting significance: His ideas and his acumen as a diplomat.
> —*Henry L. Roberts, 1953.*

The Great Terror accomplished the near total destruction of that talented and urbane corps of diplomats organized under Commissars Chicherin and Litvinov. The new Ministry of Foreign Affairs which emerged from the purges differed radically from its predecessor in the nature of the personnel, in the style of the diplomacy and in their relationship to the political leadership of the state.
> —*Teddy J. Uldricks, 1979.*

I. THE NEW DIPLOMACY

A. Changing International Environment

World War I had brought about far-reaching changes in international relations and in the conduct of diplomacy. The old imperial systems of continental Europe collapsed under the impact of war, revolution, and the rising forces of democracy. The Bolsheviks took over in Russia; and professing a new revolutionary doctrine of social change that promised the "liberation" of the masses, they set out to transform Russia and the world by revolutionary means into a new totalitarian order.

Elsewhere in Europe new states emerged, spurred on by the Wilsonian democratic principle of self-determination, while the older established democracies of the West found strength and sustenance in their war victory and in the vitalization of democratic principles, and new hope and expectation in the promise of the League of Nations.

In brief, the war created a new distribution of power and a new spirit of internationalism; in so doing, it imposed new requirements on the evolving diplomatic method.

B. Undermining of the Old Diplomacy

1. IMPACT OF WORLD WAR I

World War I discredited the old diplomacy. This was perhaps one of the most significant diplomatic results of the war. Much of the blame for the war was placed upon secret diplomacy, and the professional diplomat could not avoid the stigma of responsibility.[1]

A counterpoint to secret diplomacy was Wilson's injunction of "Open Covenants Openly Arrived at" in his Fourteen Points. The central theme of Wilson's egalitarianism applied internationally was the democratization of diplomacy. The impact of this distrust upon diplomacy was most evident in the role of the diplomat; he was looked upon with suspicion, not with trust and confidence. As a member of the British House of Commons somewhat prophetically said in March 1918: "The old Ambassadorial system has failed and is discredited in the eyes of most people. After the war, the old diplomacy of Court and upper classes will be in the eyes of most people, obsolete and inadequate."[2]

Thus, the war exposed perhaps the most serious weakness of the old diplomacy; namely, unwarranted secrecy, a weakness that even Nicolson, a devout believer in the old diplomacy, was compelled to admit.

This habit of secretiveness was a major factor in its downfall.[3]

2. POLITICAL, ECONOMIC, AND TECHNOLOGICAL CAUSES

More subtle were the deeper political, economic, and technological factors that gradually undermined 19th century diplomacy. The spread of democracy and the growing belief in the need for democratic control of foreign policy created new requirements that transformed the structure, style, and values of diplomacy. Institutions, once rigidly adapted to the absolutism of another era, had to give way and meet the new and changing needs of emerging democratic societies. (Witte understood how these changing forces affected the United States, particularly the role of public opinion, and adapted himself to it; hence his success.) Diplomacy was no longer the strict domain of the king and his ambassadors, but rather that of elected officials and the popular constituencies from which they were elected. Accordingly, the idea of secrecy and the exclusive role of the diplomat had to be revised. Diplomats had to account for their diplomacy. In the process a new form of diplomatic method emerged.[4]

The spread of colonialism also contributed to the downfall of the old diplomacy. Rivalries among European nations became magnified and globalized with the spread of imperialism into Asia and

---

[1] Craig and Gilbert, Diplomats, p. 6.
[2] Quoted in, Pearson, Diplomacy in the Nuclear Age, p. 7.
[3] As late as 1914, Nicolson noted, the French Assembly was unaware of the secret clauses in the Franco-Russian Alliance; and Sir Edward Grey, "a man of scrupulous integrity," saw no wrong in concealing from the British Cabinet the exact nature of military arrangements reached between the French and British General Staffs. "Confidential negotiations that lead to secret pledges," he declared, "are worse even than the televised diplomacy that we enjoy today." (Nicolson, Evolution of Diplomatic Method, pp. 77-78.)
[4] Craig and Gilbert, Diplomats, p. 5.

Africa. A balance of power that once could be managed in a Concert of Europe was, in Nicolson's words, "complicated and compromised by new and uncontrolled appetites, by much flagrant hypocrisy, by fresh jealousies and suspicions, and by the perversion * * * of the doctrine of a just equilibrium into a conspiracy for the sharing out of loot." [5] Forces, spurred on by colonialism, got out of control, disrupted the balance of power, and produced a devastating world war in which the old diplomacy was a prime loser.

Economic and technological change produced by the industrial and communications revolutions also had a part in transforming 19th century diplomacy. The internationalization of business imposed new requirements on representatives abroad so that the diplomat, whose functions had once been largely political, had to compete with specialists in trade and economics.[6] Finally, the revolution in communications created another competitor for the diplomat; namely, the foreign office and its head. No longer was the Ambassador free to carry out instructions with virtually complete independence—as was the case of Townsend Harris, the first U.S. Minister to Japan, who in time with patience, persistence, skill, and alone, achieved a brilliant diplomatic success by negotiating a treaty that established Japanese-American relations on a sound basis. The effect of the revolution in communications was to reduce still further the Ambassador's role in diplomacy.[7]

C. NEW DIRECTIONS OF DIPLOMACY

1. A NEW INTERNATIONALISM

Diplomacy in the aftermath of World War I bore the marks of Wilsonian egalitarianism. A new era opened up, professing a new faith, the democratization of diplomacy. Believers held that the ideas and conduct of internal affairs in a liberal democracy could be applied to external affairs.[8] Harking back to the rationalism and functionalism of Grotius, this new era stressed a diplomacy by conference according to the rules of democratic government within a new internationalism that was symbolized by the League of Nations.

Europe remained the center of international politics, as the United States withdrew into isolationism. The Versailles system prevailed as a sort of one-sided concert of victorious European powers designed to contain Germany and by so doing maintain the peace. Germany and Russia, the troublemakers of Europe, were the outsiders.

2. ROLE OF DIPLOMAT

The role of the diplomat was substantially changed as the diplomacy of Europe entered this era of new directions. Reduced in importance by forces beyond his control, the diplomat seemed to become riveted to a regime of conference diplomacy and was inexorably faced with the institutional problem of the ascendancy of the foreign office and central government in the foreign policy process. Compared to his

---

[5] Nicolson, Evolution of Diplomatic Method, p. 80.
[6] Craig and Gilbert, Diplomats, pp. 4–5.
[7] Nicolson, Evolution of Diplomatic Method, pp. 81–82.
[8] Ibid., p. 84.

power and influence of former years, he probably came close to being what critics of the old diplomacy would call the antiquated, superfluous man.

Moreover, secrecy, the bane of the old diplomacy, did not disappear, and suspicions of the diplomat and diplomacy lingered on in the popular mind. Added to this burden was the popular impression that the diplomat was something of an anachronism, forming part of a social tradition that belonged to another age.[9]

Still, Jules Cambon, the noted French diplomatist, cautioned that the changes brought about by the new diplomacy were only superficial and that the essential functions and purposes of diplomacy remained. He believed that:

Expressions such as "old diplomacy" and "new diplomacy" bear no relation to reality. It is the outward form,—if you like, the "adornments"—of diplomacy that are undergoing a change. The substance must remain the same, since human nature is unalterable; since there exists no other method of regulating international differences; and since the best instrument at the disposal of a Government wishing to persuade another Government will always remain the spoken words of a decent man. * * *[10]

Implied in what Cambon was saying seemed to be that the specific role of the ambassador, as it was known in times of classical diplomacy, may have been altered, but the essential tasks of diplomacy remained. What was occurring, therefore, was not a diminution of diplomacy but rather an increasing shift of the burdens of diplomacy from the ambassador to other centers of power and decision in the home government.

---

[9] Craig and Gilbert, Diplomats, pp. 6–7.
[10] Quoted in, Nicolson, Evolution of Diplomatic Method, pp. 83–84. Nicolson expanded on the important role of the resident ambassador despite external changes brought about in the modern era. (See pp. 82–83.)

II. IMPACT OF BOLSHEVIK REVOLUTION ON RUSSIAN DIPLOMACY

A. Diplomacy Ideologized and Revolutionized

1. GESTATION OF SOCIALIST DIPLOMACY

Neither the old nor the new diplomacy had any immediate appeal to the Bolsheviks. In the early days of the revolution they cared nothing at all for the values, forms and procedures or any of the accepted norms of formal diplomacy. They had revolutionary goals conceived in an irrepressible ideological struggle between world capitalism and communism which were simply to transform the international social order using socialist Russia as the starting point. The unity of the masses under the banner of proletarian revolution led by the Bolsheviks precluded the use of diplomacy and its traditional methods. For them, diplomacy was part of the capitalist superstructure, like the nation-state. Revolutionaries would know how to deal with themselves as the advanced national states perished in the upsurging world revolution. What was needed was only the means to stimulate the lethargic masses of Europe and their dependencies abroad and to spread and even complete the world revolution.[1]

2. BOLSHEVIK DECREE OF PEACE, NOVEMBER 8, 1917 AND TROTSKY'S DICTUM

Accordingly, the Bolshevik regime in Russia began life on the international scene by abolishing diplomacy. In effect, it declared that it was withdrawing Russia from the Western diplomatic community; that it intended to repudiate all legal ties established by the Czarist Government with other nations; and that it would no longer conform to the rules and procedures then existing in international relations. Soviet purposes were made clear in the Bolshevik Decree on Peace, passed by the second All-Russian Congress of Soviets on November 8, 1917, and by Trotsky's statement 2 weeks later on the occasion of publishing the secret treaties. Caught up in the highly charged emotion of the revolution, he proclaimed the abolition of the old diplomacy and "its intrigues, codes, and lies" and promised the inauguration of an "honest, popular, truly democratic foreign policy." Henceforth, the decree stated, negotiations would be conducted "absolutely openly before the entire people." It was implied that negotiations between governments would be minimal, particularly after the restora-

---

[1] Von Laue, Theodore H. Soviet Diplomacy: G. V. Chicherin, Peoples Commissar for Foreign Affairs, 1918–20, in Craig and Gilbert, Diplomats, pp. 235–236. Teddy J. Uldricks, a student of the Soviet Foreign Office, wrote: "In the early days of the Soviet regime, the very conception of 'Bolshevik diplomacy' seemed impossible to both friend and foe of the revolution. Could bomb-throwing revolutionaries suddenly don striped pants and sit down to tea with the representatives of imperialism?" (Uldricks, Teddy J. The Soviet Diplomatic Corps in the Cicerin [Chicherin] Era. Jahrbucher fur Geschichte Ost Europas, 23, No. 2, 1975, p. 213.)

tion of peace, and that the Bolshevik regime, as a people's government, would direct its appeals and messages to all peoples rather than to the rulers.[2]

3. ABOLITION OF CZARIST DIPLOMATIC APPARATUS

With diplomacy thus abolished, the old Russian diplomatic apparatus was rendered unnecessary. The Soviet Foreign Office, named the Peoples Commissariat of Foreign Affairs (the acronym in Russian, Narkomindel), was intended to be little more than an agency for disseminating propaganda and the publication of the secret treaties. Trotsky, the first head, described its functions when responding to an inquiry from a Bolshevik colleague about the function of diplomacy in a Communist state: "I will issue a few revolutionary proclamations to the peoples of the world and then shut up shop." [3]

Selection of personnel was done very simply. Upon Trotsky's arrival to take over the Foreign Office, he ordered the entire staff to assemble and announced to them curtly: "Those for us go to the left, those against us go to the right." The bureaucrats, after deliberating, went to the right; only the "menials" greeted Trotsky with a handshake. Shortly thereafter all Foreign Office personnel overseas were recalled or repudiated. Within 2 months the Foreign Office numbered about 200, including the revolutionary guards from the Siemens-Schuckert works and a nearby pipe-rolling mill. Style and organization were wanting in that chaotic beginning; the mood and the mode were revolutionary. Even after Chicherin's arrival, wrote Theodore H. Von Laue, an authority on Soviet diplomacy, "the organization and routine of the new People's Commissariat reflected for some time the shiftlessness of that hectic phase of Soviet rule." [4]

B. NEGOTIATING AT BREST-LITOVSK

1. AN INITIATION IN BOLSHEVIK NEGOTIATING TACTICS

The West had its initial exposure to the new socialist diplomatic style, first in Trotsky's barrage of revolutionary appeals to the peoples of the belligerent nations and to the subject nationalities of the East, and then more dramatically in the unorthodox Bolshevik tactics at the peace conference at Brest-Litovsk in the winter of 1917–18.

Formally, the conference was intended to establish peace between the Bolshevik state and the Central Powers. It did achieve this purpose, but in a manner unlike any such conference held in the past; for the Bolshevik delegates violated all approved procedure and protocol. Their predecessors Orlov, Shuvalov, and Witte came to their conferences as representatives of a defeated power, seeking the best terms in a bad situation. Not the Bolsheviks. They did not want to negotiate a peace settlement at all; rather they wanted to negotiate for time, time to permit the upsurge of revolution abroad. Hence their demand for a "peace without annexations and indemnities"—ludicrously excessive,

---

[2] Craig, Techniques of Negotiation, p. 361.
[3] Uldricks, Soviet Diplomatic Corps in Cicerin Era, p. 214. Trotsky accepted the post because, as he said, "I want more leisure for party affairs."
[4] Von Laue, Soviet Diplomacy Under Chicherin, p. 248.

perhaps, given the military conditions at that time. But as Trotsky wrote later, "We began peace negotiations in the hope of arousing the workmen's parties of Germany and Austria-Hungary as well as those of the Entente countries. For this reason we were obliged to delay as long as possible to give the European workmen time to understand the main fact of the Soviet revolution itself and particularly its peace policy." [5]

Thus, the Bolshevik delegation rejected the traditional behavior of negotiations. They negotiated as revolutionaries, directing their speeches not to their negotiating adversaries across the table but to the revolutionary working classes across their borders to Central and Western Europe.

2. ASPECTS OF BOLSHEVIK REVOLUTIONARY BEHAVIOR

The formal aspects of the conference and its protocol bore the clear marks of the new Bolshevik approach to diplomacy. After arriving at Brest, Trotsky refused to observe any of the superficial, but, nonetheless, meaningful amenities of the old diplomacy. In the first place, the Bolshevik delegation was hardly the kind that a European great power would have put into the field as negotiators. It consisted of a representation of Bolshevik leaders in addition to a worker, sailor, soldier, and a peasant. Trotsky set the radically changed mode of behavior, insisting that the delegation dine alone, rejecting all invitations from their hosts, dispensing with the forms of courtesy customary in diplomatic intercourse, and even going to the extent of deleting the word "friendship" from the preamble to the draft treaty. "Such declarations," Trotsky said on this point, "copied from one diplomatic document into another, have never yet characterized the real relations between states." But Trotsky had a purpose in this seemingly petty behavior. Such tactics were designed to establish the Bolshevik reputation for commonsense, love of truth, and plain speaking that presumably would appeal to the masses everywhere. [6]

The Bolshevik negotiating tactic of delay had its effect, notably in setting the pattern of the negotiation on Soviet terms—a tribute to their resourcefulness and tactical elasticity. "Why should we submit to the Russian style?" exclaimed German General Hoffmann in an angry outburst. Soviet cunctator tactics were, however, only momentarily successful; for increasing German pressure (they launched a new military offensive at midpoint in the negotiations) and the failure of the expected revolution abroad, forced them to accept the punitive territorial settlement they had hoped to avoid. Trotsky's efforts to escape this end by improvising the formula "no war, no peace"—the cessation of hostilities without a peace treaty—startled the other negotiators, and Hoffmann's cry, "Unheard of!" convulsed the Bolshevik delegates. But Trotsky's was an empty gesture that could neither deflect the overwhelming reality of German military power nor change the German decision to impose extremely harsh peace terms on the young Bolshevik state. [7] The Bolsheviks learned their first lesson

---

[5] Craig, Techniques of Negotiation, p. 362.
[6] Ibid., p. 363.
[7] Ibid., p. 363.

in diplomacy, that one cannot win at the conference table what was lost on the battlefield.

C. Trotsky's Legacy of Revolutionary Diplomacy

Trotsky's performance at Brest-Litovsk dramatized the new Bolshevik approach to diplomacy and in many ways set the mold for the future. This approach was a radical departure from both the old and the new as it was then taking shape; it was, as Nicolson said, "something else." It ignored the premises and the values, the style and the ethics of traditional European diplomacy and declared its own based on a uniquely designed revolutionary Marxist-Leninist ideology. It set for itself revolution as a primary goal and linked this ultimate purpose to a radical negotiating style. In brief, it made diplomacy an instrument of revolution, and negotiations one more weapon in the arsenal of the class struggle. Trotsky symbolized this new revolutionary era of Socialist diplomacy by closing shop, as he said, on the old, and looking to the future for the new in an upsurge of world revolution.

III. CHICHERIN IN COMMAND

A. CHICHERIN: ARISTOCRAT, DIPLOMAT, AND REVOLUTIONARY

1. SHIFT TOWARD TRADITIONAL DIPLOMACY

Defeat at Brest-Litovsk; disillusionment with the failure of revolution abroad; fear generated by the unexpected recovery and consolidation of the bourgeois governments in Europe after 1918; the isolation of a Soviet Russia weakened by war, revolution, and civil war, making it vulnerable to what was perceived as the capitalist encirclement"; an awareness of economic interdependence as a necessity for Russian recovery—all of these factors forced the Soviet leaders to reassess their utopian goals for the immediate future pushing them further on in the timespan of history, to reevaluate their earlier repudiation of traditional diplomacy and withdrawal from the Western diplomatic community, and to reconsider a policy of engagement with the West.

Russia was to make its first great concession to reality: A shift from its overtly aggressive revolutionary mode to a defensive policy of engagement.

Trotsky, the theoretical revolutionary, now urged the resumption of normal relations with the other powers as a matter of practical policy.[1] But it was upon George V. Chicherin, aristocrat, diplomat, and revolutionary that fell the task of returning Soviet Russia to the European community and rebuilding the Russian diplomatic service along more traditional lines. In brief, Chicherin was to restore the disconnection between the diplomatic traditions of Imperial and Soviet Russia.

2. THE MAN AND HIS CAREER

Born into the aristocracy, Chicherin enjoyed all of its privileges and advantages—a degree from St. Petersburg University, a career in the government service, and the social amenities of his class. A diplomat in a family of diplomats, Chicherin could look back upon a solid and distinguished family tradition in diplomacy, virtually preordaining his future career. His father served as a counselor at the Paris Embassy, and an even more notable maternal grandfather was the Russian Ambassador at Vienna at the time of the Congress of Vienna.

But somewhere along the way, Chicherin developed a quest for social justice in a society where the needs were great. After 1904, the two lines of his interest, diplomacy and social justice, separated but to be rejoined in 1918. Resigning from the diplomatic service where he was an archivist and diplomatic scholar, Chicherin joined the Rus-

---

[1] Ibid., pp. 363–364.

sian Social Democratic Party. Within 3 years he assumed the important post of secretary of the party's foreign bureau, a clear indication
of his ability. During World War I, he pursued an active revolutionary
career, participating in various organizational and antiwar activities
abroad. After the Bolshevik Revolution, he was arrested and imprisoned in England as a Socialist propagandist, but was returned to
Russia in January 1918 in an exchange for the British Ambassador
to Russia, Sir George Buchanan. Immediately, Chicherin joined the
Bolshevik Party, and since he was the only Bolshevik with diplomatic
experience, in addition to having excellent linguistic abilities, Lenin
assigned him to the Foreign Office. Even before Trotsky resigned as its
head in March 1918, Chicherin had assumed control at the age of 45,
opening, as he later wrote, a new page of his life." [2]

As a person and a personality, Chicherin was considered something
of an oddity. A shy, timid little man with an intelligent and gentle
glance, negligent of dress, an aesthete and hypochondriac, he had little
of the outward sophisticated appearance usually associated with a
diplomat. Yet, he was a man above pettiness and party intrigue, and
as Von Laue observed, "almost too fragile for the rude hurly-burly of
Bolshevik politics." [3] Noted for his unorthodox methods of work and
particularly as a stickler for detail, he often turned the Foreign Office
into a state of confusion. Still, everyone who knew Chicherin respected
his abilities as a diplomat, particularly, as Von Laue noted, "his
brillant mind, his sharp repartee, and that amazing memory which
made foreign diplomats wince." [4]

B. Soviet Foreign Office and Diplomatic Service

1. REQUIREMENTS OF A NEW ERA

Chicherin would have ample opportunity to exercise his much respected diplomatic abilities; for the 1920's had placed a heavy burden
on Soviet diplomacy and its fledgling diplomats. Their overriding task
was to preserve Soviet power in a hostile world environment. As
representatives of the first Socialist state, Soviet diplomats had to
exploit with skill and persistence the fissures and blunders within the
imperialist camp in order to deflect what they perceived as the destructive onslaught of world capitalism. Self-protection was a first priority.
Buying time for the maturing of revolution in the West was for the
true believers another essential task. [5]

Still another was the need to use diplomacy defensively in a two-fold
way: To establish political and security arrangements with European
states; and to rebuild a weakened Russia by drawing upon the resources of the West through trade and technical assistance.

To accomplish these formidable goals required the services of an
educated, talented and highly professional diplomatic service. The
Soviet leaders realized this and accordingly set to work building one.
"The diplomatic service which emerged," wrote Teddy J. Uldricks,

---

[2] Von Laue, Soviet Diplomacy Under Chicherin, pp. 248–251.
[3] Ibid., p. 249.
[4] Ibid.
[5] Uldricks, Soviet Diplomatic Corps in Chicherin Era, p. 211.

a student of the Soviet diplomatic service, "was unique both among Soviet commissariats and among European foreign offices." [6]

2. BUILDING A NEW DIPLOMATIC SERVICE

The first generation of Soviet diplomats beginning with the Chicherin years was for the most part made up of revolutionary and cosmopolitan oriented members of the old Russian intelligentsia. "Despite a certain proletarian tendency at the beginning," wrote Boris Meissner, a West German specialist on Soviet diplomacy, "this group continued to set the tone for the foreign service." [7]

In his studies on the Soviet diplomatic service, Uldricks has brought together an impressive array of data that justified his conclusions with respect to its high quality. Suggestive is this selection that gives a limited but reasonably accurate profile. During the early years, the foreign office had drawn about 70 percent of its personnel from the middle classes and a significant 17 percent from the aristocracy. Workers and peasants made up only a minute fraction of 5 percent and 8 percent, respectively, of the service. [8]

In educational background, the Chicherin foreign service was, as Uldricks noted, "extraordinarily impressive." A third of the foreign office had studied in graduate or professional schools, and another third had received a college education. Degrees from Russian schools and leading universities in Europe and the United States in medicine, law, and the liberal arts, were quite common. [9]

These achievements can best be appreciated when compared to the educational standards of the party and the nation as a whole. Fully 50 percent of the general Russian population over the age of 8 was at that time illiterate. The Bolshevik Party itself was experiencing a steep decline in the overall educational level of its members, owing to severe war casualties and heavy recruiting among the proletariat and peasantry. [10] Clearly, the party leadership was making a great investment in the diplomatic service from its very small pool of educated members.

Thus, in the Chicherin years, the Soviets had succeeded in building an impressive diplomatic service, men from the czarist intelligentsia, well educated, competent in foreign languages, and at ease in foreign cultures having lived abroad. Like Chickerin himself many had that mixture of an aristocratic and revolutionary background, while others from the tsarist diplomatic service continued to serve as a patriotic duty. Uldricks made this significant appraisal:

Thus, the Soviet foreign service was called into being. By 1930, despite the Bolsheviks' initial distaste for the devious arts of bourgeois diplomacy and in spite of the almost total lack of experienced personnel, the Soviet Union possessed a fully functioning and reasonably effective Commissariat of Foreign Affairs as well as a large, able, and increasingly professional corps of diplomats. * * * The U.S.S.R. now possessed a foreign service capable of defending the country's interests with all the wiles of the diplomat's art. The Soviet state had put an extremely large amount of its limited talent resources into diplomatic

[6] Ibid., p. 215.
[7] Meissner, Boris. The Foreign Ministry and Foreign Service of the U.S.S.R., Aussenpolitik, v. 28, No. 1, 1977 :61.
[8] Uldricks, Teddy J. The Impact of the Great Purges on the People's Commissariat of Foreign Affairs. Slavic Review, vol. 36, June 1977 : 195.
[9] Uldricks, Soviet Diplomatic Corps in Chicherin Era, p. 195.
[10] Ibid., pp. 218–219.

work, thus reemphasizing the importance of traditional diplomacy to the Bolsheviks in the 1920's.[11]

3. SOVIET FOREIGN OFFICES: ORGANIZATION, POWER, AND CONFLICTING PURPOSES

The reversion to traditional diplomacy did not bring with it the aura of prestige as in tsarist days. The foreign office remained fairly low in the hierarchy of power. It never had the impact on Kremlin politics as the Politburo, party secretariat, secret police, and even the Gosplan. Chicherin was, after all, a former Menshevik, an early opponent of the Bolsheviks, and accordingly could never be wholly accepted by Bolshevik purists. He was, therefore, never a part of the inner circle of power; not until 1925 did he become a member of the party's Central Committee—still a comfortable distance from the center.[12]

By and large the foreign office reflected Chicherin's status. It was a low prestige institution, and in some respects it became a "dumping ground" for oppositionists, though this has been a disputed point.[13] Neither Lenin nor Stalin held the institution and its leader in high esteem. Von Laue described the attitude of the party leadership toward the foreign office as one of "tolerance because of a limited usefulness but not respect." [14]

Whatever the varying social and political hues of the foreign service personnel, there was little or no opportunity for real independence; the party was in firm control. The overwhelming majority of diplomats and higher officials in the central apparatus were party members

---

[11] Ibid., p. 223. Craig notes that a number of Western studies of diplomacy, including Sir Ernest Satow's, "Guide to Diplomatic Practice, and Jules Cambon's "Le Diplomate," were translated into Russian and used in training courses. (Craig, Totalitarian Approaches to Diplomatic Negotiation, p. 118.)
In summing up his profiles of the Soviet diplomatic corps during the Chicherin years, Uldricks said : "Veterans of the European socialist movement who were at ease in Western European languages and culture, and who were familiar with social and political conditions throughout Europe and North America, formed the core of this group. Almost all of these men were Communist Party members, but a significant minority had formerly belonged to other Russian revolutionary or reformist movements. Great Russians predominated among the group, but a number of Jews, Ukrainians, and other nationalists as well were to be found in the Soviet corps diplomatique. Although few of its members had any formal training in diplomacy, the educational level of the Narkomindel staff was probably higher than that of any other (nonacademic) government agency." (Uldricks, Soviet Diplomatic Corps in Chicherin Era, p. 223.)
[12] Ibid., pp. 219–220.
[13] Von Laue wrote : "In the years of Stalin's rise, assignment to the diplomatic service became a favorite method of isolating potential opponents, a practice which reflects again the relatively inferior position of diplomacy." (Von Laue, Soviet Diplomacy Under Chicherin, p. 257.) On the other hand, Uldricks contended : "A number of oppositionists saw service in the Narkomindel and it seems that several prominent Soviet political figures received diplomatic posts abroad as a means of eliminating them from domestic struggles. That much is certain. Suggesting that the Narkomindel was a hotbed of oppositional activity and intrigue, however, and that the principal role of the Commissariat was to serve as a 'dumping ground' for political casualties seems to stretch the argument beyond what the evidence will bear." (Uldricks, Soviet Diplomatic Corps in Chicherin Era, p. 221.)
[14] Von Laue, Soviet Diplomacy Under Chicherin, p. 256. Von Laue noted : "In many ways, an early uncomplimentary characterization of the Narkomindel as 'just a diplomatic chancellery attached to the Central Committee' stated the simple truth. And as a true clerk it was not necessarily admitted into the secret purposes of its masters." (p. 247) With respect to Chicherin's relationship with Lenin and Stalin. Von Laue wrote : "Even foreigners knew how much he depended upon Lenin in all major decisions. An early tiff with Stalin over the nationality question, in which he lost out, may have also shown him his powerlessness. His timidity toward the chief leaders increased with the years ; rarely did he dare to assert himself." (p. 247.) Lenin's private opinion of Chicherin was evident in a letter to Trotsky after Chicherin had suggested that substantial concessions be made at the Genoa Conference : "Send Chicherin at once to a sanitarium." (Ibid.)

under party discipline, and a number of the most prominent Bolsheviks were in the foreign office. Decisionmaking and control were thus
firmly in the hands of the central authority.[15]

The actual functions of Soviet diplomats were complicated by the
revolutionary arm of Soviet power that worked side-by-side with them
in overseas operations, the Communist International or Comintern.
This dicotomy of functions has remained a central problem in Soviet
diplomacy. Von Laue explained it this way:

> One can imagine the difficulties of Chicherin as Soviet Russia's chief diplomat
> in such a setting. The Soviet Foreign Office had lost the monopoly over the
> conduct of foreign relations. In the Comintern, it always had a jealous rival
> and one which was closer to the ears of its superiors. Traditionally, the Foreign
> Minister had always enjoyed a leading position in the government, and the
> Foreign Office was an honored branch of the government. There had been notable
> exceptions to the undisputed monopoly of foreign relations in the hands of
> Foreign Offices, but never had diplomacy fallen to such a humble and suspect
> position as it now did. In an avowedly revolutionary society, diplomacy was an
> anomaly, a standing contradiction to the essential spirit of the regime. Its
> imitation of the formalities practised by other states was—even while patently
> insincere—disconcerting and unpleasant to the hard-bitten professional revolu-
> tionaries who dominated the government.[16]

The incompatability of revolutionary and diplomatic purposes became readily apparent. Revolutionaries and diplomats resided in the
same Soviet foreign missions, and their relations were said to be "often
stormy." As Von Laue noted, "Nowhere else was their rivalry so keen
and so intimate." [17] Many times disputes over disciplinary rights of
the diplomat reached the Politburo. The position and influence of the
subversive Comintern agents in Soviet embassies and trade missions
were reduced, even though they had greater prestige than the diplomats, but with strong backing from Moscow, individual agents defied
Foreign Office regulations and controls. Diplomatic immunity was too
essential for the Comintern's work.[18] Diplomats themselves were sometimes compromised, and while they might resist pressures at the risk
of their careers, nonetheless, diplomatic mail pouches would carry
dynamite, weapons, propaganda, or money for revolutionary purposes.
And the couriers of the Foreign Office were all said to be secret police.[19]

In a similar fashion the secret police complicated the professional
role of the Soviet diplomat. As part of the subversive machinery
abroad, the secret police constituted an equally compromising part of
foreign missions. Even Chicherin's office was bugged.[20]

Patterns of organization and conflicting purposes appeared to become fairly well set in this early period and were carried on into the
future: The party apparatus controlled diplomacy and its diplomats
from the center; the Foreign Office was merely an administrative
appendage and the diplomats, as Hayter said of Chicherin and other

---

[15] Uldricks, Soviet Diplomatic Corps in Chicherin Era, p. 220. For details on the
foreign office's organization, see, Meissner, Foreign Ministry and Foreign Service of
U.S.S.R. pp. 53–55.
[16] Von Laue, Soviet Diplomacy Under Chicherin, p. 246.
[17] Ibid., p. 255.
[18] In noting the low prestige of the Foreign Office, Von Laue cited the fact that other
government departments paid their officials three to four times as much. "By comparison
the experts of the Comintern, mostly pampered foreign comrades, lived like kings."
(Ibid., p. 253.)
[19] Ibid., p. 255.
[20] Ibid.

Soviet Foreign Ministers, were "men of little or no political standing internally, experts acting under orders from the holders of real power;" and finally, the conduct of traditional diplomacy and the pursuit of revolution were in essence missions in conflict.[21]

4. FAVORABLE APPRAISAL AND DURABLE DILEMMAS

That the Soviets had succeeded in building a respectable diplomatic service there seems to be little doubt. The early leaders realized the requirements of the time and built a diplomatic establishment accordingly. As Uldricks concluded:

> * * * G. V. Chicherin and his assistants built a large and efficient commissariat which closely paralleled the British Foreign Office or the Quai d'Orsay in form and function. The construction of a dedicated and able foreign service, whose representatives could hold their own in negotiations with the most experienced European diplomats, must be ranked as one of the greatest accomplishments of the revolutionary regime.[22]

Notwithstanding these accomplishments, Soviet diplomats and Soviet diplomacy were burdened with an irresolvable dilemma. In brief, Soviet diplomats had the impossible task of serving two causes, two professions, two masters: One of revolution, the other of diplomacy. Essentially, they had to bridge the enormous gap between a revolutionary Soviet regime with its Marxist-Leninist perception of reality and the capitalist governments to which they were accredited whose values, indeed existence, they were committed ideologically to destroy. In diplomatic method they had to reconcile the tenets of De Callières and Nicolson with the tactics and goals of Lenin and Stalin. By accenting the revolutionary commitment, they limited their usefulness to their own government in alienating the host country. By accenting the professional commitment to diplomacy, requiring the customary functions of the diplomat, they ran the risk of being accused of falling victim to the enemy. As a party member and representative of the Soviet Government, they could not expect to gain the confidence of the host government. Yet, this was a primary requirement of the diplomat. Caught in this impossible bind, they could not honestly and clearly convey the policies of the Politburo, for these expressed only the surface segment and concealed the deeper purposes of Soviet foreign policy. Then, if they reported accurately and understandingly on the intentions and policies of their host governments, they ran the danger of being accused of disloyalty and lacking in revolutionary purity.[23]

One student of diplomacy most aptly described this dilemma when he wrote:

> As a Communist, he knew that the end justified lying, cheating and double-dealing, as a diplomat, he knew that the tactics he was from time to time ordered to

---

[21] Hayter, Sir William. The Diplomacy of the Great Powers. New York, Macmillan, 1961, p. 23.

[22] Uldricks, Impact of Great Purges on People's Commissariat of Foreign Affairs, pp. 187–188. In describing the Soviet change to reliance on playing "the game of diplomacy by the old rules," Sir William Hayter observed: "They had no great difficulty in conforming to these rules, and soon their representatives, once again called Ambassadors or Ministers, installed in many cases in splendid Embassies or Legations inherited from Tsarist Russia, were operating outwardly at least much like any other diplomats." Included among these diplomats, he noted, were "some of the ablest diplomats of the inter-War years, notably Maisky in London and Troyanovsky in Washington, men who operated the traditional methods of winning friends and influencing people, establishing informal personal relationships, entertaining agreeably, avoiding too open connextions with foreign Communist parties." (Hayter, Diplomacy of Great Powers, pp. 21–22.)

[23] Von Laue, Soviet Diplomacy Under Chicherin, pp. 259–260.

employ created nothing but suspicion and distrust and destroyed all hope of building good relations between the soviet Union and the outside world. The dilemma was constantly with him, and the strain was often immense.[24]

Faced with this irresolvable dilemma, the safest way out for the Soviet diplomat was to forget professional standards and as a diplomatic technician adapt himself to the outlook that was required, at whatever cost to Soviet interests and world peace. This tactic of inner migration is amply recorded in the chapters below.

C. Conduct of Soviet Diplomacy

1. DEFENSIVE POLICY OF ENGAGEMENT

Despite the dilemma of trying to reconcile the disruptive spirit of the revolutionary with the professionalism of the diplomat and cope with the difficulties this engendered, the defensive policy of engagement had many successes. Normal relations were established with the Great Powers, the succession states in the Baltic, and other countries of Europe. Traditional diplomatic interests in the Middle East and Far East were revived and political activities resumed. Soviet security was enhanced by developing a network of neutrality and nonaggression treaties with its neighbors in Europe. The United States persisted in its formal policy of political nonrecognition, but nonetheless famine relief was extended on a vast scale, trade relations expanded, and extensive private technical assistance programs initiated. Failure of the German Revolution in 1923 accelerated the trend in which diplomacy came into its own in preference to revolutionary activism. By the mid-1920's, wrote Von Laue, Soviet foreign policy "had moved toward greater moderation. The original predominance of revolutionary agitation was ended; diplomacy had risen to equal rank." [25]

In general, Soviet Russia tried to exaggerate its doubtful position of a great power during the Chicherin period, though it was a very weak and underdeveloped country hard pressed to match its utopian dreams with reality. In compensation, its leaders conducted a policy of negative power politics, a policy counting less on material power and more on exploiting the divisions, unrest, and disunity among its opponents. Developing techniques of propaganda (that had reached a new level of perfection in World War I) and building political strength within revolutionary organizations abroad, it depended on fluctuations in Western parliamentary politics, the turn of the business cycle, local, social, and economic conditions, and other factors not controlled by foreign governments. Thus, Soviet Russia was to perfect

---

[24] Rotter, Diplomatic Art, pp. 106–107. An aspect of this dilemma was described by Harriman on recounting a visit to Soviet Russia in the mid-1920's: "I had pointed out to the Soviet commissars in 1926 that the difficulty in American public opinion regardng recognition was, first and foremost, the support and money coming from Moscow for Communist subversive activities in the United States. They insisted that the Soviet government had nothing to do with this, that the Communist Party was entirely independent of the Soviet Government. I would have none of it. I asserted that the Communist Party and the Soviet Government were one and the same." Harriman was to become one of the Nation's most seasoned negotiators with the Soviets, particularly with Stalin. (Harriman, W. Averell. America and Russia in a Changing World. New York, Doubleday, 1971, p. 10.)

[25] Von Laue, Soviet Diplomacy Under Chicherin, p. 273. But Von Laue continued: "the extreme hopes of some Soviet diplomats for a return by their government to prerevolutionary power politics and a settlement of spheres of influence with the leading colonial powers, were not fulfilled: although with clipped claws, revolutionary agitation continued. And furthermore, the preferment of diplomacy did not imply greater tractability on the part of the Soviet masters. It only meant a partial shift back to European standards in the choice of foreign policy instruments."

revolutionary techniques that could give them some means of control over these neglected areas in power politics. Moreover, it sought to intensify its impact abroad by manipulating foreign contacts and putting to maximum use whatever sympathies and loyalties it could find. In its weakness, the Soviets developed new resources for diplomacy that were ignored by the stronger countries.[26]

2. SOME ASPECTS OF EARLY SOVIET NEGOTIATING BEHAVIOR

Soviet successes were achieved in the main by patient negotiations and skillful use of the techniques of classical diplomacy, particularly the art of playing upon differences among other powers or appealing to their avarice or fears. In these early years and later, Soviet negotiators demonstrated abilities equal to their adversaries, sometimes to the latter's surprise. In preparing their negotiating positions, in mastering the agenda and the technicalities of the subject matter, and in devising negotiating strategies and tactical skills to exploit the legal aspects of existing agreements under negotiations, they sometimes gave a superior performance.[27]

But a recitation of these negotiating skills and admirable qualities tells only part of the story. In many respects Soviet behavior in formal negotiations with bourgeois states bore some resemblance to the Russians of the 16th and 17th centuries. Only reluctantly, and out of self-interest, did the Soviets join the Western diplomatic community; but they never became members in a real sense. Ideological differences were too deeply rooted and the impulse to exploit by any means was too strong to establish a mutually acceptable negotiating frame of reference. In the early 1930's, a British negotiator wrote in exasperation that it was impossible to get anywhere with the Soviets because they were "completely unable to see themselves in any other light than that of an aggrieved power struggling for their noble ideals against a world of political, financial, and commercial conspirators." [28] The Soviets could not rid themselves of a conspiratorial mentality that saw evil purposes in their adversaries and even within their own system.

In all dealings with the Western powers, the Soviet attitude was one of inveterate suspicion that took on many forms. Like the earliest Russian diplomat, rigidity and legalisms became hallmarks of Soviet negotiating technique. Soviet diplomats were bound as tightly by instructions as any of those in the days of Peter the Great and his predecessors. Soviet stubbornness in holding negotiating positions became proverbial. Less inclined to make concessions than their negotiating adversaries, the Soviets even looked upon concessions of the latter with uncertainty and distrust, suggesting insincerity in their original position and suspicion that they were plotting some sinister anti-Soviet move.[29]

Such negotiating tactics and strategies, both positive and negative, were in gestation during the Chicherin years; but they took on forms and characteristics that became commonplace in subsequent years. For

---

[26] Ibid., pp. 279–280.
[27] Craig, Totalitarian Approaches to Diplomatic Negotiation, pp. 118–119.
[28] Craig, Techniques of Negotiation, p. 365.
[29] Ibid., pp. 365–366.

Russia's was a diplomacy from weakness, and like its Byzantine ancestors, it became a diplomacy of artifice, intrigue, and deception.

3. GENOA CONFERENCE AND RAPALLO TREATY, 1922

(a) *Purpose of Genoa Conference*

The West got its first major exposure to Soviet negotiating behavior, at least its more positive aspects, at the Genoa Conference in April 1922. Briefly, this conference failed in its declared purposes, but it had the unintended effect of creating conditions for rapprochement between Soviet Russia and Germany. The results were significant and far reaching.

The principal purpose of the Genoa Conference was to devise an arrangement for the economic reconstruction of Europe, something of a Marshall plan for an earlier era. It was to be the first major international summit conference since Versailles. Both Germany and Russia, the outcasts of Europe, were invited. It was expected that Russia would be included in the reconstruction process and in dealing with the problem of German reparations and war debts. By this time the Russians had reverted to their new economic policy, a modified form of socialism that admitted elements of capitalism. The West misread this temporary change as having a "deep and symbolic meaning" and as heralding "a change in conviction." [30] The Soviets played on these high expectations in negotiating at the conference to their advantage.

The Soviets welcomed the invitation to the extent that it gave them access to economic aid from the West; but they were fearful of facing a united Western front of capitalist creditors since the prospect of commercial relations might be contingent upon settling the claim debt question. Because the French ruled out any discussion of German reparations, the conference was left with the Russian problem. [31]

(b) *Russian-German meeting at Berlin*

Chicherin and his Russian delegation that included Maxim Litvinov went to Genoa with the single-minded purpose of splitting Western unity and eliminating Germany from any future connection with the allies. In pursuing this goal, they had superior leverage in Germany's fear of Russia's joining the allies' reparation drive (the bill of 132 billion gold marks had been presented in 1921), increasing its economic burden and sealing its political isolation in Europe. Chicherin played on these fears. The opportunity was created by French insistence upon article 116 of the Versailles Treaty that had left open for Russia (hopefully a democratic Russia) the matter of reparation claims against Germany. [32]

Such an arrangement could satisfy the claims of French investors against the Russians who in turn could collect reparations from the Germans.

Secret negotiations between the Russians and Germans had been underway for some 2 years on military matters in what Kennan called

---

[30] Fischer, Louis. The Soviets in World Affairs, Princeton, N.J., Princeton University Press, 1951, pp. 320–321.
[31] Kennan, George F. Russia and the West under Lenin and Stalin. Boston, Little, Brown, p. 210.
[32] Ibid., p. 213.

"the purest and coolest expediency." [33] Other informal connections laying the groundwork for Rapallo had been made by Karl Radek and other agents of Trotsky since 1919.[34] But the time had now come for the Soviets to push their advantage and confront the allies with a fait accompli. On the way to Genoa, Chicherin conferred with German authorities in Berlin and drafted a treaty that was along the lines of the one finally concluded at Rapallo. The pro-Russian "Easterners" in the German Foreign Office were enthusiastic, but signatures were delayed because the pro-Western faction still hoped for a reduction in reparations at Genoa.[35]

(c) Negotiations at Genoa; treaty at Rapallo

The opening of the much-publicized summit conference at Genoa on April 10, 1922, marked the first time that a Soviet representative appeared at a major international conference. Chicherin and the Soviet delegation, wearing the formal attire of European diplomats, top hats, and cutaways, no doubt shocked those attending diplomats and journalists who may have expected the prototype of the bewhiskered, bomb-throwing Bolsheviki. Chicherin spoke perfect French, the diplomatic language, and then himself translated his statement into English. With impeccable manners, he seemed to convey more the image of a retiring scholar than that of a revolutionary.[36]

In his opening statement drafted with Lenin, Chicherin gave a classic definition of peaceful coexistence, and then proceeded to lay before the assembled delegates, and more importantly the world beyond Genoa, Soviet demands for general limitations on armaments, complete abolition of weapons of mass destruction and a world economic conference attended not only by governments by also by labor unions.[37]

But the real negotiations began after the opening plenary session when the conference broke up into subcommittees. And as Kennan wrote, "Here it was to be demonstrated that ideological passion on the part of the Soviet delegation was not at all incompatible with extremely shrewd and hard-boiled diplomacy." [38]

Briefly, the conference failed, and it did so on the claims question. As hard bargaining negotiators, the Russians would discuss the allied claims of $13 billion in return for considering counterclaims of $60 billion growing out of the allied blockade and intervention. They might even reduce this clearly inflated sum to $25 billion. But, no meeting of minds was possible, and the conference broke down.[39]

[33] Ibid., p. 211.
[34] Craig, Techniques of Negotiation, pp. 364–365.
[35] Fischer, Soviets in World Affairs, pp. 322–323.
[36] Fischer, Soviets in World Affairs, pp. 333–334. Kennan has a remarkable characterization of Chicherin in which he said, "a more appealing character from the ranks of the Russian revolutionaries I do not know. He believed—as I see it—in many of the wrong things ; but he believed in them for the purest of motives. And when I try, as a historian, to follow the progress of the political cause he represented, my sympathies are often with him, even when they are not with it." (Kennan, Russian and West Under Lenin and Stalin, p. 216.)
[37] Ibid., pp. 216–217.
[38] Ibid., p. 217.
[39] Bailey, American Faces Russia, p. 256.

At Genoa, the allies made a serious mistake; and the Soviets shrewdly capitalized on it. In the course of the conference, informal negotiations took place at British Prime Minister Lloyd George's residence, Villa Alberti: The Russians were invited; the Germans were not. As in so many aspects of international political life at that time, the Germans were ostracized, oftentimes in most humiliating ways.[40]

Lloyd George, for example, would not meet with German Foreign Minister Walter Rathenau who in the first week of the conference asked for an appointment three times. Obsessed by fears of an Allied-Russian arrangement on reparations—some historians spoke of a "conspiracy," the Germans were thus easy prey for the clever Soviets who, like Iago playing on the jealousy of the much tormented Othello, exploited the magnifying fears and anxieties of the Germans. The Russians were careful not to disabuse them of their perceptions, particularly when the Germans were misinformed that an agreement had been reached. These German fears had been aggravated, it must be borne in mind, not only by the heavy reparations bill handed them just a year before but also by the loss of the mining and industrial area of Upper Silesia to Poland, a source from which they could pay the reparations. At a critical moment in the conference, on Easter Sunday April 16, the Germans responded to the Russian request for a treaty after an all-night meeting of Foreign Office officials (called the "pajama party"), and failing to get a response from the British whom they wanted to contact to convey their decision, signed the Treaty of Rapallo.[41]

The treaty instrument itself was nothing extraordinary. It was not an alliance treaty; nor did it contain secret clauses or protocols. The treaty merely provided for the establishment of full diplomatic relations; mutual renunciation of claims, thus relieving the Germans of their article 116 nightmare and the Russians of any claims against them from German nationals; and the extension of the most-favored-nation treatment in commercial matters and in the treatment of nationals.[42]

News of the treaty was received in London and Paris, as Kennan wrote, with "utter stupefaction" and a "crescendo of indignation." The London Times referred to it as an "unholy alliance," and "an open defiance and studied insult to the Entente Powers." Action was demanded "to teach Germans and Bolshevists alike that the allies are not to be defied or flounded with impunity." Lloyd George's official biographers were to look upon this incident in later years as an example of the "most cold-blooded German treachery." And the New York Herald-Tribune referred to it as "an alliance of hatreds."[43]

---

[40] Kennan wrote: "In 1922, these feelings were very much in evidence; and it was difficult for the Germans to maintain anything resembling normal diplomatic contact with the allied delegations at Genoa." (Kennan, Russia and West Under Lenin and Stalin, p. 218.)

[41] Ibid., pp. 218–222, and Fischer, Soviets in World Affairs, pp. 335–342.

[42] Kennan, George F. Soviet Foreign Policy, 1917–41. Princeton, N.J., Van Nostrand, 1960, p. 47. The treaty is reproduced as Document No. 13 in the appendix.

[43] Quoted in Kennan, Russia and West under Lenin and Stalin, p. 221, and Bailey, America Faces Russia, p. 257.

An acrimonious exchange of notes between the Allied Powers and Germany followed. The allies charged Germany with negotiating a secret treaty with Russia behind their backs in violation of the purposes of the conference; the Germans accused the allies of having "initiated separate negotiations with Russia" that could have imposed "oppressive" reparations demands on Germany from Russia.[44]

(d) Significance of Rapallo and evaluation of Soviet performance

Western reaction to the treaty inversely provided an accurate measure of the magnitude of Soviet Russia's success at Rapallo: Kennan called it a "triumph" and a "first great victory" for Soviet diplomacy.[45]

For Russia, the treaty had profound significance; for it accomplished many things through diplomacy and negotiations. The treaty:

—Ended Soviet isolation in Europe, having robbed the allies of their most effective political weapon and brought Russia into the active politics of Europe;

—Drove an entering wedge into a united European front against Russia, politically and particularly economically where its weakness was the greatest;

—Created a momentum and set a pattern for diplomatic recognition and resumption of trade relations between Russia and the West;

—Detached Germany decisively and finally from the ranks of those pressing Russia for payment of debts owed from past governments and compensation for foreign property nationalized by the Bolshevik regime;

—Ended German isolation, giving it immediate and permanent benefits, particularly a flexibility it did not have before in dealing with the allies; and finally, it

—Constituted an unspoken protest by the anti-Versailles revisionist outcasts of Europe against the Versailles powers who were striving to maintain the status quo.[46]

A diplomatic triumph of this magnitude naturally reflected favorably upon the performance of Chicherin and his fellow negotiators. In striving for maximum effect, Chicherin outwardly adapted to the style and protocol of European diplomacy, and by attire, demeanor, and speech melted into the European diplomatic scenery without difficulty. His opening speech was clearly a remarkable example of a style of Soviet conference diplomacy that was to become commonplace: The use of an international platform to give Soviet policy global exposure.

But Chicherin proved to be more than an astute propagandist; he was a clever negotiator. Really not expecting solutions at Genoa,

[44] Toynbee, Arnold J. Survey of International Affairs, 1920–23. London, Oxford University Press, 1925, pp. 30–31.
[45] Kennan, Soviet Foreign Policy, 1917–41, p. 47, and Kennan, Russia and West Under Lenin and Stalin. p. 222.
[46] The significance of Rapallo is discussed in, Kennan, Soviet Foreign Policy, 1917–41, p. 47; Kennan, Russia and West Under Lenin and Stalin, p. 222; Fischer, Soviets in World Affairs, pp. 342–344; and Hilger, Gustav and Alfred G. Meyer. The Incompatible Allies: A Memoir-History of German-Soviet Relations, 1918–41. New York, Macmillan, 1953, p. 80.

the Soviet delegates were hard bargainers, holding their own ground in negotiations and yet wisely, from their view, stringing out the private informal discussions and thus allowing time for the buildup of German suspicions. Most importantly, they knew how to take advantage of German ostracism and exploit German vulnerabilities by feeding on their suspicions of a conspiracy between Russia and the Allied Powers against them. At what seemed to be the precise moment of maximum effect, the Russians made their bid for a separate treaty, and the Germans accepted.

Thus Rapallo was more than a striking example of successful Soviet negotiating technique; it was an exercise in psychology, a lesson in its impact upon the negotiating process, and ironically a demonstration of the successful use of diplomacy to overcome one of Russia's most serious disabilities in negotiations with foreigners, a self-awareness of its own weakness.[47]

D. Importance of Chicherin: A Bridge From Czarism to Bolshevism

To sum up, Chicherin's was an era of great importance in the formation of Soviet diplomacy and negotiating style. Grounded in the traditions of realpolitik and traditional European diplomacy, he gave Russian foreign policy a substantial overlay of European traditionalism that did much to conceal the revolutionary coloration of the regime. As a Marxist-Leninist, he exploited and aggravated the cleavages within the capitalist West; as a practitioner of realpolitik, he sided with the revisionist powers in a linkage of the weak against the strong in the manner of a firm believer in the balance of power; and as a Russian nationalist, he could obscure the revolutionary component of Soviet foreign policy in achieving the traditional foreign policy goals of Russia.[48]

In substance as well as in the form and style of diplomacy, Chicherin was able to convince the Bolshevik leaders that the aristocratic tradition had at least defensive uses in the new Soviet state.[49] He was a builder of the new Soviet diplomatic service, and as Rapallo had shown he had a unique capacity for adjusting the machinery and methods of diplomacy to the needs of contemporary society. He was, as Lloyd George said, "a splendid diplomat". At the same time as a revolutionary, he could draw upon multiple channels available to

---

[47] In an appraisal of Soviet diplomacy under Chicherin, Uldricks noted that at its best, "Soviet diplomacy could be superb. Chicherin's rebuttals at Genoa to the arguments of Lloyd George on the question of tsarist debts were examples of the highest diplomatic skill." Uldricks quoted the British Prime Minister as later telling Ivan Maisky: "It wasn't easy for Chicherin at Genoa: one against us all! But he maneuvered superbly and at the same time firmly defended the positions of his government. Though no agreement was reached, Chicherin personally proved himself a splendid diplomat." The great English economist J. M. Keynes, who was also at Genoa, similarly praised Chicherin as one of the most accomplished diplomats in Europe. In a larger appraisal of the Foreign Commissariat, Uldricks wrote: "Beyond Chicherin, in Litvinov, Krasin, Rotshtein, Maiskii and Dovgalevskii, the Narkomindel possessed diplomats of the first rank." (Uldricks, Teddy J. Diplomacy and Ideology: The Origins of Soviet Foreign Relations, 1917–30. London/Beverly ·Hills, Sage Publications, 1979, pp. 154–155. Professor Uldricks very kindly sent the writer the galley-proofs of his upcoming book for which he is most grateful.)
[48] Von Laue, Soviet Diplomacy Under Chicherin, pp. 263–264.
[49] Craig and Gilbert, Diplomats, p. 8.

diplomacy in this revolutionary age that accordingly was to add a new element to the evolution of diplomatic method.[50]

Von Laue probably best summed up Chicherin's overall accomplishments when he concluded his biographical analysis:

> Chicherin's main contribution * * * should be sought, not so much in the history of international relations in the 1920's, as in the changing formulations of Soviet foreign policy among the inner circles of the party. He stood for a continued validity of Realpolitik in the tradition of Metternich and Bismarck at a time when the professional revolutionaries were all but throwing diplomacy overboard. In his efforts to preserve the Staatsgedanke [the grand design] of Russia, he carried over into the new regime the heritage of Tsarist diplomacy. He was responsible for the element of continuity which links Tsarist and Soviet foreign policy and which, despite the great contributions of Leninism, seems to grow stronger as the years go by.[51]

---

[50] Craig, Techniques of Negotiation, pp. 364–365.
[51] Von Laue, Soviet Diplomacy Under Chicherin, pp. 280–281.

IV. ERA OF THE UNITED FRONT

A. Ascent of Litvinov, 1930–39

1. NEW REQUIREMENTS FOR CHANGING TIMES

Changes on the international scene in the 1930's were profound and far reaching; they created new requirements for diplomats and their diplomacy. New forms of organization of state power emerged in Germany and Italy with the rise of nazism and fascism, and the democracies found themselves confronted with a new totalitarianism which, along with Soviet Russia, denied the validity of the laws and values they professed. The emergence of a militaristic Japan, seeking a "New Order in East Asia," added to the spreading wave of totalitarianism.

International anarchy was thus in the ascendancy in the 1930's; universal respect for the rule of law, as it became symbolized in the League of Nations, was in decline. The forces of revisionism, gaining strength, sought to overturn the Versailles system and restructure Europe according to their own preferences. The end of this policy was World War II in 1939.

These changing conditions created new requirements for Moscow, and its response was the United Front. Accordingly, Soviet Russia emerged from its inner-directed policy of "building Socialism in one country" and reaching out sought to create counter-balances of power against the threats to its security in Europe and the Far East. This meant establishing close linkages with the democracies of Europe, the United States then deep in isolation, the League of Nations, and other international bodies, and in general with all forms of resistance to fascism. During the 1930's Russia was to be an activist in partnership with those who strove to maintain a system of collective security against the forces of revisionism.

The rise of totalitarianism produced a new diplomacy, or as Craig and Gilbert noted, "an older diplomacy than the New Diplomacy demanded in the democracies."[1] Reverting to patterns reminiscent of the despotism of the Italian City States and 18th century Europe, diplomacy became imbued with the same spirit of raison d'etat and realpolitik, and addicted to the indiscriminant, unrestrained exercise of power. Again, as in the age of despotism, the diplomat became virtually the personal representative of the dictator to the government to which he was accredited. This relationship created dilemmas in representation comparable to those experienced by Soviet diplomats who had to function in two worlds, one of totalitarianism and one of democracy.[2]

---

[1] Craig and Gilbert, Diplomats, p. 6.
[2] Ibid.

2. ENTER MAXIM LITVINOV

It was in this international environment then only taking shape that Maxim Litvinov entered as Peoples Commissar for Foreign Affairs. In the late 1920's, Soviet policy under Stalin was moving in two directions: One toward a greater concentration on internal development, notably industrialization; the other toward a cautious rapproachement with the West. Chicherin, who had always insisted on the defense of Soviet state power in critical border areas, opposed this far-reaching subordination of foreign policy to domestic reconstruction. Moreover, he was always opposed to the League of Nations. Basically, he grounded his policy on the German connection which the new Stalin approach, calling for anti-German agitation, would weaken. Litvinov, more atuned to the totalitarian style of Stalin and a supporter of the new policy direction, was in the wings as Deputy Commissar, having filled in for the ailing Chicherin for a year and a half. Finally, in July 1930, Chicherin was removed from his position by the 16th Party Congress, and Litvinov named as successor.[3]

An inveterate revolutionary, Litvinov was born Meyer Wallach in 1876, joined the Social Democratic Party in 1898, and then the Bolsheviks in 1903. Travelling throughout Europe on behalf of the Bolshevik cause, he was expelled from France and Britain for his revolutionary activities. After the Bolshevik Revolution, Litvinov was sent to England, but was quickly arrested; he was returned to Russia on an exchange for Bruce Lockhart, a British diplomat.

During the interwar period, Litvinov was undoubtedly the most widely and familiarly known Soviet diplomat. As Henry L. Roberts, a specialist on Soviet foreign policy, wrote: "At international conferences and at sessions of the League of Nations his chubby and unproletarian figure radiated an aura of robust and businesslike commonsense that was in striking contrast to the enigmatic brutality of the Politburo or the conspiratorial noisiness of the Comintern."[4] It was perhaps to Litvinov more than any other person, Roberts continued, "may be traced the impression that revolutionary Russia was returning to the family of nations and could be counted upon as a force for stability and peace." The most perplexing problem in Litvinov's career was the relationship between his diplomatic role as an advocate of collective security and close connections with the West to the totality of aims and intentions of the Soviet regime.[5]

The incongruity of diplomatic style and ideological beliefs was no doubt especially puzzling to Americans. For Litvinov had made a very favorable impression on Americans, and at critical times in Soviet-American relations, he was called on as a symbol and reality of friendship. Harry Hopkins, wartime aide to President Franklin D. Roosevelt, touched the roots of understanding this relationship when he explained Roosevelt's preference for Litvinov over Molotov as Foreign Minister. For 7 years the President had been accustomed to dealing with Litvinov: "he had a western kind of mind and an understanding of the ways of the world that Roosevelt knew."[6]

[3] Von Laue. Soviet Diplomacy Under Chicherin, p. 278.
[4] Roberts, Henry L., Maxim Litvinov, in Craig and Gilbert. Diplomats, p. 344.
[5] Ibid.
[6] Standley. William H. Admiral, and Arthur A. Ageton, Rear Admiral. Admiral Ambassador to Russia. Chicago, Henry Regnery, 1955, p. 452.

Similarly, Dean Acheson, longtime Govenment official and Secretary of State, found Litvinov appealing as a diplomat, particularly his genial style of diplomacy. Writing of Litvinov in 1943 and the founding of the United Nations Relief and Rehabilitation Administration (UNRRA), he expressed sentiments of respect when he wrote:

Maxim Litvinov, an old Bolshevik but an old-school Russian as well, also understood the forms and uses of courtesy, as some of the new types in the Soviet establishment did not. Roly-poly, short, and voluble, he presented an amusing antithesis to Lord Halifax [the wartime British Ambassador to the United States], never bothering to cloak stubbornness, but making his points clearly and courteously.[7]

B. Soviet Foreign Office and Diplomatic Service

1. SUBSERVIENCE OF FOREIGN OFFICE AND ITS HEAD

Litvinov's term as Foreign Affairs Commissar coincided with the blackest period of Soviet history, the consolidation of Stalin's power and the Great Purge of 1936–38. Leaders in the party, government, and military services, indeed persons in all walks of Soviet life, were arrested, summarily tried, executed or sent to labor camps. No Soviet institution was spared as fear and anxiety gripped the whole nation. As discussed below in a separate section, the purge devastated the Foreign Office, and that Litvinov survived was something of a miracle. Thus, in contrasting the Chicherin years with the Stalin era in the matter of accessibility of foreign diplomats to the Foreign Office, Kennan, while absolving Litvinov of blame for changing practices, could make a judgment that had more universal application to Soviet diplomatic methods: "The most that may be said is that Chicherin's aristocratic background and personality gave to Soviet diplomacy, in the years of his greatest activity as Foreign Commissar, a polish, a flexibility, and an adaptability which it was never to enjoy during the Stalin era." For in Stalin's scheme of things "such normal diplomatic contact had no place." [8]

Stalin wielded total power, and the Foreign Office and its head were totally subservient to him and his Politburo. Though an "Old Bolshevik," for years a member of the Central Committee, and, as second in command, possibly the "Bolshevik guardian" over the former Menshevik Chicherin, Litvinov was still, like Chicherin, on the fringes of power, not at the center. In the long run his party status was not higher than Chicherin's, a fact that would affect his influence within the system, and may have even been lower.[9]

Foreign affairs was, moreover, on the fringes of Stalin's interests in this period, giving it a lower priority that inevitably affected the status and influence of the Foreign Office and its head. Soviet energies were directed inward; diplomacy and foreign relations were ranked below domestic concerns; and even in the field of foreign relations, the diplomatic arm never had the prestige of the revolutionary and military arms. Owing to the sensitivity of foreign policy decisions, moreover, the Politburo maintained a close, direct, and continual relation-

---

[7] Acheson, Present at Creation, p. 68.
[8] Kennan, Russia and West Under Lenin and Stalin, p. 233.
[9] Roberts, Maxim Litvinov, pp. 370–371.

ship with the Foreign Office. Consequently, the Foreign Affairs Commissar did not carry a great deal of weight in the Soviet system.[10] Neither as its head nor as party member, therefore, was Litvinov able to follow his own policy or even initiate policy, though he may have disagreed with his superiors.[11] That he understood his subservient role and that of the Foreign Office was evident in a rather sour remark attributed to him late in his career: "You know what I am. I merely hand on diplomatic documents." [12]

2. DEVASTATION OF THE FOREIGN SERVICE IN THE GREAT PURGE

(a) Continuation of the Chicherin tradition

Under Litvinov, the Chicherin tradition of quality and professionalism in the diplomatic service was carried forth, at least until the full impact of the Great Purge was felt. Intellectuals for whom raison d'état took precedence over the goal of world revolution were added to the corps. Perhaps one of the best abbreviated characterizations of Soviet diplomats in the Chicherin-Litvinov tradition came from Gustav Hilger, a German diplomat who had specialized in Soviet affairs. Hilger wrote:

With all their differences of background, personality, and policy orientation, Litvinov, Chicherin, and most of their collaborators in the Foreign Commissariat belonged to the same type of Bolshevik intellectual who had spent years of exile in Europe. On the average these men and women were well educated, highly cultured and sensitive people; many of them were Jews, and a few came from the highest strata of the old society. * * * As a rule, these people possessed initiative, imagination, cleverness, and negotiating skill. Many of them had mastered several foreign languages and had learned to adapt themselves to the Western mentality. Thus they were invaluable as diplomats and trade representatives, and contact with them was a rewarding experience, even though the non-Communist could never overcome the feeling that, fundamentally, these Marxist intellectuals looked down with a certain condescending pity on us poor blundering representatives of the doomed bourgeois class.[13]

But the Great Purge thinned the ranks of this Chicherin-Litvinov generation.[14] Only a trickle of men entered the Foreign Office between 1931 and 1936 that fit the requirements of the later post-purge Molotov generation; namely, servility and ruthlessness.[15] Until that time the professionalism of the Chicherin-Litvinov tradition was by and large maintained.

(b) Impact of the Great Purge

(1) Extent of devastation

When the Great Purge struck between 1936 and 1938, it struck with a devastating fury that impacted upon every institution within the Soviet Union. In this greatest of Soviet purges, over an estimated 1 million people were executed (600,000 were party members, according

---

[10] Ibid., p. 370.
[11] Ibid., pp. 364–365.
[12] Ibid., p. 371. An indication of the tight control Stalin held over the diplomatic corps was the admonition he made to Gregory Bessedovsky as he set out for Tokyo as ambassador: "Talk to the Japanese as little as possible and telegraph us as often as possible. And don't think yourself the cleverest of us all." (Quoted in, Von Laue, Soviet Diplomacy Under Chicherin, p. 259.)
[13] Hilger, Incompatible Allies, p. 114.
[14] Meissner, Foreign Ministry and Foreign Service of U.S.S.R., p. 61.
[15] Uldricks, Impact of Great Purges on People's Commissariat of Foreign Affairs, p. 197.

to the Soviet dissident physicist Andrei Sakharov); about 7 million arrested; and over 8 million imprisoned in labor camps (in which an additional 550,000 to 600,000 party members, according to Sakharov, died, or about one-half the total party membership). Over the whole Stalin period not less than 12 million were estimated to have died in the camps.[16]

The Great Terror decimated the Soviet diplomatic service, and in Uldricks' words, "completely smashed" the Foreign Office organization in Moscow.[17] Stalin's victims read like a who's who in Soviet diplomacy: Deputy Foreign Commissars N. I. Krestinsky and G. Ia. Skolnikov, as well as former Deputy Commissar and then Ambassador to Turkey L. M. Karakhan; the Ambassadors to Finland, Hungary, Latvia, Poland, Norway, Germany, Turkey, Rumania, Spain, Afghanistan, Mongolia, and Denmark; department heads in the Foreign Office, such as the Chief of Protocol, the press chief, the heads of the Second Western Division and the Central Asian Division, as Uldricks wrote, "to name only a few of the more prominent officials." Some legations, like the one in Spain, were completely decimated.[18]

Diplomats abroad were recalled without warning; some defected, most returned obediently; those in the Home Office often simply vanished—arrested and either executed or imprisoned in the labor camps. In his study of the impact of the Great Purge on the Soviet diplomatic corps, Uldricks estimated that at least 34 percent of the entire Foreign Office staff was purged (purge meaning arrest, execution, imprisonment, or exile, not demotion). With respect to the elite of the Foreign Service (that is, Commissars, Deputy Commissars, Collegium members, and ambassadors, numbering over 100 for the 1920's), 44 percent were definitely purged, while another 18 percent were likely victims since they disappeared at the height of the terror, making a minimum total of 62 percent of the top echelon. Only 16 percent seemed to have remained at their posts while another 14 percent either defected or died before the purge occurred.[19]

Thus, the U.S. Embassy in Moscow could report in 1939, specifically with respect to the Foreign Ministry, that "with only few exceptions, almost the entire staff of the Commissariat has changed since Molotov assumed the functions of the Commissar for Foreign Affairs. * * * Among the minor officials of the Foreign Office at least 90 percent have been replaced since the appointment of Molotov."[20]

And Uldricks could conclude:

The Great Terror accomplished the near total destruction of that talented and urbane corps of diplomats organized under Commissars Chicherin and Litvinov. The new Ministry of Foreign Affairs which emerged from the purges differed

[16] Conquest, Robert. The Human Cost of Soviet Communism. U.S. Congress. Senate. Committee on the Judiciary. 92d Congress, 1st session. Washington, D.C. U.S. Government Printing Office, 1971, p. 17.
[17] Uldricks, Impact of Great Purges on People's Commissariat of Foreign Affairs, p. 188.
[18] Ibid., p. 188.
[19] Ibid., p. 190.
[20] Ibid., pp. 191–192. In describing the extent of the purge in the Soviet diplomatic service, Fischer went down the roster of those purged and executed, even to the secretaries, translators, and Litvinov's private secretary who were arrested in Litvinov's own office. "With the exceptions of Maisky in London, Suritz in Paris, and Boris Stein in Rome—Stein was removed later—" he wrote, "all Litvinov's appointees as heads of Soviet foreign missions had been replaced, and replaced not by foreign office men but usually by GPU agents. The Soviet diplomatic service is now dominated by the secret service." (Fisher, Louis. Men and Politics. New York, Duell, Sloan and Pearce, 1941, pp. 495–496.)

radically from its predecessor in the nature of its personnel, in the style of its diplomacy and in its relationship to the political leadership of the state.[21]

(2) Litvinov's survival

To contemporary observers, Litvinov's survival of the purges was something of a surprise and miracle. Old Bolsheviks, of which he was one, were, as Roberts wrote, "dropping like flies." Litvinov headed the Foreign Commissariat which, along with the embassies abroad, was swept clean. "Inexplicably," wrote Alexander Barmine, a Soviet diplomat who defected and lived to write about it, Litvinov survived "all his friends and collaborators." Two of his four assistants were executed; the third imprisoned; and the fourth disappeared. Old friends and protégés, heading embassies abroad, disappeared. Almost all the heads of departments in his Ministry and leading diplomatic personnel abroad, which he recruited and trained during 15 years of service, were shot. But, as Roberts noted, Litvinov "continued to smile enigmatically," saying, "They were traitors; all is well !" [22]

Theories abounded as to why Litvinov survived, but the most satisfactory explanation seemed to lay in Stalin's multiple approach to problems, particularly the emerging foreign policy problem; namely, the pursuit of collective security, identified with Litvinov as its advocate and possibly even formulator, or revival of the German connection. In this competition of policies which Stalin viewed within the unfolding of events, the failure of the former gave him the option of the latter. Hence, Litvinov's resignation in May 1939 and the conclusion of the Nazi-Soviet Pact in August 1939. By this time the purge had been spent.[23]

(3) The new Molotov generation of diplomats

The few survivors of the terror provided at best a bare minimum of continuity between the two generations affected by the purge, but they served to train the new generation of diplomats, novices all with little preparation for the burdens of diplomacy. The loss of talent was, however, enormous and probably could only be measured by the loss of a generation that was comprised of seasoned diplomats, well trained and highly intellectual. The purge had thrown open the diplomatic corps to an entirely new generation. Between 1937 and 1944, a new Stalinist Foreign Ministry was created, as the Chicherin-Litvinov generation of diplomats almost entirely passed from the scene.[24]

This second generation did not measure up to the first. By and large, the Foreign Office was flooded with inexperienced but eager recruits who quickly assumed responsible positions and today still dominate the Soviet diplomatic corps. From this group came Andrei Gromyko, Valerian Zorin, Nikolai Federenko, Iakov Malik, Arkady Sobolev,

---

[21] Uldricks, Diplomacy and Ideology, p. 181.
[22] Roberts, Litvinov, p. 371. Pope defended Litvinov's role in the purges and the purges themselves. Litvinov felt, in Pope's words, that "they deserved liquidation," and that "he did not feel personally humiliated" since a number of his associates were convicted some of whom "he had implicitly trusted." (Pope, Litvinoff, pp. 418–420.)
[23] Roberts, Litvinov, pp. 374–375. Ilya Ehrenburg, a close friend of Litvinov, was puzzled as to why he was spared while his whole organization was destroyed. "Why, having put to death almost all of Litvinov's assistants, did he (Stalin) not have the obstreperous Maxim himself shot? It is extremely puzzling, certainly Litvinov expected a different ending. From 1937 until his last illness he kept a revolver on his bedside table because, if there were to be a ring at the door in the night, he was not going to wait for what came after." (Quoted in, Uldricks, Impact of Great Purges on People's Commissariat of Foreign Affairs, p. 193.)
[24] Uldricks, Impact of Great Purges on People's Commissariat of Foreign Affairs, pp. 193–194.

and Fedor Gusev—all familiar names in postwar foreign affairs. A sprinkling of high-ranking Stalinists (for example, Andrei Vyshinsky, the prosecutor in the Great Purge trials) and seasoned journalists leavened this batch of inexperienced young men in order to provide what Uldricks called, "a crucial minimum of leadership and knowledge of the outside world." [25]

The profile of this young Molotov generation (average age, 33) differed remarkably from the corps of the Chicherin-Litvinov era. Largely sons of workers and peasants, this new group had only limited educational background. Many had no postsecondary education, and those with advanced training had attended various kinds of technical institutes. Few had a background in the liberal arts; almost none had attended foreign universities. Great Russians comprised fully 80 percent of the new corps, giving it, perhaps, a more nationalistic coloration; while the older corps had only 43 percent and the Commissariat included nationalities from all important ethnic groups (Jews 17 percent and Ukrainians 10 percent), conceivably, along with other factors, giving it a certain cosmopolitanism.[26]

But the most important generational difference was in their contrasting formative experiences. The Chicherin-Litvinov corps was comprised of genuine European intellectuals who had lived in foreign lands—Litvinov had lived in England for many years and had an English wife—spoke many foreign languages; and suffered the joys and sorrows of the revolution, civil war, famine, and of building socialism in Russia. In sharp contrast, this new "Gromyko cohort" were children during the revolution; spent their formative years under the stresses of early Stalinism; had extremely limited proficiency in languages and even less experience in foreign travel. Prior to entering the service, their careers had been in industry, education, the military, other branches of the government bureaucracy and the party apparatus. A large proportion had only recently joined the party, some as late as 1938. "In all these respects," observed Uldricks, "the second generation of diplomats shared the same social, political, and educational profile as other members of the post-purge generation who were flooding into the sorely depleted ranks of the government and the party." [27]

---

[25] Ibid., p. 194.
[26] Ibid., p. 195.
[27] Ibid., p. 196. Charles E. Bohlen, career diplomat, specialist on Soviet affairs and former U.S. Ambassador to Moscow, made the following observations on this generational change from his perspective in Moscow: "As time went on, it became apparent that the entire staff of the Soviet Foreign Office had been changed immediately after the removal of Litvinov. Most of the new officials seem to have been selected because of their nonexperience or nonconnection with foreign affairs. Among the new officials mentioned in an Embassy dispatch was Andrei Gromyko. This was the first time, I think, that anyone had heard the name Gromyko in the foreign service of the Soviet Union. During this period, he came to lunch at Spaso House, and I think it was the first time he had ever had a meal with foreigners. It was quite apparent that Gromyko, a professor of economics, had virtually no knowledge of foreign affairs. He was ill at ease and obviously fearful of making some social blunder during the luncheon." (Bohlen, Charles E. Witness to History, 1929–69. New York, W. W. Norton, 1973, p. 65.)
In support of Bohlen's observations respecting the "nonexperience or nonconnection" of the new generation with foreign affairs it can be noted that Ambassador Dobrynin graduated with a degree in engineering from the Aviation Institute. "His subsequent assignment to the Narkomindel," wrote Uldricks, "came as a complete and apparently not altogether pleasing surprise." Malik graduated from the Kharkov Institute of National Economy, while Sobolev was awarded a diploma from the Leningrad Electrical Engineering Institute. Careers were also unrelated to foreign affairs. N. I. Charonov, the new ambassador to Greece and Albania, had directed the chartering of foreign steamers for Soviet use; V. K. Dereviansky, the ambassador to Finland, was a manager of an electrode factory in Moscow. (Uldricks, Impact of Great Purges on People's Commissariat of Foreign Affairs, pp. 195-196.)

(4) Effects of the Great Purge on Soviet diplomacy

The effects of the Great Purge on Soviet diplomacy and the foreign service were far-reaching and profound. The radical turnover in personnel combined with the climate of terror had an acute demoralizing effect that made the normal functions of diplomacy very difficult if not impossible. American diplomats in Moscow reported a state of paralysis gripping the Soviet Foreign Ministry that made its representatives unreliable in adequately explaining Soviet policies or in conveying foreign views to the Soviet leaders with any precision.[28] Uldricks well expressed this condition of paralysis when he concluded: "In the main, the devastated Commissariat of Foreign Affairs was hard pressed to carry out even the most elementary diplomatic tasks." [29]

More important, perhaps, were the larger institutional effects of the purge. Servility and ruthlessness became the prevailing mode and mood as Stalinism impacted upon the foreign policy establishment. Centralization of power into Stalin's hands, the institutionalization of totalitarianism, and the total ideologization of society became the goals of the leadership, the party and the state. Whatever latitude Litvinov may have been able to exercise was now radically reduced as Molotov became totally subservient to Stalin.[30] The style of leadership permeated the entire foreign policy apparatus. And as it will be seen in the next chapter, Soviet diplomatic officials could be reduced to complete immobility out of fear of taking any independent, unauthorized action. The Foreign Ministry was further removed from the center of power as its decisionmaking role in foreign affairs was lessened still further as Stalin took unto himself the formulation of policy, the conduct of diplomacy, and the negotiations with the wartime powers. Under the impact of the purges the Foreign Office was also drawn more deeply into espionage work. In the Chicherin Litvinov years until about 1937, Soviet career diplomats were relatively unencumbered by compromising entanglements with either the Comintern or covert intelligence activities. But now the secret police (NKVD) moved into the Foreign Ministry in force and apparently began to involve foreign service personnel directly in their clandestine activities.[31]

In brief, Soviet diplomacy, the diplomatic service, and the foreign policy institutions became Stalinized. This was the most significant effect of the Great Purge. As Uldricks concluded:

> Thus it can be seen that the Great Terror accomplished the near total destruction of that talented and urbane corps of diplomats organized under Commissars Chicherin and Litvinov. The new Ministry of Foreign Affairs which emerged from the purges differed radically from its predecessor in the nature of its personnel, in the style of its diplomacy, and in its relationship to the political leadership of the state.[32]

---

[21] Loy Henderson, the American charge in Moscow, reported that "some of the officials of the People's Commissariat for Foreign Affairs are so patently in abject terror that one must pity them. They fear to talk on almost any subject and apparently dread meeting foreign visitors, particularly those from the local diplomatic corps." (Quoted in, Uldricks, Impact of Great Purges on People's Commissariat of Foreign Affairs, p. 192.)

[29] Ibid., p. 192.

[30] Ibid., p. 198.

[31] Ibid.

[32] Ibid., p. 199.

3. PERSISTING DILEMMA OF PURPOSES

Problems other than the Great Purge troubled Soviet diplomats of the 1930's. Like those of the 1920's, they faced the same dilemma inherent in the pursuit of professed revolutionary goals while maintaining the professionalism of their diplomatic craft—the persisting two-master problem of the Comintern versus the Soviet Government. No doubt the advocacy of collective security in juxtaposition to the subversive activities of the Comintern magnified this connection.

The Comintern had never really concealed its hard revolutionary core, and the often energetic behavior of the comrades under the new "popular front" line caused Litvinov perpetual embarrassment. In 1936, for example, French Ambassador Robert Coulondre complained to Litvinov that Comintern interference in French internal affairs was imperiling the Franco-Soviet pact. In response, Litvinov assured him that the Soviet Union had no intention of interfering and that the Soviet Ambassador in Paris was instructed accordingly; but he was obliged to fall back on the old deception that the Comintern had nothing to do with the foreign policy of the Soviet Government. Nonetheless, Coulondre felt that Litvinov was well aware that this customary disclaimer of responsibility for the Comintern was unconvincing. "But the question went beyond him," Coulondre observed, exposing the roots of the dilemma facing Soviet diplomats. "It concerned the other side of the double ladder on the top of which sat Stalin alone." [33]

C. ASPECTS OF SOVIET POLICY AND NEGOTIATING STYLE

1. TRANSCENDING POLICY THRUST: COLLECTIVE SECURITY

(a) A reflection of Litvinov, the diplomat

The policy that Litvinov and the Soviet diplomatic corps were commanded to carry out could best be summed up in the words, "collective security." This was the transcending thrust of Soviet policy in the 1930's, elements of which were detectable in the late 1920's but did not come into full bloom until 1933.

The characteristics of this policy reflected very much the substance and style of Litvinov as a diplomat. Like Litvinov, the spirit of the policy was fundamentally pragmatic; it had a tone of "unrevolutionary reasonableness," as Roberts described it, a sort of commonsense and businesslike approach to international politics that remained a permanent trademark of Litvinov's diplomacy; it favored practical accommodation with the West as opposed to creating and abetting revolution, disturbance and international disorder.[34] In brief, this policy called for commitment to and involvement in the West, peace and stability in international relations, and a "united front" in International Communism.

The rationale underpinning collective security was simply Soviet weakness and insecurity. Russia was vulnerable internally and externally. Internally, it was undertaking a total reconstruction of the

---

[33] Quoted in, Roberts, Maxim Litvinov, p. 368.
[34] Roberts, Maxim Litvinov, pp. 346 and 367.

nation on a socialist basis; the step backward into modified capitalism came to an end; the time had come to take the two steps forward to socialism. Industrialization and collectivization were the main instrumentalities for this giant leap to modernity. The cost was enormous in human life (an estimated 3.5 million in the collectivization drive, 1930–1936) and in internal stability.[35] Externally, the rise of Hitlerian Germany in Europe and the aggressions of a militaristic Japan in the Far East posed a two-front threat of the first magnitude. The combination of external threats and internal weakness made the search for new power balances imperative, and the Russians looked to Western Europe and America.

(b) The critical year 1933, the turning point

Since the late 1920's, Soviet policy began a slow orientation toward the West, notably in the direction of the League of Nations and in modifying somewhat its revolutionary impulses.[36]

But 1933 was the critical year, the turning point, and for the next 2½ years Litvinov, in Roberts' words, "proceeded in high gear down the road of collective security and cooperation with the peace-loving Powers." These were the years Soviet Russia joined the League, signed mutual assistance pacts with France and Czechoslovakia, established relations with the United States, and when Litvinov made some of his most constructive pronouncements on the means for preserving peace which he now declared was "indivisible." [37]

German, Italian, and Japanese aggression proceeded apace, however, with little disposition in the West to check it. Doubts of Soviet sincerity respecting the "United Front" were magnified by continued suspicions, and the onset of the Great Purge weakened Western confidence in the character and stability of the regime. From 1936 until the Munich Conference in 1938, the high point of appeasement, it became clear that collective security as a policy was a failure.[38]

2. U.S. RECOGNITION OF THE SOVIET UNION

(a) Initiation into Litvinov's negotiating style

Negotiations for establishing diplomatic relations between the United States and the Soviet Union was an important component of Soviet Russia's collective security policy; it was also the first major official encounter by American leaders with the Soviet negotiating style, particularly Litvinov's, for as Foreign Commissar he was the chief Soviet negotiator in the proceedings that took place in Washington during November 7–16, 1933.

Like most Soviet diplomats, Litvinov had a reputation for being a very tough and stubborn negotiator who resorted excessively

---

[35] Conquest, Robert. Casualty Figures for the Stalin Terror. Reprinted from Conquest's "The Great Terror," in, U.S. Congress. Senate. Committee on the Judiciary. The Human Cost of Soviet Communism. 92d Congress, 1st session. Washington, U.S. Government Printing Office, 1971, p. 32.

[36] Von Laue, Soviet Diplomacy Under Chicherin, pp. 278–279. Von Laue described the gradual shift in Soviet policy then taking place, quoting Stalin at the 16th Party Congress in July 1930 in which he insisted that, "We do not seek a single foot of foreign territory, but we will not surrender a single inch of our territory either." Von Laue interpreted this statement as implying: "We will not seek any foreign revolution even during the tempting opportunities of a world depression."

[37] Ibid., p. 354.

[38] Ibid., p. 357.

to the conventional tactic of inflating the asking price, hoping to gain more than what could be expected. Arthur Upham Pope, his eulogistic biographer, charged that Litvinov's enemies accused him of having brought into international negotiation the "bazaar technique" of demanding at the start of a negotiation "an exorbitant price so that even with substantial concessions he could still make a good profit." If this was his method, Pope wrote in defense, then "it was justified" by its aims, results, and the conditions that other countries imposed on him. "No matter how often his proposals were rejected," Pope noted approvingly of this spirit of reconciliation, citing the case of the United States, presumably in negotiations for recognition, "he always tried again, always came back with new offers." Litvinov's negotiations, he assured, "were not secret, and were never complicated by efforts to save face." [39]

In a more detailed commentary on Litvinov's recognized negotiating skill, Pope made these observations:

Some of his colleagues abroad were even afraid of him, and all knew his power as a negotiator. It is always difficult, without offering substantial concessions, to get him to commit himself. He is like absorbent cotton; when pressed, he apparently gives way, conceding and retreating in a sensible and disarmingly agreeable way; yet when the time comes for final commitment, there he is in good shape; he has not given way at all. Nor has there ever been any feeling of tension or bitterness, or hint of trickery or bad faith in his dealings. His tranquil detachment, complete freedom from anxiety, his ready laughter and deliciously ironic wit all have helped. He has invariably been confident, conciliatory, unhurried, cool, giving the impression that he had all the time in the world to wait. Count Werner von der Schulenburg, the German Ambassador to Moscow, once said, "I have the toughest diplomatic job in the world and the most agreeable opposite number." In reality there was no harder fighter, no more incessant worker than Litvinoff in those years * * *.[40]

In an afterthought on Litvinov's negotiating style, Pope added a little more color to this portrait. Litvinov was "most flexible" in negotiation, he wrote. He knew "when to drop the unessentials, when to give way, and when to allow his opponent the relief of a strong affirmation." "Skill at playing a waiting game, in which he does not waste the waiting interval but uses it for review, new planning and adjustments," Pope continued, "is only a corollary of his intelligence and his patience." [41]

More critical diplomatic practitioners who jousted with Litvinov across the negotiating table underscored his inflexibility and stubbornness in holding to positions. "Anyone accustomed to dealing with Mr. Litvinov," Sir Esmond Ovey wrote from his diplomatic post in Moscow during December 1929, "will remember how he frequently appears to be on the point of agreeing to suggestions made to him, but in practice, when pressed for any definite statement, he invariably reverts to his original point of view." [42] Similarly, Acheson, while praising Litvinov's jovial spirit, was nonetheless critical of his stubbornness in negotiation which he never bothered "to cloak." [43] Presumably, this display of inflexibility and stubbornness, a tactic common among later Soviet negotiators, was designed in part to pressure

[39] Pope, Maxim Litvinoff, p. 189.
[40] Ibid., p. 191.
[41] Ibid., p. 493.
[42] Quoted in, Craig. Totalitarian Approaches to Diplomatic Negotiation, p. 121.
[43] Acheson. Present at the Creation, p. 68.

a negotiating adversary into making greater and more important concessions.[44]

(b) Proceedings in Washington, November 7–16, 1933

(1) Converging interests

Negotiations to establish diplomatic relations with Soviet Russia gave American negotiators their first exposure to Litvinov's style. A convergence of interests brought about the negotiations: Common fears of Japanese aggression in the Far East; mounting mutual concern for Hitler's rise to power in Europe; Soviet need for credits; and American expectations of an expanding market in Soviet Russia to relieve its economic depression.[45]

(2) Hull's preliminary assessment of Litvinov

Both nations were thus favorably disposed toward recognition, but the Soviets more so. Preliminary formal and informal contacts led President Roosevelt to believe, as Secretary of State Cordell Hull said, that the Soviets were "eager" for recognition.[46]

At the London Economic Conference in July–August 1933, Hull met Litvinov for the first time. He found him "a thoroughly capable diplomat and international statesman" with "an agreeable personality." Hull was impressed by Litvinov as "one of Russia's principal peace advocates" who was later "to become a world figure by reason of his constructive support of peace at Geneva." At London Hull assessed Litvinov as being "more interesting in conversation and in his ideas than the average diplomat," though guarded in his conversations. While in London, Hull succeeded in establishing the groundwork for negotiations on recognition 3 months later.[47]

(3) Preparations for negotiations

After much discussion of the recognition question within the administration, President Roosevelt decided to take the initiative, and on October 13, 1933, he sent a proposal directly to the Soviet leaders (revealing in this early period his preference for dealing at the top) to explore outstanding questions between the two nations. No promise of recognition was made; the word did not even appear in the letter.[48] The Soviets responded favorably and sent Litvinov as their chief negotiator.

Before Litvinov's arrival on November 7, the State Department made the most extensive and careful preparations for the negotiations,

[44] Craig cited the case of negotiations in 1939 between British Foreign Secretary Lord Halifax and Soviet Ambassador Maisky to illustrate Soviet stubbornness in negotiations and reluctance to compromise. The Western powers were seeking an agreement with the Soviets to check Hitler's march of aggression. The Soviet attitude, wrote Craig, "proved an almost insuperable barrier to profitable exchanges." The Soviet negotiators demanded Western concessions on the very points on which the West was most reluctant to give way; and attempts to conciliate the Soviets by giving way on lesser points. Craig noted, merely whetted their appetite to believe that by persisting the West would yield on major points also. During the negotiations, Halifax asked Maisky "point blank whether the Soviet Government wanted a treaty at all; to which M. Maisky said that of course they did, and why did I ask the question? Because, I replied throughout the negotiations the Soviet Government has not budged a single inch and we had made all the advances and concessions. * * * Saying 'No' to everything was not my idea of negotiation." (Craig, Techniques of Negotiation, p. 366.)

[45] Browder, Robert Paul. The Origins of Soviet-American Diplomacy. Princeton, N.J., Princeton University Press, 1953, pp. 108–112.

[46] Hull, Cordell. Memoirs. N.Y., Macmillan, 1948, vol. 1, p. 295.

[47] Ibid., pp. 293–294.

[48] Ibid., p. 298.

particularly in studying the experiences of other nations and the treaties that were concluded. In a memorandum for the White House on recognition, Robert F. Kelley, the Chief of the Department's Division of Eastern European Affairs and an astute student of Soviet affairs, analyzed all facets of the recognition problem and particularly cautioned the President that a satisfactory settlement on outstanding matters such as debts should be reached before recognition was extended. "Until a substantial basis of mutual understanding and common principles and purposes has been established," he wrote, citing the experiences of other governments, "official intercourse, with its increased contacts is bound to lead to friction and rancor." [49]

In a later memorandum to the President, Hull reiterated the points Kelley made and directed the President's attention to "two powerful weapons" the United States possessed in the negotiation: Soviet Russia's great desire for credits and for recognition.[50]

Litvinov was also preparing for the negotiations, at least laying the groundwork psychologically. In a press interview prior to embarking for America, he remarked that agreement would be reached in "a half an hour." The remark was widely publicized in the United States where it made a most unfavorable impression. Critics noted that negotiations for recognition required more than a half hour and that extensive preliminary negotiations were indispensable. Litvinov had expected a prolonged conference, as had the American officials; but, it was reasoned, after the remark, extensive negotiations appeared to be a compromise, a concession by Litvinov, thus giving him an initial advantage.[51] At a press conference upon his arrival, Litvinov repeated his previous assertion that the negotiations should take only a half hour. "Perhaps less," he added.[52]

(4) Deadlock and Roosevelt-Litvinov "summit" meeting

Negotiations took place in Washington between November 7 and 16, 1933. No stenographic record or reports of negotiations were made, and in the critical negotiations between Litvinov and Roosevelt, where the vital decisions were taken, no one else was present, and no Presidential report or memorandum was made on the proceedings.[53]

Briefly, the U.S. approach was, as Kelley recommended, negotiations first on outstanding problems, then diplomatic recognition. The key issues, as the American negotiators saw it, were: Protection against Soviet propaganda and subversive activities in the United States; freedom of worship and protection of the legal rights of Americans in Russia; and satisfactory settlement of the Russian debts.

The Soviets reversed the order: Recognition first, and then negotiations. Litvinov insisted on this sequence "right off," as Hull wrote, but he was quickly disabused. Thereafter, negotiations proceeded according to the American plan.[54]

---

[49] Browder, Origins of Soviet-American Diplomacy, pp. 105–106.
[50] Ibid.
[51] Pope, Litvinoff, p. 294.
[52] Browder, Origins of Soviet-American Diplomacy, p. 129.
[53] Ibid., p. 130.
[54] Ibid., pp. 130–133, and Hull, Memoirs, vol. 1, p. 300.

But not for long. Deadlock set in very quickly. As the British Ambassador to Washington notified his Home Office:

M. Litvinov had proven somewhat of a surprise to the State Department. I learn on good authority that he has been showing himself the toughest of negotiators. He has evinced no trace of any ambition to achieve a personal success. He has had the blandest, but firmest, of retorts ready for any question, and has appeared quite ready to depart emptyhanded at any moment.[55]

After a series of fruitless meetings at the State Department in which progress was reached only on some aspects of subversive activities, the negotiations were turned over to the White House where Litvinov, as the Americans suspected, and Roosevelt wanted them in the first place. To the Americans at this point, Litvinov had proven to be a very tough, stubborn, highly uncooperative, and suspicious negotiator.

In mid-summer, Roosevelt had considered the method of personal negotiation which he eventually used. "If I could only, myself, talk to one man representing the Russians," he said to Henry Morgenthau, the Secretary of the Treasury, "I could straighten out the whole question." With this "plan in mind," as Roosevelt said, he conferred with Litvinov in the presence of some of his aides, and in what was described as "his most affable and winning manner" drew the threads of the negotiations together thus far, expressed sincere U.S. interest in a just settlement and to break the ice injected some humor. By the end of the hour, Litvinov had "noticeably thawed," and at Roosevelt's suggestion they agreed to meet alone that evening, as he jokingly said, to insult each other with impunity. Litvinov laughed heartily. "The Roosevelt touch had succeeded," wrote Robert Paul Browder, a student of Soviet-American recognition, "and the prospects for continued and profitable negotiations were greatly enhanced." [56]

That evening Roosevelt and Litvinov were closeted alone for 3 hours during which the question of religious freedom and propaganda activities were apparently resolved satisfactorily. On the evening of November 11, Roosevelt and Litvinov met again for 2 hours. A subsequent break of a few days in negotiations took place, presumably to get Moscow's approval of the proceedings up that that point.[57]

The remaining unresolved issue was the debts owed by the pre-Bolshevik Russian Provisional Government totalling over $187 million. The State Department had strongly recommended, it should be emphasized, that a definite settlement be reached before recognition, citing the unhappy allied experience. Apparently, this course was being followed, but the negotiations had gone on longer than anticipated, and Litvinov adamantly refused to make a specific commitment. Thus, it was decided to draw up a declaration of intent "in principle" that could be the basis for future negotiations after recognition. Roosevelt and Litvinov conferred on November 15 in order to draft the memorandum. Thus, the United States abandoned its initial negotiating strategy of recognition as a lever for settlement. Subsequently, Roosevelt and Litvinov initialed a "gentleman's agreement" to ne-

[55] Quoted in, Craig, Totalitarian Approaches to Diplomatic Negotiation.
[56] Browder, Origins of Soviet-American Diplomacy, pp. 102 and 133.
[57] Ibid., p. 134.

gotiate the difference between the Soviet figure of $75 million and the U.S. figure of $150 million after relations were resumed.

Recognition and the mutual commitments accompanying it were embodied in an exchange of 11 letters and a memorandum. Briefly, in return for recognition, the Soviets pledged to grant freedom of worship to Americans in Russia and to discontinue propaganda and subversive activities in the United States. Consideration of the debt matter was postponed to a later date.[58]

(5) *Litvinov's performance assessed*

In considering strictly Soviet negotiating behavior in this first encounter with the United States, it is difficult to fault Litvinov's performance. The stubbornness and persistence for which he had been noted paid off: He negotiated alone with the President, apparently one of the undeclared purposes in his negotiating strategy; and he won the recognition he sought. In the process he made concessions, but on matters that the Soviets did not take seriously, as future protests by the United States against Soviet subversive activities indicated.[59] Most importantly, perhaps, Litvinov forced a shift in U.S. negotiating strategy on the debt issue that cleared the way for the recognition he sought. In this case the United States seemed to have underestimated the strength of its "leverage" of recognition.

Thus, after speaking at the National Press Club in Washington and addressing the American-Russian Chamber of Commerce and the American-Russian Institute in New York, Litvinov, who seemed to have a fine public relations sense, could leave the United States on November 25, 1933, "in a very happy mood," as Pope wrote, and feeling, in the words of Browder, "that he had completed a successful mission." There had been concessions, on paper at least, but they seemed worth the gaining of what he later termed "not merely one more recognition * * * by a great power, but the fall of the last position, the last fortress in the attack on [the U.S.S.R.] * * * by the capitalist world, which after the October Revolution took the form of nonrecognition and boycott."[60]

(6) *Lessons for U.S. negotiators*

As for the United States—again strictly with respect to negotiating procedures—this first encounter with the Soviets revealed short-

[58] Ibid., pp. 141–148. The documents on recognition can be found in. Browder's book on recognition, appendix B, pp. 225–238. and in. U.S. Congress. House. Foreign Relations of the United States. 1933–39, Soviet Union. Washington, U.S. Government Printing Office, 1952. pp. 25–37.

[59] The subversive problem is discussed in Beloff, Max. The Foreign Policy of Soviet Russia, 1929–1941. London, Oxford University Press, 1947, vol. 1, p. 126, and by Hull in his memoirs on p. 305. The occasion was the All-World Congress of the Comintern in the summer of 1935. American Communists attended and participated in discussions and plans for the development of the CPUSA. "Here was a flagrant violation of the pledge of noninterference given us on Nov. 16, 1933, and we could not let it pass without protest." Hull wrote. He summarized the protest note.

The seriousness with which the Soviets took this pledge may be seen from the remarks by former American Communist leader Benjamin Gitlow. According to Gitlow, the CPUSA was concerned about the effect of the pledges against subversive activities on the organization. He noted that the Soviet secret police apparatus (OGPU) in the United States arranged a meeting between Litvinov and the Party Secretariat in New York at which Litvinov assured the American members that the commitments in no way affected the activities of their party and its relations with the Comintern. Browder commented: "It seems very surprising that Litvinov would risk such a meeting." (Browder, Origins of Soviet-American Relations, p. 150, ff. 57.)

[60] Ibid.. p. 152.

comings; namely, imprecise drafting of diplomatic documents, conceding on a critical point of leverage, and failing to have a stenographic record or full report on the proceedings.

Kelley and the other aides to the President were meticulously careful in drafting the documents and preparing exhaustively for the negotiations. But the critical "gentleman's agreement" and its reference to a declaration of intent "in principle," which Browder termed "unfortunate" and a "mistake" because it gave up vital American negotiating leverage, was "badly worded" and gave the Soviets, who have long demonstrated an ability of taking advantage of broad agreements "in principle," the opportunity to draw a different meaning in the future than intended by the negotiators. "The phraseology," Browder wrote, "would indicate that Roosevelt simply wrote the memorandum down at the moment or perhaps called in a secretary and dictated it. So vital a document should have been carefully worded by experts in the State or Treasury Departments." [61]

Finally, the failure to have an accurate stenographic record or any reports of the meetings, particularly at the "summit" level, could have been a source of problems in the future. While this may not have been true in this instance (although a record of conversations on reaching the "gentleman's agreement" may have provided useful clarification), it was true during the wartime conferences when the United States did not have a complete record.

In the negotiations Litvinov also revealed a tactic that has become fairly standard operating procedure for Soviet negotiators. Judging from Browder's detailed account of the proceedings, Litvinov did not lay on the negotiating table any detailed Soviet proposal but rather reacted to those initiated by the American side.[62]

Future American negotiators were to find this procedure virtually established practice. The burden of negotiations was thus placed firmly on the American negotiators to define the problems, establish the negotiating framework, and devise formulas ultimately acceptable to the Soviet Union.

Understandably, advantages could be gained by assuming this initiative. But Russian negotiators coped with this possibility in two ways: By using the "bazaar technique" of making counterproposals

---

[61] Ibid., pp. 140–141. With respect to the imprecise formulation of this agreement, Charles E. Bohlen, a long-time Soviet specialist in the State Department and Ambassador to the Soviet Union, wrote in his memoirs : "The trouble was that the memo of understanding on the debts was a carelessly drafted document—a fault which, repeated later, was to cost the U.S. heavily in its world War II dealings with the Soviet Union. The memo (it remained secret until 1945) referred to a 'loan' to be credited to Moscow by Washington. In his discussions with Bullitt [William C. Bullitt, the first U.S. Ambassador to the Soviet Union] in the spring, summer, and fall of 1934, Litvinov insisted that the word 'loan' meant that the United States had promised to extend to the Soviet Union funds to use wherever and however it chose. The United States always held the contrary view that any money made available to the Soviet Union would be in the form of a credit to be spent in the United States. The memorandum was also deficient in that it made no reference to the Export-Import Bank's control of credits to the Soviet Union." (Bohlen, Charles E. Witness to History, 1929–1969, New York, W. W. Norton, 1973, p. 32.) Hull told Soviet Ambassador Trovanovsky in a meeting on Mar. 26, 1934, that "Litvinov has offered a contention and version of the debt understanding entirely different from anything our officials thought they were discussing. It is entirely different from anything they were thinking about." (Hull, Memoirs, vol. 1, p. 303) For other commentaries, see Farnsworth, Beatrice. William C. Bullitt and the Soviet Union. Bloomington, Ind., Indiana University Press, 1967, pp. 105–106.

[62] Browder wrote, for example, "The experts in the Department were engaged in work on the agreements which were to be presented to the Russians for approval before recognition." In some cases as many as 20 drafts of proposed texts were drawn up in an effort to achieve wording that "would be binding and at the same time acceptable to Litvinov." (Browder, Origins of Soviet-American Diplomacy, p. 128.)

that widened the negotiable gap and thus forced the adversary to compromise at some point of expected profit; and by using an elusive and totally passive "counterpunching" technique of rejecting proffered proposals without making counterproposals, thus placing the adversary in the position of negotiating with himself. Underlying this tactic was a Soviet awareness of the American negotiating psychology and political habit of seeking a rational compromise. Thus, Soviet stubbornness and inflexibility had a political purpose.[63]

In the arms control negotiations over 3 decades later U. Alexis Johnson, the chief American negotiator, faced the same Soviet tactic which he found "very bothersome." By rejecting U.S. proposals, he said, the Soviets would compel the American side to modify its position, running the risk, as Johnson noted, of "negotiating with ourselves." Where to draw the line, he said, was a real problem.[64]

For American negotiators, therefore, the diplomacy of recognition had important lessons, none perhaps more significant than what to expect from their Soviet counterparts in the future. Secretary of State Hull seemed to have summed this up convincingly when he concluded the chapter of his memoirs on the diplomacy of recognition:

During the years following our recognition, Russia did not pursue a stable course based on fundamental policies. The comparatively new Soviet regime seemed at this stage not to have settled on a solid, permanent, straightforward course in the conduct of its foreign policies. We noticed a careless or indifferent observance by the Soviet Government of some of the agreements and understandings our two Governments had entered into. There was a disposition to haggle over little things and to debate seriously and interminably over wholly minor matters which developed numerous pinpricks. Some questions of major importance were also to arise on which Russia's attitude was difficult to understand.

Negotiating with Russia, therefore, was not like negotiating with other great powers. In every approach to Moscow I had to bear these facts in mind.[65]

D. Litvinov, Diplomat and Negotiator: A Summing Up

As a diplomat and negotiator, Litvinov was uniquely suited to the era of the United Front, and the respect that he received in the West stemmed largely from his advocacy of the policy of collective security against fascism. Never a firebrand or theoretician, he manifested a

---

[61] This tactic was apparent in Litvinov's design to negotiate with Roosevelt and not just with his aides. When Litvinov met Roosevelt privately, only minor textual changes were made to satisfy the former's objections, thus supporting the explanation of Litvinov's earlier obduracy suggested by Hull and others; namely, that he wanted to negotiate with the President. (Ibid., pp. 133–134.)

[64] Johnson, U. Alexis. What Is SALT All About? A Review of Soviet Negotiating Tactics, George Washington University, Institute for Sino-Soviet Studies, Washington, D.C., Oct. 4, 1977. (Whelan, Joseph G. Notebook No. 6, pp. 53–54.)

[65] Hull, Memoirs, vol. 1, p. 307. William C. Bullitt went to Soviet Russia with great expectations as the first U.S. Ambassador. However, he became disillusioned with the prospects of establishing a viable relationship and eventually became, in Bohlen's words, a "bitter * * * enemy" of the Soviet Union. In a message written on Apr. 20, 1936, Bullitt gave this final advice to Hull on relations with Soviet Russia which, Bohlen said, "still makes sense":

"We should neither expect too much nor despair of getting anything at all. We should take what we can get when the atmosphere is favorable and do our best to hold on to it when the wind blows the other way. We should remain unimpressed in the face of expansive professions of friendliness and unperturbed in the face of slights and underhand opposition. We should make the weight of our influence felt steadily over a long period of time in the directions which best suit our interests. We should never threaten. We should act and allow the Bolsheviks to draw their own conclusions as to the causes of our acts.

"Above all, we should guard the reputation of Americans for businesslike efficiency, sincerity and straightforwardness. We should never send a spy to the Soviet Union. There is no weapon at once so disarming and effective in relations with the Communists as sheer honesty. They know very little about it." (Bohlen, Witness to History, p. 34.)

practicality and businesslike commonsense in diplomacy; and while in negotiation he was tough, resourceful, and effective, still he conducted Soviet diplomacy in a tone of "unrevolutionary reasonableness," as Roberts described it, that attracted the West.[66]

Yet, Litvinov was a Marxist-Leninist, and he carried with him all the ideological baggage that the term implies. His Western orientation and conception of collective security did not transform his internal ideological beliefs. For him, peaceful coexistence was not a permanent order of things; the world was still divided into two camps with the Fascist belonging to that of capitalism; nor were the motives inducing certain capitalist powers to be peace-loving necessarily fundamental and enduring. As Roberts cautioned, "Litvinov's collective security is not to be identified with the idealism of some of his Western admirers." [67]

Nor was the Soviet diplomat in Litvinov's view to be anything less than what ideology and the Soviet Union demanded. "I cannot imagine a typical Soviet diplomat and I hope there is not," Litvinov once said when asked if there was a Soviet diplomatic "type." He explained that the Soviet diplomat tried in peacetime to perform the tasks of the Red Army in wartime—a reversal of the classic dictum of Clausewitz:—"War is the continuation of politics with other means"—that is to say, "Diplomacy is the continuation of war by other means." [68]

And Litvinov could be a sycophant to Stalin, as evident in his response to Stalin on the occasion of his 60th birthday in 1936 from a congress in Montreux:

* * * If I look back I am chiefly proud of having done my whole Party work of 40 years under the immediate guidance of our great leaders and teachers, Lenin and Stalin. If there are any successes in my diplomatic work they must be attributed to the strong and wise leadership of the man who is responsible for the successes in all fields of socialist reconstruction—Stalin.[69]

All things considered, Roberts concluded, Litvinov has claim to two things of lasting significance: "his ideas and his acumen as a diplomat." Whatever the aims of Soviet foreign policy or Litvinov's connection with those aims, the ideas expressed in his major League of Nations speeches were "important in themselves." And Litvinov's ability to detect the major trends of the 1930's and to anticipate the course of events indicated, in Roberts' judgment, "an extraordinary understanding of that decade." [70]

Ironically, it was Litvinov's ideas and pro-Western orientation that were ultimately to be his undoing. For with the failure of collective security to halt the onrush of fascism, Stalin removed Litvinov

[66] Roberts, Litvinov, pp. 345–346.
[67] Ibid., p. 364.
[68] Pope, Litvinoff, p. 190.
[69] Quoted in, Pope, Litvinoff, pp. 190–191.
[70] Roberts, Litvinov, p. 376. Roberts concluded his study of Litvinov with the following assessment by F. P. Walters from his two-volume history of the League of Nations: "No future historian will lightly disagree with any views expressed by Litvinov on international questions. Whatever may be thought of the policy and purposes of his government, the long series of his statements and speeches in the Assembly. the Council. the conferences, and committees of which he was a member between 1927 and 1939 can hardly be read today (1952) without an astonished admiration. Nothing in the annals of the League can compare with them in frankness, in debating power, in the acute diagnosis of each situation. No contemporary statesman could point to such a record of criticisms justified and prophecies fulfilled." (p. 377.)

on May 3, 1939, ended the pro-Western policy identified with him, and, reviving the Rapallo spirit, established a new connection with Hitlerian Germany with Molotov as Foreign Commissar. From this new connection emerged the Nazi-Soviet Non-Aggression Pact of August 23, 1939. This pact effectively neutralized Russia, ending any possibility of a united front with Britain and France against Germany and clearing the way for Hitler's invasion of Poland on September 1, 1939. This ultimate aggression was followed in rapid succession by a British and French declaration of war on Germany on September 3. World War II had begun.

CHAPTER IV—NEGOTIATIONS UNDER STALIN: DURING WORLD WAR II, 1939–45

Part I—International Setting, Soviet Diplomacy and Negotiations for Lend-Lease and Military Cooperation

Harriman did not realize it at the time, but he was to learn on several later occasions that this first experience of a major conference in Moscow set a pattern which was to be followed time and again: Extreme cordiality at the start of the conference, changing to disagreeable and even surly hostility at the second meeting—and then harmonious agreement and a jubilantly triumphant banquet with innumerable toasts to Allied cooperation at the finish.

*—Robert E. Sherwood on W. Averell Harriman's
first wartime conference with Stalin, 1948.*

My observation of the psychology of the individuals who are conducting Soviet foreign policy has long since convinced me that they do not and cannot be induced to respond to the customary amenities, that it is not possible to create "international good will" with them, that they will always sacrifice the future in favor of an immediate gain, and that they are not affected by ethical or moral considerations, nor guided by the relationships which are customary between individuals of culture and breeding. Their psychology recognizes only firmness, power and force, and reflects primitive instincts and reactions entirely devoid of the restraints of civilization. It is [I am] of the opinion that they must be dealt with on this basis and on this basis alone.

*—U.S. Ambassador Steinhardt to
Secretary of State Hull, June 17, 1941.*

I. DIPLOMACY IN WARTIME

A. Radical Change in International Environment

World War II brought about a radical change in the international environment. At last the forces of repudiation and revision, joined by Fascist Italy and with a Soviet Russia on the sidelines free to seize Eastern Poland, the Baltic States, Bessarabia and Northern Bukovina, set out to redraw the map of Europe on their terms and according to a new distribution of power. In political terms, the war was the final challenge to the Versailles system in Europe and an expressed determination to establish a new order.

Conclusion of the Tripartite Axis Pact on September 27, 1940 among Germany, Italy, and Japan universalized their common purposes militarily and politically: It linked together the forces of aggression and revision in Europe and the Far East in a new global purpose of conquest and revision. The German invasion of Russia on June 22, 1941 and the Japanese attack on Pearl Harbor six months later were politically the ultimate challenge to the old international order and the maximum expressed determination to establish a new order.

The political effects of this Axis military effort seemed to have been threefold: It globalized diplomacy as never before, particularly as this truly world war spawned new problems and created new needs; it marked a major step in the gradual shift of the center of international relations away from Europe and toward an awareness of other power centers in the world; and it created the ingredients of what was to be a new historical synthesis arising out of the defeat of the Axis powers that produced the decline of the European colonial empires and their metropolitan centers in Europe, the rise of new nation-states in what came to be known as the Third World, and the emergence of communism as a new contender for power on a global scale.

B. As Soviets Face War and Diplomacy

1. STALIN, THE DECISIONMAKER

(a) Concentration of power

World War II was the catalyst of change that was to set the course of international relations into new and unexpected directions. For the Russian people and particularly for the Soviet regime this was a war of survival, one that conjured up all the deeper and darker national traits of insecurity, suspicion of foreigners, and a profound feeling of inferiority arising from their vulnerability and weakness. Stalin reflected many of these characteristics as the Soviet Union faced the problems of war and diplomacy. And the concentration of power in his hands and the total exercise of that power in an enveloping climate of fear tended to radiate and reinforce these characteristics to those below who were carrying out his policies and orders.

Wartime American negotiators discovered very quickly that the real decisionmaker in the Soviet system was Stalin. Little could be achieved, it was found after much frustration and misspent energy, without his imprimatur. Once while waiting to see Stalin, Ambassador Standley reflected on what many diplomats discovered to be a truism: "I was beginning to learn. Every question, of even the most minor importance, eventually passed up to Stalin for decision." [1]

Such centralization of power and authority produced two effects on wartime negotiations. When negotiating with Stalin himself, as it will be shown below, decisions could be made immediately and problems often resolved without unnecessary delay. Though a tough negotiator and often rude, Stalin could be surprisingly affable, congenial, moderating, even pliant in some instances, as observers at Yalta and other wartime conferences have reported. James F. Byrnes, wartime Director of Economic Stabilization, adviser to President Roosevelt at Yalta and later Secretary of State under President Truman, found Stalin, as other negotiators had who dealt with him, "a very likable person." [2]

In Moscow, the direct approach was usually rewarding. Ambassador Harriman's intercession with Stalin made it possible on many occasions for General Deane, as head of the U.S. military mission in Moscow, to cut through the bureaucratic redtape and get decisions on supply matters that were being interminably delayed. Fear of de-

---

[1] Standley and Ageton, op. cit., p. 115.
[2] Byrnes, James F., Speaking Frankly. Westport, Conn., Greenwood Press, 1947, pp. 44–45.

cision by subordinates paralyzed administration of problems dealing with foreign officials.

At the same time this concentration of power imposed an inflexible rigidity that made negotiations extraordinarily difficult, sometimes impossible. A common theme running through accounts of wartime negotiating experience was that of Gen. John R. Dean, head of 'he U.S. Military Mission in Moscow and administrator of lend-lease at the Soviet end. Deane wrote:

> In negotiations with foreign nations, one may be sure that Soviet representatives come to the conference table without authority to make any departures from their instructions—only one man in the Soviet Union can make "on the spot" decisions and he is Joe Stalin. The Molotovs, Vyshinskys, Gromykos, and Maliks are little more than messengers.[3]

Gustav Hilger, an experienced German diplomat who negotiated the Nazi-Soviet Pact with Molotov, made a similar observation about Molotov who he said "never showed any personal initiative, but seemed to keep strictly to the rules laid down by Stalin. When problems came up, he would regularly say that he had to consult his 'government.' "[4]

Rigid control from the center reduced the effectiveness of negotiations on both sides. Soviet diplomats were handicapped by their narrowly limited power of decision that prevented them from exploring new developments or taking new initiatives. Unable to use their own discretion, they were put in a negotiating straitjacket by their superiors in Moscow. Western diplomats were also handicapped by this rigidity in that they were restricted from probing hard and soft spots in the Soviet positions, making progress in negotiations, if at all, painful and slow moving. Yet this rigid process relieved the Soviet negotiator of responsibilities that he often willingly did not want to bear.[5]

(b) Value of diplomacy to Stalin

In diplomacy as in everything else Stalin concentrated power within himself. He personalized diplomacy because he understood that despite its transformation over the years diplomacy's importance as an instrument of national power was in no way diminished. Stalin did not make Hitler's mistake of casting aside this valuable instrument and believing, as he did from 1937 to 1939 and in 1941, that triumphs could be won and power augmented only with the sword.[6]

An irrationality that devalued diplomacy governed Hitler's policy toward Russia leading to the invasion of June 1941. During the previous 22 months the Nazis had won great concessions from the Soviets by combining negotiations with subtle menaces. On every contested

[3] Deane, John R. Negotiating on Military Assistance, 1943–45, in, Dennett, Raymond and Joseph E. Johnson. Negotiating with the Russians. Boston, Mass., World Peace Foundation, 1951. p. 27.

[4] Hilger and Meyer, op. cit., p. 290.

[5] Ikle. How Nations Negotiate, pp. 123–124. In a letter to President Truman, Harriman stressed the importance of dealing solely with Stalin. The occasion was the Moscow visit of Harry Hopkins in June 1945. Harriman wrote: "I told you, I believe, that I was certain that Molotov did not report to Stalin accurately and in fact truthfully in all cases. This was brought out again in our talks. It is clear also that Molotov is far more suspicious of us, and less willing to view matters in our mutual relations from a broad standpoint, than is Stalin. The fact that we were able to see Stalin six times and deal directly with him was a great help. Many of our difficulties could be overcome if it were possible to see him more frequently * * *." (Harriman, W. Averell and Elie Abel, Special Envoy to Churchill and Stalin, 1941–46. New York, Random House, 1975, p. 474.)

[6] Craig. Totalitarian Approaches to Diplomatic Negotiation, pp. 116–117. On Aug. 22, 1939, Hitler admitted his preference for solutions through war when he told his generals: "Now Poland is in the position in which I wanted her * * * I am only afraid that at the last moment some swine or other will yet submit to me a plan for mediation."

point in the partition of Eastern Europe that was agreed to in the Nazi-Soviet Pact, the Soviets yielded. Stalin had actually gone to greater lengths in appeasing Germany than Britain and France during the years from 1933 to March 1939; and he was even preparing, the Germans believed, to make further concessions. But, as Craig noted, "Hitler the warrior had superseded Hitler the negotiator."[7]

Stalin, like Lenin and Trotsky before him and for that matter even his Imperial predecessors, valued diplomacy, especially in times of weakness. Far from preferring the arbitrament of arms to decisions at the conference table, Stalin's was in many ways a Russian perception of diplomacy, one that generally valued it for its defensive utility and its ability to win great triumphs at small risks. Accordingly, as Craig pointed out, the Soviets "have shown virtuosity, not only in mastering its procedures and forms, but also in devising formidable negotiating techniques of their own."[8]

In World War II, Stalin used diplomacy within the Grand Alliance as an instrument for strengthening the Soviet Union politically and militarily, for securing its conquests, and finally for establishing its position as a world power.

2. MOLOTOV AND HIS FOREIGN POLICY CADRES

(a) The Molotov generation of diplomats

Stalin may have valued diplomacy as an instrument of national power but he faced the problems of war and diplomacy with a much demoralized, untrained and generally unprepared diplomatic establishment and with a Foreign Minister noted more for Bolshevik stolidiness and obstinancy than for brilliance and tactical skill in negotiations. For 1939 has come to be looked upon as a "major watershed" in the personnel policies of the Foreign Affairs Commissariat and its devastation by the Great Purge as a strictly negative contributary factor in the catastrophe that engulfed Soviet Russia in 1941. As Robert M. Slusser, a specialist on Soviet diplomacy, observed, the Commissariat of Foreign Affairs had lost "its capacity to serve effectively as an intermediary between Russia and the outside world," a crucial indictment of any foreign diplomatic establishment.[9]

The novice Soviet diplomats of the wartime period, untrained and with little experience, floundered on occasion, and adopting a hypercautious approach to diplomacy, exasperated their foreign colleagues in negotiations.[10] Hemmed in by a predominating NKVD presence and distanced still further from policymaking than their predecessors by an autocratic Stalin, they were reduced to the level of a suppressed and isolated minority within the Soviet bureaucracy and diplomatic community.[11]

---

[7] Ibid., p. 117.
[8] Ibid.
[9] Slusser, op. cit., pp. 230–232.
[10] Uldricks, Impact of Great Purges on People's Commissariat of Foreign Affairs, p. 197. See also, Slusser, op. cit., p. 230 for a comment on the lack of training and diplomatic skills within the Commissariat.
[11] Hayter, Diplomacy of Great Powers, pp. 22–23. Hayter observed that the "diplomats of Molotov's school are iron civil servants. Indeed, even Molotov himself, despite his authentically revolutionary and old Bolshevik past, is something of an iron civil servant, and he has formed many in his image, primarily Gromyko." Hayter noted further that Soviet diplomats in the Stalin era were "denied all social life, other than the most formal, by orders from Moscow, and the vast staffs of Soviet Embassies lived, like an enclosed monastic order, shut off by the high walls literal and metaphorical, from the ordinary life of the country around them."

Comprised mostly of Great Russians (with a sprinkling of Ukrainians, Byelorussians, and Armenians, but very few Jews) generally of peasant and working-class stock, they were somewhat clumsy socially, not intellectuals in the Western sense, but, in Hayter's judgment, "very technically able." [12]

This new Molotov generation had manifested an intense nationalistic attitude (that is, Great Russian), having been exposed to a unique wartime experience that witnessed a revival of Great Russian nationalism, renewed emphasis upon Russia as a great power, and a resurrection of prerevolutionary traditions. [13]

Molotov was more "an iron civil servant," as Hayter termed it, than a revolutionary hero, and he molded many within his foreign policy cadre accordingly in his image, particularly Gromyko. [14] He wanted a foreign service staffed by others like himself. The casualness that characterized Russian administration under both the Tsarist and Soviet regimes had to be eradicated. For Molotov everything had to be just so. As Roetter described him, "With his pince-nez and pedantic fussiness which caused Western diplomats to refer to him as 'Aunti Moll,' he pursued his goal with the determined air of a maiden aunt who could not stand untidyness, and he succeeded." [15]

In one sense, Molotov was fortunate. He began with a clean slate, thanks to the Great Purge. When he took over the Foreign Commissariat, the first generation of young men educated entirely under the Soviet regime were leaving the universities, academies, and institutes to begin their careers. Though untrained as diplomats, they were malleable. Too young to have been active in the revolution and untouched by the bitter ideological battles and arguments of that period, they were truly products of the regime with passions and emotions uninvolved in these earlier struggles. They were bureaucrats, careerists whose primary concern, like Molotov's, was to make things work. Such pliable, submissive young men were, according to Roetter, "ideal material for the kind of Service" Molotov wanted. [16]

Accordingly, he set out to recruit a new breed of diplomats, in Roetter's words, with this criteria—"efficient, capable, ruthless, tough, and unquestioningly loyal to all and any orders from the Kremlin." [17]

And Molotov succeeded, particularly in transforming the Commissariat under the rubrics of Stalinism. For after 1939 unity under Stalin's command was successfully imposed at the top party level at the cost of eliminating any opportunity for the expression of views at vari-

---

[12] Ibid., p. 23.
[13] Meissner, Foreign Ministry and Foreign Service of U.S.S.R., pp. 60–61. Meissner also discussed the formal changes made in the Soviet diplomatic establishment during the wartime period.
[14] Hayter, Diplomacy of Great Powers, p. 22.
[15] Roetter, op. cit., p. 108. Flt. Adm. William D. Leahy, wartime Chief of Staff and aide to the President, referred to "Molly" arriving for his first visit with President Truman in April 1945. (Leahy, William D., Flt. Adm. I Was There. New York, McGraw-Hill. 1950, p. 349.) Bohlen recalled the incident at a party in the Waldorf Astoria Hotel in 1946 when celebrating the completed treaties with the East European countries Molotov did not know what to do when "a merry Ernie Bevin [the British Foreign Minister] linked arms with him and [Secretary of State] Byrnes and began to sing 'Sweet Molly Malone,'" an old Irish ballad about a Dublin fishmonger. Bohlen continued: "Knowing he looked awkward, but not wanting to break away. Molotov wore a silly smile and moved his lips slightly, as if joining in the song. He seldom tried to be funny, and when he did the result was usually elephantine. * * *" (Bohlen, op. cit., pp. 379–380).
[16] Ibid., pp. 108–109.
[17] Ibid., pp. 107–108.

ance with Stalin's intended policy. As Slusser observed, "The Commissariat of Foreign Affairs under Molotov's direction—its internal staff and its diplomatic representatives abroad thoroughly purged—functioned in perfect accordance with the Communist theory of centralized, monolithic policy formulation and execution." [18]

After the formation of the Grand Alliance, the role of the Commissariat (renamed Ministry in 1946) was reduced to a secondary level of importance as Stalin assumed immediate responsibility for the formulation and conduct of Soviet foreign policy.[19]

(b) Characterization of Molotov as diplomat and negotiator

Characterizations of Molotov suggest his strengths and weaknesses as a diplomat and negotiator. Lenin once dismissed him as "the best filing clerk in Russia" and referred to him as the "iron behind." Karl Radek nicknamed him "Stone Bottom," presumably for his stubbornness. Churchill described him as being carved from cold Siberian granite. "A man of outstanding ability and cold-blooded ruthlessness," he was "above all men, fitted to be the agent of the policy of an incalculable machine." [20]

Hilger regarded him as "a highly efficient administrator, a capable executive of policies that are handed down to him, and an experienced bureaucrat." But unlike Litvinov, he had "no creative mind." [21]

Paul Schmidt, another German diplomat who observed Molotov at close range, saw in Molotov "a certain mathematical precision and unerring logic in his way of speaking and presenting arguments. In his precise diplomacy he dispensed with flowery phrases and, as though he were teaching a class, gently rebuked the sweeping vague generalities of Ribbentrop and, later, even of Hitler." [22]

Wartime encounters with Molotov among American negotiators by and large produced realistic and often favorable appraisals. In meetings with Molotov, President Roosevelt was "unusually uncomfortable" and "his style was cramped," noted Harry Hopkins, his close wartime adviser. The language barrier had something to do with it, but Roosevelt had never encountered such a person like Molotov. He lacked that "Western kind of mind and an understanding of the ways of the world that Roosevelt knew," a characteristic he found in Litvinov. Rather than being appalled by this "new and strange problem in human relations that Molotov presented," as Robert E. Sherwood, White House aide to Roosevelt and historian of the Roosevelt-Hopkins relationship wrote, he looked upon it as a challenge "to discover the common ground which, he was sure, must somewhere exist." The tenor of this first meeting in May 1942 was, in Sherwood's words, "marked by a somewhat unexpected frankness and amiability" on Molotov's part, leading to the supposition that since the Soviets wanted something "very seriously," Stalin had given the word "to be somewhat more agreeable than is Mr. Molotov's custom." [23]

[18] Slusser, op. cit., p. 231.
[19] Ibid., pp. 232–233.
[20] Ibid., p. 108, and Bohlen, op. cit., p. 380.
[21] Uldricks, Impact of Great Purges on People's Commissariat of Foreign Affairs, p. 198.
[22] Craig, Totalitarian Approaches to Diplomatic Negotiation, p. 118, ff. 48.
[23] Sherwood, Robert E., Roosevelt and Hopkins: An Intimate History. New York, Harper, 1948, p. 561.

Secretary Hull found Molotov "to be a quiet-mannered, very agreeable man who confined his talk strictly to the serious emergency matters pending." Though not easy to approach at their first meeting where he "seemingly kept a reserved attitude," at Moscow in 1943 "he became more affable. He early impressed me with his ability, shrewdness, and resourcefulness." [24] But Acheson wrote Molotov off: "he was tough, but a poor diplomatist, outmaneuvered by Ribbentrop, and unprepared for the massive Nazi offensive mounted against the Soviet Union." [25] Without further explanation, Adm. William D. Leahy, a participant in many wartime summit conferences and member of the Joint Chiefs of Staff, said that judging from his observations at Teheran and Yalta, he "did not have a very high opinion of the Soviet Foreign Minister." [26]

In contrast, Ambassador Standley, a sharp critic of the Soviet Union, wrote most favorably about Molotov, stressing the kindness and courtesy that marked their many encounters in Moscow. Standley probably best summed up his attitude when he said to Secretary Hull immediately before Hull's departure for the Moscow Foreign Ministers Conference of October 1943: "I have always found Mr. Molotov scrupulously polite and correct. At no time do I recall that he treated me unpleasantly, even though he was sometimes called upon to tell me unpleasant things. But he is a completely humorless, dedicated man, devoted to Party principles and wholeheartedly loyal to the boss." [27]

And finally Bohlen, who observed Molotov at close range as interpreter-adviser to the President at the wartime summit conferences and later as Ambassador, gave a balanced appraisal of Molotov as a diplomat and negotiator, stressing particularly the word "impassive" in his description, a word that invariably was used by those attempting to describe him. On the occasion of the Moscow Conference on October 1943, Bohlen wrote:

Like almost all Soviet leaders a man of mystery, Molotov maintained that air at the conference. Although he was obviously trying to be affable, he had a hard time smiling, and his face remained impassive throughout most of the talks. This first close-up impression of Molotov as a careful, sober negotiator, the epitome of an intelligent Soviet bureaucrat, deepened the more I came in contact with him, and I had many an hour with him over the next dozen years. [28]

Bohlen fleshed out this characterization of Molotov in a later appraisal of his career as Foreign Minister. He wrote:

Molotov was the perfect assistant to Stalin. He was not more than five feet four inches tall, fitting the pattern of associates who would not physically dominate the dictator. Molotov was a fine bureaucrat. Methodical in his procedures, he was usually thoroughly prepared to argue his case. He would carry out his orders no matter how ridiculous he might appear to other Foreign Ministers. * * *
In the sense that he relentlessly pursued his objective, he was a skillful diplomat. He never initiated policy on his own, as Hitler found out at their famous meeting. Stalin made policy; Molotov executed it. He was an opportunist, but only within the framework of his instructions. He plowed along like a tractor. I never saw him pull off any delicate maneuver; it was his stubbornness that made him effective. [29]

[24] Hull, Memoirs, vol. 2, p. 1174.
[25] Acheson, Dean A. Sketches from Life of Men I Have Known. New York, Harper, 1959, p. 85.
[26] Leahy, William D., Fleet Admiral. I Was There. New York, McGraw-Hill, 1950, p. 349.
[27] Standley and Ageton, op. cit., p. 497.
[28] Bohlen, op. cit., p. 130.
[29] Ibid., p. 380.

In brief, Molotov, as a diplomat and negotiator, was the consummate Soviet bureaucrat and lieutenant to Stalin: A true believer, methodical, precise, logical, ruthless, fiercely realistic, cold and calculating, able, a follower of orders, and utterly loyal to his chief. His was not a creative mind but one that pursued diplomatic objectives with the stubbornness and persistence of a mule. Lacking facility of mind, originality, and quickness of maneuver, essential assets in negotiations, he, nonetheless, possessed the Communist virtues of being able to accept appraisals of Soviet interests and goals as defined by his mentor and work diligently, often effectively, within those prescribed limits. A dedicated Communist believer whose speech was permeated with the flavor of Marxist-Leninist verities and whose actions were dedicated wholly to achieving its single-minded purposes, Molotov was a tough negotiator who, nonetheless, won a grudging respect from his diplomatic adversaries.[30]

3. SOVIET AMBASSADORS TO THE UNITED STATES

(a) Oumansky, "a walking insult"

Secretary Hull may have thought kindly of Molotov, but he regarded Constantine A. Oumansky, the Soviet Ambassador to the United States, as "a walking insult when at his worst." [31] Oumansky was a tough, abusive, ruthless negotiator, in contrast to Hull, himself a genial dignified elder statesman. Hull gave this estimate of Oumansky as a diplomat:

Oumansky was one of the most difficult foreign diplomats with whom we ever had to deal. He was insulting in his manner and speech, and had an infallible faculty for antagonizing those of us with whom he came in contract. Overbearing, he made demands for concessions as if they were a natural right, and protested our acts as if they were heinous offenses. In my opinion he did much harm to Russian-American relations.[32]

Acheson shared Hull's views. In describing the difficulty in adapting to the changed relationship from one of hostility during the period of the Nazi-Soviet Pact to that of friendship after the German invasion, Acheson noted that Oumansky belonged to "the new school of offensive Soviet diplomats." Never learning the manners of the old Russian Foreign Office as had Chicherin, Litvinov, and Maisky, these new men "cultivated boorishness as a method of showing their contempt for the capitalist world, with which they wished minimum contact." In Acheson's estimation, Andrei Vishinsky, the Deputy Foreign Minister, was "a natural blackguard, but cultivated and amusing; Gromyko's gaucheness was relieved by a grim, sardonic humor." But, Oumansky "had no redeeming qualities." Acheson admitted that "to frustrate him with icy politeness" had been a source of "considerable pleasure." So, Acheson acknowledged, "it was difficult to reverse course and, as policy cleared, to begin helping instead of hindering Russian procurement in the United States." [33]

But Acheson, then concerned with lend-lease problems as Assistant Secretary of State, did not have to bear this burden for long. Ou-

[30] Bohlen, op. cit., p. 381.
[31] Hull, Memoirs, vol. 1, p. 809.
[32] Ibid., p. 743.
[33] Acheson, Present at the Creation, p. 34. For a summary of U.S. policy toward Soviet Russia on the eve of the German invasion, see, Hull, Memoirs, vol. 2, pp. 972–973.

mansky's removal came about during Harriman's first mission Moscow in September–October 1941. In a talk with Stalin the subject of ambassadors came up. Harriman, who was well aware of American displeasure with Oumansky, told Stalin, rather politely, that "he was overzealous in watching out for Soviet interests in the United States" and that he thought those interests "would be best served by a man who knew us and how to get along with us." [33a]

Not long thereafter Oumansky was replaced by Litvinov, transferred to Mexico where he was killed in a plane crash of suspicious cause.[34]

(b) *Litvinov, "a morning coat * * * dusted off"*

In contrast to the inhospitable Oumansky, Litvinov was most hospitable and, indeed, had become Soviet Russia's symbol of a political reorientation westward. Ambassador Standley viewed his diplomatic career as a barometer for reading the current state of Soviet-American relations and its future course. When President Roosevelt sent Hopkins to Moscow in July 1941 to confer with Stalin on lend-lease, Litvinov, who had "disappeared into the vast silences after the Nazi-Soviet pact" as Sherwood put it, resurfaced to act as interpreter. As Hopkins later said, in Sherwood's words, "he seemed like a morning coat which had been laid away in mothballs when Russia retreated into isolation from the West but which had now been brought out, dusted off and aired as a symbol of completely changed conditions." [35] When the Harriman-Beaverbrook mission went to Moscow 2 months later, Litvinov returned to Washington as ambassador in one of the mission's planes.[36]

As Ambassador, Litvinov apparently made a most favorable impression in the United States.[37]

Secretary Hull had earlier described him as "a thoroughly capable diplomat and international statesman," and presumably this estimate was enhanced still further in their wartime dealings in Washington.[38] Leahy found Litvinov to be "alert, energetic, and, for a Russian of the present regime, attractive." [39] Acheson acknowledged that Litvinov "understood the forms and uses of courtesy" unlike other new types in the Soviet diplomatic establishment.[40] And Standley, who on a number of occasions on his return to Moscow lunched with Litvinov followed by bridge, said that his was "one of the most pleasant associations I had with a Russian official while I was in Moscow," and that he "enjoyed" Litvinov for his "sharp intellect and for his pleasant personality." Standley hoped to maintain this friendly relationship.[41]

[33a] Harriman, American and Russia, p. 164.
[34] Acheson, Present at the Creation, p. 34. Sherwood referred to Oumansky as "that tough proposition" with whom Roosevelt had "few personal contacts' leaving that to Hull and Sumner Welles, the Under Secretary of State. (Sherwood, op. cit., p. 561.) Oumansky seemed to have adapted to the changed relationship after the German invasion. Hull wrote in August 1941 on the occasion of a meeting with the Soviet Ambassador: "Oumansky's attitude was now quite different from what it had been at our last interview." (Hull, Memoirs, vol. 2, p. 974.)
[35] Sherwood, op. cit., p. 333.
[36] Standley and Ageton, op. cit., p. 451.
[37] In January 1943, Standley had an audience with Stalin who asked him about Litvinov's popularity or lack of popularity with the American people. This was the first indication Standley had that Litvinov was on his way out. Standley replied: "I think that the attitude of the American people toward Mr. Litvinov is reflected in the great wave of sympathy for the Russian people which has swept over the United States." (Ibid., p. 454.)
[38] Hull, Memoirs, vol. 1, p. 294.
[39] Leahy, op. cit., p. 148.
[40] Acheson, Present at Creation, p. 68.
[41] Standley and Ageton, op. cit., pp. 464 and 471.

After the decisive victory of Stalingrad in early 1943, Standley detected a shift and hardening in Soviet policy toward the West, signaled by the recall of Litvinov from Moscow and Maisky from London. Thereafter, Litvinov assumed a low profile in Moscow undertaking such low-level chores as a greeter of dignitaries and interpreter in conferences with American negotiators.[42]

According to Molotov, the recall of Litvinov and Maisky was linked to Stalin's desire to have them close by as advisers. But Standley had a different reading. When Litvinov failed to appear at a grand diplomatic reception at the Spaso House, the official Embassy residence, in September 1943, and concerned "as to the fate of the most friendly 'Old Bolshevik' I had met," Standley, with his Embassy Counselor, made a courtesy call at the Foreign Office. There, they "found him crowded into a 'cubbyhole' of an office with his English-speaking secretary. Neither one of them looked happy. There were no chairs for us to sit, so all four of us stood during our brief visit." When asked about his next assignment, Litvinov shrugged expressively. "That has not been decided," his secretary replied for him. Asked about bridge the next day, Litvinov and his secretary exchanged glances, and he responded, "I'm not going out at present." Litvinov did return Standley's call, and the Ambassador, acknowledging that he was taken in by the Russians, recorded, "I should have recognized that the frock coat 'was being put back in mothballs,' that the diplomatic freeze was on again."[43]

After the war, Litvinov sank further into obscurity. At his death on December 31, 1951, he was accorded the honors of a minor Soviet hero—with members of the Foreign Ministry as pallbearers, but no one from the Politburo.[44]

C. Problems for Diplomacy and Negotiators

1. Major Problems in Wartime Negotiations

For the Soviet Union, World War II was a test of national survival, a test of its military prowess, and a test of its skill in diplomacy. Entering the war in the wake of the Great Purge that had weakened its military arm and devastated its diplomatic establishment, the Soviet Union faced the problems of war and diplomacy hardly from a position of strength.

The major problems of diplomacy that Soviet and American negotiators had to cope with during the war arose from three sources: The conduct of the war, the maintenance of the coalition, and the structure of the peace.

The first problem concerned mainly the selection and negotiation of military priorities in the conduct of the war—for example, the prece-

---

[42] On the occasion of the Foreign Ministers Conference in Moscow during October 1943, General Deane wrote: "On Vishinsky's right was Maxim Litvinov, erstwhile Foreign Minister and Ambassador to the United States. I gained the impression at the Conference that although Litvinov was present he had been definitely relegated to the background. As time went on this impression was strengthened in the fact that his principal duties seemed to consist of greeting visiting dignitaries upon their arrival in Moscow." (Deane, John R., General. The Strange Alliance: The Story of Our Efforts at Wartime Cooperation with Russia. New York, Viking Press, 1946, p. 16.) Other accounts of wartime conferences record Litvinov's presence as an interpreter.

[43] Standley and Ageton, op. cit., p. 472.

[44] Roberts, op. cit., p. 375.

dence of the European theater over the Pacific and the strategy of the second front.

The second problem of coalition maintenance focused on such specific matters as lend-lease, coordination of allied cooperative efforts (for example, shuttle bombing), and resolving disruptive military issues that potentially had far-reaching consequences as in the case of the Bern incident in early 1945 when Stalin suspected the Western Allies of negotiating a separate peace with the Germans.

The final problem, the structure of the peace, centered on political arrangements for the occupation of the defeated powers, postwar government in the Soviet conquered areas of Eastern Europe, and the founding of the United Nations.

Probably two of the most transcending problems in the Grand Alliance arose from Soviet insistence on the second front and the Polish question: the first involved sharing the military burden very early in the war; the second concerned conflicting perceptions of security needs on the Soviet side and the requirements of a democratic government in Poland on the Western side. The problem of Soviet responsibility for the Comintern that had plagued its relations with the West in the past was at least momentarily set aside with the ostensible dissolution of the Comintern in 1943.

The wartime experience in the context of diplomacy was unique in three aspects: It represented a time of maximum need and convergence of vital interests for the three major powers; it provided a test as never before of Soviet behavior in negotiating and carrying out agreements; and it revealed the interaction, indeed integration, of military and political affairs within problems of diplomacy as the implications of one impinged almost indistinguishably upon the other. For the essence of coalition diplomacy in World War II was the pursuit of war by political as well as military means.

2. RENEWAL OF SUMMIT DIPLOMACY

The renewal of Summit diplomacy, reminiscent of the Versailles Peace Conference ending World War I, was perhaps the most significant characteristic of wartime negotiations. Major decisions were made at the top as a matter of necessity and preference. Stalin would neither delegate authority nor devolve decisions upon underlings on wartime issues and interests so vital to Soviet security. Nor was it in Churchill's character to do so. And Roosevelt, who like the others held in his hands the reins of power in war and diplomacy, believed in a special chemistry in personal contacts that enhanced the possibility of reaching agreements, as the negotiations for recognition demonstrated. He was convinced that Stalin was "getable," meaning apparently that through his power of persuasion Stalin could be brought into an integrated community in peace as in war.[45]

Furthermore, as Sherwood wrote, "it was a cause of wonderment" to Roosevelt that the Russian leaders seemed to be so inadequately informed as to conditions in the United States or the character of public opinion. Presumably, he felt that direct contact would provide some

---

[45] Sherwood, op. cit., pp. 798–799.

remedy for deficiencies in the flow of information into Moscow from the multiple Soviet sources in the United States.[46]

Yet, the ambassadors were not left out entirely; they played a many-faceted and very important role in wartime negotiations. Ambassador Harriman, British Ambassador to Moscow Sir Clark Kerr, and Litvinov's successor as Soviet Ambassador to the United States, Andrei Gromyko, participated in the Yalta Conference. Harriman was at Teheran. As Ambassador, Harriman, who enjoyed a special relationship with Roosevelt, played a remarkable role in Moscow, as the data below will indicate. In Washington, Gromyko had won the praise of Secretary Hull for his contributions at the Dunbarton Oaks Conferences in 1944. Earlier, Hull had spoken to Molotov with "warm praise" of Gromyko, noting the favorable impression made "by his practical judgment and efficiency."[47] Similarly, Lord Halifax in Washington and John G. Winant in London were exceptional in their respective ambassadorial tasks. Winant, for example, was a principal U.S. negotiator on the European Advisory Commission that was charged with drawing the occupation zones in Germany, while Halifax, as Hull's memoirs records, was deeply and continuously involved in the multiple negotiations carried on in Washington. And the extraordinary wartime career of Ambassador Robert D. Murphy recorded in his autobiography was remarkable for its contributions to the conduct of American foreign policy.[48]

In brief, major decisions may have been made at the Summit, but there was sufficient work to be done at the lower echelons of diplomacy, as a review of the wartime literature reveals, to satisfy the most ambitious envoy.

3. DOWNGRADING OF THE STATE DEPARTMENT

For the United States a unique institutional change occurred during the war that adversely affected the State Department and impacted upon the traditional conduct of diplomacy. There were two aspects of this change: The downgrading of the Secretary of State, and thus the State Department; and the prominence of Hopkins as the President's alter ego in foreign policy matters.

During the early years of the Roosevelt administration, the President tended to ignore Secretary Hull and turn to what Acheson called "other, more energetic, more imaginative, more sympathetic collaborators." Accordingly, Hull, as senior Cabinet officer (Secretary Seward had even referred to himself as "Premier"), became in Acheson's words "one of the least influential members at the White House." Even in the field of diplomacy and the State Department, the Secretary's influence was diluted by Roosevelt's preference for Assistant Secretary Sumner Wells as the principal liaison with the White House on foreign policy

---

[46] Ibid., p. 796.
[47] Hull wrote: "I concluded the conversation by complimenting Gromyko very highly on his excellent showing as head of his delegation. I expressed this compliment in all sincerity, for the Russians had in general shown an admirable cooperation from the first day of the conference." (Memoirs, vol. 2, pp. 1253 and 1681.)
[48] Murphy, Robert D. Diplomat Among Warriors. Garden City, N.Y., Doubleday, 1964, 470 pp.

questions. This downgrading of the Secretary and the State Department was furthered by Hull's inclination to defer to the military during the war and opt for a passive role within the administration.[49]

Contributing further to the shift of power in foreign policy away from the Secretary of State was the President's preference for a personal foreign policy adviser, and this he found in Harry Hopkins. In the course of the war Hopkins accrued increasingly greater power in foreign policy to the extent that Sherwood could write of him in 1942 that "Hopkins was now more than ever 'Roosevelt's own, personal Foreign Office.'"[50]

This combination of factors contributed to the shift of power, decisionmaking, and execution of policy on the most important foreign policy matters away from the State Department to the White House. And as a result, most of the wartime negotiations with the Soviets were carried on by the President himself, Hopkins as his personal diplomatic aide, and Harriman as his special envoy to Moscow.[51]

---

[49] Acheson, Present at Creation, pp. 11–12. For Kennan's criticisms of this development, see Kennan, George F. Memoirs, 1925–50. Boston, Little & Co., 1967, pp. 172–174.

[50] Sherwood, op. cit., p. 640. At Teheran, wrote Admiral Leahy, "Harry Hopkins was acting informally as a sort of Secretary of State for the President, attending meetings with Molotov and Eden" in the absence of Hull. (Leahy, op. cit., p. 207.) When Joseph E. Davies urged the President to appoint Hopkins Ambassador to the Soviet Union upon the return of Standley, Roosevelt "flatly rejected this suggestion," wrote Sherwood, "for he did not want Hopkins to be away from Washington for any length of time." (Sherwood, op. cit., p. 733.)

[51] Sumner Welles expanded on Roosevelt's dislike of specialists in general and Foreign Service officers in particular. He pointed out that the President was unwilling to dictate any memorandums of his conversations with foreign statesmen and diplomats for the information of the State Department and that he harbored a "deep-rooted prejudice against the members of the American Foreign Service and against the permanent officials of the Department of State." He very rarely "could be persuaded to bring into White House conferences on foreign policy any of those State Department specialists who had devoted a lifetime to the study of some particular country or region." Welles noted that during the Cairo Conference and the meeting at Yalta the President did not have at his side a political adviser on Far Eastern affairs and yet both conferences focused in large measure on the Far East. (Quoted in, Kertesz, Stephen D. American and Soviet Negotiating Behavior. In, Stephen D. Kertesz and M. A. Fitzsimons, ed. Diplomacy in a Changing World. South Bend, Ind., University of Notre Dame Press, 1959, chapter 10, pp. 162–163.)

II. NEGOTIATING FOR LEND-LEASE

A. THE HOPKINS MISSION, JULY 30–31, 1941

1. BACKGROUND AND PURPOSE OF THE MISSION

The first major wartime negotiation with the Russian leadership was the Hopkins mission to Moscow during July 30–31, 1941. German military successes in Soviet Russia provided the background for the mission. Germany had invaded Russia on June 22, 1941, and within weeks its armies had pushed deep into the country. The Soviets and the British were now allies in a common purpose, to defeat Hitler's forces. On March 11, 1941, the Lend-Lease Act had been passed, making the United States the main arms supplier to Britain. The question now arose as to how the United States could assist the Russians.

Within a week after the invasion and after preliminary discussions in Moscow, the Soviets requested military assistance from the United States and placed a detailed order.[1]

The President was determined to give all possible aid to the Russians. At the time, Hopkins was in London conferring with Churchill on political understandings and military assistance in the war. Realizing the importance of making certain that the Soviets maintained a permanent front even though defeated in the immediate battle, Hopkins sent word to the President on July 25, suggesting, "If Stalin could in any way be influenced at this critical time, I think it would be worth doing by a direct communication from you through a personal envoy." The President at once authorized Hopkins to go on to Moscow as the bearer of a personal message to Stalin confirming this Nation's willingness to aid Soviet Russia.[2]

The purpose of the Hopkins mission was threefold: To determine whether the Russian military situation was as disastrous as pictured in the War Department, especially as depicted in cables from the U.S. military attaché in Moscow; and, as Hopkins told Stalin in their first meeting, to determine what aid Russia would require that the United States could deliver immediately, and what the Soviet requirements would be on the basis of a long war.[3]

2. HOPKINS CONFERS WITH STALIN

After an arduous and dangerous flight over enemy-controlled waters and over an expanding Russian front, an ailing and very tired Harry Hopkins landed in Moscow on July 29, 1941. On the following day, Hopkins met with Stalin from 6:30 to 8:30 p.m. in the company

---

[1] Jones, Robert Huhn. The Roads to Russia: United States Lend-Lease to the Soviet Union. Norman, Okla., University of Oklahoma Press, 1967, p. 37.
[2] Feis, Herbert. Churchill-Roosevelt-Stalin: The War They Waged and the Peace They Sought. Princeton, Princeton University Press, 1957, pp. 11–12.
[3] Sherwood, op. cit., pp. 327–328.

of Ambassador Laurence Steinhardt and an Embassy staffman acting as interpreter.

Emphasizing that he came as the President's personal representative and was speaking on his behalf as if he were there, Hopkins expressed the President's confidence in a Soviet victory and asked what the Soviet requirements were at that moment and for the long haul. In reply Stalin referred to the list already presented in Washington and enumerated specifically the types, sizes, and numbers of weapons he needed along with supplies of gasoline and aluminum for planes. In addition to other matters they discussed the means and routes of delivery.[4]

On July 31, the following day, Hopkins conferred with Molotov at which time they discussed Japanese aggression in the Far East. Nothing more substantive was discussed. In April 1941, the Soviets had concluded a neutrality pact with Japan but with the German-Russian war underway they became apprehensive lest the Japanese strike into Siberia. Molotov hoped that the United States would issue a warning to Japan as a deterrent. Hopkins responded that the U.S. position toward Japan was a reasonable one and that "we had no desire to be provocative in our relations with Japan." [5]

That evening Hopkins conferred alone, and for the last time, with Stalin from 6:30 p.m. to 9:30 p.m. with Litvinov acting as interpreter. In response to Hopkins' request for the briefing on the war that the President wanted, Stalin elaborated in great detail and with apparent objectivity on the military situation as he appraised it, stressing particularly German strength and Soviet military needs. He also underscored the importance of an American declaration of war against Germany and invited the presence of an American army on the Russian front. Hopkins doubted American interest in this proposal, but agreed to send the message to the President.[6]

3. CONSIDERATIONS ON THE MISSION

(a) *As a negotiating experience*

As a negotiating experience the Hopkins mission was unique. The United States had all the bargaining chips, but it did not bargain: it asked for nothing, only a shopping list. The sole U.S. objective was to keep Soviet Russia in the war, and it was willing to pay the price without asking for anything more than what the Soviets might have been only willing to pay; namely, to fight the Germans.

The Soviets were in the weakest possible bargaining position. Their only leverage was a determination to fight Germany; for them it was a matter of survival. But Soviet-American interests coalesced in absolute terms, having the effect of leveling the inequities in bargaining.

Despite their weakness, however, the Soviets assumed an aggressive negotiating stance: Stalin called for a war declaration and U.S. participation on the Russian front; Molotov pushed for an American warning against Japanese aggression in the Soviet Far East. Neither course was in the interests of the United States, and owing to its stronger negotiating position, it could and did reject them outright.

---

[4] Ibid., pp. 328–329.
[5] Ibid., p. 332.
[6] Ibid., p. 343.

Subsequent negotiating experiences revealed that this type of aggressive negotiating behavior from a position of weakness was a distinctive Soviet characteristic.

Another important point in this first wartime negotiating encounter was the role of interpreters. In the first meeting with Stalin, a U.S. Embassy staffman acted as interpreter; at the second, Litvinov interpreted. However much at home Litvinov may have been in the English language, still the fact remains that Hopkins was receiving Stalin's thoughts and transmitting his own through the filtering system of a Soviet mind. Hopkins was thus placed in double jeopardy; words, meanings, and perceptions passed in a two-way direction, but through a mind uniquely formed by Soviet ideology, experience, training, and thought processes. Subsequent American participants and observers at future conferences with the Soviets, particularly Dr. Philip E. Mosely, the noted American teacher and specialist in Russian affairs, have strongly emphasized the risks created by interpreters and translators. In the business of diplomacy where precision of language and clarity of meaning are extremely, even vitally, important, every precaution has been urged to lessen the risks of imprecision and error in communication.

(b) On the preeminence of Stalin

In negotiating with Hopkins, Stalin revealed neither by his actions nor his words the real weakness and peril of the Soviet Union; but he made it very clear who was in charge in the Soviet Union. Hopkins, deeply impressed by Stalin, came away convinced that the Soviets would fight on to victory, a judgment quite at odds with prevailing opinion in the United States and Britain, and so carried a message of optimism home to the President.[7]

Impressed by the presence and preeminence of the Soviet dictator, Hopkins was also convinced that, as he said in his report, "There is literally no one in the whole Government who is willing to give any information other than Mr. Stalin himself." [8] Hopkins recorded an instance of meeting General Yakovlev who refused to make any comment on the suggestion of establishing a permanent Soviet military mission in Washington, replying that it would have to be taken up with Stalin. "This was Hopkins' first real encounter with the limitations imposed on the lower levels (which meant any level below the very top) of the Soviet system," observed Sherwood; "they did not dare to utter a word on any topic beyond the prescribed agenda." [9] Hopkins had thus seen

---

[7] Sherwood, op. cit., p. 344. Later Hopkins drew a verbal picture of Stalin who, he said, talked "straight and hard" with "no waste of word, gesture, nor mannerism." Talking to him, Hopkins declared, was "like talking to a perfectly coordinated machine, an intelligent machine." His questions were "clear, concise, direct"; he knew "what he wanted, knew what Russia wanted, and he assumed that you knew." Hopkins continued: "No man could forget the picture of the dictator of Russia as he stood watching me leave—an austere, rugged, determined figure in boots that shone like mirrors, stout baggy trousers, and snug-fitting blouse. He wore no ornament, military or civilian * * *. He's about 5 feet 6, about 190 pounds. His hands are huge, as hard as his mind. His voice is harsh but ever under control." Hopkins observed that if he wanted to soften an abrupt answer or a sudden question, "he does it with that quick, managed smile—a smile that can be cold but friendly, austere but warm. He curries no favor with you. He seems to have no doubts. He assures you that Russia will stand against the onslaughts of the German Army. He takes it for granted that you have no doubts either. * * *" Stalin "laughs often enough, but it's a short laugh, somewhat sardonic, perhaps. There is no small talk in him. His humor is keen, penetrating."
[8] Ibid., p. 342.
[9] Ibid., p. 330. In their conversation Yakovlev gave little information and no judgments. In a most circumvoluted manner he noted that the Russians could use extra tanks and antitank guns and that the United States could provide them. But he quickly added, "I am not empowered to say whether we do or do not need tanks or antitank guns."

the "awful fear," as Sherwood put it, which was part of the respect any subordinate, even a general like Yakovlev, regarded his superiors.[10]

(c) *An encounter with Soviet suspicions*

For Hopkins, this mission was his first encounter with Soviet fears, suspicions, and antiforeignism. Steinhardt confided to Hopkins that he and other diplomats in Moscow had been continually frustrated in their attempted dealings with Soviet authorities because of the prevailing attitude of suspicion toward all foreigners which in turn produced an obsession with secretiveness. But Hopkins was determined, as Sherwood wrote, "somehow or other to break through this wall of suspicion." [11]

While his talks with Yakovlev may have given him doubts about his success, at least those with Stalin seemed to have been reassuring. As Sherwood noted, "In 2 days he had gained far more information about Russia's strength and prospects than had ever been vouchsafed to any outsider." [12] But Hopkins knew, as he told the President, that Stalin was the only source of any important information and was, therefore, aware of the depth of suspicions and fears below.[13]

(d) *Mission accomplished*

Hopkins came away from Moscow with some misgivings: He was depressed by this first exposure to totalitarianism. As a believer in liberal democracy, Communist Russia was hard to take. Nonetheless, he left Moscow "elated" with his "two long and satisfactory" talks with Stalin. "I feel ever so confident about this front," he told the President. "The morale of the population is exceptionally good. There is unbounded determination to win." [14] Thus the President got the assessment he sought which was the main purpose of the mission.

Confident of Soviet staying power in the war and impressed by Stalin's strength of personality, firmness of decision, and totality of control, Hopkins could now feel secure in the future development of the anti-Hitler coalition, particularly in the decision to give lend-lease assistance. Sherwood called the mission a "turning point" in the wartime relations of the United States and Britain with the Soviet Union. "No longer would all Anglo-American calculations be based on the probability of early Russian collapse," he wrote, "after this, the whole approach to the problem was changed." [15] To Feis it marked rather the "point of no return." Hopkins' report to the President gave a firm basis for an already strong inclination. Up to that point the United States responded to Soviet requests for assistance without assuming any obligation; on August 2, 1941, in an exchange of notes with Moscow, it made an official commitment to give all practical economic assistance to strengthen the Soviet Union in its "struggle against armed aggression." [16]

[10] Ibid., p. 345.
[11] Ibid., p. 327.
[12] Ibid., p. 343.
[13] Ibid., p. 342.
[14] Ibid., pp. 344–345. Also, Hopkins to the President, the Secretary of State and the Under Secretary, Moscow, Aug. 1, 1941, 3 p.m., received 8:50 p.m., Foreign Relations of the United States, 1941, General: The Soviet Union, vol. 1, p. 814.
[15] Sherwood, op. cit., p. 343.
[16] Feis, Churchill-Roosevelt-Stalin, p. 13.

And finally Hopkins was able to give the President a close-up reading, his first one, on Stalin as a personality, a leader, and a negotiating adversary under great stress. This was a one-on-one negotiating encounter, unstructured and informal, but direct and intimate, frank and revealing. Its effect was to establish a direct and highly significant connection between Roosevelt and Stalin, a connection that formed the basis for the Big Three conferences yet to come.

B. The HARRIMAN-BEAVERBROOK MISSION, SEPTEMBER–OCTOBER 1941

1. BACKGROUND AND PURPOSE

(a) German military successes, Soviet peril

During the 3 months following the Hopkins mission the German armies continued to mark up extraordinary successes, advancing rapidly eastward before the retreating Russians and enveloping great swatches of territory more than twice the size of France. As autumn approached Stalin hoped that the Russian winter would slow down the German advance. But one-half the Ukraine was now in German hands; Leningrad was in a state of siege; Russia's chief source of iron ore, the Krivoi Rog Basin, had been lost. Industrial plants in European Russia producing aluminum, aircraft, trucks, and tanks had to be evacuated to safety behind the Urals. Seven or eight months would pass before production could be resumed. In the last hours of the Harriman-Beaverbrook mission the Germans were within some 30 miles of Moscow as the anxious Russians quickly concluded the conference, sent the delegates on their way and prepared to evacuate foreign embassy staffs to the provincial city of Kuibyshev on the Volga before the onrushing Germans enveloped the Soviet capital.

In brief, Soviet Russia faced "a mortal menace," as Stalin wrote Churchill on September 4, 1941, in an appeal for Western assistance. Only a second front in the Balkans or France, he felt, could draw off sufficient German divisions in the east to bring relief, and he asked for supplies of aluminum, airplanes, and tanks from the West to keep Russia going.[17]

(b) Agreement on purposes at Roosevelt-Churchill Argentia meeting

Such was the background of the Harriman-Beaverbrook mission, a follow-on to the Hopkins mission of July. On his return from Moscow, Hopkins joined Churchill aboard the HMS *Prince of Wales* then preparing for a rendezvous with Roosevelt aboard the *Augusta* at Argentia off the coast of Newfoundland where from August 9 to 12, 1941, aid to Russia was a primary topic on the agenda.

Now the two leaders had before them Hopkins himself and his convincing report that the Russians could hold out until winter, that they could then rebuild their armies, improve their defenses, complete the relocation of industries, increase weapons production and improve their military equipment. Impressed and hopeful, Roosevelt and Churchill decided, on Hopkins' suggestion, to send a joint mission to Moscow. Having reached agreement on the purposes of the mission,

---

[17] Harriman and Abel, op. cit., pp. 81 and 107.

they dispatched a proposal to Stalin on August 15; he welcomed the invitation. Churchill told the President that he would send Lord Beaverbrook, a noted British journalist and Minister of Aircraft Production. Hopkins, who had already begun to assume control over the allocation of war supplies, was the logical choice as the U.S. representative, but ill health stood in the way. The President appointed Harriman who was then in London in charge of U.S. military aid to Britain. In that capacity Harriman had won the confidence of Churchill and other British leaders and in addition had much experience in administering aid programs.[18]

In the next 2 weeks Anglo-American fears of a Russo-German negotiated peace magnified as the German military successes mounted, despite Stalin's assurances that nothing of the kind would take place.[19] Upon returning from Argentia, Roosevelt set out to organize the supply mission. His thinking on this matter of aid to the Soviet Union, at that time and in the years ahead, was clearly set forth in a letter of August 30 to Secretary of War Henry L. Stimson in which he wrote: "I deem it to be of paramount importance for the safety and security of America that all reasonable munitions help be provided for Russia not only immediately but as long as she continues to fight the Axis powers effectively. I am convinced that substantial and comprehensive commitments of such character must be made to Russia by Great Britain and the United States at the proposed conference." [20]

The President was, however, very concerned whether American public opinion would accept the idea of aid to Communist Russia and whether Congress would appropriate funds through lend-lease if Russia were added to the bill. Isolationist sentiment was still strong in the country, and anti-Soviet attitudes were deeply rooted. For these reasons he urged Harriman to get some qualifying statement from Stalin on the matter of religious freedom that might assuage opposition in the American religious quarter.[21]

Thus when the U.S. delegation left Washington for a preliminary meeting with their British counterparts in London, and then on to Archangel aboard the HMS *London* on September 21, the main purpose of the mission had been clearly defined: To discuss thoroughly a continuing program of allocation and supply of assistance for the Soviet forces.[22] Stress was to be placed on Anglo-American support for the duration of the war, not merely for the immediate crisis. Harriman had the additional directive to explore the religious question with Stalin, hoping for a Soviet modification. The matter of financing was left open; Roosevelt, with potential congressional opposition in mind, had not yet decided whether to bring the Russians under Lend-Lease.[23]

[18] Feis, Roosevelt-Churchill-Stalin, pp. 13–14, and Jones, op. cit., pp. 51–54.
[19] Ibid., p. 57.
[20] Quoted in, Feis, Churchill-Roosevelt-Stalin, p. 14.
[21] Ibid., p. 15.
[22] Ibid., p. 14.
[23] Jones, op. cit., p. 59. Admiral Standley, a member of the delegation, gave this definition of the Mission's purpose: "We were to do everything within the power of our two nations to keep the Russians fighting until spring, when, rather optimistically, we hoped the Allied potential power could be applied in sufficient strength to draw off some of the pressure on the Soviets." (Standley and Ageton, op. cit., p. 68.)

2. CONFERENCES WITH STALIN

(a) First meeting: Elation

The Harriman-Beaverbrook mission arrived in Moscow on September 28, 1941; the first meeting with Stalin took place in the Kremlin that evening, lasting 3 hours from 9 p.m. to after midnight. Litvinov acted as interpreter. (Harriman was not a novice in negotiating with Soviet leaders; he had his first experience in 1926 when he conducted a successful negotiation with Trotsky on the subject of an American manganese mining concession in the Caucasus.) [24]

Cordiality and frankness marked the first meeting, as Stalin discussed the military situation and his urgent needs, and Harriman and Beaverbrook outlined what was available from American and British sources. Stalin began the meeting with a review of the military situation in the same frank and objective manner that he had with Hopkins. He credited Germany with superiority in airpower by a ratio of 3 to 2, in tanks by 3 or 5 to 1, and in numbers of divisions, 320 to 288. He graded the quality of the Nazi satellite divisions, commending the Finns as the best fighters, and citing the others in descending order: The Italians, Rumanians, and Hungarians. Then he discussed Soviet military needs, with tanks heading the list, followed by antitank guns, medium bombers, antiaircraft guns, armor plate, fighter and reconnaissance planes, and barbed wire. Again Stalin stressed the necessity of the second front and asked for a commitment of British forces to fight in the Ukraine. In response, Beaverbrook mentioned the possibility of some British forces being dispatched to the Caucasus, but Stalin countered sharply: "There is no war in the Caucasus but there is in the Ukraine." [25]

Harriman raised the question of the Siberian airports and the possibility of the delivery of American aircraft to Russia via Alaska. At first Stalin warmed to the subject but quickly cooled when the use of American pilots was mentioned, saying, it was "too dangerous a route." Harriman concluded that Stalin did not want to provoke the Japanese with whom the Soviets had a neutrality treaty.[26]

Stalin asked about peace objectives, and when Beaverbrook mentioned the eight points of the Atlantic Charter just proclaimed by Roosevelt and Churchill, Stalin brought up the matter of German reparations—"What about getting the Germans to pay for the damage?" Beaverbrook replied, "We must win the war first." [27]

Harriman turned to a discussion of religion in the Soviet Union and mentioned Roosevelt's concern for American public opinion, notably of the Catholics, on this issue, stressing particularly the President's anxiety that it might adversely affect aid to Russia. The President envisioned a favorable impact on public opinion if the Soviet Constitution meant what it said about religious freedom. Stalin claimed to have no knowledge of American public opinion toward Russia, gave the impression that he had no interest in the subject, and intimated that it would best be taken up with his subordinates. Harri-

[24] Harriman, "America and Russia," pp. 2–5.
[25] Sherwood, op. cit., Harriman, "America and Russia," pp. 387–388 and pp. 18–19.
[26] Sherwood, op. cit., pp. 387–388.
[27] Ibid.

man did not press the issue but promised a memorandum at some future time.[28]

The hour was late and the first meeting adjourned after midnight in a spirit of great cordiality. Harriman and Beaverbrook left the Kremlin "more than pleased," as Harriman noted, with this "extremely friendly" first encounter with Stalin. So confident was Beaverbrook that he felt the whole complicated negotiation could be quickly wrapped up and then head for home. But Harriman took exception. Having come a long way with a high-powered delegation, he wanted to discover Russia's actual needs.[29]

(b) Organizational meeting of delegations

Prior to the second meeting with Stalin on September 29, delegates of the Harriman-Beaverbrook mission conferred with Molotov in the afternoon on specific arrangements for the work of the conference. Molotov explained that agreement had been reached in preliminary talks on setting up six committees: aviation; army and military supplies; navy; transport; raw materials and equipment; and medical supplies and Red Cross. Plenary sessions were to be held as needed, and since time was precious, the work of the conference would be most valuable, he said, if carried forth "successfully and speedily."[30]

Beaverbrook and Harriman followed with statements of purpose. Harriman stressed that the United States, like Britain, had the same objective, to aid Russia in resisting the German attack. The U.S. mission had come to Moscow, he continued, "not only as friends but because the United States had a vital and lasting interest in the outcome of the struggle." Harriman concluded, again in Steinhardt's words, with a pledge from the President to the Soviet people, its delegation and Government to give "the fullest possible assistance not only today but as long as the struggle lasted—until ultimate victory."[31]

The meeting ended in an agreeable spirit.

(c) Second meeting: Depression

Such was not the case in the second meeting with Stalin that evening at 7 o'clock. For 2 hours Stalin was rude to the point of insult, as he had been in previous correspondence with the British—"surly, snarly, grasping, and so lately indifferent to our survival," Churchill wrote.[32] It was "very rough going," Harriman recalled. Stalin gave the impression of extreme dissatisfaction with what was being offered. He seemed to question the good faith of Harriman and Beaverbrook, openly charging that they wanted to see Hitler destroy the Soviet regime or else they would have offered more help. At one point Stalin coldly dismissed the Anglo-American efforts of help in these words: "The paucity of your offers clearly shows that you want to see the Soviet Union defeated."[33]

According to Harriman, Stalin "showed his suspicion in a very blunt way." It was difficult to fathom, he said, whether this behavior

[28] Ibid.
[29] Harriman and Abel, op. cit., p. 88.
[30] Steinhardt to Secretary of State, Moscow, Sept. 29, 1941, U.S. Foreign Relations, 1941, Soviet Union, pp. 837–838.
[31] Ibid., p. 838.
[32] Feis, Churchill-Roosevelt-Stalin, p. 15.
[33] Harriman and Abel, op. cit., p. 89.

was a negotiating ploy, "to smoke us out, or whether he had discussed our offer with his associates and they had said it was not enough * * *." Only once did Stalin show any positive response and that was when Harriman, who himself countered Stalin's bluntness in kind, offered to supply 5,000 jeeps. Stalin accepted the offer and asked for more, but rejected brusquely the parallel offer of armored cars, charging that they were death traps, and he didn't want them.[34]

Beaverbrook recorded other signs of Stalin's fury at this meeting. "Stalin was very restless," he reported to Churchill, "walking about and smoking continuously, and appeared to both of us to be under an intense strain." Stalin was also rude, Beaverbrook reported, as when he handed him a letter from Churchill, and after opening the envelope, barely glanced at it and left it on the table during the meeting. When Harriman and Beaverbrook were preparing to leave, Molotov called Stalin's attention to the unread letter, but in a demonstrable put-down gesture, Stalin proceeded to push the letter back in the envelope and handed it to a clerk.[35]

So little was accomplished at this second meeting that Harriman and Beaverbrook asked for a third, and to their great relief Stalin agreed. Neither could account for Stalin's surly and disagreeable behavior. Both left the Kremlin "disheartened, puzzled and somewhat discouraged," as Harriman recalled.[36] Standley described their mood as one of "indigo blue" when he saw them the next morning.[37]

But apparently on reflection Harriman came up with three possible explanations for Stalin's conduct. Though still confessing ignorance as to the real reason, he suggested in a message to the President that Stalin may have been "concerned over military news, or * * * considered that he would get more if he was rough with us, or * * * was just moody over something he heard of the meetings of the committees of the conference, or some incident in his entourage. * * *"[38]

(d) Third meeting: Elation

At the third meeting in the evening of September 30, Stalin's mood had radically changed. Deeply depressed by the previous session and concerned about the burden of failure, Beaverbrook suggested to Harriman that he take the initiative at this final meeting. Harriman agreed.[39]

Beginning the meeting on a sober note, Harriman explained the importance of concluding this conference quickly, successfully and to the satisfaction of all. Stalin agreed, remarking with some amusement that Nazi radio propagandists were already predicting failure and indicating that it was for the three of them to prove Goebbels a liar.[40] Methodically the three negotiators went over a list of 70 items the Soviets had requested while Harriman explained which the United States and Britain were prepared to supply and in what quantities.[41]

---

[34] Ibid., p. 89.
[35] Ibid.
[36] Ibid., and Harriman, America and Russia, p. 19.
[37] Standley and Ageton, op. cit., p. 67.
[38] Harriman and Abel, op. cit., p. 93.
[39] Ibid., p. 90.
[40] Sherwood, op. cit., p. 389.
[41] Harriman and Abel, op. cit., p. 90.

Amity and agreement after some give-and-take in the bargaining process prevailed throughout the proceedings. As Harriman wrote, Stalin made an effort to sound "reasonable and not too exacting." [42] By and large Stalin raised few objections. Sensing the changed atmosphere, Beaverbrook asked Stalin if he were pleased with the offer of assistance. Stalin smiled and nodded. At that point, Litvinov, who was interpreting, bounded out of his chair and out of his modest role as interpretor and "cried with passion," as Beaverbrook wrote: "Now we shall win the war!" [43]

Questions on the conduct of the war in Europe and the Far East were discussed. Ways of communications among the three leaders were explored. And when Stalin again raised the political issue of Allied peace aims and the proposal of extending the Anglo-Soviet military alliance into a postwar treaty, Beaverbrook replied that it would be enough to win the war, and Harriman added that the Atlantic Charter constituted a peace program subscribed to by Britain and the United States, implying presumably that this was sufficient. Other lesser important matters were also discussed. [44]

The meeting went well; it broke up "in the most friendly fashion possible," Harriman reported. Stalin made no effort "to conceal his enthusiasm," giving Harriman the impression that "he was completely satisfied that Great Britain and America meant business." Harriman believed that Stalin had been frank with them and "if we came through as had been promised, and if personal relations were maintained with Stalin, the suspicion that has existed between the Soviet Government and our two governments might well be eradicated." [45] A mark of Stalin's pleasure with this third meeting was an invitation to the two negotiators to have dinner the next evening. They accepted to what turned out to be a sumptuous banquet.

(e) Plenary session and protocol

Meanwhile, the six committees explored with their Soviet counterparts the nuts-and-bolts side of managing the problem of needs and supply in aiding Russia. This first exposure to Soviet indecision at the lower levels in a negotiating mode no doubt mystified the Anglo-American delegates, clogged the work of the committees, and created considerable frustration within the delegations. "One of my colleagues," noted Admiral Standley, head of the committee on naval matters, "described our committee meetings as exercises in frustration." [46]

On October 1, Harriman and Beaverbrook met with their delegates to review the reports of the six committees, some in only very sketchy form ("none of our committees had more than scratched the surface," wrote Standley), and then rushed off to see Molotov about the protocol that the Soviets wanted signed to mark the successful conclusion of the conference. [47] Molotov pressed Harriman and Beaverbrook to record

[42] Ibid., p. 90.
[43] Ibid.
[44] Ibid., pp. 90–92.
[45] Ibid., p. 92.
[46] Standley went on: "Certainly, the Naval Committee, which I headed for the American delegation, could get nowhere at all. We made various proposals for a program of naval supplies but Adm. Nikolai Kuznetsov, Commissar for the Navy and my opposite number in the Russian delegation, wouldn't even comment. I never felt that this indicated a lack of desire to cooperate as much as a lack of information and indecision." (Standley and Ageton, op. cit., p. 67.)
[47] Ibid., pp. 68–69.

their agreement in writing and in a formal protocol. Beaverbrook saw no need for such formality, arguing that the British signed no documents when they worked out their initial lend-lease arrangements with the United States and that protocols were only glorified memorandums. But Molotov was under firm instructions from Stalin; he persisted in the protocol. "You [the British and Americans] didn't have a conference," he said, rejecting the parallel. "A conference must terminate with a protocol." [48]

Without specific instructions from Washington, Harriman was placed in an awkward position. Furthermore, provisions were yet to be made to include the Soviet Union in the Lend-Lease Act. After clarifying a very sticky point on the interpretation of the words to "make available" weapons and materials for the Soviet Union, the protocol was approved for signing on the following day.

In his message to the President, Harriman said he explained to the Soviets that financial arrangements were not worked out in the United States and that "all we are undertaking to do at the present time is to allow them to buy and export from America." [49] The protocol contained 70 principal items and more than 80 items in medical supplies, from tanks, planes and destroyers down to Army boots (the Soviets asked for 400,000 a month) and shellac (300 tons monthly). [50] All of this material and more was promised in the protocol without requiring full information about total Soviet needs or Soviet stocks (or for that matter resources)—information that was required of every other country seeking lend-lease assistance. [51]

3. CONSIDERATIONS ON THE HARRIMAN-BEAVERBROOK MISSION

(a) From a negotiating perspective

(1) No quid pro quo

From a strictly negotiating perspective, the Harriman-Beaverbrook mission was, like that of Hopkins', very much a case of one-sided bargaining or self-bargaining. The Americans did not really come to bargain, but only to find out what the Soviets needed and how those needs could be supplied. Again the assumption of the negotiations, as stated by Roosevelt and Harriman, was that keeping Soviet Russia in the war satisfied vital American interests and that alone was sufficient. The negotiating criteria was, in Harriman's words, "Give and give and give, with no expectation of any return, with no thought of a quid pro quo." [52]

Beaverbrook shared the same view, much to the chagrin of Sir Stafford Cripps, the British Ambassador, and others at the British Embassy. Exasperated beyond endurance by the Russian passion for secrecy, they wanted to break down this wall of secrecy by hard bargaining, trading supplies for detailed information about Russian pro-

---

[48] Harriman and Abel, op. cit., p. 97.
[49] U.S. Foreign Relations, 1941, vol. 1, Soviet Union, p. 841.
[50] Ibid. and Sherwood, op. cit., p. 394.
[51] Feis, Churchill-Roosevelt-Stalin, p. 17. For a more detailed listing of lend-lease requirements, see Harriman to Roosevelt and Hopkins, London, Oct. 10, 1941, and Harriman to Roosevelt, Moscow, Oct. 3, 1941, U.S. Foreign Relations, 1941, vol. 1, Soviet Union, pp. 844–846 and pp. 841–842. See also, Harriman's final report to the President of Oct. 29, 1941 on pp. 849–851.
[52] Quoted in, Standley and Ageton, op. cit., p. 63.

duction and resources. But Beaverbrook was adamant. "They were not going to Moscow to bargain but to give," he said, when designing his negotiating strategy aboard ship. "The Mission must not only offer supplies. It must offer them in such measure that the Russian leaders would be satisfied and encouraged." He explained further to critics in Moscow:

The one way to break down the suspicious attitude which had given rise to Russian secrecy was to make clear beyond a doubt the British and American intention to satisfy Russian needs to the utmost in their power, whether the Russians gave anything or not. It was to be a Christmas-tree party, and there must be no excuse for the Russians thinking they were not getting a fair share of the gifts on the tree.[53]

On the American side, President Roosevelt regarded the religious question in the context of lend-lease, in Harriman's words, as a matter of "the highest domestic priority." It was for him a matter of human rights and of practical politics in dealing with the Congress. Here was a negotiating point; the United States had all the leverage; all that was being asked in return was a Soviet expression of consideration for religious freedom. Harriman attempted to negotiate this point with Stalin, but got nowhere. Subsequent discussion with Molotov, Oumansky, and lesser officials failed to get the satisfaction the President wanted beyond a well-hedged comment by a Soviet official at a press conference. At this meeting with the press, Commissar of Information Solomon A. Lozovsky in effect affirmed with additional explanations the President's comment at his press conference on October 1 in which he stressed only the positive side of guarantees of religious rights under the Soviet Constitution. The President was very displeased with Harriman's performance in Moscow on this matter, hoping that he would get more solid assurances, and, as Harriman later recalled, "took me to task upon my return." [54]

(2) Stalin's tactic of abuse

Most extraordinary in the negotiation, at least from the benign view of the American negotiator, was the pattern of Stalin's behavior, particularly the tactic of abuse interspersed with cordiality. Though the Soviet Union was then facing its greatest peril in its brief history as the German armies were approaching within 30 miles of Moscow, and though its needs for Allied assistance in great quantities were immediate and most acute, still Stalin was the tough-minded negotiator who could and did, by employing the tactic of abuse, throw off balance his negotiating adversaries. By placing them on the defensive, he reversed the roles of petitioner and donor, thus creating a psychological mood and relationship that could give greater assurance that his needs would be met. Perhaps on no other occasion was Stalin able to demonstrate more dramatically this historic Russian negotiating tactic of successfully using diplomacy to create a negotiating position of

---

[53] Taylor, A. J. P. Beaverbrook. New York, Simon and Schuster, 1972. p. 487. Standley deplored the tactic of no quid pro quo. Writing of the negotiation, he noted: "Certainly, we gave a vast amount of naval supplies in those 3 days. But we had been instructed to ask for no quid pro quo. The only exchange of information we received was due to the personal influence of Admiral Kuznetsov; we took home with us Russian hydrographic codes which our Naval attachés had been vainly trying to obtain for months." (Standley and Ageton, op. cit. p. 67.)

[54] Harriman and Abel, op. cit. pp. 103–104.

strength out of one of weakness. "Harriman did not realize it at the time," wrote Sherwood—

but he was to learn on several later occasions that this first experience of a major conference in Moscow set a pattern which was to be followed time and again: Extreme cordiality at the start of the conference, changing to disagreeable and even surly hostility at the second meeting—and then harmonious agreement and a jubiliantly triumphant banquet with innumerable toasts to Allied cooperation at the finish.[55]

(3) Future agendas and the politics of war

Finally, Stalin revealed in these negotiations a Soviet penchant for viewing the war in a political context and for seeking to establish very early an agenda for future negotiations. The Harriman-Beaverbrook negotiations demonstrated beyond doubt that Stalin was clearly looking beyond the current peril to political arrangements in the future when he pressed for a discussion of war aims, peace objectives and politics in general, as he did at the first and third meetings. Both Harriman and Beaverbrook fended off the initiative with counter-arguments that the war had to be won and that the Atlantic Charter established the principles the Allies were fighting for.

But Stalin was dissatisfied with this response. Within weeks after the departure of Harriman and Beaverbrook from Moscow (and notably after the Soviet recapture of Rostov, the first point of importance in reversing the German advance), Stalin persisted in pressing his political point. As Sherwood wrote, "Stalin was not content to drop the embarrassing subjects that he had raised with Beaverbrook."[56]

This diplomatic episode revealed two important characteristics in Soviet negotiating behavior: It revealed their desire to get political issues on the agenda well in advance for future negotiations, giving them the advantage of the initiative in designing the dimension of the problem; it also revealed the Soviet perception of war as an extension of politics by other means, whatever the vicissitudes of the occasion, though military success, as at Rostov, gave title to greater demands. In brief, the Soviets thought of war politically, in sharp contrast to the Americans who tended to reverse the order, downgrading war's political aspects while giving precedence to the military.

(b) Views of Soviet leaders

(1) Harriman on Stalin

This was Harriman's first of many negotiating encounters with Stalin in the next 4 years, and clearly Stalin had made a lasting im-

[55] Sherwood, op. cit., p. 395.
[56] Sherwood, op. cit., p. 401. Sherwood continued: "He apparently felt that the time had come to fix the borders between the Soviet Union and Finland, Poland, and Rumania, and the status of the Baltic states of Estonia, Latvia and Lithuania, and even to reach agreement on such far-flung subjects as the future of the Rhineland, Bavaria, and East Prussia, the restoration of the Sudetenland to Czechoslovakia, and numerous territorial adjustments affecting Greece and Turkey." Since the United States was not yet in the war, these were matters for negotiation primarily between Moscow and London, but the British kept Washington constantly informed since U.S. interests were clearly involved. However, with the recapture of Rostov, "the situation became so tense," Sherwood wrote, that it was decided that Anthony Eden, the British Foreign Secretary, should go to Moscow and attempt "to smooth out relations in general, to explore the possibility of some kind of political agreement, and to discuss certain postwar problems." In a dispatch from Hull to Ambassador Winant, the Secretary reiterated the Harriman argument that the postwar problems had been "delineated in the Atlantic Charter which today represents the attitude of Great Britain and the Soviet Union as well," and noted that it would be "unfortunate for any of the three governments" to enter into commitments regarding specific terms of the postwar settlement. "Above all," he concluded, "there must be no secret accords * * *."

pression on him. Shorter and broader than he had imagined, Stalin had a heavy black mustache, speckled with gray, and wore a simple tunic without decorations, mottled in the color of brown. A man of few words, he seemed almost detached except when he became interested; then, as Harriman recalled, "he showed strong attitudes, sometimes emotion, at times brutally blunt, at others emphatically frank." At times he evaded the direct look; at others, "particularly when he wanted to see your reaction, he looked straight at you with a cold and penetrating stare." In conferences with foreigners, Stalin doodled, and his favorite figure was the wolf, presumably a reflection of his unappeasable suspicions. At one time during the Harriman-Beaverbrook negotiations when he appeared annoyed, Harriman observed, Stalin "drew pictures of wolves and then filled in the background with red pencil," while waiting for Litvinov's interpretation. Others were to record the same habit.[57] Yet Stalin could be cordial and expansively congenial as at the dinner for Harriman and Beaverbrook where he generously toasted the B–24 pilots who brought the U.S. delegation to Moscow, and, as Harriman recalled, sitting between Beaverbrook and Harriman, Stalin chatted "amiably as if not a harsh word had been uttered during the negotiations."[58]

Harriman's first meeting with Stalin affirmed Hopkins' judgment as to where the power and authority lay in the Soviet Union. Harriman reported to the President: "There can be no doubt that Stalin is the only man to deal with in foreign affairs. Dealing with others without previous instruction from Stalin about the matters under discussion was almost a waste of time."[59]

What Harriman seemed to bring out in his characterization of Stalin are important qualities of the successful negotiator: toughness in pursuit of negotiating goals; controlled emotion enabling displays of disinterest and detachment, anger, and cordiality when called for; an awareness of the psychological impact of externals upon negotiating adversaries, as in the intimidating implications of the red penciled wolves that suggested deeper and unstated meanings sufficiently visible to be observed and recorded; but most of all, the power of decision of the negotiator.

(2) Molotov and the Ambassadors

Harriman had no such respect for Molotov as a negotiator and diplomat. At the first meeting with Stalin, Molotov impressed Harriman "by his silence." Stalin did all the talking, he noted, and occasionally when Molotov tried to put in a word, Stalin would "brush him aside." Throughout the meeting Harriman got the impression that Molotov was "not in a secure position," a fact he attributed to the failure of the Molotov-Ribbentrop pact.[60] Upon returning to Washington, Harriman, who now became convinced of the importance of personal relationships in influencing the affairs of nations, confided in

---

[57] Harriman, America and Russia. p. 18; Harriman and Abel. op. cit., p. 87 and 92; and Sherwood. op. cit., p. 391. In recalling his long talks with Stalin in 1941 and 1942. Harriman referred to "the great weight of suspicion to be overcome." (Harriman and Abel. op. cit., p. 224.)

[58] Ibid., pp. 98–99.

[59] Sherwood, op. cit., p. 391. Beaverbrook even found Stalin "a kindly man" who "practically never shows any impatience at all." Harriman later wrote: "Beaverbrook's unquenchable exuberance carried him a long way beyond the plain facts." (Harriman and Abel. op cit., p. 92.)

[60] Harriman and Abel, op. cit. p. 87.

Roosevelt that Stalin ought to be signaled in various subtle ways which "of his people we liked to deal with and to avoid building up those like Molotov who seemed antagonistic" while Stalin was in a cooperative mood. But Roosevelt ignored Harriman's advice and invited Molotov to Washington in the spring of 1942, much to Harriman's displeasure.[61]

The conference also provided the occasion for the removal of the ambassadors in Moscow and Washington. In a very frank exchange Stalin expressed his dislike of Steinhardt as a defeatist and rumormonger, while Harriman expanded on the grievances Oumansky created in official Washington. Both were recalled.[62] Litvinov returned to Washington with Harriman as Oumansky's replacement; Admiral Standley was to replace Steinhardt.[63]

(c) Conference procedures

(1) Planning without information

The procedures of the conference produced problems that were unique in negotiating with the Soviets. The Russian passion for secrecy clearly created difficulties in planning. According to Harriman, the mission was able to proceed to Russia, after preconference meetings in London, "with a well formulated program," a first essential in negotiating strategy.[64]

However, the Soviets, as the British Embassy staff complained, failed to come forth with information on stocks or resources; hence, their plea for hard bargaining in the negotiation.[65] But none took

---

[61] Ibid., p. 94. Harriman's "own distaste for Molotov, born at their first encounter in 1941, increased upon closer acquaintance over the years that followed. It was Harriman's impression that as Molotov became more sure of his position he also grew more overbearing and unpleasant. He found Molotov a man of great energy, totally lacking in humor or flexibility, literal-minded and less open to compromise than Stalin himself." Harriman recalled reporting to Roosevelt on his return "that we would have great difficulties with the Soviets as long as Molotov was an important factor." (p. 94.)

[62] Ibid., p. 94.

[63] That Steinhardt was not at all ingratiating to the leadership is revealed in this excellent appraisal of Soviet negotiating behavior:

"* * * As I have urged in my telegrams to the Department I have been convinced for quite some time that a firm policy such as outlined is best calculated to maintain our prestige in Moscow and to prepare the ground for the important developments with which we will ultimately be confronted. My observation of the psychology of the individuals who are conducting Soviet foreign policy has long since convinced me that they do not and cannot be induced to respond to the customary amenities, that it is not possible to create 'international good will' with them, that they will always sacrifice the future in favor of an immediate gain, and that they are not affected by ethical or moral considerations, nor guided by the relationships which are customary between individuals of culture and breeding. Their psychology recognizes only firmness, power and force, and reflects primitive instincts and reactions entirely devoid of the restraints of civilization. It is [I am] of the opinion that they must be dealt with on this basis and on this basis alone. I feel fortified in these views, which I arrived at independently, by conversations with Count von [der] Schulenburg, who has on several occasions told me quite frankly that more considerate treatment was accorded German interests and the German Government by the Soviet authorities during the period when the violence of the German campaign against the Soviet Union was at its height than at any time prior or subsequent to that period. It has been my own experience that on every occasion that either the Department or the Embassy has made concessions to the Soviet Government, or has approached it in a spirit of friendly cooperation or good will, these gestures have been received by the Soviet authorities with marked suspicion and a disposition to regard them as evidence of weakness, whereas on each occasion that our attitude has stiffened the Soviet authorities have regarded our demeanor as evidence of self-confidence and strength and have promptly reacted by a more conciliatory attitude which has noticeably increased our prestige. Nor have I found any evidence of resentment or bitterness at the reciprocal application of unpleasant measures. As in the case with all primitive people it is important, however, that retaliation should not be carried to the point at which it may be regarded as provocation, and every such act should be clearly identifiable in each instance as retaliation for something the Soviet Government has done or failed to do. If so identifiable, it does not appear to provoke further retaliation, but on the contrary, frequently results in a relaxation or complete withdrawal of the action which provoked the retaliation." (Steinhardt to Secretary of State, Moscow, June 17, 1941. U.S. Foreign Relations, 1941, vol. 1, Soviet Union, pp. 764–765.)

[64] Harriman to Roosevelt, London, Oct. 29, 1941, U.S. Foreign Relations, 1941, vol. 1, Soviet Union, p. 849.

[65] Taylor, op. cit., p. 487.

place, at least on the Anglo-American side. Therefore, the final protocol, as Feis pointed out, provided for this massive aid in material, weaponry, and other supplies without requiring full information about Soviet needs or stocks—information required from all other lend-lease recipients.[66] Thus, as Standley exclaimed in an air of grievance, "We went to Moscow, not knowing what we had to give that they might want, and ended by promising them everything they asked." [67]

Soviet secrecy, therefore, and no doubt the exigencies of the time, impeded what would have been considered normal planning procedures. (In keeping with this mode of behavior it is significant to note that in arms control negotiations, as in SALT I, the Soviets did not provide information on their own weapon systems which, like those of the United States, was the heart of the negotiation, but rather relied on that provided by the United States.)

(2) Interpreters: relying on the Soviets

Selection of a Soviet interpreter was a disputed point within the Harriman-Beaverbrook mission. Beaverbrook felt that they should not bring their own interpreters from the British or the American Embassies in their meetings with Stalin but rather should rely on the Soviets to provide one. Evidently, he believed that Stalin would construe this gesture as a mark of trust and that it would elicit greater frankness from Stalin in the discussions. Harriman assented with some misgivings.[68]

Accordingly, the Soviets sent word that Oumansky would interpret. Harriman objected; he did not trust Oumansky. Both Harriman and Beaverbrook had confidence that Litvinov would provide an accurate translation and asked for him. Within 3 hours of the meeting he was produced.[69]

How accurately Litvinov interpreted the meetings with Stalin cannot be determined, though the same problem of transcultural communication, as noted above, existed. But there were problems. At one critical point in the negotiations to frame the protocol, Litvinov had great difficulty in conveying to Molotov the subtle nuances in the meaning of the words "make available" war supplies—a very essential point in the agreement. Harriman recalled that Litvinov's English was still somewhat rusty, and even with the help of Charles Thayer, a Third Secretary at the U.S. Embassy, Litvinov spent much of the meeting which lasted some 40 minutes struggling with the idea before Molotov, after repeated explanations by Harriman, understood.[70]

While this episode might cast doubt upon Litvinov's proficiency as an interpreter, particularly since he was still somewhat rusty in his

---

[66] Feis, Churchill-Roosevelt-Stalin, p. 17.
[67] Standley and Ageton, op. cit., p. 76.
[68] Harriman and Abel, op. cit., pp. 86–87, and Harriman, America and Russia, p. 17.
[69] Harriman and Abel, op. cit., p. 87. Harriman perceived that Litvinov had fallen on hard times. "I was somewhat shocked by Litvinov's appearance," he recalled. "His clothes and shoes were shoddy and, I remember, his waistcoat and trousers did not meet to cover the expanse of his shirt front. I had the impression that he had been in disfavor since the time he was thrown out and replaced as Foreign Minister by Molotov."
[70] Ibid., p. 97. Apparently, Harriman had good reason not to trust Oumansky. At the banquet that was marked by interminable, but politically important, toasts, Oumansky provided some of the translations. In his report to Roosevelt, Harriman wrote: "There is no doubt that Oumansky did not translate all the toasts accurately. Stalin even commented on this to Litvinov in Beaverbrook's hearing" (Sherwood, op. cit., p. 392.)

English, it nonetheless underscored the difficulties in capturing the nuances of meaning in translation; hence the stress by American specialists on the importance of having one's own corps of trained, professional interpreters.

(3) Record of meetings with Stalin

Another crucial point in the conference proceedings was the keeping of records at the meetings with Stalin. Apparently, no complete stenographic account was made. A. J. P. Taylor, the noted British historian and biographer of Beaverbrook, noted that Harriman, "who himself knew shorthand," kept the formal record of the meetings.[71] Secretary of State Byrnes and U.S. diplomat Robert Murphy were expert at shorthand and kept their own records in conferences, but the sources examined do not reveal this proficiency in Harriman. Apparently, Harriman took notes of the meetings from which he dictated his reports to Washington.

Beaverbrook did not even bother with formal notes, as was his habit in all business dealings. "Once set on an affair," Taylor observed, "he could carry all the details in his head." [72]

However accurate the notetaking of Harriman and the memory of Beaverbrook, still the absence of a complete official stenographic record could have caused problems of misunderstanding and misinterpretation at some future time on what had been agreed to or said at these meetings.

In this connection it is significant, and characteristic, that Molotov had insisted upon a written document in the form of a protocol of the agreements reached. Beaverbrook saw no need for this and downgraded the idea, arguing that it had not been done in the British case. But Molotov persisted in conforming to a procedure that has been a marked characteristic of Soviet negotiating behavior.

(4) Committee system and Soviet intransigence

Six committees were set up to study in detail the problems of needs and supply. This was normal operating procedure in international relations. But the Soviets were not at all cooperative. As Admiral Standley complained, the "committees met, organized, and planned procedure, but we accomplished no real work." [73] By the end of the conference, he said, "none of our committees had more than scratched the surface of the possibilities of extending lend-lease aid." [74]

At an intermission of the Swan Lake ballet at the Bolshoi, Harriman complained to Deputy Foreign Minister Vishinsky that according to members of the delegations the detailed talks in the working committees were not going well. He cited the case of the Soviet representatives in the committee on transportation who refused to answer any more questions or to attend any more meetings with their British and American counterparts. Nor had the Soviets responded to his request that General Burns be permitted to visit the area of northern Iran,

---

[71] Taylor. op. cit., p. 488.
[72] Ibid. Taylor continued: "On each item—whether weapons or raw materials—he could say at once how much Great Britain could supply or was prepared to sacrifice from her share of American resources. Afterward he dictated from memory the agreement which had been reached, and his figures were never wrong."
[73] Standley and Ageton, op. cit., p. 66.
[74] Ibid., p. 68.

then under Soviet control, to survey the proposed lend-lease supply route through the Persian Gulf.[75]

Vishinsky, supported by Oumansky, assured Harriman that this display of intransigence was no cause of worry. They urged him not to be disturbed by Soviet officials who had yet to receive their instructions.[76]

What the negotiators at the working committee level were going through was characteristic of an aspect of Soviet negotiating behavior that Harriman and other Americans were to face throughout their negotiating experience: It might be called the tactic of immobility. Lower level officials could not act on their own, and without instructions from above, in many instances from Stalin himself, they had three possible options: To temporize, while awaiting firm instructions; to counter proposals with rejections as a way of keeping the discussions going; or, as in the case of the transport committee representatives, to refuse to respond to questions or even to attend the meetings.

Such conduct was most frustrating to the Anglo-American negotiators, but this was only a foretaste of the future. What the negotiators were then experiencing had its root cause in the fear of Soviet negotiators of breaching secrecy by sharing information (information which in this case was necessary), in the deeply engrained bureaucratic habit of strict adherence to instructions from above, and in a system where the decisionmakers may not have yet made up their minds.

(d) Conference results and significance

As a negotiating experience, the Americans and British undoubtedly came away from this first encounter with Stalin, Molotov, and lesser Soviet officials much the wiser and more knowledgeable in the strategy and tactics of Soviet negotiating behavior. At a time of extreme peril, they were able to see the Soviets perform under the most extraordinary kind of pressure, and despite their visible weakness, their imminent danger, and their desperate need for Anglo-American assistance, their performance in negotiations revealed a persisting behavioral pattern uniquely Stalinist: Toughness and calculated ruthlessness in negotiation; a penchant for employing variations of emotions to the greatest psychological effect; a determination of purpose and a resoluteness in achieving ultimate victory; unyielding in sharing information and uncooperative in areas where even their interests would be best served; a passion for secrecy that when bureaucratized created intolerable frustrations, delays and inaction; a tightly bound bureaucratically managed negotiating structure rigidly controlled by Stalin—all negotiating characteristics on display in their most acute form and in the most aggravated setting. For Standley who was to become Ambassador in Moscow and for Harriman who continued as Roosevelt's special envoy in high-level dealings with the Russians until his appointment as successor to Standley, this experience was clearly the opening of the door to a new political reality.

Initially, the American and British negotiators viewed the conference, as Harriman reported to the President, "with some question,"

---

[75] Harriman and Abel, op. cit., p. 96.
[76] Ibid.

but he assured Roosevelt that "the results have been accepted with undisguised enthusiasm by Stalin and all others connected with the dicussions." [77]

And well they might, for in retrospect the conference succeeded in setting into motion the machinery of lend-lease that was to be an essential factor in the Soviet victory on the eastern front. For the immediate crisis Feis believed it probable that the Anglo-American support "helped to make the defense so unyielding." [78]

Diplomatically, the conference broadened the base of cooperation among the United States, Britain, and the Soviet Union by the sheer necessity of negotiating lend-lease allocations, by expanding military and political relationships, and by the concurrence at Moscow to establish direct and personal communications among Roosevelt, Churchill, and Stalin.

In his final report on October 29, 1941, Harriman expressed the "conviction of the mission that Russia can make every effective use of the latest types of American equipment and that Russia will continue to fight even in retreat * * * that her continuation as an active belligerent is of paramount importance and that every effort should be made to assist her and assist her promptly." [79]

On October 30, as the fighting intensified around Leningrad and Moscow and the southern front was near collapse, Stalin urged the Soviet people to make a supreme effort to save the fatherland. On the same day, President Roosevelt sent a message to Stalin approving the work of the conference and pledging immediate military assistance through lend-lease to the amount of $1 billion in value. [80]

C. Hazard on Negotiating Under Lend-Lease: From the Perspective of Washington

1. ORGANIZATIONAL STRUCTURE FOR LEND-LEASE

With completion of the Harriman-Beaverbrook mission and the subsequent Presidential decision to bring the Soviet Union under lend-lease, the administrators in Washington were now faced with the task of establishing the machinery for processing Russian war supplies. Briefly, there were three major subdivisions in which lend-lease was administered: The Army, Navy, and the civilian agencies represented by the Office of Lend-Lease Administration. Multiple points of contact at all levels between the Russians and Americans where negotiations took place were inevitable under this arrangement. This was particularly the case where the categories in allocating supplies were ambiguous. One such point was the Division for Soviet

---

[77] Harriman to Roosevelt, Moscow, Oct. 3, 1941, U.S. Foreign Relations, 1941, vol. 1, Soviet Union, p. 842.

[78] Feis, Churchill-Roosevelt-Stalin, p. 17.

[79] Harriman to Roosevelt, London, Oct. 29, 1941, U.S. Foreign Relations, 1941, vol. 1, Soviet Union, p. 851.

[80] Roosevelt to Stalin, Washington, Oct. 30, 1941, U.S. Foreign Relations, 1941, vol. 1, Soviet Union, pp. 851-852. In a reply Stalin wrote: "The Soviet Government accepts with sincere gratitude your decision, Mr. President, to grant to the Soviet Union a non-interest bearing loan to the extent of $1,000,000,000 with which to pay for supplies of armaments and raw materials for the Soviet Union, as exceptionally substantial assistance to the Soviet Union in its great and difficult struggle against bloodthirsty Hitlerism, our common foe." Stalin closed with an expression of satisfaction to do everything possible to establish "personal direct contact * * * immediately * * * between us." (Stalin to Roosevelt, Moscow, Nov. 4, 1941, Ibid., pp. 855-856.)

Supply in the Office of Lend-Lease Administration, and it was from this perspective and that of successor agencies that Dr. John N. Hazard, Professor of Public Law at Columbia University and noted American authority on Soviet law, observed Soviet negotiating behavior during the war years.[81]

2. PROBLEMS IN NEGOTIATING WITH THE SOVIETS

(a) Binding bureaucratic control

Negotiations on lend-lease matters at the working level varied greatly depending upon the characteristics of the individual negotiators. On both the American and Soviet sides temperaments ranged from the patient to the impatient; from the mind precise and methodical to the inexperienced and confused; from the organizational operator who sought personal aggrandizement to the self-effacing worker whose goal was simply to do a good job with a minimum of fanfare.

But there was one crucial difference, and here was the rub: Soviet negotiators were conditioned by a society that instilled excessive organizational discipline so that progress in negotiations was delayed and precious time lost—time particularly vital in expediting much-needed wartime supplies. A binding bureaucratic control proved to be a problem of the first magnitude.

The Americans, by nature free-wheeling organizational activists, imbued with a spirit of individualism that valued improvisation, and unburdened by an oppressive bureaucratic system, sought results, directly and immediately, without necessarily referring questions to a higher authority for approval. In contrast, the Soviet negotiator, molded by different values, conditioned by a spirit of collectivism, and fearful of self-initiatives, operated directly, and safely, under strict orders from a superior. Any deviation in that order required a conference with a superior who himself might or might not have to seek approval from still another higher authority, and so on, before accepting a proposed plan of action. Acheson's experiences with lend-lease negotiations with the Russians paralleled those of Hazard. "Our clients * * * were clumsy and difficult," he complained. "Not daring to depart in the smallest particular from their instructions, they had no flexibility, no feel for the possible." [82]

This rigid bureaucratic control caused great frustration and exasperation among American negotiators at the working level. For these wartime negotiators the experience was particularly painful because they were noncivil servants, brought into the government from the outside for the duration; they had no careers to protect and thus were inclined to operate freely and unencumbered according to the rules of their own private world.

As a result of this clash in negotiating styles and procedures, conferences usually came to be looked upon, not as places where decisions were made, but only as a means for imparting information to a Soviet negotiator to be transmitted to his superior. "Decision," as Hazard observed, "had to be saved for another day." [83]

[81] Hazard, John N., Negotiating Under Lend-Lease, 1942–45. In, Dennett and Johnson, Negotiating with the Russians, ch. 2, pp. 31–46.
[82] Acheson, Present at Creation, p. 34.
[83] Hazard, op. cit., pp. 32–33.

(b) *Communication difficulties*

Difficulty in communicating with the staff of the Soviet Purchasing Commission, which had a questionable knowledge of English, was another problem in negotiationg lend-lease, but ironically in this case the delay in conference negotiations described above worked at least to one advantage.

Personnel policy of the Lend-Lease Administration prevented the tapping of the large supply of Russian-Americans in the United States who could have been interpreters. To avoid the possibility of partiality in lend-lease allocations, former citizens of the receiving nations could not be employed in the agency. As a result the few native Americans who had learned Russian for some professional reason were employed and did what they could with interpreting.

Communications between negotiators were in English. In instances where doubts existed as to whether the Soviet interpreter would give the desired tone or emphasis to a letter addressed to the Chairman of the Soviet Purchasing Commission, who knew no English, a Russian-speaking American would deliver the letter personally and make an oral statement explaining its contents.

To insure accuracy, it became customary to write the substance of a communication being made in conference in the form of a letter or memorandum. It was given to the Soviet negotiator after the conference ended, and he would be told that it contained the substance of the conference discussion. Because decisions were not made immediately at the conference but after approval by higher authority, this procedure worked well. However circumvoluted the system may have seemed, at least it insured accuracy in communications between negotiators which is a very important principle in effective negotiations.[84]

(c) *Suspicion and its adverse impact on negotiations*

Other misunderstandings and difficulties arose from incompatibility of ideological perceptions which aroused Soviet suspicions and in turn impacted adversely on negotiations.

Soviet officials approached negotiations with Americans with considerable ideological indoctrination in their own schools. As a consequence, they looked at Americans through the distorted prism of the Marxist-Leninist stereotype. Their presumption that American officials were capitalists or lackeys of capitalists aroused suspicions of their motives. Americans could not be genuine friends, it was believed, but were really assisting the Soviet Union only for self-serving ends. The suspicion persisted that Americans hoped for a weakened Soviet Russia by the war—as sort of "bleed the Russians white" theory—in order to strengthen the postwar position of the United States. "As a result of this attitude springing from their Marxist training," Hazard noted, "the Soviet negotiators from top to bottom approached their opposite numbers on the American side with a certain suspicion. They tended to impute motives to every suggestion of the American officials." [85]

---

[84] Ibid., pp. 33–34.
[85] Ibid., p. 34.

In many instances this imputing of American motives had little effect, except in creating a lack of mutual good will in personal relationships. But in some cases it was a serious obstacle to quick decisions. Delays or rerouting of convoys because of German activities at sea made quick decisions imperative, but Soviet officials, doubting American good faith, would assume some sinister motive with the result that they hesitated to concede or adjust to changed plans. Serious matters involving convoy schedules required discussions at the upper echelons in the White House or the Embassy in Moscow.[86]

Even in cases of lesser decisions the same suspicion intruded to make operations difficult. In such cases it was found that sometimes casting American proposals in Marxist terms tended to enhance their acceptability and reduce somewhat the suspicion of motives.[87]

Nonetheless, suspicion of American motives, inculcated through intensive political and ideological indoctrination, remained an impediment to negotiations and to the carrying out of lend-lease assistance.

(d) On understanding the American system: Minuses and pluses

Failure of the Soviets to understand the workings of the American system created problems in negotiating for lend-lease procurement, but there were some pluses. American officials made every effort to provide Soviet negotiators with sufficient background information. Changes in shipping procedures by the Association of American Railroads that resulted in increased costs was an occasion for extensive explanations to the Soviets. Soviet negotiators could not understand why the U.S. Government was not sufficiently powerful to request the railroads to act as directed and perform according to the commitments undertaken with the Soviet Union.[88]

Problems of costs constantly plagued negotiations. Americans correctly assumed that the final lend-lease bill would be calculated at a considerably lower cost to the Soviet Union and final settlement would be negotiated accordingly after the war. Cost-conscious Soviet negotiators from Amtorg, the official purchasing agency early in the war, haggled over price on the assumption that their Government would eventually be charged with the full cost. Not until the Soviets, acting upon an American suggestion, established the Soviet Purchasing Commission in Washington headed by a Soviet general was the pricing problem resolved, at least with respect to military supplies. Occasional flurries still occurred in negotiations over the cost of steel, nickle, aluminum, copper, machine tools, and food. Hazard stated that "the cost approach marred the friendliness of some discussions and frayed tempers on both sides." [89]

Though lack of knowledge of the American system hampered negotiations for lend-lease, Soviet resourcefulness in finding persons who had authority to act on their requests within the American administrative apparatus was remarkable. The Soviets carefully studied routing procedures within the U.S. Government and sought out the person to whom a request would be sent for opinion as to availability of supply or relation to the war effort. Though some of these persons had

[86] Ibid., p. 35.
[87] Ibid.
[88] Ibid., p. 35.
[89] Ibid., p. 38.

modest positions, they could, nonetheless, make the decisions approving or denying the Soviet requests. Accordingly, the Soviet Purchasing Commission engaged in an extensive series of informal luncheons and dinners pairing persons according to hierarchy from both sides in order to lobby for their requests.[90]

Soviet lawyers with the Soviet Purchasing Commission also proved to be skillful in mastering U.S. Government regulations and in negotiating for requested items for quick action on the basis of those regulations. "Let no one who deals with Soviet agencies think that they do not know what is happening," concluded Hazard, a specialist in Soviet law. "Their legal staffs are composed of able men who read everything and who are prepared to argue forcefully, although sometimes mistakenly, for their point of view."[91]

The most extensive negotiations with Soviet lawyers occurred when preparations were underway for an agreement to terminate Lend-Lease. The lawyer sent from the Commissariat of Foreign Trade in Moscow to handle the matter, Hazard wrote, "proved to be as meticulous as the best products of the American law firms." His ideas were often excellent and accordingly were readily accepted by the American lawyers. Others seemed to stem from a sense of suspicion. Changes were made to suit him, and upon returning another day after consultations with his superiors, still another change would be requested. "Patience beyond belief was required on the part of the American negotiators," Hazard noted, "but in the end their work was rewarded. A workable agreement was reached."[92]

In brief, Soviet failure to understand the American system proved to be a detriment in negotiating lend-lease procurement, but as products of the Soviet bureaucracy where skills in political manipulation were a premium and generally universally applicable, Soviet negotiators demonstrated great resourcefulness in manipulating the American administrative apparatus to achieve their interests. And Soviet lawyers, in the judgment of one of this Nation's leading specialists on Soviet law, proved to be remarkable and knowledgeable negotiators.

(e) On expecting gratitude

Soviet failure to understand the American system was compounded by a studied lack of gratitude for American lend-lease assistance, either at the person-to-person working level or in the official Soviet press. Consistent throughout the literature on wartime negotiations is the warning by seasoned negotiators neither to expect gratitude nor favors from the Soviets in return for a good deed. Negotiators have cautioned with consistency that "one cannot bank good-will with the Soviets."

American lend-lease negotiators, in Washington dealing with their Soviet counterparts on an hourly basis and in the detailed work of the operations, were on many occasions exasperated by constant pressure for speed when everything possible was being done and for the lack of a grateful response. "Nothing seemed to please them," wrote Hazard, "and almost no heroic effort to push something ahead of what had come to be accepted as the inevitable delays of a large Govern-

[90] Ibid., p. 41.
[91] Ibid., p. 42.
[92] Ibid., p. 43.

ment operation met with open appreciation in the form of a 'thank you.' " [93]

Some Americans who had dealt with the Russians before the war advised the Soviet officials that Americans were happy to assist but were used to being thanked when doing something extraordinary. On one occasion a Soviet air force general called for the fifth time asking why his request for much needed munitions had not been acted upon. When the request was finally met, the American officer responsible for the work called to tell him of the affirmative decision. No expression of appreciation was forthcoming in the general's response but rather the immediate request about the status of another request, "rather antagonizing his American colleague," Hazard wrote. Later at a luncheon the general was asked why there was no expression of gratitude. In reply, he simply said that if the Soviet Army stopped to celebrate at every recaptured village, opportunities would be lost for taking the next village. The general was told, according to Hazard, "that his approach might be the best way to win a war against the enemy, but it was not equally effective in dealing with Americans." [94]

That this lack of gratitude for lend-lease extended beyond Washington to Moscow and that it may have been more of a studied position than had seemed apparent was revealed by the remarks of Ambassador Standley on Soviet ingratitude for lend-lease and the other forms of American aid, Russian Relief and Red Cross. When the Second Lend-Lease Protocol was pending congressional approval early in 1943, Standley had attempted to get some Soviet public statement of acknowledgement and gratitude from the Soviets in order to insure passage of the measure. In an informal press conference with American reporters on March 8, 1943, Standley explained how he had failed to get any evidence that American supplies were being used by the Russians. "The Russian authorities seem to want to cover up the fact that they are receiving outside help," Standley observed, adding, "Apparently they want their people to believe that the Red Army is fighting this war alone." On the following day he wrote the State Department: "* * * I do not feel that we should remain silent and continue to accept the seeming ungrateful attitude of the Soviet leaders. * * *" [95]

Standley's statement made headlines in the American press and created a general uproar first of disapproval and then approval. Sumner Welles wanted Standley relieved; Roosevelt took a wait-and-see attitude. Harriman reported from London that many of his friends, both British and American, were "secretly pleased at the way Standley spoke out in Moscow even if this was an indiscretion." [95a] On March 10,

[93] Ibid., p. 43.

[94] Hazard went on to say that the experience with Soviet manners in Lend-Lease matters had an "amusing sequel." Soviet officials began to preface every meeting with a lengthy statement of appreciation for all that was being done for them "almost to the point of that official's embarrassment at such fulsome praise." At one meeting a loquacious member of the Soviet delegation was asked why so much "palaver." "He replied, perhaps with his tongue in his cheek," wrote Hazard, "that Americans seemed to like it, and if they did, who were the Soviets not to provide compliments to please them!" Hazard himself recalled only one occasion of rudeness from a Soviet official. His tone of voice in making a request was that used by a superior talking to an inferior officer in the Army. This tone was often heard among officials in the Soviet Purchasing Commission but it had not been used previously in talking to Americans. The offending officer was advised that nothing would be done for him when he approached the matter in such a way. His superior was notified of the difficulty. "The offender apologized later," Hazard wrote, "and no similar incident was subsequently reported." (p. 44.)

[95] Standley and Ageton, op. cit., pp. 341 and 343.

[95a] Ibid., p. 347.

Standley conferred with Molotov at which time he explained his grievances against Soviet ingratitude. For 3 days there was no comment in the Moscow press; then, as Standley wrote, "there came a veritable rash of statements about American aid to Russia." [96]

Standley's seemingly "last-straw" reaction was the culmination of nearly 11 months of frustration and exposure to difficulties in dealing with the Soviets of which their ingratitude for American aid was only one. His patience had clearly been drawn to the breaking point.

3. RULES FOR NEGOTIATING WITH THE SOVIETS

(a) On keeping one's self-control

In reviewing Soviet negotiating behavior at the procurement end of lend-lease in Washington, Hazard laid down five rules for American negotiators. But he cautioned, first of all, that his experience at the working level had one limitation as a learning process; namely, that the United States was the donor, the Soviet Union the recipient, and in this inequity of roles "it paid to cater to the wishes and even whims of the Americans concerned." This experience might offer little guidance, therefore, in situations where the United States was on the asking end of the relationship.[97]

The first rule in negotiating with the Soviets—"elementary," Hazard noted—was to keep one's self-control. A display of temper was a good negotiating device so long as it was done at the appropriate time and under proper control; it ought never to appear at the wrong time or blind the negotiator who failed to keep it in check. "It takes a mind untouched by temper or other dulling forces to deal with the usual competent Soviet official who approaches the table," he cautioned.[98]

(b) Patience as a virtue

Patience is a cardinal virtue in negotiating with the Russians. Hazard cautioned, "He who rushes can be lost." While this advice did not rule out applying pressures on the Soviets to influence their actions, it nevertheless required "a controlled pressure exercised on the part of a man who utilizes it with care rather than the unreasoning pressure of the exasperated." [99]

A full understanding of Russian history and Soviet administrative practices would help in dealing with situations which, Hazard noted, "seem to drag on forever." As many American negotiators were to find out, delays were not always indicators of a Soviet unwillingness to negotiate but rather the result of some administrative or personal deficiency within the bureaucracy such as a failure to get a superior's attention or an insensitivity to the timeliness of a particular action.[100] For example, in dealing with Admiral Kuznetsov during the Harriman-Beaverbrook mission, as noted above, Standley came to realize that Kuznetsov's intransigence in sharing information needed to de-

[96] Standley continued: "The Stettinius Report was published in full. Daily, the papers mentioned American war material issued on this or that sector of the front or praised the generosity of the American people for some gift of Red Cross or Russian Relief supplies. At last, millions of Russians were finding out for the first time of the generosity and genuine friendliness of the American people." (Ibid., pp. 347-348.)
[97] Hazard, op. cit., p. 45
[98] Ibid.
[99] Ibid., p. 45.
[100] Ibid.

sign a program for naval supplies was caused by deficiencies in the bureaucracy—lack of information and indecision—and not in Kuznetsov's unwillingness to cooperate. Patience in this instance paid off to some extent when in another related naval matter Kuznetsov passed on to Standley Soviet hydrographic codes which the naval attachés at the U.S. Embassy had been vainly trying to obtain for months.[101]

(c) On understanding Communist theory and value of the direct approach

An appreciation of Communist theory can be an asset to the American negotiator, particularly, as Hazard noted, to one "who wishes to take advantage of every opportunity to press his case." "Imputation of false motives," he continued, "can sometimes be avoided by one who knows what motives might be imputed from actions which might seem innocent enough to the American." [102] Hazard did not explain, but clearly knowledge of the inbred hostility toward capitalism that Communist ideology instills probably could have enabled American negotiators in lend-lease operations to appreciate the depth of Soviet suspicions with respect to American motives in aiding Soviet Russia. With this knowledge they may have been able to better cope with Soviet suspicions as a realistic problem in day-to-day working relations.

Moreover, the direct approach has its value. "Straight answers given without an effort to evade the real reason," Hazard emphasized, "can make for pleasanter relationships with the Soviet negotiator, even though he seems to be evasive at times." Evidence that the Soviets understand the direct approach in the manner Hazard suggested abounds in the literature on negotiations. Harriman seems to have followed this rule meticulously during his stay in Moscow, and as a result, his dealings with Stalin were generally successful. A direct and extremely sharp encounter with Stalin occurred in mid-April 1945 when an American airman had smuggled out a young Pole in a GI uniform from the Poltava "shuttle-bombing" base in the Ukraine. At that time Soviet-American relations were being sorely tried over the Polish question. In a meeting with Harriman, Stalin accused the American Air Forces of having conspired with the anti-Communist Polish underground against the Soviet Army. Harriman "thundered back," as his memoirs put it: "You're impugning the loyalty of the American high command and I won't allow it. You are actually impugning the loyalty of General Marshall." The tough-minded Patrick J. Hurley, the U.S. Ambassador to China, who was present, was shocked by Harriman's blunt words. But Stalin replied in a mollifying tone: "I would trust General Marshall with my life. This wasn't he but a junior officer." [103]

While the Harriman-Stalin exchange did not occur in a negotiating setting, nevertheless, it does underscore the effectiveness of the direct approach in dealing with the Soviets.[104]

---

[101] Standley and Ageton, op. cit., p. 67.
[102] Ibid., p. 45.
[103] Harriman and Abel, op. cit., p. 445.
[104] Also illustrative of the direct, unevasive approach was Standley's meeting with Molotov over the issue of Soviet failure to publicly acknowledge American assistance. The Ambassador very frankly laid the whole case on the line before the Soviet Foreign

(Continued)

(d) On avoiding "mudslinging contest"

Hazard cautioned American negotiators against returning in kind the same abuse that Soviet negotiators handed out as a way of pressuring them into adopting a desired attitude. "The sad truth," he noted, "seems to be that in a mudslinging contest with a Soviet official the latter proves to be better equipped than the American. He can exceed anything the American could imagine." Accordingly, it would be better never to begin the contest but to meet any uncouthness "with efforts to clear the air of it, rather than outdo it unless one expects eventually to take to arms." "Negotiating under such conditions," Hazard acknowledged, "is not easy and requires the utmost in diplomatic skills with which few are adequately endowed." [105]

(e) On standing by decisions

Hazard's final word of advice to American negotiators was to stand by decisions once made until circumstances required a change on grounds presumably that vacillation meant uncertainty which in turn revealed an exploitable weakness. Unless new evidence could be presented, the negotiator was "lost" if he changed his mind without reasonable cause. "The mind which is ever ready to change," he said, "will be subjected to endless argument and constant attack by the Soviet colleague who is quick to sense the opportunity." Once this weakness was detected, Hazard cautioned, "pressure from Soviet negotiators will be redoubled and may result in complete exhaustion on the part of the American so that he comes to the point at which he feels that he never wants to see a Russian again and is thoroughly miserable in the performance of his job." Thus, Hazard concluded, "For his own peace of mind, if for no other reason, the American negotiator would do well to act carefully and advisedly and then stand by his decision until circumstances have changed." [106]

4. A SUMMING UP

To sum up, negotiating lend-lease with the Russians in Washington revealed significant characteristics in Soviet negotiating behavior that appear again and again in most wartime experiences and that arose from the problems Americans experienced:

—The binding bureaucratic control that centralized decisionmaking, momentarily immobilized conference activity, and generally hampered progress.
—Difficulties in language communications, due partly to the insufficient number of American interpreters, that created problems of comprehension and precision and inevitably bogged down the proceedings;

(Continued)

Minister, stressing particularly Soviet failure to acknowledge Russian Relief and Red Cross aid which was especially important to him, as he said, because it was, being of a private and personal nature, "a matter of good will and friendship between the American and Russian peoples." Molotov defended the Soviet side with equal force, but the favorable outcome was indicated by Molotov's response to Standley's admission that his remarks to the press were "actuated by that thought alone" : "I'm afraid, then, Mr. Ambassador, that far more importance is being given to your remarks than appears justified. I regret the misinterpretation that has been placed on them and the resulting bad publicity in the United States." (Standley and Ageton, op. cit., p. 346.)
[105] Hazard, op. cit. p 46.
[106] Ibid., p. 46.

—Inbred Soviet suspicion in dealing with foreigners that created doubts of American motives in the war and prevented a free-and-easy exchange in negotiations and operations which normally should have been the case with wartime allies;

—Soviet failure to understand the American system that created unnecessary difficulties and strung out negotiations, though in some instances they achieved personal advantages by applying techniques universal in bureaucracies; and finally

—The lack of Soviet gratitude that had a spoiling effect on personal relationships, adversely affecting negotiations and efficiency in operations.

From this experience, which was unique in that the United States was on the giving and not taking end of the relationship, Hazard laid down a set of general rules for future American negotiators. Hazard's commandments emphasized:

—The importance of self-control and patience;

—The wisdom of understanding Communist theory as a guide in avoiding pitfalls and exploiting negotiating opportunities;

—The value of the direct approach;

—The necessity of avoiding "mudslinging contests" in which Americans would be the losers; and finally

—The importance of standing by decisions once made and not vacillating before the Soviet negotiator until circumstances required change.

D. DEANE ON NEGOTIATING LEND-LEASE AND MILITARY COOPERATION: FROM THE PERSPECTIVE OF MOSCOW

1. NEGOTIATING ENCOUNTERS WITH THE SOVIETS

(a) Deane's role, his attitude, and mission in Moscow

(1) Purposes of Deane's mission

The task of managing lend-lease and the multiple forms of military cooperation at the receiving end in Moscow fell to Maj. Gen. John R. Deane, U.S. Army. As chief of the U.S. military mission, Deane was responsible for the administration of lend-lease assistance to Soviet Russia, which he placed at a money value in supplies and services at some $11 billion. He was also responsible for the coordination of land, sea, and air activities of the United States with those of the Soviet Union.[107] He served almost exactly 2 years, from October 18, 1943 to October 31, 1945, "under circumstances," he said, "which forced a closer contact with the Soviet Government than is afforded to most foreigners. * * *"[108] From this close-in perspective, Deane recorded his observations of Soviet behavior, particularly in negotiations, as he perceived it through the day-to-day operations of his mission.[109]

(2) His attitude toward the Russians

Deane approached his new tasks with a favorable mental attitude toward the Russian people and the Soviet leadership. He greatly admired their "gallant battle," as he said, against the Germans. Upon

---

[107] Deane, Strange Alliance, p. 95.
[108] Ibid., p. 289
[109] In addition to Strange Alliance, Deane wrote, Negotiating on Military Assistance, 1943-45, in Dennett and Johnson, op. cit., ch. 1, p. 328.

leaving Washington, Gen. George C. Marshall, the Army's Chief of Staff, instructed him to be frank and open in his military discussions and to overcome "Soviet suspicion" if collaboration was to be effective. "In brief," wrote Deane, "I went to the Soviet Union full of good will, ready to bubble over with honesty and frankness, and prepared to be lavish in my recommendations for the delivery of American supplies to the Soviet Union." [110] This sympathetic and friendly attitude toward the Russian people persisted throughout Deane's stay in Moscow, though he clearly came away at the end of the war with serious misgivings about the intentions of the Soviet leadership.[111]

On the Soviet side of the equation the official attitude toward Deane was positive. Once when Harriman asked Stalin how he felt about Deane, he was greatly reassured by Stalin's reply that the Soviet generals held him in the highest respect.[112] When Deane made his only permitted visit to the front, the Soviet officers were most friendly—"our interest and curiosity were satisfied by a frank response that denied suspicion of our motives," he wrote.[113] And on the few occasions when he was able to mix with the Russian people, as in the opening of the Poltava "shuttle bombing" air base and during the visit of General Eisenhower to Moscow, the popular reaction was always favorable, even enthusiastic.[114]

(3) Range of negotiations for military cooperation

The range of military cooperation was extensive, requiring hard bargaining and persistent negotiations seemingly at every step. Typical of the American proposals that Deane and the U.S. Mission negotiated with the Soviets with respect to the European theater were: use of Soviet bases by American bombers; coordination of strategic and tactical plans of military forces; maintenance of liaison between Soviet and British-American forces, on ground and in the air; methods for preventing clashes between Soviet and Anglo-American air forces; care of liberated prisoners-of-war; improved signal communications; establishment of Air Transport Service between the Soviet Union and the United States; and exchange of information on the enemy.[115]

In the Far East, the mission's efforts were directed toward the long-range problem of bringing the Soviet Union into the war against Japan and preparing for that occasion. Among the questions negotiated were: Coordination of strategic plans; use of Soviet bases for American aircraft; creation of a Soviet strategic bombing force; the build-up of reserve supplies for the Soviet Army in the Far East; and the maintenance of Pacific sea routes.[116]

---

[110] Deane, Negotiating on Military Assistance, p. 5.
[111] Deane gave this appraisal of the Russian people: "From my observation I believe that the average Russian of today [1946] is a strong virile individual inured to hardship that has been the heritage of centuries; an individual who is generous, sympathetic, and full of human understanding as the result of generations of common suffering and oppression, and who can get satisfaction from life through the simplest material advantages and the capacity for spiritual fulfillment and lighter pleasures which is within himself. The average Russian is just a youth in his national self-consciousness. He has all the unsophistication and naivete that goes with youth. He is capable of tremendous accomplishment if the spirit moves him, but he can be a silent and subtle obstructionist when it does not. He is docile to authority, but intensely curious and thoughtful. Intellectually he is growing with the increased opportunity of education. In the war he has just fought he was inspired first by the urge of self-preservation and later by revenge. In his invasion of foreign soil he has had a glimpse of how the rest of the world lives. * * *" (Deane, Strange Alliance, p. 318.)
[112] Harriman and Abel, op. cit., p. 352.
[113] Deane, Strange Alliance, p. 220.
[114] Deane wrote about the Eisenhower visit: "* * * we encountered huge masses of people and small groups of people. We could almost physically feel the attitude of kindliness with which they regarded us" Deane, Strange Alliance, p. 220.)
[115] Deane, Negotiating on Military Assistance, pp. 8–9.
[116] Ibid., p. 9.

Most revealing in these negotiations was the Soviet attitude toward wartime cooperation: Initiatives were strictly one-sided, from the Western side; and in general the Soviets were not very friendly, particularly when acting in their official capacity as negotiators. In Europe, there were many opportunities for cooperative action that if taken could have been mutually beneficial to both sides. "Yet I know of no action initiated by the Soviet Union," Deane wrote, "that was designed to facilitate the task of her Western allies. In every instance in which the efforts of the Soviet Union were coordinated with ours, the proposal was originated by the British or the Americans." [117]

Furthermore, the Soviets maintained a cool and distant attitude toward their Western allies. There never was what Deane called "the free and easy feeling of partnership" which characterized Anglo-American relations. "Every effort to collaborate," he noted, "was a negotiation which had to be bargained out." [118]

In many respects Soviet behavior was determined by Soviet needs. Lend-lease was the only major leverage the United States had in negotiating with Soviet Russia, though it was never really used as such. It commanded Soviet respect and attention in negotiations only until the end of the war was in sight and when lend-lease deliveries ceased. "As long as lend-lease was operative," Deane observed in contrasting Soviet wartime and postwar behavior, "Soviet leaders were forced to indulge in international and personal good manners, sufficient, at least, to keep us sweet." Discussions leading to agreement and decision could take place, but with the end of the war in view and the closing down of lend-lease, the "Soviet leaders quickly divested themselves of the strain imposed by ordinary courtesy." [119]

Deane had some successes, not all entirely satisfactory, in negotiations that were often long and difficult. Among them were: The Soviet decision to allow American pilots to escape who had been interned after bombing Japan, having landed on neutral Soviet territory; arrangements for cooperation between the Soviet and U.S. intelligence services, the NKVD and the Office of Strategic Services, which President Roosevelt suspended indefinitely for domestic political reasons; exchanges of weather information in Europe (but not in the Far East); and the establishment of the shuttle-bombing base at Poltava.

Yet Deane soon learned after his first encounter with Vishinsky in October 1943 that it should not come as a surprise that agreements could be successfully negotiated with Soviet leaders—"the surprise comes," he said, "when they do what they have agreed to do." [120] Deane and the U.S. mission experienced many disappointments in their dealings with the Soviets, and they are recorded with the appropriate flavor of frustration and anguish in Deane's book, "The Strange Alliance." Two major efforts, detailed by Deane in the Dennett-Johnson work on negotiating with the Russians, concerned negotiations for a repatriation agreement on the return of Soviet-liberated American POW's and Allied-liberated Russian nationals, and on the acquisition

---

[117] Ibid., p. 8.
[118] Deane, Strange Alliance, p. 83.
[119] Deane, Negotiating on Military Assistance, pp. 3–4. A common complaint of Standley, Deane, and Harriman was the failure of the administration to use lend-lease as a leverage for getting more cooperation from the Soviets, particularly in matters of getting information. From the beginning the directive had been not to insist upon a quid pro quo in negotiating for lend-lease.
[120] Ibid., p. 7.

of airbases in Soviet Siberia. Both are illustrations of Deane's overall experience.

(b) Negotiations on Soviet-liberated American POW's

(1) Problem of POW's: Differing perceptions

As the Soviet Army moved westward into Eastern and Central Europe during the summer of 1944, Deane became concerned about the welfare of American POW's, particularly those known to be in camps located in eastern Germany and western Poland who would be liberated by the Russians. Those American POW's numbered about 75,000. A somewhat parallel problem arose as the Western allies moved from west to east into Germany with respect to the 3 to 5 million former Soviet citizens who were either taken as POW's, inducted into forced labor, or had defected and fought with the Germans against the Soviet Army.[121]

The problem arose from the differing perceptions of POW's on both sides: Deane was convinced that the Soviets suspected the loyalty of any POW (Solzhenitzyn's "Gulag Archipelago" has since abundantly documented the soundness of that judgment); the Americans assumed the loyalty of their POW's, hence Deane's anxiety to get them safely into the West.[122]

(2) Deane takes initiative

Deane first approached the Soviet Army General Staff on this question in a letter to Gen. N. V. Slavin on June 11, 1944. He provided Slavin with lists of camps known to be in the path of the advancing Soviet armies and the names of Americans in them. Slavin gave assurances that the Americans would be well cared for. However, Deane came away believing that this was the first time that the General Staff had ever given thought to the problem and actually had no plans for coping with it.[123]

On August 30, Deane pressed the matter further. He prepared two identical letters and asked Ambassador Harriman to send one to Molotov while he sent the other to Gen. A. E. Antonov, Chief of the General Staff. Deane proposed an agreement, providing for the anticipated return of POW's to their respective homelands, requiring an exchange of information on POW camps and access of each other's officers of POW's and the assumption of their control over them, and permitting identification, substantiation and quick repatriation of those claiming either Soviet or American nationality. Neither Harriman nor Deane received a response to these letters for several months, although they kept pressing for one. Meanwhile, they began making plans for the return of the liberated American POW's.[124]

General Eisenhower's staff now became concerned about the failure of a Soviet commitment on this matter. Gen. Bedell Smith reported to Deane that Soviet repatriation officials were at allied headquarters and were being given every facility for their work. He urged restriction on their activities until some positive action was taken on the American request. Deane rejected Smith's advice, arguing that in a "competition of discourtesy" the odds would be against the Americans, an attitude he was to regret. As he later wrote, Smith's proposal

---

[121] Deane, Strange Alliance, pp. 162–183.
[122] Deane, Negotiating on Military Assistance, pp. 9–10.
[123] Ibid., p. 10.
[124] Ibid., pp. 10–11.

"would have been exactly the type of quid pro quo that Soviet leaders respect." [125]

Impatient for action Deane approached General Slavin in early November 1944. The general responded that all was being done to assist the Americans. He then launched a verbal attack on Deane, laying out a series of unsubstantiated complaints against the U.S. handling of the Russians liberated in the West. "It was an attack typical of Soviet leaders," Deane noted, "when they realize fully the insecurity of their own position." [126] Pravda picked up the attack on November 9 with an expanded list of complaints by Col. Gen. Felip Golikov. Molotov added his protests through diplomatic channels. They charged, among other things, that Russians, forced to fight for the Germans and would have deserted at the first opportunity to return to their units, were being imprisoned with German POW's. "Actually the Russians knew as well as we that their complaints were unfounded," observed Deane. The Russians referred to were those fighting with the Germans when taken in action against American forces and had doubtful friendship for either the Soviets or the Americans.[127]

But this offensive was the conventional Soviet negotiating tactic of abuse and attack in order to disguise a vulnerable position. The "turn-coat" POW's were certainly a profound embarrassment for the Soviets, and the severity of the retribution taken against returning POW's, whatever the conditions of their capture, was a true measure of this embarrassment. Pure and simple they were regarded as traitors. Deane explained this negotiating tactic:

* * * the situation was one perfectly adapted to Soviet negotiating technique. Under the guise of solicitude for Soviet nationals, we were accused of mistreating Russians, while at the same time urging proposals for proper care of liberated Americans. The implication was that when we mended our ways, our proposals could be considered. At the same time, we were being needled to segregate and return every Soviet national to Soviet authority, regardless of the wishes of the individual or the circumstances under which he was apprehended.[128]

(3) Agreement at Yalta; failure in compliance

Finally, on November 25, 1944, Molotov responded to Harriman's letter of August 30, agreeing "in principle" to Deane's proposals and promising to have the proper Soviet authorities confer on details for an agreement. Further Soviet delays provoked another Harriman letter on December 28, urging the promised discussions. Molotov responded affirmatively, and the first meeting was held on January 9, 1945, more than 6 months after the subject was first raised. At this meeting Col. Gen. K. D. Golubev, head of the newly formed Repatriation Commission, presented a completed plan for carrying out the proposals Deane had made in August. For Deane it was a "reasonable plan," and with a few minor changes it embodied what he had hoped to accomplish. The agreement was signed at Yalta a few weeks later.[129]

Thus, despite the long and calculated delays and the intensity of the abuse—as Deane said, during the negotiations "Soviet authorities from Stalin down poured forth a continuous stream of accusations regarding the treatment of liberated Soviet citizens," the final negotiations for the agreement went smoothly.[130] "The agreement was a good

[125] Ibid., p. 11.
[126] Ibid.
[127] Ibid.
[128] Ibid., p. 12.
[129] Ibid., pp. 13–14.
[130] Ibid., p. 18.

one," wrote Deane, "but so far as the Russians were concerned it turned out to be just another piece of paper." [131] Since the main emphasis in this study is on negotiations and not compliance (though oftentimes compliance only comes after applying pressures in further postagreement negotiations), suffice it to say, in Deane's words, that the "implementation of our agreement was the most dismal failure that I encountered during my stay in the U.S.S.R.—so much so that the matter was the subject of a bitter exchange between President Roosevelt and Stalin just prior to the President's death." [132]

(c) Negotiating for airbases in Soviet Siberia

(1) The problem

General Deane's efforts to negotiate with the Soviets for airbases in Siberia were met with similar calculated delays, frustrations, and ultimately with failure. As in the case of the POW issue, agreement was not the problem, compliance was. [133]

American war planners assumed that Soviet participation in the Pacific War was imperative once the war in Europe had ended (the atomic bomb had not bet been developed), and this assumption formed the basis of the wartime Soviet-American relationship and accounted for much of the seemingly excessive American concessions. Deane's main task was to lay the groundwork in negotiations with the Russians for strategic planning and combined operations in the Far Eastern theater. One of his major tasks was to convince the Soviets of the need for American airbases in Siberia, and, as he wrote, "I spent 2 years trying." [134]

Part of Deane's problem stemmed from Soviet fears of a two-front war which were shared by the Western allies who wanted no diversion of Soviet power from the European theater. The neutrality pact with Japan was their best insurance against this threat. Hence Soviet caution. For the United States, airbases in Siberia were considered vital because the Soviet Union had no strategic air force. Bases in Siberia would enable the United States to launch air strikes against Japan and give support to Soviet ground forces in Manchuria.

(2) Agreement with Stalin

At the Teheran Conference in November 1943, Stalin announced that the Soviet Union would enter the Japanese war once Germany had been defeated. At Harriman's request, President Roosevelt asked Stalin during the conference for facilities in Siberia to operate 1,000 American bombers. On February 2, 1944, Stalin agreed to the proposal, noting that additional facilities would have to be built in order to accommodate that number of bombers. Stalin also told Harriman that he had ordered high-ranking air force officers to return from the Far East to undertake preparations and discussions with Deane. But they

---

[131] Ibid., p. 14.

[132] For Deane's summary of Soviet violations, see pp. 16 and 17. For example, American authorities were never allowed to contact the prisoners until they reached Odessa from eastern Germany and western Poland. Many of those first liberated followed the Soviet advice to "go East" and hitch-hiked across Poland. Apparently, no attempt was made to care for the sick and wounded. Deane referred to the liberated POW's being "herded like animals into vile prisoner of war camps in eastern Poland and the western U.S.S.R. and shipped in boxcars to Odessa, the port of embarkation." (p. 14.)

[133] This section is based on Deane's account of "Negotiating on Military Assistance." For a detailed discussion of his efforts to negotiate with the Soviets on a wide range of cooperative agreements relating to the Far East, see his Strange Alliance, Chapters 13 and 14.

[134] Deane, Negotiating on Military Assistance, p. 19.

never showed up. As Deane put it, they were always "en route" or "just about to start." [135]

Delays on the base question continued until the Churchill-Stalin meeting in October 1944. Because of primary U.S. interest in the Pacific war, Harriman and Deane were asked to participate, particularly in matters referring to Japan. At the second session, Deane gave a full briefing to the assembled leaders and their staffs on the war against Japan. At the conclusion Deane asked Stalin directly about Soviet intentions with respect to Japan and among other things asked what proportion of the Trans-Siberian Railroad's capacity could be devoted to the build-up of the American strategic air force bases in Siberia. Stalin gave no answer. Upon leaving the conference Churchill acknowledged Deane's nerve in asking Stalin but expressed his doubts to Deane that Stalin would provide the information. [136]

At the next meeting Stalin came fully prepared with maps on which he pointed out where the airbases would be located, Soviet troops concentrated, and military supplies stockpiled. "He answered questions freely and committed the Soviet Union to a degree of cooperative effort," Deane noted, "that had never been attained in the war against Germany." [137] Stalin expressed the further wish to meet with Harriman and Deane to work out details in the joint effort against Japan. Perhaps the only negative note was Stalin's strong opposition to putting the agreement in writing, arguing the danger of security leaks from stenographers and secretaries. [138]

At the final session negotiations were completed and the agreement fully developed. Stalin would permit the bases, but the United States had to agree to sending 1 million tons of supplies, in addition to that already being sent for use in the German war, as a reserve stockpile for the Soviet Army's future operations against the Japanese in Manchuria. The supplies were to reach the Soviet Union not later than June 1945. [139]

In recalling the transaction, Deane later wrote with uncharacteristic bitterness:

When presenting us with his bill of goods, Stalin agreed to almost every proposal we had made. We could have airbases; we could count on the same priority as to use of transportation and other facilities as was given to the buildup of the Red Army; we could have Petropavlovsk as a naval base; we could send small parties to survey our prospective airbases; and most important of all, we could proceed at once with joint Soviet-American detailed planning.

"Looking back," Deane continued, somewhat sardonically, "it is difficult to see how Stalin kept a straight face because the end result of the negotiations was that the Russians got their supplies and the United States got nothing but a belated, last minute, undesirable Soviet attack against the Japanese." [140]

(3) Stalin as a negotiator

In this first of many meetings with Stalin, Deane came away with some very vivid impressions that were deepened by subsequent encounters. Seeing him in the company of the Politburo, comprising

---

[135] Ibid., pp. 19–20.
[136] Ibid., pp. 22–23.
[137] Ibid., p. 23.
[138] Ibid., p. 24.
[139] Ibid.
[140] Ibid., pp. 24–25.

such men as Molotov and Mikoyan, he was convinced that the power of decisions was with him alone. Isolated to a "startling degree" from both Russia and the outside world, he was dependent upon the flow of news dispatches and advice from his advisers for information. With respect to the latter, he listened but also brushed aside undesired arguments and made up his own mind. He was a master of detail, a characteristic that impressed others who dealt with him. Unprepossessing in appearance, he had a lack of color or desire for it that was his "greatest strength." Completely indifferent to the opinion of others, he paid little or no attention to the social graces. Though he could indulge in the Soviet ritual of rudeness, he generally betrayed little emotion; his manner was neither pleasant nor unpleasant: It was "markedly indifferent." Deane had seen him smile but never heard him laugh. He had never seen him unduly agitated. In brief, as a negotiator Stalin had "all the attributes of a good poker player." [141]

(4) Soviet failure to comply

Immediately after the close of the Churchill-Stalin conference, the United States set out to fulfill its commitment. Within a month after Harriman's agreement with Stalin on the Siberian stockpile, supplies began to flow across the Pacific. By June 30, 1945, the United States succeeded in delivering the promised supplies to the item, despite the lack of full cooperation on the Soviet side. [142]

In contrast, the Soviets set out to sabotage their commitment, creating for the United States a postagreement situation of negotiating for compliance. First, the appointment of Soviet officers for planning purpose was delayed until January 1945. Even when the appointments were made, planning, in Deane's words, "proved to be impossible." [143] After the first meeting, which proved to be a social encounter in the Russian tradition of first getting acquainted with the consumption of great quantities of vodka, the planners got down to business. But the Soviets insisted on circling the problem and not getting to the heart of it. When matters of substance were even raised, they always pleaded that such things were beyond their authority to the extent that they could not even be discussed. Soon it was evident that the Soviets had no intention of undertaking any joint planning for the war against Japan. This was made clear to Deane in December 1944 when General Antonov called him to his office to say without embarrassment or hint of apology that, "The Soviet Government wishes to inform the United States Government that requirements of the Red Air Force will not permit granting the use of airbases in the Maritime Provinces to the American Air Forces." By this time much of the promised 1-million-ton stockpile had been delivered and the balance in the pipelines. [144]

Protests at all levels from the President on down failed to induce Stalin to comply with the agreement. To keep supplies flowing, Stalin finally did agree to American airbases to be situated in the far north in the Amur River area of Siberia. Only B–29's could be used there because the sites were so far north and distant from their targets. The United States had sufficient B–29 bases to the south and east of Japan. The utility of the bases, as first conceived, was clearly diminished.

[141] Ibid., p. 22.
[142] Ibid., p. 25. Apparently. Deane must have had more complete information when he wrote this account in 1951, because in "The Strange Alliance," written in 1946, he noted that only 80 percent of the supplies had been delivered by that time. (p. 249.)
[143] Deane, Negotiating on Military Assistance, p. 25.
[144] Ibid., p. 25.

Besides, doubts were being expressed in the spring of 1945 that the bases might not be needed at all.[145]

Still, U.S. planners wanted a "look-see" at the Siberian sites. But the Soviets closed the door. An American reconnaissance party was dispatched to inspect the area; they got as far as Fairbanks, Alaska where they were to meet their Soviet escorts. But the escorts never arrived as excuse after excuse, in Deane's words, "more fatuous than the one preceding," was made. Finally, the United States gave up in despair and abandoned the idea of airbases in Siberia.[146]

2. SOVIET NEGOTIATING BEHAVIOR: CHARACTERISTICS AND PROBLEMS

(a) Ingredients of fear: Insecurity, suspicion, secrecy, and xenophobia

Negotiations on the POW issue and the airbases in Siberia were in microcosm the sum of Deane's total experience in Moscow. Revealed in both his published works was one overarching characteristic that could probably be reduced to the word, "fear"—a fear that combined an obsession with insecurity, an excess of suspicion, a passion for secrecy, and an addiction to antiforeignism. It was fear that sprang out of the circumstances of the war, the persisting reality of Russia's historical past, and the totalitarian nature of the governing system.

In countless ways fear had lain at the root of Soviet obstructionism in negotiations and compliance; it seemed to permeate the national psyche from Stalin and his ruling elite on down to the simple Russian folk, as for example, Deane's cook, housekeeper, and chauffeur; it was this fear, displayed in its many manifestations, that suffused the negotiating process and impacted upon Deane's performance and activities as head of the U.S. military mission.

It was because of these deep-rooted characteristics, revealed in the negotiating process, that the Soviets,

—Rejected the American proposal for the Siberian airbases that would have required some 50,000 Americans on Soviet soil;

—Frustrated efforts by Deane and other American officials to contact, visit, and personally assist the liberated American POW's wherever they were in European Russia as provided by the repatriation agreement;

—Only reluctantly provided an airbase at Poltava in the Ukraine for the shuttle-bombing venture, evinced, as Deane noted, "nothing but a desire to sabotage the venture," and made everything difficult for the Americans, including "approval of visas, control of communications, selection of targets, and clearances for landings and departures, and in the end * * * literally forced [the Americans] out of Russia by restrictions which had become unbearable";[147]

—Failed to cooperate closely on air operations and to give navigational assistance for the huge allied bomber formations over

---

[145] Ibid., p. 26. In the spring of 1945, Deane had his staff undertake a study of the need for the projected Amur River bases and their expected contribution to the bombing of Japan along with other related war matters. It was learned that the net increase of putting four groups of B–29's in the Amur River district would be 1.39 percent of the total bomb tonnage the United States could place on Japan without using Russian bases. Deane wrote: "This was convincing proof that the slight increase in our bombing effort and the advantage of an added direction of approach for our bomber formations were not at all commensurate with the logistical effort involved in establishing our forces in Siberia. In addition, it was evident that we would not carry out the project without prompt, continued, and wholehearted Soviet cooperation—this in itself was sufficient proof that the venture should not be tried." (Strange Alliance, p. 263.)

[146] Deane, Negotiating on Military Assistance, p. 26.

[147] Deane, Strange Alliance, pp. 124–125.

Germany, the latter for the "silly reason" of interference to Red Army radio communications, the "real reason" being, "that the stations would require 1 American officer and 20 American enlisted men to operate them" (the 6 base stations requested to be established on Soviet territory would have required a total of 126 Americans) ; [148]

--Rejected any attempts to coordinate military operations on land that required the intermixing of troops, in Deane's words: "As I look back over the pattern of Russia's collaboration with the Western allies, there emerges constantly evidence of Russia's desire to avoid any entanglements from which she would have difficulty in extricating herself in the postwar world"; [149]

—Refused "in her darkest days" to allow a group of allied bombers to base in the Caucasus in order to assist besieged Stalingrad ; [150]

—Refused to permit Deane's staff from moving freely about the country (Deane was permitted only one visit to the front) so that they, acting in the mutual interests and for the benefit of both countries, could get first-hand information on lend-lease requirements, as Deane wrote: "We could have done so much more had we been allowed to see the picture, but no, we were dreaded foreigners who must be kept under close surveillance in Moscow"; [151]

—Refused to extend full, extensive, and close-in cooperation as Americans extended to the Russians in the United States, at allied staff headquarters, and in the field, or to share technology as was done by the Americans, in Deane's words: "This generosity, or at least attitude, was never reciprocated by the Russians except after endless argument, negotiation, and delay"; [152]

---

[148] Deane wrote: "Aside from the shuttle-bombing bases we were allowed to have in the Ukraine, which were reduced in effectiveness because of Soviet restrictions, none of our requests for assistance to our Air Forces was approved. We sought bases at which our disabled aircraft could land when forced to come down behind the Russian lines. We were told they could land anywhere, which was not much help to a disabled pilot looking for a runway. A considerable number of our planes which did land behind the Soviet lines in fairly good condition were not returned to us, and when I left Russia it was not at all unusual to see an American Flying Fortress or Liberator with a red star on it parked on a Soviet airdrome." In contrast, Deane wrote of the American response to Soviet requests: "While Soviet requests for American assistance were few, those which were made were invariably granted." (Deane, Strange Alliance, pp. 140–141.)

[149] Ibid., p. 142.

[150] Ibid., p. 296.

[151] Ibid., p. 100. During his only visit to the front where on 1 occasion he met Colonel General Krylov, Deane made this observation: "Krylov, his staff, and our small party gathered round the conference table, and Sid Spalding [Maj. Gen. Sidney P. Spalding, head of the supply section of the mission,] quizzed them on the use and effectiveness of American equipment. As was the case with all the field commanders, they were enthusiastic about the supplies that were being sent from America. The meeting was a fruitful one, and Sid and I were able to get firsthand evidence of how some of our equipment should be altered to meet their needs. The corrective action we were able to take after we returned to Moscow more than repaid the Red Army for any inconvenience that accrued from our visit to the front. If we could only have gone more freely and without such elaborate preparations, we could have done much more." (Ibid., p. 211.)

[152] Ibid., p. 49–50. Deane wrote: "In contrast to Soviet secrecy was American openness. We had thousands of Soviet representatives in the United States who were allowed to visit our manufacturing plants, attend our schools, and witness tests of aircraft and other equipment. In Italy and later in France and Germany, Russian representatives were welcomed at our field headquarters and allowed to see anything they desired of our military operations. Our policy was to make any of our new inventions in electronics and other fields available to the Russians once we had used such equipment ourselves, had exploited the element of surprise, and were satisfied that the enemy had probably gained knowledge of the equipment as the result of its having fallen into his hands. Each month I would receive a revised list of secret American equipment about which the Russians could be informed in the hope that, if it could be made available, it might be used on the Russian front. We never lost an opportunity to give the Russians equipment, weapons, or information which we thought might help our combined war effort." The United States not only offered the Norden bombsight to the Russians but actually set up a training program of key engineers in Moscow (after some difficulty) to train core instructors. The Soviets failed to cooperate to the extent required so that the enterprise was a failure. (pp. 236–237.)

—Persisted in their deep suspicion of foreigners and their motives, as Deane observed: "Whatever the cause, suspicion existed and was evidenced by close surveillance of all foreigners [even to an NKVD presence in negotiations], a search for the hidden motive behind all foreign proposals, and, above all, by maintaining a veil of secrecy over the means and methods by which the Soviet Union was waging war against the common enemy"; [153]

—Frowned upon and indeed prevented the development of personal relationships between officials and foreigners, as in Deane's case who was never invited into the home of a Soviet official with whom he was working, as he said in a letter to General Marshall: "I have yet to see the inside of a Russian home. Officials dare not become too friendly with us, and others are persecuted for this offense"; [154] and finally

—The Soviets failed to widely publicize the magnitude of lend-lease (and did so only under pressure) on grounds of the need for secrecy.[155]

(b) Changing cycles in cooperation

Another key determinant in Soviet negotiating behavior was the changing cycles in the Soviet attitude toward cooperation. From his close-in vantage point Deane was able to chart these moods in general and in their specifics, and assess more realistically his expectations in negotiations.

Clearly the victory at Stalingrad in January 1943 and the thrust into Eastern and Central Europe in the spring of 1945 were decisive points in the cycle of Soviet cooperation. Power and politics were accordingly correlated and integerated into the negotiating process. Mounting military successes were reflected in Soviet behavior as their improved position of strength, integrated into the larger conception of the correlation of forces, encouraged stiffer demands at the negotiating table and a greater reluctance to cooperate.[156] Thus in the spring of 1945 when Soviet-American relations became increasingly tense over Soviet repressive actions in Poland in violation of the Yalta agreement, Soviet pressures were applied against the American base at Poltava, and characteristically negotiations, such as those on joint action in the Far Eastern war, took a rapid downward turn. American activities in the Soviet Union came to a complete halt; repercussions were felt on the international scene, notably in organizing the United Nations at San Francisco.[157]

---

[153] Ibid., p. 48. Other observations by Deane emphasized this excessive suspicion in contacts with foreigners: "Throughout my stay in Moscow i was constantly impressed by evidence that Soviet leaders were determined to defeat any joint enterprise that involved close contact with foreigners" (p. 295) ; and, "The greatest deterrent to full collaboration lies in Soviet distrust of foreigners." (p. 302).

[154] Ibid., p. 85.

[155] Ibid., p. 102.

[156] Deane described the changing cycles in the context of lend-lease : "l.. the early days of the program their attitude was not only understandable but essential. Russia had her back to the wall, and the news indicated that it was problematical if she could remain in the war. It is not necessary to go into the disasterous effect that Russian capitulation would have had on the allied effort. And it was right that we should give Russia every material and moral support of which we were capable. However, when the tide finally turned at Stalingrad and a Russian offensive started which ended only at Berlin, a new situation was created. We now had a Red Army which was plenty cocky and which became more so with each successive victory. The Soviet leaders became more and more demanding." (Ibid., p. 90.)

[157] Deane wrote with respect to Poltava : "When the Polish dispute occurred, Soviet displeasure was reflected in all branches of government and many restrictions were placed on American activities in Poltava. Our aircraft were unnecessarily grounded, rescue crews were refused permission to service American planes known to have force-landed in Poland, seriously injured American airmen were not allowed to be moved from Poltava to our

(Continued)

The orchestration of Soviet behavior and its correlation with negotiations in fluctuating cycles were well described by Deane in his first
encounter with Marshal Klementy Voroshilov and General Antonov
after taking over the mission in November 1943. At the Foreign Ministers Conference in October, which had ended on a high note of optimism with respect to allied cooperation, Deane had become friendly
with Voroshilov who, he described as a "short round" man with a "red
cherubic face." But at their subsequent meeting soon after, "he was
still short and round and his face was red, but not cherubic." Voroshilov knew that Deane had come to pin down an agreement "in principle" regarding shuttle-bombing and other matters. At once, Voroshilov "assumed a cold demeanor, a scolding attitude, and went at
once on the offensive," complaining about the ease with which the Germans were shifting reserve divisions to the Russian front and sharply
criticizing the Anglo-American inability to contain the Germans on
the Italian front. A very long and heated argument ensued. Deane
was later to write about this encounter, projecting it against the larger
background of his 2-year experience:

> At my initial meetings with Voroshilov and Antonov they conformed to a
> pattern of Russian behavior that should be recognized in future relations with
> Soviet officials. They illustrated a phase of the cycle that has characterized our
> military and political relations with the Soviet Union. Periods of accord are
> invariably followed by periods of dissension. It is difficult to know when or
> why such periods are to start or end. Moreover, the attitude of the moment is
> reflected in all agencies of government. At the time that I was being attacked
> with regard to our Italian efforts, Ambassador Harriman was receiving the same
> complaints from Molotov, who indicated Stalin's displeasure in the matter. Just
> as the accord of the Moscow Conference was followed by coolness with regard to
> our Italian operations, the Yalta Conference was followed by dissension over
> Poland and the Potsdam Conference by a complete failure in the Council of
> Foreign Ministers in London a month or so later.[155]

*(c) Tough bargainers: On the offensive with abuse and counter
charges*

In the nitty-gritty of negotiations Deane, like so many other Americans, discovered that the Soviets were very tough bargainers and that

(Continued)
general hospital at Teheran and Russian women were not allowed to associate with
American men. Russian airmen, who were undoubtedly simply carrying out instructions
from Moscow in applying restrictions, incurred the resentment of the American soldiers.
Morale and friendliness waned rapidly. Russians began to loot American warehouses."
(Ibid., p. 123.)
In describing Soviet reaction to differences over Poland, the negotiations at Bern, and
air incidents, Deane noted that it followed a pattern of behavior experienced in the past
and could be expected to occur in the future. "A complete stop was put to all American
activities within the Soviet Union," he wrote. "Word seemed to have been passed to all
agencies of the Government to suspend action in all ventures in which Americans were
involved. We were hardest hit in connection with the evacuation of prisoners of war * * *.
The blackout on Americans extended elsewhere. We had been promised that we would
be permitted to study the German submarine experimental station at Gdynia as soon as
it was captured. We were not allowed to do so on the grounds that the city was unsafe
until it had been cleared of mines. We were promised air bases at Budapest, but after
permitting one reconnaissance trip by General Hill the Russians refused to issue the
necessary instructions to implement the plan. The American group that was to be allowed
to survey the Amur River Valley was delayed at Fairbanks for 21 days before we gave
up in disgust. The Civil Air Administration refused to continue discussions concerning
the establishment of a connecting air route between the United States and the Soviet
Union." On the political side, Deane observed, "the situation was perhaps even worse."
and he cited the case of Molotov's refusal to appear at the United Nations Conference in
San Francisco. The only area where relations were at all amicable was in connection with
deliveries of lend-lease supplies to Russia, but even there "the American task was not
made easier by any marked degree of Soviet cooperation." (Ibid., p. 294, pp. 293–294.)
155 Ibid., pp. 33–34. Deane described an encounter with Mikoyan on his refusal to grant a
request for shipments of aluminum and nickel without a justification that reflected a
chilling mood from the top: "My letter to Mikoyan brought a prompt response in that I
was asked to come to his office to discuss the matter. I was received coldly, and the chilli-
ness even extended to his interpreter, ordinarily a most affable individual. I was always
amazed at the speed with which the attitude of the moment would permeate not only
within but among the various branches of the Soviet Government. When it was 'Kick-
Americans-in-the-pants' week even the charwomen would be sour." (Ibid., p. 97.)

the relative weakness of their negotiating position was conversely proportionate to the intensity of their abuse and the outrageousness of their countercharges. As Deane observed, "It is almost axiomatic that the vigor, vindictiveness, spleen, and outright dishonesty of Soviet argument increases in direct ratio with the weakness of its position." [159]

The incident with Voroshilov and Antonov regarding arrangements for shuttle-bombing was characteristic of Soviet toughness in negotiations and their penchant for the ritual of rudeness. Both knew that the Soviet Government had committed itself to making detailed arrangements for shuttle-bombing, but, as Deane wrote, "they had no intention of doing so until it suited their purposes." A diversionary attack was called for; hence the verbal offensive against Deane by berating the Anglo-American performance on the Italian front. [160]

Similarly, in negotiating the POW-repatriation issue the Soviets responded to Deane's pressure for negotiation with a string of verbal abuse and countercharges against alleged allied mistreatment of liberated Russians. As Deane wrote, "During the entire course of our negotiations, Soviet authorities from Stalin down poured forth a continuous stream of accusations regarding the treatment of liberated Soviet citizens. All accusations were investigated and all proved to be unfounded." [161] It is significant to point out that the Soviets were in the weakest and most embarrassing position in these negotiations.

Deane's experiences with A. I. Mikoyan, the Commissar of Foreign Trade, revealed another aspect of Soviet negotiating behavior, the tendency to haggle even to the point of jeopardizing their own interests. Mikoyan, an Armenian by birth, prided himself on his skills as a trader. As a principal negotiator in the lend-lease program from the Soviet side, he elaborately entertained foreign representatives, especially those remotely connected with providing supplies to Soviet Russia. Visitors usually paid some tribute to Mikoyan's shrewdness as a negotiator in responding to toasts. "This always delighted Mikoyan's vanity," Deane observed, "but the foreigner was usually dismayed during negotiations to find that the playful jest of his toast was in fact stark reality. Unless one was constantly on guard, Mikoyan would take his shirt." [162]

In contrast to others, Deane always felt that Mikoyan was just "too shrewd," and he cited an incident in which his shrewdness reacted against the interests of the Soviet Union. The incident involved Mikoyan's haggling over the interest rate of 2⅜ percent over a period of 25 to 30 years for industrial equipment that would probably have

[159] Deane, Negotiating on Military Assistance, p. 27.
[160] Deane, Strange Alliance, p. 34. In describing his first meeting with General Antonov, Deane observed: "I have never had a reception of more studied coldness. There was not the slightest spark of cordiality as he shook hands and asked me to be seated. I explained that the purpose of the Military mission was to provide a group through which operational coordination could be effected. He seized on this to berate me about our efforts in Italy, reciting in detail the German divisions that had recently appeared on the Russian front from the west. By this time I had become thoroughly chilled except under the collar and recited a few plain truths. I pointed out that we had liquidated Rommel's forces in Africa, forced Italy out of the war, taken on a second front in the Pacific without the help of our great Ally, and, at the same time, run the gauntlet of the German submarine menace to deliver supplies to Russia. With that he asked me if I had any further business, indicating that our conference was concluded. This time when we shook hands there were two pairs of eyes which belied any cordiality in the process." Deane went on to note that subsequent meetings with Antonov were "extremely pleasant" and that he attained "the utmost admiration for his intelligence and ability." However, at the close of their first session he was "greatly disheartened and held little hope for success" (p. 33).
[161] Deane, Negotiating on Military Assistance, p. 18.
[162] Deane, Strange Alliance, p. 92.

to be delivered after the war valued at $300 million under the third protocol and over $1 billion in the fourth protocol. Mikoyan insisted on 2 percent which the United States would not meet, thus delaying agreement for more than a year. The agreement was concluded after the war. As a result, much of the industrial equipment was not produced. Deane did not doubt that Mikoyan's haggling delayed Russia's postwar industrial recovery.[163]

(d) Centralized decisionmaking and a binding bureaucracy

The principle of centralized decisionmaking and the obstructionism of a binding bureaucracy were for Deane two inescapable facts of life in negotiating with the Russians. There was no mistaking that Stalin was the man; he was the principal decisionmaker; negotiators were merely "specialized messengers," as Deane observed, carriers of his word and doers of his will. Deane put it simply: "only one man in the Soviet Union can make 'on the spot' decisions and he is Joe Stalin." [164]

Soviet negotiators could not, therefore, negotiate in the American sense. A Soviet response to an American proposal had to await another meeting, as Hazard noted, so that new instructions could be drawn up. A proposition under consideration, Deane recalled, was consequently "seldom explored thoroughly and agreed upon objectively." Deane was never able to confer with the Soviet Chief of Staff, thrash out a problem, and arrive at an acceptable solution. Soviet negotiators could "only advocate a predetermined point of view" and could "never recognize any validity in an adversary's argument." Detailed approval at every step of a constantly changing negotiating environment was a Soviet operating principle that applied, as Deane said, "not only to basic decisions, but also to the numberless supporting decisions which might be called for in carrying them out." Thus, he concluded, "It is a system that is not conducive to close collaboration." [165]

American negotiators, such as Deane, were, therefore, at the mercy of a binding Soviet bureaucracy, be it political, diplomatic, military, or a combination of all, that inevitably produced delays, frustrations, and, in so many cases, intended and unintended failure. For negotiations did not stop with agreement, a normal procedure in the American mode, but proceeded on through the compliance stage where each step forward, or backward, was a new opportunity for further negotiations and bureaucratic obstructionism. In the joint planning for Soviet entry into the Pacific war, Deane discovered that while the decision could be quickly and expeditiously made by Stalin in conference with Churchill and Roosevelt, it was quite another matter at the operating levels where the details had to be worked out. At this level Soviet bureaucratic habits could and frequently did virtually paralyze continuing negotiations and procedures.[166]

American proposals for shuttle-bombing, the POW-repatriation issue and countless other forms of cooperation were subject to the same

---

[163] Ibid., pp. 92–93.
[164] Deane, Negotiating on Military Assistance, p. 27.
[165] Deane, Strange Alliance, pp. 300–301.
[166] On the matter of joint planning Deane wrote: "The Russians met us reluctantly, coming to the discussions under all of the handicaps of the Soviet system of centralized authority, and with the conviction that it was all a waste of time. They knew full well that they had not the power to make any firm agreements with the American group. In fact, it was necessary for them to get clearance from above before talking about each new subject as it was raised. They were so inhibited in their freedom of thought and expression that they could not answer even the most inconsequential questions at the meetings in which the questions were asked." (Ibid., p. 258.)

double jeopardy of negotiating the agreement and then endlessly negotiating its compliance within the environs and under the control of a formidable Soviet bureaucracy. For the Soviets the bureaucracy was clearly a defense mechanism against unwanted or reluctantly accepted collaboration with the Americans. Deane's negotiating experience of 2 years bears testimony to this.[167] It also bears testimony to a great many lost opportunities when Soviet interests were clearly not served as their totally bureaucratized system got in its own way.

Ironically, a way was found to circumvent the huge Soviet bureaucracy by taking initiatives in certain situations that spared the Soviets the burden of decision. In brief, it was a tactic that applied the time-honored salesmanship principle of the time-honored "Fuller-Brushman"; namely, "to assume the order." It worked very well in the case of establishing the bombing line in the Balkans. From his early experiences Deane knew that to request Soviet approval or cooperation for a particular action would require many weeks of negotiations and delay, a self-defeating process given wartime situations when time was of the essence. Cooperative arrangements had to be made quickly as the Soviet armies moved into the Balkans in the fall of 1944 in order to avoid accidental allied bombing of Russian troops. In one instance a group of American fighter planes accidentally attacked a Soviet column in Yugoslavia killing Russian soldiers, including a general. Informal arrangements had already been established in the case of local commanders of the Second Ukrainian Army, and it worked well; information was exchanged and operations proceeded. Lt. Gen. Ira Eaker, commander of the Allied Air Forces in the Mediterranean, wanted to expand the arrangement to include two other armies. Though Deane had misgivings about its success if he conferred with the General Staff in Moscow, he still felt that it should be done. His worst suspicions were confirmed: the General Staff was shocked by the knowledge of the informal agreement and not only rejected the proposal for its extension but immediately discontinued the arrangement with the Second Ukrainian Army.[168]

Further negotiations with the Soviets in Moscow on establishing the bombing line got nowhere. After several weeks of still further negotiations, an impatient General Eaker finally took the initiative and sent a message to Deane and his British counterpart in Moscow, announcing that effective at 2 o'clock on Sunday morning, December 3, 1944, the Mediterranean Air Forces would confine their bombing activities west of a certain line that he designated. Deane informed General Slavin orally and in writing of Eaker's action. "Surprisingly enough," wrote Deane, "Slavin and his chief, General Antonov, took Eaker's pronounced very well."[169]

Eaker's action confirmed a long growing suspicion in Deane's mind that relations with the Soviet authorities would be improved if a "tougher attitude on our part" was taken.[170] This display of initiative and toughness may have had a positive effect, but even as Deane observed, "there was little they could do about it."[171] A more subtle aspect of this episode than its self-enforcing nature and the demonstrated value of toughness seems to lie in the relationship between

[167] Ibid., pp. 302–303.
[168] Ibid., pp. 136–138.
[169] Ibid., p. 137.
[170] Ibid., p. 138.
[171] Ibid., p. 137.

Eaker's decision to take affirmative action and the passive response of the Soviet bureaucracy. What Eaker had done was in fact to relieve the Soviet side of the burden of decision that it seemed clearly unable to take in the ongoing negotiations. It spared Slavin and Antonov the further task of having to resort to higher authority, in this case Stalin, the Politburo, and the General Staff. The bureaucracy was, therefore, circumvented and, as the local Soviet commanders had rightly judged in their earlier understanding, Soviet-American interests were mutually well served.

A reading of Deane's experiences suggest that the combination of centralized decisionmaking and a binding bureaucracy inhibits individual initiatives, encourages the "bucking up" of decisions through the bureaucratic ladder, and induces a type of built-in conservatism that creates delays, frustrates negotiators, impedes progress in negotiations, and ultimately can cause failure—a positive attribute when failure is intended, but a decidedly negative and self-defeating one when it is not.

(e) On agreements "in principle"

Another aspect of Deane's education in Soviet negotiating procedures was the real meaning of agreements "in principle." Much to his surprise and chagrin Deane discovered very quickly that the term meant "exactly nothing." [172]

During the Moscow Foreign Ministers Conference in October 1943, Deane presented three proposals for cooperation with respect to shuttle-bombing, the exchange of weather information and improvement of signal communications, and the improvement of Soviet-American air transport. Two days later Molotov announced that after due consideration the Soviet Government approved of the proposals "in principle." Details were to be worked out between Deane's military mission and the Soviet General Staff.

For days a much-elated General Deane waited patiently and optimistically for a call from the Soviet General Staff. But none came. "Alas," he wrote, "it was the first of a great many such vigils I was to have in the insuing 2 years." Not until February 1944 were negotiations actually started on the proposals and then only after continuous pressure was applied by the President on Stalin, by Harriman on Molotov, and by Deane on the Soviet General Staff. [173]

Presumably Molotov's agreement "in principle" was only intended to create the illusion of an agreement, a way of clearing it off the agenda of a conference that could then be given the patina of success. The hard bargaining was to come later, if at all.

(f) On not taking initiatives

Deane was also to discover that the Soviets did not take the initiative in negotiations for cooperation but rather reacted to proposals from the other side. He could recall no action that was initiated by the Russians, he wrote, "that was designed to facilitate the task of her western allies." In every instance of wartime cooperation the proposals were originated by the British or the Americans. [174] As Deane said with respect to information made available to General Eisenhower:

[172] Ibid., p. 20.
[173] Ibid., pp. 20–21.
[174] Deane, Negotiating on Military Assistance, p. 8.

All the information Eisenhower had concerning the Red Army's plans was the result of our initiative in seeking to obtain it, and then it was only obtained after continuous pressure at the highest levels. Not once during the war did Stalin or his subordinates seek a meeting with British or American authorities in order to present proposals for improving our cooperative effort. It was either the President or the Prime Minister who proposed Teheran, Yalta, and Potsdam.[175]

Even in actual negotiations, as revealed in Deane's writings, the Soviets seemed not to have taken the initiative in presenting proposals. Always they seemed to react to those put forward by Deane, as in the case of the POW-repatriation issue. Deane did not attempt to explain this aspect of Soviet negotiating behavior. But conceivably, the Soviets, themselves, had no proposals to make, either due to a lack of knowledge or because they just had not thought about it—as seemed to be the case when Deane first approached Slavin on the POW matter. This hesitancy to take initiatives probably could be partly explained by the built-in ultraconservatism of a fear-ridden bureaucracy. Whatever the reason, the Soviets seemed inclined to leave the initiatives to Deane. This passive procedure gave them time to analyze the problem, sort out their interests and objectives, formulate a negotiating position, and instruct their negotiators accordingly.

(g) Problems and language and concepts

(1) Special problems with translators and interpreters

Finally, Deane faced a special problem in negotiating with the Soviets with respect to language barriers and conflicting concepts. Deane acknowledged that some American differences with the Russians sprang from language difficulties. He explained that Russian was a more precise language than English and that it was more likely to have a word to express each different shade of meaning. The same word in English had not only different meanings but inflections on words and their relationship to words in the context connoted different thoughts. As a result, a Russian translation into English often appeared, as Deane observed, "blunt and unnecessarily offensive," while an English translation into Russian was likely to result in an unintended interpretation. Deane recalled an instance when a Russian-American committee was to be established and would be in "continuous session." To the Russians, this meant that the members would never leave the committee room. After arguing the point, "with mounting suspicion on both sides for a half hour," it was agreed that the committee should always be available to meet immediately upon the call of the chairman.[176] While this example had no earthshaking importance, still it does suggest the potential pitfalls of language when negotiating subject matter of very great importance. This is particularly the case when considering the different perceptions of words and agreements. "We lay stress on the spirit of agreements," wrote Deane; "the Russians recognize only the written word."[177]

Whether or not Deane used his own American interpreter in negotiations with the Russians is not clear. But it is significant that during the very important briefing to Stalin and Churchill on the plans, strategy, and history of the Pacific war during their October 1944 meeting, he used Pavlov who was Molotov's interpreter. Deane found

---

[175] Deane, Strange Alliance, p. 160.
[176] Ibid., p. 301.
[177] Ibid.

it easy to speak through an interpreter, he said, "especially one as good as Pavlov," because delays for translation gave him time to observe the audience and see the impression made by the thought just expressed and to formulate what he was to say next. At least in this instance no question was raised with respect to the accuracy of translation, but the potential pitfalls of depending upon a Soviet interpreter remained.[178]

(2) Conflicting concepts in ideology and military planning

Equally as difficult as the language barrier in negotiating with the Russians was perhaps the wide gap in conceptual perceptions, both ideological and institutional. In explaining the ideological differences, Deane put it simply: "We differ in our beliefs concerning the four freedoms, and each of us is amazed at those of the other. We differ in our interpretation of the meaning of words." [179] From those differences flowed a stream of problems in perceptions that inevitably complicated Soviet-American negotiations.

But the problems were more than ideological; they were institutional; this was evident in attempts at joint planning. Differing perceptions of joint planning doomed such efforts to failure. As Deane recalled, "They preferred to operate independently rather than in conjunction with us." [180] Americans approached combined operations with the Russians in a matter-of-fact, problem-solving commonsense way: Combine operations where possible to bring maximum weight to bear on the enemy. In contrast the Soviets believed agreement should be only on separate tasks that were to be performed independently of each other. "I think this accounts for the difficulty Harriman and I encountered in our efforts to initiate detailed planning," Deane explained.[181]

In attempting to devise some joint planning with Russia in the Pacific war, Deane ran into innumerable difficulties: Problems of centralized control that prevented a free-and-easy exchange of ideas; lack of freedom of thought, expression and of action that prevented Soviet negotiators from responding to the most inconsequential questions and taking even the most modest initiatives; in brief, the absence of a consensus on the ways and means and thinking on cooperative measures for winning the war. Here was the root of the problem. The only solace that Deane could find for this failure in negotiations was from the fact that joint planning, as he described it, "was a new experience for the Russians, and they did not have the vaguest idea of how to go about it or what it implied." [182] Deane explained what amounted to an ideal joint planning environment: Freedom of planners to study their problems objectively and try to reach the best solution with an open mind, without regard to national or service interests, and without being hampered by prior instructions. "It seems almost ridiculous," con-

---

[178] Ibid., p. 245.
[179] Ibid., p. 301.
[180] Ibid., p. 231.
[181] Ibid., p. 255. In commenting on the fierce Soviet attitude of·"going-it-alone," Deane wrote further: "As I look back over the pattern of Russia's collaboration with the Western Allies, there emerges constantly evidence of Russia's desire to avoid any entanglements from which she would have difficulty in extricating herself in the postwar world. Russia wanted to fight and end the war with none of the heterogeneous mixture of troops, divided responsibilities, and mutual obligations which the British and Americans were prepared to accept with regard to each other. Russia's position at the end of the war was to be that which she herself had won—a position which Russia would control free of obligations to and interference from her allies." (p. 142.)
[182] Ibid., p. 258.

cluded Deane, "to have expected objective planning for Soviet-American operations in the light of the known Soviet penchant for centralized control." [183]

3. PRECEPTS AND GUIDELINES FOR NEGOTIATING WITH THE SOVIETS

(a) On the value of firmness, quid pro quo and leverage

In the expectation that others could benefit from his experiences, Deane suggested here and there in his writings certain precepts and guidelines for negotiating with the Soviets. Perhaps the most important was singly or in combination the value of firmness, of insisting on a quid pro quo and having leverage. An unchanging line in Deane's thinking was the necessity for firmness; this was what the Soviets respected. For him the "most outstanding lesson" emerging from efforts to coordinate air operations was the effectiveness of General Eaker's firm action in drawing the bombing line after 8 months of futile negotiations.[184] Accordingly, Deane strongly recommended to the U.S. Chiefs of Staff that Soviet military authorities be informed of actions to be taken but to ask for their consent or concurrence only when necessity to do so was "plainly indicated." "This suggestion," wrote Deane, "was motivated by the conviction that Soviet leaders have respect only for strength."[185] Linked to firmness was the value of pressure which Deane found to be a cardinal virtue. All the information that General Eisenhower's headquarters had on the Red Army's plans was "only obtained after continuous pressure at the highest levels."[186] This could probably be said about every negotiating encounter he had with the Soviets. At the same time Deane stressed the importance of openness and frankness. Distrust of foreigners was the "greatest deterrent" he found to full collaboration, but he believed that it could be overcome "to a limited degree by complete frankness."[187]

Dealing on a quid pro quo basis intelligently applied was "the only basis upon which we can establish reasonably good relations" with the Soviet leadership.[188] Agreements should be reached on this basis, Deane advised, "with the quid running concurrently with the quo." And he further cautioned against agreements in which "we pay in advance," warning that, "Honesty is not a virtue of present-day Soviet leadership."[189]

Implied in this advice is the third precept; namely, the importance of leverage in negotiations. Like Harriman, Deane was not at all happy with the open-ended, no-justification-asked, no-strings-attached approach the administration had taken toward lend-lease, mainly because it deprived the United States of important leverage in negotiating for other interests. Consequently, the United States was in the position, as Deane wrote General Marshall, "of being at the same time the givers and the supplicants. This is neither dignified nor healthy for U.S. prestige."[190] Nor, as Deane found out, was it conducive to a strong negotiating position in dealing with a political sys-

---

[183] Ibid., pp. 258–259.
[184] Ibid., 141.
[185] Ibid., p. 300.
[186] Ibid., p. 160.
[187] Ibid., p. 302.
[188] Ibid., pp. 296–297.
[189] Deane, Negotiating on Military Assistance, p. 27.
[190] Deane, Strange Alliance, p. 85.

tem and leadership that respected strength and firmness and viewed relationship in a spirit of cold realism.[191]

(b) On building good will and expecting gratitude

Deane was particularly emphatic in warning that, "There is no such thing as banking good will in Russia," or, as he wrote General Marshall, "Gratitude cannot be banked in the Soviet Union." "Each transaction is complete in itself without regard to past favors," he said, adding, "The party of the second part is either a shrewd trader to be admired or a sucker to be despised." [192] In explaining the American expectation of Soviet gratitude for lend-lease, considering that allocations were made at sacrifice to American forces and the Western allies and delivery was made at great risks by American seamen, and the negative Soviet response, Deane wrote:

> It was my experience that Soviet officials are intelligent and shrewd traders. They do not permit sentiment to play a part in negotiations in which the interests of the Soviet Union are involved. There is no such thing as banking good will in Russia. Each proposition is negotiated on its merits without regard to past favors.
>
> Unfortunately in the early part of the war the United States was in a position where it had to meet all Soviet demands without question in order to keep Russia in the war. It might have been expected that our attitude of helpfulness and generosity would arouse a feeling of friendliness or gratitude on the part of the Soviet authorities which would influence them favorably toward the United States in subsequent negotiations. On the contrary, American generosity was taken as a sign of weakness, and the Soviet leaders became increasingly overbearing and demanding. They persisted in this attitude long after the urgent need for American aid ceased to exist. We continued our appeasement policy long after it was necessary to do so. Whenever we did take a firm stand during the war, our relations took a turn for the better. I believe it can be said with some degree of certainty that Soviet officials are much happier, more amenable, and less suspicious when an adversary drives a hard bargain than when he succumbs easily to Soviet demands.[193]

(c) On expecting delays in procedure and discriminating targets for cooperation

Like Hazard, Deane cautioned that nothing could be accomplished at the first meeting with a Soviet official, particularly if he were to receive unexpected proposals. Deane explained, citing his conference with Generals Slavin and Golubev on the POW issue. An NKVD representative was present to take notes on what transpired, a practice that Deane said made negotiations difficult if not futile. The Soviet negotiator dared not agree with any argument advanced by the other side, however sound, that did not accord with his prior instructions. Hence, nothing could be accomplished if there were disagreement until the Soviet negotiator received new instructions. Under these circumstances Deane advised that it was best not to press for agreement since it would not be obtained, and, as he wrote, "it evokes fantastic argument from the Soviet officials, from which it is difficult and embarrassing for him to recede at a later meeting if he is permitted to do so after reporting to his superiors." [194]

---

[191] For Deane's views on this problem, see Ibid., 90–91 and 97–98.
[192] Ibid., pp. 85 and 297.
[193] Ibid., p. 297. Note that Deane was specifically referring to Soviet officials with respect to expressions of gratitude. "Among the Russian military forces, especially those outside of Moscow who were using American equipment daily," he wrote, "I believe there was a considerable feeling of gratitude to America." He noted that Harriman had been received outside of Moscow with acclaim. After Roosevelt, he was looked upon by the Russian people as "the father of American aid." (p. 103.)
[194] Deane, Negotiating on Military Assistance, p. 13.

In targeting areas for cooperation Deane urged the greatest discrimination. The basic differences between the centralized Soviet system and the decentralized American system created problems when the American side sought to establish an agency-to-agency relationship. The result was an inflow of requests to Deane for cooperation on the most inconsequential matters, some of which, such as the proposal for joint study of 300 German industrial sites and experimental stations as soon as the Soviets seized them, had no chance of winning approval. Often the Soviets had no comparable agency for cooperation, and if they did, it would have been idle to expect that they would cooperate freely with Americans. Consequently, persistent Soviet refusals carried over to proposals that were of real importance. "For this reason," advised Deane, "we should resign ourselves to seeking Soviet cooperation only on the broad aspects of any joint enterprise and refrain from seeking it at all unless the results expected are essential to our interests." [195]

(d) Deane to Marshall: Prescription for negotiations

On December 2, 1944, Deane filed a frank, detailed but balanced report to General Marshall on the Soviet attitude toward cooperation with the United States and on future expectations of the relationship. The report amounted to a prescription for negotiating a stable relationship.

Deane stressed the importance of collaboration "now and in the future" based on "mutual respect and made to work both ways." He cited the imbalance in cooperation to the disadvantage of the United States and urged a change in policy. He elaborated on the unique Russian characteristics already discussed, such as suspicion, insecurity and the hard-headed realism of Soviet authorities in negotiations, and acclaimed the virtue and valor of the Russian people.

Deane perceived few conflicting interests with the Soviet Union, adding that "there is little reason why we should not be friendly now and in the foreseeable future." Deane then proceeded to recommend a revision of American policy along lines which clearly reflected his negotiating experience with the Russians:

—Continue to assist the Soviet Union, provided assistance was requested, and that it contributed to winning the war;
—Insist upon Soviet justification for American assistance in all cases, rejecting assistance upon failure of compliance;
—Insist upon a quid pro quo in cases where American assistance did not contribute to winning the war;
—Present proposals for collaboration that would be mutually beneficial and then leave the next move to them;
—"* * * act as we think best and inform them of our action" when American proposals for collaboration were unanswered within a reasonable time; and
—Stop "pushing ourselves on them and make the Soviet authorities come to us. We should be friendly and cooperative when they do so."

Deane concluded that there was something here worth fighting for and that it was simply "a question of the tactics to be employed." American interests would suffer for a period were his recommendations followed, this he acknowledged. However, Deane was "certain

---

[195] Ibid., p. 299.

that we must be tougher if we are to gain their respect and be able to work with them in the future." [196]

(a) Prospects for the future

Deane left the Soviet Union in late 1945 feeling that his mission was "scarcely * * * an outstanding success." "We had barely scratched the surface of the possibilities that existed for a full Soviet-American partnership in the prosecution of the war," he said. While maintaining a "deep affection" for the Russian people, Deane came away with "high skepticism" about the possibility of future cooperation with the Soviet leaders. [197] Still, he believed that the United States could establish an on-going workable relationship, but under these conditions:

We can get along with the present Russian leaders if we recognize them for what they are. We can, if we are stronger, smarter, and at least as certain of our objectives as they are of theirs. We must appreciate that we are dealing with individuals who are motivated by realism and not by sentiment. We must be shrewd enough to get value received for concessions we make. We must be certain that our own hands are clean in our relations with Soviet leaders. We must be motivated by principles in which we believe rather than by retaliation against principles which we abhor. Above all, we must abandon the hopes that go with the weakness of appeasement. We are dealing with people who respond only to strength. It may not be a happy relationship, but it can be a workable one. Leadership is a transient thing, and beneath the oppression of the present Soviet regime is a people with whom we shall someday be proud to march into a happier future. [198]

(b) Soviets as negotiators

Deane confessed to recognizing the futility of trying to discover what made the Soviet negotiator what he was; but he did not underrate him as a negotiator. He had, Deane said, certain characteristics in negotiations and in compliance with agreements. When they are seen as part of a technique, then, Deane said, "we discover the dog to be more a barker than a biter. Its barking is endless, but biting is attempted only when the victim is helpless." [199] In a more sweeping statement on the Russians as negotiators, Deane observed:

Soviet leadership will meet with an enemy when it is expedient to do so in progressing to the ultimate objective. It will bargain shrewdly; it will bluff at every opportunity; it will stop and wait whenever and wherever the enemy is stronger; its objective is not one to be reached in a day, a year, a generation; attainment will come through patient and unremitting pressure and by taking full advantage of the soft spots in the enemy's armor. [200]

(c) Deane as a source

A great deal of emphasis has been placed on Deane's observations in this study. And for good reason. After the passing of 33 years, his writings remain perhaps the most valuable source on Soviet negotiating behavior as seen from the American perspective and through American eyes. Except for a few slight strictures here and there, they

---

[196] Text of letter is reproduced in, Strange Alliance, pp. 84–86.
[197] Ibid., p. 285.
[198] Ibid., p. 304.
[199] Deane, Negotiating on Military Assistance, p. 27.
[200] Deane, Strange Alliance, p. 304. "There is perhaps no more futile occupation than endeavoring to discover what makes the Soviet negotiator what he is," wrote Deane. "Averell Harriman and I spent many a long evening before his fireplace in Moscow advancing and shattering theories on the subject. I suppose that no one, including the Soviet leaders themselves, could fully give the answer." (Deane, Negotiating on Military Assistance, p. 27.)

are restrained, objective and balanced, betraying none of the bitterness that has marked the works of so many other close-in observers. As a result, his analysis and judgments, penetrating and judicious, have enhanced his credibility as a source. Moreover, Deane negotiated in depth and at many levels, high to low, and did so on a day-to-day basis. Few Americans have probably ever been so deeply involved in the negotiating process with the Russians. Thus he was able to observe the process of negotiation and compliance not only at close range and on a continuing basis but in a setting of great peril and threat to the Soviet Union—a setting that tended to resurrect all the deeply held Russian traits of insecurity, suspicion, secrecy, and xenophobia. It is this aspect of his experience that has value in giving insights to Soviet negotiating behavior in the Nuclear Age, for the 1970's and 1980's is a time of perhaps even potentially greater peril for Russia as well as the United States and the West.

CHAPTER V—NEGOTIATIONS UNDER STALIN: DURING WORLD WAR II, 1939-1945

Part II—Major Wartime Conferences: From the Moscow Conference of 1942 to Yalta in 1945 and Descent Into the Cold War

Watch for their self-interest. And take care of our own. They're mighty skillful negotiators, with all the trumps. * * * They don't ever give anything away, Mr. Secretary, not even for something.

—*U.S. Ambassador Standley to Secretary of State Hull on the eve of the first Foreign Ministers Conference, October 1943.*

* * * Soviet officials are intelligent and shrewd traders. They do not permit sentiment to play a part in negotiations in which the interests of the Soviet Union are involved. There is no such thing as banking good will in Russia. Each proposition is negotiated on its merits without regard to past favors.

—*General John R. Deane, 1946.*

III. MAJOR WARTIME CONFERENCES

A. CHURCHILL-HARRIMAN MEETING WITH STALIN, AUGUST 12–15, 1942

1. PURPOSE OF THE CONFERENCES

(a) *Major wartime conferences*

Beyond specific negotiations for lend-lease and the various types of military cooperation, wartime diplomacy, notably at the Summit, focused mainly on military and political problems of maintaining the coalition, conducting a global war, and devising political arrangements for the postwar world. Major wartime conferences of the allied leaders were held in Moscow (1942), Teheran (1943), Yalta (1945), and Potsdam (1945). The Foreign Ministers of the Grand Alliance met in special conferences in 1943 and again in September and December 1945. This chapter examines in some detail three of these conferences, the Churchill-Harriman meeting with Stalin in 1942, and the Summit conferences at Teheran (1943) and Yalta (1945) in which Churchill, Roosevelt and Stalin were the principal negotiators.

(b) *Decision against second front*

Prime Minister Winston S. Churchill conferred with Stalin in Moscow during August 1942. On Churchill's insistence, Harriman, then in London as a coordinator of military assistance to Britain, participated on behalf of President Roosevelt.[1]

Briefly, Churchill's purposes in the conference were to explain to Stalin the compelling reasons why the cross-Channel invasion could not take place in 1942 as the Soviets had fully expected in order to relieve pressure on their front, and to explain the value of the North

---

[1] Feis. Churchill-Roosevelt-Stalin, p. 73.

African operation designated Torch that was planned for the autumn of 1942. Churchill had hoped that such explanations would end Soviet suspicions that the British and Americans were not fully cooperative in the war and accordingly improve the political basis for the future conduct of the war.[2]

2. FIRST SESSION: SOMBER BUT FRIENDLY

(a) *Churchill gives bad news, then good news*

Less than 3 hours after arriving in Moscow together from Cairo and Teheran on August 12, Churchill and Harriman began their talks with Stalin in the Kremlin. The first session, lasting nearly 4 hours and ending near midnight, went unexpectedly well, though the first 2 hours, by Churchill's account, were "bleak and somber." [3]

Churchill's negotiating strategy was first to give the bad news, then the good news: the bad news being that there would be no second front; the good news, an explanation of Torch. Churchill explained his case against the second front, as he said, "frankly" and invited "complete frankness" from Stalin—which he eventually got.[4] Other aspects of the European war were also discussed by the leaders, and Churchill, in an apparent effort to assuage Stalin's disappointment, held out prospects of expanding military operations in 1943.

Stalin remained grim—"very glum," Churchill wrote—and unconvinced by Churchill's explanations. According to Harriman, he took issue with the Prime Minister at every point "with bluntness, almost to the point of insult," making such strictures as, "You can't win wars if you aren't willing to take risks" and "You must not be so afraid of the Germans." [4a] Not until Churchill discussed the morale-breaking aspects of the air war over Germany and the strategic value of Torch did the tension ease and Stalin's manner become more friendly.[5]

(b) *Ending on happy note*

And so, on this happy note the first session ended. Both Churchill and Harriman were delighted with the talks and said so on leaving the Kremlin. Churchill, who was meeting Stalin for the first time, termed it the most important conference of his long life and expressed his pleasure and gratitude to Harriman for helping him over some of the "rough spots." [6] At midnight Ambassador Standley joined the pleased but tired negotiators for dinner, along with some British officials. Standley reported that both were "elated at the cordiality of the conversations" and both seemed impressed by Stalin's intelligence and grasp of the strategic implications of Torch. "Tomorrow comes the freeze," warned Standley sourly and prophetically, drawing, as he said, from "the depth of my own experience with the Russians." Harriman looked at him sharply. "Oh, not at all, Admiral, not this time." Both were recalling the previous Harriman-Beaverbrook encounter with Stalin.[7]

---

[2] Ibid.
[3] Churchill, Winston S. The Second World War: The Hinge of Fate. Boston, Houghton Mifflin, 1950. p. 477, and Harriman and Abel, op. cit., p. 152.
[4] Churchill, Hinge of Fate. p. 477.
[4a] Ibid., and Harriman and Abel, op. cit., p. 152.
[5] Ibid., p. 152–153 and Churchill, Hinge of Fate, p. 481.
[6] Harriman and Abel, op. cit., pp. 154–155.
[7] Standley and Ageton, op. cit., pp. 210–211.

3. SECOND SESSION: STALIN'S TACTIC OF ABUSE

(a) *Nocturnal meetings, a calculated negotiating ploy?*

The initial elation and optimism of Churchill and Harriman were, as Standley predicted, quickly shattered at their second meeting with Stalin on the next day, August 13. As customary with Stalin the time for the meeting was late in the evening, at 11 o'clock—a time quite exceptional from the working habits of most Britons and Americans. Standley perceived a calculated intent behind this late scheduling that was designed to adversely affect Western negotiators. As he observed, it was a "working schedule to which the Russians were accustomed, but one designed to exhaust the most rugged Western diplomat." [8] The implication was that fatigue made the negotiating adversary vulnerable.

(b) *Stalin's negotiating offensive*

Churchill described the second meeting as "most unpleasant" and Harriman as "an unexpectedly tough encounter" as the negotiators argued for about 2 hours.[9] Stalin took the offensive: He handed each a formal aide-memoire in which he accused the British and Americans of violating a pledge allegedly made to Molotov in London to launch a cross-channel invasion in 1942 and expressed dissatisfaction with the decisions he seemed to accept at their first meeting. In a recourse to his tactic of abuse, Stalin verbally reiterated the points made in the memoire, saying, in Churchill's words, "a great many disagreeable things." He charged the British with cowardice in failing to fight the Germans; he rebuked both allies for reneging on lend-lease supplies (a devastating U-boat attack had required a temporary halt); and in general he laid down a barrage of harshly uttered complaints that were directed as much at the Americans as the British.[10]

(c) *Churchill-Harriman repulse*

Churchill repulsed all of Stalin's contentions "squarely," as he said, without resorting to taunts. Much to his surprise, Stalin, who he confidently felt was not used to repeated contradictions, became neither angry nor animated. At one point in the bitter exchange Harriman passed a note to Churchill recalling Stalin's tactics during the Harriman-Beaverbrook mission 1 year ago when on the second night he was "equally rough." Harriman cautioned that this show of hostility should not be taken seriously.[11] Both negotiators denied breaking a pledge that was in fact never given and said so again in subsequent memoires to Stalin. Other matters relating to the conduct of the war were discussed including Harriman's proposal for delivery of lend-lease planes via Alaska and Siberia which Stalin curtly rejected, though he had previously agreed to it; final plans were then underway.[12]

(d) *Churchill's gloom*

Churchill came away from the second meeting in what Harriman described as a "deeply depressed mood." He kept Harriman up until 3:30 in the morning analyzing Stalin's behavior. Both guessed that the Politburo had more power than supposed in the West and that this

---

[8] Standley and Ageton, op. cit., p. 211.
[9] Harriman and Abel, op. cit., p. 155, and Churchill, Hinge of Fate, p. 486.
[10] Harriman and Abel, op. cit., pp. 156–157.
[11] Ibid.
[12] Ibid., p. 159.

was a negotiating ploy by Stalin to assuage the disappointment of its members and make easier their acceptance of the decision against the second front.[13] Harriman cabled the President a reassuring message explaining Stalin's negotiating behavior that reflected an optimism Churchill was eventually to share:

The technique used by Stalin last night resembled closely that used with Beaverbrook and myself in our second meeting last year. I cannot believe there is cause for concern and I confidently expect a clear-cut understanding before the Prime Minister leaves.[14]

4. KREMLIN DINNERS: SATISFACTION AND AFFABILITY

(a) Harriman's prediction proved correct

Harriman's prediction that Stalin did not want a breakdown in negotiations and that the conference would end on an upswing proved to be correct. The icebreaking gesture occurred when at the conclusion of the second meeting Stalin invited his guests to an official Kremlin dinner on the next evening, August 14.

Harriman judged the mood at the Kremlin dinner to be "sober," but Churchill's gloom gradually gave way to a certain affability so that he could report to Roosevelt 3 days later that the atmosphere was "very friendly." [15]

Stalin toasted many of his Soviet guests; and among the foreigners, he toasted only President Roosevelt; the honor of toasting the others present fell to Molotov. In describing Stalin's demeanor at the dinner Harriman reported to the President that he appeared "entirely oblivious of the unpleasant discussions of the night before." [16]

(b) Churchill meets Stalin in private apartment

As if to confirm the success of the conference Stalin invited Churchill to dine with his family in his private apartment on August 14, the day before his departure—a gesture never accorded other foreign leaders. Records of the meeting suggest that the private meeting was "extraordinarily cordial throughout." [17] The two leaders talked until near daybreak over a wide range of subjects, notably the conduct of the war. "This convivial night," wrote Feis, "did not induce any new decisions nor lasting trust, as time was soon to show. But it extracted the thorns of argument and made the associates in the same cause comfortable with each other again." [18]

---

[13] Ibid., p. 159. At a luncheon on Aug. 14 with Churchill and Harriman, the question of Stalin's behavior was discussed. Harriman reiterated the point that he and Churchill had discussed with respect to the role of the Politburo. "Whenever Stalin gets tough with us," he said, "it's the Politburo attitude he's expressing, not his own views on the major subject at issue." Harriman also noted that Stalin used the same tactic of abuse with Foreign Minister Eden a year before. Standley, whose memoirs clearly reflect a certain dissatisfaction with Harriman, had been thinking a great deal about the matter, and he said: "I can't agree with you Averell. . . . From my experience, I believe it's a Soviet technique for negotiation—first day, all smiles, enthusiasm, visitors on top of the world; second day, the big freeze, nothing right, insults, visitors in depths of gloom, got to give Stalin something to make him happy again; third day, with or without concession, a big thaw, sunny skies, everything fine with the world. Today you had the freeze, tomorrow, the thaw." Churchill remarked, "Interesting," but Standley didn't think that he believed him. (Standley and Ageton, op. cit., pp. 213–214.)
[14] Harriman and Abel, op. cit., p. 159.
[15] Harriman and Abel, op. cit., p. 160, and Churchill, Hinge of Fate, p. 494.
[16] Harriman and Abel, op. cit., p. 160.
[17] Ibid., p. 163.
[18] Feis, Churchill-Roosevelt-Stalin, p. 97.

5. RESULTS OF THE CONFERENCE

(a) As a negotiating experience

(1) Stalin's tactic of abuse

The Churchill-Harriman conference revealed again the tactic of abuse that Stalin employed in negotiations. (In his personal report to the President, Harriman referred to "those long, reproach-filled sessions at the Kremlin.")[19]

At the time, both Churchill and Harriman tried to fathom its meaning, and both were convinced that in this instance it was related to internal Soviet politics, a ploy, so to speak, to ease the acceptance of a disagreeable decision. In retrospect, Harriman had second thoughts: He viewed it as a means of pressure on Churchill to underscore Soviet desperation in the war. At that time the Soviet Union was caught up in a grave crisis with the Germans advancing on Stalingrad and still besieging Leningrad, by then for 350 days. Harriman explained:

Stalin's roughness was an expression of their need for help. It was his way of trying to put all the heat he possibly could on Churchill. So he pressed as hard as he could until he realized that no amount of additional pressure would produce a second front in 1942. He had the wisdom to know that he could not let Churchill go back to London feeling there had been a breakdown.[20]

Reflecting the analysis at the time, Churchill reported to the war cabinet that he believed Stalin, knowing that the decision on the second front was correct, may have been compelled to speak as he did and might later make amends. The implication was that the tactic had an internal political purpose. Feis countered with this analysis: "But it was the British and Americans who tried the harder in that way, seeking to get their Soviet associates to appreciate how much they were doing and proposed to do to take the burden of war away from the Russians and unto themselves." [21]

Whatever the explanation, this negotiating episode revealed the Soviet ability to use the tactic of abuse to put their adversary on the defensive, to magnify their own needs and interests, and ultimately to try to create a debtor-creditor psychological relationship in which the Western Allies were in debt to the Soviet Union.

(2) On the technical military talks

If the talks at the summit were successful, such was not the case at the lower level. The Anglo-American negotiators collided head-on with the same negative Soviet behavior revealed in Deane's experience. In a typically British understatement, Churchill wrote that the technical military discussion "had not gone well." The British generals asked all sorts of questions, he said, to which the Soviets claimed they were not authorized to reply. They demanded only, "A second front now." The British reply was, in Churchill's words, "rather blunt, and the military conference came to a somewhat abrupt conclusion." [22]

[19] Harriman and Abel, op. cit., p. 169. Harriman recounted that Roosevelt listened closely to his report on these latest talks with Stalin and that he seemed to enjoy hearing about Churchill's discomfiture during the the Soviet leader's verbal assaults.
[20] Harriman and Abel, op. cit., p. 159.
[21] Feis, Churchill-Roosevelt-Stalin, p. 79.
[22] Churchill, Hinge of Fate, p. 495.

Harriman was somewhat more successful, but only after applying pressure at the top. Almost daily he had tried to arrange a meeting with the Soviet general in command of the armored forces. He wanted a first-hand performance report on the American light and medium tanks. This information was vital: Only the Soviets could provide it because they had used the tanks in combat; the Americans had not, and Torch was in the offing. Apparently fearing to take the initiative and distrustful of foreigners, the Soviet officials parried Harriman's requests, and only when he interceded with Stalin did discussions take place with the technical military staff. As a result many useful Soviet criticisms were incorporated in later tank models.[23]

(3) Technical conference matters

With respect to the technical aspects of the conference, the sources revealed no outstanding problems. Churchill had his own interpreters, though he never felt comfortable with them. When Dunlop, his first interpreter, failed to keep up with the expansive flow of Churchillian English, he was replaced by Maj. A. H. Birse who apparently was much more competent.[24] Presumably on some occasions, as at the official Kremlin dinner, he relied on Pavlov, Stalin's interpreter.[25]

(b) For the conduct of the war

The conference had great significance for the conduct of the war. Stalin accepted the decision against the second front and supported the strategy of Torch. He had little choice; he would not disrupt the alliance; hence, as Feis put it, "Mutual need prevailed over grievances."[26] Also a closer relationship between Churchill and Stalin emerged from the conference that had much to do with establishing a more stable political basis for the conduct of the war.[27] As recorded in Harriman's memoirs, Churchill came away from Moscow "greatly pleased and relieved over his new intimacy with Stalin."[28]

B. Moscow Foreign Ministers Conference, October 1943

1. CONFERENCE PURPOSES AND STANDLEY'S ADVICE TO HULL

(a) Participants and purposes

The first of a long series of Foreign Ministers Conferences was held in Moscow during October 18–30, 1943. Stalin proposed the conference as a preliminary step to his much-postponed first meeting with Churchill and Roosevelt.[29]

The principals at this conference were Secretary of State Hull, British Foreign Secretary Anthony Eden, and Soviet Foreign Commissar Molotov. The subject matter particularly important to each participant suggested the main purposes of the conference: For Molotov, it was to pressure the Western Allies into a firm commitment on the cross-channel invasion; for Hull, it was to gain acceptance of his four-power declaration on war aims and postwar international organization; and for Eden, it was to get agreement on machinery

[23] Harriman and Abel, op. cit., p. 164.
[24] Ibid., pp. 157 and 163.
[25] Churchill, Hinge of Fate, p. 493.
[26] Feis, Churchill-Roosevelt-Stalin, p. 78.
[27] Sherwood, op. cit., p. 622.
[28] Harriman and Abel, op. cit., p. 164.
[29] Harriman and Abel, op. cit., p. 235.

for intraallied consultation on war-related questions of Europe. In addition, Molotov sought a Soviet voice in Italian affairs; Hull, a strong advocate of liberal trade policies, pressed for consideration of economic questions; and Eden wanted to discuss a number of European problems with Molotov.[30]

With respect to the first category of purposes, Eden observed, "All these major objectives were realized," and on the second, he noted, "We made uneven progress." Among the successes was the agreement to reestablish a free and independent Austria.[31]

(b) Standley's advice to Hull

Ambassador Standley returned from Moscow in September 1943 with his initially high expectations of improving relations considerably lowered and himself somewhat disillusioned by his Soviet experience. As he recorded, "I was glad to be rid of the whole Russian business. * * *"[32] During October 4, 5, and 6, Standley conferred with Hull and gave him a reading on long-term Soviet foreign policy goals, the Soviet leadership and their negotiating techniques, and an assessment of the possible conference results.

In sketching out the larger design of Soviet foreign policy, Standley told the Secretary:

> We must face up to the realities of the situation in negotiating with Mr. Stalin and Mr. Molotov. The present world struggle has resulted from the efforts of the [democratic] Allies to prevent an ideology contrary to their own being thrust upon them by the use of military power. When this war has been won, we will find our country faced with an equally vital and grim struggle in the economic field. We will be competing with the enormous, *unfled* power of the Communist Soviet Union. *This economic struggle will be just as bitter and unrelenting as the military struggle has been.*[33]

Standley concluded: "A grim challenge, but a realistic one!" The Secretary had leaned forward, resting his chin on one palm, his eyes closed. "A grim challenge, indeed, Admiral," he agreed looking out at Standley suddenly from under his bushy eyebrows.[34]

Standley went on to describe the now familiar Soviet negotiating tactic of alternating abuse and affability as experienced by Harriman, Beaverbrook, and Churchill.[35]

When asked to comment on Molotov and Stalin, he gave the stereotyped characterization of Molotov as "a completely humorless, dedicated man, devoted to party principles and wholeheartedly loyal to the Boss," noting also that with him Molotov had been "scrupulously polite

---

[30] Eden, Anthony, Sir. The Memoirs of Sir Anthony Eden, Earl of Avon: The Reckoning. Boston, Houghton Mifflin, 1965, p. 476.
[31] Ibid.
[32] Standley and Ageton, op. cit., p. 493.
[33] Ibid., p. 496.
[34] Ibid.
[35] Ibid., p. 497. Standley explained the procedure starting with the reception at the Moscow Airport "with considerable fanfare" and the "full treatment, with honor guard, plush accommodations, probably at Number Eight guest house." Turning to the conference sessions, he gave this picture:
"The first meeting of the Conference, everything will be wonderful. You will feel that the Soviets will agree to anything. Mr. Molotov can be the most pleasant and ingratiating person you have ever met, when it serves his purposes. You will wonder why anyone ever said that the Russians are hard to get along with.
"The second meeting, you will be thrown into a maelstrom that resembles a pack of caterwauling cats. Nothing will be right. All the progress of the first meeting gone by the board, even less prospect of agreement than before you met. You will leave the conference table in a mood of the deepest gloom.
"That may be the night you are invited to the Kremlin for the usual grand banquet. You will probably find Mr. Stalin affable and pleasant. In conversation, he will make some offhand remarks which may or may not amount to commitments.
"If the Russians have decided to agree to anything, everything will be sweetness and light. In any case you might as well pack your bags and come home."

and correct" and at no time treating him "unpleasantly." With respect to Stalin, he said:

> Mr. Stalin is a different sort of character—he can be calculating abrupt or rude, sometimes downright offensive. Then, with that rare Georgian humor, he can smile and let his eyes warm up. You might even get to thinking he likes you. But he doesn't. I know much more about both Mr. Stalin and Mr. Molotov than I did two years ago but I don't feel that I know either one of them, not really, that is, as one person makes an impression on another here in America. They are both still an enigma to me, even after all the times I have met and talked with them.[36]

On October 7, Standley saw Hull off at the airport in Washington. "Well, Bill, any last-minute advice for an Alice-in-Soviet-Wonderland?" Hull asked. Standley urged him not to "overdo," cautioning that the "trip can be mighty rugged." "So I understand," said the 72-year old ailing Secretary. "But seriously, any advice?" And then Standley said: "Well, yes, sir, if you insist. Watch for their self-interest. And take care of our own. They're mighty skillful negotiators, with all the trumps." As the Secretary turned to leave, Standley added: "They don't ever give anything away, Mr. Secretary, not even for something." [37]

2. PRINCIPAL SUBJECTS ON THE AGENDA

(a) Soviet pressure for the second front

(1) Molotov's proposals

At the first session of the Moscow Conference on October 19, Molotov circulated draft copies of an agenda that placed at the top his proposals for shortening the war, a euphemism for the second front. (Hull's proposal for a four-power declaration on war aims and international organization had been first but was displaced and excluded by Molotov. At Hull's request, and the concurrence of Molotov and Eden, it was made point 2.) [38]

There were three points in the Molotov proposal: (1) To affirm the validity of the Roosevelt-Churchill statement at the Quebec Conference in August 1943 to the effect that the cross-channel invasion would begin in the spring of 1944; (2) to suggest jointly to the Turkish Government that it enter the war immediately; and (3) to demand the neutral Swedish Government to place air bases at the disposal of the Allies. The first point was the most crucial.[39]

(2) Anglo-American reaction to affirmation of second front provisional decision

In response, Hull and Eden declared that they would have to consult their respective governments on the matter of the second front. They did so hurriedly. The return instructions from the U.S. Joint Chiefs was clear: The Soviets could be told emphatically that the Quebec statement remained valid.[40]
.But the British response was less definite and dissimilar: It seemed to confirm the provisional decision made at Quebec and stressed the conditions for the operation, but the reply from Churchill reflected his doubts about the prospect of the invasion and his desire for alternative ways to defeat Germany.

[36] Ibid., p. 497.
[37] Ibid., p. 500.
[38] Hull, Memoirs, vol. 2, p. 1279.
[39] Feis, Churchill-Roosevelt-Stalin, pp. 224–225.
[40] Ibid., p. 225.

On October 20, General Deane and British Gen. Sir Hastings
Ismay elaborated on the Anglo-American military operations and
plans before the assembled Foreign Secretaries. Molotov tried to pin
Hull and Eden down on the direct point of acceptance or rejection of
the Soviet proposal. Both avoided a direct response and reiterated the
essence of the Ismay-Deane statement. Molotov seemed satisfied, but at
a subsequent meeting Marshal Voroshilov probed the matter of conditions for the invasion; for example, that the Germans should have
no more than 12 divisions of mobile troops in northwest Europe on
the day of the invasion.

Again Molotov pressed Eden and Hull for a specific reply on the
validity of the Quebec statement. Eden responded that it was valid
under certain conditions; Hull limited himself to subscribing to the
Ismay-Deane statement. Molotov accepted the fact that an unqualified
promise was not in the cards but proposed that the discussion be part
of the written record of the conference protocol. Eden saw no problem,
but Hull was more cautious, not wishing to commit the United States
beyond the Ismay-Deane statement.[41]

(3) Protocol of the conference

The conference protocol gave effect to Molotov's proposal on the
second front. It reproduced Molotov's original memorandum and recorded in parallel columns the views expressed by the Anglo-American
representatives and the comments by the Soviet representatives. "The
entry in the Soviet column was temperately trustful," wrote Feis, "being merely to the effect that Molotov had noted the American and
British statements, and expressed the hope that the plan of invasion of
northern France in the spring of 1944 would be carried out on time."[42]

(b) Four-power declaration on war aims and international organiza-
tion

(1) Hull's proposal

For Secretary Hull, one of the main purposes of the conference was
to gain acceptance of his brainchild, the Four-Nation Declaration on
General Security. At the third session of the conference on October 21,
Hull presented the declaration as a prescription for victory and a
design for postwar peace.[43] Eden supported Hull's presentation, and
Molotov encouraged both by saying that, "the Soviet Government was
very favorably disposed toward the principles set forth in this declaration and therefore welcomed it."[44]

(2) Substantive sections of declaration

The framework of principles making up the four-nation declaration issued by the conference was, in Feis' words, "vaguely magnificent
rather than sturdy."[45] In the preamble the four powers vowed to
continue the war until the enemy surrendered unconditionally. Under
the main substantive sections, the Allies pledged that they would—
—Cooperate to maintain peace and security as they had cooperated
in the war;
—Cooperate in matters relating to the surrender and disarmament
of the common enemy;

---

41 Ibid., pp. 226–227.
42 Ibid., p. 228.
43 Hull, Memoirs. vol. 2. p. 1280.
44 Feis, Churchill-Roosevelt-Stalin, p. 207.
45 Ibid., p. 207.

—Recognize the necessity of establishing a general international organization for maintaining international peace and security and open to all nations large and small;

—Consult together and when necessary with other United Nations members "with a view to joint action on behalf of the community of nations" until a new system of general security was in being; and

—Not to use their military forces within the territories of other states except for the purpose envisaged in this declaration and after consultation." [46]

(3) Molotov's objections; Hull's firmness

To get concurrence on the declaration, Hull had to make concessions, notably on the last point which Molotov objected to vigorously as it was stated in the original draft. Initially, Hull used the term "joint consultation and agreement." The Soviet Union would accept consultation, but not agreement or, in effect, Western veto power over Soviet troop movements in Eastern Europe. [47]

But Hull would not concede on Molotov's objection to China as an originating sponsor of the declaration, and in this effort he had Eden's support. For a week Molotov balked on this point, making what Feis termed, "quite a lot of trouble." [48] Much to Harriman's displeasure, Hull expended a great deal of energy, and leverage, on this matter which he felt would have been better employed in working out agreements to safeguard the independence of Poland and other East and Central European states whose liberation was foreseen in a few months. [49]

Privately, Hull warned Molotov that failure to include China could have "the most terrific repercussions" not only in the Pacific theater but in American public opinion. He hinted that aid then being sent to Russia might be diverted to China. Molotov backed down. [50]

(c) Problems of Europe

(1) Setting up the European Advisory Commission

At the fourth session on October 22, Eden presented his proposal to set up the European Advisory Commission (EAC) with headquarters in London to deal with all European problems affecting the Three Powers. [51] Agreement was, apparently, reached without difficulty. An American-devised plan for the postwar control of Germany was discussed at the conference and won the acceptance of the Russians, at least as a minimum but not maximum proposal. The plan was later turned over to the EAC for detailed study. [52]

(2) Confederation of Europe

Eden also pushed a number of measures broadly designed to forestall the division of postwar Europe into separate spheres of influence. One proposal, presented on October 26, would have encouraged the smaller countries of Central and Eastern Europe to form federations

[46] Ibid., pp. 207–208.
[47] Harriman and Abel, op. cit., p. 237.
[48] Feis, Churchill-Roosevelt-Stalin, p. 210.
[49] Harriman and Abel, op. cit., p. 236.
[50] Feis, Churchill-Roosevelt-Stalin, pp. 210–11, and Hull, Memoirs, vol. 2, p. 1282.
[51] Ibid., p. 1283.
[52] Ibid., p. 1287. For a more detailed discussion, see Feis, Churchill-Roosevelt-Stalin, pp. 220–223.

"in order to increase their mutual welfare by the establishment of institutions on a wider scale than each can separately maintain." Eden counseled the American delegation that the small, weak countries, inheritors of the collapsed Austro-Hungarian Empire, could only gain stability and prosperity by pooling their resources.[53]

But Eden got no support from Hull who expressed no opinion, noting only that he was there to agree on general principles; the details could come later. Molotov vigorously opposed the idea after giving the conference his personal "guarantee that there was no disposition on the part of the Soviet Government to divide Europe into * * * separate zones." He argued further that premature discussion could hurt the interests of the smaller countries and of European stability.[54]

3. OTHER CONCERNS AT MOSCOW

Other concerns preoccupied the Foreign Ministers at Moscow. Among them were: Successful arrangements for the Teheran meeting of Churchill, Roosevelt, and Stalin; Stalin's pledge to Hull that the Soviet Union would enter the war against Japan as soon as the Germans were defeated; a mutual pledge against a separate peace; agreement on establishing a free and independent Austria, and discussion but failure to reach agreement on pressuring Turkey into the war.

4. RESULTS AND SIGNIFICANCE OF THE CONFERENCE

(a) As a negotiating experience

(1) Formal atmosphere of cordiality

A predominating characteristic of this negotiating experience was its apparent formal cordiality. Deane described the atmosphere at the sessions of the Foreign Secretaries as being "idyllic—no serious differences developed," and the atmosphere of the conference as a whole as one of "goodwill and cordiality." [55]

No doubt the milieu of the conference proper and the external formalities such as the Stalin banquet, contributed much to insure its success. In this sense the apparent traditionalism and style of the old diplomacy, at least superficially, seemed to give the conference an aura of reasonableness, sensibility, and hope for the future. And thus was encouraged the belief that it was possible to establish a stable relationship with the Soviet regime and to conduct diplomacy in the normal traditional manner.

(2) Hull's hopeful assessment

For Secretary Hull this negotiating experience was most gratifying. The account in his memoirs exudes a spirit of great satisfaction and high expectation for the future. Hull came away from an audience with Stalin impressed by this "very cordial and affable" man.[56]

---

[53] Harriman and Abel, op. cit., p. 244.
[54] Ibid.
[55] Deane, Negotiating on Military Assistance, p. 5, and Strange Alliance, p. 26.
[56] Hull, Memoirs, vol. 2, p. 1293. Hull made this observation on Stalin after shaking hands to leave the official banquet: "I had an impressive experience with Stalin as we parted. After the usual expressions of leave-taking, he shook hands with me and said 'Goodbye' in Russian. Then after walking three or four steps away from me, he suddenly turned and walked back and shook hands a second time to a rather protracted extent, but without saying a word. Then, with serious demeanor, he turned and walked away. I thought to myself that any American having Stalin's personality and approach might well reach high public office in my own country." (p. 1311.)

He was similarly impressed by Molotov who in the course of the conference became "increasingly pleasant and communicative," enabling their conversations to become "freer and more outspoken." "In all my contacts with him in the course of the conference proceedings," Hull recalled, "I was more and more impressed with his broad grasp of the questions entering into the discussions." [57]

The four-power declaration was, in Deane's words, the "crowning achievement" of Hull's career.[58] And so the Secretary regarded it. In a conversation with the Chinese Ambassador in Moscow Foo Ping-sheung, Hull remarked that throughout the conference "all Russian officials had been exceedingly cordial and that, when matters of difference were under discussion, they had talked them out with us in a thoroughly agreeable spirit." And then he gave this hopeful reading of the future:

> This is a splendid state of mind with which to launch our great forward movement of international cooperation, with Russia for the first time a full-fledged member of it without reservations of any kind. All signs indicate that Mr. Stalin and his Government are opposed to isolation and are wholeheartedly in favor of the movement of international cooperation launched by this conference, with Russia as a full partner with the United States, Great Britain, and China.[59]

As Hull boarded the plane for home, he felt "very strongly that great things had been accomplished" at this conference in Moscow. In summarizing its achievements, he recalled:

> We had agreed on the creation of the international organization that became the United Nations. Russia agreed to be a member of that organization and to work closely with the Western Powers in many other respects. We had agreed on a policy toward Italy and toward Austria. We had created the European Advisory Commission and the Advisory Council for Italy. We had exchanged numerous ideas on the postwar treatment of Germany, on our attitudes toward France, and on the economic policies to pursue after the war. And, apart from the conference, Stalin had agreed to enter the war aganst Japan, once Hilter was defeated.
>
> Russia, moreover, never once raised the question that had disturbed us the previous year; namely, the settlement at this time of postwar frontiers.[60]

(3) Aggressive Soviet behavior and dilatory tactics

(a) *Upstaging Hull on the agenda.*—Soviet behavior was not so benign and passive as Hull's account seemed to portray. On at least two occassions the Secretary had to go to the mat with Molotov. Characteristically, Molotov tried to engineer the agenda to the Soviet advantage: He excluded discussion of Hull's four-power declaration and placed Soviet demands for a second front first. Hull opposed this ploy. Molotov conceded and agreed to giving Hull second place.

(b) *Opposition to China in the four-power declaration.*—More meaningful was Hull's insistence on including China as a sponsoring nation in the Four-Power Declaration on General Security. Molotov played this very tough, opposing Hull all along the way. Though Hull's account seems benign, still he too played it tough and pressured Molo-

[57] Ibid., p. 1283.
[58] Deane, Strange Alliance. p. 23.
[59] Ibid., pp. 1312–1313. Hull's confidence in a positive relationship with Russia in the future was no doubt buoyed up by Molotov's reaction to his comments at their first session: "I then said I wanted to tell Molotov what I had already told Eden, that I envisaged cooperation among the three countries on an entirely equal footing and that there should therefore be no secrets between any two of us. Molotov heartily agreed." Hull continued: "Since I was convinced our three countries could engage in close cooperative action not only during the war but in the postwar period as well, I said it was important that misunderstandings or suspicions that might exist between our peoples should be steadily and progressively broken down, and I was prepared to devote the closing period of my life to facilitating such collaboration. Molotov said he was prepared to do everything he could toward the same end." (p. 1279.)
[60] Ibid., p. 1313.

tov with the implied threat of a reduction in lend-lease. According to Deane, the Secretary "outplayed and outwaited the Soviet contingent and, with the support of Eden, won the day." [61] In this instance, lend-lease was clearly proven to be a powerful leverage in negotiating with the Soviet Union, a view that Harriman and Deane never ceased to impress upon the administration but without effect.

(c) *Deane's sideshow with Vishinsky.*—The full display of really tough Soviet negotiating behavior took place away from the main arena of the conference and in a sideshow encounter between Deane and Vishinsky. As Deane recalled in 1951, he was "singled out to be given in private the abuse that we have come to expect our representatives at such conferences to receive in public." "My whipping," he went on, "was at the hands of Vishinsky * * *." [62]

Toward the end of the conference Molotov proposed steps to bring Turkey into the war. Eden and Hull objected on grounds of Turkey's declining geographical importance in the war and the unwise diversion of military supplies and energy. Molotov seemed to accept the rejection in good grace, and the subject was dropped.

In the course of the conference Deane had made proposals for military cooperation, already discussed above in chapter IV. But Molotov now refused to allow these proposals to become a part of the conference minutes. Hull protested, and an arrangement was made for Deane to meet with Vishinsky and work out a solution.

Deane, a new arrival in Moscow, had been impressed by what he termed, "the serenity of the main conference"; but he was "totally unprepared for the vigor of Vishinsky's attack." Deane recalled the attack in these words:

Neither the United States nor the United Kingdom were seriously opposing Hitler or Gitler, as he was called po Rooske (in Russian). If Garriman (Averell) or Dyen (me) believed that the Soviet Union was deluded by the false promises of a second front, we were both sadly mistaken. The Soviet Union alone was carrying the war to the Germans and the western allies objected to the U.S.S.R. receiving what little help Turkey might be able to offer. What matter if Turkey were overrun by Germans—that would at least divert some German effort from the Russian front. The idea of coming to Turkey's aid was absurd. Their neutrality thus far had already made them deserving of any fate that might befall them. And, as for the United Kingdom and the United States! What were they doing to take pressure off the glorious Red Army? On and on and on—the most violent and vituperative abuse! The spleen that was let loose was all the more shocking because the events of the conference—my first few days in the Soviet Union—had made me believe that we were in fact among friends. [63]

For Deane the meeting with Vishinsky was "an eye-opener." They had met for the single purpose of reaching agreement on including his military proposals in the conference minutes. He was surprised to learn that the Soviet delegation had no real objections to including them or the favorable action on them as part of the conference report. For the heat of Vishinsky's attack and the heat of Deane's reaction precluded reaching a solution on that day, but on the following day Molotov readily agreed to the American request. [64]

Deane gave this explanation for the bad behavior of the Soviet negotiator:

The real Soviet purpose in arranging the meeting between Vishinsky and me was to let the British and American delegations know, through me, their true

---

[61] Deane, Strange Alliance, p. 23.
[62] Deane, Negotiating on Military Assistance, pp. 5–6.
[63] Ibid., p. 7.
[64] Ibid.

feelings about Turkish participation in the war, their displeasure with regard to the delay in opening a "second front" and other matters about which they had been relatively tranquil during the conference in the interest of harmony.[63]

Thus the Vishinsky incident was for Deane a "personal baptism" into at least two techniques used by Soviet negotiators—

One, a vigorous offensive with no regard for the truth; the blatancy of their misstatements makes rebuttal seem so absurd as to be embarrassing, hence untruth is frequently unchallenged—second, the devious approach as exemplified in the Soviet expression of displeasure with British and American actions and policies by upbraiding me, an unimportant member of the American delegation at a private and informal meeting. Of course, to me, the victim of Vishinsky's onslaught, the sincerity, friendliness and spirit of cooperation that had characterized the Soviet delegation during the conference became doubtful indeed.[65]

(d) *Soviet dilatory tactics.*—Molotov employed the usual Soviet dilatory tactics at this conference; he did not readily concur in proposals that had clearly reached the point of decision in the negotiating process. For about a week, Eden recalled, the conference had been "churning along ever more slowly, until I began to wonder whether anything would be finally settled." Hull, also disturbed by the delays, conferred with Eden during an adjournment of one of the sessions and complained, while gesticulating with his pince-nez, that they were getting nowhere and were being "strung along." [67]

Eden shared Hull's sentiments and confided that in an audience with Stalin, expected in a day or two, he would raise the matter with him. Hull agreed. On October 27, Eden conferred with Stalin and during an interval in the proceedings told Stalin of his talks with Hull on the delays in the conference. "What do you want?" Stalin asked. "Decisions on the subjects we have been discussing for more than a week," Eden replied. Stalin nodded, and said he would talk to Molotov.

For 2 days Eden waited hopefully and expectantly, but there was no change—"the next 2 days were as abortive as their predecessors and when we had finished I had to tell Hull that evidently I had failed." On the afternoon of October 30, however, the atmosphere suddenly changed. And, as Eden described it, "Molotov became brisk and businesslike, he was always a superb workman, as skillful at disentangling as at stalling. In an hour or two we had reached conclusions on all the 10 days' discussions." [68]

(b) *In achieving its purposes: An "enormous success"*

That the Foreign Ministers Conference had achieved more than its major purposes, there seems little doubt, as Hull, himself, noted above.

---

[65] Ibid., pp. 7–8.
[66] Ibid., p. 8.
[67] Eden, "Reckoning", pp. 480–481.
[68] Ibid., p. 481. That Molotov could use the tactic of abuse with positive effect was revealed in an encounter with Eden in discussions on whether the Czechoslovak Government-in-exile should conclude a 20-year defensive alliance with the Soviet Union alone or whether the building of any regional system against the revival of German aggression should be postponed until the three major allies could resolve the problem by joint decision. Early in the discussion a concrete question of fact arose between Eden and Molotov. In a conciliatory manner Eden began by saying, "I may be mistaken, but —". Before he could complete the sentence Molotov broke in harshly, "You are mistaken." Eden was, of course, resorting to a convention of the old diplomacy wherein one pretended not to notice the artifices employed by an adversary and accepted the verbal formulas which one covered them with. As Mosely observed: "His abrupt riposte was effective. Eden's presentation was disrupted. By this tactic, and by constant accusations that the Western Powers were trying to rebuild a cordon sanitaire in Eastern Europe, Molotov succeeded in evading any probing discussion of the nature and purpose of the Soviet program of building up a security belt of its own and won British approval and American acquiescence for the first step, the conclusion of the Soviet-Czechoslovak alliance, which was signed at Moscow 2 months later." (Mosely, Philip E. "Some Soviet Techniques of Negotiation." In, Dennett and Johnson, op. cit., ch. 10, pp. 282–284, and Craig, Totalitarian Approaches to Diplomatic Negotiation, p. 122.)

Sherwood referred to the "enormous success" of the conference and "its consequent profound effect on congressional opinion." (As Hull was returning from Moscow, the Senate on November 5 approved the Connally resolution providing for postwar collaboration to secure and maintain peace and for establishing an international organization that was to become the United Nations. In brief, the United States had taken, by this act, a major step away from isolationism and toward accepting a new internationalism.) [69]

Many of the hard issues, such as the future of Eastern Europe, were postponed for later consideration. But this conference had set the stage for the Teheran meeting of Churchill, Roosevelt, and Stalin; it maintained the political integrity and unity of the wartime alliance; and in the larger sense it laid the foundation for postwar collaboration between East and West to maintain the peace through international organization. To this extent, the conference, and in particular the four-power declaration, reasserted the principles of Wilsonianism which Hull very much represented and encouraged the revival of the idealism and hopes that it had once engendered. [70]

In so doing, the participating Foreign Secretaries overlooked many of the hard power realities that were suppressed at the conference but were to surface as the war came to an end. [71]

At this Moscow Conference, therefore, the Allied consensus was sustained in pledges based upon commonly shared interests. But the four-power declaration was a promise of fulfillment not fulfillment itself, a pledge of future behavior according to a set of principles that took on a different meaning with changing times, changing interests and conflicting ideological perceptions. For a time at least under the pressures of war Russia was brought into a vision of the future as perceived by men such as Roosevelt and Hull whose public life had bridged the era of Wilsonianism with hopeful expectations of a new era of internationalism. [72]

[69] Sherwood, op. cit., p. 575.
[70] On Hull's attitude toward the Soviets and his role in creating the "grand design" of the postwar world, Robert Murphy wrote : "Hull often was depicted as the most anti-Soviet member of the Roosevelt Cabinet, whereas he was virtually cocreator with the President of the 'grand design' for the postwar world, a plan which assumed that the United States and Soviet Russia could become partners in peace because circumstances had made them partners in war." (Murphy. op. cit., p. 208.)
[71] Bohlen, who was Hull's adviser and interpreter at the Moscow Conference, believed that Hull "had only a limited understanding of political currents in the world. He did not understand, and indeed, true to American tradition. rejected the concept of power in world affairs. His view of the enemy as a skunk in the barroom was to become the basis of his approach to all dictators. They were wicked men who had to be stopped if there was to be any decency or peace in the world." (Bohlen, op. cit., p. 129.)
[72] For a commentary on various perceptions of the Conference's results. see Feis. "Churchill-Roosevelt-Stalin," pp. 237–239. Feis spoke of Hull's "undue optimism" in thinking that postponement of the hard issues of the postwar frontiers was advantageous and that "as relations between the Allies deepened into trust, Russia would be less intent on particular frontier lines." An extract from Hull's speech to the Congress indicated his unanchored idealism : "As the provisions of the four-nation declaration, are carried into effect, there will no longer be need for spheres of influence, for alliances, for balance of power. or any other of the special arrangements through which, in the unhappy past, the nations strove to safeguard their security or to promote their interests." Feis discussed the favorable reaction of Roosevelt and Churchill to the Conference but noted the skepticism of Harriman. Bohlen. and other officials in the State Department concerned with Soviet affairs. Stalin and his associates, he noted, confirmed both the hopes and the cautions respecting the Conference. Stalin had acclaimed the Conference as a mark of a firm fraternity among the Allies. but a talk by Litvinov to representatives of other United Nations in Moscow indicated that the Soviets may have wanted to impress upon them the idea that the frontiers had not been discussed : that the Soviet frontiers were "untouchable and defended only by the Red Army :" and that the British and Americans "had not objected to the idea of demanding unconditional surrender from the German satellites."

C. Conference at Teheran, November 28–December 1, 1943

1. SUBSTANTIVE ISSUES

(a) *Background and purposes of the conference*

The Moscow Conference of Foreign Ministers had set the stage for the meeting of Churchill, Roosevelt, and Stalin. The question was: Where was it to be held? A reluctant Stalin finally agreed to the meeting but only if it took place in Teheran, close to the Soviet border where communications could be maintained. Important military operations were then underway, and as supreme commander of the Soviet Forces (and total dictator over the Soviet political system), Stalin did not want to be out of touch with his commanders.

Roosevelt, anxious to confer with Churchill and Stalin and to lay the foundation of a postwar partnership with Stalin, would have willingly traveled 60,000 miles for this meeting. Feeling that the Conference had the greatest possible importance for the success of the war and the establishment of a postwar peace for generations to come, Roosevelt acceded to Stalin's wishes.[73] The meeting would be in Teheran.

By October–December 1943, the war had reached the point where consultation among the Allied leaders was essential in preparation for the final great move against Germany. The Americans and British, having defeated the Germans and Italians in North Africa and having successfully invaded Italy and brought about its capitulation, were building up their forces in preparation for the cross-channel invasion, termed Overlord. The Russians were mounting a massive counteroffensive which, though temporarily stalled near Kiev, was in 1944 to bring them into eastern and central Europe. The Foreign Ministers Conference had stressed the importance of Overlord and projected the design of postwar cooperation but had deferred discussion of territorial claims. The time had now come for the Big Three to sit down together and discuss matters of common interest.

The Teheran Conference, it finally turned out, had many purposes. The foremost was military; namely, to nail down firmly the Western commitment to Overlord. Others included the initiation of preliminary discussions on such political matters as the Polish boundaries and the structure of what was to become the United Nations Organizations. For Roosevelt, Teheran was to be what Bohlen called a get-to-know-you meeting—unlike Churchill, he had never met Stalin.[74]

(b) *Questions of military strategy: Overlord*

(1) *Overlord, the central question*

The meeting at Teheran during November 28–December 1, 1943, was primarily a military conference. Military questions relating to bringing neutral Turkey into the war,[75] pressuring Finland, Germany's ally, out of it,[76] and assisting Tito's Partisans in Yugoslavia[77] were decided and action proposed. But the central question was Overlord.

[73] Feis, Churchill-Roosevelt-Stalin, pp. 240–241.
[74] Bohlen, op. cit., p. 139.
[75] Feis, Churchill-Roosevelt-Stalin, p. 266, and Churchill, Winston. The Second World War: Closing the Ring. Boston, Houghton Mifflin, vol. 5, pp. 371–372.
[76] Feis, Churchill-Roosevelt-Stalin, pp. 268–269.
[77] U.S. Foreign Relations, 1943, Cairo and Teheran Conferences, p. 652.

At the Quebec Conference in August 1943, the United States and Britain made the preliminary decision to launch Overlord in May 1944. At the Moscow Foreign Ministers Conference in October, they reaffirmed this decision, but under guarded conditions. Stalin came to Teheran determined to nail down this commitment clearly and unequivocally.

(2) *Churchill's ambiguity; Roosevelt's and Stalin's solidarity*

Differences in strategic concepts governing American and British thinking on the conduct of the war continued, despite the preliminary decision taken at Quebec. The American view was firm on the commitment; the British ambiguous. Simply put, the Americans advocated a cross-channel invasion of France as the best way to strike at the heart of Germany; the British, whose forces were predominant in the Mediterranean, held to the Churchillian concept of a strike at the soft underbelly of Europe, that is, diversionary operations in the eastern Mediterranean, the Aegean, and southern Europe. Lingering fears of the great British losses in the trenches of World War I were believed to have colored British thinking in this enterprise.

For Churchill, therefore, "the most important task" of the Conference was to decide which of the many mooted plans to adopt—"increasing the strength of our attack in Italy, the Balkans, the Aegean, Turkey, and so forth." "The governing object," he later wrote, "would be for the Anglo-American armies to draw the greatest weight off the Soviet forces." [78]

In pleading his case at Teheran, Churchill did not propose to renege on the Overlord commitment—only its timing—but rather to use the time between the fall of 1943 to the spring of 1944, Overlord's deadline, to engage the Allied forces in the Mediterranean in other military operations that would keep them occupied and their military skills honed and at the same time draw off German forces from the Russian front. He was opposed to any rigid timing of Overlord, presumably suggesting to critics the tentativeness of his commitment. [79]

In brief, Churchill wanted flexibility to engage idle troops for other strategic purposes; Overlord would have to pay some undetermined price. But it was a price that neither Roosevelt nor Stalin wished to pay.

Roosevelt was opposed to such diversionary thrusts on grounds that involvement in the eastern Mediterranean might pin down military forces larger in size and for a longer time than expected, thus delaying Overlord. He suggested consideration of a diversionary invasion of Southern France (later called Anvil) to be launched 2 months before Overlord. [80]

Arguing from the successful Soviet experience of a two-directional military thrust rather than a solitary one, Stalin subscribed to the American concept. Not only did he dismiss Churchill's proposal for military operations in the Mediterranean as really only diversionary but pressed extremely hard for the designation of a specific date for Overlord and the naming of a commander before the Conference ended. [81]

[78] Churchill. Closing the Ring, p. 349.
[79] Ibid., p. 357.
[80] Ibid., pp. 356–369.
[81] Ibid. and Harriman and Abel, op. cit., p. 273.

Discussion of Overlord at Teheran focused generally within the perimeter of these positions.

(3) Recommendations by the combined military staffs

For Churchill, Teheran was his last chance to further his strategic principle; he argued his points forcefully, but in vain, at plenary sessions and in bilateral talks with Stalin. The matter of Overlord and its timing was finally turned over to the combined American and British military staffs for discussion and recommendations.[82]

At the third plenary session on November 30, they reported their recommendations, and accordingly Roosevelt announced that Overlord would be launched in May 1944 in conjunction with a supporting operation against the south of France.[83]

Stalin received the announcement with great satisfaction and promised that the Red Army would open a series of offensives simultaneously on the eastern front to prevent any shift of German forces to the west. Stalin asked when the commander would be named and was told by the President "in 3 or 4 days."[84]

The main issue of the Conference was thus laid to rest.

(c) Political questions: Laying the foundations of the postwar world

(1) The matter of territorial claims

Future disputes among the three Heads of State, if they did occur, would most likely take place over conflicting territorial claims. At Teheran, the views of each began to surface in forms that were to suggest future negotiating positions.

In the Far East, Stalin wanted an ice free port (i.e., Darien), the other half of Sakhalin, and all the Kurile Islands.[85] In Europe, he sought roughly the areas held during the period of the Nazi-Soviet pact, part of East Prussia, and from Finland points close to Leningrad. Feis summed up the Soviet attitude: "* * * if it could get what it wanted, the United States and Great Britain could take what they wanted, provided it was not something that the Soviet Union wanted. This was its rule, not the restraining precepts of the Atlantic Charter to which the Soviet Government had professed to adhere."[86]

In contrast, the United States view was, as Feis noted "virtuous but ineffectual." It stressed the importance of governing principles that were fair and wanted to avoid responsibility for any wartime territorial settlements. Hence, it tried to persuade its allies to leave territorial questions open until the war was won when military considerations would not have to be taken into account and decisions might be more farsighted.[87]

The British approach was more flexible. It took a "pliant view," Feis wrote, toward such Soviet wishes that seemed reasonable in light of

---

[82] Churchill, Closing the Ring, p. 357.
[83] Ibid., p. 382.
[84] Harriman and Abel, op. cit., p. 274. Other military matters came up at Teheran. In a bi-lateral meeting the President handed Stalin a memorandum outlining three cooperative military projects discussed above: the shuttle-bombing project, exchange of weather information, and the use of Soviet bases in the Far East by the U.S. Air Force and Navy. The proposal had been accepted in principle a month earlier by Molotov, but the Soviet General Staff seemed to be in no great hurry to discuss it. In presenting the memorandum, Roosevelt emphasized the importance of getting started on secret planning so that the American Air Force could bomb Japan from Soviet territory in the Far East and the Navy could operate jointly with the Russians from Soviet port facilities in the North Pacific. Stalin promised to study the documents. On Dec. 1, however, he told Roosevelt that he had not been able to find the time but assured the President he would take the matter up with Harriman upon returning to Moscow (pp. 269–270)
[85] Feis, Churchill-Roosevelt-Stalin, p. 255.
[86] Ibid., p. 272.
[87] Ibid.

history, security, and any other acceptable basis. At a luncheon on November 30, Churchill emphasized that the nations who would govern the postwar world should be satisfied and have no territorial or other ambitions. If that question could be settled to the satisfaction of the great powers, he said, the world would remain at peace. Soviet claims respecting its western frontier were thus unobjectionable. But in areas of unjustified Soviet intrusion, as in Western Europe, the Middle East and the African coast, the British Government showed, what Feis termed, "a front of resolute denial." Disturbed that Soviet territorial ideas might reduce Europe to a collection of small dependencies—a "pulverized" Europe—Churchill and Eden sought ways to counter this tendency by advocating councils, federations, and alliances.[88]

At Teheran, therefore, the Big Three approached territorial matters from differing perspectives. In time, elements of these views were to take on more concrete form in serious negotiating encounters. Meanwhile, as Stalin replied to Churchill when he tried to draw him out on Soviet territorial ambitions in the war: "There is no need to speak at the present time about any Soviet desires; but when the time comes, we will speak." [89]

(2) *The problem of postwar Germany*

Foremost among the specific political questions raised at Teheran was the problem of postwar Germany. The subject was discussed frequently and at great length. Out of these discussions emerged essentially three contrasting positions. Common to all was agreement on the dismemberment of Germany and an arrangement for close control in the future.

Roosevelt's plan envisioned a Germany divided into five autonomous states: (1) Prussia (reduced), (2) Hanover and northwest, (3) Saxony and Leipzig area, (4) Hesse-Darmstadt, Hesse-Kassel, and the area sought south of the Rhine, and (5) Bavaria, Baden, and Wurttemberg. The Kiel Canal, Hamburg, the Ruhr, and the Saar were to be under United Nations control.[90]

Churchill agreed that Prussia should be separated from the rest of Germany but proposed that the detached southern states become part of a Danubian confederation. Stalin scoffed at this idea, arguing forcefully against any arrangement that could offer a good chance of a German revival. He felt that unless Germany were held under strict control, such as assured by the occupation of key strategic points, it could revive in 15 or 20 years. Stalin was not enthusiastic about either proposal but of the two he preferred Roosevelt's.[91]

The discussion on Germany was inconclusive. It was finally decided to turn the matter over to the European Advisory Commission for further study.[92]

(3) *Poland's frontiers*

Poland, with all its complexities, was another prime political subject for discussion at Teheran. Churchill and Stalin were particularly concerned about settling the frontier issue, at least in a preliminary way. Roosevelt, who absented himself from territorial discussions, seemed

[88] Ibid.
[89] Harriman and Abel. op cit.. p. 274.
[90] Sherwood, op. cit., p. 797.
[91] Ibid., p. 798.
[92] Ibid.

more concerned about the unfavorable impact of the Polish question on the next Presidential election, though he supported the idea of moving the eastern border further west and the western border even to the Oder River.[93] In brief, Churchill and Stalin reached a preliminary agreement in principle on the Polish boundaries which under certain conditions and pending further study would be between the Curzon line in the east to the Oder in the west, including East Prussia and Oppeln.[94]

(4) On the United Nations organization

Preliminary discussions were also undertaken on a postwar world organization. In a second private conversation with Stalin on November 29, Roosevelt threw out for discussion his concept of a world organization based on the United Nations to preserve the peace. The organization was to compromise three main elements: (1) An assembly of world states to discuss problems and make recommendations to two smaller bodies for decision and action; (2) an executive committee consisting of the four signatories of the Moscow declaration and six other selected countries to make recommendations for settling disputes; and (3) a group called the Four Policemen (United States, Soviet Union, Britain, and China) empowered to act immediately in the event of a threat to the peace.[95]

In the ensuing discussion Stalin raised numerous questions, for example, the resentment of small nations to the power of the Four Policemen, and suggested as an alternative to the global organization a regional structure of two committees, one in Europe and another in the Far East, an idea Churchill also had, with some variations.

Subsequently, Roosevelt indicated the preliminary nature of the suggestions to Stalin, saying it would be premature to consider his proposal for the world organization with Churchill at Teheran. Further study was required on the policing body. Stalin indicated a change of mind, now preferring a world organization to regional committees. The entire matter was, however, relegated into the future with the understanding that each of the three leaders would continue to examine the complexities that surfaced in the discussions.[96]

2. TEHERAN AS A NEGOTIATING EXPERIENCE

(a) Organization and procedures
(1) General characteristics of the conference

Bohlen described the Teheran Conference as "quite informal and somewhat disorganized." [97] Indeed it was, and firsthand accounts by other Conference participants bear this out. For Teheran was a loosely

---

[93] Feis, Churchill-Roosevelt-Stalin, p. 285.
[94] Ibid., pp. 283–287; Churchill, Closing the Ring, p. 403; and Harriman and Abel, op. cit., p. 280. Harriman was sharply critical of Roosevelt's policy of deferring territorial matters until after the election. "The crucial flaw in Roosevelt's approach, as he saw it," according to the Harriman-Abel account, "was that once the Red Army had taken physical possession of Poland and other neighboring countries, it might well be too late for a negotiated settlement. But the President was looking at the practical politics of the Polish question. He knew that any compromise on the eastern boundary would almost certainly be rejected by the Polish government in exile, which in turn could raise a great outcry among the Polish-American voters in Buffalo, Detroit, Chicago, and other centers across the country. * * * The 1944 election was fast approaching and he preferred to postpone the Polish outcry until after the votes were counted, leaving Churchill to take the lead meanwhile." (Pp. 279–280.)
[95] Feis, Churchill-Roosevelt-Stalin, pp. 269–270.
[96] Ibid., p. 271. See also, Sherwood, op. cit., pp. 785–786.
[97] Bohlen, op. cit., p. 138.

structured conference: Its procedures were flexible and its tone informal, reflecting Roosevelt's preference for the casual approach to international negotiations and diplomacy. Bilateral private meetings among the three leaders were held in which conversations ranged over the globe. Diplomatic business was also carried on in luncheons and dinners which on the surface seemed, as Bohlen wrote, "like victory banquets but whose laughter was undercut by sarcastic references to differences and distrust." [98] For Churchill the talks at these luncheons and dinners that interspersed the formal Conference were "even more important. * * * Here there were very few things that could not be said and received in good-humour." [99] Plenary sessions were held, but they were formal in name only.

A reading of the major accounts of Teheran, those by Churchill, Bohlen, Harriman, Sherwood, and Leahy, suggest a conference with many arenas all concentrated in Teheran's Soviet Embassy compound where Roosevelt and Stalin were quartered for security reasons. (Churchill remained in the British Legation, as he wrote, a walk of only "a couple of hundred yards to reach the Soviet palace, which might be said to be for the time being the center of the world.") [100] This close proximity permitted the tasks of diplomacy and negotiation to go forth expeditiously, with a certain intimacy, and with little wasted motion. Improvisation seemed to be the order of the day as the three leaders, in varying modes of contact, exchanged ideas and information on the conduct of the war and the shape of the political world in its aftermath.

In brief, Teheran was the type of diplomatic encounter that Roosevelt seemed most to enjoy—recall his meeting with Litvinov in 1933. And while such casualness and informality can elicit a cost in imprecision, still it has the value and virtue of encouraging the breakdown of barriers that often impede full and complete interaction. This seemed to be the case at Teheran. Negotiations at Teheran thus abjured the formal style of hard give-and-take international collective bargaining for the sake of informality. Issues were resolved, and those that were not, were defined and deferred for future negotiations.

(2) *Agenda, staffing, records, and interpreters*

(*a*) *No agenda.*—The informality of the Conference was marked first by the lack of an agenda, apparently at Roosevelt's insistence.[101] For the formalistic Molotov it must have come as a surprise when Harriman advised him that the President had no formal agenda to offer. He wanted to start with the strategic plans for the defeat of Germany. After that, Harriman said, he would be prepared to discuss any political topic that Churchill or Stalin wished to raise. Molotov had expected a more formal conference, but, as Harriman noted, "he made no specific objection." [102]

(*b*) *Imbalanced staffing.*—Harriman also insisted that the United States had no delegation when Molotov asked for their names. "I gave him the names of the Chiefs of Staff, Admiral Leahy and Mr. Hopkins," he noted, "but explained that there was no American delegation.

---

[98] Ibid.
[99] Churchill, Closing the Ring. p. 359.
[100] Churchill, Closing the Ring. p. 344.
[101] Bohlen, op. cit., p. 139.
[102] Harriman and Abel. op. cit., p. 263.

The President considered that the meeting was a personal one between him, Marshal Stalin, and Churchill with their respective advisers." [103]

The American "party," as it was officially termed, was in fact a formidable one, comprising over thirty with a heavy accent on the military some of whom were among the Nation's leading officials.[104] The British also came well staffed with their military specialists in addition to Foreign Secretary Eden.

In contrast, the Soviet delegation was exceedingly thin: Stalin, Molotov, Voroshilov and two interpreters. In fact, Stalin seemed embarrassed by the lack of military staff in discussions on war operations. When it was agreed that the military staffs would confer on Overlord, Stalin observed that he had not expected that military questions would be discussed at the Conference and thus had not brought his own military specialists with him. Nevertheless, he said, Marshal Voroshilov would do his best.[105] Voroshilov was not a professional soldier but rather a politician, an old Bolshevik who had risen to the top having more the form of high position than the substance of power.

(c) *Absence of sufficient record.*—Both Harriman and Bohlen were greatly disturbed by the organizational failures in the Roosevelt delegation, notably the lack of proper records.[106] Bohlen was "somewhat startled" to discover that no provisions had been made for taking the minutes of the proceedings, a failing that Bohlen remedied by acquiring four American soldiers with stenographic skills from the American Army camp. No one was in charge of organizing the meetings, setting up schedules, or handling the numerous technical procedures of the Conference. The President had no position papers on questions to be discussed. This was Bohlen's first experience with Roosevelt's "informal method of operation." As he wrote, the President "did not like any rules or regulations to bind him. He preferred to act by improvisation rather than by plan." [107]

Fortunately, Bohlen kept detailed notes when interpreting for the President at his meetings with Stalin. From these notes he would immediately thereafter dictate his report. Consequently, Bohlen's record is probably the most complete coverage of the Conference along with those by the several military notetakers. However, Bohlen was not needed during the Churchill-Roosevelt private talks. Thus, as Bohlen recalled, "Since Roosevelt did not like to keep records, there was almost no American account of these conversations." In contrast, Churchill "painstakingly made a complete record of his recollection of talks and reported them at length in his books on the war." [108] Like the Americans, the Soviet record was made and kept by the interpreter. According to Bohlen, "the published Russian record of the Conference is considerably less complete than the American. Apparently, the Soviets deleted quotations that did not fit the Soviet line." [109]

In reflecting upon the absence of a sufficient conference record, Bohlen made these exceedingly instructive observations:

The absence of records is dangerous. Joint records and joint minutes of meetings would have simplified the problem, since what was decided or said could be

---

[103] Harriman and Abel. op. cit., p. 263.
[104] U.S. Foreign Relations. 1943. Cairo and Teheran Conferences, p. 462.
[105] Churchill, Closing the Ring, p. 359.
[106] Well aware from his Teheran experience "how disorganized a Roosevelt delegation could be," Harriman, in the weeks prior to Yalta, "took upon himself the job of scheduling, recordkeeping and coordinating the work of the conference on the American side." (Harriman and Abel, op. cit., p. 384, and Bohlen, op. cit., p. 136.)
[107] Ibid.
[108] Ibid., p. 137.
[109] Ibid., pp. 137–138.

put down at once as understood by both sides. In most of the wartime conferences, there were no joint minutes. Each side kept its own. This oversight was quite harmless when Roosevelt and Churchill were dealing with each other. The Soviets, however, were literal-minded and painstaking in drafting the actual text of any agreement. As we subsequently discovered, they went quite far in interpreting a generalized statement or even absence of a statement as implying a tacit agreement. Therefore, a clear record what was or was not said was important in conducting business with the Soviet Union.[110]

(d) *The interpreters.*—The President had the advantage of having in Bohlen a man who combined many gifts: He was skilled in the Russian language; he, along with Kennan, was among the first Foreign Service officers trained as a Soviet area specialist in the State Department; and he was a seasoned professional diplomat whose later career affirmed his earlier recognized potentialities. And in the President, Bohlen had a speaker who was respectful of the rules of interpreting that made his tasks much easier and accordingly reduced the risk of error.[111] By common agreement Churchill also had in Major Birse an "excellent interpreter," to quote Bohlen, but unfortunately Churchill lacked the consideration of Roosevelt in pacing his utterances.[112] Stalin's principal interpreter was Pavlov, his personal secretary. Occasionally, V. M. Berezhkov substituted. Judging from accounts of previous conferences, Pavlov was a very able interpreter.

Thus, the conferees at Teheran had the services of their own professional interpreters. In Bohlen, the Americans had the best combination of linguist, specialist, adviser, and diplomat.

Still, problems rooted in interpreting could arise as apparently one did on the matter of Poland. Stalin and Molotov had construed a statement by Roosevelt on moving Poland's eastern border further west as accepting the Curzon line—which Roosevelt did not do. The President was later puzzled and troubled by what should be done about Lwow and the oil region. "When this misunderstanding was revealed," wrote Feis, Ambassador Harriman "wondered whether the meaning of what the President had said in their informal private talk at Teheran might have been accidentally twisted in translation." [113]

(3) *Shortcomings at Teheran, a summing up*

Organizational and procedural shortcomings at Teheran appeared to justify the criticism of Harriman and Bohlen. Whatever the value of the informal approach, these advantages would have to be weighed against known costs in negotiating with the Soviets. Due to inadequate coordination, for example, General Marshall and Gen. H. H. Arnold,

---

[110] Ibid., p. 138. Clearly from the perspective of an artist and writer, Sherwood made the following comments on the Teheran records: "The official records of these meetings were written with so much circumspection that the inherent drama was largely obscured; but it was far too big to be totally disguised. One cannot read these deliberately dry and guarded accounts without feeling that here were Titans determining the future course of an entire planet." (Sherwood, op. cit., p. 789.)

[111] Bohlen wrote: "In the few minutes I had with President Roosevelt before his first meeting with Stalin, I outlined certain considerations regarding interpreting. The first and most important was to ask if he would try to remember to break up his comments into short periods of time. I pointed out that if he talked very long, his Russian listeners, not understanding what was said, would inevitably lose interest. On the other hand, short periods of 2 or 3 minutes of conversation would hold their attention and make my job infinitely easier. Roosevelt understood, and I must say he was an excellent speaker to interpret for, breaking up his statements into short lengths and in a variety of ways showing consideration for my travails." (Bohlen, op. cit., p. 136.)

[112] Bohlen noted: "Churchill was much too carried away by his own eloquence to pay much attention to his pleasant and excellent interpreter, short, baldish Arthur H. Birse. There were occasions when Churchill would speak for 5, 6, or 7 minutes, while poor Major Birse dashed his pencil desperately over the paper, trying to capture enough words to convey the eloquence into Russian." (Ibid., pp. 136–137.)

[113] Feis Churchill-Roosevelt-Stalin, p. 285.

the Air Force chief, missed the first plenary session. (There were a total of three.) No one in the President's personal entourage remembered to alert them, and so they went on a sightseeing tour of Teheran.[114]

Judging from Bohlen's account, the records of the Conference were inadequate. Poor housekeeping of records was also evident. The declaration on Iran was actually lost. Signed by the Big Three, this very important document bound the signatories to respect the territorial integrity and sovereignty of Iran then occupied by elements of the Soviet, British, and American forces. Soviet hesitation in withdrawing its forces provoked one of the first crises in the cold war early in 1946. After much searching, the document was finally located in a White House file 1 year later.[115]

A final point is the absence of an agenda. Such an absence throws open the field to a wide range of discussion which may be valuable when negotiating at the summit where the subject matter of discussion is not the details of planning but the larger design of policy. Yet, this advantage would have to be weighed against the inability of the other participants to be adequately prepared for a negotiation. This was surely the case with Stalin. He was not prepared to discuss detailed military matters in the absence of military advisers and had to throw in a weak reserve, Marshal Voroshilov. Yet, the strategy of the war, specifically Overloard, was the principal subject for discussion. Much the same could perhaps be said for the failure of an immediate Soviet response at Teheran to General Deane's proposals for military cooperation.

(b) Negotiating with Stalin

(1) Stalin's toughness on Overlord

Stalin came to Teheran for one singleminded purpose, to get a firm Anglo-American commitment on the date for Overlord. He pursued this goal with characteristic persistency, toughness, and bluntness. At Teheran, Stalin put on display perhaps his most distinctive negotiating tactic, the tactic of abuse and intimidation. He pushed and badgered Churchill who tended to cloud the issue, insisting several times that the Americans and British should concentrate primarily on Overlord and not be tempted by diversionary thrusts elsewhere. As General Deane recalled, "Stalin appeared to know exactly what he wanted at the Conference * * * [he] wanted the Anglo-American forces in western, not southern Europe." In pressuring Churchill, he "made no attempt at oratory nor did he search for words that would satisfy diplomatic niceties." He was terse and to the point.[116]

Time and again, Stalin declared emphatically that the Soviet Government was vitally concerned about the date for Overlord. He linked with this operation the progress of the Soviet offensive, the morale of the Soviet soldiers and nation itself, and the success of the war. Churchill, the equivocator, became his prime target. On one occasion after the Prime Minister had put on a remarkable forensic display,

---

[114] After that incident, the much-distressed Harriman took personal responsibility for the organization of the President's party. "I saw Molotov daily," Harriman recorded in a note on the conference, "and made with him the arrangements for the day in accordance with the President's wishes, and conveyed to the President Molotov's messages from Stalin." (Harriman and Abel, op. cit., p. 267.)

[115] Sherwood, op. cit., p. 798.

[116] Deane, Strange Alliance, pp. 43–44.

Stalin asked if the British were only "thinking" of Overlord in order to satisfy the Soviet Union. And when Roosevelt and Churchill urged the formation of an ad hoc committee of the Chiefs of Staff to study the issue, Stalin declared, "What can such a committee do? We Chiefs of State have more power than a committee and the question can be decided only by us."[117] At one point in the discussion of Overlord, Stalin looked across the table and said bluntly to Churchill, "I wish to pose a very direct question to the Prime Minister about 'Overlord.' Do the Prime Minister and the British staff really believe in 'Overlord'?"[118] And once after a long speech by Churchill, Stalin asked seemingly with a mixture of impatience and anger, "How long is this Conference going to last?"[119]

Once Stalin got his verbal commitment on the date for launching Overloard, he pressed relentlessly for the name of the commander. He was determined to nail down this whole question before leaving Teheran.

It was with such tactics of abuse and intimidation and such a display of persistency in mind that Sherwood was to describe Stalin's negotiating style at Teheran: "Stalin wielded his bludgeon with relentless indifference to all the dodges and feints of his practiced adversary"; and to record Roosevelt's view of Stalin by the end of the Conference: He "had found Stalin much tougher than he had expected and at times deliberately discourteous. * * *"[120]

Bohlen left this picture of Stalin, the negotiator—perhaps one of the best—when he was pressing for a decision to launch Overlord in May 1944. Stalin exclaimed, "I don't care if it is the 1st, 15th, or 20th, but a definite date is important." Bohlen continued:

> While Overlord was of passionate interest to the Soviets, Stalin's words came out in an almost matter-of-fact tone. It was a typical performance for him. Stalin would occasionally read from a prepared document, but most of the time he spoke extemporaneously, doodling wolf heads on a pad with a red pencil, and pausing considerably so that the interpreter could translate. He never showed any agitation and rarely gestured. Seldom consulting his only advisers, Molotov and Voroshilov,[121] Stalin sat quietly, cigarette in hand, concentrating on the discussion.

On issues other than Overlord, Stalin seemed to be a negotiator in the traditional mode. As Admiral Leahy recorded, in his approach to mutual problems Stalin was "direct, agreeable, and considerate of the viewpoints of his two colleagues"—and other sources support this judgment; but when some points were advanced that he perceived to be detrimental to Soviet interests, "then he could be brutally blunt to the point of rudeness."[122]

---

[117] Ibid.
[118] Churchill, Closing the Ring, p. 373. Churchill replied: "Provided the conditions previously stated for 'Overlord' are established when the time comes, it will be our stern duty to hurl across the Channel against the Germans every sinew of our strength."
[119] Deane, Strange Alliance. p. 44. Deane continued: "Soviet bluntness is new in diplomatic procedure but at times it is refreshing and who can say that it has not been successful?"
[120] Sherwood, op. cit., pp. 789 and 798.
[121] Bohlen, op. cit., p. 145.
[122] Admiral Leahy gave this description of Stalin's negotiating style: "The talk among ourselves as the meeting broke up was about Stalin. Most of us, before we met him, thought he was a bandit leader who had pushed himself up to the top of his government. That impression was wrong. We knew at once that we were dealing with a highly intelligent man who spoke well and was determined to get what he wanted for Russia. No professional soldier or sailor could find fault with that. The Marshal's approach to our mutual problems was direct, agreeable, and considerate of the viewpoints of his two colleagues—until one of them advanced some point that Stalin thought was detrimental to Soviet interests. Then he could be brutally blunt to the point of rudeness." (Leahy, op. cit., p. 205.)

(2) *Roosevelt's approach in negotiating with Stalin*

Roosevelt's approach in negotiating with Stalin at Teheran could be summed up in his belief that the Soviet dictator was "getable"—meaning presumably that he could be influenced, as Sherwood wrote, "despite his bludgeoning tactics and his attitude of cynicism toward such matters as the rights of small nations." Roosevelt believed, according to Sherwood, that "when Russia could be convinced that her legitimate claims and requirements—such as the right to access to warm water ports—were to be given full recognition, she would prove tractable and cooperative in maintaining the peace of the postwar world."[123] The President seemed convinced—Murphy called it "an article of faith to him"—that in negotiating with Stalin he could build a relationship of trust and confidence that could encourage a cooperative spirit.[124] "I have just a hunch," he told Bullitt in 1942, "that Stalin doesn't want anything but security for his country, and I think that if I give him everything that I possibly can and ask nothing from him in return, noblesse oblige, he won't try to annex anything and will work for a world of democracy and peace."[125]

Accordingly, the President made every effort to win Stalin's confidence at Teheran, even to the extent of avoiding the appearance of "ganging up" on him by distancing himself from Churchill, much to the annoyance of the British.[126] Perhaps, Sherwood best described Roosevelt's approach as mediator between Stalin and Churchill when he wrote that "Roosevelt sat in the middle, by common consent the moderator, arbitrator, and final authority. His contributions to the conversations were infrequent and sometimes annoyingly irrelevant, but it appears time and again—at Teheran and at Yalta—that it was he who spoke the last word."[127]

Both Roosevelt's negotiating style and his approach to Stalin have been criticized by close observers at the wartime conferences. Bohlen admired the President's genius for improvisation and his instinctive grasp of problems which worked so well in domestic affairs. But this was not the case, he noted, in foreign affairs, particularly in dealing with the Soviets. To Bohlen, this style meant "a lack of precision" which was "a serious fault."[128] Harriman also noted that Roosevelt was never "much of a stickler for language." Even at Teheran, he said, when his health was better, "he didn't haggle with Stalin over language." Harriman explained: "It was my impression that as long as

---

[123] Sherwood, op. cit., p. 799.
[124] Murphy, op. cit., p. 209.
[125] Quoted in, Ikle. How Nations Negotiate, p. 89. Harriman wrote: "Above all, he believed that the intimacies the war had forced upon us could, and should, be used to establish the basis for postwar collaboration.... He was determined, by establishing a close personal relationship with Stalin in wartime, to build confidence among the Kremlin leaders that Russia, now an acknowledged major power, could trust the West." (Harriman and Abel, op. cit., p. 170.)
[126] Churchill's account of Teheran suggests his annoyance at this tactic. Eden "could not fathom the apparent American unwillingness to make ready with us for the Conference in advance." (Eden, Reckoning, p. 497.) Bohlen was very critical of the President on this point. He wrote: "I did not like the attitude of the President, who not only backed Stalin but seemed to enjoy the Churchill-Stalin exchanges. Roosevelt should have come to the defense of a close friend and ally, who was really being put upon by Stalin ... Roosevelt never explained his attitude in my presence, but his apparent belief that ganging up on the Russians was to be avoided at all cost was, in my mind, a basic error, stemming from Roosevelt's lack of understanding of the Bolsheviks. Russian leaders always expected and realized that Britain and the United States were bound to be much closer in their thinking and in their opinions than either could conceivably be with the Soviet Union. In his rather transparent attempt to dissociate himself from Churchill, the President was not fooling anybody and in all probability aroused the secret amusement of Stalin." (Bohlen, op, cit., p. 146.)
[127] Sherwood, op. cit., p. 789.
[128] Bohlen, op. cit., p. 210.

he could put his own interpretation on the language, he didn't much care what interpretations other people put on it." [129] Yet, language is the principal tool of negotiations and diplomacy, and precision is by common agreement imperative.

More serious was Bohlen's criticism of the President for his lack of understanding the ideological gap between the United States and the Soviet Union. On this point Bohlen wrote:

As far as the Soviets were concerned, I do not think Roosevelt had any real comprehension of the great gulf that separated the thinking of a Bolshevik from a non-Bolshevik and particularly from an American. He felt that Stalin viewed the world somewhat in the same light as he did, and that Stalin's hostility and distrust, which were evident in the wartime conferences, were due to the neglect that Soviet Russia had suffered at the hands of other countries for years after the Revolution. What he did not understand was that Stalin's enmity was based on profound ideological convictions. The existence of a gap between the Soviet Union and the United States, a gap that could not be bridged, was never fully perceived by Franklin Roosevelt.[130]

(3) Churchill's approach in negotiating with Stalin

In contrast to Roosevelt, Churchill was far more realistic and less trusting in his approach to negotiating with Stalin. A sense of realism pervades Churchill's account of Teheran and those of others reporting Churchill's performance. His bilateral discussions with Stalin on the Polish frontiers, for example, suggest a highly rational and realistic approach to perhaps one of the most difficult and passion-filled political problems of the war. Perhaps, Harriman best summed up Churchill's approach when he recalled:

Churchill had a more pragmatic attitude [than Roosevelt]. He, too, would have liked to build on the wartime intimacy to achieve postwar understandings. But his mind concentrated on the settlement of specific political problems and spheres of influence. He despised Communism and all its works. He turned pessimistic about the future earlier than Roosevelt. And he foresaw much greater difficulties at the end of the war.[131]

---

[129] Harriman and Abel. op. cit., p. 399.

[130] Bohlen. op. cit., p. 211. For a sobering assessment of Soviet-American relations and what might be expected in the postwar era. see Standley's audience with Roosevelt, in Standley and Ageton. op. cit., pp. 498–499. The meeting took place on Oct. 4, 1943, prior to the President's departure for Teheran. Among Standley's predictions was that the Soviets would not make a separate peace but the Red Army "will push right on across the German border to Berlin, just as fast as it can get there"; that in the postwar era Stalin would cooperate "for a while, anyway, to get our help in rehabilitating his country" as a matter of Russian self-interest; and that Stalin "will insist that the Soviet Union has a priority of interest in the Balkans and other Eastern European nations" and that Stalin "will try to set up buffer states along the Russian border which he can control, to help promote the security of the Soviet Union." Standley recalled that the President remained silent for a long time, looking down at his plate. "Presently, he took a cigarette from a pack on the desk and put it into his long holder. I got up to give him a light but he beat me to it. His face was suddenly tired and drawn, as it had been the week before. He drew on his cigarette and exhaled with a force that was like a sigh."

[131] Harriman and Abel. op. cit.. p. 170. British realism in their approach to Stalin was revealed in an episode at a formal dinner in Teheran. Stalin, in completing a toast begun by Roosevelt. accused General Sir Alan Brooke. Chief of the Imperial Staff. of failing to show real feelings of friendship toward the Red Army. that he was lacking in a true appreciation of its fine qualities. and that he hoped in the future Brooke would be able to show greater comradeship toward Soviet soldiers.

Brooke was "very much surprised" by these unfounded accusations, as he later wrote to Churchill. "I had however seen enough of Stalin by then to know that if I sat down under these insults I should lose any respect he might ever have had for me." he recalled. "and that he would continue such attacks in the future." Hence. Brooke got up. thanked President Roosevelt "most profusely for his very kind expressions." and then turning to Stalin remarked that he was surprised he should have found it necessary "to raise accusations against me that are entirely unfounded." Brooke proceeded to recall a discussion in the morning concerning cover plans and camouflage for great offensives in order to divert the enemy. "Well. Marshal." said Brooke. "you have been misled by dummy tanks and dummy aeroplanes. and you have failed to observe those feelings of true friendship which I have for the Red Army. nor have you seen the feelings of genuine comradeship which I bear towards all its members."

As these remarks were being translated by Pavlov. Stalin's expression was inscrutable. but at the end he said. in Churchill's words. "with evident relish": "I like that man. He rings true. I must have a talk with him afterwards."

(Continued)

That Churchill maintained throughout a healthy skepticism of Stalin was clearly revealed in the episode concerning the execution of 50,000 German officers and technicians as a way of insuring Germany's good behavior in the future. Churchill failed to see a joke in Stalin's comment—"Fifty thousand must be shot"; nor did he appreciate the President's jocular reference to making it 49,000, presumably to reduce the matter to ridicule and thus head-off any embarrassing confrontation. Churchill, deeply angered, said he would "rather be taken out into the garden here and now and be shot myself than sully my own and my country's honour by such infamy." At that he left the dinner table in a huff and went into the next room. Stalin, with Molotov at his side, followed, and putting his arm around his shoulder, eagerly declared, as Churchill wrote, that "they were only playing, and that nothing of a serious character had entered their heads." But Churchill got no such meaning. He wrote:

Stalin has a very captivating manner when he chooses to use it, and I never saw him do so to such an extent as at this moment. Although I was not then, and am not now, fully convinced that all was chaff and there was no serious intent lurking behind, I consented to return, and the rest of the evening passed pleasantly.[132]

3. RESULTS AND SIGNIFICANCE OF THE CONFERENCE

Teheran has rightly been seen as the "high tide" of the Grand Alliance.[133] Churchill, Roosevelt, and Stalin came away with feelings of satisfaction with their work.[134] With the decision taken on the timing of Overlord, the strategic pattern of the war was given its final shape. Soviet affirmation of their pledge to enter the Pacific war after Germany's defeat signalled their intent in that quarter but also contained faint hints of what was expected in return.

Political discussions contained a number of disquieting indications of Stalin's thinking at that time, particularly with respect to the future of Poland. The dismemberment of Germany was now a clear prospect. A world organization was tentatively accepted and its general design at least projected in preliminary discussions. Warm water ports were clearly in the offing as part of Stalin's claims in a postwar settlement.

(Continued)

And talked with Brooke he did. Brooke, having been comforted by the Prime Minister's favorable reaction to his toast as having "the right effect on Stalin," decided, as he said, "to return to the attack in the anteroom." Brooke went up to Stalin and told him again how surprised he was, and grieved, that he should have found it necessary to raise such accusations against him in a toast. Stalin replied, "The best friendships are those founded on misunderstandings," and he warmly shook Brooke by the hand.

Churchill concluded his account of the episode with this evaluation : "It seemed to me that all the clouds had passed away, and in fact Stalin's confidence in my friend was established on a foundation of respect and good will which was never shaken while we all worked together." (Churchill, Closing the Ring, p. 386–388.)

[132] Churchill, Closing the Ring, p. 374. That Stalin could be charming and gentle was a characteristic often reported by observers. Bohlen noted : "Stalin gave me the impression of a man to whom pity and other human sentiments were completely alien. He was not immoral; he was simply amoral. He did not understand any of the elements of Western thought or behavior which Churchill and Roosevelt expressed to him during the wartime conferences." After analyzing the historical, and ethnic roots of his personality, Bohlen continued : "There was little in Stalin's demeanor in the presence of foreigners that gave any clue to the real nature or character of the man. Many persons have tried, but have been unsuccessful in discerning the real man behind the swarthy face and black mustache. At Teheran, at Yalta, at Potsdam, and during the 10 days I saw him during the spring of 1945 with Hopkins, Stalin was exemplary in his behavior. He was patient, a good listener, always quiet in his manner and in his expression. There were no signs of the harsh and brutal nature behind this mask—nothing of the ruthlessness with which he ordered the slaughter of millions of Russians. He was always polite and given to understatement." (Bohlen, op. cit., pp. 339–340.)

[133] Harriman and Abel, op. cit., p. 284.

[134] Feis, Churchill-Roosevelt-Stalin, pp. 276–279.

Thus, Teheran was in many respects a forerunner of Yalta. While many of the ideas discussed were so inchoate and informal as not to constitute decisions, still they at least set the direction of thought among the wartime leaders. Teheran generated a feeling of great optimism within the Grand Alliance, perhaps even euphoria, but elements of potential discord were there in the Conference record, suggesting to the hopeful but discerning observer the reality of trouble ahead.[135]

D. YALTA CONFERENCE, FEBRUARY 4–11, 1945

1. BACKGROUND AND PURPOSE OF THE CONFERENCE

(a) Approaching victory, emerging discord

By February 1945, when Churchill, Roosevelt, and Stalin were to confer at Yalta in the Russian Crimea, military victory was clearly approaching, but elements of discord had already begun to surface within the Grand Alliance.

The Soviets approached the Conference in a militarily, and thus politically, strong position. Their forces had occupied Bulgaria, Romania, parts of Hungary and Yugoslavia in the south and Poland in the north. They were preparing for a final thrust at Berlin while continuing to envelop eastern and southeastern Europe. In brief, eastern Europe was fast falling under their sway.

In contrast, the Allied Forces in the west, having successfully invaded Normandy in June and rapidly moving across France and into Germany, had suffered a severe military setback in the Battle of the Bulge in mid-December. By the time of Yalta, they had yet to cross the Rhine and were advancing ever so slowly in northern Italy. In the Pacific, preparations were underway for the invasion of Iwo Jima and the Philippine campaign was going forward, but the American forces were still a long way from Japan proper.

By the end of January 1945, the German armies were thus compressed virtually within their own territory except for a brittle hold in Hungary and northern Italy. "The whole shape and structure of postwar Europe," wrote Churchill, "clamoured for review." How was defeated Germany to be treated? Was the Soviet Union to join in the defeat of Japan now that the American Forces were successfully penetrating the outer perimeter of its defenses (they captured Manila during the Conference)? And once the military objectives had been achieved, could the three Heads of State devise an international arrangement to preserve world peace and provide some structural form for world governance? Discussions at Dumbarton Oaks on a world organization had ended in disagreement, and in the smaller but no less vital sphere of Poland negotiations between the Soviet-sponsored "Lublin Poles" and their Western-backed "London Poles" had reached an impasse that was to bode ill for the future of the Grand Alliance.[136]

---

[135] Bohlen returned to Moscow full of hope after what he called "the most successful of the wartime Big Three conferences." But "a realist on Soviet policy always has his doubts," he noted, and accordingly made this pessimistic but reasonably accurate assessment of things to come : "Germany is to be broken up and kept broken up. The states of eastern, southeastern and central Europe will not be permitted to group themselves into any federations or association. France is to be stripped of her colonies and strategic bases beyond her borders and will not be permitted to maintain any appreciable military establishment. Poland and Italy will remain approximately their present territorial size, but it is doubtful if either will be permitted to maintain any appreciable armed force. The result would be that the Soviet Union would be the only important military and political force on the continent of Europe. The rest of Europe would be reduced to military and political impotence." (Bohlen, op. cit., pp. 153–154.)

[136] Churchill, Winston S. The Second World War : Triumph and Tragedy. Boston, Houghton Mifflin, 1953, pp. 331–332.

The view from Moscow was far from reassuring. From about the spring of 1944, Ambassador Harriman began sending storm signals to Washington, warning of a changing Soviet attitude toward the United States and somewhat prophetically predicted the pattern of postwar Soviet behavior. For Harriman, Poland was to become a "touchstone" of Soviet behavior, the first test of Stalin's attitude toward his less powerful neighbors.[137]

As early as April 20, 1944, Harriman reported to the State Department "startling" tendencies in Soviet policy toward "aggressiveness, determination and readiness to take independent action."[138] Harriman was outraged at Soviet refusal to support the Warsaw uprising during August through October and to permit the American and British Air Forces to drop relief supplies, referring to Soviet behavior as a "dirty business."[139]

It was against this background of the uprising that Harriman cabled to the President and Secretary Hull in late August that judging by recent conversations with Vishinsky and particularly with Molotov "these men are bloated with power and that they expect that they can force acceptance of their decisions without question upon us and all countries."[140] And then in a personal letter to Hopkins on September 10, Harriman described what he called a "starting turn" in Soviet policy against meaningful cooperation. He was convinced that the trend could be diverted only by a material change in U.S. policy. America's generous attitude, he noted, had been misinterpreted as "a sign of weakness, and acceptance of their policies." The time had come to make clear what was expected "as the price of our goodwill." And he warned:

Unless we take issue with the present policy there is every indication the Soviet Union will become a world bully wherever their interests are involved. This policy will reach into China and the Pacific as well when they can turn their attention in that direction. No written agreements can be of any value unless they are carried out in a spirit of give and take, and recognition of the interests of other people.[141]

Not all was tranquil, therefore, when Churchill, Roosevelt, and Stalin began preparations for Yalta. The time was ripe for discussions at the summit as victory in Europe approached and the defeat of Japan was given a new priority, but beneath the surface lay the discordant issue of Poland's future—the "touchstone" of Soviet behavior—that was to break the unity of the Grand Alliance.

(b) Goals and purposes at Yalta

Only after some delay was Yalta finally settled on as the site for the second wartime summit meeting. For reasons of health Stalin, undisturbed by the delays, had steadfastly refused to meet elsewhere than at some point in the Soviet Union. Roosevelt, who looked forward to the reunion but vacillated on the site, finally agreed to a meeting at Yalta after inauguration on January 20. Churchill, indifferent to the location but anxious for a meeting out of fear of growing fissures

---

[137] Harriman and Abel, op. cit., p. 317.
[138] Ibid., pp. 306–307.
[139] Harriman wrote to General Eaker: "I realize it is essential that we make every effort to find a way to work with them and, in spite of disagreements, I am still hopeful. But one thing is certain, that when they depart from common decency we have got to make them realise it." (Ibid., p. 342.)
[140] Ibid., p. 341.
[141] Ibid., p. 344.

within the alliance, was willing to go wherever the President wished.[142] And so the place was Yalta in the Russian Crimea.

The goals and purposes of Churchill, Roosevelt, and Stalin at Yalta became more clearly defined as the Conference proceeded and the issues under discussion took on their own priority treatment. For Stalin, the central issue was Poland. Vitally concerned about future Soviet security, Stalin insisted upon an arrangement that would insure Soviet predominance in Poland. Roosevelt seemed to have two major goals: To finally nail down the Soviet commitment to enter the Far Eastern war, and to win Stalin's final agreement on the creation of the United Nations. Preservation of the British Empire along with insuring a stable balance of power on the European continent with the revival of France and a Germany intact as a counterweight to the Soviet Union seemed to be among Churchill's most important concerns.

2. GLOBAL ISSUES IN A GLOBAL WAR

(a) Range of issues

World War II was a global war that produced global issues. While the range was far reaching, the issues themselves fell principally within two major categories, military and political. Among the military matters discussed and negotiated at Yalta were: American and British strategy in the final defeat of Germany; coordination of their offensive operations with those of the Red Army in the east; Soviet entry into the Pacific war; Soviet-American military cooperation in the Pacific northwest, such as, American use of Siberian air bases; and repatriation of Soviet and American nationals.

Among the political issues negotiated were: The conditions for Soviet entry into the Pacific war; the future of Poland; organizing for world peace with the United Nations; plans for a defeated Germany; and a declaration of intentions with respect to the countries of Eastern and Central Europe liberated from German control.

(b) Poland and Soviet security: Stalin's major concern

(1) Military power and Soviet negotiating leverage

Stalin's major concern at Yalta was the future of Poland. More than any other issue, perhaps excepting the German problem, it was Poland that went directly to the heart of Soviet security interests. Stalin was determined, therefore, to insure Soviet predominance. By the time of Yalta this predominance had been made virtually a certainty by the presence of the Red Army. For events had overtaken the politics of the problem. Accordingly, the Soviets had all the negotiating leverage; the Americans and British had little: The best that Roosevelt and Churchill could expect, as Harriman believed, would be to moderate the new order in Poland, and this they tried to do.[143]

(2) Negotiating Poland's frontiers

(a) Test between conflicting perceptions of security, political systems, and ideologies.—The Polish question was, in Feis' words, "a disheveled presence" in every meeting at Yalta. It was discussed in private talks among Churchill, Roosevelt, and Stalin; in meetings of the Foreign Ministers; and in all but one plenary session.[144] It was

---

[142] Feis, Churchill-Roosevelt-Stalin, p. 489.
[143] Harriman and Abel, op. cit., p. 405.
[144] Feis, Churchill-Roosevelt-Stalin, p. 521.

enmeshed in the complex negotiations of all issues and in variable settings. The British record contained an interchange of nearly 18,000 words among the three leaders on this subject.[145]

The Polish question became the testing ground between Soviet Russia and the West, between two conceptions of security, between two basically conflicting ideologies and political systems.

For the negotiators at Yalta, the Polish question was divided into two parts: (1) What were Poland's boundaries to be? and (2) who was to govern Poland? At issue was whether or not a Poland restored within new and enlarged boundaries was to be a revolutionary state permanently fixed in the Soviet zone of control.

(b) *Stalin firm on eastern boundary.*—At Stalin's insistence, the eastern boundary of Poland had been rather firmly set along the Curzon Line at Teheran. Churchill concurred but Roosevelt equivocated, hoping to persuade Stalin to allow Lwow and its oil deposits to remain in Poland. Roosevelt had talked with Harriman earlier in November 1944 about personally arbitrating this boundary dispute and handing down a decision within a year of the armistice. At the time Harriman noted critically:

> He has no conception of the determination of the Russians to settle matters in which they consider that they have a vital interest in their own manner, on their own terms. They will never leave them to the President or anyone else to arbitrate. The President still feels he can persuade Stalin to alter his point of view on many matters that, I am satisfied, Stalin will never agree to.[146]

At Yalta, Roosevelt made the effort to persuade Stalin to give up Lwow to the Poles in a plea rather than an argument. The American people generally favored the Curzon Line, he said, but adjustments allowing Polish possession of Lwow and the oil deposits in Lwow Province would have a very salutary effect. Churchill concurred, noting that the British accepted the Curzon Line as the eastern boundary. But he added that a magnanimous concession suggested by Roosevelt would be most prized.[147]

Harriman proved to be right. Stalin would make no such concession; he rejected the Roosevelt proposal. Stalin explained the Soviet case for a strong independent Poland on security grounds; namely, that a weak Poland had in the past jeopardized Soviet security. Poland was the corridor through which the Germans attacked Russia twice in 30 years, he said. Stalin argued further that the Soviet Union was entitled to Lwow and Lwow Province which was east of the Curzon Line. To compensate Poland, Stalin made the counterproposal of extending the western frontier to the more westerly of the Neisse Rivers.[148]

Churchill, who perceived the necessity of a strong independent Poland as part of the general European balance of power against Russia, nonetheless, opposed this territorial extension on grounds that Poland should not be given more land than it could properly handle. Moreover, the transfer of large numbers of the German population, he argued, would be difficult and would provoke strong opposition.[149]

Roosevelt conceded to the Curzon Line with small changes in Poland's favor as suggested by Molotov. He also agreed to compensate

[145] Churchill, Triumph and Tragedy, p. 365.
[146] Harriman and Abel, op. cit., pp. 369–370.
[147] Feis, Churchill-Roosevelt-Stalin, p. 522.
[148] Ibid., pp. 522 and 523, and Churchill, Triumph and Tragedy, pp. 369–370.
[149] Feis, Churchill-Roosevelt-Stalin, p. 523.

Poland in the west at the expense of Germany. But he saw little justification for extending the western frontier to the western Neisse River.[150]

(c) *Resolution of the frontier issue.*—The frontier issue was still unresolved when the negotiators reached the end of the Conference. They now had to determine whether anything should be said about the frontiers in the Declaration on Poland which was to be part of the Conference report. Churchill believed that something should be said or otherwise suspicions of a secret arrangement would be aroused. All three had seemed to agree on the eastern boundary, he noted. A plus factor. He also approved compensation to Poland in the west up to the Oder River. But the War Cabinet had registered its firm opposition to Stalin's proposal for a boundary further west.[151]

Roosevelt resisted any mention of the boundaries on the somewhat inexplicable grounds that it exceeded his constitutional authority to do so. But Stalin and Churchill persisted: Stalin argued that mention should be made of the eastern frontier; Churchill suggested compensation by the accession of substantial territory to the north and west pending final decision by the Poles. Roosevelt did not object in principle but asked that the draft proposal be put in writing. The Foreign Ministers produced a draft which, after certain changes indicating that the Declaration represented only an expression of views of the heads of government, was made part of the Conference communique.[152]

At a last final try, Molotov pressed for further changes that specified the accessions to Poland in the north and west in these words, "with the return to Poland of her ancient frontiers in East Prussia and on the Oder." A negative reaction from Roosevelt and Churchill, expressed in a humorous way, forced Stalin to withdraw the proposal.[153]

(3) Poland's future government

(a) *Soviet's negotiating advantage.*—The second part of the Polish question facing the Yalta negotiators was the creation of a provisional Polish Government. To simplify this most complex problem, suffice it to say that their principal task was to create a representative provisional government of national unity until elections could be held from the Soviet-supported Communist "Lublin Committee" in Poland and the Polish Government-in-exile in London which was supported by the Western Allies. The Lublin group, set up by the Soviets in July 1944 to govern liberated Poland, had the supreme advantage of being in control at home with the support of Soviet military power. In advancing their cause at Yalta, therefore, the Soviets had all the leverage.

At Yalta, the Americans and British abandoned the idea of fusing the Lublin and London Poles, believing that the only solution possible was through the creation of a new and more representative government in Poland pledged to hold free and unfettered elections as soon as conditions permitted.[154]

A crucial problem in the negotiations arose from Soviet insistence that the Lublin Committee was the nucleus of the provisional government as a government-in-being, that a "new" government could not be

[150] Ibid., pp. 523–524 and Churchill, **Triumph and Tragedy,** pp. 376–377.
[151] Ibid., pp. 385–386, and Feis, **Churchill-Roosevelt-Stalin,** p. 524.
[152] Ibid., p. 525.
[153] Ibid.
[154] Ibid., p. 525.

constituted, and that other elements could only be added on to this nucleus.

(*b*) *Pledge for free elections.*—Stalin was not prepared to concede his advantage, as Harriman had predicted some months before, and in the course of negotiations resisted all reasonable efforts to create a fair and viable solution that would encompass not only the Lublin Committee but the interests and aspirations of the genuinely democratic Poles at home and abroad. In the final agreement reached by the negotiators, the provisional government was "pledged to the holding of free and unfettered elections as soon as possible on the basis of universal suffrage and secret ballot." "Whatever chance remained that the Polish people might be free to choose their government and determine their national policies," wrote Feis, "was deemed to depend on this pledge." And it was, as he observed, about "as firm and clear promise as could be had." [155]

Efforts to provide some means for supervising the elections—the only practical safeguard against arbitrary actions—(for example, through the commanding presence of the ambassadors of the three powers in Warsaw) came to nothing. As Churchill said when he unsuccessfully tried in a last-minute plea with Stalin to retain the original American proposal on the free movement of ambassadors which was substituted by a meaningless statement, "This was the best I could get." [156]

(*c*) *Soviet entry into the Pacific war: Roosevelt's major objective at Yalta*

   (*1*) *Stalin takes the initiative*

If securing predominant Soviet interest in Poland was Stalin's major objective at Yalta, pinning down Stalin on the timing and extent of Soviet participation in the Pacific war was Roosevelt's.[157] The basis for the President's policy was the memorandum of the Joint Chiefs dated January 23, 1945, in which they declared that "Russia's entry at as early a date as possible consistent with her ability to engage in offensive operations is necessary to provide maximum assistance to our Pacific operations." [158] Soviet entry in the Pacific war became a vital American interest.

But Stalin had his own objectives in the Far East, and in December 1944, he had laid out his conditions for entering the war to Harriman. Briefly, they were: Return of South Sakhalin and the Kuriles; leases on the ports of Darien and Port Arthur as well as on the Manchurian railways; recognition of the status quo in Outer Mongolia; and a promise not to interfere with Chinese sovereignty over Manchuria.[159]

On February 8, at Yalta, Stalin took the initiative in a private meeting with Roosevelt, announcing that he wished to discuss his political conditions as earlier explained to Harriman. Roosevelt said that Harriman had filled him in and then proceeded to give his views. Roosevelt saw no problem about returning South Sakhalin and transferring the Kuriles. He recalled that at Teheran he said the Soviet Union should have a warm water port at Darien. While he could not speak for Chiang

[155] Ibid., p. 528.
[156] Ibid., p. 529.
[157] Bohlen, op. cit., p. 177.
[158] Harriman and Abel, op. cit., p. 397.
[159] Ibid., p. 397.

Kai-shek with respect to a lease, he expressed his preference for Darien as a free port under an international commission. He also preferred a joint Russian-Chinese operation of the Manchurian railroads.[160]

Apparently dissatisfied with the price Roosevelt was offering, Stalin pressed harder. Unless his conditions were met, Stalin said, it would be difficult for the Soviet people to understand why they went to war against Japan. If the political conditions were met, the matter could be better understood by the people and the Supreme Soviet in terms of the "national interest involved." [161] (According to Bohlen, the idea of referring issues to the Supreme Soviet, an institution without any power, as if it were an important political institution in the country, was a frequent Stalin gambit. At Yalta, no one disputed him as a matter of courtesy.) [162]

Roosevelt explained that he had not conferred with the Chinese because they could not keep a confidence and that the information confided would be around the world and known in Tokyo within 24 hours. Stalin saw no need to rush into talking with them and told the President he would present his conditions in writing before the Conference ended.[163]

(2) Stalin's first draft of conditions

At Molotov's request, Harriman called at the Soviet residence on February 10, to receive and discuss Stalin's first draft of conditions. Harriman was a principal in these negotiations and one of the very few Americans at Yalta privy to the agreement. Harriman told Molotov that the President would have to ask for three amendments. Two days earlier, he noted, Stalin had agreed that Port Arthur and Darien should be free ports; that the Manchurian railroads should be operated by a joint Russian-Chinese commission; and that Chiang's concurrence would, he felt certain, have to be received. All of these amendments would have to be incorporated into the Soviet draft.[164]

Harriman returned to Roosevelt with the Soviet draft along with the suggested amendments. Roosevelt promptly approved them, and Harriman resubmitted them to Molotov. Later that day after a plenary session the matter was finally settled when Stalin told Roosevelt that he agreed with the appropriateness of his amendments though Port Arthur, being a naval base, would have to be acquired under a lease arrangement. Roosevelt concurred with the changes and took upon himself the responsibility for informing Chiang Kai-shek upon receiving a signal from Stalin.[165]

(3) Harriman's reservations on Soviet linguistic initiatives

Harriman was not pleased with the final Soviet text submitted for signing by Roosevelt, Churchill, and Stalin on February 11. Without prior discussion, the Soviets added into the section on the Manchurian ports and railroads a provision that the "pre-eminent interests of the Soviet Union shall be safeguarded." Harriman disliked the term "pre-eminent interests" and told the President so. But Roosevelt saw no

---

[160] Ibid., p. 398.
[161] Ibid.
[162] Bohlen, op. cit., p. 197.
[163] Harriman and Abel, op. cit., p. 398.
[164] Ibid., p. 399. See also, Feis, Churchill-Roosevelt-Stalin, pp. 503-515.
[165] Harriman and Abel, op. cit., p. 399.

reason to fuss over words that to him simply meant that the Soviets had a larger interest in the area than the Americans and the British.[166]

Harriman also questioned the paragraph providing that Soviet territorial claims in the Far East "shall be unquestionably fulfilled after Japan has been defeated." But again to Roosevelt it was just language, and he was not disposed to quarrel with Stalin over it. Other matters were more important, such as getting Stalin's cooperation in establishing the United Nations and settling the matter of Poland; Roosevelt did not want to waste his negotiating assets.[167]

(4) Tieing up the package

The Joint Chiefs approved the agreement without change. "This makes the trip worthwhile," was the reaction of Admiral Leahy, for, as the Americans viewed the matter, the Soviets were now locked into an agreement to wage war against Japan some 2 or 3 months after the surrender of Germany and to conclude an alliance with China for the purpose of warring against Japan. (The best military judgment was that the Pacific war would continue for another 18 months after the defeat of Germany. The atomic bomb, still under development, was not factored into this evaluation.) Because the Soviets feared a preemptive Japanese attack before sufficient forces could be transferred to the Far East, the agreement was kept secret. The State Department and even Secretary of State Edward R. Stettinius, Jr. were kept in the dark.[168]

For Churchill, the problem of the Far East was, in his words, "remote and secondary," and accordingly he played no part in the negotiations. Against Eden's opposition (he called the agreement "a discreditable by-product of the Conference"), he signed the agreement without question on grounds that British authority in the Far East would suffer otherwise.[169] Churchill's major concern at Yalta was not the Far East but Europe where he sought to maintain a balance of power in order to prevent Soviet domination. Accordingly, he fought hard to insure a respectable postwar role for France, to block the dismemberment of Germany, and, as seen above, to guarantee an independent Poland.

(d) Plans for a defeated Germany

(1) Areas of agreement

At Yalta the three heads of state agreed on one common criterion with respect to plans for a defeated Germany; namely, their decisions should be governed by the desire to prevent the rise of a hostile Germany and not cruel revenge. Thus, they shared the common belief that National Socialism as an institution, ideology, and system of life and government should be abolished; that war criminals should be punished; and that reparations should be imposed as acts of justified retribution. They tended to diverge, however, on the severity of measures to be taken to keep Germany weak and its people peaceable.[170]

Agreement was quickly reached on the terms of surrender which were summed up in the words, "unconditional surrender." This entailed disbandment of the military establishment, eradication of Na-

---

[166] Ibid., p. 399.
[167] Ibid.
[168] Ibid., p. 401. For the text of the agreement, see U.S. Foreign Relations, 1945, Conferences at Malta and Yalta, p. 984.
[169] Churchill, Triumph and Tragedy, pp. 388–389, and Eden, Reckoning, pp. 594–595.
[170] Feis, Churchill-Roosevelt-Stalin, p. 530.

tional Socialism as a regime, party, and ideal, and the submission of the German people to the orders in all spheres of the United Nations in reconstituting the life of the nation. With equivalent speed agreement was reached on the control of defeated Germany through three zones of occupation and the mechanism of the Allied Control Council. In this arrangement the right of zone commanders to act separately in the event of disagreement on any principal matter of policy was preserved.[171]

(2) The role of France: Stalin's concessions

Differences emerged on the role that France was to play in the postwar control of Germany. The issue of zones of occupation for the United States, Britain, and the Soviet Union had been settled. The question was now whether France should be allocated a zone and a seat on the Allied Control Council. It was understood, as the negotiations proceeded, that the French zone would be formed from the American and British zones and that the Soviet zone would not be reduced.[172]

Churchill came forth as the strongest advocate of a role for France. His reasoning was based on larger balance-of-power considerations already noted and on a specific desire to protect Britain against the rise of a hostile Germany in which case the British might again be confronted by the specter of German forces at the channel ports. The British could count on France but not on the Americans whose military presence in Europe was, in Roosevelt's judgment, not to last more than 2 years. This factor, which made some impact on Stalin, provided added incentive for Churchill to strengthen the role of France.[173]

Stalin resisted the admission of France to the occupation machinery until the Conference had nearly ended. Ostensibly, he was concerned that other countries, following the French example, might also claim a role in the occupation. But Stalin was also deeply prejudiced against the French for their small contribution to the war effort and for their overall poor performance in the war.

What bothered Stalin most was not so much the allocation to France of a zone as the assignment of a position on the Council. The conduct of business would be made much harder, he said, since France would have its own interests to protect and bargain for. De Gaulle was even then causing annoying problems for the Allies. Stalin might concede the assignment of a zone carved out of the American and British zones but only with the understanding that France would have no role in the Council.[174]

Roosevelt accepted Stalin's proposal, but not Churchill and Eden, who argued that France could cause more trouble off than on the Council. Ultimately, Roosevelt changed his mind after the intervention of Hopkins and Harriman and supported Churchill on grounds that on the Council it would be easier to get de Gaulle to go along with other agreements reached at Yalta, such as the Declaration on Liberated Europe. Stalin, who had just won very much of what he wanted with respect to Poland, finally conceded.[175]

[171] Ibid., pp. 530–531.
[172] Feis, Churchill-Roosevelt-Stalin, p. 531.
[173] Ibid.
[174] Ibid., p. 532.
[175] Ibid., p. 532 and Harriman and Abel, op. cit., p. 402.

(3) Problem of German economic recovery and reparations

The conflict in Anglo-Soviet perceptions and evaluations of the German problem emerged clearly in considerations on the pace of German economic recovery and the related issue of reparations. The heads of state agreed that the Germans could not become wards of the victorious Allies; that they had to take care of themselves; and that they be reduced to the same standard of living of other Europeans they had made to suffer in the war. But the British, presumably mindful of the warnings of Keynes in the 1920's when Germany was over-burdened with reparations to the point of economic collapse, was more interested than either the Americans or Soviets in preserving enough of the existing German economic organization and structure to maintain themselves at this or a somewhat better level. In contrast, the Soviets were determined to destroy the German economic capacity to make war and to impose on them severe reparation payments.[176]

Little or no attempt was made at Yalta to define precisely the allowable levels of German industry and what industries or sections thereof were to be suppressed. The final text of the Conference report expressed only the determination to "eliminate or control all German industry that could be used for military production." [177]

Differences surfaced in full view, however, over reparations. The American asked for no reparations beyond retention of German assets in the United States and perhaps raw materials. The British wanted some German equipment and products to repair their war damage more quickly; but they were willing to adjust demands to other policy considerations. In contrast, the Soviets sought heavy reparations.[178]

In the course of negotiations these differences were reduced to clearly defined conflicting positions. The Soviets, taking the initiative on this issue, insisted that the reparation bill should not be paid in money but in kind (with the removal of some 80 percent of German industry within 2 years) and labor services at a value of $20 billion with 50 percent going to the Soviet Union. The time for payment was placed at 10 years.[179]

Churchill and Eden protested that the figure was excessive, that it could not be collected, that it could impoverish Germany and require the United States and Britain to subsidize Germany so that ultimately other countries would be paying Russia for German reparations. They urged that no decision be made on the total reparations bill and that the time of payment be shortened.[180]

Stalin, speaking with great emotion, engaged the British in a bitter debate over this issue, suggesting sarcastically at one time that if the British felt the Russians should receive no reparations they should say so frankly.[181]

Roosevelt played the role of mediator in this dispute. He opposed excessive reparations demands, warning of the danger that Germany would become a burden to the rest of the world. In the final session he suggested that the matter be left open for the Reparations Commission

---

[176] Feis, Churchill-Roosevelt-Stalin, pp. 534–536.
[177] Ibid., p. 534.
[178] Ibid.
[179] Ibid., p. 535.
[180] Ibid.
[181] Ibid., p. 536. See also, Stettinius, Edward R., Jr. Roosevelt and the Russians: The Yalta Conference. Garden City, N.Y., Doubleday, 1949, p. 263.

that was to begin work in Moscow. In a compromise arrangement it was finally agreed that the protocol of the Conference would state that the Commission would take "as a basis for discussion" (an American formulation) the total sum set by the Soviet Union and that the British believed that, pending consideration of the Commission, no figure should be mentioned.[182]

The dispute ended in a standoff, but not completely, for the Soviets, after the President's death, put their own construction on the words "as a basis for discussion" in order to claim support for their demand for $10 billion in reparations.[183]

(4) Dismemberment of Germany, a lingering notion

Preliminary arrangements for governing a defeated Germany were based on the premise of a single German state reduced in size but a solitary German state nonetheless. Still, the notion of a divided Germany, discussed by Churchill, Roosevelt, and Stalin on earlier occasions, lingered on and was superficially, perhaps tentatively and somewhat cautiously, explored at Yalta.

Viewing continental politics with an eye for the future balance of power, Churchill accepted the principle of a Germany partitioned but reconstituted in the form of a confederation. In October 1944, he discussed the various possibilities with Stalin in Moscow, even to the formation of a Danubian Basin Confederation. Personally, Churchill believed that the isolation of Prussia—he called it, "The tap root of all evil"—and the elimination of its power would remove the central cause of trouble, and that a South German state, with a capital in Vienna, might indicate the dividing line.[184] But Churchill was perplexed by the great and many problems that would have to be considered before a final decision could be made (for example, what to do about the Ruhr and Saarland). Certainly, the brief airing at Yalta was not sufficient, and so he pleaded for time to study the matter, suggesting delay until the occupation before deciding.[185]

Roosevelt seemed to side with Churchill on the idea that a delayed decision would be better so that actual conditions existing in postwar Europe would be known. But, as Bohlen confessed, Roosevelt's real view on dismemberment remained "somewhat of a mystery."[186] There were indications in his remarks, however, that if they delayed, the answers to their problems would emerge and the Germans themselves might separate into several states before or during the occupation. Personally, the President thought Germany should be divided into five or seven parts to prevent it from breaking any future peace. But as the discussion developed Roosevelt seemed to lose interest in dismemberment and, as Bohlen recorded, "He was just giving lip service to a dying idea."[187]

Stalin wanted no delay; he pressed for a decision then and there; he advocated dismemberment. Detecting shared views among all three, Stalin suggested that agreement be reached and recorded on the principle of dismemberment, and accordingly instruct the Foreign Ministers to work out the details. To forestall any German complaint when

---

[182] Ibid., pp. 263–264 ; Feis, Churchill-Roosevelt-Stalin, p. 537 ; and Harriman and Abel, op. cit., pp. 403–404.
[183] Ibid., p. 405.
[184] Ibid., p. 401 and Feis, Churchill-Roosevelt-Stalin, p. 538.
[185] Ibid.
[186] Bohlen, op. cit., p. 183.
[187] Ibid., and Feis, Churchill-Rosevelt-Stalin, p. 539.

the plan was put into effect, he proposed that a clause calling for dismemberment be added to the terms of surrender, already drafted by the European Advisory Commission in London. Though Churchill believed this to be superfluous, all acceded to the proposal and the phrase was added.[188]

When the Foreign Ministers considered the matter, Molotov pressed for more far-reaching language, but in the end he and Stalin conceded to counterpressures from the other sides and accepted the single word "dismemberment." [189] There the matter ended because the committee proposed at Yalta never met.[190]

3. YALTA AS A NEGOTIATING EXPERIENCE

(a) Organization and procedures

(1) General characteristics and tone of the conference

Judging from the various accounts of the Yalta Conference, the tone, mood, and general atmosphere of the proceedings were by and large cordial. Illustrative was the observation by Bohlen, perhaps the closest observer, who recorded that despite the differences and disappointments of the negotiations "The atmosphere remained pleasant throughout the conference." [191] And as he noted elsewhere, "There were moments of irritation and bitterness during the succeeding days, but the overall mood of good feeling continued right to the last dinner, given by Stalin." [192]

Moments of tension and stress were offset by displays of cordiality, particularly when toasts were made by the three Heads of State at dinners and luncheons.[193] On occasion Stalin displayed his toughness as a negotiator, especially on the issue of Poland, and in a burst of sarcasm could try to needle Churchill as on the reparations issue; but there was no resort to the tactic of abuse so evident in past conferences. On occasions, as Churchill recorded, Stalin could be "in a most cordial mood." [194] Byrnes described Stalin as "a very likeable person." [195]

Informality was also a marked characteristic as the Conference took on the style most favored by the President.[196] And despite pressures and counterpressures of negotiations, a cooperative spirit seemed to prevail.[197] Accounts of the Conference, such as Eden's, convey the general feeling of a traditional negotiating environment with expected tensions in the give-and-take of negotiations as the participants sought to achieve their own purposes. Tough and complex issues were re-

---

[188] Article 12 of the surrender terms read : "The United Kingdom, the United States of America, and the Union of Soviet Socialist Republics shall possess supreme authority with respect to Germany. In the exercise of such authority they will take such steps including the complete disarmament, demilitarization *and the dismemberment* of Germany as they deem requisite for future peace and security." (Italics added.) Ibid., p. 539.
[189] Harriman and Abel, op. cit., p. 401.
[190] Bohlen, op. cit., p. 183.
[191] Bohlen, op. cit., p. 179.
[192] Ibid., p. 182.
[193] In one toast to President Roosevelt, Stalin, quite unprecedently, cited "lend-lease as one of the President's most remarkable and vital achievements in the formation of the anti-Hitler combination and in keeping the Allies in the field against Hitler," as Bohlen's minutes described it. (Yalta Documents, p. 798.)
[194] Churchill, Triumph and Tragedy, p. 391.
[195] Byrnes, op. cit., p. 45.
[196] Yalta Documents, p. 574.
[197] Stettinius recorded the "whole spirit" of one meeting of the three Heads of State as being "most cooperative." (Stettinius, op. cit., p. 111.)

solved, often according to existing power realities; some were only discussed; others were deferred.

That a generally favorable spirit prevailed at the proceedings was perhaps most evident by the hopeful expectations reflected in the attitudes of the participants upon leaving Yalta for home. Yet the cordiality of the Conference was counterbalanced by the seriousness of its business. As Bohlen recorded, "Underneath this gloss of goodwill, the three leaders were waging a fierce struggle on the shape of the postwar world." [198]

(2) Aspects of Conference support and organization

(a) *Procedure and agenda: Order and confusion.*—At Yalta, there was both order and confusion. A strong advocate of informality in international negotiations, President Roosevelt set the stage when he proposed at the opening first plenary session on February 4, which he chaired, that the talks be conducted, in the words of Bohlen's minutes, "in an informal manner in which each would speak his mind frankly and freely, since he had discovered through experience that the best way to conduct business expeditiously was through frank and free speaking." [199]

Organizationally, Yalta was a multilevel conference with many sessions going on often simultaneously among the military chiefs, the Foreign Ministers and the Heads of State. In addition, business was carried on at luncheons and dinners and at private meetings between any of the leaders. Plenary sessions were held every day at 4 p.m. and meetings of the Foreign Ministers and military chiefs every morning. [200]

No orderly discussion and resolution of each problem by the leaders occurred in any systematic way. Instead, as Bohlen noted, "issues were brought up, discussed, then shunted off to the Foreign Ministers or military chiefs or just dropped for a few hours." [201] Accounts of the Conference suggest a good deal of administrative and organizational disarray, a constant interaction among participants on virtually all levels. As Bohlen wrote, "It is a wonder that any agreements could emerge from such confusion. But the constant switch from one subject to another kept tempers cool." [202]

In keeping with Roosevelt's stress on informality, the Conference did not seem bound to a strict agenda. It was understood before the meeting that each of the leaders would be free to raise any subject for discussion. No formal order of business was prepared in advance of Yalta. Informality was to prevail, much in the spirit expressed by the President in an earlier message to Stalin on November 18, 1944: "We understand each other's problems and as you know, I like to keep these discussions informal, and I have no reason for formal agenda." [203]

The records suggest that at least the American and British staffs had discussed issues beforehand, independently and together (for example, briefly at Malta); and it can be assumed that the Soviets had also staffed-out the problems to be considered. [204]

---

[198] Bohlen, op. cit., p. 182.
[199] Yalta Documents, p. 574.
[200] Leahy, op. cit., p. 297; Bohlen, op. cit., p. 179; and Stettinius, op. cit., pp. 327–330. Stettinius included in the appendix of his book a summary of the major diplomatic meetings, giving the date, place, participants, and subject matter discussed.
[201] Bohlen, op. cit., p. 179.
[202] Ibid.
[203] Feis, Churchill-Roosevelt-Stalin, p. 497.
[204] Bohlen, op. cit., p. 171.

The Conference issues were known, but the order of priority seemed to take on the preferences of the three leaders as the Conference proceeded. At the end of each plenary session the major subjects for discussion on the following day would be agreed to and announced. For example, after the first meeting it was agreed that on the following day the leaders and their Foreign Ministers would meet to discuss the political treatment of Germany. The military chiefs were also to meet.[205]

Agendas were created quickly when issues were turned over by the three leaders to the Foreign Ministers for discussion.

In brief, the agenda and the organizational structure of the Conference seemed to be fairly loose, allowing for a full airing of issues within some semblance of procedural order.[206]

(b) *Staffing and briefing.*—Unlike Teheran, the Yalta Conference had a sizeable support staff. Some 700 American and British support personnel and officials were flown into Yalta from Malta among whom were representatives from both the diplomatic and military establishments. In contrast to Teheran, where the State Department had no voice except through Ambassador Harriman, State had a large representation at Yalta.[207] Again, Bohlen acted as interpreter and counselor to the President, and at times participated in policy discussions with the President and his foreign policy aides.[208]

The Soviets also had a formidable delegation of both diplomatic and military leaders. Unlike Teheran, all sides, therefore, seemed well staffed to cope with the problems at hand.

A unique characteristic on the American side was the preparation of briefing papers for the President. According to Bohlen, State Department participation meant much better preparation for the Conference. A series of "black books," covering the subjects to be discussed at Yalta, were prepared for the President. Bohlen himself helped in their preparation and upon seeing the final series, as he recalled, he was "impressed with their thorough and competent analysis of every problem likely to come before the Conference and the recommendations of the U.S. positions."[209]

To what extent the President, who was noticeably ill at the time, studied the "black books" is a matter open to question. Byrnes, who accompanied him to Yalta, noted that the President "had made little preparation for the Yalta Conference."[210] Discussions among the President, Byrnes, and Admiral Leahy did take place on four or five occasions usually at dinner aboard the U.S.S. *Quincy* during the voyage to Malta. But not until the day before landing at Malta did Byrnes

[205] Yalta Documents, p. 580. Churchill wrote after this meeting on Germany: "We then arranged to meet next day and consider two topics which were to dominate our future discussions, namely, the Dumbarton Oaks scheme for world security and Poland." (Triumph and Tragedy, p. 353.)

[206] That Harriman had assumed a great deal of the organization responsibility at Yalta was revealed by the following: "Kathleen Harriman, in the role of hostess for her father, saw to the room assignments and the general housekeeping. While the Ambassador, well aware from his Teheran experience how disorganized a Roosevelt delegation could be, took upon himself the job of scheduling, recordkeeping and coordinating the work of the conference on the American side." (Harriman and Abel, op. cit., p. 384.)

[207] Bohlen, op. cit., p. 171.

[208] Bohlen wrote: "My role * * * included both interpreting for and advising the President" (p. 179); "From my position at Roosevelt's side, I witnessed almost all the important exchanges with the Soviet Union" (p. 182); "Because of the better arrangements and because I knew Roosevelt, Hopkins, and Stettinius, I took part in many discussions of policy, especially on Germany and Eastern Europe" (p. 179).

[209] Ibid., p. 171.

[210] Byrnes, op. cit., p. 23.

hear that the U.S. delegation had on board "a very complete file of studies and recommendations prepared by the State Department." Upon making an inquiry with the President, he was told they were in the custody of a Lt. William M. Rigdon. Byrnes observed:

Later, when I saw some of these splendid studies I greatly regretted they had not been considered on board ship. I am sure the failure to study them while en route was due to the President's illness. And I am sure that only President Roosevelt, with his intimate knowledge of the problems, could have handled the situation so well with so little preparation.[211]

Bohlen was more critical of the President. He recorded how Roosevelt had sparred and bargained with Churchill and Stalin still believing, as at Teheran, "in improvising solutions to difficulties." But this time he had backup support from his military advisers as well as a State Department staff of about a dozen officers. "As the conference progressed," Bohlen recalled somewhat ruefully, "it became obvious that Roosevelt had not studied the 'black books' as much as he should have, but they undoubtedly helped him." [212]

(c) *Official records at Yalta.*—Except for the official documents, Bohlen's minutes of the Conference and those of other staff members constitute the official American record. Members of the American delegation, such as H. Freeman Matthews, head of State's European Affairs Division, and Alger Hiss, Deputy Director of State's Office of Special Political Affairs, also kept their own personal notes.[213] Matthew's notes, published in the Yalta Documents, compare favorably with Bohlen's which are, as at other conferences, quite remarkable; but in comparison to both those by Hiss appear to be primitive and elliptical, suggesting their personal nature.[214] Edward Page of the U.S. Embassy in Moscow was an interpreter and notetaker at the Foreign Ministers meetings.[215]

According to Bohlen, who, prior to Yalta, had been named liaison from State to the White House, Hopkins "had become alarmed at Roosevelt's tendency to hold meetings of the utmost importance without keeping any official record." One of the functions Hopkins assigned to Bohlen was, therefore, to keep the Conference record.[216] Accordingly, Bohlen was prepared. Unlike at Teheran, he had a full stenographic staff to take his dictation. (His practice was to dictate the minutes after the meetings.) Bohlen was the official notetaker for all plenary sessions; he also recorded the conversations at luncheons, dinners, and all private meetings between Roosevelt and Stalin.[217]

The British and Russians apparently followed the same general procedure as before. Pavlov interpreted for the Russians, and Birse for the British. Sir Edward Bridges took notes in shorthand for the British.[218] Since it was the general practice to interpret after each sentence or paragraph, it was presumably possible for all to make a fairly complete record.

Stettinius was not at all satisfied with these arrangements for recordkeeping. "There was * * * no single official record of the meetings, nor

---

[211] Ibid., p. 23. Admiral Leahy wrote: "Throughout the 10 days on the Atlantic, the President held daily conferences at which we talked over the problems that would be faced at the Crimea meeting." (Leahy, op. cit., p. 292.)
[212] Bohlen, op. cit., p. 178.
[213] Stettinius, op. cit., p. 104.
[214] Feis, Churchill-Roosevelt-Stalin, p. 524, ff. 35.
[215] Stettinius, op. cit., p. 104.
[216] Bohlen, op. cit., p. 165.
[217] Ibid., p. 179.
[218] Stettinius, op. cit., p. 103.

was there any stenotypist recording every word," he complained.[219] He would have preferred a single translation for all delegations, as was done at the League of Nations (and presently at the U.N.). A single official record of proceedings could then be distributed and approved by all delegations. The record would be complete, accurate, and mutually acceptable. As it was, separate records were kept at Yalta, allowing for possible variations in meanings in the official account of each participating nation.

The military chiefs followed a different procedure at Yalta from that of the diplomats. Each delegation had its own notetaker; their notes were then cleared with each other and all participants, insuring an accurate report of the proceedings.[220]

The official documents of the Conference, as Stettinius noted, "should appear the same in all the minutes, and the final agreements reached were identical, since Eden, Molotov, and I, with our respective staffs, prepared the official protocol with great care." [221]

Official records of negotiations have great value, particularly for future reference in instances of conflicts over interpretations and nuances of meanings in official translations. The records also provide an invaluable source for the diplomatic historian. But in the case of Yalta, the official records were particularly important when, in the 1950's, the Conference became the subject of a fierce national controversy.

(b) Negotiating with Stalin

(1) General appraisals of Stalin's style

Perhaps no American was at once better qualified and in a better position to appraise Stalin as a negotiator than Charles Bohlen. A professional diplomat trained in the language and culture, the politics and ideology of Russia and of Stalin's Soviet system, Bohlen was uniquely qualified to pass judgment on the negotiating skills of its chieftain. This was his appraisal:

Stalin was a shrewd and skillful negotiator. He was always calm and unruffled and almost always courteous in his mood and manner. He was particularly adroit and effective in defensive diplomacy. When the subject under discussion dealt with an area under Soviet control, such as Poland or the Eastern Balkans, he showed himself to be a master of evasive and delaying tactics with no great regard for facts. He had done his homework on the principal issues, but he did not hesitate to cite events and actions which Churchill and Roosevelt, to say nothing of the rest of us, profoundly disbelieved but could not refute. On matters not under his control, Stalin was less skillful and did not vigorously push his position. He was ably backed up by Molotov, the faithful follower.[222]

Less a Soviet specialist but more a seasoned professional diplomat than Bohlen, Anthony Eden could draw upon a rich and valued experience and training as a high-ranking British diplomat in making his appraisal of Stalin as a negotiator. From the prospective of being Churchill's right arm at Yalta and a close-in observer of Stalin in action, Eden wrote:

Marshal Stalin as a negotiator was the toughest proposition of all. Indeed, after something like 30 years' experience of international conferences of one kind and another, if I had to pick a team for going into a conference room,

[219] Ibid.
[220] Ibid., p. 104.
[221] Ibid.
[222] Bohlen, op. cit., p. 178.

Stalin would be my first choice. Of course the man was ruthless and of course he knew his purpose. He never wasted a word. He never stormed, he was seldom even irritated. Hooded, calm, never raising his voice, he avoided the repeated negatives of Molotov which were so exasperating to listen to. By more subtle methods he got what he wanted without having seemed so obdurate.[223]

(2) Stalin's toughness and shrewdness

By the common judgment of many diplomatic practitioners, Stalin was a tough and shrewd negotiator, qualities that were well demonstrated at Yalta. Eden understood this when he wrote of the three Heads of State in January prior to going to Yalta, Stalin was the only one "who has a clear view of what he wants and is a tough negotiator." [224] "Churchill's eloquence and skillful maneuvering," Stettinius observed, "were generally answered by the Marshal in blunt and direct remarks." [225] He spoke in "forceful language," noted Stettinius on the occasion of Stalin describing the Soviet war effort against the Germans, "and at one point he rose from his chair and emphasized his points with dramatic gestures." [226]

Stalin employed the same mode of behavior in his discourse on the Soviet Union's claims in Poland. Stalin based his claims on security grounds, expounding to the conferees on the historic problems of Russia's vulnerability to invasion from Germany through Poland. To Churchill's assertion that Poland's future was to the British a matter of honor (the British had declared war when the Germans invaded Poland), Stalin responded that to the Soviet state Poland was a matter of life and death. "A sure clue to the gravity of the problem," noted Bohlen, "was Stalin's getting up and walking up and down behind his chair while expounding his points." According to Bohlen, Stalin's best debating skill was most conspicuous on the Polish question.[227] For he faced the diplomatic task of retaining a tight grip on Poland without causing an open break with the Western Powers. "In this regard," wrote Bohlen in an appraisal of Stalin's negotiating performance:

Stalin displayed a considerable astuteness, an extensive knowledge of the geographic elements of the problem, such as the location of the frontiers, and a tenacity in beating back one Western attempt after another to create conditions for a genuinely democratic government.[228]

Stalin displayed the same emotion and behavior when the German reparations question was discussed. Like the Polish issue, this question went straight to the heart of Soviet security interests. According to Stettinius, Stalin spoke with "great emotion * * * in sharp contrast to his usual calm, even manner." On several occasions, when he was elaborating on Soviet suffering at the hands of the Germans during the war, "he arose, stepped behind his chair, and spoke from that position, gesturing to emphasize his point." Stalin did not orate, nor did he even raise his voice, but, as Stettinius noted, "he spoke with intensity." [229] It was on this occasion that Stalin rebuked Churchill with a sarcastic remark to the effect that if the British felt the Soviets

[223] Eden, Reckoning, p. 595.
[224] Eden, Reckoning, p. 583. Eden continued: "P.M. is all emotion in these matters, F.D.R. vague and jealous of others."
[225] Stettinius, op. cit., p. 104.
[226] Ibid., p. 107.
[227] Bohlen, op. cit., p. 187. When Roosevelt said that he wanted the Polish election to be pure, like Caesar's wife, Stalin commented, "They said that about her but in fact she had her sins."
[228] Ibid.
[229] Stettinius, op. cit., pp. 263–264.

should not receive reparations at all it would be better for them to say so frankly.[230]

Clearly, Stalin's behavior in these instances, markedly different from his general conduct during Yalta, was intended to underscore his profound concern when negotiating issues that bore directly on vital Soviet security interests.

That Stalin could combine shrewdness, indeed calculated deception, with toughness, was also demonstrated at Yalta. During the negotiations on conditions for Soviet entry into the Pacific war, an understanding had been reached. However, when the final Soviet text was submitted for signing by Roosevelt, Churchill, and Stalin, the Russians had written into the section concerning the Manchurian ports and railroads a provision that "the preeminent interests of the Soviet Union shall be safeguarded." This phrase had not been discussed at prior meetings. Harriman, a principal negotiator of the agreement, was greatly disturbed by this sleight-of-hand maneuver because of the implications of acquiescence in Soviet predominance. Not disposed to fuss over words, the President acceded, apparently without comment.[231]

(3) Concessions by Stalin

(a) *A prevailing compromising spirit.*—Despite Stalin's displays of emotion, pressure, and power on the Polish issue and German reparations, Yalta was by no means a one-sided affair. Accounts by participants at the Conference and other sources suggest a common theme; namely, that Yalta was a genuine and quite normal negotiating experience characterized by a good deal of hard bargaining, give-and-take in which the Soviets did make concessions contrary to popularly held views at one time. Stettinius stated categorically, "The record of the Conference shows clearly that the Soviet Union made greater concessions at Yalta to the United States and Great Britain than were made to the Soviets." He then proceeded to summarize what he perceived to be significant Soviet concessions.[232]

Similarly, Admiral Leahy acknowledged that Stalin's views on many political questions usually differed from the American, but "he spoke quite frankly in presenting the Russian attitude. He was friendly, and seemed in many instances willing to compromise in order to reach an agreement." [233]

And in a note scribbled to the President at a moment of deadlock on the reparations issue suggesting a compromise formula, Hopkins observed, "The Russians have given in so much at this conference that I don't think we should let them down." [234]

(b) *Concessions on France.*—On the matter of French participation in the occupation of Germany as a full allied partner, Stalin resisted until the last. When after the intervention by his staff Roosevelt changed his position and so announced it at a plenary session, Stalin raised his arms above his head and said, "I surrender." To the surprise of all, he accepted France as an occupying power and a member of the Control Council.[235]

[230] Feis, Churchill-Roosevelt-Stalin, p. 536.
[231] Harriman and Abel, op. cit., pp. 398–399.
[232] Stettinius, op. cit., pp. 295–304.
[233] Leahy, op. cit., p. 322.
[234] Harriman and Abel, op. cit., p. 404.
[235] Bohlen, op. cit., p. 185.

However, when Roosevelt switched to Churchill's position, there was little that Stalin could do without arousing French hostility. Bohlen perceived in this concession a significant insight into Stalin's negotiating tactics. The concession on France reinforced Roosevelt's notion, first of all, that he had great personal influence over the Soviet leader, presumably which Stalin could manipulate to his advantage. None of the Western negotiators, moreover, questioned whether Stalin's concession merited a quid pro quo response. But, according to Bohlen, "Stalin may have thought in terms of such a tactical maneuver." And he explained:

> When he saw that he could not win on an issue, he sometimes gave in, hoping to affect the Western negotiators, and, indeed, it is possible that Stalin's acquiescence on France may have affected Roosevelt's views on German reparations.[236]

(c) *U.N. participation and less weighty concessions.*—In the case of voting procedures in the U.N. Security Council and the question of U.N. membership, Stalin made concessions.[237] These questions had become stalemated at Dumbarton Oaks. At Yalta where the creation of the United Nations was a prime objective of President Roosevelt, the Soviets accepted the American formula limiting the veto of the permanent members of the Security Council to plans of action. As a result of this concession, the creation of the United Nations could go forward. They also conceded on the issue of demanding membership for 16 Soviet republics and finally acquiesced into accepting 2. Bohlen referred to agreement on voting procedures in the Security Council as "the one solid and lasting decision of the Yalta Conference." [238]

Less weighty were Stalin's concessions on the issues of Poland and German reparations.[239] On the Polish question, Stalin held all the cards and commanded a negotiating position that rested solidly (and immovably) on Soviet military power in place. What concessions he made (for example, expanding political representation in the provisional government) were by and large for cosmetic purposes; the essentials of Soviet power and control were not conceded.

On the reparations issue, the Soviets did make a basic concession. They had insisted on a bill of $20 billion with 50 percent going to the Soviet Union. In the face of British and American opposition they accepted the Roosevelt compromise formula, devised by Hopkins stating that the Soviet figure would be accepted as a "basis for discussion" in the "initial studies" of the Reparation Commission. Stalin insisted, however, that this figure be mentionel in the Conference protocol. But, later Molotov purposely misstated the President's formula and intention, with respect to the Soviet share, insisting that he had agreed to the 50 percent Soviet share.[240]

(4) *Roosevelt's health and effects on negotiations with Stalin*

Within 8 weeks after Yalta, President Roosevelt died. Subsequently, rumors spread throughout the Nation, particularly among critics of

---

[236] Ibid.
[237] Feis, Churchill-Roosevelt-Stalin, ch. 57.
[238] Bohlen, op. cit., pp. 193–194.
[239] Stettinius, op. cit., pp. 300–303.
[240] Ibid., pp. 299–300 and Harriman and Abel, op. cit., pp. 404–405. During the negotiations Hopkins had suggested a way out of the deadlock in a note he scribbled to the President during the final Yalta meeting: "The Russians have given in so much at this conference that I don't think we should let them down. Let the British disagree if they want to— and continue their disagreement at Moscow. Simply say it is all referred to the Reparations Commission with the minutes to show the British disagree about any mention of the $10 billion."

the Yalta decisions, raising the question whether he had been physically and mentally competent at the time of the Conference.[241] That the President was a sick man at Yalta, there seemed to have been little doubt. That his impaired health had adversely affected his negotiations with Stalin has remained a disputed question.

Byrnes was "disturbed" by Roosevelt's appearance aboard the U.S.S. *Quincy*, but noted that he had "improved greatly" by the time they had reached Malta.[242] In contrast, Bohlen was "shocked" by the President's physical appearance when he boarded the ship. And he continued:

His condition had deteriorated markedly in the less than two weeks since I had seen him. He was not only frail and desperately tired, he looked ill. I never saw Roosevelt look as bad as he did then, despite a week's leisurely voyage at sea, where he could rest. Everyone noticed the President's condition, and we in the American delegation began to talk among ourselves about the basic state of his health. I was relieved somewhat, however, to note that his illness did not affect his speech.[243]

Eden, who met Roosevelt at Malta, noted in his diary that the President "gives the impression of failing powers." [244] Upon returning from Yalta and meeting the President for the last time, Churchill observed: "The President seemed placid and frail. I felt that he had a slender contact with life." [245]

Opinion differed on the effect of the President's health on the negotiations with Stalin. As an historian of the period, Feis recorded that among the American group he seemed tired in prolonged discussions and seemed to want to avoid sustained argument. But, he noted, "decisions did not seem to burden him as they would a sick or extremely worried man." [246]

Admiral Leahy acknowledged that the President "looked fatigued as we left, but so did we all." The intense pressures of the Conference were suggested in Leahy's remark that "it was one of the most strenuous weeks I had ever had. * * *" Nonetheless, he felt that Roosevelt conducted the Conference "with great skill and that his personality had dominated the discussions." [247]

In 1951, Harriman testified before the Joint Senate Armed Services and Foreign Relations Committee that the President was "unquestionably * * * not in good health and the long conferences tired him." But, having thought out and discussed the matters at hand and blocked out definite objectives, "he came to Yalta determined to do his utmost to achieve these objectives and he carried on the negotiations to this end with his usual skill and perception." [248] In a retrospective assessment, following publication in 1970 of the clinical notes by the President's attending physician, Harriman made this revision:

* * * He seemed to tire when conversations wore on too long. I used to say that Roosevelt had a Dutch jaw—and when that Dutch jaw was set you couldn't move him. At Yalta, I believe, he didn't have the strength to be quite as stubborn as he liked to be. I suppose that if FDR had been in better health, he might have held out longer and got his way on a number of detailed points. But I can't believe that it would have made a great difference on, say, the Polish question. At the time of Yalta, the Red Army was in full control of the country and no

[241] Harriman and Abel, op. cit., p. 389.
[242] Byrnes, op. cit., p. 22.
[243] Bohlen, op. cit., pp. 171–172.
[244] Eden, Reckoning, p. 592.
[245] Churchill, Triumph and Tragedy, p. 397.
[246] Feis, Churchill-Roosevelt-Stalin, p. 557.
[247] Leahy, op. cit., p. 321.
[248] Harriman and Abel, op. cit., p. 389.

amount of careful drafting could have changed that. If Stalin was determined to have his way, he was bound to bend or break the agreements, even if they had been sewn up more tightly.[249]

Eden appeared to have struck something of a balance on this question when he observed: "I do not believe that the President's declining health altered his judgment, though his handling of the Conference was less sure than it might have been." On one occasion when Eden had become especially concerned, Hopkins said to him: "The President's not looking very well this afternoon." He replied: "We'd better adjourn now before we get into serious trouble." Adjourn they did. Eden reminded those who attributed Roosevelt's decisions to illness that "though the work of the Conference was strenuous enough to keep a man even of Churchill's energy occupied, Roosevelt found time to negotiate in secret * * * an agreement with Stalin to cover the Far East."[250] Presumably, the imagination, intellectual and physical energy required to negotiate an agreement with Stalin on so vast and so politically complex an area was for Eden a measure of his mental acuity and physical strength as a negotiator.

In his final assessment, Bohlen came to the same conclusion. He acknowledged that the President's physical state "was certainly not up to normal," but he insisted that "his mental and psychological state was certainly not affected." Roosevelt was "lethargic," Bohlen noted, "but when important moments arose, he was mentally sharp." And he concluded: "Our leader was ill at Yalta, the most important of the wartime conferences, but he was effective. I so believed at the time and still so believe."[251]

(c) Some lessons from the Yalta negotiations

(1) Absence of a negotiating strategy

One of the criticisms of the President by Conference principals was the absence of a meaningful negotiating strategy, particularly with respect to America's closest ally, the British. The reasons for this absence were rooted in the President's preference for his free-and-easy informal negotiating style and in his careful concern for arousing Stalin's suspicion by seeming to act in concert with the British. As at Teheran, the President did not want to give Stalin the impression that he and Churchill were "ganging up" on him.

Roosevelt's informal approach was based on his continued belief that he could personally accomplish more in a man-to-man talk with Stalin than Churchill, the State Department, or the British Foreign Office, and to succeed in this Stalin would have to be in a receptive state of mind.[252] This belief led him to shunt aside any suggestion of developing a preconference negotiating strategy with the British that could rob him of flexibility in negotiations and the confidence of Stalin. Hence, at Malta, Roosevelt virtually ignored the British except for exchanges of social amenities, much to Eden's displeasure.[253] Even at

[249] Ibid., pp. 389–390.
[250] Eden, Reckoning, pp. 593–594.
[251] Bohlen, op. cit., p. 172.
[252] Harriman and Abel, op. cit., pp. 390–391.
[253] Eden found it impossible "even to get near business" at a planned working dinner. "I spoke pretty sharply to Harry [Hopkins] about it, when he came in later," wrote Eden in his diary, "pointing out that we were going into a decisive conference and had so far neither agreed what we would discuss nor how to handle matters with a Bear who would certainly know his mind." (Reckoning, p. 592.)

Yalta the President put off seeing Churchill alone until the fifth day of the Conference.[254] "The outcome of this," concluded Eden in criticism both of Roosevelt's behavior and his long-range vision, "was some confusion in Anglo-American relations which profited the Soviets."[255]

(2) *Imprecision in drafting*

Imprecision in drafting Conference documents was another criticism of negotiating procedures followed by the U.S. delegation in dealing with the Russians at Yalta. The effect of this deficiency was to create future opportunities for the Soviets to exploit.

In the case of Poland, two paragraphs in the final agreement on Poland's political future were, in Bohlen's words, "not specific enough and bore the mark of hasty drafting." He explained:

The number of non-Lublin Poles from within and without Poland is not even indicated. The phrase "in the first instance" seemed clear enough to us at Yalta and still does. But Harriman, Clark Kerr [British Ambassador to the Soviet Union], and Polish emigree representatives soon discovered that the Soviets were interpreting "in the first instance" to mean that the negotiations in Moscow should only be with the members of the Lublin government, and not to mean, as the English text clearly indicates, that the first meeting should be in Moscow rather than Warsaw. I do not believe the Soviets put the words "in the first instance" in the agreement with the idea of misinterpreting them later. Rather, I believe the Russians, in studying the text afterward, saw in this phrase a loophole allowing them to promote their own cause. The fact that we did not spot the loophole is another example of the lack of care that the Western Allies occasionally showed in their dealings with the Soviets, to whom even the last comma had meaning. Too often, we were more concerned not to appear to be nit-picking than with defending a position by carefully watching small points.[256]

Imprecision in drafting was also evident in the Far Eastern agreement. Clearly by design and without prior discussion the Soviets had insisted on the phrase "the preeminent interests" of the Soviet Union being "safeguarded" in the sections of the agreement pertaining to the Soviet presence and role in Port Arthur, Darien, and with respect to the Manchurian railroads. Roosevelt, overruling Harriman who opposed acceptance of the term, acceded to it. Accession to the word "preeminent," wrote Bohlen, was "unfortunate" since the choice of this word "provided the Soviets with the legal basis to assert all sorts of interests and positions in Manchuria."[257] Feis concluded: "This was a lax and hazy treatment of demands on which for almost half a century grave quarrels had centered."[258]

(3) *The matter of the Kurile Islands*

Disposition of the Kurile Islands raises two questions with respect to procedures at Yalta; namely, an apparent lack of preparation for

---

[254] Harriman and Abel, op. cit., p. 390. This account continued: "The President still believed that Stalin would prove more tractable if the Western powers did not appear to be acting in unison. In his private meetings with Stalin, Roosevelt talked openly about his differences with Churchill, and on more than one occasion, poked a little fun at the Prime Minister for his old-fashioned attachment to the Empire." For an attempt to analyze Roosevelt's behavior in this matter, see Bohlen, op. cit., p. 172.

[255] Eden, Reckoning, p. 593.

[256] Bohlen, op. cit., pp. 191–192. At the time Harriman felt that the language was "far too vague and generalized." Both he and Bohlen agreed before leaving Yalta that "there was bound to be trouble ahead." "There was an expression we used at the Embassy at the time—that trading with the Russians you had to buy the same horse twice," Harriman recalled. "I had that feeling about the Polish agreement and said as much to Bohlen. He agreed that the whole negotiation we had just completed at Yalta would have to be developed again from the ground up. We had established nothing more than the machinery for renegotiation." (Harriman and Abel, op. cit., p. 412.)

[257] Ibid., p. 198.

[258] Feis, Churchill-Roosevelt-Stalin, p. 513. See footnote 19 for an explanation of the historical context.

negotiations and imprecision in drafting a highly important agreement.

Dr. George H. Blakeslee, an American specialist on the Far East and consultant to the State Department, had prepared a briefing paper for the "black books" that in particular dealt with the Kurile Islands. Another concerned Southern Sakhalin. The memoranda showed that Japan had seized only Southern Sakhalin in the 1904 war and that it had obtained the Kuriles in a 1875 Treaty of Commerce and Navigation with Imperial Russia. This material was never included in the "black books;" nor was there evidence that it was brought to the attention of President Roosevelt and Secretary of State Stettinius. No explanation has been given for this omission.[259]

In negotiating the conditions for Soviet entry into the Pacific war, Roosevelt told Stalin that Harriman had already filled him in on their previous talks on this question and that he foresaw, in the words of Bohlen's minutes, "no difficulty whatsoever in regard to the southern half of Sakhalin and the Kurile Islands going to Russia at the end of the war." [260] This stipulation was one of the conditions laid down by Stalin. Apparently, Harriman, a principal in negotiating this agreement, demurred on Stalin's claim to the Kuriles.

According to the Harriman and Abel account, "Roosevelt dismissed Harriman's reservations on this point before signing the agreement," adding that the "Kuriles seemed to him a minor matter measured against the larger benefits of a Russian helping hand against Japan." [261]

Bohlen implied in his memoirs that because the President had not done his "homework" and the Americans "were napping" at Yalta, the Soviet Union obtained the Kurile Islands which Japan had obtained not by force but by peaceful treaty.[262] But, judging from the Harriman account, this seems to be a misreading of the facts known to the President.

It is not a misreading, however, that an error was made in the Kuriles matter due to imprecise drafting. The agreement merely stated that the islands would be "handed over to the Soviet Union." It did not specifically list the islands. Later in 1945 when the Russians entered the Pacific war, the Red Army seized four islands that Japan insisted were not part of the Kuriles, but of a different group, the Northern Territories, which had always been Japanese. Not until 1972 did the Soviets consent to talk about returning these islands.[263]

4. RESULTS AND SIGNIFICANCE OF THE CONFERENCE

(a) Achievements of negotiators

For the three principal negotiators, Yalta was a success, at least in the short term: Each had achieved his main purposes. Stalin, the hard realistic bargainer, achieved his primary goal; namely, to maintain control over Poland's future destiny, for the Soviets a most

---

[259] Yalta Documents, pp. 379 and 385. See also Feis, Churchill-Roosevelt-Stalin, p. 511, ff. 17.
[260] Yalta Documents, p. 768 and Bohlen, op. cit., p. 196.
[261] Harriman and Abel, op. cit., p. 400.
[262] Bohlen, op. cit., p. 197. .
[263] Ibid., pp. 197–198.

vital security interest. Stalin achieved this goal without immediately disrupting the wartime alliance.[264]

Roosevelt, the neo-Wilsonian and political idealist, the improviser and arbiter between Stalin and Churchill at Yalta, achieved his main purposes.[265] At a price Roosevelt was willing to pay for victory in the Far East, Stalin agreed to enter the Pacific war in what was then (before the atomic bomb was developed) perceived by the Nation's leading military strategists to be a vital American interest. Stalin also moderated his position on the United Nations, clearing the way for the realization of Roosevelt's dream of building what was hoped would be an international structure for world peace.

Churchill, a political realist whose negotiating style was suffused with rhetoric and emotion, achieved his purposes, particularly in reconstructing elements of what would be a new balance of power in Europe and in preserving the integrity of the British Empire.[266]

In brief, the success of negotiations at Yalta, however transitory, lay in the ability of the negotiators to satisfy their immediate interests, to maintain the unity of the alliance so necessary in the pursuit of the war to the end (it was expected to go on against Japan for 18 months after the surrender of Germany), and to establish some essential elements of the postwar political world.

(b) Prevailing mood: Optimism and hopeful expectation

No wonder, therefore, that the prevailing mood when the conference broke up seemed to be one of optimism and hopeful expectations for the future. Sherwood described the mood of the American delegation, including Roosevelt and Hopkins, as "one of supreme exultation." [267] Others evoked similar sentiments.[268] Toasts by the three leaders in the closing days of the Conference exuded a spirit of good will that nourished this optimism. "We really believed in our hearts," Hopkins was to later recall "that this was the dawn of the

---

[264] On this security issue Bohlen explained : "To Stalin, the aim was far more than the understandable one of preventing Germany, when she recovered, from mounting a third invasion of Russia. Stalin was a Bolshevik, and his principal aim was to protect the Soviet system. Thus he felt he could not depend on capitalist Britain or the United States to help him, even though their immediate wartime interests coincided. Nor could Stalin count on an international organization, where the Soviet Union was sure to be outnumbered, to give Moscow what it wanted. The Soviet Union would have to protect the Soviet system herself, and that meant the establishment of satellite governments all through Eastern Europe." (Bohlen, op. cit., p. 178.)

[265] Bohlen wrote of Roosevelt's negotiating style: "The Roosevelt who sparred and bargained with Churchill and Stalin still believed, as he had at Teheran, in improvising solutions to difficulties." (Bohlen, op. cit., p. 178.) Admiral Leahy emphasized a characteristic in Roosevelt's style that others had noted: "Since he was the presiding officer, and most of the arguments were between Stalin and Churchill, he played the role of arbiter at many of the daily sessions." (Leahy, op. cit., p. 321.) Mrs. Roosevelt gave this description of her husband's negotiating style: "Franklin had high hopes that at this conference [Yalta] he could make real progress in strengthening the personal relationship between himself and Marshal Stalin. * * * He knew that negotiation invariably involved some give and take, but he was a good bargainer and a good poker player, and he loved the game of negotiation. I am sure that even at the Yalta conference, the necessity of matching his wits against other people's stimulated him and kept him alert and interested, no matter how weary he may at times have been." (Quoted in, Harriman and Abel. p. 388.)

[266] Bohlen wrote: "Churchill's style in negotiation was based in large measure on his debating experience in the House of Commons. His arguments were always well reasoned but were often based on emotional appeal, which left Stalin cold." (Bohlen, op. cit., p. 178.) Eden commented on Churchill's style with respect to "a meeting of the three great men" : "P.M. is all emotion in these matters, F.D.R. vague and jealous of others." Stalin, he noted, was "the only one of the three who has a clear view of what he wants and is a tough negotiator." (Eden, Reckoning. p. 583.)

[267] Sherwood, op. cit., p. 69.

[268] Byrnes quoted from the American press the widespread enthusiasm created by what was judged to be the success of Yalta and added: "That was how I felt about it. There is no doubt that the tide of Anglo-Soviet-American friendship had reached a new high." (Byrnes, op. cit., p. 45.)

new day we had all been praying for and talking about for so many years." [269]

"In short," concluded Bohlen, "there was hope, as we left Yalta, of genuine cooperation with the Soviet Union on political questions after the war." A gloomy assessment by Kennan which he had received on his first day at Yalta predicting the coming cold war "had not yet proved correct." And Bohlen continued: "It would take Stalin's refusal to carry out his bargain on Poland, his disregard of the Declaration on Liberated Europe, and other actions to extinguish our hopes for Soviet cooperation." [270]

---

[269] Sherwood, op. cit., p. 870.
[270] Bohlen continued his assessment of Yalta: "Even with all the advantages of hindsight, however, I do not believe that the Western allies could have walked away from the attempt to reach an understanding with the Soviet Union. Nor do I believe that through harder bargaining we could have struck a better deal with Stalin. Certainly spheres of influence were not the answer. The fault was not the agreements at Yalta, but something far deeper. Regardless of all that was said or not said, written or not written, agreed to or not agreed to at the Yalta Conference, there was nothing that could have prevented the breakup of the victorious coalition and the onset of the cold war once Stalin set his course." (Bohlen, op. cit., pp. 200–201.)

IV. DESCENT INTO THE COLD WAR: THE VIEW FROM MOSCOW

A. Early Signals from Harriman and Kennan in Moscow

The descent into the cold war had long been anticipated by Ambassador Harriman and his closest adviser in Moscow, George Kennan. In the summer and autumn of 1944, Harriman began sending signals to Washington, reporting a change in the Soviet attitude toward cooperation with the United States. For Harriman, Poland was the "touchstone" of Soviet policy, and the ill-fated Warsaw uprising, the "dirty business," as he said, of the Soviet refusal to come to their aid or to allow Anglo-American relief, was for him perhaps the clearest and most decisive indicator of expected Soviet behavior in the future.[1] Harriman confided his confirmed suspicions to Hopkins in a personal letter on September 10, 1944, in which he reported the growing Soviet tendency of noncooperation. He urged a change of policy to divert this trend, noting that the Soviets "have misinterpreted our generous attitude toward them as a sign of weakness, and acceptance of their policies. Time has come when we must make clear what we expect of them as the price of our good will." And he then warned:

Unless we take issue with the present policy there is every indication the Soviet Union will become a world bully wherever their interests are involved. This policy will reach into China and the Pacific as well when they can turn their attention in that direction. No written agreements can be of any value unless they are carried out in a spirit of give and take, and recognition of the interests of other people.[2]

Kennan was also becoming considerably apprehensive as he and Harriman observed from Moscow the expansion of Soviet power and the assertion of its control as the Red Army advanced further into Eastern and Central Europe. Kennan sent a personal letter to his long-time friend and professional colleague Bohlen at Yalta in which he poured out his anxieties about the future. The letter reflected Kennan's mood of brooding pessimism. Kennan recognized that Russia's "masterful" and "effective" effort in the war "must, to a certain extent, find its reward at the expense of other peoples in Eastern and Central Europe." But he failed to see why "we must associate ourselves with this political program, so hostile to the interests of the Atlantic community as a whole, so dangerous to everything which we need to see preserved in Europe." As a possible remedy, Kennan urged, among other alternatives, a "decent and definitive compromise" by dividing Europe into spheres of influence that would in effect limit Soviet expansionism.[3] Neither Bohlen nor Harriman were sympathetic with this view, but its value here lies in reflect-

---

[1] Harriman and Abel, op. cit., p. 342.
[2] Ibid., p. 344.
[3] Bohlen, op. cit., pp. 175–176.

ing Kennan's early and indeed prophetic appraisal of expected Soviet behavior in the postwar era.[4]

Taking the larger view of the global war effort and the need for Soviet cooperation in the postwar world, the administration in Washington was not prepared to follow the advice of its representatives in Moscow. Central to American policy was the imperative need for Soviet participation in the Pacific war. All considerations, however negative, such as General Deane's difficulties in administering Lend-Lease and in getting Soviet cooperation in agreed bilateral military programs, were subsumed beneath this overriding principle. This prevailing attitude, along with the great expectations of the United Nations as a keeper of the postwar peace, seemed to underpin the President's approach to and performance at Yalta. Yet in the weeks after Yalta as aggressive Soviet behavior in Eastern Europe, particularly in Poland and Rumania, became more visible and as other tension-creating incidents emerged within the Alliance (for example, the Berne incident in which Stalin charged the President with seeking a separate peace with the Germans)—all buttressed by Harriman's continuous warnings from Moscow, Roosevelt himself became doubtful about his earlier optimism. On March 23, 1945, 19 days before his death and at the height of the Berne incident, Roosevelt confided to Anna Rosenberg, "Averell is right. We can't do business with Stalin. He has broken every one of the promises he made at Yalta." The President voiced to Anne O'Hara McCormick of the New York Times similar doubts of Stalin's fidelity on the day he left Washington for Warm Springs.[5]

B. Soviet Change to a "Unilateral", "Isolationist" Policy

1. Deadlock at London's Foreign Ministers Conference

By autumn of 1945, characteristics associated with Soviet behavior in the cold war had become more clearly manifested and understood. (By then American public opinion polls had registered a decided downturn in attitudes on the possibilities of cooperating with the Russians.) Illustrative was the Foreign Ministers Conference that met in London during September to draft peace treaties for Germany's former allies. The Conference broke down ostensibly over minor procedural matters, but its collapse was in fact the product of much deeper

---

[4] Ibid., p. 176 and Harriman and Abel, op. cit., pp. 414–415. For a full exposition of Kennan's views, see, Kennan, George F. Memoirs, 1925–50. Boston, Little, Brown, 1967, vol. 1, pp. 224–231. Kennan began: "Several weeks of life and work in Moscow during that summer of 1944 sufficed to dispel these uncertainties. What I saw during that time was enough to convince me that not only our policy toward Russia, but our plans and commitments generally for the shaping of the postwar world, were based on a dangerous misreading of the personality, the intentions, and the political situation of the Soviet leadership." He proceeded to summarize his essay entitled, "Russia—Seven Years Later."

[5] Harriman and Abel, op. cit., p. 444. Bohlen gave the following account of Stalin's reaction to Roosevelt's death and of his esteem for the President: "The Russians were deeply affected by Roosevelt's death. When Ambassador Harriman went to the Kremlin to convey the news officially, he found Stalin upset. There is no reason to believe this was an act; Stalin did have a regard for Roosevelt, and on a number of occasions at the wartime conferences I saw the Marshal show genuine feeling toward the President. He rarely argued with Roosevelt, and his refusals of Roosevelt's requests were always made with regret. I do think Stalin respected Roosevelt as a man who genuinely believed in democratic liberalism. Stalin obviously did not agree with or even understand democratic liberalism and therefore did things in accordance with his Marxism commitments. But on balance, I think he had a higher regard for Roosevelt than he did for Churchill. It is conceivable that Stalin did not consider Roosevelt to be as difficult or as tough an adversary as Churchill, but he did respect the President." (Bohlen, op. cit., p. 209.)

disagreements over the governments being established in Eastern Europe through Soviet intervention and pressure.[6] At the Conference Secretary of State Byrnes had become increasingly alarmed at what was described as Molotov's aggressive and arbitrary behavior.[7] A subsequent and more productive Foreign Ministers Conference was held in Moscow during December 1945, which provided insights not only into Soviet negotiating behavior but also into that of the new Secretary of State.[8]

2. HARRIMAN'S CONVERSATION WITH STALIN AT GAGRA

That the Soviet Government had undergone or was undergoing a policy change became reasonably certain to Harriman after he met Stalin at Gagra in the Crimea on October 24, 1945. In the course of their conversation in which Stalin expressed his displeasure with the arrangements for the occupation of Japan and the role assigned to the Soviet Union, Stalin suggested for the first time that the Soviet Union might pursue a go-it-alone policy. It might be better if the Soviet Union stepped aside, Stalin suggested, and let the United States do as it wished in Japan. Recalling the isolationists in the United States, Stalin expressed his opposition to the policy but indicated that perhaps the Soviet Union should now adopt it. There was nothing wrong with such a policy, he said.[9]

To Harriman, Stalin was not referring to the American brand of isolation but rather to a Soviet policy of unilateral action. Stalin would never entrust the real security of the Soviet Union to collective security arrangements which in the final analysis, Harriman reasoned, rested on the good will of other nations. Accordingly, Harriman felt that Stalin's policy of isolation meant maintaining Soviet domination over Eastern Europe, using Communist parties in Western Europe and elsewhere as a means for expanding Soviet influence,

---

[6] Kennan, Memoirs, vol. 1, pp. 283–284.

[7] Harriman and Abel, op. cit., pp. 507–508.

[8] Kennan, who attended this Conference, gave the following characterization of Molotov as a negotiator: "Molotov, conducting the meeting, sat leaning forward over the table, a Russian cigarette dangling from his mouth, his eyes flashing with satisfaction and confidence as he glanced from one to the other of the other foreign ministers, obviously keenly aware of their mutual differences and their common uncertainty in the face of the keen, ruthless, and incisive Russian diplomacy. He had the look of a passionate poker player who knows that he has a royal flush and is about to call the last of his opponents. He was the only one who was clearly enjoying every minute of the proceedings." (Kennan, Memoirs, vol. 1, p. 287.)

Of Secretary Byrnes as a negotiator Kennan wrote: "I sat just behind Byrnes and could not see him well. He plays his negotiations by ear, going into them with no clear or fixed plan, with no definite set objectives or limitations. He relies entirely on his own agility and presence of mind and hopes to take advantage of tactical openings. In the present conference his weakness in dealing with the Russians is that his main purpose is to achieve some sort of an agreement, he doesn't much care what. The realities behind this agreement, since they concern only such people as Koreans, Rumanians, and Iranians, about whom he knows nothing, do not concern him. He wants an agreement for its political effect at home. The Russians know this. They will see that for this superficial success he pays a heavy price in the things that are real." (Ibid., pp. 287–288.)

Kennan made two observations in his diary for December that reflect on Soviet behavior. After the Foreign Ministers meeting referred to above, Kennan had supper with Frank Roberts, a British diplomat, and Harrison F. Matthews, an American diplomat. He recorded this in his diary: "By the end of the evening, Matthews looked so crestfallen at the things that he had heard from Roberts and myself that I felt sorry for him and had to try to cheer him up. In the introduction of newcomers to the realities of the Soviet Union there are always two processes; the first is to reveal what these realities are, the second is to help the newcomer adjust himself to the shock." (Ibid., p. 288.)

On December 21, 1945, Kennan noted in his diary that he had lunch with Roberts, Sir Alexander Cadogan and two or three other people from the British delegation, and commented: "Chip [Bohlen] was there and I think he and I rather shook Cadogan's composure with our observations on the technique of dealing with the Soviet Government." Kennan did not explain, but later he elaborated on rules for negotiating with the Russians which will be summarized in the next chapter. (Ibid.)

[9] Harriman and Abel, op. cit., p. 514.

and neither relying on the United States and the West for economic assistance nor depending on their military cooperation in the future.[10]

Harriman came away from Gagra feeling that Stalin's comment added further evidence to the belief that the Soviet leadership had discussed and settled on a new policy of increased militancy and self-reliance. Reflecting on Molotov's obstreperous behavior at the London Foreign Ministers Conference over seemingly minor points of procedure, Harriman, accordingly, was persuaded that the Soviet Foreign Minister had been acting in conformance to Stalin's new policy.[11]

3. OMINOUS WARNING FROM LITVINOV

Signs of the coming cold war were increasing during the autumn of 1945. The political climate in Moscow was described as "notably bleak and chilly." On the evening of November 22, while attending a Moscow theater, Harriman met Litvinov and had what the Ambassador called "a most disquieting conversation of a few sentences." [12] By this time Litvinov was clearly on the outside, but not quite a nonperson.

Litvinov was disturbed by the international situation, emphasizing, as Harriman reported to Washington, that "neither side knew how to behave toward the other." This was the underlying reason for the breakdown of the London Foreign Ministers Conference and the subsequent difficulties, he said. To the suggestion that time might cool the aroused strong feelings, Litvinov replied that in the meantime other issues were developing. To the suggestion that the atmosphere might clear if an understanding were reached on Japan, he replied that "other issues would then confront us." When asked what the United States could do about it, Litvinov replied, "Nothing." When asked what he could do about it, Litvinov replied, "I believe I know what should be done but I am powerless."

"You are extremely pessimistic," Harriman remarked.

"Frankly, between us, yes," Litvinov replied softly.

For Harriman, this direct suggestion by Litvinov that matters were bound to get worse regardless of what the United States did in its relations with Russia, was significant, and accordingly reported it to Washington.[13]

Other signs of a new hard-line policy were evident in the press and at party meetings. Propaganda attacks against "an aggressive new American policy" toward the Soviet Union were emerging. Still, Harriman saw no reason for despair, though he passed on the following tentative but somber interpretation to Washington:

To sum up the above, together with Stalin's comment that the Soviet Union may have to pursue an isolationist policy, it appears that since Molotov could not get what he wanted at the London conference, the Soviet Government * * * has been pursuing to the fullest extent a policy of unilateral action to achieve their concept of security in depth.

After citing evidence of a stiffening Soviet policy in Bulgaria, Rumania, Iran, and eleswhere, Harriman concluded:

Thus it would appear that Molotov's policy following the London breakdown has been to seize the immediate situation to strengthen the Soviet position as

---

[10] Ibid., p. 515.
[11] Ibid.
[12] Ibid., p. 518.
[13] Ibid.

much as possible through unilateral action and then probably to agree to another meeting of the Foreign Ministers. We would at that time be faced with a number of entrenched Soviet positions and faits accomplis.[14]

4. SOURCE OF SOVIET AGGRESSIVENESS : "THEIR OLD FEELING OF INSECURITY"

(a) Effect of the atomic bomb: Andreychin's estimate

Increased aggressiveness in Soviet policy tended to create a new siege mentality within the ruling elite. Harriman's own assessment of the rationale behind this behavior was confirmed during a surreptitious visit to Spaso House on October 30, 1945, by George Andreychin, a Bulgarian-American revolutionary whom Harriman had first met as Trotsky's English-language interpreter in 1926.

Andreychin attributed the change in Soviet policy primarily to American possession of the atomic bomb. Filled with pride over the Red Army's strength at the end of the war in Europe, the ruling elite was shocked to learn, Andreychin explained, that American possession of the bomb once again exposed Russia's comparative weakness. Soviet aggressiveness, he declared, was intended to conceal this weakness.[15]

(b) Harriman's assessment confirmed

Andreychin's analysis carried the stamp of authenticity because of his revolutionary credentials and his seemingly close ties with Soviet authorities.[16] It reinforced Harriman's own views with respect to the crucial effect of the atomic bomb on the Soviet leadership and its causal effect on the shift to a more aggressive policy. On November 27, 1945, Harriman passed on his personal assessment to Secretary of State Byrnes.

Briefly, Harriman explained the "almost constant state of fear or tension," induced by internal and external forces, that the Soviet leadership had lived with since the Bolshevik Revolution. This fear culminated with the German invasion that "all but destroyed them." Victory in the war had given them "tremendous relief" and "confidence in the power of the Red Army and in their control at home, giving them for the first time a sense of security, for themselves personally and for the revolution, such as they had never before had." But Stalin had no illusions for whom the people were fighting. As he told Harriman in September 1941, they were fighting as they always had "for their homeland, not for us," meaning the Communist party. Stalin would make no such statement today, Harriman declared, explaining that the war had assisted in consolidating the revolution in Russia. They had determined, he went on, that the Red Army should be kept

---

[14] Ibid., pp. 518–519.
[15] Ibid., pp. 519–520. Andreychin and Harriman carried on their conversation in the bathroom with the water rushing from the faucet in order to make the conversation inaudible through any listening device. Harriman gave assurances that the Embassy had been checked and rechecked, but Andreychin wanted this precaution because he knew devices had been installed before Bullitt's arrival in 1934 and that part of the evidence used against him by the Russians had been based on recordings of conversations with Bullitt. Andreychin told Harriman that Molotov and Vishinsky had become the makers of Soviet foreign policy because Stalin had no independent sources of information about the outside world. He suggested that the United States establish shortwave radio broadcasts to the Soviet Union in order to offset Soviet propaganda to the people who. Andreychin assured Harriman, remained friendly to the United States. Harriman passed along the suggestion to William Benton, Assistant Secretary of State for Public Affairs, where it was well received and the idea eventually evolved into the Voice of America.
[16] Andreychin was being sent to Bulgaria where he was to offer his advice to the American mission in Sofia. Harriman met Andreychin again at the Paris Peace Conference in 1946 where he reappeared as a member of the Bulgarian delegation staff. (Ibid., p. 520.)

strong and industry developed to support it "so that no power on earth could threaten the Soviet Union again." Political measures had been taken, Harriman noted, to obtain "defense in depth" without regard for the desires or interests of other peoples.

"Then, suddenly, the atomic bomb appeared and they recognized it as an offset to the power of the Red Army," Harriman declared, adding, "This must have revived their old feeling of insecurity. They could no longer be absolutely sure that they could obtain their objectives without interference." Molotov's aggressiveness at the London Foreign Ministers Conference could be explained partly by this attitude. In keeping with this new militancy, "the Russian people have been aroused to feel that they must again face an antagonistic world. American imperialism is included as a threat to Russia."

Harriman concluded by saying that his message was not intended to suggest any course of policy or action, but only to partially explain "the strange psychological effect of the atomic bomb on the Soviet leaders' behavior." [17]

What makes Harriman's assessment significant for the purposes of this study is that it brings to the surface once again a theme that has persisted in Russian diplomacy and was particularly characteristic in Stalin's wartime negotiations; namely, that aggressive Russian behavior has been intended to conceal their own weakness and a deep feeling of insecurity.

Scholars today substantiate what was to Harriman essentially an intuitive reading of Soviet alarm over the U.S. development of the atomic bomb. According to David Holloway, a British historian and specialist on the Soviet weapon-building system, Stalin initiated the first Soviet effort to develop the bomb with the issuance of the Soviet State Defense Committee decree in December 1942. This decree ordered that a nuclear research laboratory be started with the leading Russian nuclear physicist Igor Kurchatov as its head. But this effort received a low priority, owing to the exigencies of the war, until August 1945

[17] Ibid., p. 521. The seriousness of Stalin's concern for the atomic bomb was underscored at a Kremlin banquet in December 1945 on the occasion of the Moscow Foreign Ministers Conference. Up to that time the Soviets had publicly denigrated the importance of the bomb. Stalin had issued a statement declaring that the weapon would only frighten the weak-willed. At the banquet, Molotov, following that line, treated the nuclear weapon in a jocular fashion, suggesting in a toast that Dr. James B. Conant, President of Harvard University and a member of the delegation who had been intimately involved in the development of the atomic bomb, might have in his waistcoat pocket a piece of fissionable material. Bohlen gave this account of Stalin's reaction: "Stalin rose and said quietly that nuclear fission was much too serious a matter to be the subject of jokes. He praised the American and British nuclear scientists for their accomplishment. There in the banquet hall of the Kremlin we saw Stalin abruptly change Soviet policy, without consulting his number two man. The humiliated Molotov never altered his expression. From that moment on, the Soviets gave the atomic bomb the serious consideration it deserved." (Bohlen, op. cit., p. 249).

Of interest also is Harriman's final assessment of Stalin at the end of his assignment as Ambassador in Moscow. When Harriman left the Kremlin after his last visit with Stalin on the evening of January 23, 1945, his mind was still in conflict about Stalin's enigmatic character. Since the autumn of 1941, they had talked dozens of times and under extreme conditions of near defeat and certain victory. Harriman saw that Stalin could also be a very brutal man, as in his harsh treatment of Poland, and also "bitterly abusive time and again" as in his criticism of the United States and Britain during the war. Yet, in personal relations with Harriman, according to the Harriman-Abel account, "Stalin was never less than courteous and at times totally disarming." Harriman had seen both sides of the Soviet dictator and on reflection made this final assessment: "It is hard for me to reconcile the courtesy and consideration that he showed me personally with the ghastly cruelty of his wholesale liquidations. Others, who did not know him personally, see only the tyrant in Stalin. I saw the other side as well—his high intelligence, that fantastic grasp of detail, his shrewdness and the surprising human sensitivity that he was capable of showing, at least in the war years. I found him better informed than Roosevelt, more realistic than Churchill, in some ways the most effective of the war leaders. At the same time he was, of course, a murderous tyrant. I must confess that for me Stalin remains the most inscrutable and contradictory character I have known—and leave the final judgment to history." (Harriman and Abel, op. cit., pp. 535–536.)

after the bombing of Hiroshima and Nagasaki. At a Kremlin meeting in mid-August 1945 in which Kurchatov attended along with the Soviet munitions' chief, Stalin reportedly made this statement which reflects the extent of his concern for Russia's security at that time:

A single demand of you, comrades: Provide us with atomic weapons in the shortest possible time. You know that Hiroshima has shaken the whole world. The equilibrium has been destroyed. Provide the bomb—it will remove a great danger from us.[17a]

C. Somber Messages to the American People

Thus, the three principal American observers in Moscow, Harriman, Kennan, and Deane, brought home on their return somber messages of a cold war already under way. With the closing of the U.S. military mission in October 1945, General Deane returned sounding warnings of the coming breakdown in relations with the Soviet Union.[18] Ambassador Harriman returned with his message of pessimism for future relations, reinforcing his skeptical views to the press on an earlier visit by supporting the thesis of Kennan's long telegram and by encouraging its dissemination throughout the upper echelons of the administration.[19]

Kennan's was perhaps the most effective message; for his 8,000-word dispatch, dated February 22, 1946, and prepared in response to a State Department request for an explanation of current Soviet behavior, laid out the nature of the Soviet threat and the responding theory of containment. After returning home in 1946, Kennan subsequently published his thesis in the famous "X" article appearing in the Foreign Affairs periodical. Kennan's concept of containment provided the theoretical basis for the American response to Soviet post-war expansionism.[20]

Clearly, the signs were ominous for the future conduct of diplomacy and negotiations with the Soviet Union.

[17a] Pincus, Walter. Soviets Had Chance to Develop First A-Bomb. Historian Says. The Washington Post, July 27, 1979, p. A2. This press account was based on a paper that Holloway had presented in July 1979 at the Smithsonian Institution's Wilson Center. Holloway, a lecturer in politics at the University of Edinburgh, has been a research fellow at the Wilson Center for the past year. For four years he has been engaged in a specialized study of the Soviet weapons-building system. He is writing a book on the Russian atomic program.

[18] In his book written in 1946 and published in 1947, Deane observed: "In my opinion there can be no longer be any doubt that Soviet leadership has always been motivated by the belief that communism and capitalism cannot coexist. Nor is there any doubt in my mind that present-day Soviet leaders have determined upon a program pointed toward imposing communism on those countries under their control and, elsewhere, creating conditions favorable to the triumph of communism in the war against capitalism which they consider to be inevitable." (Deane, Strange Alliance, p. 319.)

[19] At a meeting with the press in May 1945 described as "hotly argumentative", Harriman said: "We must recognize that our objectives and the Kremlin's objectives are irreconcilable. The Kremlin wants to promote Communist dictatorships controlled from Moscow, whereas we want, as far as possible, to see a world of governments responsive to the will of the people. We have to find ways of composing our differences in the United Nations and elsewhere in order to live without war on this small planet." Two of Harriman's listeners, Walter Lippmann and Raymond Gram Swing, were "so shocked," according to the Harriman-Abel account, "that they got up and left the room." Harriman was amazed at the reaction, noting that he spoke "calmly" and "understated the case as I saw it." (Harriman and Abel, op. cit., p. 457. For comments on Kennan and his dispatch, see pp. 547–548.)

[20] For an early commentary on Kennan's containment theory, see, Whelan, Joseph G., George Kennan and His Influence on American Foreign Policy, Virginia Quarterly Review, vol. 35, Spring 1959: 196–220. In recent years an extensive literature has emerged on this question. See, for example, Wright, C. Ben. Mr. "X" and Containment, Slavic Review, vol. 35, March 1976: 1–31: also Kennan's reply in the same issue (pp. 32–36), and Wright's reply in issue of June 1976, pp. 318–20.

CHAPTER VI—NEGOTIATIONS UNDER STALIN: DURING THE COLD WAR, 1946-53

A single demand of you, comrades: Provide us with atomic weapons in the shortest possible time. You know that Hiroshima has shaken the whole world. The equilibrium has been destroyed. Provide the bomb— it will remove a great danger from us.

—Stalin to his scientists and munitions chiefs, mid-August 1945.

* * * we had doubts of our own about Stalin's foreign policy. He over-emphasized the importance of military might, for one thing, and consequently put too much faith in our armed forces. He lived in terror of an enemy attack. For him foreign policy meant keeping the antiaircraft units around Moscow on a twenty-four-hour alert.

—Khrushchev, Khrushchev Remembers, 1970.

I. INTERNATIONAL SETTING

A. Emergence of Bipolarity

The cold war was a creation of multiple forces that issued from three major sources: World War II and its aftermath; Soviet great power dynamism and the Soviet ideological commitment to expand its power and further the goals of communism; and America's determination to protect its vital interests by countering the Soviet outward thrusts, a determination underpinned by the same great power dynamic and a unique historical commitment to expanding and preserving the concepts of liberal democracy.

World War II brought about a profound change in the structure of international relations. The distribution of world power shifted from the main actors in world affairs during the 1930's to those who heretofore had played only limited roles. Destruction of the wartime Axis powers combined with the voluntary and involuntary liquidation of the British, French, Dutch, and later the Belgian imperial systems created vast power vacuums in the world. New states and new constellations of power emerged, and the alinement of world forces changed radically as a consequence. This was the beginning of the era of bipolarity and global confrontation between the United States and the Soviet Union. Around both powers were alined clusters of allies in what came to take on the shape of a politically bipolar world. The principal objective of the United States was to preserve a world order acceptable to the common interests of free peoples and committed to the principle of orderly democratic change; the U.S.S.R. sought to destroy this order through violent revolutionary change and transform it into the Soviet image with its distinctive governmental and economic form and totalitarian, mechanistic value systems. The resulting clash of interests and forces produced the cold war.

The 7 years from 1946 to Stalin's death in 1953 was a period of acute confrontation between the Soviet Union and the United States. Consolidation of Soviet power in Eastern Europe clearly signaled by the founding of the Cominform (Communist Information Bureau) in 1947 and the Czech coup in February 1948; Soviet attempts to expand its influence into Western Europe through its disciplined Communist parties; Soviet pressures on Iran and Turkey and support for the Communist revolutionary forces in Greece; the grave Soviet challenge to the Western political position in Berlin—all were perceived as serious threats and were met by vigorous Western counteractions. The established cold war pattern of oscillating movements of action-counteraction, challenge and response brought on war in Korea, Southeast Asia, and a revolutionary upsurge in other parts of the Third World.

An essential element in the Soviet approach to the cold war was the Stalinist ideological formulation of the "two-camp thesis." This concept perceived the world as divided clearly and unequivocally into capitalist and Communist "camps," and it accepted as a theoretical verity the principle that wars were inevitable. This belief produced a Soviet spirit of revolutionary renewal in the world and its effects as manifested in the cold war were to create a climate of acute and seemingly unrelenting pressure and tension in the whole of international relations.[1]

B. Impact of the Cold War on Diplomacy and Diplomats

The impact of the cold war on diplomacy and diplomats was far-reaching: It depreciated both the institution of diplomacy and the craft of its practitioners.

For Prof. Hans J. Morgenthau, the noted authority on international politics, the cold war accelerated the decline of traditional diplomacy which he perceived had set in at the conclusion of World War I. "Since the end of the Second World War," he lamented, "diplomacy has lost its vitality, and its functions have withered away to such an extent as is without precedent in the history of the modern state system.[2]

Four factors, it will be recalled, accounted for that decline: The technological developments in modern communications, the condemnation of secret diplomacy and the stigma of power politics arising from the World War I experience, the democratization of diplomacy and the

---

[1] Churchill's speech at Fulton, Mo., in March 1946, has often been cited as marking the beginning of the cold war. It was in that speech that the term "iron curtain" became prominent, though Churchill had actually used it once before in a message to President Truman on May 12, 1945, describing aggressive Soviet behavior in occupied Europe. (See Bohlen, op. cit. p. 216.) Often overlooked was Stalin's speech of Feb. 9, 1946, that in effect has been regarded as proclaiming the new Soviet political and ideological offensive. How American foreign policy officials viewed this speech was clearly reflected in this commentary by Acheson: "Evidence had been accumulating that Stalin was steering foreign policy of the Soviet Union on an ominous course. On Feb. 9, 1946, before a vast 'election' audience in Moscow, he stated with brutal clarity the Soviet Union's postwar policy. Finding the causes of the late war in the necessities of capitalist-imperialist monopoly and the same forces still in control abroad, he concluded that no peaceful international order was possible. The Soviet Union must, therefore, be capable of guarding against any eventuality. * * * This grim news depressed even the ebullient spirits of Secretary of State [Byrnes]. They were soon to be depressed even further [by the arrival of Kennan's February dispatch]." (Acheson, op. cit., pp. 150–151.) Later Acheson observed: "Stalin's offensive against the United States and the West, announced in his speech of February 9, 1946, had begun in Poland in 1945 and would reach its crescendo in Korea and the 'hate America' campaign of the early 1950's. This was the start of the 'cold war,' and was to condition the rest of my official life." Acheson then proceeded to describe the evolution of the Soviet offensive and the American response. (Ibid., p. 194.) For a commentary by an American diplomat on the transition from the idealism that marked the American attitude toward Russia during World War II to the realism of the cold war, see Murphy, op. cit., pp. 435–436.

[2] Morgenthau, Hans J., Politics Among Nations: The Struggle for Power and Peace. New York, Knopf, 1973, 5th ed., p. 525.

foreign policy process, and the emergence of diplomacy by parliamentary procedures as in the League of Nations and, since World War II, in the United Nations. Morgenthau added two other causes for the decline: "The peculiarly untraditional approach of the two superpowers to the issues of international politics, and the very nature of world politics [in] the second half of the twentieth century." [3]

That the nature of contemporary world politics, notably the cold war, has impacted adversely on diplomacy there seems to be little doubt. Morgenthau explained it in terms of conflicting universalisms advocated by the superpowers:

Imbued with the crusading spirit of the new moral force of nationalistic universalism, and both tempted and frightened by the potentialities of total war, two superpowers, the centers of two gigantic power blocs, have faced each other in inflexible opposition. They could not retreat without giving up what they considered vital to them. They could not advance without risking combat. Persuasion, then, was tantamount to trickery, compromise meant treason, and the threat of force spelled war.

Morgenthau concluded that given the nature of the power relations between them and the mind sets of each in their relationship:

* * * diplomacy had little with which to operate and tended to become obsolete. Under such moral and political conditions, it was not the sensitive, flexible, and versatile mind of the diplomat, but the rigid, relentless, and one-track mind of the crusader that guided the destiny of nations. The crusading mind knows nothing of persuasion and compromise. It knows only of victory and of defeat. [4]

The craft of the diplomat was similarly depreciated by the impact of the cold war. The untraditional behavior of the Soviet diplomat, amply recorded thus far, was deepened, broadened and indeed hardened by cold war conditions. Specialists in Soviet affairs have attributed much of this behavior to the paranoia of Stalin and his leadership. By the early 1950's, Stalinism had reached new heights of extreme internal repression, making productive negotiations and normal diplomatic intercourse virtually impossible.

Some American foreign policy specialists have asserted that the United States also had its own deficiencies that contributed to the depreciation of the diplomat. Morgenthau asserted that when Roosevelt left the scene, "there was no man or group of men capable of creating and operating that intricate and subtle machinery by which traditional diplomacy had give peaceful protection and furtherance to the national interest." [5]

He attributed this deficiency to the Roosevelt style of diplomacy by improvisation and to the President's almost single-handed control over American foreign policy for 12 years.

For Kennan, the fault lay in the overmilitarization of U.S. foreign policy and that of the West which had "probably" caused an intensification of Soviet military preparations and accentuated their "habitual preoccupation with questions of internal security." The effect, he wrote in 1952, was to weaken "what little usefulness might otherwise have been present in the institution of diplomatic relations between Russia and the West. It had, in other words, further impaired that cushion of

---

[3] Ibid., p. 529.
[4] Ibid., pp. 530–531.
[5] Morgenthau continued: "Nor could that small group of able and devoted public servants who knew what foreign policy was all about rely upon the public understanding of, and popular support for, the rational and intricate processes of foreign policy, without which foreign policy in a democracy cannot be successfully conducted." (Ibid., p. 529.)

safety that normally existed in the ability of governments to talk with one another over the diplomatic channel." [6]

At the more mundane level, the tasks of American diplomatic practitioners in dealing with their Communist adversaries were complicated by the cold war. With the rise of fears and anxieties in the Nation generated by the cold war, the diplomatic establishment became the target of criticism for past failures and current deficiencies in diplomacy. The prestige of the Foreign Service and the State Department suffered accordingly.

Thus, the cold war dealt a severe blow to the evolution of diplomacy. On the Soviet-side, diplomacy became an instrument of political warfare and the diplomat a means for achieving the aggressive revolutionary goals of Stalinism. As instrumentalities for serious negotiations aimed at maintaining a balance of interests they were debased and the level of their purposes reduced to the primitive revolutionary diplomacy of the early Bolshevik era. Soviet behavior, therefore, precipitated this rapid decline in diplomacy. For there is a fundamental contradiction in the purposes of revolution and the ideals of diplomacy: The former seeks radical, often violent, change; the latter seeks change by consensus and gradualism.

---

[6] Kennan, George F. Memoirs, 1950–63. Boston Little, Brown, 1972, vol. 2, p. 139. In his memoirs, Acheson frequently complained of the "shrinking place" that the State Department had in the foreign field during World War II. This was attributed to the President's primary role in formulating foreign policy and his preference to be his own Secretary of State, the dominating role played by the White House, notably Hopkins, and the acquiesence by Hull. Referring to his own role Acheson referred to the comment by Abbe Sieyez when asked what he did during the French Revolution, "I survived." (See Acheson, Present at Creation, p. 39 and p. 88.) Presumably with the onset of the cold war and the development of military programs in response to the perceived Soviet threat, the State Department had an uphill struggle in reclaiming its rightful role in the foreign policy process. This experience contrasts sharply with that of Secretary of State Seward whose role as policymaker was magnified rather than reduced during the Civil War and its aftermath.

II. CHARACTERISTICS OF SOVIET COLD WAR DIPLOMACY

A. GENERAL CHARACTERISTICS OF SOVIET BEHAVIOR

1. DIPLOMACY OF ABUSE AND HOSTILITY: A RETURN TO THE BREST-LITOVSK STYLE

Perhaps Craig best characterized Soviet diplomacy in the cold war when he termed it a return to the style of Brest-Litovsk and for much the same reasons that prompted Bolshevik behavior in those early years of revolution.[1] For all practical purposes negotiations and and diplomacy in the traditional sense were suspended.[2] As in the early days of the Soviet era, propaganda in its most distorted and vitriolic form became one of the principal arms of Soviet diplomacy and espionage a significant part of the diplomatic infrastructure.[3]

As the spirit of the cold war gathered momentum, the United Nations and other international bodies were transformed into arenas of political combat quite opposite from their intended purpose of reconciling differences and reaching agreement through negotiations and diplomacy.[4]

---

[1] Craig, Techniques of Negotiation, p. 367. Craig drew this analogy: "Once more it has seemed to be confident that the victory of Communism on a world scale could not be long delayed and that all confrontations between Soviet and Western negotiators must be used to encourage the forces of revolution. Once more negotiation has been used not as a means of promoting agreement but as a weapon to discomfit enemies and reveal to the world their weaknesses, the falseness of their professions, and the injustice of their claims. Once more the very act of negotiation has been transformed into a dramatic performance designed to entertain and instruct a wider public with a spectacle of enlightened Soviet representatives battling manfully against the forces of capitalism and imperialism."

[2] In what Craig termed a "melancholy survey" of post-World War II diplomacy, Lord Vansittart, the former British Permanent Under Secretary for Foreign Affairs, wrote in 1950: "I have 'done' many conferences in my life but never went into one without some hope of fairly quick result. No one could say the same today. Results are often not expected, and often not even desirable." (The Decline of Diplomacy, Foreign Affairs, vol. 28, 1950 : 184, quoted in Craig, Techniques of Negotiation, p. 367.)

[3] Bohlen gave this characterization of Soviet propaganda: "The cold war was turned against America as a part of the basic and unwaivering hostility which the Bolsheviks have always displayed against capitalist countries. The United States was selected as target number one simply because it was the chief source of power left in the non-Communist world after the war." He continued: "In the 40 years that I have been reading the Soviet press, I have never seen any worthy or decent sentiments attributed to the United States government. Any action we have taken, no matter how civilized or progressive, is judged on the basic premise that all capitalism is evil and anything good that comes out of it is only apparently so. This is the basis for the cold war." (Bohlen, op. cit., pp. 272–273.)

Frederick Osborn, the U.S. Deputy Representative on the U.N. Atomic Energy Commission during 1947–1950, remarked in a commentary on Vishinsky's angry abuse during debate in the U.N. General Assembly: "We were forced to the conclusion that the Soviet delegates were more interested in propaganda than in negotiations, and that their propaganda was directed almost entirely to the emotions of the people on their side, rather than to the intelligence of their audience." (Osborn, Frederick, Negotiating on Atomic Energy, 1946–1947, in, Dennett and Johnson, op. cit., chapter 8, pp. 230–231.)

[4] Acheson's speech at Berkeley in March 1950 gave some indication of the dismal state of diplomacy at that time. He summarized the speech in his memoirs, noting what the Soviets could do to make coexistence "a great deal tolerable to everyone" and went on to record: "Perhaps on the most primitive level of international intercourse—the treatment of diplomatic representatives and the language of international communication—some improvement in debased Communist standards might be possible." But Acheson saw no evidence that the Soviet leaders "will change their conduct until the progress of the free world convinces them that they cannot profit from a continuation of these tensions." (Present at the Creation, p. 380).

Negotiating tactics reminiscent of Brest-Litovsk diplomacy were reactivated in this Stalinist renewal of revolutionary elan. Latter-day American and West European negotiators soon became familiar with,

—The Soviet practice of universalizing their own position in appealing to a global audience, hoping that peoples of the colonial areas, the Third World, and significant parts of the West would identify themselves with it; [5]

—The resort to the tactic of abuse and the display of open hostility and bad manners in which Gromyko and Vishinsky were proven to be masters of invective, as British Foreign Secretary Ernest Bevin said after one session of the Foreign Ministers Conference in London during December 1947: "I did not dream we would have insults and abuse inflicted on our countries in the manner we have had them this afternoon"; [6]

—The methods of obfuscation, as Craig wrote, "practiced so blatantly that they are often more insulting than some of the speeches made by Soviet negotiators"; [7]

—The tactic of calculated delays intended to exhaust the negotiating adversary, undermine his position and in other ways make him an extended target of abuse and ridicule; [8] and

—The inclination of seeking not agreement but to make a record for propaganda purposes and self-protection so necessary in a political system that was dominated by institutionalized fear. [9]

---

[5] Craig, Techniques of Negotiation. pp. 367–368.

[6] Quoted in, Craig, Techniques of Negotiation, p. 372. Craig continued: "In subsequent years Western statesmen ceased to show or feel surprise when their opposite numbers engaged in egregious assaults upon the laws of elementary courtesy and taste. In the armory of Soviet negotiating weapons bad manners had been one of the most frequently used, and it is always used coldly and with calculation, with two main purposes in mind. The first is to disconcert the other side, throw it off balance, and betray it into ill-considered statements or actions. The second is to demonstrate to peoples around the world who have real or fancied grievances against the Western powers that the Soviet Union is contemptuous of the West and is honest enough to say so publicly."

Acheson made this observation on Soviet manners: "It seems almost as though Russians going abroad went to a school of dialectics. where naturally coarse manners were made intentionally offensive. and where the students were trained in a technique of intellectual deviousness designed to frustrate any discussion." (Acheson, Sketches from Life, p. 91.) In a comment on Soviet refusal to conclude an Austrian peace treaty. Acheson remarked: "For 5 months the Soviet Union did not deign to notice our proposal, and then merely refused to discuss it. I have often wondered who convinced the foreign offices of Communist countries that bad manners were a basic requirement for the conduct of international relations. Marx or Engels? Whoever did so. it was a great pity." (Acheson. Present at the Creation, p. 634.)

[7] Craig, Techniques of Negotiation, p. 370.

[8] Roetter described this tactic as it applied to disarmament. He wrote:

"On disarmament, for instance. negotiations have been started. abandoned and restarted any number of times since 1945. and their pattern has always been the same. After an imposing opening ceremony, at which the chief Soviet delegate would voice the loftiest principles in the most general terms, the Russians would, once public interest had moved to some other event, put forward a plan which they knew to be completely unacceptable to the West. They would then leave it to the West to keep the negotiations going by putting up a series of counterplans.

"Usually the Russians would not reject those out of hand, at least to begin with. Indeed, they would never address themselves to a plan as a whole. They would take one aspect out of it, discuss and debate the point for weeks and months, and then, quite suddenly, leave the whole matter hanging in the air. ignore the fact that no conclusion had been reached, and move on to another point. frequently to repeat the same process. This would go on until the moment when, often after years of patient negotiation. there would seem to be a prospect of an agreement somewhere on the horizon and a likelihood that the Soviet Union would have to commit itself in detail on a system of effective controls.

"At that moment. the Soviet delegates would either walk out of the negotiations. accusing the other side of bad faith, or would demand that the negotiations should continue in Geneva instead of London or New York, or vice versa,. or would suggest that the negotiations would have to begin again in another body with a larger or smaller membership.

"Even conferences that begin under the most auspicious circumstances eventually become bogged down in some mysterious way and just go on and on." (Roetter, op. cit.. pp. 121–122.)

[9] Osborn made this observation with respect to the desire of Soviet negotiators to make a record when their performance was reviewed in Moscow:

"During all the discussions on atomic energy the Soviet delegates maintained a remarkably hostile attitude. It was clear that what they said was dictated to them from Moscow. and a good many of us came to the conclusion that they emphasized the hostility because

In brief, Soviet negotiating behavior became very much a form of guerrilla warfare without lethal weapons but within the respected and internationally recognized institutions and forms of diplomacy. In this spoiling environment for the much-cherished and long-evolving customs and traditions of diplomacy there could be no real basis for personal relationships let alone those on the official level among diplomats.[10]

Verbal invective, bad manners, ridicule, humiliating the adversary, calculated delays, walking out of conferences—these and more were some of the tactics Soviet diplomats employed not to further the purposes of genuine peace through negotiations but rather to nourish the revolutionary spirit and to seek its advance internationally.[11]

2. VIEWS ON SOVIET LEADERS AND PRACTITIONERS OF DIPLOMACY

(a) Bohlen on Stalin

In many respects these highly negative characterizations of Soviet behavior in diplomacy and negotiations during the cold war were reflections of the Soviet leaders themselves. Bohlen, the closest American observer of Stalin during negotiations, recorded the positive side of his personality: his affability, his "exemplary" behavior, his self-control. According to Bohlen, Stalin was "patient, a good listener, always quiet in his manner and in his expression;" "he was always polite and given to understatement." "There were no signs of the harsh and brutal nature behind this mask," he noted, "nothing of the ruth-

---

they wanted to be sure they would never be reported to the Kremlin as being lukewarm in their efforts. The verbatim records of the debate would show what they actually said; but the reports of their colleagues would give a further proof of their zeal. We have already noted Dr. Skobeltzyn's defensive harangue in Committee No. 2 when he found that the work of the committee had progressed further than he had previously realized.

"There were many other similar outbursts whose only purpose seemed to be to give the individual a strong record with which to defend himself.

"The behavior of the Soviet delegates to each other at times seemed to indicate that they were afraid of each other and of what each might say about the other. Skobeltzyn was quite evidently afraid of Gromyko." (Osborn. op. cit., pp. 229–230.)

[10] Recalling his long associations with Soviet diplomatic officials. Acheson made this observation: "Why is it that so many of us who have dealt with Russian officials find that personal recollections are pretty much restricted to anecdotes, sardonic or ridiculous, to discussions, frustrating and boring? It is, I think, because no real personal relations are possible. Either those Russians with whom we have had to deal do not dare open their minds, or those who dare have nothing in them to disclose." Acheson quoted Sir William Hayter as writing that it was not "possible to establish any kind of lasting or genuine personal relationship" with individual Russians and with "the real rulers of Russia * * * it was the distressing experience of all Ambassadors that these great men had no more to say in private than in public; the same series of gramophone records was played on every occasion; nothing emerged from these private conversations that could not just as well be gleaned from the pages of Pravda." (Acheson, Sketches from Life. p. 91.)

[11] Osborn seemed to sum up the experience of others in negotiating with the Soviets when he made these generalizations with respect to his 3 years on the U.N. Atomic Energy Commission: "Gromyko, Malik, and Skobeltzyn could all be very charming socially, and on all the many formal social occasions when they met with the other delegates seemed to take a certain pride in showing us this side of their characters. But their behavior in the meetings of the Commission was entirely different. It was stylized to the extreme. It showed careful training. Of the three men, only Skobeltzyn ever came close to a departure from it, and he was an elderly scientist who had spent much time in Paris. The few times he seemed to be making a departure from the approved Soviet style, he was quickly put back on the track by Gromyko, or by one of his aides." Osborn went on to say that "At no time did any of these men give any honest clarification of their proposals; at no time did they indicate any possibility of compromising any issue, though there were plenty of times when they made compromise proposals, patently fraudulent to the other delegates, for purposes of propaganda. At no time did they discuss the proposals of the other delegates on their merits." Osborn contrasted this behavior with the positive behavior of the Western delegates. "They were there to reach a solution to a problem : the international control of atomic energy," he wrote. "The Soviet representatives were there to make certain proposals, and to make propaganda if the proposals were not accepted." In concluding his chapter Osborn asked in conclusion : "Was this a negotiation? Certainly it was not in any ordinary sense of the term. I think that at the end of the 3 years all of us came to believe that we had not been negotiating, except among ourselves." (Osborn. op. cit.. pp. 235–236.)

lessness with which he ordered the slaughter of millions of Russians." Little in Stalin's demeanor in the presence of foreigners gave any clue to the real nature and character of the man.

"Judged by his actions," wrote Bohlen, "I believe he ranks high on the list of the world's monsters." Count Leo Tolstoy had what Bohlen termed "a moment of real prophecy" when he said of Stalin, "Imagine Genghis Khan with a telephone!" To Bohlen, Stalin gave the "impression of a man to whom pity and other human sentiments were completely alien. He was not immoral; he was simply amoral." [12]

(b) On Molotov

Rude behavior, inscrutability, secretiveness, "innately suspicious," the prototype of the impassive Soviet bureaucrat—these seem to be the common characteristic diplomatic observers have found in Molotov. At the Moscow Conference in 1943, Bohlen discovered that Molotov was "like almost all Soviet leaders a man of mystery." Though he tried to be affable, "he had a hard time smiling, and his face remained impassive throughout most of the talks." "This first close-up impression of Molotov as a careful, sober negotiator, the epitome of an intelligent Soviet bureaucrat," wrote Bohlen, "deepened the more I came in contact with him, and I had many an hour with him over the next dozen years." [13]

Molotov's ruthless diplomatic technique was clearly revealed in an encounter with Jan Masaryk, the Czech Foreign Minister, during the U.N. Conference at San Francisco in 1945. "Bohlen," asked Masaryk upon their meeting at the bar of the Fairmont Hotel, "what can one do with these Russians?" Not waiting for a reply, he continued, "Out of the clear blue sky I got a note from Molotov saying Czechoslovakia must vote for the Soviet proposition in regard to Poland, or else forfeit the friendship of the Soviet government." Masaryk paused and then asked another rhetorical question, "What kind of a way is that to behave to a country that is trying to be friendly?" Bitterly, he commented on the crude Soviet diplomatic technique: "You can be on your knees and this is not enough for the Russians." Czechoslovakia voted with Moscow on the Polish issue but the motion did not pass.[14]

Herbert L. Matthews emphasized the suspicious side of Molotov's personality. In describing his behavior at the London Foreign Ministers Conference in 1945, Matthews wrote: "He is innately suspicious. He seeks for hidden meanings and tricks where there are none. He takes it for granted that his opponents are trying to trick him and put over something nefarious." [15]

(c) Acheson on Vishinsky

To those with a memory of the cold war, Vishinsky seemed to have represented something of the composite of Soviet diplomatic characteristics. Acheson's appraisal of him was simple, direct and uncom-

---

[12] Bohlen, op. cit., pp. 338–340. Bohlen attributed much of Stalin's cruelty and ruthlessness to his Georgian ancestry: "The roots of Stalin's inhumanity can be found in his ancestry. Russians are not sadistic. They are not like the Nazis. They are too primitive for that. They are cruel, they are ruthless, but they are not inhuman, and not pathological cases. Stalin was not a Russian. He did not have a drop of Slavic blood in him. He was a Georgian, and Georgian history has been marked by vengeance, conspiracy, deceit, and cruelty, although obviously there are many fine people among them. They are mountain folk, with characteristics more like the people of the Near East than of Russia." (p. 339.)

[13] Ibid., p. 130.
[14] Ibid., p. 214.
[15] Quoted in Craig, Totalitarian Approaches to Diplomatic Negotiations, p. 12.

plimentary: "Vishinsky was a natural blackguard, but cultivated and amusing." [16] Short and slim with "quick, abrupt gestures and rapid speech," he gave the impression of "nervous tension." An outsider from the inner circle of Soviet power, he was "an instrument," as Acheson wrote, "not a source of power." [17]

Bohlen found Vishinsky "sometimes abrasive as a negotiator"; Acheson found in him serious shortcomings as a diplomat. "I was braced for a dangerous and adroit antagonist," Acheson wrote on the occasion of their first encounter at the Paris Foreign Ministers Conference in 1949, "but neither then nor later did I find him so. Instead he proved to be a long-winded and boring speaker, as so many Russians are. His debate held no surprises or subtleties; his instructions evidently left him little latitude." [18] Acheson concluded: "No, Mr. Vishinsky was not a formidable opponent. He was not equipped, as is Khrushchev, to use debate, discussion, and negotiation for their chief function in Soviet strategy." [19]

(d) On Soviet diplomats

That the personalities, style, behavior, and values of the Soviet leadership in diplomacy had a strong influence on the practitioners of diplomacy, there seemed to be little doubt, Roetter gave the following portrait of Soviet diplomats that had been recruited and trained during the Molotov era:

After the war, the world saw more products of Molotov's recruiting policy. They all seemed to be cast in the same mold. They functioned with extreme skill and precision in exact accordance with their instructions from Moscow. They hurled passionate insults one moment and exuded charm the next. They stomped out of conferences in a towering rage one day and returned a day later as if nothing had happened. Their speeches were sweetly reasonable and rudely obstructionist in turn. Their own feelings throughout these remarkable performances never showed through. They remained remote and had a few social contacts. [20] They were the utterly dedicated instruments of "an incalculable machine."

Another impressive composite portrait of the Soviet diplomat and negotiator in action was that by Osborn who wrote in describing his 3 years experience on the U.N. Atomic Energy Commission:

The Soviet representative was quite evidently under specific instructions both as to what he was to say and as to his conduct. He was at all times to question the motives of the others; he was to try to split the other nations apart from

[16] Acheson, Present at Creation, p. 34.
[17] Ibid., p. 294.
[18] Bohlen, op. cit., pp. 130–131, and Acheson, Present at Creation, p. 294.
[19] Acheson, Sketches, p. 103. Vishinsky had been the prosecuting attorney at the Soviet purge trials of the mid-1930's. "Whenever I looked into those pale eyes," wrote Bohlen who was present at those proceedings. "I saw the horrible spectacle of the prosecutor browbeating the defendants at the Bukharin trial." (Bohlen, op. cit., p. 130.) Acheson recounted an incident at the Paris Foreign Ministers Conference in which Bohlen told Vishinsky that he had first seen him "at the Bukharin trial." Bukharin had been a friend of Vishinsky's who was instrumental in his being condemned to death. Acheson wrote: "As Bohlen pronounced the name, Vishinsky turned deathly white. 'Oh,' he said, 'that was not a diplomatic job.' Then hastily getting up, he said that it was late and he must be off. From the look of him, Bukharin's ghost went home with him." (Acheson, Sketches, pp. 87–88.)
Of his meeting with Vishinsky, Murphy wrote: "Vishinsky's reputation led me to expect a steely eyed, ice-cold individual, but he proved as approachable in private relations as Bogomolov [the Russian member of the Advisory Council for Italian and Balkan affairs during the war]. His public career seemed to have nothing to do with Vishinsky personally. His manner was a Bolshevik device, put on and off like robes of office." According to Murphy, Vishinsky's strong point "was not international conferences, which are mostly talk, but undercover maneuvers." He cited Vishinsky's success in laying the foundation for Soviet policy in Western Europe and for his work in effectively organizing several satellite governments in Eastern Europe. (Murphy, op. cit., p. 211.)
[20] Roetter, op. cit., pp. 109–110.

each other, but never to conciliate the smaller nations, to whom he was always to be arrogant and truculent; he was never, under any circumstances, to concede a point except on specific instructions from the Kremlin, and then only in the exact language given him; and, finally, he was to talk as much as all the others put together, to delay, to confuse, and never to admit his true intent or to tell the truth. The representative of the satellite was under his orders, and was to repeat the same thing in much the same words but at somewhat less length, and with new variations of bitterness and accusation.[21]

3. ONE-SIDED NEGOTIATIONS: AN INVITATION TO FAILURE

(a) Osborn's appraisal of the UNAEC experience

After 3 years of frustrating negotiations with the Soviets on the U.N. Atomic Energy Commission, Osborn could rightly ask, "Was this a negotiation?" To which he replied directly and unequivocally: "Certainly it was not in any ordinary sense of the term. I think that at the end of the 3 years all of us came to believe that we had not been negotiating, except among ourselves." For Osborn the lesson of these 3 years was simply, "that the word negotiation should not be used to define meetings in which only one of the parties is actually attempting to negotiate. Such a 'negotiation' must inevitably fail, and it is not always easy to make it clear to the public who was to blame for the failure." [22]

(b) Simmons' similar experience in "negotiating" cultural exchanges

Prof. Ernest J. Simmons, the noted American authority in Russian literature at Columbia University, experienced the same frustrations in his efforts to negotiate a cultural exchange agreement. Many efforts, detailed in Simmons' chapter on negotiating with the Russians, had been made during the war and early in the postwar years to establish a program of cultural exchanges (and some scientific exchanges), but to no avail. Often no acknowledgments were made to official proposals. Only a small number of exchanges actually took place. As Simmons wrote, "the actual successes in promoting cultural relations over 1946 were gratifying but still quite meager." [23]

A long series of proposals for exchanges were subsequently communicated to Molotov by Ambassador Walter Bedell Smith in Moscow, but, as Simmons wrote, "the net results were outright rejections, evasions, or specious excuses for failure to accept these offers." [24]

Having failed at the official government level, it was decided to use private channels. Briefly, the American Council of Learned Societies invited Simmons to undertake a cultural mission to Moscow in the

---

[21] Osborn, op. cit., pp. 234–235. The extent to which Soviet diplomats had a conspiratorial cast of mind was revealed in an exchange between Gromyko and Osborn before the former returned to Moscow. Osborn and other Western delegates had concluded that the Soviets were "personally quite sincere" in their belief that the United States was run by a small group of Wall Street conspirators and that it was not just part of their propaganda line. "Government by conspiracy was the only kind of government they could imagine," he wrote. "They knew nothing else. Such an attitude would, of itself, make them difficult to deal with." On the occasion of Gromyko's return to Moscow, Osborn sought him out in the lounge and asked if they could go over atomic energy matters before his departure. Osborn noted that they had worked together for 3 years; that he was sincere in his desire to seek a solution; and that he also felt that Gromyko also believed in his sincerity. Osborn thought that he would be able to give Gromyko a better idea of the U.S. Government's position in such a private talk than in the public debates of the Commission. Gromyko looked quietly at Osborn for a moment and then said, "Mr. Osborn, you may be sincere, but governments are never sincere." The talk never took place. (p. 230.)
[22] Ibid., pp. 235–236.
[23] Simmons, Ernest J. Negotiating on Cultural Exchange, 1947, in, Dennett and Johnson, op. cit., ch. 9, p. 251.
[24] Ibid., p. 252.

winter of 1947 for the purpose of negotiating exchanges on a wide-range of cultural and educational matters. He went in July 1947, at the time of the formulation of the new Zhdanov cultural policy "line" that corresponded to the "hard" aggressive line being carried out domestically and internationally. Criticism of the West had already begun to surface in August 1946, but it was not until the summer of 1947 that, in Simmons' words, "the violent condemnation of virtually everything Western and particularly American broke out in all its fury." [25]

The Simmons mission was a failure; there was really nothing to negotiate. In American parlance he was given "the run around" by Soviet cultural authorities and only when Ambassador Smith intervened was he able to see not Vishinsky as requested but Vice-Minister of Foreign Affairs Y. A. Malik. The results were predictable: A one-sided negotiation, wholly negative. There were in fact no real negotiations, only proposals from the U.S. side which the Soviet Foreign Ministry acknowledged receiving and indicating that they were being forwarded to the proper Soviet organization for study.

Thus, writing in 1951 when the cold war was perhaps at its worst, Simmons concluded:

Obviously, there can be no further hope of negotiating cultural relations with the Soviet Union for the time being. A thin façade of relations will be maintained by the Soviets for the understandable purpose of obtaining the vast quantities of American printed matter and information which they very much want through library exchanges and their official agents here, a situation in which we are at a great disadvantage in our efforts to procure similar Soviet materials. And in any possible future development of a free interchange of ideas, peoples and cultures, there will always be the obstacle of Soviet fear of standing comparison with American achievements. At any rate, such a future development will be possible only when the Soviet Government becomes convinced that it will be in their own interests to achieve it. If such a time ever comes, they will make it abundantly clear, and then there will be no great difficulty in negotiating cultural exchanges with the Soviet Union.[26]

(c) Acheson's diagnosis of the problem

One-sided negotiations appeared to be a general characteristic of Soviet diplomacy in the cold war. Failure was, therefore, preordained, for it is elementary that for any successful negotiation there must be first and foremost a will to negotiate and the beginning must be in the minds of the negotiators.

Acheson understood this first rule of negotiations and so expressed it early in 1950. He explained that in the Western tradition "negotiation was bargaining to achieve a mutually desired agreement;" in the Communist, "it was war by political means to achieve an end unacceptable to the other side." In both cases, "it was a means to an end, but in the latter case the ends were, if understood, mutually exclusive." Acheson explained further that he had found that "the most useful negotiation was by acts rather than words, and stability was better and more reliable than verbal agreement." Four years of trial, he noted, "had convinced us that agreement with the Kremlin was not then possible." The reason, he inferred, was the absence of a positive will on the Soviet side. There were those, he said, who believed that good will and negotiation would solve all problems if only President

<hr />

[25] Ibid., p. 268.
[26] Ibid., p. 269.

Truman and Stalin would "get their feet under the same table" and that they could iron out any and all international difficulties. But Acheson's response was: "The problem lay not in where the leaders' feet were but where their minds were. We had tried most earnestly to get Kremlin minds running toward cooperation and failed."[27]

4. LEITES ON SOVIET BEHAVIOR: FEAR FOR SECURITY

Osborn attributed the behavior of the Soviet negotiator to a number of possible sources: Ignorance; "a very real and deep seated suspicion of his foreign 'adversaries' (the Soviet delegates always acted like men who were being conspired against);" "his own fears and sense of inferiority;" or it may have been "a studied behavior taught him in the Communist schools for diplomats."[27a] But Nathan Leites, an American social scientist, attributed it to a single cause, fear for security.

In an extensive study on the "spirit of Bolshevism," Leites attempted to analyze the behavior of the Soviet elite as revealed through Bolshevik writings since its early beginnings.[28] He elaborated on the central point of the Bolshevik fear of annihilation and their resort to the tactic of "a generally offensive posture" as a way of concealing their own vulnerabilities. "By reinforcing its verbal attack on the threatening enemy," he wrote, "the party heightens the enemy's estimate of its strength and determination, and weakens the enemy's own 'mass basis.' " With this concept in mind, Leites gave the following explanation of Soviet behavior in the cold war:

> Thus the Politburo believed after the end of the second war that a new crisis was beginning to develop: In some form or other the unified enemy would at some future date take the offensive against the Soviet Union. There was not much that the Politburo felt it could do to modify this course of events. But at least the Party leadership—transforming passivity into activity, as it likes to do—could conduct a preventive counter-offensive in the sphere of words and other symbols against the enemy who was as yet merely preparing his more devastating attacks and who had perhaps not yet decided on their timing and details. By appearing brazen when it was deeply apprehensive, the Politburo could attempt to impress upon the enemy that it expected these attacks and was ready to meet them. From the Politburo's verbal aggressiveness the enemy was supposed to conclude—as the Party would, in the inverse case—that if he proceeded to war, he would encounter full and effective resistance. Having been induced to overestimate Soviet strength—did the Politburo not have to be strong to be as aggressive as it was?—he might be deterred from undertaking an all-out attack at a moment when it would lead, the Politburo feared, to its retreat or collapse. If the Politburo was not certain that these favorable effects would occur, it was confident that it had little to lose on adopting the posture which I described.[29]

Leites went on to explain that negotiation for the Soviets was a form of political warfare intended "to decrease the chances of the party being annihilated, to increase the chances of its annihilating its enemies." Stalemate of the struggle produced conditions for an effective agreement which he defined as "the result of overt conflict pursued up to the very last moment." It compelled the enemy to substitute negotiation for war, whether hot or cold. Leites continued:

> The struggle by negotiation, in its turn, proceeds in the same fashion: The exertion of pressure on each other by both sides—including the threat to break

[27] Acheson, Present at Creation, pp. 378–379.
[27a] Osborn, op. cit., 238.
[28] Leites, Nathan C. A Study of Bolshevism. Glencoe, Ill., Free Press, 1953. 639 pp. See particularly, "Prologue: The Politburo and the West." Also, Leites, Nathan C. The Operational Code of the Politburo. Rand Corporation. New York, McGraw-Hill, 1951, 100 pp.
[29] Leites, Bolshevism, pp. 37–38.

off negotiations and actual rupture—is apt to foster the conclusion of an agreement. The more pressure one has exercised not only before, but also during the negotiations, the more favorable will the final agreement be. At any point it is the "sharpening" of conflict which is likely to increase the chance of a favorable settlement. If the issue is important—and which is not, directly or indirectly?—the conflict is likely to be protracted.[30]

Excerpts from Leites' analysis suggest his perception of some aspects of the Soviet approach to negotiations during the cold war:
—"They strive to push to the limits of their strength, using verbal assault as one of their means and trying hard and long for all objectives, whether big or small"; [31]
—"They fiercely resist anything which seems to be a concession unless a condition of duress requires them to retreat—then, perhaps, quite substantially"; [32]
—"The Soviet delegates elaborate or change their position in strict isolation and then present it in dogmatic fashion. They rarely take account of the views and objections of the other side, and frequently affirm and repeat points which the other side (they know) as well as they themselves regard as grossly false, without bothering to furnish evidence"; [33] and
—"Bolsheviks * * * react against the temptation to believe that enemies can be persuaded by appeals to their morality or their real interests, and their enmity thus reduced." [34]

Though Leites' work bears the impress of the cold war era (he was a member of Rand Corp., the U.S. Air Force "think tank," which sponsored his study), its value today appears to lay at three levels; as a pioneering work in behavioral studies; in its influence in the American community of scholars and policymakers during the 1950's; and, for the purposes of this study, in relating aggressive Soviet behavior in diplomacy and negotiations not to strength but rather to Soviet weakness, vulnerability, and an abiding sense of insecurity.

B. IN THE VORTEX OF THE COLD WAR: SMITH AND KENNAN IN MOSCOW

1. WALTER BEDELL SMITH, SOLDIER AND DIPLOMAT

(a) Dominating presence of the cold war

Scholars such as Leites had to draw mainly upon written Soviet sources for their analyses of the Soviet Union in the cold war, but practitioners of diplomacy like Ambassadors Walter Bedell Smith (1946–1949) and George F. Kennan (1952), caught in the vortex of the cold war at its source, could give a unique and authentic account from their perspective in Moscow.

Diplomatic life in Moscow during the cold war was perhaps not much different from that described by Harriman in giving his first wartime impression: It was "grim" and "about as close to prison as anything outside bars." [35] Briefly, Ambassador Smith's memoirs, "My Three Years in Moscow," reflect the dominating presence of the cold war.[36] In his mind the Soviet leaders had made a deliberate choice" at

[30] Ibid., p. 60.
[31] Ibid., p. 60.
[32] Ibid., p. 61.
[33] Ibid.
[34] Ibid.
[35] Harriman and Abel, op. cit., p. 95.
[36] Smith, Walter Bedell. My Three Years in Moscow. Philadelphia, Lippincott, 1950, 346 pp.

the end of World War II to resume the struggle against capitalism
and its foremost leader, the United States. This decision that contrasted sharply with the expectations of the American people but
not their Soviet specialists produced a world divided into two hostile
camps just as Lenin and Stalin had long predicted. Smith, whose
tenure had coincided with the Berlin blockade of 1948–49, was
witnessing Marxist-Leninist predestination being carried out in
reality.[37]

Under these conditions the normal functions of the diplomat were
most difficult if not impossible to perform. At his first audience with
Stalin in early 1946, during the emerging crises in Iran and Turkey,
Smith probed deeply Soviet intentions and goals. "How far is Russia
going to go?" he asked. Stalin replied, "We're not going much further," and then proceeded to explain the Soviet demand for a base
in the Dardanelles as "a matter of our security."[38] Though Stalin
pledged his ready assistance to Smith in carrying out his duties as
Ambassador—"I am at your disposal at anytime," Smith conferred
less than "a score of times, and to talk at length to Stalin only four
times" during his 3-years tenure. Still, these encounters—"four
lengthy talks and one or two brief social meetings"—were more than
any other Western diplomat had.[39]

Contacts with Molotov were apparently more frequent, for the
Soviet Foreign Minister never refused Smith a prompt audience on
request.[40] But the relationship was hardly friendly and took on the
uniform hostility that was de rigueur during the cold war.[41] Molotov's
personality was "unattractive", and though "always correct and
courteous," he was "repellingly colorless" and seemed always ill at
ease in the presence of foreigners. In dealing with foreign representatives, he was "systematically aggressive, stubborn, and unyielding." At times in conferences he seemed "deliberately to bait
and irritate his opponents." His criticism of the United States in
party statements, according to Smith, were "particularly sarcastic
and bitter," and "his stubbornness in negotiations justifies his party
name (Molot means 'hammer'—his real name is Skriabin)."[42]

[37] For Smith's perception of the cold war, see his memoirs, pp. 309, 316–17. With respect
to the American expectations, Smith explained their hopes that collaboration established
during the wartime conferences could be continued and cordial relations expanded. In contrast, Russian specialists in the State Department, he said, "felt that the Soviet Union,
owing to its peculiar structure and the political philosophy which motivated it, was almost
incapable of collaborating with other governments in the manner which Americans have in
mind. * * * These officials were of the opinion that the Soviet Union had no intention of
permitting anything like the number of personal contacts between the two peoples which
would be required to lead to a broad basis of confidence and collaboration." (p. 30.).
[38] Ibid., pp. 53–54.
[39] Ibid., pp. 53–55. Smith made the now familiar observations about Stalin : "* * * Stalin
is not by any means the unattractive personality which some writers have depicted. Indeed,
he has genuine charm when he chooses to exercise it" (p. 59) ; "The most attractive feature
of Stalin's face is his fine dark eyes, which light up when he is interested. They did not
impress me either as 'gentle,' as one observer thought, or 'cold as steel,' as others have
remarked, but they are alert, expressive, and intelligent. His manner is calm, slow, and
self-assured, and when he wishes to warm up during a conversation he seems at times
actually benign. There is no question but that he can be brutally abrupt. * * *" (p. 60) :
a Georgian, not a Russian, he was, "courageous but cautious ; suspicious, revengeful and
quick to anger, but coldly ruthless and pitilessly realistic ; decisive and swift in the execution of his plans when the objective is clear, but patient, deceptive and Fabian in his
tactics when the situation is obscure. * * * he is, as one of my most experienced officers
put it, 'like a true Georgian hero—a great and good friend or an implacable dangerous
enemy. It is difficult for him to be anything in between.' " (pp. 62–63.)
[40] Ibid., pp. 41–43.
[41] For Smith's observations on the inability of Soviet officials to be "a free agent in terms
of Western individualism," see his memoirs, p. 109.
[42] Ibid., p. 73.

Smith's view of Vishinsky, who was the Soviet Foreign Office's overseer of American affairs, conformed generally to those of other Americans. As Chief of Staff to General Eisenhower during World War II, Smith had first met Vishinsky at a meeting of the Mediterranean Commission. Vishinsky could be charming, Smith recalled, and had a "lively sense of humor," but Smith soon found out as they got down to business that Vishinsky's "outstanding characteristic is a brusque truculence." [43]

(b) Soviet obsession with security

The cold war exacerbated the traditional Soviet obsession with security; Ambassador Smith could hardly escape this reality. In recalling the flight from Berlin to Moscow to assume his post, he observed from the air, with the eye of a General in the U.S. Army, part of "the vast plain, completely lacking in major geographical obstacles and exposed to invasion from every direction." In light of history, the General continued, "it was easy * * * to understand why the government of the Soviet Union was so preoccupied with providing security against invasion, and why it was so intent upon constructing a security belt around its borders through a chain of buffer states." [44] As he explained, "Russia has suffered severely from the lack of natural defense frontiers to protect her from the incursions of hostile people upon her borders," and depending on the tactic of "defense in depth" to wear out the enemy. Russia "has had a tendency to push out her frontiers as far as possible whenever she has been in a position to do so." [45]

Smith believed that the chief causes for the excessive concern of the Soviet leadership for security was "directly or indirectly connected with the fear of war—foreign or civil." This fear, he suggested, was heightened by three factors; namely, (1) an awareness of Soviet vulnerability and a fear of defeat in a major war when they had "no margin of safety"; (2) by fear of a preemptive strike to crush the Soviet Union, should the outside world know "Russia's weakness and her ultimate objective"; and (3) the conviction that "the capitalist world was implacably hostile to the Soviet Union." [46]

Thus Smith's exposure to the Soviet environment convinced him that behind Russian policy for centuries had lain "the age-old sense of insecurity of an agricultural people reared on an exposed plain in the neighborhood of fierce, nomadic tribes." And with this in mind he asked these rhetorical questions:

Would this sense of insecurity now become a permanent feature of Russian psychology? Would their psychology provide the basis for successful expansion of the new areas to the East and West? And, if initially successful, would it know where to stop? Might it not be inexorably carried forward, by its very nature, in a struggle to reach the whole—to attain complete mastery of the shores of the Atlantic and the Pacific? [47]

---

[43] Ibid., p. 17.
[44] Ibid., p. 37.
[45] Ibid., pp. 311–312. Smith quoted Lord Palmerston who said a century ago in relating Russian security to expansionism: "It has always been the policy and practice of the Russian Government to expand its frontiers as rapidly as the apathy or timidity of neighboring states would permit, but usually to halt and frequently to recoil when confronted by determined opposition; then to await the next favorable opportunity to spring upon its intended victim."
[46] Ibid., p. 312.
[47] Ibid., p. 30.

For Smith, the Soviet obsession with security explained other extraordinary aspects of their behavior which inevitably influenced Soviet diplomacy and the quality of their negotiations:

—The excessive concern for secrecy as shown in the constant surveillance of foreigners and in other manifestations of suspicion; [48]

—The isolation of the Soviet people from all foreigners, including limitations on contacts between foreign and Soviet officials; [49] and,

—The institutionalized fear existing within the Soviet bureaucracy that created a reluctance to assume responsibility and induced excessive caution in dealing with foreigners.[50]

(c) Prospects for the future

"The general outlook is one of friction, disputes, recrimination and tension"—such was the estimate of Ambassador Smith upon his departure from Moscow.[51] A combination of historic Russian expansionism and ideological conviction of fulfilling the goals of Communism were the driving force behind Soviet policy.[52] The danger of war, accepted by the Soviets as inevitable, continued to exist even though the Soviet leadership pursued a policy of seeking goals without great risk and seemed to expect peace "for several years." [53] Fear of imminent war for the past 3 years was "deliberately fostered" by the Soviet Government for three reasons: "To impede the economic recovery of the West, to spur the Soviet people to greater industrial effort, and to hide present Soviet weaknesses." [54] The best assurance of peace, Smith believed, was the "strength and determination to support our convictions, and our strength must exist and be apparent. * * *" [55]

In this cold war environment negotiations and diplomacy could serve little purpose beyond limiting the damage to the relationship caused by confrontations and crises as in the Berlin blockade.

2. KENNAN IN ISOLATION

(a) Lower depths of the cold war

Kennan's tour as Ambassador in Moscow during 1952 coincided with the darkest days of the cold war. In the spring, Communist

---

[48] American ambassadors, for example, were always under constant surveillance when they left the Embassy.
[49] Smith wrote: "We were completely cut off from the great bulk of the Russian people by constant police surveillance, by propaganda and by the fear of punishment." (p. 98) ; "On the Ambassadorial level, our professional contacts with top Russian officials was limited to not more than two or three a month, on the average. Socially, we saw them even less frequently." (p. 99) ; "I now realize that any Soviet and most Communist officials are immune to feelings of personal liking or gratitude toward any individual foreigner, and indeed would receive immediate and severe disciplinary punishment if they betrayed such feelings" (p. 109).
[50] Smith wrote: "* * * we all shared in common * * * the same difficult problems of attempting to do business with a vast bureaucratic machine, where all policy emanated from the Kremlin and where a subordinate official, or even a cabinet minister, found it safer—both professionally and personally—not to give the slightest indication of his reaction or possible action until the most precise orders had been received *in writing* from the men at the top of this monolithic structure." Smith recounted an incident when a memorandum on "a routine unimportant matter" was sent from the Foreign Office to the Embassy by mistake. It bore the penciled notations of half a dozen Foreign Office officials increasing importance with "an official OK" at the bottom signed by Vishinsky (pp. 108–109).
[51] Ibid., p. 326.
[52] Ibid., pp. 309–314.
[53] Ibid., pp. 326–27 and 307–08.
[54] Ibid., pp. 307–308.
[55] Ibid., p. 329.

propaganda attacks against the United States reached new heights with charges of bacteriological warfare in Korea. A "new crescendo" with added themes of atrocities was reached, Kennan noted, soon after his arrival and continued through the summer.[56] He referred to the "chorus of vituperation, directed against the United States, which for sheer viciousness and intensity has no parallel, so far as I know, in this history of international relations. The wartime anti-Allied propaganda of Joseph Goebbels paled, as I can testify, beside it." [57] So serious had become the state of relations that by the autumn of 1952 Kennan accepted war as "inevitable, or very nearly so—that the only alternative to it lay in the collapse of our political position in Europe," and he further lamented that he would have to return to Moscow and "live through further weeks and months of exposure to foul, malicious, and insulting propaganda * * *." [58]

As Ambassador, Kennan lived virtually in total isolation, referring in his memoirs to the Spaso House as "my gilded prison" and to his "miserable months" in Moscow.[59] He presented his credentials on May 14, 1952 without instructions for the Soviet Government so low had relations degenerated.[60] He never had an audience with Stalin, not wishing to suffer the same humiliation of his British colleague, Sir Alvary Douglass Frederick Gascoigne, who at that time had been waiting several months in vain for a reply to his own request for such meeting.[61] And only seldom did he have occasion to visit the Soviet Foreign Office; when he did, the various officials were correct and reserved, but the response to inquiries into political matters was predictable, making such visits unsatisfying. Hence the Embassy staff was left to derive their impressions of Soviet attitudes from the official press and other media.[62]

The isolation of Kennan, aggravating in itself, was further aggravated by continuous surveillance, eavesdropping, the terrorization of the Soviet staff at the Embassy (Kennan referred to the servants as being "wholly terrorized"),[63] the cutting off of social contacts with

---

[56] Kennan, Memoirs, vol. 2, pp. 122–123.
[57] Ibid., p. 122.
[58] Ibid., p. 162.
[59] Ibid., pp. 116 and 168.
[60] Ibid., pp. 119–120.
[61] Kennan acknowledged that his failure to do so may have been a mistake, but he noted, "God knows what impression was produced by it on the aging and semi-mad dictator." (Ibid., p. 122.) In an earlier characterization of Stalin, Kennan wrote: "The teeth were discolored, the mustache scrawny, coarse, and streaked. This, together with the pocked face and yellow eyes, gave him the aspect of an old battle-scarred tiger. In manner—with us, at least—he was simple, quite, unassuming. There was no striving for effect. His words were few. They generally sounded reasonable and sensible; indeed, they often were. An unforewarned visitor would never have guessed what depths of calculation, ambition, love of power, jealously, cruelty, and sly vindictiveness lurked behind this unpretentious facade." Kennan noted that "Stalin's greatness as a dissimulator was an integral part of his greatness as a statesman. * * * He possessed unbelievably acute powers of observation and, when it suited his purposes, imitation. * * * By the same token he was, of course, a great, if terrible (in part: great because terrible), teacher of politics. Most impressive of all was his immense, diabolical skill as a tactician. The modern age has known no greater master of the tactical art. The unassuming, quiet facade, as innocently disarming as the first move of the grand master at chess, was only a part of this brilliant, terrifying tactical mastery. * * * When I first encountered him personally, I had already lived long enough in Russia to know something about him; and I was never in doubt, when visiting him, that I was in the presence of one of the world's most remarkable men—a man great, if you will, primarily in his iniquity; ruthless, cynical, cunning, endlessly dangerous; but for all of this—one of the truly great men of the age." (Memoirs, vol. 1, pp. 279–280.)
For a good example of what can be achieved in a personal exchange between an ambassador and a Head of State, see Kennan's final interview with Tito at the end of his term as Ambassador to Yugoslavia, Memoirs, vol. 2, pp. 310–311.
[62] Ibid., p. 122.
[63] Ibid., p. 11.

Soviet officials, and numerous other indignities and repressive measures that in all "tell on the nerves," as Kennan wrote, and generally made life difficult and diplomacy impossible.[64] For Kennan the "last straw" came when a Soviet guard at the Embassy would not permit little Soviet children to play a child's game with his son through the fence that surrounded the Embassy grounds. As Kennan wrote:

It was a small episode, but it came at the end of a difficult and nerve-wracking summer. And something gave way, at that point, with the patience I was able to observe in the face of this entire vicious, timid, medieval regime of isolation to which the official foreigner in Moscow was still subjected. Had I been the perfect ambassador it would not, I suppose, have given way. But give way it did; and it could not soon be restored.[65]

Subsequently, while in Berlin, Kennan was asked at a press conference whether the Embassy staff had many social contacts in Moscow. An annoyed Kennan responded, "Well I was interned here in Germany for several months during the last war. The treatment we received in Moscow is just about like the treatment we internees received then, except that in Moscow we are at liberty to go out and walk the streets under guard." [66] For this remark Kennan was declared persona non grata.

(b) Soviet "congenital sense of insecurity"

At this time Kennan was perhaps the most knowledgable and articulate American diplomat and specialist in Soviet affairs. His dispatch of February 1946, hailed by Acheson as "truly remarkable" and referred to above, had an impact upon official American thought and upon public opinion as a whole (through his "X" article) as perhaps few other documents in the history of American diplomacy.[67]

An idea central to Kennan's thought expressed in this dispatch and elsewhere on Soviet aggressive behavior in the early stages of the cold war was the traditional Russian obsession with security. In this telegraphic dispatch, he elaborated on this theme which is important not only as an analytical concept but also for the purposes of this study in explaining Soviet negotiating behavior.

"At the bottom of the Kremlin's neurotic view of world affairs," Kennan wrote in 1946, "is traditional and instinctive Russian sense of insecurity." This insecurity had its historical origins in "a peaceful agricultural people trying to live on vast exposed plain in neighborhood of fierce nomadic peoples." Added to this uncertain historical undergrowth of insecurity was "fear of more competent, more powerful, more highly organized societies in that area" when Russia came into contact with the economically advanced West. This latter type of insecurity afflicted the Russian rulers rather than the people; for "Russian rulers have invariably sensed that their rule was relatively archaic in form, fragile and artificial in its psychological foundation, unable to stand comparison for contact with political systems of Western countries." For this reason, Kennan continued:

They have always feared foreign penetration, feared direct contact between Western world and their own, feared what would happen if Russians learned the truth about world without or if foreigners learned truth about world within. And they have learned to seek security only in patient but deadly struggle for total destruction rival power, never in compacts and compromise with it.[68]

---

[64] Ibid., pp. 119 and 145–152.
[65] Ibid., pp. 157–158.
[66] Ibid., p. 159.
[67] Acheson, Present at Creation, p. 151.
[68] Kennan, Memoirs, vol. 1, pp. 549–550.

In another long dispatch of September 1952 from Moscow on the Soviet Union and NATO, less known and less influential, Kennan reemphasized the same idea of insecurity—"their congenital sense of insecurity," he termed it, in the context of a rationale for maintaining large ground forces. Kennan explained that Russian insistence on the excessively large ground forces was a tradition in both the Soviet and Tsarist Governments. It was practiced again in the 1920's and 1930's when Russian ground forces were superior numerically until German rearmament. The prompt reversion to the same pattern after World War II, Kennan noted, was "the resumption of a practice which seemed quite normal to Soviet leaders." And he went on to explain, linking the traditional desire for large ground forces with the deeply embedded historic feeling of insecurity:

If one looks at the psychological basis of this practice one finds a welter of considerations and explanations. For various reasons, Russian forces have generally appeared—have often, in fact, been deliberately caused to appear—more formidable to outsiders, particularly from the standpoint of possible offensive employment, than they appeared to their masters within Russia. Russian political leaders have usually operated against a background of uncertainty and anxiety with respect to domestic political and economic conditions which heightened their congenital sense of insecurity and caused them to wish for a larger margin of numerical safety in armed strength than would be thought necessary elsewhere. The maintenance of land armies in Russia has generally been cheap financially, and has had certain domestic political advantages insofar as it kept a good portion of the young male population in a regimented and controlled status. Finally, the Soviet leaders, interested in extending their real power by measures short of general war, have not been oblivious to the possibilities of such things as threats and intimidation—the possibilities of the use of the shadow of armed strength rather than its substance—as a means of influencing the political behavior of people elsewhere. In the wake of World War II, the maintenance of large land forces (with the number of divisions somewhat inflated by their relatively small size) served this purpose excellently, particularly in the face of the extreme nervousness of the war-shocked and terrorized populations of Western Europe.[60]

What is significant about this analysis is that the seminal idea is an historic one; namely, Russian obession with the idea of insecurity. Other aspects of motivation and behavior spring from this seed.

(c) *Diplomacy, negotiations, and the cold war: Paradox of Soviet purposes*

While not denying the genuineness of the Russian obsession with insecurity, still it is paradoxical that objectively their behavior produced the very conditions that in reality deepened rather than lessened their insecurity. For Stalin rejected the only real instrumentalities of peace, that is to say, diplomacy and negotiations. "In the real sense," wrote Kennan in his dispatch of September 1952, on the Soviet Union and NATO, "the Soviet leaders have broken diplomatic relations with the Western world." Existence of diplomatic missions in Moscow and theirs in Western capitals did not alter this fact. "The Western missions in Moscow," he went on, "have been isolated as completely and effectively as though they were on enemy territory in wartime." Diplomatic missions ceased to be used by the Soviets "as vehicles for any real exchange of views with the Western governments." "The fact remains," Kennan noted, "that during these past years diplomatic relations in the normal and traditional sense, which existed between the Soviet Union and the Western powers on a partial scale and in an im-

⁶⁰ Kennan, Memoirs, vol. 2, p. 331.

perfect form in the twenties and thirties as well as during World War II, ceased entirely to exist." What this meant, Kennan noted, was that "There is no longer the usual diplomatic cushion between impact and reaction" in the Soviet Union and the West to military events and impulses. Possibilities did not exist to explain in a normal way the meaning of individual moves or to know if they produced serious misunderstanding in the Soviet mind. "If these last should provoke countermoves actually dangerous to peace," he warned, "there is little the diplomat can do to prevent deterioration of the situation." And in the absence of diplomatic influence, the Western powers would be unable "to bring pressure to bear on the Soviet Government by any means other than the demonstration of a readiness to go to war over a given issue." [70]

Kennan's was a plea for diplomacy and negotiations, for what he was describing in brief was that Soviet behavior in the cold war had removed that "cushion of safety" that diplomacy and negotiations provided. As he concluded, with this evolving international condition an "added and unique delicacy" was given to all questions of military preparations especially those relating to the territories of third countries, "for in the absence of any diplomatic language such moves, and the reactions to them become in themselves a form of communication between the two camps, and one replete with opportunities for misunderstanding." [71]

[70] Kennan, Memoirs, vol. 2, pp. 344–345.
[71] Ibid. Kennan felt that for specific domestic reasons the Soviet leaders "had no desire, at the close of World War II, to become involved in another major foreign war for the foreseeable future, and this—in terms of Soviet policy determination—meant anything up to 15 or 20 years" (p. 328). By 1952, however, Kennan seemed to grow apprehensive that serious misunderstandings could lead to war though the Soviets did not necessarily seek it. As he wrote, "In the threat that unquestionably hovered over the peoples of Western Europe, and of which they had now become extensively conscious, the accent simply did not lie on the prospect of open aggression by the Red Army: it lay on the continuation of sharp political pressure by a variety of much more subtle and insidious devices" (p. 335).

III. SOVIET NEGOTIATING TECHNIQUES

A. Commentary by Mosely, Scholar and Negotiator

1. Mosely's Credentials as Observer of Soviet Negotiations

Diplomacy and negotiations may have reached their nadir during the cold war, but efforts were made by scholars, diplomats and other American officials who had negotiated with the Soviets to record their experiences and offer some suggestions for coping with Soviet negotiating behavior. The Dennett-Johnson compendium, published in 1951 under the sponsorship of the World Peace Foundation and entitled "Negotiating With the Russians," was the most prominent and comprehensive effort. A major theme in the work was the value of negotiations, even though little in the way of positive results could be expected in dealing with the Russians. Nonetheless, for thoughtful Americans, the editors wrote, these experiences conveyed "both a lesson and a warning." [1]

Perhaps one of the best commentaries on this subject was included in this volume and that was the chapter by Professor Philip E. Mosely entitled, "Some Soviet Techniques of Negotiations." A renowned Russian specialist and pioneer in this field of study, Mosely was professor of International Relations at Columbia University and director of its Russian Institute. From 1942 to 1946, he served in the State Department in various capacities including that of adviser to the U.S. Delegation at the Moscow Conference of 1943, and political adviser to the U.S. Delegation on the European Advisory Commission, 1944–1945, at the Potsdam Conference of 1945 and at the meetings of the Council of Foreign Ministers at London and Paris in 1945 and 1946. In addition, he was the U.S. representative on the Commission for the investigation of the Yugoslav-Italian boundary in 1946. [2]

Thus, Mosely brought to this commentary a wealth of negotiating experience with the Russians combined with impressive credentials as a teacher and scholar in Russian studies.

2. A Summary of Observations Drawn from Experience

(a) *Soviet negotiator, "a mechanical mouthpiece" for Moscow*

In summing up Mosely's personal observations on Soviet negotiating behavior during and immediately after the war, a few characteristics stand out. Perhaps the most prominent is that the Soviet diplomat could hardly be called a "negotiator" in the traditional sense. He was rather, as Mosely noted, "a mechanical mouthpiece for views and demands formulated in Moscow." Unlike the Western diplomat who acts as the channel for exchanging ideas and information between his

---

[1] Dennett and Johnson, op. cit., p. xi.
[2] Mosely, Some Soviet Techniques of Negotiations, p. 270.

government and the one to which he is accredited, the Soviet diplomat was "deliberately isolated from the impact of views, interests, and sentiments which influence foreign governments and peoples." Through fear of being accused of "falling captive to imperialist and cosmopolitan influences," the Soviet diplomat served "as a block to the transmission of foreign views and sentiments, rather than as a channel for communicating them to his government." [3]

Hence, Mosely's Soviet negotiator was a thoroughly disciplined functionary deeply committed to the Bolshevik ideology and as such was an inflexible advocate for his government, not a searcher for common ground among negotiating adversaries. Unlike his Western counterpart, he was not schooled in the techniques of what Mosely termed "continuous negotiations," a procedure where negotiating staffs would be divided into "working groups" and informally through mutual exploration of positions and instructions seek out areas of flexibility for eventual agreement at the higher level.[4] No such organizational device existed; no such individual flexibility was possible in this monolithic operation of Soviet diplomacy.

(b) Bound to rigid instructions

As a first principle of negotiations, the Soviet negotiator was inflexibly bound to rigid instructions from his mentors in Moscow, and no changes, even in the nuance of language, could be made without Moscow's direction. Consequently, as Mosely noted, "each point at issue, large or small, then becomes a test of will and nerves." Rather than seeking to reduce points of difference, the Soviet negotiator often appeared to take pride in "finding the maximum number of disputes and in dwelling on each of them to the full." [5] Owing to this strict control from the center, dilatory tactics were often not exercises in intended frustration but rather the only tactic possible in the absence of instructions from Moscow.[6]

(c) "Treasuring of grievances" and the "head-against-stone-wall" technique

Another tactic that Soviet negotiators resorted to was what Mosely called the "treasuring of grievances" and the "head-against-stonewall" technique. The former was intended to cover up the Soviet's own aggressive behavior by piling on grievances, real or imaginary, against the negotiating adversary usually amid disconcerting ripostes and accusations of bad faith.[7] In employing the latter technique the Soviet negotiator would persistently pursue points, no matter how minor, with a fierce determination, and when deadlock was reached, he would shift to the next item and pursue it again to deadlock.[8] It could not be determined whether the number or duration of these attempts were prescribed by instructions or whether the individual negotiator was to decide, as Mosely said, "when he has built up a sufficiently impressive and protective record of having beat his head against a stone wall." [9]

---

[3] Ibid., p. 272.
[4] Ibid., p. 275.
[5] Ibid., p. 281.
[6] Mosely cited the example of his negotiating experience on setting up the European Inland Transport Organization. See, pp. 278–281.
[7] Ibid., p. 282.
[8] Ibid., p. 285.
[9] Ibid., p. 285.

(d) Pitfall: Reaching "agreement in principle"

This fixation to detail and persistency in pursuit of negotiating goals opened up one of the main pitfalls for the Americans and British during the wartime negotiations; namely, the tendency to accept "agreement in principle." Impatient and frustrated Western negotiators, strung out by the long, strenuous debates with the Soviets and, as Mosely noted, "studded with charges, accusations and suspicions," found great relief in this generality which on the surface could pass for agreement. As a result, they sometimes gained the "principle" of their hopes, as Mosely put it, but only found out later that "in practice" the Soviets continued to pursue their original aims.[10] (Recall General Deane's experience.)

(e) Compromise anathema to the Soviet negotiator

Strict adherence to instructions radically limited the range of flexibility in negotiations; it also reinforced the Soviet revulsion against compromise. Soviet negotiators were extremely apprehensive about recommending to Moscow a change in instructions fearful that such requests would open them to the charge of "falling captive to imperialist insinuations." Consequently, he was unwilling to take initiatives in seeking reasonable meeting grounds for conflicting viewpoints.[11] For compromise in the Western sense was foreign to the Bolshevik mentality. As Mosely explained:

One of the difficulties of Soviet-Russian vocabularly is that the word "compromise" is not of native origin and carries with it no favorable empathy. It is habitually used only in combination with the adjective "putrid." "Compromise for the sake of getting on with the job" is natural to American and British people, but it is alien to the Bolshevist way of thinking and to the discipline which the Communist Party has striven to inculcate in its members. To give up a demand once presented, even a very minor or formalistic point, makes a Bolshevik-trained negotiator feel that he is losing control of his own will and is becoming subject to an alien will. Therefore any point which has finally to be abandoned must be given up only after a most terrific struggle. The Soviet negotiator must first prove to himself and his superiors that he is up against an immovable force. Only then is he justified in abandoning a point which plainly cannot be gained and in moving on to the next item, which will again be debated in an equally bitter tug-of-wills.[12]

Similarly foreign to the mentality of the Soviet negotiator was the Western concept of a quid pro quo and "good will" as lubricants in the negotiating process. (Recall Harriman's warning that one cannot "bank goodwill" with the Soviets.) Mosely explained:

The Soviet negotiator takes a minor concession as a sign that his principles are stronger and his will is firmer than those of his opponent. He does not believe in "good will." He is trained to assume the ill-will of the "capitalist environment." If an "imperialist" negotiator asserts his will for peace, it means at best, that he is consciously in favor of peace but is unconsciously a tool of

---

[10] Ibid., p. 289.
[11] Ibid., p. 292. From February to July 1946, the writer was on the Secretariat of the Far Eastern Commission, an international body ostensibly intended to establish policy for the occupation of Japan. As a secretary on the Committee on the Disarmament of Japan, I took notes at a subcommittee meeting of two delegates, one a Soviet admiral. The Executive Secretary of the Secretariat also attended. The purpose of the meeting was to resolve a disagreement over some aspect of the policy document then under consideration. At one point in the discussion the admiral suggested a compromise solution which was acceptable to the other delegate, but he insisted that it be recorded as coming from the other delegate. A most good-natured Georgian who resembled the Russian-American actor Akim Tamiroff, the Admiral smiled and ran his finger across his throat as he made this proposal. The meaning was clear, though nothing more was said.
[12] Ibid., p. 295.

uncontrollable forces which work for war and for the final clash between "two worlds." At the worst, it means that he is trying to deceive and gain time while mouthing words of "peace." To a Bolshevik even a momentary "loss of vigilance" may have fatal consequences. The Soviet diplomat feels himself like a traveler by night in the forest who must be constantly on the watch for the smallest sound or sight of treachery. He must be unceasingly on guard against his own human tendency to "fall into complacency" and thus to underestimate the dangers which surround both him and the regime which he serves.[13]

3. ADVICE IN NEGOTIATING WITH THE SOVIETS

(a) Determine the Soviet negotiating position

"A grim picture," Mosely called his portrait of the Soviet negotiator who he summed up as a person "tight as a spring, deeply suspicious, always trying to exert the Soviet will-power outward and to avoid reflecting non-Soviet facts and aspirations inward, a rigid agent knowing only the segment of policy which he must carry out with mechanical precision." Acknowledging that negotiations under such conditions were "a very limited affair and very difficult and unrewarding," they were, nonetheless, "both possible and essential." [14]

But such negotiations required a special approach. Knowledge of the language with its Soviet nuances was important. Equally important was an understanding of the role of the Soviet negotiator in relation to his government and its ideology. With this beginning, Mosely instructed, the negotiator should "determine whether the Soviet negotiators have no instructions, have definite instructions, or merely have instructions to build up a propaganda position." Soviet intentions were much more fathomable, he noted, in the original language without the handicap of "the opaque veil of translation." In addition, Mosely continued, the negotiator "should review each document exchanged or each statement made in the light of its clear rendering into Russian." The purpose here was to understand the exact meanings being conveyed in both languages.[15]

(b) Establish a "single clear position"

Next it was important to establish at the beginning of a negotiation, in Mosely's words, "a single clear position, one which can be upheld logically and politically during long discussions." Not until that position had been tested by verbal assaults from all sides would it be reported to Moscow by the Soviet delegation. The American negotiator could expect an "indefinite repetition of arguments" as an inevitable preparation to negotiate. Ordinarily, he would make a single presentation and then become impatient when the Soviet representative expressed misunderstanding or disbelief. Not believing what he had heard, the Soviet negotiator "listens for undertones of firmness or uncertainty which tell him whether or not he is shaking the determination of his adversary." According to Mosely, an effective response to this technique was "strong but controlled feeling, rather than impatience or anger." [16]

Once firmly established, a position should be put in writing in a special memorandum rendered in clear idiomatic translation to make sure of its accuracy when reported to Moscow, the source of any new

---

[13] Ibid., p. 296.
[14] Ibid., p. 297.
[15] Ibid., pp. 297–298.
[16] Ibid., p. 298.

instructions. Unlike oral statements, which might not be transmitted, it was probable that written ones would be. Again, Mosely stressed the importance of avoiding ambiguity in translation even to the point of rephrasing the English to accommodate the inflexibility of the Russian to a literal rendering of a concept or phrase in English.[17]

(c) Uphold position "in detail, and for a long time"; avoid constant modifications

When a position had been firmly established, Mosely continued, the non-Soviet negotiator "must be prepared to uphold it in detail, and for a long time." The Soviet negotiator would be confused by the technique, effective in the Western style of negotiations, of trying out variations on proposals; he would suspect some new trick at each new variant and subject each to exhaustive interpretation. Constant modification of a position or in the manner of presentation placed the Soviet negotiator at a loss to determine which was solidly based and accordingly should be reported to Moscow. Even slight shifts in position or wording, Mosely cautioned, would increase "his belief that the adversary's position is a shaky one and thus encourage him to hold out that much longer for the full Soviet position." While Western negotiators usually could accept minor adaptations, Soviet negotiators had to report back to Moscow the slightest variation for decision.[18]

Nor did the Soviet negotiator have the latitude of his Western counterpart who generally could comment at once on new proposals or statements. He would always be free to raise innumerable objections and criticisms but not to concur in any part without instructions from Moscow. Even "program statements," Mosely noted, had to be reviewed or written in Moscow before delivery, making such Soviet presentations at conferences often seem unrelated to the current flow of discussion.[19]

Mosely also cautioned against pressing the Soviet delegate to commit himself to a new proposal or draft once a negotiation was actually underway. When a redraft or new proposal was first presented before the European Advisory Commission, he would attempt to clarify its meaning and implications through questions and take the initiative in saying that he would consult with his government. This procedure relieved the Soviet delegate of either declining to comment or building up a series of negative statements against it.[20]

When under instructions on a new point at issue, Mosely would also on occasion confer with his Soviet counterpart, providing details of the American position. When an agreement seemed apparent, this procedure often proved effective, or seemed to, in reducing the number of divergences by giving Moscow the full background of the problem before it had taken a position which could later be modified, Mosely noted, "only by a long and exhausting tug-of-wills." Such informal talks in Russian often provided Mosely an occasion to learn or sense often unforeseen Soviet objections and suspicions and attempt to eliminate or alleviate them at an early stage.[21]

(d) State position "in terms of a definite material interest"

Mosely cautioned against the use of general or broadly stated principles, noting that when used as an essential part of the position to

---

[17] Ibid., p. 299.
[18] Ibid., p. 299.
[19] Ibid.
[20] Ibid., p. 300.
[21] Ibid., p. 300.

remember they were not shared by the Soviet side. Nonetheless, such principled statements, anchored in the historic experience of one's people and explained in that context, could have a certain impact on Soviet thinking and make policymakers accept them as fact and take them into account, though disbelieving and not sharing them.[22]

Thus, Mosely urged that wherever possible "it is more useful to state one's position in terms of a definite material interest * * *." "Soviet-trained negotiators," he explained, "pride themselves on identifying material interests and can therefore more readily visualize them as facts to which a certain adjustment can be made." [23]

A case in point, Mosely continued, was the repatriation of POW's as World War II was coming to an end. Soviet fulfillment of the agreement fell far short of American expectations, as explained in chapter IV. The source of the problem was differing perceptions of POW's and the care they deserved. Mosely suggested that had American authorities based their case on grounds that the imprisoned soldiers and airmen were needed immediately in the war against Japan, the Soviets probably would have been more cooperative in caring for and returning them to the West. Because, as Mosely reasoned, "they would have been impressed by the direct material interest involved." [24]

4. A ROLE FOR NEGOTIATIONS IN THE COLD WAR

Mosely acknowledged that wartime negotiations were "extremely difficult and frustrating" and that none of the agreements on postwar cooperation worked out as hoped—"even against hope." He also acknowledged that in a period of Soviet expansion and intentions of further expansion, negotiations "could have only the purpose of confusing and dividing the nations which opposed its pressure." And he recognized that since the war the Soviet purpose in negotiations was not to reach agreement with strong opponents but "to intimate weaker and adjacent countries and to undermine the stamina of its principal potential adversaries." Mosely further acknowledged the American inclination of reluctantly thinking of the possibility of war in times of peace and ignoring the political goals of peace in times of war. In contrast, the Soviets, whose Leninist-Stalinist thinking was suffused with the theory of Clausewitz (war is a continuation of politics by other means), made no such distinction—the "struggle" continues under both conditions.[25]

Still, Mosely did not rule out a role for negotiations in the cold war. He pleaded the case for a Western policy of building "positions of strength" and using negotiations, both going "hand in hand." Negotiable issues were admittedly held in abeyance, but

the art of policy will be to recognize, from a position of strength, future potentialities of negotiation, not with an expectation of bringing about a lasting or worldwide relaxation of Soviet ambitions, but as a means of alleviating individual sources of tension and thus of strengthening the free world. And if negotiation must go in harness with consistent and purposeful building of strength, the art and technique of international dealings must also be broadened to take full account of the peculiar character of the Soviet approach to negotiation.[26]

---

[22] Ibid., p. 300.
[23] Ibid.
[24] Ibid., p. 301.
[25] Ibid., pp. 301–302.
[26] Ibid., pp. 302–303.

B. Kennan's Rules of Behavior

1. IMPOSSIBIILITY OF CLOSE FRIENDSHIPS

Like Mosely, Kennan also contemplated the matter of Soviet behavior. Though he did not have Mosely's extensive practical experience in negotiating with the Soviets, still he understood the Russian national character and recorded in his private papers what he terms "a useful set of rules for dealing with the Stalin regime." [27] Some of these rules, written during the winter of 1946 in a direct informal style without extended elaboration, relate to various suggested approaches in dealing with the Soviets.

"Don't act chummy with them"—this was Kennan's first rule. To do so "only embarrasses them individually, and deepens their suspicions." "Russian officials," he continued, "abhor the thought of appearing before their own people as one who has become buddies with a foreigner. This is not their idea of good relations." [28]

2. CONFLICTING "COMMUNITY OF AIMS"

"Don't assume a community of aims with them which does not really exist"—the second rule. Kennan advised against trying "to swing Russians into line" by references to common purposes such as strengthening world peace or democracy to which both had given "lip service." Both purposes were in conflict, he said: "For them it's all a game. And when we try to come at them with arguments based on such common professions, they become doubly wary." [29]

3. GOOD WILL GESTURES AS CAUSE OF "PERPLEXITY AND SUSPICION"

"Don't make fatuous gestures of good will"—the third rule. "Few of us have any idea," Kennan explained, "how much perplexity and suspicion has been caused in the Soviet mind by gestures and concessions granted by well-meaning Americans" who sought to convince the Soviets of their frendship. Such gestures of good will "upset all their calculations and throw them way off balance." Kennan elaborated:

> They immediately begin to expect that they have overestimated our strength, that they have been remiss in their obligations to the Soviet state, that they should have been demanding more from us all along. Frequently, this has exactly the opposite effect from that which we are seeking. [30]

4. ON MAKING REQUESTS AND SHOWING DISPLEASURE ON REJECTION

"Make no requests of the Russians unless we are prepared to make them feel our displeasure in a practical way in case the request is not

---

[27] Kennan, Memoirs, vol. 1, p. 291.
[28] Ibid.
[29] Ibid.
[30] Ambassador Smith observed that "any Soviet and most Communist officials are immune to feelings of personal liking or gratitude toward any individual foreigner, and indeed would receive immediate and severe disciplinary punishment if they betrayed such feelings." This is the source of the statement by many Americans that one cannot "bank goodwill" with the Russians. Smith related an incident concerning General Marshall—the "only plaintive note" he had ever heard from him. It was a wire from China complaining that on an important question of Japanese repatriation he had received no reply to his repeated inquiries directed to Soviet Ambassador Petrov, "in spite of having loaned him a jeep." Smith concluded: "At the time, it was somewhat comforting to realize that Soviet practice was no respecter of persons, and was applied as rigidly to our most distinguished representative abroad as it was to me." (Smith, op. cit., pp. 109–110.)

granted"—the fourth rule. Such an approach required "imagination, firmness, and coordination of policy." Should these qualities be absent in U.S. foreign affairs, then "we should begin to prepare for serious trouble." [31]

5. ON DEALING WITH THE SOVIET BUREAUCRACY

"Take up matters on a normal level and insist that Russians take full responsibility for their actions on that level"—Kennan's fifth rule. Failing to achieve satisfaction for requests at the lower level should not be cause to resort to the higher levels. Such procedures "merely encourage the Russian bureaucracy to be uncooperative and cause our relations with high-level Soviet authorities to be encumbered with matters of second-rate importance." Kennan stated that "retaliatory or corrective action" should be taken "promptly and unhesitatingly" when satisfaction was not obtained on the lower level. "It is only in this way," he noted, "that we can teach the Russians to respect the whole range of our officials who must deal with them." Failure to support subordinate U.S. officials made it difficult to accomplish anything in the intervals between high-level meetings. "This works in the interests of the Russians and prejudices our interests," he said, and went to the heart of many American failures in the last 2 or 3 years. According to Kennan,

> The top level is physically incapable of encompassing the whole range of our dealings with the Soviet Government and of assuring the collaboration which we are seeking. Agreements reached there can be—and frequently are—sabotaged successfully and with * * * [impunity] on the lower levels. We must train the Russians to make their whole machine, not just Stalin, respond sensibly to our approaches.[32]

6. ON INITIATIVES FOR HIGH LEVEL CONFERENCES

"Do not encourage high-level exchanges of views with the Russians unless the initiative comes at least 50 percent from their side"—the sixth rule. According to Kennan, "Russians can be dealt with satisfactorily only when they themselves want something and feel themselves in a dependent position." Only when these conditions prevailed, he said, should the United States deal with them on a high level.[33]

7. ON THE VALUE OF OVERKILL

"Do not be afraid to use heavy weapons for what seem to us to be minor matters." For Kennan this seventh rule was "very important" but one that many Americans would receive with skepticism. While in general it might be bad practice "to take a sledgehammer to swat a fly," it was sometimes necessary in dealing with the Russians. Kennan explained:

> Russians will pursue a flexible policy of piecemeal presumption and encroachment on other people's interests, hoping that no single action will appear important enough to produce a strong reaction on the part of their opponents, and that in this way they may gradually bring about a major improvement in their position before the other fellow knows what's up. In this way, they have a

[31] Kennan, Memoirs, vol. 1, p. 562.
[32] Ibid., pp. 562–563.
[33] Ibid., p. 563.

stubborn tendency to push every question right up to what they believe to be the breaking point of the patience of those with whom they deal. If they know that their opponent means business, that the line of his patience is firmly established and that he will not hestitate to take serious measures if this line is violated even in small ways and at isolated points, they will be careful and considerate.

According to Kennan, the Soviets disliked a showdown unless they had "a great preponderance of strength." But they were "quick to sense and take advantage of indecision or good-natured tolerance." Thus Kennan cautioned, "Whoever deals with them must therefore be sure to maintain at all times an attitude of decisiveness and alertness in defense of his own interests." [34]

8. ON THE VALUE OF BEING UNPLEASANT

"Do not be afraid of unpleasantness and public airing of differences"—the eighth rule. According to Kennan, the Russians "don't mind scenes and scandals. Were they to discover that someone else (a negotiating adversary, for example) did mind and would go out of his way to avoid them, "they will use this as a form of blackmail in the belief that they can profit from the other fellow's squeamishness."

Kennan advised that if the United States was to reestablish its prestige with the Soviet Government and gain respect in Russia, it had to be prepared to undertake a "taming of the shrew" which was "bound to involve a good deal of unpleasantness." No need to fear, he said, that occasional hard words would have a permanent bad effect on relations. "The Russian is never more agreeable than after his knuckles have been sharply rapped," Kennan declared, adding, "He takes well to rough play and rarely holds grudges over it." And he cited the case of Stalin's first reaction when he met Nazi Foreign Minister Ribbentrop: "It was to joke good-naturedly and cynically about the bitter propaganda war which had been waged for so many years between the two countries."

Kennan concluded with this aphorism: "The Russian governing class respects only the strong. To them, shyness is a form of weakness." [35]

9. OTHER INSIGHTS, OTHER INSTRUCTIONS FOR THE NEGOTIATOR

(a) *Their value: Durability and relevance*

Other insights and lessons with respect to Soviet behavior that could be instructive to the negotiator can be found in Kennan's memoirs. While some of these observations and commentaries, like the rules above, were written during the cold war, still they seem to contain a certain durable wisdom that makes them relevant today. The first relates to the impact of Russian history on Soviet behavior in diplomacy; the second, to calculations of Soviet interests; the third, to power and its connection with Soviet behavior; the fourth to the Soviet attitude toward agreements; and the fifth, to a response to a Soviet negotiating initiative in times of extreme American adversity.

(b) *Impact of history on Russian behavior in diplomacy*

Historically, the foreign affairs of Russia have developed along lines entirely different from those of the United States. Our most important foreign relations, historically speaking, have been along the lines of peaceable overseas trade.

---

[34] Ibid., p. 563.
[35] Ibid., pp. 563–564.

These have set the pattern of our thinking on foreign affairs. The Russians, throughout their history, have dealt principally with fierce hostile neighbors. Lacking natural geographical barriers, they have had to develop, in order to deal with these neighbors, a peculiar technique (now become traditional and almost automatic) of elastic advance and retreat, of defense in depth, of secretiveness, of wariness, of deceit. Their history has known many armistices between hostile forces; but it has never known an example of the permanent peaceful coexistence of two neighboring states with established borders accepted without question by both peoples. The Russians therefore have no conception of permanent friendly relations between states. For them, all foreigners are potential enemies. The technique of Russian diplomacy, like that of the Orient in general, is concentrated on impressing an adversary with the terrifying strength of Russian power, while keeping him uncertain and confused as to the exact channels and means of its application and thus inducing him to treat all Russian wishes and views with particular respect and consideration. It has nothing to do with the cultivation of friendly relations as we conceive them.[36]

(c) *On calculations of Soviet interests*

* * * Everyone in the Soviet Government must assume that foreign governments act only in their own interests, and that gratitude and appreciation are unknown qualities in foreign affairs.

In this way, the machinery by which Soviet foreign affairs are conducted is capable of recognizing, and reacting to, only considerations of concrete Soviet interest. No one can argue any proposition in the councils of the Soviet Government unless he can show concretely how the interests of the Soviet Union stand to gain if it is accepted or to suffer if it is rejected. This principle is applied with the most serene objectivity. In examining a position taken by a foreign state, the Russians make no effort to look at it from the standpoint of the foreign state in question or from any fancied community of aims on the part of themselves and the state involved. They assume it is dictated by purposes which are not theirs, and they examine it only from the standpoint of its effect on them. If the effect is favorable, they accept it without gratitude; if it is unfavorable, they reject it without resentment. We could make it much easier for them and for ourselves if we would face these facts.[37]

(d) *Power and Soviet behavior*

I have no hesitation in saying quite categorically, in the light of some 11 years' experience with Russian matters, that it would be highly dangerous to our security if the Russians were to develop the use of atomic energy, or any other radical and far-reaching means of destruction, along lines of which we were unaware and against which we might be defenseless if taken by surprise. There is nothing—I repeat nothing—in the history of the Soviet regime which could justify us in assuming that the men who are now in power in Russia, or even those who have chances of assuming power within the foreseeable future, would hesitate for a moment to apply this power against us if by doing so they thought that they would materially improve their own power position in the world. This holds true regardless of the process by which the Soviet Government might obtain the knowledge of the use of such forces, i.e., whether by its own scientific and inventive efforts, by espionage, or by such knowledge being imparted to them as a gesture of good will and confidence. To assume that Soviet leaders would be restrained by scruples of gratitude or humanitarianism would be to fly in the face of overwhelming contrary evidence on a matter vital to the future of our country.[38]

(e) *On the Soviet attitude toward agreements*

For the Russians, and for Stalin in particular, there were agreements and agreements, just as there were negotiations and negotiations. Highly specific agreements, relating to military dispositions and control over territory, were more likely to be respected by them than vague subscriptions to high moral principles. Agreements founded in an obvious and concrete Soviet interest of a political and military nature were more likely to be respected than ones based on an

---

[36] "The United States and Russia," (Winter 1946), Kennan, Memoirs, vol. 1, p. 560.
[37] Ibid., p. 561.
[38] Dispatch of Sept. 30, 1945, Kennan, Memoirs, vol. 1, pp. 296–297. Kennan explained: the tenor of the dispatch "was strictly negative, the reflection only of an anxiety lest this matter be handled on the basis of the same effort to curry favor with the Stalin regime that seemed to me to have inspired our other policies up to that time."

appeal to international legal norms or to the decisions of multilateral international bodies. Agreements negotiated quietly and privately, representing realistic political understandings rather than public contractual obligations, were more apt to be respected by Moscow, so long as the other party also respected them, than were agreements arrived at in negotiations conducted in the public eye (the Russians called these *demonstrativnye* negotiations) where the aim was, or appeared to be, to put the other party in a bad light before world public opinion.[39]

(f) *Response to Soviet negotiating initiative in times of extreme American adversity*

Any approach to the Russians simply asking for an immediate cease-fire in Korea and not connected with any political agreements about the future of Korea or other Far Eastern problems would probably be taken by the Kremlin leaders as a bid for peace by us on whatever terms we can get.

They would regard this as confirmation that we were faced with the alternative of capitulation, on the one hand, or complete rout and military disaster on the other. In such a situation their main concern would be to see that the maximum advantage, in terms of damage to our prestige and to non-Communist unity, should be extracted from our plight. This being the case, they would see no reason to spare us any of the humiliation of military disaster. They would not be interested in promoting a cease-fire unless it were on terms at least as damaging to our prestige as a continuation of military operations might be expected to be. * * *

The present moment is probably the poorest one we have known at any time in the history of our relations with the Soviet Union for negotiations with its leaders. * * * The prerequisite to any satisfactory negotiation about the local situation in Korea is the demonstration that we have the capability to stabilize the front somewhere in the peninsula and to engage a large number of Communist forces for a long time. If we are unable to do this, I see not the faintest reason why the Russians should wish to aid us in our predicament. * * * Any approach we make to them without some solid cards in our hand, in the form of some means of pressure on them to arrive at an agreement in their own interests, may simply be exploited by them for the purposes of spotlighting our weakness and improving their own position in the eyes of other peoples. * * *

The prerequisite to any successful negotiation on political subjects would be a posture of unity, confidence and collected strength on our side.[40]

---

[39] Kennan, Memoirs, vol. 2, pp. 50–51.
[40] Kennan Memorandum to Acheson, Dec. 3, 1950, Kennan, Memoirs, vol. 2, pp. 28–29. The occasion for this memorandum, prepared by Kennan with the assistance of long-time colleagues in the State Department, was the near collapse of the U.S. military effort in Korea after the intervention by Chinese military forces in November–December 1950. Withdrawal of American forces from the Korean Peninsula was being suggested by some officials at this extreme moment of crisis in the face of what then seemed to be imminent disaster. Kennan, who was on leave at Princeton, was called to Washington for consultation. "What was wanted from me," Kennan wrote, "was an opinion as to the prospects for direct negotiations with the Russians, as a possible escape from our military embarrassment." This memorandum, four pages, single-spaced and "of the bleakest and most uncomforting prose that the department's files can ever have accommodated," Kennan wrote, was his response.

IV. SIGNIFICANT NEGOTIATING ENCOUNTERS

A. Negotiations by Semaphore: Lifting the Berlin Blockade, 1949

1. SOVIET PURPOSES IN BERLIN CRISIS OF 1948–49

(a) Some successful negotiations: FEC and Nuremberg trials

Early in the cold war some negotiations with the Soviets were successful, mainly because they had little or no leverage to apply or they shared common negotiating goals with the other side. The former was the case in reorganizing the Far Eastern Advisory Commission (later named the Far Eastern Commission) ostensibly to provide for Soviet participation in this policymaking machinery for the occupation of Japan. Only by U.S. sufferance, but under great Soviet pressure, were provisions finally made to give the Soviets at best a nominal role.[1] The latter case concerned the Nuremberg trials. The wartime allies shared the common goal of punishing the Nazi war criminals. Their problem, therefore, was not one of ends but of means; namely, to accommodate through negotiations the contrasting forms and traditions of Anglo-American common law with the continental based Russian law. This was successfully done.[2]

But these successful negotiations were exceptions, for negotiations became virtually impossible as the impact of the cold war produced and uncompromising spirit of hostility and alienation between East and West.

(b) Berlin, the ultimate threat

The Soviet offensive in the cold war reached its outer limits in Europe during the late 1940's with the Berlin blockade between June 1948 through the spring of 1949. The West perceived the blockade as a direct threat to its security and an ultimate test of policy and national nerve. Beset by serious foreign policy failures (e.g., Tito's defection) and concerned by the countervailing measures taken by the West in West Germany as East-West relations worsened, Stalin was determined, in President Harry S. Truman's words, "to get us out of Berlin."[3]

In brief, Berlin became the fulcrum, then and in subsequent crises, for Soviet efforts to change the balance of power in Germany and thus in Europe by unilaterally reducing the Western role in violation of its legal rights, by imposing its own diktat, and by neutralizing a demoralized Germany as a power factor in Europe. As Truman wrote, "What was at stake in Berlin was not a contest over legal rights, although our position was entirely sound in international law, but a struggle over Germany and, in a larger sense, over Europe."[4]

---

[1] Blakeslee, George H. Negotiating to Establish the Far Eastern Commission, 1945, in Dennett and Johnson, op. cit., ch. 5.
[2] Alderman, Sidney S. Negotiating on War Crimes Prosecutions, 1945, in, Dennett and Johnson, op. cit., ch. 3.
[3] Truman, Harry S. Memoirs. Garden City, N.Y., Doubleday, 1956, vol. 2, p. 122.
[4] Ibid., p. 123.

The ostensible Soviet reason for the blockade was allied currency reform in West Germany, but Stalin's real purposes were far more serious and impinged directly on Western security interests.

Efforts to negotiate a settlement through the remainder of 1948 proved unsuccessful as the Soviet leadership seemed confident that the Berlin airlift, taken as a countermeasure to insure Berlin's survival, would fail and allied policy in Germany collapse amid spreading demoralization. It became clear to Ambassador Smith after a series of discussions with Stalin and Molotov that the Soviet price for lifting the blockade, never addressed directly but through the veiled issue of currency reform, was a reversal of Western policy in West Germany.[5] This policy was designed to counter Soviet unilateral policy in Eastern Germany by establishing a separate German Government in the Western zones of occupation.[6] In the United Nations, Vishinsky vetoed a resolution in October 1948 proposed by six neutralist nations to lift the Soviet blockade and allied counterblockade and call upon military commanders to meet and set up currency controls.[7]

In this environment of threat and blackmail negotiations had no chance to succeed. Stalin's destructive purposes were clear. Thus, during June 1948 through the spring of 1949 Berlin became the dominant issue in international relations.[8] So serious was the impact of this issue on East-West relations that observers close to the scene, such as Gen. Lucius D. Clay, the U.S. commander in Berlin, and Ambassador Smith in Moscow, reported growing alarm over the Soviet threat to Berlin and a deepening war psychosis within the Soviet leadership. The fear of war, a World War III, brought on by some untoward incident in Berlin, became a source of great concern.[9] So grim was the U.S. perception of the threat that General Clay, with Murphy's support, even recommended that the blockade be challenged with an armed convoy, a recommendation that was turned down by Washington.[10] The risks of war were high; this was the feeling in the West.

2. AN EXCHANGE OF SIGNALS

(a) Stalin's interview by Kingsbury Smith

With formal diplomatic relations for all practical purposes severed (Smith had left for home in the latter part of 1948), prospects seemed

---

[5] Smith, op. cit., pp. 252–253.
[6] Stebbins, Richard P., et al. The United States in World Affairs, 1949. Published for the Council on Foreign Relations. New York, Harper, 1950, pp. 8–9.
[7] Bohlen, op. cit., p. 282.
[8] United States in World Affairs, 1949, pp. 8–9.
[9] Ibid., pp. 8–9. See also, Clay, Lucius D. Decision in Germany. Garden City, N.Y., Doubleday, 1950, p. 345. In the weeks prior to imposing the blockade, Clay reported to his superiors in Washington an intuitive feeling of the impending change in Soviet policy. Allies of the United States were concerned about the risk of war. While conferring with British Foreign Secretary Bevin in London, Bohlen recorded that he told him, "I know all of you Americans want a war, but I'm not going to let you have it." He spoke in a "semijocular fashion," Bohlen noted, "but still put a good deal of conviction in his statement." The French Ambassador Rene Massigli also expressed fear that hasty American action would precipitate a war." (Bohlen, op. cit., p. 279.) At the United Nations Australian Foreign Minister Herbert Evatt told Dr. Philip Jessup, the U.S. Deputy Representative at the United Nations, in Bohlen's presence, "So you want to start another war, do you? Well, we're not going to let you do it." (Ibid., p. 282.) And Smith observed, presumably in 1949: "At present, beyond question, there appears to exist a war psychosis among Soviet leaders. The constant and violent charges with which they assail the West are simply a manifestation of the Communist characteristic of loudly accusing others of the acts which they themselves are committing, or intend to commit." (Smith, op. cit., p. 305.)
[10] Clay, op. cit., p. 374, and Murphy, op. cit., pp. 316–317.

dim for negotiating a settlement on Berlin. However, negotiations were initiated after an exchange of signals betweeen Moscow and Washington in what might be termed "negotiations by semaphore."

Early in 1949, observers noted several signs of a Soviet peace offensive. For example, the Soviet Government lifted restrictions on the entry of foreign correspondents into the Soviet Union. It was speculated that the Soviet signals might have been designed to test the validity of press commentary that General Marshall's resignation and Acheson's appointment as Secretary of State signified a new "soft" line by the second-term Truman administration.[11]

Whatever the motivation, the Soviets sent their subtlest, perhaps most cryptic, signal on January 30, 1949, a week after Acheson took office. In January, Kingsbury Smith, an American correspondent and European director of the Hearst's International News Service, had submitted a series of questions to Stalin, one of which pertained to Berlin. This was a common practice: Sometimes Stalin responded, if it were to his advantage; more often he ignored them. Smith asked:

Third Question: If the Governments of the United States of America, the United Kingdom and France agree to postpone the establishment of a separate West German state until the convocation of a session of the Council of Foreign Ministers devoted to the examination of the German problem as a whole, would the Government of the USSR be prepared to remove the restrictions introduced by the Soviet authorities on communications between Berlin and the Western zones of Germany?

On January 30, Stalin replied:

Reply: If the United States of America, Great Britain and France observe the conditions stipulated in the third question, the Soviet Government sees no obstacle to a removal of transport restrictions provided, however, that the transport and trade restrictions introduced by the three powers are removed simultaneously.[12]

(b) Acheson's response: Signal to use private channel

The Stalin-Smith interview caused a sensation in the press. Bohlen, who was then a special assistant to the Secretary, had been on the lookout for any signal from Moscow. He perceived in Stalin's reply on the Berlin question an important omission: There was no reference to the currency reform issue, ostensibly the cause of the Soviet blockade in the first place. A quick consultation with Acheson and the Berlin group of specialists led to the conclusion that this was, in Acheson's words, a "cautious signal." To this group the signal meant that Stalin was ready to lift the blockade, but for a price. Further sounding had to be made to determine what that price was. For Acheson, abandonment of tripartite plans for unifying the three zones of Germany was clearly too high a price to pay.[13]

With the President's approval Acheson proposed to signal back to Moscow, as he said, "through a bland and relaxed press conference" that the message was received and then to follow through with a secret inquiry into the Soviet negotiating terms. On February 2, 1949, at a regular press conference Acheson gave a carefully studied reply to the questions raised in the Stalin-Smith interview. With reference to Stalin's specific response to the inquiry on Berlin, Acheson signaled

[11] Smith, Gaddis. Dean Acheson. New York, Cooper Square, 1972, pp. 83–84. (Series: The American Secretaries of State and Their Diplomacy.)
[12] U.S. Foreign Relations, 1949, vol. 5, Eastern Europe and the Soviet Union, p. 562.
[13] Bohlen, op. cit., pp. 203–204, and Acheson, Present at Creation, p. 267.

the U.S. message: "There are many ways in which a serious proposal by the Soviet Government * * * could be made. * * * I hope you [the press] will not take it amiss if I point out that if I on my part were seeking to give assurance of seriousness of purpose I would choose some other channel than the channel of a press interview." [14]

Acheson had two purposes in this approach: To play down Stalin's interview, as he said, in order to avoid any "premature hardening" of the Soviet position; and to signal Stalin that if he wanted serious discussions, he should use a more private channel. Acheson avoided comment on press inquiries with respect to the absence of any mention of the currency reform on grounds of being speculative. [15]

3. JESSUP-MALIK SECRET MEETING AT THE U.N.

(a) *Initial contact, February 15, 1949*

As intended, Acheson's press conference remarks dampened public speculation about the Stalin-Smith interview and soon Stalin's cryptic overture was forgotten in the press. [16] For U.S. policymakers the central question was the Soviet leader's intention in omitting the reference to the currency reform as a condition for lifting the blockade. The task of finding out fell to Dr. Philip C. Jessup, the Deputy American Representative to the U.N. Security Council.

The utmost secrecy surrounded Acheson's next move. Jessup conferred personally in Washington with the Secretary and Bohlen, then the State Department's Counselor, rather than telephoning, telegraphing, or writing. They concluded that a highly secret, casual approach to the Russians could be made by Jessup at the U.N. rather than through the U.S. Embassy in Moscow or by the State Department through the Soviet Embassy in Washington. Acheson reasoned that the fewer the persons involved the better and that Jessup and his Soviet counterpart at the U.N. Jacob Malik (he had just replaced Vishinsky) could act in purely personal and unofficial capacities. [17]

On February 15, 1949, Jessup waited for Malik near the entrance to the delegate's lounge at the temporary U.N. headquarters at Lake Success (and not, as other accounts have reported, in the men's room). [18] After remarks about the weather, the following conversation took place.

"By the way," said Jessup casually, "I have been interested in the omission of any reference to the currency question in Stalin's reply to the inquiry from Kingsbury Smith, and we wondered if there was any significance to it."

"I have no information on that," Malik responded.

"If you do get any information, I would be interested," Jessup said. Then the two diplomats walked into the Security Council for a routine meeting. [19]

(b) *Subsequent negotiations and agreement, May 4, 1949*

For a month the Soviet Government remained silent, and then on March 15, Malik requested a meeting with Jessup at the Soviet dele-

[14] Ibid., p. 268.
[15] Ibid., p. 269.
[16] Smith, Dean Acheson, pp. 85–86.
[17] Acheson, Present at Creation, p. 269.
[18] Bohlen, op. cit., p. 284.
[19] Smith, Dean Acheson, p. 86.

gation's headquarters in New York. There, Malik informed Jessup that the omission of the currency matter in the Stalin-Smith interview was "not accidental," that the matter was important and could be discussed at a meeting of the Council of Foreign Ministers if it could be arranged. In response to Jessup's probing, Malik pledged to make further inquiry to determine whether the blockade would be lifted before the CFM meeting or would be a question for discussion at the meeting. On March 21, Malik informed Jessup that, "If a definite date could be set for the meeting of the Council of Foreign Ministers, the restrictions on trade and transportation in Berlin could be lifted reciprocally and the lifting of the blockade could take place in advance of the meeting." [20]

As Gaddis Smith, Acheson's biographer, observed, "Here was a genuine Soviet concession. The tide was now running fast in favor of the West." [21] To which it could be added that Stalin's gambit in Berlin had clearly become counterproductive. In the weeks ahead other Jessup-Malik meetings took place to work out the final details of an agreement. There was much jockeying back and forth until final agreement was reached. All of this secret diplomacy took place against a background of great and significant diplomatic activity: The North Atlantic Treaty was signed on April 4; the movement toward establishing a West German Government continued apace; and Acheson conferred with Bevin and French Foreign Minister Robert Schuman to fill them in on the secret negotiations with Malik. Through it all, the Allied position remained firm and clear; there was to be no conditional agreement on lifting the blockade.

Failing to arrest the movement toward greater West German independence, one of the Soviet's primary objectives, Stalin acquiesced, and agreement was finally reached on May 4. On the following day, a four-power communique was issued, announcing that the blockade and counterblockade would be lifted on May 12, 1949 and that on May 23, a meeting of the CFM would be convened in Paris where questions relating to Germany and problems arising out of the Berlin issue, including the currency matter, would be considered. [22] Nothing was said about suspending the movement toward establishing a West German Government, the first major step in the direction of integrating West Germany into the West European Community.

4. COUNCIL OF FOREIGN MINISTERS CONFIRM JESSUP-MALIK AGREEMENT

As agreed, the Council of Foreign Ministers, established at the Potsdam Conference with offices and staff in London, met in Paris on May 23, 1949, and, as Acheson wrote, "wearily" ended its deliberations on June 20, never to meet again. [23] The Conference accomplished little more than to formally liquidate the Berlin blockade. [24] Discussions on Germany's future revealed only profound differences between East and West and on the Soviet side particularly confusion and ambiguity respecting future policy in Germany. [25] Some progress was

---

[20] Ibid., p. 87.
[21] Ibid., p. 88.
[22] Acheson, Present at Creation, p. 274.
[22] Ibid., p. 300.
[24] Bohlen. op. cit., p. 286.
[25] United States in World Affairs, 1949, pp. 38–41.

made on an Austrian peace treaty, an occasion for a serious breach of imposed Soviet bureaucratic discipline by Vishinsky.[26] But as Acheson told President Truman upon returning from Paris, "I don't think we really accomplished too much." [27]

This was not the case with respect to Berlin, however; for the Conference had accomplished a great deal. Amid renewed Soviet threats of traffic restrictions vigorously countered by the Western negotiators, the Conference, as the communique recorded, confirmed in general the Jessup-Malik agreement lifting the blockade and counterblockade. It also advised the occupation authorities in Germany to take the necessary measures to insure the normal operation of transport and communications facilities and to initiate four-power consultations for the purpose of mitigating the effects of divided Germany and Berlin.[28] The Soviets rejected a Western effort to gain jurisdiction over the autobahn through East Germany to Berlin with Soviet control of the bridges over the highway, arguing that they wanted no Danzig corridors (a remainder of the prewar arrangement respecting Germany and Poland).[29]

5. RESULTS AND SIGNIFICANCE OF THE BERLIN NEGOTIATIONS

(a) As a negotiating encounter

(1) Risks and dangers magnified in the absence of diplomacy

Many lessons were to be learned in the negotiations to lift the Berlin blockade and one of transcending importance was that this first major crisis in the cold war revealed the danger to world peace when the diplomacy of the great powers was suspended.

The void between East and West broadened and deepened during the year of the blockade. Stalin's diplomacy of threat, coercion, and intimidation gave the West no other choice than to respond as it did, with displays of counterforce and power. As a consequence, normal channels for diplomatic communications were effectively destroyed. Stalin's aggressively intended action produced a real possibility of war, even though Western policymakers and other foreign policy observers judged that war was not his intent.

What magnified the danger to world peace was not only the risks of war by accident but the absence of a diplomatic connection through which to work out an acceptable negotiated settlement. But diplomacy had been forsaken in this intense cold war encounter, and the risks of war were magnified accordingly.

[26] Smith, Dean Acheson, p. 98. Bohlen noted that Vishinsky had made a serious slip by agreeing to a provision in the Austrian treaty without getting certain safeguards the Soviet Government regarded as important. American negotiators along with the French knew about the incident because the French had monitored a telephone call from Gromyko in Moscow to Vishinsky in Paris in which, as Bohlen recorded, "Gromyko used as rough and abusive language as it is possible to imagine." Bohlen noted that the call demonstrated the difference between a Communist Party position and a government position in the Soviet Union. Vishinsky was Foreign Minister, Gromyko only a Deputy Foreign Minister, yet, as Bohlen noted, "Gromyko's position in the Party was so much better than Vishinsky's that he felt perfectly at ease in abusing his superior." Vishinsky's effort to get a rectification of a sentence in the comunique failed. He dropped the subject and agreed to let the sentence stand when Acheson coldly inquired if the Soviet Government was prepared to violate an agreement when it had been hardly put on paper. "His reception on his return to Moscow," Bohlen noted, "could not have been warm." (Bohlen, op. cit., p. 286.)
[27] Smith, Dean Acheson, p. 97.
[28] United States in World Affairs, 1949, pp. 41–42, and Acheson, Present at the Creation, p. 299.
[29] Smith, Dean Acheson, p. 98.

(2) *Importance of "negotiations by semaphore"*

In such conditions of virtually complete alienation, irregular channels of communications can prove useful, and so they did in the Berlin crisis when Stalin resorted to the news media to send a vital signal to Acheson.[30] A form of "negotiations by semaphore" emerged in which each side declared its willingness to parley. Here was the starting point for carrying on a series of subsequent exchanges through direct negotiations that were to bring about a solution.

The value of such diplomacy by indirection lay in the flexibility it allowed the negotiating adversaries and the opporunity it offered for making contact without commitment until conditions were right for taking the next step in negotiations. In the Berlin case, it permitted time for the sequence of action and reaction to set in and for determining negotiating positions cautiously but expeditiously. On the other hand, it placed a great burden upon the negotiators and their mentors, requiring a delicate orchestration of signals and a skillful management of the process so that misunderstandings would not arise that might blow the whole thing. The risk in such procedures would seem to lay in an excessive trust in the manipulation of forces and people not directly under one's immediate control.[31]

Whatever the value of "negotiations by semaphore"—and in the Berlin crisis it had clearly proven its worth, still compared with normal, traditional diplomatic procedure at a time of acute crisis it is hardly a substitute: At best it is a very slender thread upon which to hang the hopes of mankind for peace. Stalin's cryptic, indeed Byzantine, signaling assumed a subtlety by the receiver and a rationality of behavior in a climate of fear and tension that was not always justified by the record of miscalculation in the history of nations.

(3) *The value of secret negotiations*

"Negotiations by semaphore" places a premium on secrecy, and the Berlin crisis of 1948–49 proved to be a clasic example of secret diplomacy at its best.

For Stalin the negotiations on Berlin were the undoing of a mistake. Soviet prestige was deeply committed in this misadventure, and since prestige, the "reputation for power" as Morgenthau called it, is a vital ingredient in international politics, conditions had to be right for a graceful retreat, a strategic withdrawal without humiliation. Secrecy was vital, therefore, to insure progress in the negotiations and to avoid throwing the issue into the fury of the international arena. Once in that highly charged political environment where the Soviets had the advantage of having perfected propaganda of the most exaggerated and vitriolic kind as an instrument of their foreign policy, such a "face-saving" proceeding would have been virtually impossible.

---

[30] For a discussion of this problem, see, Davison, W. Philips. News Media and International Negotiation. Public Opinion Quarterly, vol. 38, Summer 1974 : 174–191. Davison referred to the Berlin blockade as "Perhaps the best-known" example of governments resorting to the news media for a channel of communication (p. 179).

[31] Acheson had a Herblock cartoon on May 1949 reproduced in his book, "Sketches from Life," that illustrated the point as the process went on to its conclusion. The setting is the meeting of the Council of Foreign Ministers in May. Acheson is seated at one end of the negotiating table and Vishinsky at the other, each designated respectively as U.S.A. and U.S.S.R. Each negotiator has a very long pole in his hand equipped with pinchers holding cards about to be released. A radio announcer is seated at mid-point between the two negotiators saying in the caption, "They're Playing Their Cards A Little Cautiously, Now —." (Acheson, Sketches, p. 64.)

(So secret were the negotiations that General Clay, who was on the frontline of the crisis in Berlin, first heard of the Jessup-Malik discussions in the press, much to his chagrin.) [32]

Bohlen probably best summed up the case for secrecy in such delicate negotiations when he observed:

> The success of the efforts to lift the Berlin blockade is a classic example of the value of secrecy in sensitive diplomatic negotiations. Had news of Jessup's approach to Malik leaked, all sorts of views would have been expressed in the press and elsewhere. The Soviets would have believed that we were trying to influence public opinion, not reach an agreement. It can almost be stated as a principle that when the Soviets are serious about something they do it in secrecy, and when they are not they indulge in propaganda. [33]

(4) On the value of the U.N. and conference diplomacy

The success of the Jessup-Malik secret negotiations was made possible, at least in part, by the United Nations. In this instance the United Nations played a part in dissolving a major crisis, not because of any specific role but rather because of its existence. For it provided the casual, informal setting for initiating the exercise in great power conciliation.

Similarly, the Council of Foreign Ministers, as an institution of conference diplomacy, had also made a positive contribution in dissolving this crisis. The Council placed its imprimatur of approval on what had been strictly a bilateral agreement. But equally important it had restored some kind of diplomatic contact between the powers which in retrospect seemed to have become almost hopelessly alienated. As the specialists on the Council of Foreign Relations observed, "This in itself was a major success." [34]

(5) Toughness in the Soviet negotiating style; response in kind

Negotiations in this crisis demonstrated again the characteristic of toughness in the Soviet negotiating style. Robert Murphy, veteran diplomat, the State Department's adviser on German matters, and himself tough-minded in his attitude toward the Russians, observed that when talking with Jessup his attitude reminded him of Ambassador Winant's in London 5 years earlier. Like Winant, he noted,

> Jessup felt that he had achieved an exceptionally cordial relationship with the Soviet diplomat, and he depended heavily upon Malik's good will to reach an agreement on Berlin. I did not succeed in convincing Jessup, any more than I had Winant, that Soviet negotiators cannot be influenced by personal friendships. At first Malik proposed outrageous conditions making acceptance impossible. But after weeks of talk Malik receded from this extreme position, thus giving the impression of substantial Soviet concessions. [35]

At the Paris meeting of the Council of Foreign Ministers, Acheson was also exposed to Vishinsky's toughness for his first time as Secretary of State, but a response in kind of the Foreign Ministers, led by Acheson, provided the necessary corrective.

---

[32] Clay, op. cit., p. 390.
[33] Bohlen, op. cit., p. 284. Acheson made the following observations when the Council of Foreign Ministers went into secret sessions during their meeting on the Berlin issue in May 1949 : "It had entered the stage of 'secret' meetings, meetings limited to the Ministers, with one adviser each, and the interpreters. By a gentleman's agreement, the press was not briefed on these meetings in the hope that a recess from propaganda might aid whatever chance there was of agreement. Secret meetings were a sure sign that, if the conference were to produce any result, high forceps would be required." (Acheson, Sketches, pp. 10–11.)
[34] United States in World Affairs, 1949, p. 44.
[35] Murphy, op. cit., pp. 320–321.

Soviet intransigence on the German question was revealed from the start, and the meeting, as Acheson recorded, was soon given over to Vishinsky's propaganda statements and maneuvers. Failure of the Conference, inherent, Acheson believed, in its purpose of saving face for the Russians having decided to abandon the blockade, seemed certain when it was discovered that they had not wholly abandoned the blockade as agreed. A strike of Soviet-operated railroad workers paralyzing rail traffic and the Soviet failure to remove restrictions on trade created what Acheson termed, "plainly * * * a test of resolution." [36]

Acheson, Bevin, and Schuman were agreed that the Conference was conditioned on the complete and immediate lifting of the blockade, and without that condition fulfilled, the Conference should be terminated. With the approval of their governments, the three Foreign Ministers demanded that Vishinsky join them in instructing the commandants in Berlin to conclude their negotiations and get the traffic moving in 3 days. At first Vishinsky refused, but seeing their determination to terminate the Conference, he reversed his position on grounds of having just received new information. ("Someone suggested," Acheson observed, "that it must have been an invisible note brought by an invisible pigeon.") Progress was resumed, and agreement was finally reached.[37]

(6) Acheson's appraisal of the Soviet negotiating style

For Acheson, the Berlin crisis was a crucial experience: It clearly demonstrated his ability as a negotiator in dealing with the Soviets both at a distance and in close engagement, and it also perceptibly hardened his views toward the Soviet Union.[38]

Acheson's personal commentaries revealed many aspects of this negotiating experience and others that were to follow:

—The liturgy, tactics, and traditions of the Council of Foreign Ministers meetings; [39]

—The "excruciating" tedium of triple translations; [40]

—The Soviet tactic of the agenda, attaching to it an importance "amounting almost to mystique," and insisting that the Council could not proceed from one item to another without reaching agreement on the item under discussion, "a procedure that was eminently adaptable to blackmail"; [41]

—The distortion of "what had seemed to be merely clumsy English translation of agenda items into admissions and concessions"; [42] and

---

[36] Acheson, Sketches, pp. 12–13.
[37] Ibid., p. 14.
[38] Acheson's biographer David McClellan wrote of the impact of the crisis on Acheson's attitude towards the Russians: "One lesson Acheson drew from the conference may have been unfortunate: he now held a deepening conviction that Soviet diplomacy was not amenable to persuasion or compromise, and that the situation in which each side found itself pointed in one direction only—that of competition in which the worst would only be avoided if the West was better prepared." According to McClellan, Acheson's "peculiarly mechanistic view of the future of Soviet-American relations left little room for negotiations or for the chance that Soviet policy might change or mellow. Preoccupied as he was by the immediate problems facing the West, Acheson seems not to have considered what might be done to modify Soviet behavior once the West had regained its strength. Herein lies the principal strength but also the principal weakness of Acheson's statecraft." (McClellan, David S. Dean Acheson: The State Department Years. New York, Dodd, Mead, 1976, p. 163.)
[39] Acheson, Present at Creation, pp. 292–293.
[40] Ibid.
[41] Ibid., p. 296.
[42] Ibid.

—The "typical * * * demonstration of Soviet political values and diplomatic method." [43]

On all occasions of crisis as in 1948 and those times of great stress that followed with respect to Germany, Acheson noted, "the same clumsy diplomacy resulted," which he described as follows:

An offer to abandon a long and bitterly held Soviet position was made on condition of allied abandonment of its proposed innovations. When this was firmly refused, the Soviet Union abandoned its own long-held position in the hope of dividing the allies or seducing the Germans.[44]

Acheson summed up his years of experience in negotiating with the Soviets in these words, followed by an instruction on the "Russian idea of negotiating" which was "admirably" expressed by Sir William Hayter:

What one may learn from the experience is that the Soviet authorities are not moved to agreement by negotiation—that is, by a series of mutual concessions calculated to move parties desiring agreement closer to an acceptable one. Theirs is a more primitive form of political method. They cling stubbornly to a position, hoping to force an opponent to accept it. When and if action by the opponent demonstrates the Soviet position to be untenable, they hastily abandon it—after asking and having been refused an unwarranted price—and hastily take up a new position, which may or may not represent a move toward greater mutual stability.[45]

(b) Impact of Berlin crisis on East-West relations

(1) Soviet setback; Western strength enhanced

American policymakers viewed Western success in the Berlin crisis as a major setback for the Soviet Union. As Acheson said on returning from Paris, the Western position in the "struggle for the soul of Europe" had "grown greatly in strength" while that of the Soviet Union had "changed from the offensive to the defensive." [46] Western unity was enhanced by the successful defense of its vital interests, by the creation of NATO, and by parallel preparations for the entry of West Germany into the Western community of nations.

(2) Europe divided in deepening cold war pattern

Failure of the Council of Foreign Ministers on Germany was symptomatic of the deeper problem of a divided Europe which at that time as never before was becoming a reality in East-West relations. Success in turning back the Soviet challenge had also affirmed the correctness of the Western policy of resistance to Soviet pressure and accordingly deepened the pattern of challenge and response in the cold war.

---

[43] Ibid., p. 274.
[44] Acheson continued: "In 1952 this took the form of threats to Bonn if it should sign the 1952 agreements and offers if it should not; in 1955, of signing the long-delayed Austrian State Treaty and the reunification of Austria as an earnest of what Germany might get by declining to join NATO; in 1963, the nuclear test ban as a means of staving off a multilateral force." (Ibid., p. 274.)
[45] The statement by Hayter that Acheson quoted so approvingly was as follows:
"Negotiation with the Russians does occur, from time to time, but it requires no particular skill. The Russians are not to be persuaded by eloquence or convinced by reasoned arguments. They rely on what Stalin used to call the proper basis of international policy, the calculation of forces. So no case, however skillfully deployed, however clearly demonstrated as irrefutable, will move them from doing what they have previously decided to do: the only way of changing their purpose is to demonstrate that they have no advantageous alternative, that what they want to do is not possible. Negotiations with the Russians are therefore very mechanical; and they are probably better conducted on paper than by word of mouth."
(Acheson, Present at Creation, pp. 274–275. The Hayter statement appeared in the London Observer, Oct. 2, 1960.)
[46] United States in World Affairs, 1949, p. 43.

(3) Berlin: A tactical retreat, not a new Soviet strategy

Although tension had momentarily eased, subsequent events showed that the Soviet return to the status quo ante in Berlin was only a tactical retreat rather than the forerunner of a new strategy. The struggle for Germany continued; preparations for an Austrian treaty faltered; and developments in the Far East demonstrated that opportunities for indirect Soviet expansion short of armed conflict were not exhausted.[47]

B. Initiating Negotiations for an Armistice in Korea

1. BALANCE OF MILITARY FORCES AND FAVORABLE POLITICAL CONDITIONS

Almost a year and a month to the day from the lifting of the Berlin blockade, North Korean Communist forces, created, supplied, and directed by the Soviet Union, invaded South Korea, precipitating a war that was to go on for nearly 3 years. More than any other event in the cold war the Korean war raised the greatest risk in Soviet-American relations. That risk was the expansion of this local war into World War III. But this did not occur, mainly because of eventual success on the battlefield in establishing a balance of military forces, an expressed willingness by the United States to alter its excessive war aim of unifying Korea by force of arms, an American initiative to search for a negotiated settlement, and a favorable Soviet response to bring the war to an end.

By May-June 1951, the front in Korea had become reasonably stabilized in a balance of military forces between the attacking Chinese and North Korean troops in the north and the defending American and South Koreans in the south roughly along the 38th parallel, the initial line dividing the Korean peninsula. The American forces had recovered from their near military debacle in December 1950 when the Chinese intervened full scale and threatened their security. Gen. Matthew B. Ridgway, successor to the deposed Gen. Douglas MacArthur as head of the United Nations command, successfully countered the Chinese offensive during May, throwing their forces back across the 38th parallel.[48]

By June 1951, the administration had achieved a unity of purpose, not existing heretofore, among the White House, the State Department, the Pentagon, and the Supreme Commander in Tokyo. As Acheson recorded, they "found themselves united on political objectives, strategy, and tactics for the first time since the war had started." [49] American political aims, in Acheson's words, were simply "to stop the aggression and leave the unification of Korea to time and political measures." [50] The military strategy and tactics were intended to maintain a stabilized front while severely punishing the enemy. In brief, a war of fixed positions and of attrition had set in. No longer was the American aim to unify Korea by force of arms. On the occasion of the so-called "MacArthur Hearings" before Congress in early June 1951, Acheson took great pains to clarify the American position publicly and beyond all doubt.[51]

---

[47] Ibid., p. 497.
[48] Acheson, Present at Creation, pp. 529–530.
[49] Ibid., p. 529.
[50] Ibid.
[51] Ibid., p. 531.

Both military and political conditions, therefore, seemed to be right for taking the initiative for a negotiated armistice in Korea.

2. RESORT TO SECRET DIPLOMACY

The question posed now was the means for approaching the Russians without inviting or risking humiliating rebuffs to determine if they favored such negotiation and would give them their support. A direct approach to the Chinese and North Koreans was out of the question. Ostensibly as a nonbelligerent, though the instigator of the invasion from the north in the first place, Russia was the linchpin that could unleash the forces that might bring about a negotiated armistice. Discretion was of the utmost importance, for as Kennan observed, "a public initiative on our part that produced only an insulting North Korean rebuff could be much worse than no initiative at all." [52] Exploration through the public procedures of the U.N. or, as Acheson noted, "through leaky foreign offices like the Indian would be fatal." Discreet probes in Europe and Asia had produced no effective response.[53]

Again the negotiating experience of the Berlin blockade suggested an answer—secret diplomacy in the mode of the Jessup-Malik talks. Malik was at the U.N. but Jessup was in Paris working on plans for a meeting of the Council of Foreign Ministers. At the time Kennan was on a leave of absence from the State Department and working on his historical studies at the Institute for Advanced Study in Princeton.[54]

By what seems to have been a remarkable coincidence, Stewart Alsop had written an article in the New York Herald Tribune on May 6, pointing out the consequences of a military advance beyond the 38th parallel and comparing favorably Kennan's known views on the danger of such an action with certain public statements recently made by General MacArthur. Briefly, MacArthur downgraded the possibility of Soviet intervention in Korea, indicating his disbelief that anything happening in Korea or Asia would affect the basic decision of the Soviets whether to intervene openly in the Korean war. Kennan held that the Russians were "extremely sensitive" to the security of their border in the Far East and the Manchurian border as well and "would certainly react militarily before permitting us to establish ourselves militarily in that region." (Kennan was one of the few advisers in the administration who opposed the initial crossing of the 38th parallel when the issue arose in the autumn of 1950.) Alsop pointed out that Kennan believed a real political victory in Korea might be soon possible if, in Alsop's words, "we do not again make the fatal mistake of demanding 'unconditional surrender.' If not, war may come anyway." But Alsop, interpolating Kennan's views as he continued, emphasized that "before edging into a world war by the back door, we should make a final effort, by the secret processes of diplomacy, to reach at least some temporary settlement with the real masters of the situation, the men in the Kremlin." [55]

[52] Kennan, Memoirs, vol. 2, p. 35.
[53] Acheson, Present at Creation, pp. 531–532.
[54] Smith, Dean Acheson, p. 276.
[55] Kennan, Memoirs, vol. 2, pp. 35–36.

Alsop's report was "not inaccurate," wrote Kennan, nor was it, apparently, "without effect," for 12 days later on May 18, he was called to Washington to confer with Acheson and his aides.[56]

3. KENNAN'S MISSION TO MALIK

(a) Why Kennan?

Though Acheson and Kennan had serious differences in their approaches to the cold war, particularly with respect to the integration of Germany into the Western community and the militarization of his "containment" concept, still these differences did not alter Acheson's appreciation of Kennan as a skillful diplomat with unique capabilities in the Soviet area. He seemed to look upon Kennan as an ideal pointman in undertaking this initially delicate diplomatic venture. In Acheson's judgment Kennan could bring to the enterprise his knowledge and deep interest in Soviet-American relations. Formally not part of the official establishment at that time he could maintain his "unofficial" capacity, while in reality, being a seasoned professional diplomat of many years service, he nonetheless symbolized a close and durable official connection. Hence, as Acheson noted, both Kennan and Malik "could talk seriously but without commitment." [57]

In brief, all indicators pointed toward Kennan.

(b) Acheson's purposes in the Kennan mission

That the Korean war was reaching a critical point, perhaps even beyond the control of the main actors, there seemed to be little doubt in Acheson's mind. The hostilities may have been confined to Korea and the major contestants the United States, South Korea, China, and North Korea, but at the center of the conflict was in reality the Soviet Union and the United States. "Our two countries seemed to be headed for what could be a most dangerous collision over Korea," Acheson later wrote. Such was "definitely not the purpose of American actions or policy," nor was it "hard for us to believe that it was desired by the Soviet Union." "Whether or not it was desired by Peking," he wrote, "it seemed the inevitable result of the course the Chinese were steering." [58]

Acheson believed that if the "drift to serious trouble" was to be halted, the means would seem to be through an armistice and ceasefire in Korea at the line then being held by the contestants, roughly the status quo ante bellum. The administration wanted to know Soviet views on this matter and what suggestions they might have. It also wanted to make sure that Moscow understood U.S. "desires and intentions" and if hostilities were to end this was a good time to begin negotiations. Acheson did not want Kennan to negotiate anything with respect to a final settlement but only to make American purposes and intentions "absolutely clear" to the Soviets and that "they were realistically aware of the course on which all were adrift and of its more than likely terminus." [59] Kennan was to make it clear to Malik that the mission, as he said, was "purely informal and exploratory, that neither

---

[54] Ibid., p. 36.
[57] Acheson, Present at Creation, p. 532.
[58] Ibid.
[59] Ibid.

government would consider itself committed by the results, and that nothing would be made known publicly of either the fact of our meeting or the tenor of our discussions." [60]

In brief, Kennan was instructed to sound out the Soviets secretly, informally, and unofficially on peace possibilities and if favorable to set into motion the negotiating process.

Kennan agreed to undertake the mission, as Acheson noted, "in his own way and alone." General Ridgway was informed and instructed to be prepared to advise on relevant military matters and to conduct proceedings in the field as required. [61]

(c) Kennan-Malik encounter in New York

The mission formally began when Kennan sent a note to Malik at his New York apartment through a young assistant on the U.S. delegation to the United Nations, asking to see him and requesting a reply by phone. Promptly Malik replied, and they agreed to meet at his Long Island home. Driving from Princeton, Kennan met alone with Malik on June 1. Kennan's ability to speak Russian simplified the proceedings and made this direct personal encounter most effective.

After overcoming the initial embarrassment of Malik upsetting a tray of fruit and wine on himself, the two diplomats approached, in a roundabout manner, the central question as outlined in Acheson's instructions. Predictably Malik could not respond directly but agreed to meet again after considering the matter; that is, after conferring with Moscow.

Kennan and Malik met again on June 5 at which time Malik declared that the Soviet Government wanted peace and that it wanted a peaceful solution in Korea as rapidly as possible. While the Soviets could not personally participate in ceasefire discussions, Malik personally advised Kennan to approach the North Koreans and the Chinese. [62]

While no American policymaker doubted the authenticity of Malik's message, still it had what Acheson termed "a sibylline quality which left us wondering what portended and what we should do next." [63] Clarification came on June 23, when Malik, in delivering a speech over a U.N.-sponsored radio program, said that the Soviet people believed that the Korean war could be settled. As a first step, he said, "discussions should be started between the belligerents for a ceasefire and an armistice providing for the mutual withdrawal of forces from the 38th parallel." [64]

For Acheson this statement sounded official, but doubts still persisted at home and abroad, both publicly and privately. [65] An inquiry through the American Embassy in Moscow, however, confirmed on

[60] Kennan, Memoirs, vol. 2, p. 36.
[61] Acheson, Present at Creation, p. 532.
[62] Acheson, Present at Creation, pp. 532–533.
[63] Ibid.
[64] Ibid., and Kennan, Memoirs, vol. 2, pp. 36–37.
[65] Acheson, Present at Creation, p. 533. The Malik speech was broadcast on a Saturday night while Acheson was at his farm in Sandy Spring, Md. He kept in touch by telephone. According to Gaddis Smith, "the Department issued a cool, slightly sardonic statement, quite Achesonian in flavor and very similar to Acheson's response more than 2 years before to the overtures from Stalin which led eventually to the lifting of the Berlin blockade." If "the Communists are now willing to end the aggression in Korea," it said, there were adequate means for discussion available. "But the tenor of Mr. Malik's speech again raises the question as to whether this is more propaganda." (Smith, Dean Acheson, pp. 277–278.)

June 27 that Malik's expressed views were indeed those of the Soviet Government and that the Soviets really wanted an armistice.[66]

4. ARMISTICE NEGOTIATIONS INITIATED

With the conclusion of this vital prelude to actual negotiations, everything seemed to fall into place rather quickly. Ambassador Alan G. Kirk noted in his report from Moscow of June 27 that Gromyko had suggested that the military authorities on both sides should arrange for negotiations and that political questions should not be discussed. Acheson and his aides at the State Department agreed that this suggestion had many advantages for the United States and accordingly proceeded along those lines, though, as Acheson later observed, "the military did not grasp for this responsibility * * *"[67]

For 3 days, Acheson carried on a series of complicated negotiations involving the State Department, the Joint Chiefs of Staff, and the Allied ambassadors. The ambassadors of the nations with forces participating in the U.N. Command in Korea met and approved of the opening of negotiations. Congressional leaders were also kept informed of developments. By June 29, agreement was reached within the administration on the procedures to be followed and the substance of the American position in negotiations; President Truman formally approved the statement and instructions to General Ridgway on the opening of negotiations.[68]

The means chosen for contacting the Chinese and North Korean commanders was a radio broadcast by General Ridgway on June 30, suggesting the opening of negotiations for a ceasefire and armistice. On July 2, the Communist commanders replied favorably, and on the 10th, the delegations met for the first time at Kaesong, a town between the lines.[69]

From the perspective of a diplomat and historian, Kennan gave this interpretive commentary on what was to take place for the next 3 years until an armistice was finally concluded and on the role of diplomacy and negotiations:

Stimulated by this Soviet initiative, formal talks were, as everyone knows, soon inaugurated. They were long, wearisome, and—from the American and United Nations standpoint—exasperating almost beyond belief. It must have been hard for the American negotiators, at times, to believe that their Korean opposite numbers were animated by any motive other than to drive them from the negotiating table and reopen hostilities. There was, as Mr. Acheson observed, a possibility that things might have gone better had we, for our part, been content to talk in terms of a line of division lying once again along the 38th parallel, instead of one somewhat to the north of it. But here again, for better or worse, military considerations were allowed to prevail over political ones. Whether for this reason or for others, the talks were sticky and often, from our standpoint, infuriating. Some of our negotiators, had they known of my part in making them possible, would have cursed me for the effort, and I could scarcely have blamed them.

The fact is, however, that the talks did take place. Fighting, for the most part, stopped. Eventually, a new line was established—more favorable, actually, to the South Koreans than the one that had existed before the Korean War began. And while the subsequent maintenance of this line was never for anyone on the non-Communist side a pleasant or easy task, the heavy and largely useless bloodshed that marked the unhappy years 1950–51 has not yet, mercifully, been renewed.[70]

[66] Ibid., p. 278.
[67] Acheson, Present at Creation, p. 534.
[68] For the text of these documents, see Truman, Memoirs, vol. 2, pp. 458–459. See also, Smith, Dean Acheson, pp. 278–279, and Acheson, Present at Creation, pp. 534–535.
[69] Ibid.
[70] Kennan, Memoirs, vol. 2, p. 37.

5. RESULTS AND SIGNIFICANCE OF THE KENNAN MISSION

(a) On seeking solutions through diplomacy and negotiations

Kennan modestly downgraded his role in initiating the armistice negotiations ending the Korean war as being "relatively minor;" but he acknowledged with greater assurance the "small but not negligible part" he played in what amounted to transforming the national goals in the war from a strictly military solution to one through diplomacy and negotiations. The armistice that has endured "with painful strains and stresses" seemed to Kennan to be far more preferable to the alternative; namely,

to press on with hostilities on the Korean peninsula in the pursuit of military and political objectives which, to the extent their realization was approached, would almost certainly have brought the Russians in against us and would probably have assured the outbreak, then and there, of World War III.[71]

Kennan had always viewed the Korean war with the bifocal vision of a diplomat-scholar who could clearly see the role of military power in maintaining stability and the role of diplomacy in seeking political solutions through negotiation. In addition he had a clear perception of what constituted Russian vital interests. Thus Kennan had unsuccessfully opposed the advance of MacArthur's forces beyond the 38th parallel early in the war because of the threat it posed to the vital security interests of the Soviet Union and China.

And when near disaster struck with the intervention of the Chinese in November-December 1950, he appealed for discipline and rationality, candor and nerve; he cautioned resistance to any direct approach to the Russians for a negotiated ceasefire by itself and unconnected with larger political problems in Korea and the Far East as a way out of the Nation's military embarrassment. Such an approach at a time of extreme adversity, he warned, would have been an invitation for the humiliation of the United States and a consequent blow to its world prestige. As he concluded in his memorandum of assessment to Acheson, "The prerequisite to any successful negotiation on political subjects would be a posture of unity, confidence and collected strength on our side." [72]

And then as early as March 1951, during the recovery from near defeat on the military front, Kennan suggested that a direct approach to the Soviets might be the best way to achieve an armistice.[73] This approach was undertaken with his full support and participation 3 months later when the balance of military forces had become more visibly stabilized.

What is significant and instructive for the purposes of this study in Kennan's approach to the Korean war was his perception not only of what constituted vital Soviet interests but more importantly his perception of the proper balance between military power and diplomacy: That finely tuned orchestration of the use of military power and the instrumentalities of diplomacy directed toward achieving political purposes through negotiations.

---

[71] Ibid., pp. 37–38.
[72] Ibid., p. 29. Kennan's views on when to negotiate during this period of great stress, at a time when some national leaders were advocating withdrawal from Korea, were expressed in a memorandum of Dec. 3, 1950. See his Memoirs, vol. 2, pp. 28–29, reproduced above on page 239.
[73] Smith, Dean Acheson, p. 276.

(b) The danger of overmilitarizing national policy

Also significant and instructive from this brief encounter into the negotiations on a Korean armistice are the two "morals" that Kennan drew from this experience. The first was, "the terrible danger of letting national policy be determined by military considerations alone." According to Kennan, "had the military been given their head" and had not they been restrained by the "wise discipline" exercised by President Truman, Secretary of State Acheson, and Defense Secretary Marshall, "disaster would almost certainly have ensued." [74]

Again the lesson to be drawn from this experience is the imperative need for keeping political goals in the proper perspective while maintaining the proper balance between the use of military power and the instrumentalities of diplomacy in achieving those goals. In this instance the danger, as Kennan stated, was overemphasis on the military side, but American diplomatic history has its share of imbalances on the other.

(c) On the value of secret diplomacy

The second moral, Kennan noted, was "the great and sometimes crucial value—so seldom heeded, so difficult perhaps to heed, in American statesmanship—of wholly secret, informal, and exploratory contacts even between political and military adversaries, as adjuncts to the overt and formal processes of international diplomacy." [75]

As in the case of the Berlin blockade, Kennan's mission underscored the value of secret diplomacy, and for much the same reasons. But more importantly and in a larger sense it underscored the transcending value of diplomacy and negotiations themselves as instruments for seeking and maintaining peace. Ironically, in the Kennan episode the United States and the Soviet Union had reversed diplomatic roles: In 1949, the Soviet Union was the pursuer, it took the initiative to solve its dilemma through diplomacy; in 1951, the task fell to the United States. In both instances the public media was the principal channel of communications, not formally established channels of diplomacy. Adhering to the pattern of the 1949 Berlin negotiations, the Soviets signaled their critical message of acceptance of the Korean negotiations through the media, not the press as before, but this time the radio—as did General Ridgway in his proposal to parley with the Communist commanders in the field. The value of using such informal channels of communication, as noted above, cannot be gainsaid, but the question remains as to the wisdom of making vital issues of war and peace between the great powers dependent upon such slender threads of communication rather than on the formal and more reliable channels of diplomacy.

---

[74] Ibid., p. 38.
[75] Ibid.

V. STALIN'S RUSSIA, 1953: BESIEGED AND ISOLATED

In retrospect, continuation of the Korean armistice negotiations, however prolonged and wearisome and often interrupted by fierce sporadic fighting, seemed to be the only positive sign in East-West relations, at least with respect to negotiations, as Stalin's reign came to an end. Some slight indications of an emphasis on "peaceful co-existence" have since been detected, but the overall thrust of relations was by and large characterized by hostility. Diplomacy and negotiations, as indicated earlier in this chapter, had come to a standstill as relations, such as they were, settled into perhaps the harshest period of the cold war.

The Soviet Union itself seemed to be entering a critical phase of its own history as Stalin in his final days was preparing another campaign of internal terror symbolized by the so-called "Doctor's Plot" and the spirit of which has been generally reflected in the writings of Solzhenitsyn. Fears that were widespread in the nation and percolated to the top leadership were apparent in Khrushchev's comment to Harriman in 1959 that Stalin's suspicions of his associates grew increasingly in the latter years of his life. "He trusted no one," Khrushchev said. "When we were called to his office, we never knew whether we were going to see our families again." [1]

On the international scene, Stalin's policy of revolutionary activism and adventurism abroad seemed to have reached an end as its forward momentum appeared to have become arrested and immobilism set in. The focus of attention seemed to turn increasingly inward toward continentalism. For the succession of Soviet-generated crises since the end of World War II, capped by the Korean war, had created a sequence of Communist challenge and Western response that polarized international politics and created a political world in schism and conflict. By his aggressive policy Stalin had succeeded in globalizing the cold war and ironically creating in reality a world of opposite forces—communism versus capitalism—that had once been only a theoretical formulation. The much-dreaded Stalinist fear of "capitalist encirclement" had now become a reality. For as Bohlen observed, speaking for the American side, "it was the Korean war and not World War II that made us a world military-political power." [2]

In brief, Soviet Russia had seemed to reach an end of policy by the time of Stalin's death in March 1953. His bequest to his successors was a Soviet Russia isolated and besieged and an international political world so sharply divided by confrontation, war, and Communist-instigated insurrection that the normal functions of diplomacy and negotiations were for all practical purposes suspended.

[1] Harriman and Abel, op. cit., p. 522.
[2] Bohlen, op. cit., p. 303.

CHAPTER VII—IN TRANSITION TO PEACEFUL COEXISTENCE WITH KHRUSHCHEV, 1953–64

Part I—Changes in Soviet Diplomacy and Negotiations: Context, Diplomatic Establishment, and Characteristics

Negotiations with the Russians does occur, from time to time, but it requires no particular skill. The Russians are not to be persuaded by eloquence or convinced by reasoned arguments. They rely on what Stalin used to call the proper basis of international policy, the calculation of forces. So no case, however skillfully deployed, however clearly demonstrated as irrefutable, will move them from doing what they have previously decided to do; the only way of changing their purpose is to demonstrate that they have no advantageous alternative, that what they want to do is not possible. Negotiations with the Russians are therefore very mechanical; and they are probably better conducted on paper than by word of mouth.

—*Sir William Hayter, October 1960.*

I. CHANGING CONTEXT OF SOVIET DIPLOMACY

A. STRUCTURAL CHANGES IN INTERNATIONAL RELATIONS

1. SHIFT FROM BIPOLARITY TO MULTIPOLARITY; EMERGENCE OF THE THIRD WORLD

Significant structural changes were taking place in international relations when Stalin's successors, first the so-called "Collective Leadership" and then Nikita S. Khrushchev, assumed control over Soviet foreign policy. One perceptible change was the shift from bipolarity to multipolarity as the forces of political pluralism within the major camps of the principal contenders in the cold war eroded their heretofore predominating position, diffused their power, and weakened their control. Other power centers varying in magnitude were to emerge.

Soviet acceptance of the principle of "other roads to Socialism," proclaimed within the unfolding larger revisionist policy of de-Stalinization, spawned political disorder and revolution in Poland and Hungary and set into motion forces that were to visibly weaken direct Soviet control over its East European satellites. At the same time Soviet Russia's dispute with China, simmering in the 1950's, was to break wide open before Khrushchev's era came to an end, creating a major contender for Soviet leadership within international communism and seriously dividing the unity of the movement.

The United States also felt the impact of political pluralism within the Western alliance system. A prosperous Europe, having fully recovered from wartime economic collapse, had sought a political outlet for its desire for greater independence from American control. This tendency was given renewed vigor in the Cuban missile crisis of

1962 when the United States acted unilaterally on a vital issue involving essentially the survival of Europe as well as the United States. Thereafter, serious differences over defense strategy within the alliance system came to the surface. Other differences were to arise among other countries on the general question of confronting Communist power whether it be in Southeast Asia, Europe, or Cuba.

The other structural change in international relations was the emergence of the Third World as a new force in world politics as the postwar liberation movement in the former colonial areas of Asia and Africa weakened and finally destroyed the Western imperial system and brought forth new nations and a new constellation of power onto the world scene. During the 20 years from 1944 to early 1964, 52 nations of the world, almost entirely from the Afro-Asian area, established their independence, numbering over one billion people and occupying over 11.5 million square miles of territory. The redistribution of world power on this magnitude was to radically impact upon old and new relationships and fundamentally transform the shape of world politics.

2. THE GLOBALIZING OF NUCLEAR POWER

Both structural changes occurred within an evolving international political system that witnessed the steady growth of Soviet-American thermonuclear power and, most importantly, the dawning of the Space Age. These new technological developments were to have a profound effect on world politics during the Khrushchev era, for the fusion of thermonuclear power with long-range delivery systems globalized the military capability of the superpowers, increasing enormously their power to influence not only the course of their own mutual relations but also that of world politics as a whole. The combination of this new power with the structural changes in the international environment was to create new opportunities for Khrushchev's Russia which by the end of Stalin's quarter century reign had seemed to reach a point of stagnation and immobilism.

B. Major Trends in Soviet-American Relations

1. EMERGING DÉTENTE, 1953–55

In retrospect, Soviet-American relations during the Khrushchev era could be divided roughly into three parts or timeframes. The first, from 1953–55, was one of emerging détente. Immediately after Stalin's death in March 1953 the "Collective Leadership" consisting of Malenkov, Khrushchev, Bulganin, Molotov, Kaganovich, Mikoyan, and Beria initiated a policy of gradual détente. This new policy seemed designed to fulfill the immediate need for consolidating their power at home and creating a base for new foreign policy initiatives abroad. Negotiations for an armistice in Korea, then in the second year, were concluded within 3 months. War in Indochina was brought to a halt, at least temporarily, within less than a year. In May 1955, the first major break occurred in the Soviet position in Europe with the conclusion of the Austrian State Treaty after a decade of tedious and sometimes bitter negotiations.

The first phase of this era appeared to end with the "summit" conference of Heads of Government in June 1955, the first in the postwar era. Thereafter, Soviet policy seemed to have been more intensely focused upon the Third World. Blocked in Europe by the buildup of Western power, the Soviets seemed to probe for "soft" spots in the colonial areas and former dependencies of the Western Powers. Bulganin and Khrushchev completed their extraordinary tour of southern Asia at the end of 1955. Coupled with the launching of a vigorous trade and aid campaign, this unprecedented venture into personal diplomacy demonstrated concretely the new diversionary thrust of Soviet foreign policy. In retrospect, Khrushchev had set into motion a new policy toward the Third World that was to mark a dramatic move beyond an inner directed continentalism to establishing a strong global presence. This marked the beginning of Soviet globalism.

One of the distinctive features of American policy toward the Soviet Union seemed to be a vigorous assertion of power. Energetic, and even on occasion daring, American policy sought to create counterpressures against the Communist bloc in a confrontation of power. Reflecting largely the thinking of Secretary of State John Foster Dulles, American policy, popularly termed "liberation", seemed to strive for a stage beyond containment. "Massive retaliation" was the term used to describe the general strategic conception within which American policy was to operate. Among the practical manifestations of American policy were the creation of the European Defense Community, the integration of West Germany into NATO, vigorous support for the Nationalist Chinese in their conflict with the Mainland Chinese Communists, and the creation of a system of anti-Communist arrangements in Asia, the Middle East, and the Western Hemisphere.[1]

2. A PERIOD OF ACUTE CONFRONTATION, 1956–62

The years 1956–62 was a time of acute confrontation between East and West. Assuming party leadership almost immediately after Stalin's death and using that position as a power base, Khrushchev successfully manipulated factions within the "collective leadership" so that by March 1958 he had shunted aside all major political opposition and assumed predominating power in the Soviet Union as Premier of the Government and First Secretary of the Communist Party of the Soviet Union (CPSU).

Though Khrushchev had proclaimed the doctrine of peaceful coexistence at the 20th Party Congress in 1956, his actions in foreign policy were, nonetheless, anything but peaceful, nor did they indicate a desire to coexist. For Khrushchev's perception of peaceful coexistence, contrary to that of the West, did not rule out the use of threats and military power for political purposes; the "struggle" continued, but below the threshold of actual war. Upstaging the United States with the successful launching of the first intercontinental ballistic missile (ICBM) in August 1957 and Sputnik two months later, Khrushchev initiated a series of what Mosely termed "rolling crises" in an effort to accomplish four central purposes: To undermine U.S.

[1] Whelan, Joseph G. Soviet-American Relations, 1933–60: A Brief Selective Chronology with Interpretive Commentary. In, Congressional Record, July 1, 1960: 14246–14247 (Daily edition).

prestige in the world; to reduce its power and presence in Europe; to weaken the Western defense system; and to assert Soviet superiority over its adversaries. Major tests of strength were staged to achieve these purposes in Berlin during 1958–59, again Berlin in 1961, and finally the ultimate test in the Cuban missile crisis of 1962.

In these years of "rolling crises," U.S. policy seemed directed toward four major purposes: To resist Soviet pressures generally with sufficient counterpressures, political and diplomatic, military and economic; to strengthen the Western defense system; to expand U.S. military power; and finally to take on the Soviet Union in what had come to be known as the "Space Race." The transcending American purpose was to preserve its world position and world peace.

3. RETREAT TO ACCOMMODATION, 1962–64

For Khrushchev and Soviet-American relations, the Cuban missile crisis was something of a watershed. In its aftermath Khrushchev gave the appearance of seeking a more genuine form of peaceful coexistence with the West as Soviet policy searched for accommodation with the United States. His "missile diplomacy" of threats and calculated aggravation was ostensibly forsworn, and the United States responded with the initiative to conclude the partial nuclear test ban. For a time, Soviet-American relations seemed to enter an era of good feeling.

In sum, Soviet-American relations during the Khrushchev years followed an uneven line beginning with an emerging détente, followed by acute confrontation in a series of "rolling crises", and finally ending with a retreat to détente. Significant structural changes were also taking place in international relations that had a profound effect on Soviet foreign policy.

II. THE SOVIET DIPLOMATIC ESTABLISHMENT UNDER KHRUSHCHEV

A. THE MOLOTOV LEGACY: A GRIM PROFESSIONALISM

1. BUILDING FOR THE FUTURE

If the context of Soviet diplomacy had changed radically under Khrushchev, so had the Soviet diplomatic establishment, for the pursuit of a global policy imposed new requirements on Soviet diplomacy, and to assure success, diplomatic institutions had to be adapted and personnel trained accordingly. But Khrushchev could approach this task with a decided advantage: He had the Molotov legacy of a grim professionalism upon which to build.

As Foreign Minister during 1939–49 and again during 1953–56, Molotov succeeded in developing a new diplomatic cadre of technically trained professionals. Manifesting what Meissner called a "nationalistic attitude" in the postwar era, these new diplomats combined with their professionalism a spirit of nationalism, a self-perception of historic Russia as a great power, and a revival of prerevolutionary Russian traditions.[1]

In an apparent attempt to establish continuity with the Russian past, changes were made in organization and nomenclature as the Soviets returned, at least outwardly, to the more traditional forms of diplomacy. The term "Foreign Commissariat of the U.S.S.R." with its identification with the Russian revolutionary era was dropped in 1946 for the more conventional expression, "Ministry for Foreign Affairs." [2] The training of diplomats was also expanded and intensified following World War II with the reorganization of the Higher Diplomatic School, founded in the 1930's, that complemented the work of the Moscow State Institute for International Relations for the training of Soviet diplomats.[3]

Professionalism was the hallmark of the Molotov era. The KGB presence in the diplomatic establishment, so extensive in the wake of the Great Purge, was reduced, though not eliminated for espionage and diplomacy were to remain useful tools in the total Soviet foreign policy process.[4] The appointment of strictly "political" types to diplomatic posts was also reduced.

New opportunities were accordingly opened up in the diplomatic ranks during the war and immediately thereafter for comparatively young men who were being trained by Molotov (e.g., Gromyko, Malik, and Zorin). Upon the removal of holdovers from an earlier era (e.g., Litvinov and Maisky), in what was described as a "more genteel and

---

[1] Meissner, op. cit., pp. 60–61. Vishinsky was Foreign Minister during the intervening years of Molotov's tenure, 1949–53. Dmitri Shepilov served briefly from June 1956 to February 1957, and Gromyko has been Foreign Minister since 1957.
[2] Ibid., p. 54.
[3] Ibid., p. 62.
[4] Slusser, op. cit., p. 235.

restricted" purge of the Foreign Ministry, this new breed of diplomatic technicians stepped into positions of authority.[5] "The year 1947," concluded Prof. Vernon V. Aspaturian, an American authority on Soviet diplomacy, "thus marks the completed transition from the old service to the new." From then until Stalin's death in 1953, he observed, all top appointments in the Soviet diplomatic establishment at home and abroad "were reserved exclusively for the career professionals." Molotov and Vishinsky remained the only "politicals," but even they, owing to length of diplomatic service, could have been legitimately classified as professional diplomats.[6]

2. CONTROL FROM THE CENTER

Changes even took place in Molotov's approach to negotiations after Stalin's death. "He acted with greater ease and freedom," observed Stephen D. Kertesz, the former Hungarian diplomat turned scholar. "His behavior became more like that of a Western foreign minister."[7] Bohlen, too, noted that with Stalin's death Molotov "adopted a new style" from that of being "visibly subservient to his master" to "not hesitating to express differences of opinion with Malenkov or Khrushchev, or to interrupt their conversation to express an opinion." The stodgy, impassive, dour Molotov even loosened up a bit. When Ambassador Bohlen mentioned that he had seen pictures of Khrushchev sitting on an elephant in India, Molotov responded, "Yes, an elephant sitting on an elephant."[8]

But changes did not occur in the centralization of power, and in the firm control over foreign policy from the center: That remained an immutable Stalinist legacy that has continued on through the Molotov era into that of Gromyko's of the present day. This point was well illustrated in Bohlen's account of a brief discussion at a presummit meeting during 1955 among Secretary of State John Foster Dulles, French Foreign Minister Antoine Pinay, and Molotov. The place was San Francisco; the occasion, the celebration of the 10th anniversary of the United Nations. At a dinner hosted by Dulles, Pinay was infuriated by Molotov's unwillingness to discuss any details of the coming meeting, such as its organization or agenda. "To those of us who had had more experience with the Soviets," Bohlen recalled, "the reason was plain. Molotov had no instructions from Moscow. The Presidium had not addressed itself to the subject, and he was not going to say anything that might compromise the Soviet Union in the future." Such an attitude was incomprehensible to Pinay who burst out, "Do you mean to say that you, the Foreign Minister of one of the greatest countries in the world, aren't able to discuss any details of this conference"? Molotov smiled, maintained his evasive posture, but later in the evening said to Bohlen with one of his "icy" smiles, "It is apparent that our French friend has not had much experience in dealing with the Soviet Union."[9]

[5] Aspaturian, Vernon V. Process and Power in Soviet Foreign Policy. Boston, Little. Brown, 1971, p. 635.
[6] Ibid.
[7] Kertesz, Stephen D. American and Soviet Negotiating Behavior. In, Kertesz, Stephen D. and M. A. Fitzsimons, eds. Diplomacy in a Changing World. Notre Dame, Ind., University of Notre Dame Press, 1959, ch. 10, p. 137.
[8] Bohlen, op. cit., pp. 380–381.
[9] Ibid., p. 379.

3. THE MOLOTOV PROTOTYPE

As noted elsewhere in this study, Molotov impressed his own personality on the Soviet diplomatic establishment that he was rebuilding. In emphasizing this point Aspaturian wrote, "the diplomatic house that Molotov built was largely shaped in his own image." [10]

Negotiation by negation became the distinguishing feature of Molotov's diplomatic style, and "nyet", meaning "no", was synonymous with his name. However frustrating this style may have been to their Western adversaries (for it was generally characteristic of Soviet diplomats), still it served the Soviet purpose of nullifying the integrative effects of the wartime coalition. By using this tactic, the Soviet leadership was given a considerable degree of freedom of action in the international arena. [11] But this tactical device had only a short-term value because it served to create a formidable opposing alliance system and ultimately defeated the higher purposes of diplomacy.

A party loyalist and inveterate Communist believer, Molotov was obedient to Stalin his master, fiercely stubborn in negotiation and almost pathologically suspicious by training. (Molotov was always accompanied by two or three guards, and when at the British Prime Minister's home at Chequers and at Blair House, the President's mansion for distinguished visitors, he slept with a loaded revolver by his head.) [12] Dour and impassive, Molotov represented values and projected a personality and diplomatic style that could not help but impact upon the emerging young Soviet diplomatic corps. Drawing upon the biographies and careers of some of the Soviet Union's leading diplomats of the Molotov era, Aspaturian sketched out a prototype of the young Soviet diplomat and his career in the foreign service, concluding with the following composite characterization:

The formative years of a Soviet career diplomat were spent in the atmosphere of suffocating conformity characteristic of the late Stalinist era, and to some degree he still carries the birthmarks of that period. Although he may be the Soviet version of the "organization man" and is ready and willing to express "the orthodox Soviet point of view," since Stalin's death he has found this excruciatingly elusive. If his ideological outlook was shaped by Stalinism, his personality reflects that of Molotov. The career diplomat of this vintage is generally a conformist who frowns upon frivolity, is inclined to be conservative and cautious in manner, somber in outlook, often both sour and dour in expression; he rarely smiles when working and virtually never relaxes. He expresses no personal opinions, keeps his political convictions to himself, and unlike the diplomats of the Chicherin-Litvinov era, who were often unable to resist the temptations of political intrigue and frequently failed to keep their irrepressible revolutionary enthusiasm in check when abroad as diplomats, he has managed to keep his political skirts clean and displays a fastidious passion for the requirements of protocol. He scrupulously avoids compromising his diplomatic status by engaging in "impermissible activities," such as cavorting with indigenous Communists or directing espionage and propaganda operations, although he may "innocently" look the other way as his subordinates use his embassy as a cover for both subversive and spying activities. He cultivates few personal friendships with foreigners, official or private, keeps no diary, and has no intention of writing his memoirs, and although not effusively sociable, and rarely loquacious, he can easily turn on the charm upon signal from Moscow.

In short, the diplomatic house that Molotov built was largely shaped in his own image. * * * [13]

[10] Aspaturian, op. cit., p. 638.
[11] Slusser, op. cit., p. 230.
[12] Rohlen, op. cit., p. 380.
[13] Aspaturian, op. cit., p. 638.

That Molotov had succeeded in his task of rebuilding the Soviet diplomatic establishment, there seemed to be no doubt—at least in Aspaturian's judgment. According to this longtime scholar of Soviet diplomacy, the Soviet diplomatic service had appeared to achieve an inner equilibrium by 1953, "marked by the high professional caliber of its leading personnel, a remarkable breadth of diplomatic experience at home and abroad, the establishment of high standards, the institution of a predictable system of recruitment, rotation, and promotion of personnel, and above all an apparent immunity from the effects of Kremlin intrigues and power struggles." [14] Under Molotov's direction and protection the corps was "virtually immune from criticism and its members were rarely targets of abuse by the various contending cliques and factions that surrounded Stalin." Except for Beria's ubiquitous secret police, the Foreign Office was "remarkably free of penetration by party hacks and status-seeking members of the party apparatus." And above all it was not a dumping ground for bureaucrats wounded in the power struggles and shunted off to oblivion as was the case before the war and after Stalin's death. [15] Thus, as Aspaturian concluded in 1971, "The Soviet diplomatic service today is second to none in its professional competence, and Molotov subsequently proved to be one of the outstanding diplomatists of all time, according to the testimony of his most implacable antagonists." [16]

[14] Ibid., p. 614.
[15] Ibid., p. 614.
[16] Ibid., p. 632, Secretary of State Byrnes probably gave one of the most comprehensive portrayals of Molotov as a negotiator, clearly suggesting a certain admiration for his adversary. Drawing from his many postwar encounters with Molotov. Byrnes concluded that "Russia's leaders are stubborn and resourceful negotiators." He cited his "broad experience in dealing with men" both as a trial lawyer and in public service in the process of which he had met many men with many interests and settled many issues. "But through all these years," Byrnes recorded, "I had no experience that prepared me for negotiating with Mr. Molotov." A newspaper correspondent in London, reluctant to believe that Molotov would purposely break up the Foreign Ministers conference then underway rather than conciliate his views, asked Byrnes incredulously whether the negotiators had explored every avenue of approach to the problems. Byrnes responded that he had not only explored "every avenue, but I've gone down every lane, byway and highway. I've tried everything I ever learned in the House and Senate. But there I worked with a majority rule. This is more like a jury. If you have one stubborn juror, all you can expect is a mistrial." Byrnes had always thought that negotiating with Molotov would be a good experience for a lawyer who represented a corporation constantly being sued for damages and whose task was to play for time hoping that the complainant would get weary of waiting for a trial and settle for a small part of his claim.

Byrnes noted that Molotov had extraordinary perseverance and patience, citing the instance at the close of the Moscow Conference when the protocol had been signed and at that late eleventh hour announced he had decided after consideration to accept the U.S. proposal on the Balkan issue made the previous afternoon. Byrnes continued: "If we are correctly informed about the patience exercised by Job, I am certain Mr. Molotov is one of his lineal descendants. He has unlimited patience as well as a fine mind and tremendous energy. Any exhibition of impatience or bad temper by others gives him amusement. At such times it is interesting to watch his serious, solemn expression as he protests his innocence of any provocation." To illustrate his point, Byrnes cited Molotov's cunctator tactics at the Council of Foreign Ministers meetings in September 1945 and later in 1946 with respect to the transfer of the demilitarized Dodecanese Islands from Italy to Greece: the Allies favored the transfer; the Soviets opposed it, clearly in light of the indecisiveness of the Greek civil war in which the Soviets supported the Communist forces. Every inquiry was met with Molotov's response that he would submit it to his government for consideration. Other excuses were made at the April meeting in Paris. At another session of the Council shortly thereafter Molotov said he had hoped to discuss the matter but had been informed that morning that the Greek Ambassador was going to call on Vishinsky and thus would have to await the results of that conference. Byrnes wrote: "The rest of us laughed at this newest and lamest excuse. Even Molotov smiled." Byrnes continued: "After enough problems were settled to his satisfaction, Mr. Molotov then proposed that the Dodecanese be transferred to Greece and demilitarized. And he made the proposal as if the subject were being mentioned for the first time."

According to Byrnes, Molotov liked to discuss questions of procedure in which "he has no equal." He proceeded to describe this tactic: "He will argue for hours about

B. Politicization and Professionalism in the Diplomatic Service

1. POLITICIZATION BY KHRUSHCHEV

Along with Molotov, Khrushchev also deserved credit for rebuilding the Soviet diplomatic service and improving the infrastructure for Soviet foreign policy. During the years of his rise to power (1943–1956) and finally achieving predominance (1957–1964), Khrushchev succeeded in politicizing the diplomatic service. This maneuver was by no means altogether detrimental because the presence of high party officials tended to raise the prestige of the foreign service. At the same time Khrushchev continued to improve the professionalism of the career service and expanded the intellectual infrastructure for the development of foreign policy.

what subjects should be placed on an agenda. You must not only be patient but also must watch carefully even the manner in which your own proposal is stated. If you do not, you will later spend hours trying to get your complete proposal before the council for discussion." Molotov's response would be "Nyet," meaning "no", which, Byrnes recalled, "I heard so often that I almost accept it as part of my own language. He can say in English 'I agree,' but so seldom does he agree that his pronunciation isn't very good."

"In any conference, with or without the unanimity rule," Byrnes continued, "he will win your reluctant admiration by the resourcefulness he exhibits in his delaying tactics. He will sit through it all imperturbably, stroking his mustache or spinning his pince-nez glasses as he waits for a translation and smoking Russian cigarettes in what seems to be an endless chain."

As was typical of all Soviet negotiators, Molotov suffered no embarrassment, Byrnes recalled, in executing a complete reversal of position maintained for hours when further delay would not result in further concessions and thus agreement might as well be reached. Byrnes described Molotov's behavior in such instances : "As a rule, Mr. Molotov smilingly announces that the Soviet delegation in order to bring about agreement, desires to make a proposal. He then presents your proposal, which has been the subject of controversy for weeks, with only a few unimportant changes. Having argued the question so long, the other conferees are so anxious to get rid of it that they receive the announcement with pleasure. And frequently they even express appreciation to Mr. Molotov for his doing what he should have done weeks or months before."

Byrnes cited another "well-exercised tactic" of Molotov's, the counter-offensive. Whenever Molotov suspected that the United States or any other country was going to complain about Soviet failures to comply with an agreement, such as that at Yalta on free press, free elections, etc., he would anticipate the discussion. The tactic was either to mount the attack himself or get one of the satellite representatives to do it. As in the case of Greece, he would launch the most vitriolic attack against the legitimate Greek Government, charging it with corruption, aggressive intent against peaceful neighbors (Yugoslavia, Bulgaria, and Albania), and with being dominated by British imperialists. Persons disapproved by Molotov were always described in such attacks as "Fascists" while Communists and their sympathizers were referred to as "democratic forces." So often had Molotov repeated his charges against Greece that Byrnes feared that he had come to believe them. (Byrnes, op. cit., pp. 277–281.)

Other American diplomats spoke admiringly of Molotov. Before becoming Secretary of State, Dulles remarked with respect to Molotov's skills as a diplomat, "I have seen in action all of the great international statesmen of this century and I have never seen such personal diplomatic skill at so high a degree of perfection as Mr. Molotov's." (Dulles, John Foster. War or Peace. New York, Macmillan, 1950, cited by Aspaturian, p. 632.) Bohlen also respected Molotov's skill as a diplomat and noted in his reminiscences, "I was a little sorry to see the sour little man vanishing from the world stage." (Bohlen, op. cit., p. 381.) While Churchill had perceived in Molotov a "remarkable skill in duplicity", he still made what was described as "the most trenchant and discerning tribute" : "A man of outstanding ability and cold-blooded ruthlessness * * * his cannonball head, black mustache, and comprehending eyes, his slab face, his verbal adroitness and imperturbable demeanor were appropriate manifestations of his qualities and skill. He was above all men fitted to be the agent and instrument of an incalculable machine." (C. L. Sulzberger's characterizations in The New York Times, Jan. 11, 1956, cited by Aspaturian, p. 632.)

That some of Molotov's toughness had rubbed off on subordinates was evident in Robert Murphy's description of his first encounter with Mikhail A. Menshikov on the occasion of preparing for Khrushchev's visit to the United States : "There followed weeks of sticky negotiations, which I conducted with the Soviet Ambassador in Washington. When Mikhail A. Menshikov arrived in the United States in 1957, newspapermen dubbed him 'Smiling Mike' because he customarily looked cheerful in public. But in discussions I had with him at the State Department, the Soviet Ambassador usually neglected to put on his facade and I am sure he removed it when alone with his own staff. I remember the sweaty palm of his counselor when we shook hands. The counselor must have lived in terror of Smiling Mike, whom I found a cold-blooded ruthless somebody." (Murphy, op. cit., p. 438.)

Political purposes had underlain Khrushchev's objectives in politicizing the diplomatic service. With the close cooperation of the party hierarchy he undercut Molotov's position in the Foreign Ministry by flooding the diplomatic corps with party officials.[17] At the same time he used assignments to diplomatic posts as a way of disposing of political losers in the struggle for power. Molotov, for example, who was in league with other opponents of Khrushchev in the so-called "anti-party group", was removed as head of the Foreign Ministry in 1957 and assigned as Ambassador to Outer Mongolia. As Roetter observed with respect to its capital, Ulan Bator, "very few of even the most assiduous students of international affairs had ever heard of [it] and certainly none had regarded [it] as a hive of diplomatic activity."[18] And finally, Khrushchev, who, as will be shown below, conducted personal diplomacy with the greatest intensity and in the most extraordinary manner, apparently used assignment of party officials to establish his firm control over the foreign policy establishment.[19]

Indicative of the extent of Khrushchev's politicizing maneuver was the fact that between 1953 and 1960, excluding Molotov and Vishinsky, no less than five full members and five alternate members of the party Presidium elected at the 19th Party Congress in 1952 were assigned to diplomatic work. One of these party bureaucrats was V. V. Kuznetsov who through an extended accumulation of diplomatic experience was to emerge eventually as a seasoned professional diplomat. He held the post of First Deputy Foreign Minister, functioned as one of Moscow's leading diplomatic troubleshooters, was much respected as a negotiator, while at the same time remaining a full member of the Central Committee.[20]

Kuznetsov achieved probably his highest honor, and office, in October 1977 when he was elected to the position of first deputy chairman of the Presidium of the U.S.S.R. Supreme Soviet, a position commonly referred to in the Western press as that of "Vice President" because it seemed intended to relieve Brezhnev of some of his duties as head of state.[21]

Aspaturian identified four waves in the politicization of the Soviet diplomatic services, each coinciding with sufficient changes in the party leadership. The first wave occurred within a year after Stalin's death in 1953. No less than four mmebers of the party Presidium were shunted aside into the diplomatic service for reasons having little to do with diplomacy, making this maneuver one of the most conspicuous features of the post-Stalin diplomatic service.[22]

The second wave occurred after Malenkov's removal as Premier in February 1955. Several party functionaries were reassigned to the Foreign Ministry with a coinciding demotion in party rank. P. K. Ponomarenko, a veteran member of the party leadership, had apparently sided with Malenkov; he was finally reduced, after a series of demotions, to the post of Ambassador to Poland.[23]

The third wave, coinciding with Khrushchev's emergence as party leader, occurred between the 20th Party Congress in 1956 and 1957 with

[17] Slusser, op. cit., p. 237.
[18] Roetter, op. cit., p. 54.
[19] Slusser, op. cit., p. 237, ff. 62.
[20] Aspaturian, op. cit., p. 615.
[21] Radio Liberty Research, RL 234/77, Oct. 7, 1977, p. 1.
[22] Aspaturian, op. cit., p. 616.
[23] Ibid., p. 617.

the removal of an array of leading party officials and their reassignment to diplomatic posts. The fourth wave came with the expulsion of the "anti-party group" in July 1957 and the assignment of oppositionists, notably Molotov, to diplomatic posts.[24]

According to Aspaturian, the year 1958 was the "high water mark" of party infusion into the Foreign Ministry. Two of Gromyko's First Deputy Foreign Ministers, Kuznetsov and N. A. Patolichev, and at least six ambassadors outranked him in the party on the basis of seniority, though the political fortunes of some were by that time on the wane. Thus in 1958, Gromyko's noncareer subordinates included, aside from Molotov, eight former Presidium members and two former first secretaries of party organizations in the republics. Altogether, the noncareer diplomats accounted for nine full members of the Central Committee, five alternates, and two members of the Central Auditing Commission who had been demoted from membership in the Central Committee.[25]

The division of labor among ambassadorial posts was fairly distinct: Party officials were generally assigned to posts in all Soviet bloc states, including China, while career diplomats represented the Soviet Union in most of the Afro-Asian nations, the Arabic and other states of the Middle East, the major states of Latin America, British Commonwealth, and Western Europe, and the United States.[26] Data published in 1960 indicated that party officials were posted in the Soviet bloc states but also in areas of strategic importance; namely, Iran, India, Indonesia, and Yugoslavia. Finally, and "intriguingly," as Slusser noted, party officials served in three small European states: The Netherlands, Belgium, and Switzerland.[27]

2. CONTINUATION OF PROFESSIONALISM

(a) A new breed of Soviet diplomat

Khrushchev's global policy placed global requirements on the Soviet diplomatic establishment. Under Khrushchev the diplomatic corps was expanded dramatically to meet these requirements. In the process a new breed of Soviet diplomat emerged.

As an extension of Khrushchev's personal diplomacy that heavily accented public relations as a means for influencing foreign opinion, the Soviet diplomat now had to leave the isolation of the embassy that had been imposed during the Stalin era and in effect become a public figure. Ambassador Mikhail Menshikov's untiring efforts to be amenable quickly won for him the title "Smiling Mike" among Americans. Soviet ambassadors to France now had to be especially knowledgeable in French culture as a means of ingratiating themselves with the French people and increasing their appeal.[28]

Beyond such superficial requirements, this new generation had to have unique technical abilities especially for service in the Third World, and in seeking open encounters with foreigners, whether in the advanced West or the underdeveloped Third World, they had to be well trained in the language, culture, economics, and politics of the areas to

[24] Ibid., p. 616.
[25] Ibid., p. 619.
[26] Slusser, op. cit., pp. 233–234.
[27] Ibid.
[28] Roetter, op. cit., p. 111.

which they were assigned. Expanded horizons for political activity imposed upon the diplomatic establishment the necessity of producing young diplomats not only trained in their craft but even more importantly in coping with the multiple needs of diplomacy in an emerging technological age. Accordingly, in the Khrushchev era the accent was on professionalism in the broadest sense.

That a better quality of Soviet diplomat as a technician of diplomacy was indeed emerging in the Khrushchev era, there seemed to be little doubt. In 1960, Mosely acknowledged in the preface of a reprinting of his earlier essay on Soviet negotiating techniques that "Soviet second-rank negotiators have emerged much better acquainted with the language, politics, and internal divisions of the West"; but he added this qualification, "though they still adhere closely to the doctrinal core and rigid techniques described in this essay." [29]

Aspaturian concluded his study of Soviet diplomacy in the post-Stalin era with this approving postscript on the service since 1960:

The main trends discerned in the development of the Soviet diplomatic service during the first decade after Stalin's death have not only continued into the second decade but have evolved along more sophisticated lines and appear to have been institutionalized into a distinctive division of diplomatic labor that has shaped the recruitment, assignment, and rotational patterns of diplomatic personnel. [30]

And finally, writing in 1970, Sir William Hayter, a well-qualified diplomatic observer, noted that Gromyko, as Foreign Minister, was "well supported by a solid and distinguished corps of ambassadors." He cited specifically some of Moscow's seasoned diplomats, "Men like Zorin, Kuznetsov, Malik, and Tsarapkin [who] have been around in diplomatic life for decades, holding important posts at home and abroad, at conferences and at the United Nations." [31]

(b) Expanding missions abroad

The dramatic expansion of Soviet diplomatic missions abroad was a prominent feature of developments in the diplomatic establishment during the Khrushchev era, again to accommodate the requirements of an emerging global policy. Thus within 7 years after Stalin's death, the Soviet Union added 14 countries to those which it had maintained diplomatic relations. In 1960, it had 53 embassies, 4 legations, and a permanent representation in the United Nations. Most of the expansion occurred in the newly independent countries of Africa (Libya, Sudan, Morocco, Guinea, and Ghana) and Southeast Asia (Indonesia, North Vietnam, Cambodia, Nepal, and Ceylon). Little progress was achieved in Latin America where relations were maintained with only Argentina, Uruguay, and Mexico.[32] By 1959, Soviet diplomatic representation abroad increased to 66, and by January 1965 to 95.[33] As of December 31, 1970, the Soviets had diplomatic relations with 108 countries. Subsequently, the total number increased to 113.[34]

[29] Mosely. Philip E. The Kremlin and World Politics : Studies in Soviet Policy and Action. New York, Vintage, 1960, p. 4.
[30] Aspaturian. op. cit., p. 640.
[31] Hayter, William. Russia and the World : A Study of Soviet Foreign Policy. London, Secker & Warburg, 1970, p. 33.
[32] U.S. Congress. Senate. Committee on Government Operations. Subcommitee on National Policy Machinery. National Policy Machinery in the Soviet Union. 86th Congress, 2d session. Washington, U.S. Government Printing Office., 1960, pp. 41–42 (Report No. 1204). See also the subcommittee's subsequent report, U.S. Congress. Senate. Committee on Government Operations. Subcommittee on National Security Staffing and Operations. Staffing Procedures and Problems in the Soviet Union. 88th Congress, 1st session. Washington, U.S. Government Printing Office, 1963, pp. 31–32.
[33] Aspaturian, op. cit., p. 641.
[34] Meissner, op. cit., p. 62.

A predominant trend in this expansion of missions was the specific focus on the Third World. The effect of this new direction in Soviet policy was to create a third career pattern within the Soviet diplomatic establishment, in addition to the career diplomat and the party career men; namely, the technological specialist trained, for example, in agronomy, industrial engineering, or economic planning rather than as a party professional or in conventional diplomatic skills.[35]

Furthermore, the expansion of diplomatic activity stimulated the proliferation of new departments, agencies, and desks within the Foreign Ministry bureaucracy.[36] New career opportunities opened up for the rising young diplomatic elite.

The underlying causes for the general expansion of the Soviet diplomatic establishment were fourfold:

—The emergence of the Soviet Union as a global power in the 1960's and its assumption of international obligations and commitments throughout the world;

—The emergence of newly independent states in the Third World;

—The continued expansion of Soviet participation in the organs, agencies, and activities of international organizations; and

—The revival of the Soviet consular service.[37]

(c) The KGB presence

Direct KGB influence and control in the Foreign Ministry declined after 1945, owing seemingly to Molotov's success in professionalizing the diplomatic corps and in Khrushchev's downgrading of the secret police in general in the wake of Beria's execution as part of an effort to reduce its importance as a power base.[38] Still, as Slusser, a student of Soviet diplomacy and the secret police, observed:

It must be remembered that the allocation of functions and personnel assignments between the two bodies is a matter for decision at top Party levels, in the light of what is believed to be the most effective way of promoting the general goals of the Party. Espionage and diplomacy both have their part to play in the total process of Soviet foreign policy, and the top leadership may consider that an overt separation between them will produce better results than their complete or partial merger. Yet the Soviet leadership has shown that under certain conditions it considers the gains to be obtained from a direct fusion of espionage and diplomacy to outweigh its disadvantages.[39]

---

[35] Triska, Jan F. and David D. Finley. Soviet Foreign Policy. New York, Macmillan, 1968, p. 86.

[36] For a commentary on the organization and activities of the Foreign Ministry, see, Senate Government Operations Committee, National Policy Machinery in the Soviet Union, pp. 41–42, and its subsequent report in 1963, Staffing Procedures and Problems in the Soviet Union, pp. 29–34.

[37] Aspaturian, op. cit., p. 641.

[38] Slusser, op. cit., p. 235. Aspaturian wrote with respect to the years 1940–1947: "During these years, diplomatic posts were temporarily filled by personnel drawn from other departments, particularly the Secret Police. Litvinov had been removed and Molotov had taken over the responsibilities of the Narkomindel in addition to his duties as chairman of the Council of People's Commissars. These were also the years when the shattered service was being reconstituted by Molotov with the help of a small handful of career diplomats who survived the purges and the Secret Police." (p. 613.) Later on he referred to the role of Beria's "minions", as V. K. Dekanozov, and party specialists who were placed in high positions in the Foreign Ministry to insure reliability and to substitute for the victims of the purges or those insufficiently mature to assume responsibility. "Although Vishinsky remained in the Foreign Ministry to become his chief assistant." Aspaturian continued, "Molotov was successful in sweeping out Beria's cronies. By 1947, the new professionals were ready to assume full administrative responsibilities under Molotov's direction." (p. 615.) For a commentary on Khrushchev's efforts to downgrade the KGB, see Triska and Finley, op. cit., p. 102.

[39] Slusser, op. cit., p. 235. Slusser went on to illustrate this point by the appointment of S. M. Kudriavtsev as Soviet Ambassador to Cuba in July 1960. In 1946, Kudriavtsev, then first secretary of the Embassy in Ottawa, was identified by the Canadian counterespionage service as a leading figure in the spy ring that had been transmitting secret atomic information to Moscow. The year 1960, it will be recalled, was a critical year in the consolidation of Castro's power in Cuba.

Revelations by Gouzenko in 1945 of Soviet espionage activities from the Soviet Embassy in Ottawa, by Petrov in 1954 of subversive activities from the embassy in Canberra, and by Kaznacheev in his book published in 1962 on the embassy in Rangoon provided detailed information on the KGB role at various timeframes within the Soviet diplomatic establishment.[40] Whatever the directing mechanism and responsible authority, their presence was real. As Kaznacheev disclosed, KGB personnel were recruited for training in the Soviet International Relations Institute for diplomats.[41] An estimated 500–600 of the Institute's student body of 2,000 were believed to have probably had prior KGB service.[42]

Thus, the directing role of the KGB in the diplomatic establishment may have changed and may even been reduced from the days when Dekanozov was Vice Commissar of Foreign Affairs and other Chekists held posts of responsibility, but not its presence. As Hayter noted: "Intelligence, espionage, call it what you will, plays a very extensive part in Soviet policy. There is nothing particularly reprehensible about this. Most countries do as much of it as they can afford, and the Russians seem able to afford a great deal and do it rather well." [43]

3. KHRUSHCHEV'S CONTROL OVER FOREIGN POLICY

After 1956–57, Khrushchev, in a finely orchestrated arrangement with the party Presidium, controlled the formulation and implementation of Soviet foreign policy; Gromyko and the Foreign Ministry were his instruments. In brief, power and authority remained where they have always been since Lenin, with the party and its leadership.[44]

Khrushchev's predilection for personal diplomacy, by far the most distinguishing feature of his style in diplomacy, visibly downgraded

---

[40] For the official reports by the Canadian and Australian Governments on the Gouzenko and Petrov revelations, see, Australia. Royal Commission on Espionage. Report and transcript of proceedings. Sydney, 1955, and Canada. Royal Commission to Investigate Disclosures of Secret and Confidential Information to Unauthorized Persons. Documents and Reports. Ottawa, E. Cloutier, printer to the King, 1946. See also, Kaznacheev, Aleksandr. Inside a Soviet Embassy: Experiences of a Russian Diplomat in Burma. Philadelphia, Lippincott, 1962. 250 pp.

[41] Ibid., p. 32.

[42] Triska and Finley, op. cit., p. 102. Robert Murphy gave some insight into the problem of using the Soviet Embassy for espionage purposes. As Deputy Under Secretary of State in the Eisenhower Administration, he negotiated with the Soviets on "exceptional matters," but he noted that "there was one type of diplomatic exchange which occurred so many times that it became almost routine. Every once in a while a staff member of the Soviet Embassy would be detected in an attempt to acquire secret and strategic information in flagrant violation of American law. As part of the most intensive espionage network the world has ever seen, there was nothing novel about such spying, and the procedure for handling the situation was rather well established. The Ambassador would be asked to call and I would hand him a formal note, with appropriate deprecating gestures, reciting the facts and requiring the offending Russian to depart from the United States within a day or two as persona non grata. This would elicit a strong verbal denial of any wrongdoing, and the Ambassador would leave my office after suitable emotional expressions. Then the Ambassador would send me a formal communication denying everything in positive terms. And then the offending official would depart from the United States. No further reference to the incident would be made by either the Ambassador or me when he called again on other matters. There was a sort of tacit understanding that this was part of the game. But it would be just a question of time before a member of the staff of the American Embassy in Moscow would be arbitrarily accused of a similar offense, declared persona non grata, and asked to depart from the Soviet Union. It was the regular price we paid for success by our detection agencies." (Murphy, op. cit., p. 420.)

[43] Hayter, Russia and the World, p. 21.

[44] Senate. Committee on Government Operations. National Policy Machinery in the Soviet Union, p. 40. Roetter write: "Real power, indeed, still lies where it always has—in the inner councils of the Party. All the reforms and reorganizations effected by Molotov before his enforced retirement from active politics cannot hide that fact; and as if to underline it, the new Foreign Ministry [building, "a vast skyscraper that looks rather like an overornate wedding cake"] is well away from the center of Moscow and the Kremlin." (Roetter, op. cit., pp. 110–111.)

the role of the Foreign Minister. And he made this point on many occasions at the expense and no doubt humiliation of Gromyko. Thus in an interview with Harriman in 1959 during the second Berlin crisis, Khrushchev declared that Gromyko could say nothing but "what we tell him to" and that he had been instructed to tell the West that the "days of the [Berlin] occupation are gone forever." [45]

Gromyko would be sent to the Foreign Ministers Conference scheduled for Geneva, Khrushchev noted, underscoring his Foreign Minister's subservience to him with the crude remark that if Gromyko were told to pull down his pants and sit on a block of ice, he would do so until he was told to rise—otherwise he would lose his job. Gromyko sat impassively by, saying nothing and betraying no inner feelings,[46] a response in the manner of "the most successful product of the Molotov school" of diplomats, as Hayter described Gromyko.[47]

The centralization of power and authority combined with the rigid conformity with instructions from Moscow were thus continuing realities that the Soviet diplomat and negotiator had to cope with. As Kertesz described the relationship in 1959 :

A Soviet representative executes instructions in the strictest sense and then ceases to function as a diplomat. He is aware of the weak power position of a diplomat in the Soviet state organization and accepts with grim determination the set of ideas, values, and methods imposed by ruling-party circles. He knows that the important foreign political decisions are not made in the foreign ministry, which has only formal authority and does not wield effective power. The forces which control Soviet diplomats are elsewhere. Nothing remains for him but to be a submissive conformist.[48]

Yet with the emerging technological era, particularly the explosion of information and the globalization of knowledge, it was understandable that an intelligent and informed Soviet diplomat, commanding a significant body of information vital for the formulation of foreign policy and upon which the decisionmakers depended, could have some impact upon the process. Hayter seemed to have this in mind when he described Khrushchev's and Brezhnev's dependency upon Gromyko :

Khrushchev, during his discussions with Sir Anthony Eden at No. 10 Downing Street in 1956, would whenever at a loss for a fact turned to Gromyko, whom he described as "our encyclopedia". Now he is at Brezhnev's elbow. In spite of his title of Minister of Foreign Affairs he is, in our terms, more like a permanent official. The decisions are not his. But his experience and his knowledge of the facts and the people involved must enable him to exercise considerable influence over the decisions, perhaps particularly when the party leaders are new and ignorant of foreign affairs.[49]

---

[45] Facts-on-File, July 16, 1959, p. 222D3.
[46] Aspaturian, op. cit., p. 640.
[47] Hayter, Russia and the World, p. 32.
[48] Kertesz, op. cit., pp. 141–142. Hayter, drawing from his decades of experience in dealing with Soviet diplomats, wrote in 1970: "In general it is fair to say that the diplomats with whom Westerners come into contact are mostly technicians, able and experienced in their field but without much influence over policy and seldom prepared to discuss it. The effect of this is that the normal, indeed almost invariable, response of a Soviet diplomatic official to any new proposal is 'I will consult my government'. The 'government' is in fact the party, whose leading officials are not very accessible to foreigners and are very rarely willing to discuss policy matters seriously with them. But it is in their hands that foreign policy decisions lie." (Hayter, Russia and the World, p. 33.) Murphy recalled when he assumed duties in Washington in 1953 : "At the beginning of my term there, Georgi N. Zaroubin was the Soviet Ambassador; later he was succeeded by Mikhail A. Menshikov. Both of these envoys were products of the Communist system, as were members of their embassy staffs, and sometimes I found myself actually sorry for the men and their families in the straitjacket existence required of them. Meeting these diplomats frequently on official business provided me with additional understanding of Soviet mentality and methods." (Murphy, op. cit., p. 420.)
[49] Hayter, Russia and the World, p. 32.

4. RISING PRESTIGE OF THE SOVIET DIPLOMATIC SERVICE

Politicizing and professionalizing the Soviet diplomatic establishment had the overall effect of raising the prestige of the Foreign Ministry and the Soviet diplomatic service. As the Senate Government Operations Committee study on Soviet national policy machinery concluded, the "revitalization of the ministry since Stalin's death has been accompanied by an enhancement in the prestige of diplomatic service." This rise in prestige was a byproduct of the infusion of high party officials into the Foreign Ministry; it was also fostered by a deliberate policy of the regime.[50]

In Stalin's day, few Soviet diplomats were members of the leading party organs. At the time of his death only eight were so privileged, and of them only Vishinsky was a full member of the Central Committee. At the 20th Party Congress in February 1956, six were named full members. By 1960, 19 had the prestige of holding high party rank; 9 were full members of the Central Committee.[51]

Khrushchev's globalist policy combined with the implications of his theoretical formulation of peaceful coexistence as a policy and strategy was another element that impacted favorably upon the diplomatic establishment: It increased the responsibilities of the diplomatic service and accordingly raised its prestige. Dependency of the decision-makers upon the flow of information into the center and the development of specialized expertise imperative for the formulation and implementation of a complex foreign policy with global implications made the functions of the Soviet diplomat crucial in the foreign policy process. Such a renewal and expansion of functions inevitably enhanced the role and thus the prestige of the Soviet diplomat.[52]

Khrushchev's pronouncement of peaceful coexistence as a policy and strategy had a similar effect. Implicit is this new theoretical formulation was a direct and intensive Soviet engagement with the "imperialist" camp and the so-called "zone of peace," that is, the nations of the Third World. The task of carrying out this policy fell primarily upon the Foreign Ministry as the recognized arm of the Soviet state and upon its diplomats who were trained in and who largely accepted the structure of the Western nation-state system; it did not rest upon the party activists.[53] Conditions that produced peaceful coexistence imposed special requirements upon the Soviets with the result, as Triska and Finley concluded, that "the form of the conventional Foreign Ministry embodied a more substantial content. Today it is indisputably the chief organ for administering foreign relations with the non-Communist industrial nations, and it has a major role in the formulation of policies toward those countries as well. Its role in Soviet relations with the developing countries and with the Communist

---

[50] Senate, Committee on Government Operations, National Policy Machinery in the Soviet Union, p. 44.

[51] Ibid.

[52] Triska and Finley observed : "Soviet diplomats play a crucial role among the selectors of information relevant to formulating and administering Soviet foreign policy. They likewise play a crucial role among agents for implementing Soviet policy abroad. They thus constitute an essential link between Soviet policy formulation and the external environment. Though supplemented and corroborated institutionally by additional channels of information gathering and agencies of policy implementation, Soviet diplomatic personnel are central to important functions of the decision process." (Triska and Finley, op cit., p. 86.)

[53] Ibid., pp. 79–80.

system is more complex. * * * " [54] These changing requirements enlarged both the responsibilities and, as a spinoff, the prestige of the Foreign Ministry and diplomatic service as an institution.

Hayter probably best summed up the mechanics of Soviet foreign policy and the impact of professionalism on the diplomatic corps in the post-Stalin era when he concluded:

The Communist Party apparatus is in charge of foreign policy, as it is of all other activities in the Soviet Union. The Politburo of the Party decides the policy, and has at its disposal subordinate party organs to see that its decisions are carried out. These subordinate organs may do some diplomatic work themselves, particularly in the countries of the socialist system, but most of the actual execution of policy is left to the professionals of the Ministry of Foreign Affairs. Many other agencies are also involved, more particularly the K.G.B., and these agencies have their own channels between Moscow and the missions abroad. There is a very extensive intelligence network, the products of which are probably not very well co-ordinated or evaluated. The sum total of information reaching Moscow about foreign countries is large but often unreliable. Taken as a whole, however, the Soviet diplomatic machine is a powerful and formidable instrument. [55]

C. Expanding Intellectual Resources for Foreign Policy

1. LIMITATION ON RESOURCES PRIOR TO THE KHRUSHCHEV ERA

An integral part of the rising prestige of the Soviet diplomatic establishment, indeed an important causal factor, was the expansion of the intellectual resources for foreign policy. Prior to the Khrushchev era Soviet resources were severely limited, and by comparison to the present day virtually nonexistent. Suggestive of the negative impact of these restrictions upon Soviet foreign policy was the case of American studies in the U.S.S.R. The purges of the late 1930's, the ravages of the war, and the imposed Stalinist orthodoxy on scholars during the cold war era dealt a severe blow to American studies in the Soviet Union. American studies shared in common the blight on all studies in international relations. In 1925, the Institute of World Economics and World Politics had been founded as a principal adjunct of foreign policy study; in 1947, the Institute and its journal were abolished by Stalin. Between 1948 and 1950 almost no significant books on the United States appeared in the Soviet Union and those that were published in the early 1950's exuded the intensely propagandistic spirit of the cold war, making this period the nadir of Soviet studies on the United States. [56]

That this spirit of Stalinist "know-nothingism" adversely affected the conduct of Soviet foreign policy was evident by the experiences of Americans such as Mosely who negotiated with the Soviets during the war and in the immediate postwar period. Linguistic training in the use of English or French, for example, was inadequate, making negotiations very difficult—ironic since Soviet linguists were pioneers in the development of effective teaching of languages, Mosely explained that at the close of the 1930's, the Soviets had recruited their foreign service personnel primarily among administrators and engineers, with a

[54] Ibid., p. 37.
[55] Hayter, Russia and the World, p. 25.
[56] Mills, Richard M. One Theory in Search of Reality: The Development of United States Studies in the Soviet Union. Political Science Quarterly, vol. 87, March 1972: 67–69.

sprinkling of professors. Until entering the service these neophytes of diplomacy had neither the need nor the incentive to learn a foreign language effectively and when on assignment they had neither the time nor were given the permission as Mosely observed, "to relax and absorb not only a language but the culture or way of thought which is expressed in mastering it." Special burdens were, therefore, placed on negotiators to insure that proposals and texts in negotiations were phrased in a form that could be rendered exactly into Russian for the sake of clarity and comprehension.[57]

Lack of legal training among Soviet diplomats also added to the difficulties in negotiations. Mosely recalled a problem that had arisen on the European Advisory Commission when the Instrument of Unconditional Surrender was under consideration. A serious point at issue was failure of the Soviet negotiator to understand the legal implications of the prisoner-of-war question as it pertained to German soldiers before and after the formal surrender. The Soviets perceived no distinction; the Western Allies did; the difference was crucial. The matter was finally resolved in a compromise after 5 months of negotiations.[58]

Perhaps most revealing of Soviet inadequacy in training was their failure to understand the workings of the American system. Hazard emphasized this point as an obstacle in dealing with the Russians on lend-lease negotiations. According to Mosely, Soviet negotiators usually showed little comprehension of the legal problems that normally arose in seeking an international agreement and in meeting special constitutional requirements of democratic states. He cited the case of the Paris session of the Council of Foreign Ministers. The Soviet delegation was puzzled by the presence of Senator Tom Connally (D–Tex.), Chairman of the Senate Foreign Relations Committee, and Senator Arthur M. Vandenberg (R–Mich.), the ranking Republican member of the committee. Both were the principal congressional leaders responsible for moving the United States from its prewar isolationist path to that of bipartisan internationalism in the postwar era.

One afternoon after leaving the conference room for tea, a member of the Soviet delegation approached Mosely and asked why the Senators were there. Mosely proceeded to give a brief lecture on their background, the importance of a bipartisan foreign policy in the American system, and explained that the peace treaties on which the Council was then working could be ratified by the President only upon the advice and consent of the Senate, and two-thirds at that. Hence, the need for affirmative action in order to win approval of the two most influential leaders of both parties, particularly when American parties, using Soviet terms for clarity, were "undisciplined." According to Mosely, his Soviet colleague was "frankly amazed" to learn of the Senate responsibilities. He asked incredulously, "You don't mean that the Senate would refuse to ratify a treaty that your Government had signed?" To which Mosely replied that the Senate had often refused to act at all or acted negatively on treaties negotiated and submitted by the executive. This elementary lesson in American civics was a new revelation to the Soviet negotiator.[59]

---

[57] Mosely, Some Soviet Techniques of Negotiation, p. 239.
[58] Ibid., pp. 291–292.
[59] Ibid., pp. 290–291.

No elaborate analysis could be more revealing than this simple story by Mosely to illustrate the lack of knowledge among Soviet diplomats of Stalin's era about the American system and on a matter that directly affected Soviet interests. It must be remembered that Molotov headed this delegation and Vandenberg particularly made his presence known to him during the negotiations.[60]

2. KHRUSHCHEV'S INNOVATIONS, 1956

(a) Revitalization and expansion of Soviet intellectual resources

For the development of Soviet area studies specifically and international relations in general the 20th Party Congress of 1956 was in every sense a "great awakening." Khrushchev's declaration on peaceful coexistence with its special focus on the Third World and call for engagement with the "imperialist" West, along with his corollary internal campaign of de-Stalinization had the effect of revitalizing and expanding Soviet intellectual resources for foreign policy. At the Congress Mikoyan made a devastating attack on the Institute for Oriental Studies which embraced in its purview Africa as well as Asia, ridiculing the Academy of Sciences with charges that the Institute was "still dozing" while "the whole East has awakened." [61] Other sharp criticisms of the inadequacies of Soviet intellectual resources for foreign policy were to follow.[62]

Khrushchev's impact on expanding the horizon of inquiry and Soviet intellectual resources in the international field was electrifying. Briefly, the Institute of World Economy and International Relations (IMEMO) was resurrected in April 1956 under a slightly revised name and in July 1957 began publication of the monthly, World Economy and International Relations, the principal Soviet scholarly journal on international relations.[63] The work of the Institute of Oriental Studies was revitalized and expanded.[64] Other institutes were subsequently established covering the Third World, such as, the Institute of Africa, the Institute of Latin America, and the Institute of the Far East.[65] Publications on subjects relating to international relations were expanded; translations of materials from abroad (for example, the works of some leading American international relations specialists, such as, Bernard Brodie and Robert Osgood) were undertaken; contacts of Soviet scholars with the world community of scholars were established and subsequently strengthened; and other areas of academic inquiry into the social sciences, such as, sociology, heretofore banned under Stalinist orthodoxy, were opened up.

---

[60] Mosely noted that Senator Vandenberg upset the Soviet delegation particularly. "After some especially outrageous tirade by Molotov," he recalled, "he would take his unsmoked cigar from his mouth and grin across the table most engagingly, as if to say, 'Well, well, that *is* a new angle!'" (Ibid., p. 290.)
[61] Zimmerman, William. Soviet Perspectives on International Relations, 1956–67. Princeton, N.J., Princeton University Press, 1969, p. 33. In chapter 2, Zimmerman examined the emergence of the study of international relations as a discipline in the Soviet Union.
[62] For a detailed and authoritative study on the intellectual infrastructure for Soviet foreign policy, see the recently published work by Dr. Oded Eran entitled, "Mezhdunarodniki: An Assessment of Professional Expertise in the Making of Soviet Foreign Policy." Tel Aviv, Israel, Turtledove Publishing, 1979, 331 pp. Eran describes the expansion of the infrastructure during the Khrushchev era in Book II.
[63] Mills, op. cit., p. 70.
[64] For a discussion of Soviet studies on the Middle East and elsewhere in the Afro-Asian world, see, Vucinich, Wayne S. Soviet Studies on the Middle East. In, Lederer, Ivo J. and Wayne S. Vucinich, eds. The Soviet Union and the Middle East: The Post-World War II Era. Stanford, Calif., Hoover Institution Press, 1974, chapter 9.
[65] The World of Learning, 1977–78. London, Europa Publications, 1977, vol. 2, p. 1233.

In brief, Khruschchev had engineered what in retrospect appears to have been somewhat of an intellectual revolution in Soviet studies on international relations, not a revolution in the Western democratic sense of expanding freedom of inquiry but rather expanding inquiry within the protective confines of Marxist-Leninist ideology. His purpose was realistic and pragmatic: To serve the global goals of Soviet foreign policy by, in effect, filling in the Orwellian "memory holes," those gaps of knowledge and information that were created under Stalinism. As Prof. Thomas P. Thornton explained with respect to Khrushchev's rationale as it pertained to the Third World:

The change in line did not result from any particular devotion to truth and scholarship on the part of the Khrushchev leadership. The Soviet Government found itself badly out of touch with the emerging areas and realized that measures to improve the situation were urgently required. In addition to the necessary political moves that were already under way, a new body of research and theory was needed. Even more important, a new generation of students had to be familiarized with the politics, history, customs, languages, and other aspects of the emerging countries.[66]

(b) Upgrading the training of diplomats

As suggested above, Khrushchev's global policy imposed new demands upon Soviet diplomats, requiring not only an expansion of the foreign service, but more importantly, an upgrading of its training, particularly with respect to the Third World. The Education and Training Department of the Foreign Ministry was responsible for the training of foreign service candidates and for the further training of diplomats. It also supervised the Higher Diplomatic School for the training of senior diplomats, the Moscow State Institute for International Relations (IRI), and the advanced courses in foreign languages.[67]

That the Soviet diplomat received an intensive training, meeting many of the criticism of past observers with respect to inadequacy, was revealed by Kaznacheev who had entered the service in the mid-1950's and later defected from the Soviet Embassy in Rangoon, Burma. According to Kaznacheev, the International Relations Institute, the principal Soviet school for diplomats, had "a strong reputation of being one of the most difficult schools in the whole country." [68] Triska and Finley credited it with being "one of the most competitive schools in the U.S.S.R." [69] The 6-year course was "packed to the utmost," Kaznacheev noted: 6 to 8 hours of lectures and seminars each day, 6 days a week during the entire 6 years was standard. There were no optional courses, and the 2,000 student body was subdivided into specialties according to subject areas, with notably increased interest in the Third World. There were three major categories of study: The general subjects, studied by all students, included, for example, the history of international relations, philosophy, international law, Marxism-Leninism; the area subjects included material, for example in the

[66] Thornton, Thomas P., ed. The Third World in Soviet Perspective: Studies by Soviet Writers on the Developing Areas. Princeton, N.J., Princeton University Press, 1964, p. 78. For a commentary by a Soviet scholar on the expansion of American studies, see, Bolkhovitinov, N. N. On the Present State of American Studies in the Soviet Union. In, Walker, Robert H. American Studies Abroad. Westport, Conn., Greenwood Press, 1975, pp. 101–108.
[67] Meissner, op. cit., p. 58.
[68] Kaznacheev, op. cit., p. 29.
[69] Triska and Finley, op. cit., p. 96.

Eastern division, on the history of the Orient, the economic geography of the Orient and philosophical schools of the Orient; and finally a number of highly specialized subjects required for students with individual area specializations. The Indian group, for instance, would undertake detailed studies in India's history, geography, economy, administration, art, literature and music. The daily Indian press was required reading. This academic training was supplemented by practical work with Indian students and visiting Indian delegations—"a highly useful and informative experience," Kaznacheev observed.

Extensive individual research projects were also required of students in the IRI. Some 40 percent of the IRI's program also comprised language training with the requirement that each student had to have a thorough knowledge of two foreign languages, with three being required in some cases.[70] The party and Komsomol (the Soviet political organization for young adults) maintained a strong presence. In Kaznacheev's time an estimated 30 percent of the student body were party members.[71]

In brief, judging from Kaznacheev's account and the extensive commentary by Triska and Finley, the training of Soviet diplomats was rigorous and demanding with a focus on general and specialized subjects as well as area studies, notably with increased interest in the emerging nations, and with demands placed on political indoctrination and activity. As Triska and Finley concluded, the educational requirements for entering the diplomatic service were "high" and the training program "arduous." [72]

3. IMPROVED BASE FOR CONDUCTING DIPLOMACY

The base for conducting Soviet diplomacy had thus been substantially improved during the Khrushchev era. Expansion of the institutional facilities associated with foreign policy; continued growth and improvement in the training of diplomats, scholars, and specialized technicians with skills especially useful in the Third World; the influx of foreign materials for study; and the growing tolerance of new methodologies, theories, and disciplines common in the West—all were among those factors that appreciably improved not only the resources for the conduct of Soviet diplomacy, particularly in their approach to the Third World, but also the study of the United States and international relations, with its unique accent on defense matters, as a discipline independent from the traditional linkage to historical studies. Like the Americans, the Soviets focused increasingly on problem solving and the role of theory in international relations.[73]

By any measure, the improvements in the Soviet diplomatic establishment were impressive.

[70] Ibid., p. 97 and Kaznacheev, op. cit., pp. 29–30.
[71] Ibid., p. 33.
[72] Triska and Finley, op. cit., p. 87. For a discussion of career incentives and other professional aspects of the diplomatic service, see, Senate, Committee on Government Operations, National Policy Machinery in the Soviet Union, pp. 42–45 and Staffing Procedures and Problems in the Soviet Union, pp. 32–35.
[73] Before 1956, William Zimmerman, an American specialist on Soviet foreign policy, observed, for example, that the absence of even the most rudimentary source books posed "insuperable obstacles" for the study of international relations in the Soviet Union, except to the most privileged; by the early 1960's, he noted, the absence of this "material base" for research had become "largely overcome." (Zimmerman, op. cit., p. 46.)

D. A Summing Up

To sum up, therefore, the Molotov legacy of professionalism provided Khrushchev a solid base upon which to build a strong and stable diplomatic establishment. Continuation of professionalism, combined with politicization of the service (at least in its positive aspects), and the expansion of the intellectual resources for foreign policy, proved in retrospect to have constituted a decided step forward in correcting the shortcomings of the middle and late Stalin era.

But these improvements, it must be remembered, and the Soviets would be the first to assert, were undertaken to further the ideological purposes of communism: They were not intended to ease the burdens on the West, but rather to magnify them. For the Soviets have insisted that there could be no peaceful coexistence in ideology; the struggle continues, according to the preordained laws of history.

In the short term Khrushchev misused these improved resources of diplomacy irresponsibly and dangerously to further his own aggressive foreign policy designs. Whether in the long term they will be used to serve the central and highest purpose of diplomacy; namely, to resolve international differences and maintain the peace, has remained an open question.

III. SOME CHARACTERISTICS OF SOVIET DIPLOMACY AND NEGOTIATIONS IN THE KHRUSHCHEV ERA

A. PEACEFUL COEXISTENCE: A NEW DIRECTION FOR SOVIET THEORY, POLICY, AND STRATEGY

1. THE MEANING OF PEACEFUL COEXISTENCE

The concept of peaceful coexistence largely determined the characteristics of Soviet diplomacy and negotiations in the Khrushchev era. For many decades a respectable term in Soviet political lexicon, peaceful coexistence was not raised to the level of doctrine until the 20th Party Congress of 1956. For good reason, therefore, Hayter and other authorities on Soviet affairs have judged that this congress "was indeed a turning-point in the history of the Soviet Union, both internally and in its external relations."[1]

Briefly, Khrushchev revised the traditional Soviet belief in the inevitability of war with capitalism and in the concept of "capitalist encirclement", for years a Stalinist bugaboo. The postwar expansion of Communist power, the emergence of the newly independent nations in the former colonial areas (he called it a "zone of peace"), and the decline of the Western imperial systems created, in Khrushchev's view, a new distribution of power in the world. On the assumption that the Third World was symbiotically linked to the "Socialist camp" (he used the terms "Communist" and "Socialist" interchangeably), Khrushchev held that the capitalist world and not the Socialist was now "encircled"; that the balance of power had now shifted to the world of socialism; that the overwhelming power of this combination of "peace-loving" powers would henceforth stay the hand of the Western "imperialist aggressor"; and that since war was now no longer inevitable between the two competing camps, given this correlation of power in socialism's favor, the world was, therefore, entering a new era, an era of peaceful coexistence. Khrushchev did not doubt that in peaceful competition the Socialist world would emerge victorious; this was the preordained verdict of history.

In the course of refining this doctrine, it soon became clear that peaceful coexistence, as Khrushchev perceived it, did not mean peaceful competition in the Western democratic sense. There was to be no real truce in the cold war, no genuine mutual acceptance of a "live and let live" philosophy in East-West relations. Rather, the "struggle" between the forces of capitalism and socialism was to continue on all levels, short of thermonuclear war; there could be no peaceful coexistence in ideology. Thus, while the Communist road to power through, for example, nonviolent parliamentary means was doctrinally

---

[1] Hayter, Sir William. The Kremlin and the Embassy. New York, Macmillan, 1966, p. 126.

sanctioned, this variation did not necessarily rule out the resort to violence and revolution. Nor did it rule out support for the so-called "wars of liberation," as were then taking place in Cuba and Southeast Asia. These were just wars, deserving of full Soviet support. Nor did Khrushchev rule out the use of military power-in-being in confrontations with the West to achieve specific Soviet political goals, as in the case of the Berlin crisis of 1958–59.

Inevitably, Khrushchev's definition of peaceful coexistence created a dangerous dilemma when it was practically applied, and this dilemma was not to be resolved, at least for him, until the Cuban missile crisis of 1962. The dilemma was this: How was it possible to avoid the admitted danger of thermonuclear war while simultaneously pressing the ideological and political "struggle" in a climate of unrelieved tension and confrontation that itself could invite the danger of the thermonuclear war that he sought to avoid. Time and the Cuban missile crisis were to show that he could not have it both ways.

In brief, peaceful coexistence was Khrushchev's rationale for pursuing the goals of communism and Soviet foreign policy in the thermonuclear age, an era of long-range delivery systems and atomic weapons that did not recognize the class principle; it was his strategy for breaking out of the continental isolation created in the Stalin era and taking the offensive to establish a Soviet global presence.

2. FOREIGN POLICY IMPLICATIONS OF PEACEFUL COEXISTENCE

The implications of Khrushchev's perception of peaceful coexistence for East-West relations were far reaching. For Khrushchev conducted a foreign policy, particularly after 1957, that was aggressive, highly provocative and on the false assumption that the balance of power in the world (in Soviet terminology, the correlation of forces) had actually been transformed to the Socialist, hence the Soviet, advantage. In the Hitlerian manner of the 1930's, he insisted that the United States and its allies recognize this new reality and adjust their foreign policy goals accordingly.[2] The upshot was acute confrontation along a global front in what Mosely termed a series of "rolling crises." Somewhat prophetically Mosely laid out as early as 1959 the main lines of Khrushchev's bellicose foreign policy that was to continue for the next 4 years when he concluded:

The past 3 years, since 1956, have given Soviet policy a wider range of goals, a far greater variety of instruments. The adaptation to the new environment has not been without risks and costs to Soviet policy. All of these, in Khrushchev's eyes, appear to have been compensated by the rapid progress of Soviet strategic power. * * * After a period of experimentation with the wider range of political, economic, and psychological instruments, Khrushchev seems again to be concentrating his main hopes on the deployment of Soviet military power, now arrayed in a new and even more ominous form. He seems determined, in one part of the world after another, or perhaps in several regions at once, to raise a major strategic challenge to the strength and cohesion of the free world.[3]

---

[2] For a commentary and analysis of Krushchev's view on the balance of power concept, see, Whelan, Joseph G. Krushchev and the Balance of World Power. In, Seabury, Paul, ed. Balance of Power. San Francisco. Calif., Chandler Publishing Co.. 1965. chapter 18. Reproduced from. The Review of Politics. vol. 23, April 1960 : 131–152, and U.S. Congress. Senate. Khrushchev and the Balance of World Power. Presented by Senator Hubert H. Humphrey. 88th Congress, 1st session. Washington, U.S. Government Printing Office., 1962. 16 pp.

[3] Mosely, Philip E. The New Challenge of the Kremlin. In, Kertesz and Fitzsimons, op. cit. ch. 10, p. 132.

On the larger world scene Khrushchev's pursuit of his peaceful coexistence policy was to provoke something of a revolution in international politics. He tried to establish a political connection with this emerging Third World that was deeply prejudiced against the West because of its colonial experience. The effect of this effort combined with the reality of a Soviet global presence which it entailed was to quicken the pace of the Third World's entry into world politics as a new power factor and to create new problems in East-West relations for policymakers.

B. KHRUSHCHEV'S STYLE OF NEGOTIATIONS BY THREAT AND INTIMIDATION

1. NEW RULES FOR DIPLOMACY AND NEGOTIATIONS

In diplomacy and negotiations Khrushchev threw out the normal courtesies and customs that had evolved so laboriously over the years and even came to be accepted by latter-day Soviet diplomats. In their place he introduced a style of threat and intimidation that sought not to conciliate but to frustrate, not to placate but to terrorize, not to ingratiate but to humiliate, not to seek stability but to disrupt established patterns of relationships.

This threatening style of Khrushchev's took on many forms and variations, and it was put on display in actual negotiations and in other settings less formal where diplomacy functioned, nonetheless, as in speeches at home and abroad and in informal comments to the foreign press. But Khrushchev's purposes were clear: To pressure his adversary into accepting his position, and that position was simply to recognize the predominance of Soviet power.

2. KHRUSHCHEV'S "MISSILE DIPLOMACY"

Most distinctive among the many characteristics of Khrushchev's style of negotiations was his resort to what observers called, "missile diplomacy." In August 1957, the Soviet Union launched their first ICBM, and in October, their first sputnik, before the United States. Khrushchev used these achievements for two political purposes: To threaten the West, especially the United States which was for the first time within direct range of Soviet military power, and to buttress his claim of Soviet superiority over the United States.

Khrushchev's missile threats were legion, and characteristically they were made during crises. The first occurred during the Suez crisis of 1956 when in an apparent effort to counter the British and French military action against Egypt, he reminded them of Soviet rockets and their devastating capabilities.[4]

At a critical moment in the second Berlin crisis of 1958–59, when formal negotiations were underway in Geneva, Khrushchev warned Harriman in what Harriman termed a "rough and tough" and "terrifying" interview, that he was determined to liquidate Western rights in Berlin, adding threateningly, "Your generals talk of tanks and guns defending your Berlin position. Your tanks would burn and the missiles would fly."[5]

[4] Hayter, The Kremlin and The Embassy, p. 146.
[5] Harriman, America and Russia in a Changing World, p. 62, and Eisenhower, Dwight D. The White House Years: Waging Peace, 1956–61. Garden City, N.Y., Doubleday, 1965, vol. 2, p. 404.

During the third Berlin crisis of 1961, Khrushchev warned Italian Premier Amintore Fanfani that both Italy and Great Britain were "hostage" to Soviet missiles and would be destroyed if nuclear war resulted from a Western resort to force in Berlin. Similarly, he was reported to have warned British Ambassador to Moscow Sir Frank Roberts that all Western Europe was at his mercy; that only six H-bombs would be sufficient to annihilate the British Isles; and that nine others would take care of France.[6]

The Soviet explosion of the largest H-bomb at a critical moment in this crisis seemed at the time intended clearly to intimidate the Western leaders. As the Soviet announcement put it: The Soviet Union has developed "a series of super-powerful nuclear bombs of 20, 30, 50, and 100 million tons of TNT and powerful rockets * * * capable of delivering such bombs to any point of the globe from which an attack on the Soviet Union or other Socialist countries could be launched." [7]

In all these missile threats Khrushchev's purposes were to pressure the West into accepting his negotiating terms for settling the Berlin issue. Credibility was no doubt given to these threats not only by the fact that the Soviets did indeed have this immense capability but also by the fact that they demonstrated their will to use military power by directly threatening Poland with invasion and suppressing the Hungarian revolution during the crisis of 1956.

President John F. Kennedy fully understood the purposes behind this style of diplomacy by threat and intimidation. When Secretary of State Dean Rusk commented to him on September 5, 1961, at a critical point in the Berlin crisis, that Moscow was showing little interest in negotiations, the President replied grimly, "It isn't time yet. It's too early. They are bent on scaring the world to death before they begin negotiating, and they haven't quite brought the pot to boil. Not enough people are frightened." [8]

3. DIPLOMACY BY DEADLINE: THE BERLIN CRISES

Khrushchev's behavior in the Berlin crises suggests another characteristic in his negotiating style, diplomacy by deadline. During the second crisis of 1958–59 Khrushchev imposed a deadline of 6 months in his initial note of November 27, 1958. He demanded Western compliance with what were to the Western leaders unacceptable and illegal demands—they violated the wartime agreements—or else he would turn control of communications to West Berlin over to the East German Government.

In retrospect, this ultimatum seemed to have been essentially a negotiating ploy to compel Western compliance without requiring any Soviet concessions, or at least to gain some concessions from the West, notably a summit conference that Khrushchev had been seeking at that time. Agreement was reached in the spring of 1959 on calling a Foreign Ministers Conference in Geneva. This Conference,

---

[6] The Washington Post, July 12, 1961, p. A17, and Facts-on-File, 1961, p. 278.
[7] Whelan, Joseph G. Major Developments in United States Foreign Policy During the Kennedy administration, Jan. 20, 1961–Nov. 23, 1963: A Brief Selected Chronology. The Library of Congress, Legislative Reference Service, Washington, D.C., May 18, 1967, p. 3.
[8] Schlesinger, Arthur M. Jr. A Thousand Days. John F. Kennedy in the White House. Boston, Houghton Mifflin, 1965, p. 398. At this moment in the crisis Schlesinger was writing friends abroad that he was "more gloomy" about international developments than he had been since the summer of 1939.

however, became deadlocked; the Soviets refused to negotiate seriously; Khrushchev was invited to tour the United States (not so much as a welcomed guest but as a visitor who had imposed himself on his host) and undertake further negotiations on Berlin at Camp David in September with President Dwight D. Eisenhower. After discussions at Camp David, agreement was reached on lifting the deadline in an arrangement where the President would announce in a press conference that negotiations on Berlin were not to take place under a time limit but they were also not to be prolonged indefinitely, after which Khrushchev would confirm the statement as correct in a press statement of his own. This was done. Thus, in this oblique way the deadline was lifted because Khrushchev did not want it to appear in a communique as a direct concession and because Eisenhower would concur in no further meetings on Berlin without this stipulation.[9]

Khrushchev resorted to the same device of diplomacy by deadline when he met with President Kennedy in Vienna during June 1961. In an aide memoire handed to the President, Khrushchev resurrected his former demands with respect to Berlin and a German peace treaty, setting a 6-month deadline for Western compliance. Failing to comply, Khrushchev threatened to turn the matter over to the East Germans, including negotiations on Western access rights to Berlin, in violation of the wartime agreements.

As before, the deadline was intended to place maximum pressure on the Western leaders to comply with Khrushchev's demands. Threats of missile destruction were orchestrated by Khrushchev with a buildup of tension that climaxed with the building of the Berlin Wall. But Western resistance, notably military preparations and the administration's announcement that there was no so-called "missile gap" between the Soviet Union and the United States to the advantage of the former and that American nuclear power was superior, presumably were among the major factors that led Khrushchev to lift the deadline in the autumn of 1961. Only inconclusive exploratory negotiations had taken place between Gromyko and Secretary of State Dean Rusk.[10]

4. DIPLOMACY BY HUMILIATION

(a) Collapse of the Paris Summit Conference, May 1960

Khrushchev reached perhaps the nadir of personal misconduct by a world leader in what could be called his "diplomacy by humiliation." In the wake of the U-2 incident in which an American spy plane was shot down over the Soviet Union virtually on the eve of the Paris sum-

---

[9] Whelan, Joseph G. The Problem of Berlin : A Survey from 1944 to July 1959 and Interpretive Analysis. The Library of Congress, Legislative Reference Service, Washington, D.C., July 25, 1959, 73 pp. Also. Whelan, Joseph G. Berlin : A Chronological Summary with an Analytical Commentary, July 1959 to July 17, 1961. The Library of Congress, Legislative Reference Service, Washington, D.C., July 18, 1961, 197 pp.

Washington crowds, lining the streets more in curiosity than anything else, stood in stony silence as Khrushchev's limousine passed. However, as Khrushchev toured the country, the public response became less restrained. Khrushchev, himself, seemed to have been aware of the compelling conditions of his visit. Eisenhower recorded in his memoirs : "The trip through the United States had seemingly given him a new feeling of confidence. Coming to us with an apparent suspicion that he would be treated as an unwelcome guest, he now seemed to enjoy thoroughly every exposure to the public. I felt that he had thrown off a bit of that peculiar defensive complex so noticeable in some Russian officials. At any rate he had gone in good spirits and with many warm messages for my grandchildren." (Eisenhower. Waging Peace, p. 448. See pp. 442–448 for discussions on Berlin.)

[10] Whelan, Joseph G. Berlin : A Chronological Summary with Analytical Commentary, July 17, 1961 to Dec. 31, 1961. The Library of Congress, Legislative Reference Service, Washington, D.C., Feb. 21, 1962, 193 pp.

mit conference of May 17, 1960, Khrushchev broke up the meeting after a 20 minute harangue in which he attacked the United States for the flight terming it an act of hostility, withdrew the invitation to Eisenhower to visit the Soviet Union, and demanded an apology. In response the President explained that the flights had been halted, but he would not apologize. In a press conference on the following day, as Bohlen recalled, a dissatisfied Khrushchev "gave vent to his violent feeling" in language that was "unprintable." [11] Eisenhower, who had given evidence of intense anger while Khrushchev harangued but kept his temper under control, described Khrushchev's performance at this opening session as "vehement," while the press termed the Soviet leader's press conference as "a rolling barrage of threats, menaces, and insults." [12]

So threatening was Khrushchev's behavior that two seasoned American correspondents called Bohlen to ask whether he thought Khrushchev, who was accompanied by his "glowering" Defense Minister Rodion Y. Malinovsky, was going to return to Moscow and start a war. One had said that Khrushchev's language was reminiscent of Hitler's tirades which had always preceded military action. But Bohlen, while acknowledging Malinovsky's menacing presence, discounted the possibility that the Soviets would deliberately start a war. [13]

Setting aside the rationale for Khrushchev's conduct (which had been explained by his misplaced trust in Eisenhower who had publicly assumed responsibility for the overflight but would not "save face" for Khrushchev before his Politburo associates by apologizing), the episode demonstrated Khrushchev's skill as a diplomatic spoiler when he wanted to be. As Bohlen recorded, "Khrushchev's anger and disappointment were real," and the Soviets would not get over the incident for some time. [14] But Khrushchev scored his points, and with great force, at the opening session and in his press conference, and uppermost in the recollections of this affair is the sense of humiliation that was inflicted upon the President. Still, Khrushchev was not prepared to worsen matters by staging another Berlin crisis. After leaving Paris, he went to East Berlin where he delivered what Bohlen called a "soothing speech," temporizing on the Berlin issue and calling for a new conference in 6 or 8 months. [15]

(b) Khrushchev at the U.N., September 1960

More outrageous because there was no palpable excuse as at Paris was Khrushchev's performance at the United Nations in the autumn of 1960. Khrushchev had proposed that the United Nations be reorganized, and he went to New York personally to present his plan. The plan substituted a "troika" (a three-man commission) for a single Secretary General and proposed moving U.N. headquarters from New York to Switzerland, Austria, or the Soviet Union. Presumably, the "troika" concept was intended to reflect Khrushchev's perception of the changing distribution of world power.

[11] Bohlen, op. cit., pp. 468–469.
[12] Eisenhower, Waging Peace, p. 555, and The New York Times, May 19, 1960, p. 1.
[13] Bohlen. op. cit., pp. 469–470.
[14] Ibid., pp. 470–471.
[15] Ibid., p. 470, and Whelan, Berlin Chronology, July 1959 to July 17, 1961, pp. 48–49.

Khrushchev's behavior at the U.N. General Assembly, however, drew more attention than his proposal. Before this august body of international diplomats, and the leaders of the neutralist world (Nehru, Nasser, Sukarno, Tito, and Nkrumah), Khrushchev in a major address on September 23, made what Eisenhower termed an "intemperate, vituperative" attack on the West in general, on the United Nations and on the Secretary General in particular. In subsequent proceedings, Khrushchev shouted and laughed during the speeches of other delegates and interrupted British Prime Minister Harold Macmillan's address by taking off his shoe and banging it on his desk. Three days later India's Prime Minister Nehru told Eisenhower that everyone, including himself, had been astonished at Khrushchev's attack.[16]

According to Eisenhower, few delegates had thought Khrushchev gained any propaganda advantage by this "tragicomic sideshow." "His behavior could not but have shocked every serious-minded diplomat who had come to the meeting to participate, hopefully, in earnest and intelligent discussion," he wrote. Khrushchev's failure to get U.N. support led Eisenhower to believe that by this display of "poor manners" the "only cause he hurt was his own."[17]

Yet Khrushchev's conduct was mindful of the early Russian diplomatic missions of Peter the Great described above, and while reprehensible to the Western and neutralist leaders as his conduct may have been, like that of the earlier Russians, it may have been equally calculated to underscore brutally Russian power and authority and his contempt for Russia's adversaries by humiliating them.[18]

C. KHRUSHCHEV'S OPEN AND PERSONAL DIPLOMACY: AN INNOVATION

1. KHRUSHCHEV'S PERSONAL APPROACH

(a) Open diplomacy, Soviet style

Open and personal diplomacy was one of the most distinctive characteristics of Soviet behavior in the Khrushchev era. Immediately after Stalin's death the "collective leadership" threw off the restraints of the Stalin era and instituted a unique Soviet style of open diplomacy. As Khrushchev's power grew, he expanded and refined this new style. Though hardly in the true Wilsonian sense, open diplomacy Soviet style maintained its distinctive totalitarian characteristics, but, nonetheless, it took on a veneer of populism, in the Communist context, that was in marked contrast to the sullen insularity of the Stalin years when diplomacy was conducted by Stalin strictly within the Kremlin walls. For the governing principle of this new style of diplomacy was direct personal engagement and the expansion of contacts with the leaders, their representatives, and peoples of the world, particularly in the developing countries.

---

[16] Eisenhower. Waging Peace, pp. 581 and 585.
[17] Ibid., pp. 588–589.
[18] Bohlen observed that Khrushchev's "ranting at the United Nations showed he had not recovered from his anger" brought on by the U-2 incident. Earlier, in Moscow, Ambassador Llewellyn E. Thompson had been subjected "to a number of embarrassing moments." At a reception Khrushchev began to shout at Thompson about the U-2. To make his point, Khrushchev said, "Do you think it is all right to do this?" as he stepped heavily on the Ambassador's foot. Afterwards, he told Thompson, "I didn't mean to hurt you." Khrushchev did not let up on his efforts to humiliate the President. In speaking before the Supreme Soviet, Khrushchev, who had once referred to Eisenhower as a wise statesman, declared that he lacked the character and dignity to head a great nation but that he might have been a good superintendent of schools. (Bohlen, op. cit., p. 472.)

Khrushchev epitomized this new style and indeed it was he who made it what it came to be. His frequent political barnstorming tours abroad to Southeast and South Asia, the Middle East, Eastern and Western Europe, and the United States, his direct personal relationships with the leaders of the world, his vigorous personal efforts to popularize Soviet policy and denigrate that of the West particularly in the Third World, were aspects of this new direction of Soviet diplomacy. The emphasis on informality and the direct populist approach also applied internally, as when Harriman and Khrushchev walked through Moscow greeting its citizens on the conclusion of the Nuclear Test Ban Treaty in 1963.[19]

(b) Khrushchev, "the most original diplomatic negotiator"

Because of these particular qualities, Roetter correctly called Khrushchev undoubtedly "the most original diplomatic negotiator in the postwar world." [20] But this recognition, however justified, was slow in building because Khrushchev moved on to the international scene with only a limited knowledge of foreign affairs. British Ambassador Hayter observed that when Khrushchev first came to power, he "had no previous interest in foreign affairs and was astonishingly ignorant of them." [21] The first impression, he wrote, was "alarming." He seemed "impulsive and blundering, and startlingly ignorant of foreign affairs." He had "totally failed to grasp" a simple point on the United Nations that British political leader Aneurin Bevan put to him at a Moscow reception in spite of expert interpreting and only until Malenkov explained it to him in words of one syllable did he understand. At the time Hayter reported that Khrushchev seemed to be "practical and cunning rather than intelligent, like a little bull who if aimed the right way would charge along and be certain to arrive with a crash at his objective, knocking down anything that was in his way." Khrushchev would have to be aimed in the right direction, he noted, and "it would be difficult to stop him once you had started him off." Also, Hayter did not believe that Khrushchev would be "receptive to new ideas."

But Hayter admitted that this was "a superficial judgment," and changing his evaluation, later wrote of Khrushchev:

* * * a little reflexion should have shown us that this first impression was necessarily wrong. Ignorant of foreign affairs he certainly was, but this was not surprising; he had until then been solely concerned with internal questions, and as soon as he applied his powerful intelligence and his encyclopaedic memory to foreign affairs he mastered them completely. He was loquacious, true, but his loquacity was under control; it had to be, or he could never have survived in such close proximity to the pathologically suspicious Stalin, ferociously watching for the slightest indiscretion. And indeed if one listened to his loquacity one observed that, though vivid and folksy in its expression, its content stuck to the strictest Party orthodoxy.[22]

---

[19] Harriman described the insularity of official Russian life in the Stalin years, particularly Stalin's purposeful detachment from the people. "The Kremlin was his fortress and no one was allowed in." Harriman noted "Khrushchev opened it up. It's a public park today, with women and their children playing in it and floods of visitors to the historic buildings." After initialing the treaty, Harriman called on Khrushchev at his office and suggested that they walk together to the dinner he was giving the Anglo-American group. Harriman went on: "We walked from his office through the Kremlin to the Great Palace. On the way we ran into quite a large crowd in front of the Palace of Congresses * * * Khrushchev stopped. He pinched a little girl on the cheek and patted another on the head. Then he said to the crowd, 'This is Gaspodin Garriman.' That is Mr. Harriman in Russian. 'He has just signed a test ban agreement. I am going to take him to dinner. Do you think he deserves his dinner?' He got a cheer. He talked as an American politician would with a crowd." (Harriman, America and Russia in a Changing World, pp. 98–99.)
[20] Roetter, op. cit., p. 118.
[21] Hayter, Russia and the World, pp. 30–31.
[22] Hayter, The Kremlin and the Embassy, p. 107.

President Eisenhower's memoirs and particularly the account of the meeting at Camp David seemed to reflect a certain recognition of Khrushchev's ability, at least as a negotiator. As he observed during one of their discussions:

There was no question in my mind of Khrushchev's skill as a debater. He was a master at picking up another's proposals and using them—with his own interpretations—to advance his own point of view.[23]

Ambassador Bohlen did not comment specifically on Khrushchev as a negotiator but he saw in the Soviet leader qualities that made him effective in diplomacy but also worked to his disadvantage. To Bohlen, Khrushchev was "basically a peasant;" he was no philosopher of ideology, though a "formidable" debater. Born and bred in the Bolshevik Party, he was a simple pragmatic believer who added nothing to the body of doctrine except the few pragmatic deviations inherent in his formulation of peaceful coexistence. A man of impulses, Khrushchev had "an extraordinary amount of animal energy" that while making him "not unattractive" did lead to some unfortunate incidents. "He was coarse and vulgar," Bohlen said, "given to scatological expressions in his earthy humor, and enjoyed lying to make a story better or to score a point."

In foreign policy Khrushchev was "a complete pragmatist," basing his decisions on two cardinal rules of Soviet diplomacy—"hold on to the Soviet system and avoid war." But a basic contradiction always existed in his foreign policy, notably the incompatibility of goals in foreign policy and roles as a leader. The contradiction lay in the fact that Khrushchev wore two hats, Bohlen stated, one as chief figure of the Soviet Government that sought détente with the West, and the other as leader of the Soviet bloc in Eastern Europe that sought to drive the West out of Berlin. "We continually tried to convince him that he could not have it both ways," Bohlen wrote, "but he could never make a choice. He was the prisoner of the Soviet contradiction." Finally, Khrushchev was an "impressionistic" man whose views were altered by world travels.[24]

2. EXPANSION OF SOCIAL ACTIVITIES IN MOSCOW

(a) A turnabout from Stalin's insularity and isolation

An important part of Khrushchev's open diplomacy was the expansion of social activities between the Soviet leadership and the diplomatic community in Moscow. Accounts by former ambassadors to Moscow, such as Bohlen and Hayter, along with those of other students of Soviet diplomacy, abound in commentary on the sudden upsurge in social activities in the post-Stalin period, a marked contrast to their virtual absence in the late Stalin era. The intense traffic of visiting foreign dignitaries, encouraged by the leadership's global political

---

[23] Eisenhower, Waging Peace. p. 437. Eisenhower's own assessment of the Camp David meeting clearly reflect his satisfaction with the negotiations with Khrushchev: "* * * a crisis over Berlin had been averted without the surrender of any Western rights. True, the crisis had been an artificial one of Khrushchev's own making, but on the other hand it carried with it the danger that by overstepping himself, he might have gotten into a position where a far worse situation could have developed for all nations. At least it now seemed that we should have a better atmosphere in which to approach such questions as expanding exchanges of visitors and information between East and West, finding an acceptable solution to the problem of a divided Germany, and developing mutual trust through satisfactorily enforced disarmament treaties, even though limited at first in scope." (p. 449.)
[24] Bohlen, op. cit., pp. 496–498.

tours, and the celebration of Soviet holidays and the national days of countries represented in Moscow provided ample occasions for receptions at the Kremlin and in foreign embassies. At these receptions the entire "collective leadership," and later Khrushchev and his favorite few, might be present. Hayter recorded in his farewell dispatch to the British Foreign Office that ultimately he "was able by a series of lucky chances to see more of Russia's rulers than perhaps any British Ambassador since Lord Malmesbury became the confident of Catherine the Great," and he did not doubt that his successors "have been luckier still." [25]

(b) Serving political purposes for both sides

Diplomatic receptions served the political purposes of both sides. For the Soviet leadership, they provided the opportunity for communicating with the official outside world. It also gave them a means, for example, of indicating their pleasure or displeasure with a particular nation, depending on the number and pecking order of the leaders and other high-ranking officials attending.[26]

On the other side, the receptions provided useful points of contact with the Soviet leadership for the ambassadors. Important chance remarks and personal assessments on the conduct of the Soviet leadership (particularly their heavy drinking habits) could be and were reported back to the home office. It also gave the ambassador access to the leadership and the opportunity on occasion to convey important information informally but in an official setting that would have a desired impact. A case in point was the Soviet reception of November 7, 1953, commemorating the Bolshevik Revolution, that was attended by the "collective leadership," high-ranking visiting Communists, and members of the diplomatic community in Moscow. The following excerpt from Bohlen's memoirs, filled with meaning and political nuance, illustrates the political significance of such diplomatic gatherings:

Molotov then proposed toasts to the United States, to Britain, and to France, without even an indirect attack on any of our policies. Ulbricht [East German leader] and Liu [Communist Chinese Ambassador] followed our lead and stood without drinking the toast. Having drunk to all the guests, the Russians then offered a multitude of toasts to peace. Following my usual practice, I had been sipping only a little vodka for each toast, but the alcohol lowered my inhibitions. After another toast to peace had been proposed, I rose and, with news reporters crowding around, said I would willingly drink to peace, but I would like to add two words, "with justice," since without justice in international affairs, there could be no firm peace. This reference to justice animated Soviet officials, particularly Kaganovich, who answered in a long speech to the effect that there were different concepts of justice in the world but that peace was something all people understood. Then Zhukov, who had taken Bulganin's place after the latter became drunk, got up and said, to my surprise, that he would like to support the toast to peace of the American Ambassador. I overheard Mikoyan ask him in a whisper if he did not have a toast of his own. Zhukov replied no, that he merely wanted to support the toast to justice. Later, Molotov toasted the health of military men who had arranged the parade earlier that day, and expressed the hope that they would confine themselves to parades. Although Molotov was contrasting parades to war, the toast did not please Zhukov. I am not sure why Zhukov supported my toast. One American correspondent wrote that Zhukov obviously had the case of Beria, who was in jail at that time, in mind. This was a stretch of the imagination. The most that can be said is that Zhukov was demonstrating his independence of the Kremlin's political leaders.

[25] Hayter, The Kremlin and the Embassy, p. 39.
[26] Ibid., pp. 41–42.

I was amused to watch Molotov and Mikoyan trying to restrain Kaganovich, who, as the evening wore on, lapsed more and more into Bolshevik jargon without, however, attacking the West. Still smarting from my earlier toast to justice, Kaganovich prodded me again on peace. I finally stood up again and said that it must be evident to everyone that all peoples, all governments, and all sections of the population of the countries of the world were desirous of peace. But, I emphasized, settlement of international disputes was one thing and preservation of peace was another. To preserve peace, only a simple rule of conduct by a nation was required—to avoid acts of aggression. If troops did not cross frontiers, the peace would not be broken. I then proposed a toast to the prevention of aggression. With some uncertainty, the Soviet officials drank the toast.

The reception was discussed for days in the diplomatic community. I linked the friendly atmosphere of the evening to Moscow's rejection of an American proposal for a Foreign Ministers' meeting on Germany and Austria. "In effect," I wired Dulles, "the Soviets were saying, 'We will not negotiate with you and it is all your fault, but we don't intend to fight you'." This is a characteristic stance the Soviets take when they do not want their actions to be the subject of far-reaching conclusions.[27]

(c) Limited value of diplomatic social functions; continued isolation

But such social affairs, helpful as they might have been especially compared with their dearth in the Stalin era, were not altogether satisfactory for the ambassador in carrying out his representational obligations; they were inadequate substitutes for direct diplomatic discourse. Both Bohlen and Hayter complained of their limitations. In commenting on the period following Khrushchev's de-Stalinization speech of 1956 and the subsequent liberalization in the Soviet system, Bohlen regretted that liberalization "had not given diplomats any additional tools to work with." While the Soviet leaders continued to attend receptions and there engage in conversations, still there were "no regular, serious, far-ranging discussions that are so necessary in diplomacy." "For the most part," Bohlen continued, "the ambassadors continued to rely on the controlled Soviet press for news of Soviet decisions and to cast about in the diplomatic community for additional clues, weighing rumors, exchanging opinions, and occasionally picking up an important fact." [28]

In almost identical fashion Hayter complained that his contacts at the formal receptions were "not always very rewarding." And he continued:

Like my colleagues, I had high hopes, when the Soviet leaders started their new policy of accessibility, that this would mean the beginning of normal diplomatic activity in Moscow. We would, we thought, engage in frank, confidential discussions with our new friends, in which the serious issues between the Soviet Union and the rest of the world would be sorted out in genuine dialogues. But it did not turn out like that. Each of the Soviet leaders carried his own private Iron Curtain around with him. Responses were predictable; conversations were like *Pravda* leading articles on one side and *The Times* leading articles on the other; well-grooved long-playing records went round and round.[29]

Hayter described Soviet official receptions as "always lavish," usually "too long," were "well intended," and rarely were attempts made to "force unwilling foreigners to drink more than was good for them." But Hayter believed that "they did not really contribute anything to international exchanges; the atmosphere was seldom conducive to serious talk, and the bonhomie so laboriously engendered always seemed a little synthetic." [30]

[27] Bohlen, op. cit., pp. 361–362.
[28] Ibid., p. 405.
[29] Hayter, The Kremlin and the Embassy, pp. 39–40.
[30] Ibid., p. 43.

On the personal level it remained impossible to really establish a close friendship with the Soviets. As Bohlen noted, "While the Russians could be friendlier," in keeping with the "spirit of Geneva" of 1955, "they could not become friends." [31] Citing the friendship that had developed between his wife Avis and Mrs. Gromyko, Bohlen said that the Soviet Minister's wife was not permitted to pursue this friendship and accepted invitations only to official occasions. Mrs. Gromyko had often said that she wanted to invite the Bohlens to their apartment, but she never did. "In fact, in all the years we spent in the Soviet Union," Bohlen recalled, "we were never invited to a private home." [32]

Again a parallel experience was recorded by Hayter. After cataloging all the receptions attended, Hayter concluded:

> But the results were, somehow unreal. We never really got to know any of them really well, never could make the kind of genuine and lasting friendships we had achieved in all our previous diplomatic posts, and were never once invited inside a Russian home.[33]

Life for the Western diplomatic staff in Moscow continued to be very difficult, notwithstanding the changing political climate. Despite the new openness in Soviet diplomacy, surveillance by the KGB continued as before, close and intense, and "bugging" remained a nagging problem. In all, life for the staff in Moscow continued to be pretty grim.[34]

Khrushchev's open diplomacy and policy of accessibility, as they impacted upon Moscow's diplomatic community, thus had a proven but limited value. No doubt diplomats from the non-Communist countries were still grateful for even these brief but unsatisfying encounters with the Soviet leadership.[35]

[31] Bohlen, op. cit., p. 391.
[32] Ibid., p. 344.
[33] Hayter, The Kremlin and the Embassy, p. 42.
[34] Bohlen noted: "We more or less went on the assumption that the Soviet Government had installed listening devices in our offices and heard what we were dictating or saying. When the new Chancellery was under construction in the spring of 1953, security men from the Embassy were on guard all day to prevent the installation of microphones on the two top floors—the seventh and the eighth, where I had my office. Unfortunately, because of carelessness and to save money, there was no watch at night. Several years later, long after I had left Moscow, forty-three microphones were discovered on the floors that were supposed to be the most secure in Moscow." Bohlen went on to describe how he had always taken precautions against such a possibility so as to protect the integrity of sensitive material. (Bohlen, op. cit., p. 345.)
[35] Soviet diplomats in the West, as noted previously, vigorously pursued this new style of open diplomacy. Soviet Ambassador to the United States Mikhail A. Menshikov soon became dubbed as "Smiling Mike" by newsmen because of his customary cheerful appearance in his public performances, though at closer quarters in negotiations Under Secretary of State Murphy found him "a cold-blooded ruthless somebody," "arrogant and difficult." (Murphy, op. cit., pp. 438–439.) Eisenhower referred to the Soviet Ambassador as "the genial-appearing Mikhail Menshikov" and then proceeded to cite an unpleasant incident when he tried to force his presence before American dignitaries in violation of U.S. protocol in the ceremony greeting the visiting Khrushchev. (Eisenhower, Waging Peace, p. 434.) Indicative of Menshikov's exposure in the United States was his address in 1958 to the National Press Club in Washington, the first Soviet Ambassador to do so since Litvinov's appearance in 1941. A year later he accompanied Mikoyan on his nation-wide tour of the United States.
An illustration of the sort of public relations activity Soviet diplomats in the United States engaged in under the new policy of accessibility was a meeting of the American Academy of Political and Social Science in Philadelphia in 1959. At this meeting the Commercial Counselor at the Soviet Embassy in Washington, Vladimir S. Alkimov, gave a paper on the value of East-West trade. One evening the writer and a colleague from the Library of Congress, Mr. Leon Herman, who was himself a specialist in Soviet economics, had a nearly 3-hour conversation with Alkimov over coffee at the hotel's restaurant in which we explored various aspects of Soviet-American relations and the changes in Russia since Stalin's death. What made this cordial encounter particularly satisfying to us was Alkimov's frankness and openness in discussing the Soviet side and also his willingness to receive explanations from the American view. The presentation of a formal paper at an American professional meeting and such an encounter on a person-to-person basis would have been impossible in the Stalin era. Alkimov, who was perhaps in his early 30's at the time and thus a representative of the rising new generation in the Soviet Union, has since risen to the position of Deputy Minister of Foreign Trade.

3. PROPAGANDA ROLE IN SOVIET DIPLOMACY MAGNIFIED

Finally, the role of propaganda was magnified in Khrushchev's style of open diplomacy. This was a natural development growing out of Khrushchev's impulse not just to verbally assault and intimidate the West into believing that Soviet power was superior but equally important to convince the Third World and other potential constituencies abroad that the Soviet economic system could win out in peaceful competition with the capitalist West. This was one meaning of peaceful coexstence. It was also the meaning of Khrushchev's provocative but misinterpreted statement at a reception in the Polish Embassy during November 1956, "We will bury you." As Bohlen observed, this phrase did not imply a "lethal attack", but was "merely a figure of speech expressing confidence in prevailing over the long haul—of being present at an opponent's funeral." [36] This was Khrushchev, the negotiator, at his best.

What distinguished Khrushchev's linkage of an expanding propaganda effort to diplomacy, as this statement suggested, was its identification with himself personally. He became the principal spokesman for the Soviet propaganda assaults on the West that impacted so directly on negotiations and on the conduct of Soviet diplomacy. The unity of these threats with the reality of his power of decision and the growing military might of the Soviet Union gave such threats an aura of credibility.

During the Berlin crisis of 1958–59, Khrushchev's propaganda threats of destroying the West were delivered by Khrushchev himself, as for example to Harriman personally and in public speeches to a world audience. They were intended to intimidate the West, deter its moves toward countering Soviet power moves in Europe, and ultimately to affect its negotiating position. The Soviet propaganda machine echoed Khrushchev's threats.

Khrushchev's use of space achievements for propaganda purposes centered upon himself, and his declarations on Soviet space superiority were voiced to convey the notion that Soviet science and technology, and thus Soviet power, were superior to that of the United States and the West. Space achievements were also directly connected with negotiations, as during the Berlin crisis of 1961 when Titov's spaceflight in August coincided remarkably with the deepening of the Berlin crisis. The relevance of this space feat to the Berlin crisis was interpreted as a reminder of the dominating influence of Soviet power, and was shown graphically in a cartoon at the time by David Low of the Manchester Guardian. The cartoon depicted Kennedy, de Gaulle, and Macmillan seated around a table with one empty chair at the head and a sign on the table reading, "Berlin Negotiations." A smiling Khrushchev is seen peering out of a space capsule that was orbiting the entire scene. A sign on the wall read, "As a negotiator Mr. K. is a great cosmonaut." The title of the entire cartoon was, "Orbiting the Point." Nothing more had to be said.[37]

[36] Bohlen, op. cit., p. 437.
[37] Whelan, Joseph G. Goals of the U.S.S.R. in Space. U.S. Congress. Senate. Committee on Aeronautical and Space Sciences. Soviet Space Programs : Organization, Plans, Goals, and International Implications. Staff Report. 87th Congress, 2d session. Washington, U.S. Government Printing Office, 1962, chapter 2. The cartoon was reproduced on page 40. The entire chapter discusses the Soviet use of space, including "missile diplomacy," for foreign policy purposes.

In more congenial settings, as on the occasion of the White House dinner during his visit in 1959, Khrushchev made the same point of ultimate Soviet success in outstripping the United States in peaceful competition. He did so in a toast that Eisenhower described as "a splendid example of combined propaganda and political argument." [38] The statement was cordial, but the message was clear.

D. KHRUSHCHEV'S STYLE OF NEGOTIATIONS AND OPEN DIPLOMACY: A SUMMING UP

Thus Khrushchev resorted to multiple forms of negotiations in the diplomatic process, for his was a total effort. Negotiations did not necessarily take place sitting across the table with an adversary. It was a continuing and total effort that could be carried on at a press conference, in a speech at home or in some distant country before a foreign audience, at a diplomatic reception as in the case of the Polish Embassy noted above where the flow of alcohol tended to make him more talkative, expansive, and in some instances more threatening,[39] or through formal diplomatic channels, as during the Cuban missile crisis.

In sum Khrushchev orchestrated propaganda, military and political pressure, the threats of "missile diplomacy," and those of negotiation by intimidation and deadline, the reality of genuine space achievements, boastful claims on the magnitude of Soviet power in the balance of world power, and direct personal encounters as at the Paris summit—the whole human effort he orchestrated into a singly directed purpose; namely to intimidate his adversaries and compel a change in their policy to the Soviet advantage.

Khrushchev was indeed "the most original diplomatic negotiator in the postwar world" as was said. For, while his face-to-face negotiating experience with the United States was limited to meetings with heads of government at Geneva, Camp David, Paris, and Vienna, the fact remained that in reality he never stopped negotiating. It was this unique perception of negotiations as a total and continuing effort accompanied by the application of a variety of instrumentalities that has set Khrushchev apart as an "original."

E. AMERICAN DIPLOMATS ON THE SOVIET STYLE IN DIPLOMACY AND NEGOTIATIONS

1. JOHN FOSTER DULLES, SECRETARY OF STATE

(a) *Dulles' address to the National Press Club on negotiations*

During the Eisenhower years, it was John Foster Dulles who had to cope with the formidable problem of negotiating with Khrushchev. He was perhaps one of the most seasoned negotiators among the long list of American Secretaries of State. Prior to becoming President Eisenhower's Secretary of State in 1952, Dulles had performed a long and distinguished service in American diplomacy, in addition to pursuing a successful legal career as a specialist in international law. As a public servant, he was an adviser to President Wilson at the Paris

---

[38] Eisenhower, Waging Peace, p. 439.
[39] Bohlen, op. cit., p. 437.

Peace Conference of 1919, a member of the Reparations Commission and Supreme Economic Council, a member of the U.S. delegation in founding the United Nations, a delegate to the U.N. General Assembly in 1948, special aide to Acheson at the Four-Power Foreign Ministers Conference in Paris in 1949, and Ambassador-at-Large on the mission to negotiate the Japanese Peace Treaty. Prior to his resignation and death in the spring of 1959, Dulles was the principal architect of American foreign policy in the Eisenhower administration, and as such he was the principal negotiator for the American side in the various encounters with the Soviet leadership.

In an address to the National Press Club on January 16, 1958, Dulles examined "The Role of Negotiation" in international relations. He focused mainly on Soviet-American relations with some commentary and analysis on the Soviet style in diplomacy and negotiations.[40]

(b) Place for negotiations

Dulles perceived Soviet–American relations in fairly clear-cut, black-and-white ideological terms. For him, it was simply "International Communism versus the Free World." [41] Yet, Dulles was a realist and a pragmatist who never ruled out negotiations.

In this address Dulles weighed Soviet strengths and weaknesses, acknowledging their great power; their penchant for long-range planning (a positive value); their growing economic strength, particularly their involvement in the Third World with a vigorous campaign of trade and aid; and their effective global propaganda. But he counterbalanced these strengths with such weaknesses as: The emergence of a new popular constituency that sought satisfaction in more consumer goods; the rise of a new generation of scientific and technological elites, a "new intelligentsia," that would affect policy; the innate distrust of the Third World for Soviet goals and power; and the Soviet failure to disengage from German partition and the suppression of the peoples of Eastern Europe. Faced with the reality of a power that "seeks world domination," the United States devised a "defensive and affirmative" policy, built upon military and economic strength, and a commitment to freedom as a "dynamic force." Dulles called for a cool and rational American response, seeing clearly and thinking straight while parrying Soviet strengths and exploiting its weaknesses.

Notwithstanding these fundamental differences, "What place is there for negotiations?", Dulles asked. To which he responded, "First

---

[40] Dulles, John Foster. Secretary of State. The Role of Negotiation. U.S. Department of State Bulletin, Washington, D.C., vol. 38, Feb. 3, 1958, pp. 159–168.
[41] Bohlen acknowledged that he had his difficulties with Dulles, "but he had many more virtues than defects. He had character and was capable of firmness of purpose and steadiness in execution." Bohlen credited Dulles for his strength as the "architect of the West's resolute policy in response to Khrushchev's ultimatum" in 1958–1959 on Berlin. In Moscow, Khrushchev denounced Dulles, in Bohlen's words, "as the archvillain preventing a détente." Whether the Soviets really felt that way, Bohlen could not tell. "I believe that they respected Dulles as a diplomat with a steady aim, as a skilled negotiator, and as a student of foreign affairs," he said. But Bohlen believed that Dulles "never understood Soviet policy. He was overattentive to the purely ideological aspects, not grasping the subtle relationship with Soviet national interests. He discovered Stalin late in life and read voraciously in Stalin's theoretical writings. He was obsessed with the idea that Soviet Communism was a conspiracy which all righteous people should oppose. This view of the world in black-and-white terms stemmed, I believe, from Dulles's Calvinism, and was a serious impediment to his performance as Secretary of State. He damaged our relations with the developing nations by his opposition to neutralism. He overcommitted the United States with ties to regional anti-Communist pacts. He scared our allies with his talk of brinkmanship." Bohlen concluded: "I am not sure how history will evaluate John Foster Dulles. He was a strong Secretary of State; whether he was a wise one is doubtful." (Bohlen, op. cit., pp. 456–457.)

of all, let me say emphatically that there is a place for negotiation."
For, "Negotiation is one of the major tools of diplomacy," and it would
be "the height of folly to renounce the use of this tool."

(c) Soviet toughness in negotiations on "matters of real substance"

On the basis of past experience, Dulles stated that Americans must
assume that "negotiation with the Communists, if it is to bring acceptable results, will be a long, hard task." Citing his "many days personally participating in high-level, face-to-face negotiations with the
Soviets," Dulles noted that he "had considerable education as to their
methods."

A determining factor in Soviet toughness in negotiations was
whether or not the negotiations themselves involved matters of real
substance. Dulles explained:

Whenever negotiations involve matters of real substance, the Communist go
at them in a tough, hard way. They are highly legalistic and seek to devise hidden
loopholes through which they can subsequently escape from what seem to be their
obligations. They practice inexhaustible patience, withholding what they may be
prepared to give until the last moment in the hope that they can get what they
want without giving as much as they are ready to give. They astutely take into
account any weaknesses of their opponents such as impatience to get the negotiation over or willingness to treat any "agreement" as a success, without regard to
the contents or dependability. Furthermore, the scope of possible agreement is
limited by the fact that the Communist record of performance is so poor that
never ought the United States rely on any promises by the Communists which
depend merely upon future good faith.

In emphasizing the relevance between substance and longevity of
negotiations, Dulles noted that ending the fighting in Korea took 2
years and involved 575 meetings; negotiations on the Austrian State
Treaty took approximately 8 years and some 400 meetings; negotiations on the International Atomic Energy Agency, concluded in 1956,
took almost 3 years; negotiations for an agreement on "cultural contacts," began 2½ years ago at the Geneva Summit Conference, were
still continuing in Washington; and the negotiations at Geneva with
the Chinese Communists, going on for over 2 years, produced an agreement for the release of American civilian captives.

Negotiations did not have to be so prolonged, Dulles declared, particularly when there was good will. "But always, the past record is,"
he noted, "if the negotiations involved real matters of substance, the
Communists have proceeded very carefully and with a design to gain
every possible advantage." [42]

Nevertheless, Dulles was optimistic that there should be and would
be further negotiations with the Soviets, since there were many areas
where there "could be dependable agreement in the common interest."
He also believed that the Soviet rulers, as with the Americans, "do not
want our two nations to drift so far apart that there is increased danger
that the cold war will turn into a hot war."

(d) Skepticism of summit conferences and Khrushchev's objectives

Dulles was skeptical of summit conferences, except those where careful preparations were made in advance at the lower levels to insure a

[42] At a press conference on Nov. 26, 1958, Dulles reiterated this point with respect to
negotiations on nuclear testing: "Now we don't anticipate as yet a breakdown of these
negotiations. They are difficult, they are hard; but negotiations with the Russians always
are long-drawn-out and hard. You don't get, in my experience—and I have had as much,
I think, as anybody—you don't get agreements negotiated with the Russians which are fair
and equal without a lot of hard work and a lot of preliminary sparring, and I think things
are conforming pretty much to pattern. And I am not discouraged about it at all." U.S.
Department of State. Washington, D.C. Bulletin, vol. 39, Dec. 15, 1958, p. 951.

measure of success. "There should be assurance that significant topics will be discussed and that there is a good prospect of arriving at significant agreements which will be fulfilled," he said. What disturbed Dulles about excessive Soviet pressures for a summit conference was the propaganda and political value that would accrue to them when reasonable assurance of some success was lacking and the harm it would inflict upon the West. As he said in response to a question on what Khrushchev hoped to gain from a summit conference:

I hope that the remarks I already made throw light on what are probably, I fear, his intentions, although those intentions will be tested by what goes on in the coming weeks and months. But the great gain, as I pointed out, that they could get—and which certainly they will try to get if we let them—the great gain is to have a meeting which, as I say, will utter platitudes about peace—"we are going to work together, we are all going to be friends, we are going to end all world tensions"—with the implication that there is no need any more to have this military preparation, to pay taxes in order to have a mutual security program, and the like. If Khrushchev can get that, that would be the greatest triumph of his career or indeed the career of almost anyone, because then we would come back here and the other free-world leaders would go back to countries where the people would no longer be willing to support the military programs, the economic assistance programs, the inconveniences of alliances which require people to coordinate their policies with each other. All those things, it would be believed, could be thrown away because peace has been proclaimed. But the Communist Parties will go right on.

(e) Distinction between party and government in negotiations

Finally, Dulles believed that in negotiating with the Soviets it was important to distinguish between the Communist Party and the Soviet Government. In explaining Khrushchev's objectives in seeking a summit conference, Dulles elaborated on this important relationship:

One point that always needs to be borne in mind is that, when you negotiate with the leaders of Communist-controlled states, you are not negotiating with the principals; you're negotiating with the second-class people, because the governments of these countries are all run by the Communist Party and, unless you bind that party, you haven't got an agreement which, as to broad policy, has any significance at all. I recall very well the Litvinov agreement, which we made at the time when we recognized the Soviet Union. The Soviet Government agreed that it would not tolerate the establishment on its soil of any group which was seeking to carry on subversive activities in the United States. Of course the subversive activities went on just the same, indeed were intensified. And we asked the Soviets "how come," and they said, "Oh, those are being carried on by the party. The state is not carrying those on. Therefore, what we are doing is entirely consistent with our agreement." That is the kind of thing you are up against.

(f) On the value of negotiations

For all the dogmatic rigidity in his approach to the Soviet Union and in his perception of the cold war, Dulles, nevertheless, valued negotiations and believed it possible for them to succeed when mutual interests were to be achieved. In his address he urged patience and an awareness of Soviet toughness in negotiations as a measure of their interest in matters of substance. He cautioned against familiar Soviet stratagems of obfuscation, deception, calculated delays, and subterfuge when probing for weaknesses and vulnerabilities in their adversary. He warned against engaging blindly in summitry without adequate preparation as falling for a Soviet negotiating ploy. But, he valued negotiations, praising them as "one of the major tools of diplomacy." Accordingly, Dulles could say with Talleyrand in his advice to an earlier generation of diplomats, "Il faut négocier, négocier et toujours négocier." ("One must negotiate, negotiate and always negotiate.") [43]

2. FOY KOHLER: VIEWS OF AN AMERICAN DIPLOMAT

(a) *Kohler, a seasoned diplomatic observer*

Secretary Dulles was not the only American diplomatic official to comment publicly on the Soviet approach to negotiations. In an address before the National Academy of Economics and Political Science at Brookings Institution in Washington on May 6, 1958, Foy D. Kohler elaborated still further on aspects of the Soviet style in diplomacy and negotiations within the context of Soviet-American relations. A Foreign Service officer with long service in Eastern Europe and the Soviet Union, at that time Deputy Assistant Secretary for European Affairs, and later on Ambassador to Moscow, Kohler had a wide range of diplomatic experience in dealing with the Russians along with being a student of Soviet affairs, and thus brought a specialized expertise as a student and practitioner to this unique problem.[44]

(b) *Definition of negotiation*

Kohler's was a comprehensive commentary on negotiations in Soviet-American relations at a time when the cold war was again heating up. Both analytical and descriptive, it treated the subject in a way that suggested not only the Soviet approach but also gave prescriptions for an American response.

To Kohler, the role of negotiations and the conduct of foreign relations were indistinguishable, like "an egg in an omelet." The dictionary defined it as "to transact business," more specifically "to hold intercourse with a view to coming to terms on some matter." Kohler expanded on this, giving his own interpretation:

Under this definition it is evident that negotiation is part and parcel of almost everything we do in the realm of foreign affairs. *It is not an occasional undertaking but a constant process.* It embraces an incredibly wide area of subject matter, ranging from life-and-death issues to the most trivial problems of protocol. It is necessary to the conduct of relations among friends and allies as well as among competitors and adversaries. In fact, one might say that there are basically only two ways to conduct relations among states—by negotiation or by war.[45]

(c) *Channels for negotiations*

To the impatient who viewed negotiations as "a rosy avenue of escape from the grim realities of the 20th century" and believed that solutions in Soviet-American relations could be resolved if only the Russians and Americans would sit down together and "talk things out," Kohler—as one of many Americans who spent "many long, late, and frustrating hours in the process"—responded with some feeling: "That is precisely what we have been doing for the past 15 years. * * * And it is what we are continuing to do—or at least, to try to do—every day."[46]

Negotiations employed a variety of channels and techniques, and in the 20th century, Kohler explained, these have been significantly ex-

[43] Kertesz, op. cit., p. 133.
[44] Kohler, Foy D. Deputy Assistant Secretary for European Affairs. Negotiation as an Effective Instrument of American Foreign Policy. U.S. Department of State Bulletin, vol. 38, June 2, 1958, pp. 901–910.
[45] Ibid., p. 901. Italics added.
[46] Ibid., pp. 901–902.

tended by the increase in multilateral and public diplomacy. Soviet leaders developed a "considerable aptitude" for these modern forms of negotiations and have introduced "some less than welcome variants into the older forms." Kohler called attention to such existing channels for negotiations as:
  —The elaborate embassies in Moscow and Washington that transacted a considerable amount of diplomatic business;
  —The diplomatic missions abroad that permitted diplomatic intercourse through third parties;
  —The various components and agencies of the United Nations that provided the means for detailed negotiations on a large variety of subjects;
  —The special bodies for particular negotiations, as in the case of those on Berlin;
  —The media as a source for communication of speeches, press conferences, and official statements that actually take on the form of negotiations; and finally,
  —The summit conference, a fairly modern device for the transaction of diplomatic business by the heads of governments.
Negotiations through these variegated channels have gone on "pretty steadily" with the Soviet Union for many years, Kohler reminded his audience, and through them a number of "important agreements" and "valuable results" were produced (for example, lifting the Berlin blockade, the Korean truce, and the Austrian State Treaty). Most of these successes in negotiations, Kohler observed, "involved a mixture of diplomatic methods—public and private, multilateral and bilateral—and all of them were important." [47]

But critics demanded, Kohler continued, "not merely negotiations but results;" they wanted an end to the cold war with all its burdens and accordingly proclaimed that "what we need are new techniques of negotiation, bold and imaginative new ideas, and a basic change in our attitudes." In reply, Kohler asked for specifics for achieving results, noting that the process of negotiating with the Soviets involved many difficulties and that they could not be removed by "fuzzy generalizations." [48]

(d) Channels and a will to negotiate

The problem of channels and techniques was to Kohler not "really a significant obstacle." When there was a "genuine desire to reach agreement on any point, large or small," the means for successful negotiations were readily available. This was true in the past; it would continue to be true in the future. Substance rather than form was the main criterion for Americans; they were ready to use any negotiating technique or instrumentality that gave "reasonable hope of constructive results." [49]

But Kohler acknowledged that the substance of negotiations sometimes limited the form to be used, notably the difficulty in conducting bilateral discussions on issues bearing on the vital concerns of allies. Nor could substantive issues of universal interest more suitable for the United Nations be treated as an exclusive Soviet-American con-

---

[47] Ibid., pp. 902–903.
[48] Ibid., p. 903.
[49] Ibid., p. 903.

cern. However, Kohler noted in an aside that the Soviets were not enthusiastic about conducting "serious negotiations on a broad, multilateral basis." True, the United Nations gave them an effective propaganda platform which they used skillfully as an instrumentality in the negotiating process, but they were reluctant to reach major agreements within the United Nations framework and to rely on the opinions and judgments of a U.N. majority as a basis for agreements. Soviet distaste for United Nations procedures was evident in their frequent flouting of its recommendations.[50]

The United States also recognized the limitations of the U.N. and acknowledged that many issues could be negotiated more effectively in private than in public. But Kohler reemphasized his main point; namely, that a variety of channels for negotiations were available. "Where there is a will," he told his audience, "there are plenty of ways open to both of us."[51]

(e) Other impediments to negotiations: Illusory and real

Impediments to successful negotiations there were, but Kohler made a distinction between what was illusory and what was real. He discounted notions of popular antagonism, noting that the Russian-American historical record was "remarkably free" from popular passions that have often fomented tensions and impeded agreement between nations. The Soviet reputation for being "hard bargainers" was also offset by the "tough Yankee trader" tradition in the American experience, making Americans in most situations "among the best negotiators on Earth." The argument that failure in negotiations arose from ignorance of each other and could be rectified by greater mutual understanding was not sound. As Kohler said, "it is doubtful that any major rivals ever knew each other better."[52]

But Kohler did not take lightly "the presence of deep-seated suspicion and distrust on both sides" as an impediment. They were obvious to negotiators experienced in dealing with the Russians; but he insisted that they were symptoms, not the cause of failure in negotiations. "Distrust alone will not necessarily impede successful negotiations where the other conditions of agreement are present," Kohler declared. And he continued, "Such negotiations may be successful either if it is clear that the particular agreement serves the interest of both parties or if adequate means of enforcing the agreement are available."[53]

The vital center of a successful negotiation was the reliability of the pledged word. As Kohler said, "promises represent the principal coinage of international negotiations." On this score the Soviet record was not good. and in the absence of adequate legal sanctions or an international political organization that provided the regular enforcement of international promises, he cautioned, "we must exercise unusual care in seeking to work out agreements that will be meaningful." "Where possible," Kohler declared, "we must seek promises that will be more or less self-enforcing," amplifying his remarks, "in other words, promises supported by concrete machinery or action." Kohler explained further with respect to the protracted arms control negotiations, concluding with this cautionary advice:

[50] Ibid., pp. 903–905.
[51] Ibid., p. 904.
[52] Ibid., p. 904.
[53] Ibid., pp. 904–905.

Where we are dealing with subjects that do not readily lend themselves to the application of enforcement machinery, we should try to obtain promises which the Soviet Union itself will have a definite incentive to keep, either because the promise is consistent with Soviet national interests or because of the impact of world opinion. In any case, we must always be on guard against trading concrete political, economic, and military assets of our own for the unsupported promises of the Soviet Union. We certainly cannot barter away our collective-security arrangements, weaken our military programs, or abandon our strategic positions in exchange for nothing more than promises of this kind.[54]

(f) Problem of differing political structures

Another major difficulty impeding agreement in Soviet-American negotiations was the "profound differences" in their political structures. Elaborating on this difference, Kohler explained:

—The role of public opinion in a democracy and its impact upon the American negotiator ("no American negotiator, from the President down, is a plenipotentiary in the literal sense. Everything he does and says is subject to examination and criticism at home.");

—The element of accountability which the negotiator must adhere to as agreement moves through the political and ratification process; and

—The problem of coalition diplomacy among allies of democratic states where unity must be achieved through negotiations and not diktat.[55]

In contrast, under the Soviet totalitarian system the leadership, holding a monopoly of political power, was bound by no such restrictions and elements of public accountability. Accordingly, the Soviets sought to exploit these requirements of an open society in negotiations to their own advantage. Hence, they tried to influence Western public opinion over the heads of their governments and condition the public mind into accepting their negotiating position, as in the case of building pressure for a summit conference. In general, they resorted to propaganda as a political device in exploiting the vulnerabilities of the democracies. Even so, Kohler believed such negotiating devices had only a short-term value. As he explained to the Brookings audience:

In general there is no reason for us to become especially disturbed or excited about the propaganda devices employed by the Soviet Union as standard techniques of negotiation. These techniques are inevitably made available by the very nature of our "open society." Soviet techniques sometimes produce real bargaining advantages but these are by no means certain or overwhelming. Actually Soviet efforts to foster confusion and division among the Western peoples during past years have been unsuccessful. Even the propaganda advantages achieved by their disregard of truth and their ability to make irresponsible proposals have had a distinctly short-term character. Falsehood has a nasty habit of backfiring sooner or later. In the long run the immediate advantage is usually lost in the general atmosphere of mistrust its exposure creates. The "open society" is somewhat vulnerable to psychological thrusts, but it also develops a toughness and resilience which assure durable strength.[56]

(g) Problem of incompatible purposes

The problem of incompatible purposes, primarily long-range rather than the immediate ones, was for Kohler by far the most important of all difficulties in negotiating successfully with the Soviets. Nations

---

[54] Ibid., p. 905.
[55] Ibid., p. 305.
[56] Ibid., pp. 906–907.

entered negotiations usually with multiple aims and objectives. Almost never were their aims identical, and often, Kohler noted, their objectives were quite dissimilar or even opposite. "But successful negotiation." he continued, "usually requires that the purposes of the negotiating parties be at least compatible." For Kohler this was "the core of our problem with the Soviet Union." [57]

What Kohler called "one shot" deals with the Soviets were not hard to negotiate when immediate interests coincided and the subject of the transaction had little significance in terms of ultimate purposes. But such deals were not the transcending ones that the peoples of the world sought. "What the American people would like to have," he explained, "* * * is an agreement on the basic elements of a continuing relationship." And this goal, Kohler suggested, was the most difficult because of the incompatability of purposes which viewed in the context of negotiations he summed up as follows:

Everything the Soviet rulers have done for the past 15 years and everything they are doing at the present time adds up to produce the inescapable conclusion that the Soviet Government has not deviated from its purpose of ultimate world domination. Every negotiation is conducted within the framework of this purpose. From time to time the Soviet rulers will make concessions but rarely, if ever, at the expense of their grand design. Where it is impossible for a particular negotiation to contribute directly to this grand design in a significant degree, they seek to convert the negotiating situation itself into a sort of stage setting for the pursuit of their ultimate purposes. [58]

This incompatability of purposes produced an ideological, political, economic, and psychological struggle known as the cold war. Kohler did not perceive any likely change in this war until fundamental changes occurred in long-range Soviet purposes. Kohler believed further that it was "highly unlikely that any foreseeable efforts at negotiation can eliminate this struggle." Nonetheless, he felt assured that:

Once we fully comprehend the necessity of being prepared to living calmly in a state of tension and danger for many years to come, we will be in a much better position to do the things that are needed to carry forward our search for lasting peace and security, including the conduct of meaningful negotiations with the Soviet Union. [59]

(h) Insistence on continuing negotiations

Despite this catalog of problems and difficulties in negotiating with the Russians, Kohler did not want to imply that "such negotiations are futile." "On the contrary," he said,

these negotiations are often valuable and sometimes essential. We must negotiate constantly, using every means and channel that gives promise of constructive results. We must consider the institution and continuation of all programs and activities that might help to make our negotiations more profitable. We must leave no stone unturned in the search for mutually advantageous agreements. [60]

Agreement was possible; negotiations could succeed. More than once "lengthy, laborious, acrimonious and seemingly hopeless negotiations" over months and years without sign of progress ended in sudden agreement within a matter of hours. "We can never afford to become discouraged," Kohler cautioned, "either with respect to specific issues or with respect to the general course of Soviet policy." Despite the in-

[57] Ibid., p. 907.
[58] Ibid., p. 908.
[59] Ibid., pp. 909-910.
[60] Ibid., p. 910.

compatibility of purposes at that time, Kohler believed that "even the most basic purposes can change," and he urged, "We must do all we can to encourage a change." [61]

In a concluding statement of warning against a policy of appeasement, Kohler gave the following prescription for negotiating with the Soviets:

A realistic comprehension of the difficulties inherent in negotiations with the Soviet Union affords no grounds for an abandonment of hope. It should serve only to prevent our hopes from becoming delusions. Let us realize that there are no quick and magical solutions to most international problems. Let us understand that the process of negotiation is continuous and that the art of negotiation frequently involves more perspiration than inspiration. Let us frankly recognize both the advantages and disadvantages of our negotiating position and try to avoid expecting either too much or too little. Let us constantly keep in mind the true nature of Soviet purposes and bend our imaginations to the task of finding incentives which may induce them to alter or modify these purposes. [62]

(i) On the value of Kohler's commentary

Kohler's commentary has one transcending value for the purposes of this study: It reaffirmed the importance of negotiations as a primary instrument of peace. The reminder that negotiation was not just an art but a continuing process has special importance for a relationship so volatile and unpredictable as the Soviet-American. Kohler made a careful distinction between illusory and real impediments, underscoring particularly the disruptive properties of incompatible purposes and the importance of solidifying promises in agreements with the satisfaction of national interests and the means of enforcement.

In retrospect, Kohler's address coincided with the emergence of an aggressive outward thrust of Soviet globalism. This new policy thrust correlated the Soviet search for security with the purposes of its long-range policy. Marked by the frequency of cold war rhetoric, the speech represented a perspective that held that "a considerable basis" existed for supposing that the Soviets "regard world domination as the only fully satisfactory form of security obtainable." [63] Yet, notwithstanding this seemingly uncompromising view, Kohler saw the value of negotiations and diplomacy as a mechanism for maintaining peace while encouraging a change in Soviet basic purposes. In the final analysis Kohler's was a message of hope and confidence in the healing properties of diplomacy.

---

[61] Ibid.
[62] Ibid.
[63] Ibid., p. 909.

CHAPTER VIII—IN TRANSITION TO PEACEFUL COEXISTENCE WITH KHRUSHCHEV, 1953-64

Part II—Major Negotiating Encounters: Geneva Summit, Cuban Missile Crisis, and the Nuclear Test Ban Treaty

War has failed. The only way to save the world is through diplomacy.
*—President Eisenhower to the Soviet
leaders at the Geneva Summit, July 1955.*

So let us not be blind to our differences, but let us also direct attention to our common interests and to the means by which those differences can be resolved. And if we cannot end now our differences, at least we can help make the world safe for diversity. For in the final analysis our most basic common link is that we all inhabit this planet. We all breathe the same air. We all cherish our children's future. And we are all mortal.
*—President Kennedy at American University,
June 10, 1963.*

IV. MAJOR SOVIET-AMERICAN NEGOTIATING ENCOUNTERS UNDER KHRUSHCHEV

A. The Geneva Summit Conference, 1955

1. BACKGROUND OF THE CONFERENCE

(a) Nuclear stalemate: Pressure to parley

That negotiations were the centerpiece of American policy toward the Soviet Union and not just political rhetoric was evident in three major negotiating encounters under Khrushchev: The Geneva Summit of 1955, the Cuban missile crisis of 1962, and the Nuclear Test Ban Treaty of 1963. Each encounter represented a transformation of the relationship from peaceful coexistence to challenge-and-crisis and a return to peaceful coexistence.

The leitmotiv of international politics in 1955 was the easing of tensions in East-West relations, and the prime catalyst of change was the Geneva summit conference. By the spring of 1955, the implications of thermonuclear warfare had become widespread. An awareness of the emerging "nuclear stalemate," where the massive retaliatory power of each side ruled out any attack and thus degraded the risk of general war, fostered a growing belief in Eisenhower's statement that there was "no alternative to peace" and generated an awareness that war had become "unthinkable" because it would mean the end of civilization. The view was taking hold that the time had come for the Soviet Union and the Western powers to break the deadlock that had immobilized any movement toward arms control and prevented the establishment of an assured peace. Knowledge of the rapid development in the technology of destruction contributed to building popular pressures for a summit meeting that might break this deadlock. The accent of the new succession regime in Moscow on peaceful coexistence stimulated this emerging international mood.[1]

(b) A favorable convergence of events

The idea of a summit conference was first advanced by Prime Minister Churchill in May 1953, but the newly inaugurated Eisenhower administration, notably its Secretary of State John Foster Dulles, was opposed on grounds that in the absence of tangible evidence of Soviet sincerity, failure was virtually preordained. Such failure, it was reasoned, would only deepen world pessimism and set back any chance for achieving genuine agreement. Eisenhower's stock reply to press inquiries on a possible summit was, "I would not go to a summit merely because of friendly words and plausible promises by the men in the Kremlin; actual deeds giving some indication of a Communist readiness to negotiate constructively will have to be produced before I would agree to such a meeting." [2]

For the next 2 years the idea was kept alive by editorials and commentaries in the press, creating the notion in segments of public opinion that such a meeting would "do no harm and might help." [3] The Soviets periodically voiced their support for a summit conference. They had two apparent motives: (1) To advance their newly proclaimed policy of peaceful coexistence by appealing to popular desires for a relaxation of tension; and (2) to frustrate the further integration of West Germany into NATO by holding out the promise of a new and acceptable settlement on Germany.[4]

But the time was not right.

By the end of 1954 and into the spring of 1955, however, the international scene, notably political conditions in Europe, changed radically. The London-Paris agreements were finally concluded bringing West Germany into NATO. Now the West, having achieved its long-sought goal of German rearmament and integration into its alliance system as a counterweight to the Soviet bloc, believed itself to be in a stronger position to negotiate with the Soviets on a settlement in Europe. The Soviets countered this move by establishing the Warsaw Alliance and by abrogating their wartime treaties of mutual assistance with France and Britain, but to no avail.[5]

Faced with the reality of a clear defeat in the cold war, the Soviets initiated in the spring of 1955 a demarche against a background of rising interest in a summit conference. After years of fruitless negotiations in some 379 meetings, they quickly agreed to an Austrian peace treaty (formally called the Austrian State Treaty) without prior notice. In addition, they sought a rapprochement with Yugoslavia, invited West German Chancellor Conrad Adenauer to Moscow as a prelude to establishing diplomatic relations, and offered to open discussions with the Japanese. All of these moves, and others most conciliatory but not recorded here, seemed intended to satisfy the Western demand for deeds as a prerequisite for a summit conference.[6]

---

[1] Barber, Hollis W., et al. The United States in World Affairs, 1955. Published for the Council on Foreign Relations. New York, Harper, 1957, pp. 1 and 2, and Barraclough, Geoffrey and Rachel F. Wall. Survey of International Affairs, 1955-56. Issued under the auspices of the Royal Institute of International Affairs. London, Oxford University Press, 1960, pp. 150-151.

[2] Eisenhower, Mandate for Change, p. 505.

[3] Ibid.

[4] The United States in World Affairs, 1955, p. 30.

[5] Ibid., pp. 32-33.

[6] Gerson, Louis L. John Foster Dulles. The American Secretaries of State and Their Diplomacy Series. New York, Cooper Square Publishers, 1967, vol. 27, pp. 220-221.

Because of this change in the Soviet attitude and not wishing to appear "sensely stubborn," President Eisenhower yielded to the pressures for a summit and instructed a reluctant Dulles to inform the interested parties through diplomatic channels that if they were genuinely interested in such a meeting, the United States was ready to listen to their reasoning. On June 13, 1955, after an exchange of notes, the Soviet Union agreed to a summit meeting at Geneva beginning July 18.[7]

(c) Perspectives and purposes

(1) From the Soviet side: Khrushchev and Bulganin

For the Soviets, the Geneva summit was, as Khrushchev recalled, "a crucial test": A test of the new leadership's ability to negotiate successfully in this first major diplomatic encounter with the Western leaders; and a test of their declared policy of peaceful coexistence.[8]

Khrushchev's sensitivity to this test was apparent in his critical reflections on Stalin's foreign policy in the postwar era. Stalin had led his successors to believe that they could not cope with the "imperialistic powers" after he had passed from the scene—they "will wring your necks like chickens," he said.[9] Knowing it would be futile, no attempt was made to reassure Stalin that they could manage without him. Besides, Stalin's successors, Khrushchev emphasized, had serious doubts about the overmilitarization of Soviet foreign policy under Stalin. "He lived in terror of an enemy attack," Khrushchev recalled. "For him foreign policy meant keeping the antiaircraft units around Moscow on a 24-hour alert."[10]

Hence the gravity of the challenge for the new leadership in this first negotiating encounter with the West. Their mettle was to be tested at Geneva. Khrushchev explained, asking rhetorically: "Would we be able to represent our country competently? Would we approach the meeting soberly, without unrealistic hope, and would we be able to keep the other side from intimidating us?"[11]

The Soviet approach to the Geneva summit, Khrushchev continued, was based on its fundamental policy of peaceful coexistence. But he was skeptical of the outcome. The Western powers had no desire, he said, to consider the "interests and wishes" of the Soviet Union and the other Socialist countries. They wanted to restore capitalism in the liberated areas of Eastern Europe. And they sought German reunification which, as Khrushchev said, "really meant the expulsion of Socialist forces from the German Democratic Republic; in other words, the liquidation of socialism in the German Democratic Re-

---

[7] Ibid., p. 223 and Eisenhower, Mandate for Change, p. 506.

[8] Khrushchev, Nikita S. Khrushchev Remembers. With an introduction, commentary, and notes by Edward Crankshaw, translated and edited by Strobe Talbott. Boston, Little, Brown, 1970, p. 393. Khrushchev's memoirs are one of the main sources for this chapter. With respect to their authenticity, Edward Crankshaw, a British specialist on Soviet affairs and biographer of Khrushchev, wrote in his introduction : "When I was told of the existence of Nikita Khrushchev's reminisences, my first thought was that they would prove to be a forgery. There have been a number of such documents which were in fact manufactured in the West for political or commercial reasons." But, Crankshaw continued, "I did not have to read very far * * * to feel pretty well sure that these were the real thing ; and by the time I had finished I was convinced. Here was Khrushchev himself, quite unmistakably speaking, a voice from limbo, and a very lively voice at that" (p. vii). The publisher, Little, Brown & Co., wrote in a prefatory note : "This book is made up of material emanating from various sources at various times and in various circumstances. The publisher is convinced beyond any doubt, and has taken pains to confirm, that this is an authentic record of Nikita Khrushchev's words."

[9] Ibid., p. 392.

[10] Ibid., pp. 392–393.

[11] Ibid.

public and the creation of a single capitalist Germany which would, no doubt, be a member of NATO." According to Khrushchev, the Soviet Union simply wanted to sign a peace treaty recognizing the existence of the two German states and guaranteeing the freedom of each to develop independently.[12]

Khrushchev felt that the "main thing" at the Geneva Conference was "to preserve peace." But he regretted that the Western powers were "still reluctant to take even the basic measures necessary for laying the foundations of a secure peace." Hence, he considered that the Geneva meeting, while having an acknowledged value, "was probably doomed to failure before it even began." [13]

Much the same sentiments of a desire for peace were expressed by Premier Bulganin. At a Moscow reception on April 13 he explored with Ambassador Bohlen in a half-hour private conversation the theme, in Bohlen's words, "that the future of the world in great measure depended on relations between the two great powers and that minor matters had been allowed to create serious differences." Bulganin deplored the absence of a common language between both nations, terming it a more basic question than the problems of the Far East. (The Quemoy-Matsu crisis in the Formosa Straits was then in full swing.) Bohlen complained that the absence of regular contacts in Moscow between the foreign ambassadors and Soviet leaders "made it difficult for anybody to understand clearly the exact motivation and purposes of the Soviet Government." Bulganin agreed, and promised to take the matter up with Molotov. In a reflective summary of the Soviet mood Bohlen recalled, "There was no question that the new leaders were interested in better relations with the United States." [14]

That Bohlen's judgment had ostensibly some validity was revealed in Bulganin's optimistic appraisal on the eve of the Geneva meeting at a Moscow press conference. The Soviet delegation was going to Geneva, he said,

to discuss frankly with the other great powers the most important international problems, to find a common language and by joint efforts to achieve a relaxation of international tension and the strengthening of confidence in the relations between states. * * * We will undoubtedly be able to find common ground * * *.[15]

(2) *From the American side: Eisenhower and Dulles*

(a) *Eisenhower's cautionary approach.*—By and large Eisenhower approached the Geneva summit with measured optimism but without illusions. He endorsed Bulganin's statement to the press and said that the purpose of his trip was "to attempt * * * to change the spirit that has characterized the intergovernmental relationships of the world during the past 10 years." [16]

Before departing for Geneva, Eisenhower made a nationwide address in which he noted that Presidents had gone abroad in times of war to fulfill their obligations as Commander-in-Chief and to participate in conferences at the end of a war to conclude peace treaties. He said:

But now, for the first time, a President goes to engage in a conference with the heads of other governments in order to prevent wars, in order to see whether

---

[12] Ibid., p. 394.
[13] Ibid., pp. 394–395.
[14] Bohlen, op. cit., pp. 377–378.
[15] The United States in World Affairs, 1955, pp. 60–61.
[16] Ibid., p. 61.

in this time of stress and strain we cannot devise measures that will keep from us this terrible scourge that afflicts mankind.

The President stressed the importance of preventing the drift toward the "inevitable end" of tensions and war or at least to continuing tensions that were brought on by a buildup of armaments and the growth of suspicions that conflicts in goals had produced. He expressed the American desire for peace and that of peoples everywhere, noting particularly his belief that "pessimism never won a battle." [17]

But Eisenhower had no illusions about the prospects at Geneva. As he wrote to Everett Hazlett, a longtime friend and confident, "Personally I do not expect any spectacular results" from the forthcoming conference. Nevertheless, he believed that he and Dulles should be able to detect whether the Soviets intended "to introduce a tactical change that could mean, for the next few years at least, some real easing of tensions." Failing in obtaining "some concrete evidence," he continued, "then, of course, the effort must be to determine the exact purpose of recent Soviet suggestions for conferences and easing of tensions and so on." [18]

(b) *Dulles' pessimism and skepticism.*—Dulles' approach to the Soviets contrasted sharply with that of the President: Where Eisenhower was pragmatic and somewhat optimistic, Dulles was more strictly ideological, more intensely moralistic, more deeply pessimistic. Only reluctantly did he accept the idea of a summit in the spring of 1955. For he had viewed with foreboding the relaxation among the Western Allies in the post-Stalin period and the increased pressure for a summit conference. He equated relaxation with peril. As he said:

> I'm concerned lest a summit meeting be nothing but a spectacle and promote a false euphoria. Under those circumstances we and our allies might not take the necessary steps to keep the free world together. If there's no evident menace from the Soviet bloc our will to maintain unity and strength may weaken. [19]

In a series of preconference position papers Dulles set forth American objectives, outlined probable British and French attitudes, anticipated Soviet purposes and estimated the possible outcome. In sum, he believed that the Soviets would gain more at Geneva than the West, and he foresaw the emergence of the Soviet Union as a moral and social equal with the United States. Central to his concern was an outcome that would encourage Western relaxation, weaken NATO, and delay West German rearmament. He understood the risks of the conference but also possible gains. As Prof. Louis L. Gerson, his biographer, noted, "Forced to go to the summit, Dulles wanted it to succeed." [20]

2. PREPARATIONS, AGENDA, ORGANIZATION, AND PROCEDURES

(a) *Preparations for the conference*

(1) *Meetings of the Foreign Ministers*

Fairly extensive preparations were made for this first summit conference in the postwar era, the last being at Potsdam in July 1945. The

[17] Eisenhower, Mandate for Change, pp. 509–510.
[18] Ibid., p. 506.
[19] Gerson, op. cit., pp. 221–222. See also, Hoopes, Townsend. The Devil and John Foster Dulles. Boston, Little, Brown, 1973, p. 286.
[20] Gerson, op. cit., p. 231.

Foreign Ministers of Britain, France, and the United States met informally with Molotov at the signing of the Austrian State Treaty in Vienna during mid-May to discuss preliminary preparations. Further talks among the Western Foreign Ministers took place in New York in mid-June followed by more detailed talks with Molotov at the celebration of the 10th anniversary of the United Nations in San Francisco during the last week of June.[21]

In San Francisco, Dulles and Molotov conferred privately and discussed with great candor their preferences for subjects on the agenda. These discussions came to grips with the deep differences that existed between the Soviet Union and the United States and its Western Allies on such matters as European security, German unification, and conditions in Eastern Europe. In brief, Molotov listed three items: Disarmament, European security and economic cooperation. Dulles suggested disarmament, German unification, political conditions in Eastern Europe and the highly objectionable activities of international communism (which Molotov took exception to on grounds that this was a matter of a state's internal affairs).[22]

The upshot of the meetings at San Francisco was agreement on procedures, though Molotov at first opposed them. The arrangements as presented by Dulles proposed a 5-day meeting during which, in accordance with the idea advanced initially by British Foreign Secretary Harold Macmillan, the heads of government would only attempt to define the crucial world problems and then issue directives to the Foreign Ministers of the four nations to work out details and conduct negotiations. The Foreign Ministers were to meet in the mornings where they would prepare for the session of the heads of government in the afternoons.[23] Apparently, the most that was expected at Geneva was an easing of international tensions and the inauguration of a process of negotiations for the future in which the Four Powers could come to grips with the hard problems dividing them.

(2) "Position papers" and conference logistics

President Eisenhower was sufficiently impressed by the "difficult and intricate preparation" required in staging a full-scale international conference that he commented on it in some detail in his memoirs. Writing from his experience at the Geneva summit, he noted that the "position papers" on negotiating positions to be taken had to be "carefully written and approved." In addition, agreements had to be reached with other governments on schedules of meetings, agenda, details of timing, personnel to be present in the conference room; advanced parties had to manage the logistics of arranging for offices, living accommodations, communications, press relations and security; and social activities had to be coordinated.[24]

The President seemed impressed by the care, complexity and intensity of the preparation, notably of the "position papers." Such papers could only be written, he noted, after the President had decided on what position he would take in the negotiations. In his mind, priority subjects were disarmament, reunification of Germany, East-West cul-

---

[21] For a commentary on some of these meetings, see Macmillan, Harold, Tides of Fortune, 1945–55. New York, Harper & Row, 1969, pp. 599–610.
[22] Gerson, op. cit., pp. 225–228.
[23] Eisenhower, Mandate for Change, p. 508.
[24] Ibid., pp. 506–507.

tural exchanges, "the plight of enslaved peoples behind the Iron Curtain," and the goals of international communism. Accordingly, arms control and the German question were, in his words, the "two critical 'action' items." Having reached decisions on his positions, the State Department and other staff carefully prepared 20 basic documents, with more than 150 secondary papers ready for alternate topics that might arise. In addition, more reference data and statistical analyses were made ready.[25]

Clearly, the American negotiating team went to Geneva well prepared.[26]

(b) Conference agenda

Agreement was not reached on the precise conference agenda until the day after the opening session. The conference began on July 18 at 10:15 a.m. in the Palais des Nations with Eisenhower in the chair in a setting colorfully, and critically, described by Macmillan:

The room in which we met filled me with horror the moment we entered it. The protagonists were sitting at tables drawn up in a rectangle; the space between them was about the size of a small boxing ring. But this arena was itself surrounded by rows of benches and seats which were provided, presumably, for the advisers but seemed to be occupied by a crowd of interested onlookers. The walls were decorated with vast, somewhat confused, frescoes depicting the End of the World, or the Battle of the Titans, or the Rape of the Sabines, or a mixture of all three. I could conceive of no arrangement less likely to lead to intimate or useful negotiations. The whole formal part of the conference was bound to degenerate into a series of set orations. It was only when the heads of government or Foreign Ministers met in a small room outside in a restricted meeting that any serious discussion could take place.[27]

Formal speeches took the whole day as each side set forth the main lines of its negotiating position. Eisenhower then proposed that the Foreign Ministers meet on the following morning to recommend a formal agenda; the heads of government could resume their discussions in the afternoon. It was agreed.[28]

---

[25] Ibid.
[26] Foreign Secretary Macmillan was critical of "position papers." He wrote with respect to preconference meetings in New York: "The Foreign Office had now fallen into the American habit of writing what were called 'position' papers. But the fault of the system was that both we and the State Department seemed to concentrate more on discussing what it was we wanted than considering how we were to achieve our objectives. The new word 'identification' now became the favorite piece of jargon. It soon came to be believed that if a problem could be defined, it could in due course be resolved." (Macmillan, Tides of Fortune, p. 606.)
[27] Ibid., pp. 616–617. President Eisenhower gave the following rather benign but fairly complete description of the conference setting:
"The edifice which makes an otherwise pleasant resort city a household word throughout the world is the Palais des Nations; once it housed the League of Nations. Now it provides, under auspices of the United Nations, facilities for high-level international conferences. As I entered the building, I was struck by its enormous size. It has several floors of offices, committee rooms, a library of half a million volumes, a restaurant and meeting rooms. It contained sufficient space to provide office facilities for our sizable delegations—one estimate put the total for the four nations at this conference at 12 hundred. The Council Chamber, where our conference was to be held, was in reality a square amphitheater. Around the gigantic hollow-squared table where 40 delegates would sit in 2 rows were spectator stands arranged in tiers on 3 sides of the room. On the fourth wall, facing the United States delegation, there were large glassed-in offices of the Secretariat, where minutes were kept and translations were broadcast into the earphones of the delegates.
"The decoration of the room was remarkable. On the lofty ceilings were murals done in deep bluish-gray and gold. Directly over the table itself the mural depicted figures representing five of the continents of the world in a circle, with arms clasped. The mural is so designed that the viewer sees the five figures peering down at him, as if he were at the bottom of a large well. Around the five continent-figures are scenes depicting man's successful struggle against scourges such as slavery and famine. The scenes are arranged to guide the viewer's eye from one to the next, finally reaching the one unconquered scourge, war, where subhuman beasts drop babies down the muzzles of monstrous cannons, titled at crazy angles. The mural is effective. The brutish characters remind the participant in this drama of the grim seriousness of his task. It is not a pleasant piece of art, but it is powerful and thought-provoking." (Eisenhower, Mandate for Change, pp. 513–514.)
[28] Ibid.

At the Foreign Ministers meeting Macmillan suggested an agenda based on subjects commonly referred to in the speeches on the previous day; namely, reunification of Germany, European security, disarmament, and development of East-West contacts. Molotov and Dulles suggested additions, arousing Macmillan's concern that a "long and inconclusive discussion about the agenda" would ensue. But this did not occur. Half way through the second round Molotov accepted the British proposal, and the agenda was adopted accordingly.[29] On the following day the conference got down to business.

3. ASPECTS OF THE NEGOTIATIONS

(a) General characteristics: Formality and informality

(1) Formalism and tedium

The Geneva Conference was in marked contrast to the small, informal, intimate and agendaless summit that Churchill had in mind when he first proposed it 2 years before: It was far larger, more formal, less intimate, and bound by a rigid agenda. The setting encouraged the set orations that Macmillan deplored. Little progress was made after lengthy discussions on the issues opened up the deep differences that existed between the contending negotiators. Gerson perhaps best described the tone of the conference when he noted that "the summit threatened to become a colossal bore" until Eisenhower dramatically gave it life with his "open skies" proposal on disarmament.[30]

(2) On the value of informal contacts: Eisenhower, Khrushchev, and Macmillan

Notwithstanding, the formalism and tedium of the conference did not degrade its overall value, nor did it close off other avenues of contact. Informal social gatherings proved most useful, particularly in permitting the principals to get a closer reading on one another. They could also serve as a tension-relaxer after arduous negotiating sessions. (Eisenhower had suggested that refreshments be served after each plenary session so that, as Khrushchev recalled, "we might end the day on a pleasant note. His idea was that if there had been any hard feelings or tensions aroused during the day's session, we could wash them away with martinis.") [31]

In the evening of the first day Eisenhower entertained the Soviet delegation including, Khrushchev, Bulganin, Molotov, Zhukov, Gromyko and their interpreter Troyanovsky. "For reasons of their own," Eisenhower noted, "they were seeking good will, but they obviously also had a goal." "They drank little and smiled much," except for Gromyko whose "rare smile" was given with the "greatest effort." Soviet attempts to ingratiate themselves "were carried out with precision and mechanical perfection," the first tactical move being to bring on Soviet Defense Minister Marshal Georgi K. Zhukov to engage Eisenhower in private conversation (the others quietly faded away in the background), hoping they would renew their wartime friendship and thus advance the Soviet cause of peaceful coexistence. The conversation

[29] Ibid.
[30] Gerson, op. cit., p. 234.
[31] Khrushchev, op. cit., p. 399.

was "strained but friendly and innocuous"—and, apparently, without much effect.[32]

At dinner, the conversation among the leaders became serious. Eisenhower probed his guests candidly saying that the superweapons of the day could "easily and unwittingly destroy the entire Northern Hemisphere." "War has failed," he told them. "The only way to save the world is through diplomacy." All vigorously nodded assent, but nothing of much importance was said. Nonetheless, this informal dinner, his first face-to-face informal contact with the Soviet leadership, revealed to Eisenhower the "solid front" that the leadership maintained, but more importantly it gave him a reading on what to expect in subsequent negotiations. As he wrote, "Despite my failure to induce them to reveal their true purposes and ideas, it was a useful evening in that I saw that the implacability of this quintet in a social situation would certainly be encountered in ensuing conferences and we would have to shape our own tactics accordingly."[33]

Informal social gatherings also served Khrushchev's purpose in getting a better reading on the Western leaders and in furthering the goals of Soviet policy. Zhukov had been brought along to Geneva, he acknowledged, because of his wartime friendship with Eisenhower. It was thought that this friendship might "serve as the basis for conversations that would lead to an easing of the tension between our countries." Eisenhower and Zhukov might have a chance to talk alone together, Khrushchev noted, and hopefully "they would exchange views about the need for peaceful coexistence." But, as he complained in rather colorful language, "that vicious cur Dulles", who could not tolerate peaceful coexistence, "was always prowling around Eisenhower, snapping at him if he got out of line."[34]

Khrushchev also talked informally with delegate Nelson Rockefeller, with whom he playfully joked about the possibility of getting credit from the United States on the order of $6 billion, but to no avail. Khrushchev discounted the value of courting the "friendly and hospitable" French Premier Edgar Faure—the Soviets nicknamed him "Edgar Fyodorovich"—because the rapid turnover in the French Government made it pointless. On the other hand, his informal friendly contacts with Prime Minister Eden led to an invitation to visit Britain.[35]

That British Foreign Secretary Macmillan gained some useful, indeed most penetrating, insights into Soviet policy and the behavior and thinking of the Soviet leadership was revealed in his notes made on the occasion of a dinner given by Eden for the Soviet delegation:

(a) They are very relaxed, after the removal of the tyrant, Stalin. (They said, with glee, that since 1953 they worked a normal day, instead of all night!)

[32] Eisenhower, Mandate for Change, p. 518.
[33] Ibid., p. 518.
[34] Khrushchev, op. cit., p. 398. Dulles had cautioned the President to avoid socializing with Bulganin and Khrushchev when photographers were present. Acknowledging that cameramen would be difficult to avoid, he hoped that the President would maintain an austere countenance whenever photographed with the Russian leaders. (Gerson, op. cit., p. 231.) Dulles' concerns proved to be well grounded. Much to his displeasure, Bulganin had maneuvered to sit next to the President whenever pictures of the four leaders were taken. The Soviets enlarged one picture out of proportion, eliminated Eden and Faure, and then duplicated it endlessly. According to Gerson, Dulles "was peeved when the cropped photograph of a smiling Eisenhower and an amiable Bulganin appeared at the Leipzig Fair and throughout Italy, to help the local Communist parties gain respectability." (Ibid., p. 236.)
[35] Khrushchev, op. cit., pp. 399–400.

(*b*) They do not want another Stalin—a bloody and uncertain tyrant. (*c*) Khrushchev is the boss, but not another Stalin. He controls the party and thus in a country where there is no Parliament, he controls the Government. (*d*) They are unable to accept the reunification of Germany in NATO, and will fight it as long as they can. This is partly because their public would be horrified. After all, the Germans treated them terribly and they hate them. (*e*) They do not fear war; they do not really believe that the Americans are going to attack them. (*f*) They are anxious about China. They told us so. They (like us) wish that Quemoy and Matsu could sink beneath the sea. (*g*) They may fear—in the long run—that China will be a danger to them on their eastern flank. I think they might prefer a weak nationalist or capitalist China, which they could plunder, to a Communist China, which they have to assist. (*h*) They do not want the conference to fail. They will play for a draw.[36]

(*b*) *Issues and deliberations*

(*1*) *German unification: a nonnegotiable issue*

Accounts of the summit conference by participants, other firsthand observers, and by general sources have provided detailed explanations of the sometimes intricate formal and informal deliberations among the negotiators on the major issues. Reduced to its simplest form, these deliberations, in effect, amounted to a restatement of known mutually unacceptable positions and thus a resolution of none of the fundamental differences. Only minor variations on familiar themes surfaced in the proceedings.

On the matter of German unification, Eden, with the full concurrence of the other Western Allies, proposed a plan for German unification which, according to Townsend Hoopes, a former U.S. Government official and biographer of Dulles, had about it, along with the plan for European security, "an air of logical unreality."[37] Eden's proposal would require free elections in both Germanys, followed by the creation of a unified government which then would decide whether or not to be neutral or aline itself either with NATO or the Warsaw Pact.[38]

But the Soviets rejected the plan outright, understandably fearing that their hold on East Germany could not withstand a free election and that such a loss could spread dissension throughout Eastern Europe. A united Germany opting for NATO membership would hardly assuage their fears of the Germans, nor would it soothe their deep concerns for Soviet security. Several times Eisenhower asked Khrushchev why they feared free elections. "The German people," he answered at once, "have not yet had time to be educated in the great advantage of Communism. Within a few years this will all be changed."[39]

Clearly, German unification was not a negotiable issue, though there was one brief moment of optimism within the American delegation. A committee made up of the Foreign Ministers hammered out what was thought to be a agreement setting the stage for general elections that would lead to the unification of Germany. But when the draft was submitted to the general conference, Bulganin gave the document a different interpretation that repudiated what Molotov had agreed to

[36] Macmillan, Tides of Fortune, p. 619.
[37] Hoopes. op. cit., pp. 298–299.
[38] The United States in World Affairs, 1955, p. 62.
[39] Eisenhower, Mandate for Change, p. 523.

less than an hour before.[40] No progress was made on this issue, and finally the President concluded that "the Russian stand, especially on Germany, was as before—adamant and inflexible." [41]

(2) European security, a case of conflicting purposes

Inextricably linked to German unification was the issue of European security, but the Soviets and Western negotiators approached the problem in reverse order: For the West, unification had to come first, followed by security arrangements in Europe; for the Soviets, the security issue had first priority, followed by unification. It was a case of conflicting purposes in this seemingly interminable East-West struggle over the future of Germany.

To meet Soviet apprehensions of a renascent aggressive Germany, Eden presented a three-point plan for European security: (1) A collective security pact joined by the Four Powers and Germany, (2) limitations on German forces and armaments, or (3) a demilitarized buffer zone of unspecified extent between Germany and the Soviet Union.[42]

But the Soviets again rejected the Eden plan. Contending that the security of Russia could not depend on the guarantee of particular states, Bulganin countered with a slightly revised version of their proposal of 1954 for a 26-state European security treaty. This revised plan coupled pledges of nonaggression and peaceful settlement with a general undertaking to assist any victim of attack, together with the eventual dissolution of the West European Union, NATO, and the Warsaw Pact.

The Soviet counterproposal was unacceptable to the West which had just achieved its goal of integrating West Germany into NATO and would not place its security in hostage to Soviet good will. Moreover, Bulganin was clearly aware that negotiations for such a plan would take many months, possibly years; that the West had no intention of abandoning NATO; and that the Soviet plan would delay German reunification, a high-priority goal in Western policy. By this time, particularly in the context of the Austrian State Treaty that bound Austria to permanent neutrality as a price for the liquidation of Soviet occupation, it was becoming clear that the Soviet leaders were prepared to wait their chances of getting better terms from direct negotiations with the West German Government, offering unification on conditions of withdrawal from NATO and neutralization.[43]

At Geneva the negotiators could do no more than air their differences over this issue of European security that went directly to the core of their vital national interests.

(3) Disarmament and Eisenhower's "open skies" proposal

On the arms control issue, the obstacle of inspection remained unsurmountable. Eden, again taking the lead, proposed that inspec-

---

[40] So complete was the Soviet reversal, Bohlen recalled, that the President seriously considered breaking off the conference and issuing a strong statement on Soviet duplicity. "On further thought," Bohlen wrote, "he realized that the onus would fall on the United States, and, since there was sufficient ambiguity in the document, it was possible that more might come out of it than Bulganin had indicated. Nothing more did come of it." (Bohlen, op. cit., p. 384.)
[41] Eisenhower, Mandate for Change, p. 517.
[42] The United States in World Affairs, 1955, p. 63.
[43] Ibid. See also, Eden, Anthony, The Memoirs of Anthony Eden : Full Circle. Boston, Houghton Mifflin, 1960, pp. 331–332.

tion, a longtime absolute prerequisite for the West in any arms control plan, be inaugurated first in the proposed European demilitarized zone and then gradually expanded. French Premier Faure suggested reductions in the percentages of spending on arms with savings going to technical assistance. The United States and Britain, long experienced in Soviet budgetary manipulations and duplicities, were not enthusiastic about this idea. Bulganin proposed a prohibition on the manufacture and use of atomic weapons and a limitation of 1.5 million men in the Armed Forces of the United States, the Soviet Union, and Communist China, with 650,000 allowed each to Britain and France, and 150,000–200,000 apiece for all other states.[44]

At this point in the proceedings during the afternoon session of July 21, Eisenhower took center stage and dramatically revealed his "Open Skies" plan. Looking directly at the Soviet delegation, the President pledged that "The United States will never take part in an aggressive war." The sincerity and conviction of the President's declaration impressed all present and evoked a reply from Bulganin: "We believe the statement." Addressing himself principally to the Soviet delegates because it was the weapons of the two superpowers that gave rise to fears and dangers of surprise attack, the President went on to suggest that the good faith of both parties be demonstrated by each supplying the other with complete "blueprints" of its military establishment and that each give the other freedom of photo reconnaissance over its national territory to prevent concealment of the establishment's size.[45]

The proposal was received with surprise, even by some members of the American delegation. (The plan had been worked out in secret by a task force on arms control headed by Rockefeller.) Eden and Faure approved the proposal and declared themselves ready to cooperate and open their territories to inspection, provided all participants agreed to do the same. Bulganin, speaking last, acknowledged, in Eisenhower's words, that the proposal seemed to have "real merit" and that the Soviet Government would give it "complete and sympathetic study at once." [46]

The President was encouraged by the tone of Bulganin's voice as well as by his words. His first reaction was that assurances of isolating inspection teams from the population thus eliminating the possibility of indoctrination might lead to progress toward an arms control agreement. But in the President's words, "The hope born of this development was fleeting." For after Bulganin spoke, the session adjourned for the day, apparently, all in "high good humor." As was his practice at Geneva, Eisenhower mingled with the Soviet delegation. Walking to the cocktail lounge at adjournment time, the participants customarily engaged in what Eisenhower called "an international substitute for the British hour of tea." On this occasion, Eisenhower walked with Khrushchev. "I don't agree with the chairman," he said, smiling, (meaning, of course, Bulganin, the chairman of the Soviet Council of Ministers), but as Eisenhower wrote, "there

[44] The United States in World Affairs, 1955, pp. 63–64.
[45] Idid., p. 64, and Eisenhower, Mandate for Change, p. 520.
[46] Ibid., p. 521.

was no smile in his voice." "I saw clearly then, for the first time," he recalled, "the identity of the real boss of the Soviet delegation." [47]

From that moment on to adjournment of the conference Eisenhower wasted no more time probing Bulganin but devoted himself exclusively to persuading Khrushchev of the merits of the "Open Skies" plan—but, to no avail. In the President's words, Khrushchev referred to the idea as "nothing more than a bald espionage plot against the U.S.S.R., and to this line of argument he stubbornly adhered." Though the Party Secretary General made his points laughingly, his argument was "definite and intractable." [48]

(4) Development of East-West contacts

The development of East-West contacts was the last major issue discussed in formal conclave at the Geneva summit. Other issues, such as self-determination in Eastern Europe, a matter of keen interest for the Americans, and recognition of the Chinese Communist regime, a subject raised by the Soviets, were discussed privately and informally by the interested parties, but without results.[49]

Some progress was made on the issue of East-West contacts, mainly because it coincided with the outward thrust of Soviet policy as subsequent events were to demonstrate. Cultural diplomacy combined with the diplomacy of trade-and-aid were to become a strong component of Moscow's globalist strategy of peaceful coexistence.[50]

But at Geneva the conferees confined themselves only to making general statements on lowering barriers to communications and trade. The West pressed for the free movement of people and printed materials into the Soviet bloc; the Soviets were mainly interested in the relaxation of controls over trade and the formal exchange of delegations. No significant progress was made beyond these stated generalities and the expressed desire of each to make a public record of their future expectations.[51]

(5) Negotiating the final communique

As the conference moved along, the Soviets, as customary with them, indicated an increasing interest in the final communique. From the beginning of the conference each delegation detailed a representative to a combined committee with instructions to prepare the communique. Their work continued throughout the conference. Every day each representative would report to his own delegation on emerging areas of agreement and discord.[52]

Negotiations on this document were a serious business because it entailed the public image that each participant would present to a world, and for a world anticipating an easing of tension, this was an important task. According to Eisenhower, the Soviets wanted a series of "meaningless generalities dealing with peace, coexistence, and good intentions." But, with apparently the resurrected Yalta controversy in mind, this approach was rejected in favor of one that, in Eisenhower's words, would "establish a basis for later negotiation of specific agreements—pledges made to the world, so worded that every citizen could,

[47] Ibid.
[48] Ibid.
[49] The United States in World Affairs. 1955. p. 64.
[50] Survey of International Affairs. 1955–56. pp. 76 and 159.
[51] The United States in World Affairs. 1955. p. 64.
[52] Eisenhower, Mandate for Change, p. 525.

by the later actions of the governments involved, know whether promises were being kept or broken, and who could be held responsible." [53]

Both sides debated very intensely the contents of the communique, with the Soviets adding to the extraordinary tedium of the task at the final meeting by laboriously contesting almost every word of the text.[54] Agreement was finally reached, and the communique was formally issued. The communique which focused on the key points set forth in the conference agenda took the form of a joint directive to the Foreign Ministers outlining the negotiating tasks they were to undertake in furthering the general agreements reached at Geneva.[55]

Khrushchev observed in retrospect that the communique was formulated to allow each side to make its own interpretation. Various compromises were made on both sides, making it possible for all to sign. As Khrushchev explained, "We didn't want to disperse without having anything to show for the meeting. On the other hand none of us wanted any point in the statement to be interpreted as a concession in principle or policy to the other side." [56]

4. ASSESSMENT OF THE SOVIET NEGOTIATORS

(a) Khrushchev and mutual perceptions

(1) Eisenhower, Macmillan, and Bohlen on Khrushchev

For the Americans and their Western Allies, the Geneva summit was their first major encounter with the new Soviet "collective leadership"—at least as it was then being pared down, among those present in Geneva, to Khrushchev, Bulganin, and Molotov. Perceptive observers like Macmillan and Bohlen very quickly saw that Khrushchev was "the real boss," as Eisenhower put it, and not Premier Bulganin.[57]

As titular head of the Russian delegation, Bohlen recalled, Bulganin did all the speaking in formal sessions, but Khrushchev was "the dominant Soviet figure among the Russians at Geneva." Never hesitating to interrupt Bulganin in private conversation, Khrushchev "took over completely at dinners and receptions. There was never any indication of resentment by Bulganin of Khrushchev's leading role or his boorish peasant humor." [58]

Eisenhower, who described Khrushchev as "rotund and amiable, but with a will of iron only slightly concealed," took measure of his adversary after failing to persuade him to accept the "Open Skies" proposal.[59] A world statesman concerned about peace and the well-being of humanity, he said, would find "egregiously wrong" a course of policy permitting the uncontrolled expansion of armaments that in the long run could lead to the destruction of his own country. But, Eisenhower observed, Khrushchev,

does not want peace, save on his own terms and in ways that will aggrandize his own power. He is blinded by his dedication to the Marxist theory of world

[53] Ibid., p. 526.
[54] Ibid., p. 526. Eisenhower wrote: "The final meetings were exceedingly tedious as arguments on minutiae went on interminably." Macmillan wrote: "The Russians were disposed to contest almost every word of the text, and there were some anxious moments when the President seemed to have been put into a position from which he could not retreat." (Macmillan, Tides of Fortune, p. 623.)
[55] Eisenhower, Mandate for Change, pp. 526–527.
[56] Khrushchev, op. cit., p. 400.
[57] Eisenhower, Mandate for Change, p. 521. Macmillan noted after a dinner hosted by Eden for the Soviet leaders: "Khrushchev is the boss, but not another Stalin." (Macmillan, Tides of Fortune, p. 619.)
[58] Bohlen, op. cit., p. 382.
[59] Eisenhower, Mandate for Change, p. 518.

revolution and Communist domination. He cares nothing for the future happiness of the peoples of the world—only for their regimented employment to fulfill the Communist concept of world destiny. In our use of the word, he is not, therefore, a statesman, but rather a powerful, skillful, ruthless, and highly ambitious politician.[60]

As the conference proceeded, Foreign Secretary Macmillan "felt more and more" that Bulganin, though the nominal head of the Soviet delegation, was "of minor importance" and that Khrushchev was the real source of political power. But for Macmillan, Khrushchev was "the mystery." And he asked himself rhetorically this question: "How can this fat, vulgar man, with his pig eyes and ceaseless flow of talk, really be the head—the aspirant Tsar—of all these millions of people and this vast country?" [61]

Bohlen detected the same boorish qualities in Khrushchev's behavior, recalling an incident at an American dinner party for the Russians in Geneva when Khrushchev ridiculed Bulganin in the presence of Mrs. Eisenhower by telling a story that exposed his heavy drinking habits. Through it all Bulganin maintained "the benign air of a chaplain, and said nothing", while Mrs. Eisenhower laughed politely. But it reminded Bohlen of Stalin's method of denigrating his associates in public; it also demonstrated Khrushchev's personal power. "While still not the sole master of the Kremlin," Bohlen noted, "he was able with impunity to humiliate the Premier of his country." [62]

(2) Khrushchev on Eisenhower and Dulles

In like manner, Khrushchev had some very critical comments to make on President Eisenhower and Secretary Dulles as negotiators and political leaders. Though Khrushchev had doubts about the propriety of his presence at Geneva because he held no ministerial post, he acknowledged, nonetheless, that he was "very anxious" to meet the Western leaders and participate in solving international problems, and accordingly had little difficulty in overcoming these doubts.[63]

At Geneva, Khrushchev took his measure of Eisenhower. Informed, presumably by the Soviet intelligence community, that Eisenhower was, in Khrushchev's words, "a mediocre military leader and a weak President," Khrushchev did not approach his subject with a tabula rasa. The President was "a good man," Khrushchev observed, "but he wasn't very tough." Indeed, Khrushchev found "something soft about his character," and clearly being President was "a great burden for him." [64]

In negotiations at Geneva, Eisenhower was "much too dependent on his advisors," according to Khrushchev. Dulles, not the President, was in his estimation the real determiner of U.S. foreign policy. To document this assessment, Khrushchev described Eisenhower's excessive deferential behavior toward and dependency on Dulles at one plenary session. Dulles sat next to Eisenhower who chaired this particular session; Khrushchev sat next to Dulles. Khrushchev described what transpired:

* * * I watched Dulles making notes with a pencil, tearing them out of a pad, folding them up, and sliding them under President Eisenhower's hand. Eisen-

[60] Ibid., p. 522.
[61] Macmillan, Tides of Fortune. p. 622.
[62] Bohlen, op. cit., p. 383.
[63] Khrushchev, op. cit., p. 394.
[64] Ibid., p. 397.

hower would then pick up these sheets of paper, unfold them, and read them before making a decision on any matter that came up. He followed this routine conscientiously, like a dutiful schoolboy taking his lead from his teacher.

The Soviet delegation, Khrushchev recalled, found it difficult "to imagine how a chief of state could allow himself to lose face like that in front of delegations from other countries." For them it "certainly appeared" that Eisenhower was "letting Dulles do his thinking for him." [65]

Khrushchev's assessment of Dulles was somewhat ambiguous: He deplored Dulles and his policies, referring to him once as a "vicious cur," but praised his respect for the limits of power. When later asked by India Prime Minister Nehru how he got along with Dulles in the negotiations at Geneva, Khrushchev replied that he had a chance to talk informally over dinner and found him to be "a very dry character"—"we hadn't talked about anything much except what dishes we liked most." [66]

In taking a larger measure of Dulles, however, Khrushchev spoke disapprovingly of the Secretary's oft stated goal of pushing Socialism back to the borders of the Soviet Union. Seemingly "obsessed with the idea of encirclement," Dulles extended restrictions on trade and cultural exchanges, even to preventing a Soviet delegation from attending "some sort of international convention of chefs" sponsored by the United States. But, "I'll say this for him," Khrushchev continued, "Dulles knew how far he could push us, and he never pushed us too far." He cited the case of the Syrian-Lebanese crisis in 1958 when Dulles "stepped back from the brink of war." On the occasion of Dulles' death, Khrushchev told his friends that:

although he had been a man who lived and breathed hatred of Communism and who despised progress, he had never stepped over that brink which he was always talking about in his speeches, and for that reason alone we should lament his passing. [67]

(b) Cameos of Bulganin, Molotov, Gromyko, and Zhukov

At Geneva, Premier Bulganin was, in Bohlen's words (and as others quickly perceived), "a front man for Khrushchev" about whom foreigners never thought had "any outstanding ability." [68] Even Khrushchev acknowledged that he "wasn't very well versed in foreign policy nor very adept in diplomatic negotiations." [69] Eisenhower characterized Bulganin as "a genial public relations type, slightly buoyant;" [70] while Richard H. Roevere, the historian of the Eisenhower years, contrasted the "squat, tough, loud, indelicate, and altogether self-possessed" Khrushchev with Bulganin who was "well turned out, in an almost aristocratic style" and looked like "a successful Kentucky horse-breeder." [71]

Molotov, by this time an international celebrity, "studiously maintained his reputation as 'The Hammer'," Eisenhower noted.[72] Macmillan, who observed him presumably for the first time at the Vienna

[65] Ibid.
[66] Ibid., pp. 397–398.
[67] Ibid., p. 398.
[68] Bohlen, op. cit., p. 383. In 1957, he conspired to remove Khrushchev, lost, and gradually faded from view.
[69] Khrushchev, op. cit., p. 394.
[70] Eisenhower. Mandate for Change. p. 518.
[71] Quoted in, Hoopes. op. cit., p. 296.
[72] Eisenhower, Mandate for Change, p. 518.

meeting of Foreign Ministers in mid-May, wrote that Molotov seemed smaller than supposed, and older. "He is grey, not black any more," Macmillan recorded, with a "very pale pasty face; a large forehead; closely cut grey hair." Wearing a "very respectable black suit," the British Foreign Secretary noted, he "looked rather like a head gardener in his Sunday clothes." [73] Before leaving for London, Macmillan spent a "pleasant afternoon" with Molotov, talking over a wide range of subjects including music (he was a cousin of Scriabin, the composer). According to Macmillan:

He certainly showed, that afternoon, a softer side of his character. His great round head was impressive and his heavy black mustache framed curiously dreamy eyes. On the one side he seemed just an efficient operator; on another, something of a philosopher.[74]

At the San Francisco meeting a month later, Macmillan was struck by what he called "the strange duality of his character." In spite of his reputation for "a hard, negative, brutal attitude, when one saw him alone there appeared an unexpected attractiveness and even softness." [75] And at Geneva, he observed Molotov's techniques of negotiations, the toughness, stubbornness, the "stonewalling tactics" and other observable characteristics as the proceedings moved on. After attending a dinner hosted by the Russians for the British, Macmillan made a cryptic reference to Molotov as being "already a sick man." [76]

In contrast, little attention was given to Gromyko, then Deputy Foreign Minister, in the accounts by conference participants. On the occasion of a small dinner hosted by the American delegation on the first day of the summit (and which was intended as an exploratory expedition), Eisenhower noted that Gromyko was "stern, unapproachable, unhappy, with little taste for the whole performance." When he "spared us a rare smile," Eisenhower recalled, he "did so with the greatest effort." [77]

Finally, Marshal Zhukov, though not strictly a negotiator at Geneva, had the unique diplomatic task of attempting to resurrect the friendship he once had with his wartime colleague in the hope of broadening the base of peaceful coexistence.[78] In the context of the dinner referred to above, Eisenhower described the Marshal as "a friendly catalyst, but frightened." [79]

After many "heavy-handed" Soviet hints that the President might want to confer with Zhukov, a luncheon was arranged. Eisenhower, too, had his political purposes: He hoped to get some explanation for the inconsistencies that "seemed always to characterize Russian attitudes and pronouncements." Ambassador Bohlen, who was very much on the outside at this conference (and with the administration because of his connection with the controversial Yalta Conference), acted as interpreter.[80] In contrast to the independent, self-confident military leader he knew in wartime, Eisenhower now found a "subdued and worried man." In recalling this brief encounter, the President wrote:

---

[73] Macmillan, Tides of Fortune, p. 599.
[74] Ibid., p. 601.
[75] Ibid., p. 610.
[76] Ibid., pp. 621–622.
[77] Eisenhower, Mandate for Change, p. 518.
[78] Khrushchev, op. cit., p. 398.
[79] Eisenhower, Mandate for Change, p. 518.
[80] Bohlen, op. cit., p. 381.

In a low monotone he repeated to me the same arguments that had been presented to the conference by the chairman of the Soviet delegation. This was not ordinary talk; he spoke as if he was repeating a lesson that had been drilled into him until he was letter perfect. He was devoid of animation, and he never smiled or joked, as he used to do. My old friend was carrying out orders of his superiors. I obtained nothing from this private chat other than a feeling of sadness.[81]

5. RESULTS AND SIGNIFICANCE OF THE CONFERENCE

(a) As a negotiating experience

(1) Opportunity for mutual appraisals

Perhaps the greatest value of Geneva as a negotiating experience was that it gave the leaders on both sides an opportunity, as Bohlen said with respect to Eisenhower and Khrushchev, "to size each other up."[81a] Except for Molotov and, to a very limited extent, Zhukov, the Soviet leadership was virtually an unknown quantity for the Western leaders. Not until Eisenhower got Khrushchev's informal reaction, for example, to his "Open Skies" proposal did he realize who was "the real boss" in the Soviet Union. Indeed, one of the President's main purposes in going to Geneva in the first place was to find out who was in charge. (Malenkov had been removed in February 1955 and Bulganin made Premier.)[82] Presumably the other Western leaders did not come to the same conclusion as Eisenhower until they had observed Khrushchev in action at the informal social gatherings where he apparently did not repress his preeminence. At any rate, all left Geneva clearly knowing the pecking order in the Soviet political hierarchy.

Moreover, Khrushchev's reaction to Eisenhower's "Open Skies" proposal revealed most emphatically the profound (and historic) Soviet sensitivity to matters impinging directly on their national security. As the President recalled.

His protests were, of course, spurious. Khrushchev's own purpose was evident—at all costs to keep the U.S.S.R. a closed society. He would permit no effective penetration of Soviet national territory or discovery of its military secrets, no matter what reciprocal opportunities were offered to him.[83]

In similar fashion, Khrushchev and the other Soviet leaders were also able to take a reading on the Western leaders. Khrushchev termed the summit "useful in a number of important respects," notably, "it gave the leaders of the four great powers an opportunity to see each

---

[81] Eisenhower, Mandate for Change, p. 525. In characterizing Zhukov, Bohlen wrote: "Zhukov was a Bolshevik who undeviatingly followed the Party line, but he was first a Russian patriot. He believed in the independence of the army, and one of the reasons for his eventual downfall was his attempt to throw off the political commissar system. There was a cleanliness of spirit about him that contrasted sharply to the deviousness of other Bolshevik leaders. He conveyed a tolerance, even a respect, for the United States, and there was no doubt in my mind that his affection for General Eisenhower was genuine and not put on for occasions." (Bohlen, op. cit., p. 385.)

[81a] Bohlen, op. cit., p. 388.

[82] Commenting on Bulganin's opening speech, Eisenhower wrote: "Naturally, I was disappointed. But Bulganin's speech was only an opening gambit. Rarely, in the usual tactics of diplomacy, will a diplomat expose his hand in the early moments of negotiations. It was clear that we had to be patient, watchful, and alert if we were to solve the Soviet enigma. What, we asked ourselves, do the Soviets really want? Who is really in charge among the five who face us across the table—Bulganin, Khrushchev, Molotov, Zhukov, Gromyko?" (Eisenhower, Mandate for Change, p. 517.)

[83] Ibid., p. 522. Bohlen wrote with respect to this proposal: "From my experience, I was sure that the Soviets would never tolerate any eyes prying into their secrets. Above all, they did not want to show how weak they were militarily. Furthermore, they had little to gain, because the location of our bases is printed on commercial maps available to anyone. The United States, on the other hand, had much to learn about the Soviet Union, where secrecy is a fetish." (Bohlen, op. cit., p. 384.)

other at close quarters and to exchange views informally among themselves, usually over dinner after the official sessions." [84]

How the assessments of the Soviet leaders might have affected future Soviet policy could not be determined. Bohlen felt that Khrushchev was "impressed" with the President and from then until the U-2 incident in 1960 had spoken "highly" of him. (And even Eisenhower, while wary, was impressed with Khrushchev sufficiently to agree to an exchange of visits.) [85] However, Khrushchev's own appraisal of Eisenhower as a "good man" but not "very tough," made on the basis of the Geneva encounter, might well have played some part, perhaps even a significant part, in his decision to test U.S. policy in Berlin during the crisis of 1958–59.[86]

(2) On the value of informal contacts

The summit also demonstrated the value of informal contacts among world leaders. The inflexibility of the negotiating positions was clearly understood by both sides before the opening of the conference. The plenary sessions, carried on in a large cumbersome formal setting that encouraged excessive formalism, worked against the real purposes of serious negotiations as Macmillan feared. But the informal contacts at dinners and at cocktails after the formal sessions made it possible for the process of negotiations to continue more freely and no doubt more profitably. The memoirs of Eisenhower, Macmillan, Eden, and Bohlen revealed the value of such informal channels in negotiations, if not so much in those at hand, then in the conduct of future diplomacy by all the principals.

(c) Preparations for the conference

Finally, a unique side of the Geneva summit as a negotiating experience was revealed in the intensive preparations that were undertaken. On numerous occasions during the 2 months prior to the opening of the summit, the Foreign Ministers of all four participating countries conferred on the subjects that were to be discussed and procedures to be followed at Geneva. Their preliminary negotiations provided the occasion for a searching out of agenda items, agreement on the priorities of problems facing East and West, and discussion of the conference's organization.

On the American side, President Eisenhower's memoirs provided useful insights into the extensive preparations of "position papers"

---

[84] Khrushchev. op. cit., p. 395.
[85] Ibid., p. 388.
[86] One aspect of Khrushchev's personality that apparently went undetected by the Western negotiators was his extreme sensitivity to matters of prestige. The Soviet leader recalled that the Soviet delegation found itself "at a disadvantage from the very moment" it landed at the Geneva airport. The Western leaders arrived in four-engine planes, while the Soviet delegation arrived in a "modest two-engine Ilyushin." "Their planes were certainly more impressive than ours," Khrushchev observed, "and the comparison was somewhat embarrassing." (Khrushchev, op. cit., p. 395.)

Khrushchev expressed particular annoyance on the occasion of reviewing the Swiss honor guard. Just before the ceremony began a Swiss protocol officer "suddenly stepped right in front of me and stood with his back up against my nose. My first impulse was to shove him out of the way." But Khrushchev realized that this was done on instructions from the Swiss Government to prevent him from joining Bulganin, the formal head of the delegation, in reviewing the troops. "I wasn't permitted to join in that part of the ceremony," Khrushchev noted, "so the Swiss Government very rudely had that man stand in front of me!" (Ibid.)

While these incidents at Geneva might not have seemed important, still they revealed an aspect of Khrushchev's personality that was to be one of the driving forces behind his diplomacy during his time in power; namely, his sensitivity to matters of prestige, his insistence on acceptance by the West, and even insistence on Western acknowledgment of what he judged to be Soviet superiority.

and other supporting research material that was available to American negotiators. That the American negotiating team was well prepared at Geneva was revealed particularly in the work of the Rockefeller task force on arms control that provided the ideas and background for Eisenhower's "Open Skies" proposal.

Clearly, U.S. preparations for major international conferences had come a long way by the mid-1950's when compared with those undertaken during some of the wartime conferences.

(b) Impact on the international scene

(1) An easing of international tensions, temporarily

At the time, the summit conference made a great impact on the international scene, producing, at least temporarily, what appeared to be an easing of tensions. Observers spoke of an emerging "spirit of Geneva." The Soviet press was quick to capitalize on this term in their efforts to advance the new political line of "peaceful coexistence." Reflecting what appeared to be a mood of excessive euphoria, the "spirit of Geneva" was apparently based on the popularly held assumption that the Four Powers had achieved a mutual understanding and tacit agreement that a major war could not be allowed to take place; that tensions among states had indeed eased; and, as the writers of "The United States in World Affairs" for the year 1955 observed, "that the world could thus heave a sigh of relief and get on with its normal business." [87]

This optimism persisted despite the fact that no concrete problems had been resolved at the summit meeting. The deadlock continued on all the major issues dividing East and West. At best, the leaders of the Four Powers had only momentarily come to grips with them at Geneva; they referred them to the Foreign Ministers for later negotiations.

Amid warnings of some skeptics (including Dulles), disillusionment soon set in, first with the formal Soviet rejection of Eisenhower's "Open Skies" proposal in August and then the collapse of the Foreign Ministers Conference in October.[88] At this conference, held in the same room as the summit meeting, the Soviets, as Eisenhower put it, repudiated every measure they had agreed to in July—measures, it might be added, that had created some reasonable expectations of serious negotiations.[89] Yet, the President held to the belief, despite this setback, that the "spirit of Geneva" had not faded entirely: He cited

<hr/>

[87] The United States in World Affairs, 1955, p. 3. See also, Hoopes, op. cit., pp. 300–301 and Eisenhower, Mandate for Change, p. 529.

[88] For Dulles' skeptical attitude, see Gerson, op. cit., pp. 235 and 236, and Hoopes, op. cit., pp. 301–302.

[89] Skeptical journalists had reported from Geneva at the time of the summit their doubts about the suddenness of Soviet "affability." James Reston of The New York Times wrote: "The Russians are waiting it out. They are counting on our impatience and on Europe's weariness and divisions. The prosperity in the West and the blandishments from the East, they are convinced, will work to their advantage. Meanwhile they will smile and smile, negotiate and negotiate, divide and divide." (Quoted in, The United States in World Affairs, 1955, p. 66.)

Optimists who might have expected a fundamental change in Soviet policy had been forewarned by Khrushchev who told an East German delegation on Sept. 17, 1955: "We are in favor of a detente, but if anybody thinks that for this reason we shall forget about Marx, Engels, and Lenin, he is mistaken. This will happen when shrimps learn to whistle. * * * We are for coexistence because there is in the world a capitalist and a socialist system, but we shall always adhere to the building of socialism. * * * We don't believe that war is necessary to that end. Peaceful competition will be sufficient." (Ibid., p. 68.)

the value of East-West exchanges that had their "small beginnings" at the summit conference.[90]

But the fact of the matter was, as Bohlen observed, that there had been "no real progress" at the Geneva summit and at best the calculated ambiguity of the final communique only made it possible to hope that the Foreign Ministers meeting "might pull something out of the bag." That hope proved to be "illusory," as each side put its own interpretation on the Geneva communique, notably with respect to the German question. The discussions went "round and round," Bohlen noted, and in the end the talks proved to be "as friendly and unproductive as at Geneva." [91]

Thus with the momentary expectations of some mutual accommodation in the cold war dashed, East-West relations reverted to their old pattern of hostility and tension. As Hayter described conditions in the aftermath, "There would be no war, but no concessions and no agreements." [92]

(2) A turning point in Soviet foreign policy

In many respects the Geneva summit was a turning point in Soviet foreign policy. Some observers in the West, notably Secretary Dulles, had judged the summit to be a classic example of a temporary Soviet retreat after a political setback—in this case, the integration of West Germany into NATO.[93] But not Khrushchev. For him it marked the beginning of a new offensive. Khrushchev, who came away from Geneva with heightened prestige and the status of a recognized world leader, was encouraged by the belief that the West now respected Soviet power and that, as he said:

Our enemies now realized that we were able to resist their pressure and see through their tricks. They now knew that they had to deal with us honestly and fairly, that they had to respect our borders and our rights, and that they couldn't get what they wanted by force or by blackmail. They realized that they would have to build their relations with us on new assumptions and new expectations if they really wanted peace.[94]

For Khrushchev the Geneva meeting was "an important breakthrough for us on the diplomatic front. We had established ourselves as able to hold our own in the international arena." [95]

Apparently convinced of the political opportunities presented by the nuclear stalemate and buoyed by the feeling, as he said, of having "passed the test" of successfully negotiating with the Western leaders, Khrushchev reversed the Stalinist policy of continentalism in the aftermath of Geneva and initiated a new policy of globalism. The year 1955 marked the beginning of Khrushchev's outward thrust into the Third World and the inauguration of a new era of "open diplomacy" of the Soviet kind. In many ways the Geneva summit set the stage for this radical departure in Soviet policy.[96]

[90] Eisenhower, Mandate for Change, p. 530.
[91] Bohlen, op. cit., p. 386.
[92] Hayter, "The Kremlin and the Embassy," p. 386.
[93] Hoopes, op. cit., pp. 301–302, and Gerson, op. cit., p. 236.
[94] Khrushchev, op. cit., p. 400.
[95] Ibid.
[96] For a commentary and analysis of Soviet Third World policy under Khrushchev, see, U.S. Congress. House. Committee on International Relations. "The Soviet Union and the Third World : A Watershed in Great Power Policy?" By Joseph G. Whelan, Senior Specialist in International Affairs, and William B. Inglee, Research Assistant in Soviet and East European Affairs. Congressional Research Service, Library of Congress, 95th Cong., 1st sess., Washington, U.S. Government Printing Office, 1977, pp. 17–30.

B. The Cuban Missile Crisis 1962: Negotiations by Action

1. BACKGROUND OF THE MISSILE CRISIS

(a) *The missile crisis as a negotiating encounter*

The Geneva summit conformed to the forms and modalities of conference diplomacy as it evolved in the postwar era. But there were exceptions to such normal behavior as in the case of the Berlin blockade of 1948–49 when "negotiations by semaphore" set into motion forces that were to end the crisis.

Negotiations in the Cuban missile crisis were similarly unique. Many channels and forms of diplomacy, traditional and unusual, were used in the negotiating process. But this encounter had the distinction of adding still another ingredient to the ongoing process; namely, the element of action. For the Cuban missile crisis was what Richard T. Davies, a veteran Foreign Service Officer, long-time specialist in Soviet and East European affairs, and recently the U.S. Ambassador to Poland, called, a classic example of "negotiations by action." [97]

(b) *Kennedy on negotiating with the Soviets*

(1) *From Sorensen's perspective*

President Kennedy's attitude toward negotiating with the Soviets was positive but realistic. He accepted as a reality Khrushchev's belief in the universal triumph of communism and expected him to exploit every means fair and foul in advancing toward that goal. Still, he hoped that in time the power of the United States and its allies could persuade Khrushchev, as Theodore C. Sorensen, one of Kennedy's closest advisers, wrote:

that no safe or cheap route was open to world domination, that all channels were open for true negotiation, that any real grounds for the Soviet Union's fears could be peacefully removed, and that realistic, effective steps to accommodation—enabling Moscow to devote more energies internally—would advance the interests and security of both sides.[98]

Kennedy strongly believed, more so than some of his subordinates, in the postive value of negotiating with the Soviets. As he once said, "we have nothing to fear from negotiations * * * and nothing to gain by refusing to take part in them." [99] Areas of confrontation had to be reduced through negotiations; reasonable negotiations with the Soviets were possible; and while harboring no illusions about Soviet good faith, he did not share the belief of those who held that no agreement reached with the Soviets would be kept. Nor did he share, as he said:

the illusion that negotiations for the sake of negotiations always advance the cause of peace. If for lack of preparation they break up in bitterness * * * if they are made a forum for propaganda or a cover for aggression, the processes of peace have been abused.[100]

---

[97] At a reception given by the Polish Embassy in Washington on July 21, 1978. commemorating Poland's National Day, the writer talked informally with Ambassador Davies about this study and various characteristics of Soviet behavior in negotiations. noting particularly the Berlin crisis as an example of "negotiations by semaphore." Davies, who was an active participant in the Cuban missile crisis while serving in the U.S. Embassy in Moscow as first secretary, remarked upon reflecting about this crisis that this was a case of "negotiations by action."

[98] Sorensen, Theodore C. Kennedy. New York, Harper & Row, 1965, p. 516.

[99] Ibid.

[100] Ibid.

For Kennedy, the limits of negotiations had to be carefully defined: "We cannot confine our proposals to a list of concessions we are to make," abandon commitments to the freedom or security of others, or negotiate in an environment of threats. On the occasion of the Berlin crisis in 1961 he expressed the prophetic fear that a nuclear confrontation might be needed before Khrushchev understood that his conciliation would not permit humiliation. "If he wants to rub my nose in the dirt," Kennedy said, "it's all over." On the other hand, Kennedy did not believe in advancing, what Sorensen described as, "meaningless, unattainable or obviously unacceptable proposals, or in deliberately taking ambiguous or flabby positions." [101]

Furthermore, Kennedy strongly objected to what Secretary of State Dean Rusk referred to as the "football stadium psychology" of diplomacy that measured wins or losses on a daily basis. For Kennedy, "negotiations are not a contest spelling victory or defeat." A mutual perception of improvement through a negotiated agreement was hardly an American victory; and failure in obtaining the only possible negotiated agreement that would damage American interests could hardly be called a defeat. Negotiations in seemingly endless, pointless talks were usually better than a battle. Indeed, for Kennedy the most successful diplomacy was more often dull than dramatic. Direct confrontations—what he called "collision courses"—produced drama, but, as he remarked after the Cuban missile crisis, "You can't have too many of those, because we are not sure on every occasion that the Soviet Union will withdraw." [102] Nuclear devastation, he felt, could be accomplished instantly, but peace through negotiations was a long haul, "the sum of many acts." [103]

Accordingly, Kennedy, who did not believe it possible to achieve any sweeping settlement of East-West problems in his administration, hoped that small breakthroughs could lead to larger ones until gradually through the process of negotiations a détente could be built, a "truce to terror," as he said, in which both sides could see that mutual accommodation was preferable to mutual annihilation. [104]

(2) Prelude to Cuba: Negotiating with Khrushchev at Vienna, June 3–4, 1961

Kennedy's first and only face-to-face negotiating encounter with Khrushchev took place in Vienna during June 3–4, 1961. Arthur M. Schlesinger, Jr.'s account fully justified Kennedy's description of this encounter to the American people as "somber" and to Prime Minister Macmillan as "grim." [105] The talks, according to Schlesinger, a noted American historian and adviser to Kennedy, were "civil but tough," and in laying down his ultimatum on Berlin, Khrushchev's behavior was "not quite a tirade; it was too controlled and hard and therefore the more menacing." [106] The general tenor of the negotiations was reflected in Schlesinger's description of the last informal Kennedy-Khrushchev meeting that centered on the main question, Berlin:

Khrushchev returned unrelentingly to the attack. The United States, he said, wanted to humiliate the Soviet Union. If the President insisted on occupation

[101] Ibid.
[102] Ibid., pp. 516–517.
[103] Ibid.
[104] Ibid.
[105] Schlesinger, Arthur M. Jr., A Thousand Days: John F. Kennedy in the White House. Boston. Houghton Mifflin. 1965, pp. 375 and 377.
[106] Ibid., pp. 361 and 372.

rights after a treaty and if East German borders were violated, whether by land, sea or air, force would be met by force. The United States should prepare itself for this, and the Soviet Union would do the same.

"I want peace," said Khrushchev, "but, if you want war, that is your problem." Kennedy said, "It is you, and not I, who wants to force a change."

Khrushchev said again that it was up to the United States to decide on peace or war. The Soviet Union had no choice but to accept the challenge. It must, and it would, respond. The treaty decision was irrevocable. He would sign in December.

Kennedy, parting, said, "It will be a cold winter." [107]

For Kennedy, the Vienna meeting was a bruising negotiating encounter.[108] From the beginning Khrushchev launched an unrelenting attack; he was on the offensive and maintained that negotiating posture throughout. What the President had hoped would be an occasion to establish a rational basis for accommodation, to introduce precision into each other's assessments, and, therefore, to avoid miscalculation, confrontation, and war, turned into an attempt by Khrushchev, as Schlesinger observed, "to unnerve Kennedy and force him into concessions." [109] In brief, Khrushchev's negotiating behavior was in the classical mode of totalitarian diplomacy by threat and intimidation.[110]

Kennedy came away from Vienna confident that he had met the test, indeed, more than equalled the test, for he parried Khrushchev's thrusts with skillful and telling ripostes.[111] But there could now be no doubt how vast were the ideological and political differences that divided both leaders and their nations. Still, Kennedy, who had genuinely impressed Khrushchev, appraised the encounter, as he told the American people, as valuable for keeping open the channels of communications and lessening the chances of miscalculation for each side.[112]

Despite the intensity and pressure of the negotiations and the disappointment with the results, Kennedy came away, as Schlesinger wrote, with the belief that, "He knew how Khrushchev thought and where he stood, and that was invaluable." [113] For Kennedy, Vienna was not only an occasion for taking measure of his principal adversary but also a critical time for reaffirming his faith in the value of diplomacy and negotiations as instruments of peace.

---

[107] Ibid., p. 374.

[108] Kennedy was "deeply disturbed," as Schlesinger noted, by this meeting with Khrushchev. Bohlen and U.S. Ambassador to Moscow Llewellyn Thompson thought the President had overreacted—Thompson told him Khrushchev's behavior was, "Par for the course." But, as Schlesinger observed, "Kennedy had never encountered any leader with whom he could not exchange ideas—anyone so impervious to reasoned argument or so apparently indifferent to the prospective obliteration of mankind. He himself had indicated flexibility and admitted error, but Khrushchev had remained unmoved and immovable." (Ibid., pp. 374–375.) Bohlen told the President, who was a "little depressed" at not having been able to make Khrushchev understand that he was seeking a détente based on a realistic balance of power in the world, that "there had been no hardening of Soviet policy. The Soviets always talk tough." (Bohlen, op. cit., p. 482.)

[109] Schlesinger, Thousand Days, p. 367.

[110] Khrushchev knew what he was up to; he was not there to negotiate but to intimidate. At a luncheon during the meeting he remarked in a rambling speech that he objected to the language of commercial bargaining so often employed in negotiations with the Soviet Union—"you give this and we'll give that." He asked, what was he supposed to concede? (Ibid., p. 362.)

[111] Ibid., p. 377.

[112] Kennedy was impressed both favorably and unfavorably by Khrushchev. After the first day's meeting, Schlesinger noted that "Kennedy was impressed by Khrushchev's vitality, his debating skill and his brutal candor, depressed by the blank wall of dogma." (Ibid., p. 375.)

[113] Ibid., p. 377. Khrushchev recalled: "I was very glad Kennedy won the election, and I was generally pleased with our meeting in Vienna. Even though we came to no concrete agreement, I could tell that he was interested in finding a peaceful solution to world problems and in avoiding conflict with the Soviet Union. He was a reasonable man, and I think he knew that he wouldn't be justified in starting a war over Berlin." (Khrushchev, op. cit., p. 458.)

(3) The balance of power: A predominating concept and non-negotiable conflicting perceptions

At issue in the Vienna negotiations, as in the subsequent Berlin and Cuban missile crises, was the balance of power. For both Khrushchev and Kennedy this was an all-pervading concept central to determining the course of Soviet-American relations and the ultimate success or failure of their nations in international politics.

Each interpreted the concept differently, inevitably making it non-negotiable; the consequence was conflict and crisis.

Khrushchev's belief in the shift in the balance of power and its impact upon the conduct of Soviet policy has been explained above. Suffice it to say that in 1961 he gave additional dramatic emphasis to the concept, particularly in his January 6, 1961, speech (which had a profound impact on Kennedy and the new administration) and during the Berlin crisis. The essence of Khrushchev's foreign policy position was in effect that the United States and it allies had to accept this changing power relationship and shape their foreign policies accordingly.[114]

As an historian and member of that generation much influenced by the consequences of appeasement in the 1930's, President Kennedy accepted the balance of power theory as a valid and realistic concept in international relations. His behavior during the crises in Berlin and Cuba and his perception of that of the Soviet leadership was greatly influenced by this belief. Downgrading ideology, Kennedy tended to view international conflict more in national than in ideological terms.[115] For him, national interest was the primary motivating force, not ideological abstractions.

Thus, at Vienna, Kennedy tried hard to reach an accommodation with Khrushchev that would satisfy the vital national interests of each nation. The key element in his negotiating position was a mutual acceptance of the existing equilibrium of power and thus a common perception of the status quo. Kennedy accepted social change as part of the normal historical process, but essentially peaceful change and change that did not involve the prestige or commitments of the Soviet Union and the United States or upset the balance of world power. He recognized the status quo as acceptance of the existing balance of international force, but far from advocating a freeze on the social mold of the world. he believed in political and institutional change as both inevitable and desirable. What Kennedy hoped for was a process of change that would not entail the transfer of power from one bloc to the other and would not make either side feel threatened and therefore obliged to resist change by force.[116]

Khrushchev rejected Kennedy's perception of the balance of power concept, arguing the thesis set forth in his January 6 speech; namely, that social revolution, as a global phenomenon, was preordained by history; that such revolutions, that is, "wars of national liberation," were "sacred"; and that the Soviet Union had an obligation to assist them whenever possible. For Khrushchev, the status quo meant the

[114] Whelan. Joseph G. "Khrushchev's Speech of Jan. 6. 1961: A Summary and Interpretive Analysis." U.S. Congress. Senate. Prepared at the request of Senator Alexander Wiley. 87th Cong.. 1st sess. Washington, U.S. Government Printing Office. 1961. 9 pp.
[115] Schlesinger, Thousand Days, pp. 298–299.
[116] Ibid.. pp. 363 and 366.

continued process of the conquest of power by Communist revolution on a global scale. Kennedy's conception of a global standstill was in his view an attempt to alter the status quo, not support it; it was an attempt to arrest the revolutionary process.[117]

Thus the conflicting perceptions of the balance of power concept and its implications for the status quo became entangled in Soviet-American relations, dangerously so because it meant that Soviet support for global revolutions (for example, Castro's revolution in Cuba) and refusal to recognize an acceptable balance of power (for example, in Berlin and thus Europe) would expose the great powers to the very miscalculations and confrontations that Kennedy sought to avoid. Out of this essentially ideological conflict of world views emerged the dynamic forces that produced the crisis in Berlin, and 1 year later, the Cuban missile crisis.[118]

(c) Deepening of Soviet interests and commitments in Cuba, 1960–62

Soviet interests and commitments in Cuba deepened progressively during the years from Castro's assumption of power in 1959 through 1962. Examination of the period prior to the missile crisis suggested three major trends: [119]

(1) The shift by Cuba from its political alinement with the American states to a closer association with the Communist bloc as the Castro regime adopted the Communist apparatus, took on more and more the coloration of a Communist regime, and openly declared its linkage with the world of Marxism-Leninism.

(2) The gradual expansion of Soviet commitments to Cuba in the form of political support, economic aid, and supplies of military weapons. Vigorous Soviet political support was forthcoming after diplomatic recognition in May 1960, followed by a progressive increase in economic and military aid (U.S. estimates of military aid in March 1962, $100 million) and a pledge of support against the United States in the aftermath of the ill-fated Bay of Pigs invasion in April 1961.

(3) Khrushchev's attempt to intimidate the United States and discredit its traditions and leadership position in the Western Hemisphere as a whole. On July 9, 1960, Khrushchev threatened to rocket the United States if it intervened militarily in Cuba, a threat he qualified then and later as being "figuratively speaking" and "symbolic." Three days later, he contended that the Monroe

---

[117] When reminiscing about Vienna 3 years later, Khrushchev complained to Senator William Benton that Kennedy had "bypassed" the real problem. "We, in the U.S.S.R.," he said, "feel that the revolutionary process should have the right to exist." The question of "the right to rebel, and the Soviet right to help combat reactionary governments * * * is the question of questions. * * * This question is at the heart of our relations with you. * * * Kennedy could not understand this." But Schlesinger argued that Kennedy understood it "well enough" after Khrushchev's January 6 speech and understood it "very well indeed" after the first day in Vienna. "Khrushchev's response left no doubt about the joker in the Soviet doctrine of coexistence: The idea of a dynamic status quo meant simply that the democracies had no right to intervene in the Communist world, while the Communists had every right to intervene in the democratic world." (Ibid., p. 366.) For Khrushchev's explanation of the balance of power concept and status quo, see Khrushchev, Nikita S. Khrushchev Remembers: The Last Testament. Boston, Little, Brown, 1974. pp. 495–496.
[118] In the case of Berlin, it meant that Kennedy would not accept Khrushchev's unilateral action as an attempt to radically alter the balance of power in Europe. As Schlesinger put it in explaining Kennedy's view, "If the United States surrendered to the Soviet demand, it would not be regarded as a serious country any longer." (Ibid., p. 372.)
[119] Whelan, Joseph G. The Soviet-American Crisis in Cuba: A Brief Survey. Legislative Reference Service, Library of Congress, Washington, Mar. 27, 1963, 44 pages.

Doctrine was dead—it "has outlived its time, has outlived itself, has died, so to say, a natural death. Now the remains of this doctrine should best be buried as every dead body is so that it should not poison the air by its decay. That would be the correct thing to do and this is what will happen apparently." Again he pledged support for Cuba in any "aggressive action" the United States takes against it. Such declarations intended to discredit the United States and lend support to Cuba continued through 1962.

(d) Vigorous American counterthrusts

The United States responded to the Soviet Union's aggressive policy in Cuba with vigorous counterthrusts and openly declared opposition. For what was at stake in Cuba was a vital national interest.

U.S. policies in the Western Hemisphere have been rooted in historic national traditions. Since the beginning of the Republic, Cuba had a special place in American thought. At the time of the Republic's founding, American leaders firmly established the national policy that Cuba, then a Spanish possession, could not be transferred to any other foreign power. The purpose of this principle was the need to protect vital political and strategic interests. This "no-transfer" principle, as it came to be called, was, in effect, incorporated into the Monroe Doctrine and in innumerable declarations was, therefore, reaffirmed as a cardinal principle of American diplomacy. Cuba, either under Spain or independent, was regarded as a vital national interest to be protected even at the cost of war. In pursuit of larger historic hemispheric interests, Cuba came to hold one of the highest places in the hierarchy of American foreign policy values. For Americans, Cuba was not far removed in a geographical, intellectual or an emotional sense from the vital center of their national interest; namely, preservation of the Republic itself.

To grasp this essential truth is the beginning of understanding why the United States was prepared to face nuclear war in order to remove the Soviet threat from Cuba, for the threat to this vital interest was not Castro but rather the Soviet Union which used Castro's Cuba to achieve larger and more aggressively directed political purposes. Failure of Khrushchev and others in the Soviet leadership to understand the deeper meaning of Cuba for the United States led them to a grave miscalculation.

American policy toward Cuba during the Eisenhower-Kennedy years—1959 through 1962—could be summed up as follows: [120]

(1) At first, to encourage genuine democracy in Cuba when the Castro government came to power;

(2) Later, to exercise restraint and maintain a "hands off" policy; that is, not to intervene directly but to seek Cuba's isolation;

(3) To build up political and economic counterpressures as Castro turned away from the Western Hemisphere and became more closely alined with the Soviet bloc;

(4) Through declarations to insist upon Soviet respect for traditional American policy in this hemisphere (that is, the Monroe Doctrine);

---

[120] Ibid., pp. 1, 21–25.

(5) Kennedy's addition on April 20, 1961, in the aftermath of the Bay of Pigs invasion, to resort to unilateral action if other nations of the Hemisphere failed to respond to external Communist penetration (Kennedy said in his 1961 State of the Union Message, "* * * Communist domination in this hemisphere can never be negotiated"); and another Kennedy addition on September 13, 1962, as the tempo of the missile crisis quickened; and

(6) To act swiftly against Cuba if U.S. security were seriously endangered.

American policy thus appeared to become progressively more firm and forthright as the Soviet threat in Cuba became more clearly evident.

2. PRELUDE TO THE CRISIS

(a) On a collision course in August–September 1962

(1) Khrushchev's decision and motivations

By August-September, 1962, the Soviet Union and the United States were clearly on a collision course. Sources conflict on the time when the decision was made to send in the missiles to Cuba. But Khrushchev himself recalled that the idea came to him during a state visit to Bulgaria during May 14–19, 1962. After "brooding over what to do", he conferred with others in the Soviet leadership upon returning to Moscow, and after discussions, as he wrote, "we decided to install intermediate-range missiles, launching equipment, and Il–28 bombers in Cuba." [121] In an account striking for its candor with respect to the decision and the motivations behind it, Khrushchev explained:

> It was during my visit to Bulgaria that I had the idea of installing missiles with nuclear warheads in Cuba without letting the United States find out they were there until it was too late to do anything about them. I knew that first we'd have to talk to Castro and explain our strategy to him in order to get the agreement of the Cuban Government. My thinking went like this: If we installed the missiles secretly and then if the United States discovered the missiles were there after they were already poised and ready to strike, the Americans would think twice before trying to liquidate our installations by military means. I knew that the United States could knock out some of our installations, but not all of them. If a quarter or even a tenth of our missiles survived—even if only one or two big ones were left—we could still hit New York, and there wouldn't be much of New York left. I don't mean to say that everyone in New York would be killed—not everyone, of course, but an awful lot of people would be wiped out. I don't know how many: That's a matter for our scientists and military personnel to work out. They specialize in nuclear warfare and know how to calculate the consequences of a missile strike against a city the size of New York. But that's all beside the point. The main thing was that the installation of our missiles in Cuba would, I thought, restrain the United States from precipitous military action against Castro's Government. In addition to protecting Cuba, our missiles would have equalized what the West likes to call "the balance of power." [122]

(2) Estimate of Khrushchev's motivations in the West

(a) Radically change strategic and political balance of power.— Western observers attributed a single motivation to Khrushchev in instigating the missile crisis: To radically change the strategic and political balance of power in the world. By this bold move, it was reasoned, Khrushchev could go far to redress the balance of nuclear power

[121] Khrushchev, op. cit., p. 495.
[122] Ibid., pp. 493–495.

then tipped decidedly in favor of the United States. A minimum of 64 medium-range (around 1,000 miles) and intermediate-range (1,500–2,000 miles) nuclear missiles appeared to have been contemplated for Cuba. Twenty-four medium-range and 16 intermediate-range launching pads were under construction. Thus the Soviet nuclear striking capability against targets in the United States would have been nearly doubled. Nonetheless, the United States would still have maintained at least a 2-to-1 superiority in nuclear power targeted against the Soviet Union, making the shift in the military balance of power less crucial than in the political.[123]

The impact on the political balance was the most critical element in Khrushchev's motivations. According to the estimates of qualified scholars, his success in Cuba would have undermined U.S. credibility in international relations, weakened its power position in the world, and exposed a vulnerable United States to severe Soviet political pressures along a global front. As Schlesinger explained:

Every country in the world, watching so audacious an action 90 miles from the United States, would wonder whether it could ever thereafter trust Washington's resolution and protection. More particularly, the change in the nuclear equilibrium would permit Khrushchev, who had been dragging out the Berlin negotiation all year, to reopen that question—perhaps in a personal appearance before the United Nations General Assembly in November—with half the United States lying within range of nuclear missiles poised for delivery across the small stretch of water from Florida. It was a staggering project—staggering in its recklessness, staggering in its misconception of the American response, staggering in its rejection of the ground rules for coexistence among the superpowers which Kennedy had offered in Vienna.[124]

(b) *Improve Soviet negotiating position.*—What Schlesinger was suggesting with respect to the impact of the crisis on the political balance was elaborated in detail by British Foreign Secretary Lord Hume in his defense of the U.S. action in Cuba against British critics. Lord Hume summed up Khrushchev's political motivation in the context of improving the Soviet Union's negotiating position:

Why was it done at this time? Mr. Khrushchev had been preparing for a meeting with President Kennedy on the major problems of East-West relations later in the year. But he does not wish to negotiate on equal terms with President Kennedy. What he wanted to do was to be able to confront the President with a change in the balance of nuclear power and thus to place the President at a political disadvantage. The Russian aim was to negotiate for victory over the whole field of these great problems, including Berlin. No doubt they calculated that, with every American city covered by nuclear weapons, Russia's chances of forcing concessions in substance would be greatly increased. It was a demonstration of brinkmanship with nuclear weapons to fray and test the nerves of the free world and in particular the United States. Fortunately, this plan was foiled by two things. First, by the discovery of the deception plan before the decisive shift in the balance of power could take place, and second, by the President's combination of resolution and restraint in restoring the balance.[125]

(3) *Influx of Soviet weapons and military technicians*

In early July, Khrushchev conferred with Raoul Castro, Cuba's war minister and brother of its leader. And in late July and throughout August the shipment of military equipment along with technicians, in the words of The New York Times, "suddenly poured into the island." [126] In September, further Soviet-Cuban agreements were an-

---

[123] Schlesinger, op. cit., p. 796.
[124] Ibid., pp. 796–797.
[125] United States in World Affairs, 1962, p. 96.
[126] The New York Times, Sept. 3, 1962, p. 1.

nounced on the supply of military weapons and the building of a fully equipped "fishing" port in Havana Bay, the latter arousing concern in the Defense Department for its military utility. Amid growing alarm in the country, the full extent of the Soviet buildup in Cuba known at that time was publicly disclosed by Under Secretary of State George W. Ball in testimony to the Congress on October 3.[127]

(b) Soviet program for "cover and deception"

In what Roger Hilsman, Director of the State Department's Bureau of Intelligence and Research, called a program for "cover and deception," the Soviet maintained a public and diplomatic stance of innocence.[128] As the buildup continued apace, Soviet officials gave numerous assurances through a variety of channels of their peaceful intent and their purely "defensive" purposes in Cuba. Among them were the following:

—Early in September, Soviet Ambassador Anatoly Dobrynin passed along Khrushchev's assurances to Attorney General Robert F. Kennedy, one of the key principals in the management of this crisis, and Sorensen on separate occasions that the equipment going into Cuba was "defensive in nature and did not represent any threat to the security of the United States." [129] Khrushchev gave further assurances to Robert Kennedy that he would do nothing to disrupt the Soviet-American relationship during the period prior to the coming election.

—In an official statement published on September 11, the Soviet Government stated that in light of the power of Soviet nuclear rockets there was "no need for the Soviet Union to shift its weapons for the repulsion of aggression, for a retaliatory blow, to any other country, for instance, Cuba." [130]

—In early October, Khrushchev and Mikoyan told Gorgi Bolshakov, a public information official at the Soviet Embassy in Washington, that the Soviet weapons being sent to Cuba were "intended" only for defensive purposes and that only antiaircraft missiles that could not reach American targets were being sent. On his return Bolshakov diligently passed the word around Washington, and apparently to the President and the Attorney General via a personal message from Khrushchev.[131]

—On October 13, Dobrynin assured Chester Bowles, a high-ranking official in the administration, "convincingly and repeatedly," according to Hilsman, that there were no "offensive weapons" in Cuba. Bowles had pressed the Ambassador "very hard" on this matter.[132]

—On October 16, Khrushchev gave the same assurances to Ambassador Foy Kohler in Moscow in the wake of a "storm of public suspicion," as Hilsman put it, over the agreement to build a fishing port in Cuba. Khrushchev explained that Soviet "purposes" there were wholly defensive.[133]

[127] The Congressional Record, Oct. 6, 1962, p. A7357.
[128] Hilsman, Roger. To Move a Nation: The Politics of Foreign Policy in the Administration of John F. Kennedy. Garden City, Doubleday, 1967, p. 165.
[129] Ibid.
[130] Ibid., pp. 165–166.
[131] Ibid. and Kennedy, Robert F. Thirteen Days: A Memoir of the Cuban Missile Crisis. New York, W. W. Norton, 1969, p. 27.
[132] Hilsman, op. cit., p. 166.
[133] Ibid.

—And finally, as late as October 18, 2 days after the President had concrete evidence of the missiles' presence, Soviet Foreign Minister Gromyko personally assured Kennedy in a White House meeting that Soviet aid to Cuba "pursued solely the purpose of contributing to the defense capabilities of Cuba," that "training by Soviet specialists of Cuban nationals in handling of defensive armaments was by no means offensive," and that "if it were otherwise, the Soviet Government would never become involved in such assistance." On hearing this, the President called for and read to Gromyko public statements made in September warning the Soviets against placing missiles in Cuba.[134]

(c) Growing American alarm

Notwithstanding Soviet assurances of peaceful intent and assurances on the defensive nature of their military assistance, the administration, the Congress, the press, and the American people became increasingly alarmed as Soviet ships poured into Cuba military equipment (for example, surface-to-air SAM missiles with related gear and equipment necessary for installation and operation, according to Ball) and military specialists (4,500, again, according to Ball).[135] Contributing to this increased anxiety was the lingering thought in the West as a whole of renewed Soviet pressure on Berlin in concert with a provocation in Cuba.[136]

Growing American alarm was reflected in published statements of the President and in actions by the Congress. On September 4, President Kennedy released a statement, intended to quiet fears in the Nation, in which he emphasized, among other things, the lack of evidence of any significant offensive Soviet weapons in Cuba. But, he added this warning for the Soviets, "Were it to be otherwise, the gravest issues would arise." [137] On September 7, Kennedy requested Congress for standby authority to call up 150,000 reserve troops to permit, as he said, "prompt and effective responses * * * to challenges * * * in any part of the free world." [138] On the same day Congress expressed its approval in a joint resolution that specifically authorized the use of these troops in Cuba if necessary. Other supportive congressional actions quickly followed, including a "fight if we must" resolution in the Senate (86–1) and the House (384–7) and an amendment to the reserve mobilization bill that called for defense of the Monroe Doctrine and intervention in Cuba if necessary.[139] On the 11th. the Soviets responded to Kennedy's warning of the 7th with an official statement declaring that a U.S. attack on Cuba would mean nuclear war.[140] Then on September 13, the President made his most sweeping statement of warning to the Soviets. In a major policy declaration in which he denied any intention of invading Cuba he said:

If at any time the Communist buildup in Cuba were to endanger or interfere with our security in any way, including our base in Guantanamo, our passage

[134] Ibid.
[135] Watt. D. C. Survey of International Affairs. 1962. Issued under the auspices of the Royal Institute of International Affairs. London. Oxford University Press, 1970. pp. 46–48, and Whelan, Soviet-American Crisis in Cuba. pp. 12–13.
[136] The Soviets had intensified their political offensive against Berlin and were once again endangering allied communications along the Berlin corridors. (Stebbins, Richard P. The United States in World Affairs, 1962. Published for the Council on Foreign Relations. New York, Harper & Row, 1963, p. 42.)
[137] Hilsman, op. cit.. p. 171.
[138] Whelan, Soviet-American Crisis in Cuba. p. 27.
[139] Ibid., pp. 28–29.
[140] Hilsman, op. cit., p. 171.

to the Panama Canal, our missile and space activities at Cape Canaveral, or the lives of American citizens in this country, or if Cuba ever attempt to export its aggressive purposes by force or the threat of force against any nation on this hemisphere, or become an offensive military base of significant capacity for the Soviet Union, then this country will do whatever must be done to protect its own security and that of its allies.[141]

Thus by the end of September and early October the stage was set for the Soviet-American confrontation in Cuba: The shuttle of Soviet cargo and passenger ships across the Atlantic continued apace; American air surveillance, though at times hampered by cloud cover, recorded in detail the ominous Soviet activities in Cuba; Soviet officials attempted to pacify American fears as a feeling of alarm spread throughout the country. In brief, a crisis of the first magnitude was in the making.

3. THIRTEEN CRITICAL DAYS OF CONFRONTATION, CRISIS, AND NEGOTIATIONS

(a) *Discovery of missiles; internal deliberations; decision*

Late on Monday, October 15, intelligence analysts confirmed the photographic evidence collected on the 14th by a U–2 reconnaissance plane after the lifting of a 5-day cloud cover that the Soviets were building in Cuba a medium-range missile base. In their judgment this base, when operational, would have the capability of delivering a nuclear warhead deep into the United States.[142] On the following morning at 8:45, McGeorge Bundy, a White House national security adviser, broke the news to the President at breakfast. As Robert Kennedy wrote, "That was the beginning of the Cuban missile crisis. * * *"[143]

Viewed strictly as a negotiating encounter, the missile crisis at this beginning phase had two distinctive characteristics: One was the internal deliberations on deciding what to do; the other was the necessity of secrecy.

First, the President called together a group of trusted advisers in the administration, soon to be known as the executive committee, presumably of the National Security Council—the press later dubbed it, "Excom." The committee included, among other high-ranking officials in the current and former administrations, the President, Vice President Lyndon Johnson, Secretary of State Rusk, Robert Kennedy, Secretary of Defense Robert S. McNamara, Director of CIA John McCone, Gen. Maxwell Taylor, and U.N. Ambassador Adlai Stevenson.[144] The principal task of the committee was in essence to study the problem and to recommend options for its solution to the President. In the context of negotiations the group was essentially to prepare both the initial bargaining position and a strategy for managing the crisis and negotiating its solution. The central objective of American policy was to get the Soviet missiles and other offensive weapons out of Cuba.

The second characteristic evident throughout the crisis and particularly at this initial phase was, as Schlesinger noted, "the most exacting secrecy: Nothing could be worse than to alert the Russians before the United States had decided its own course."[145]

---

[141] Ibid.
[142] Schlesinger, op. cit., p. 801 and Sorensen, op. cit., pp. 672–673.
[143] Kennedy, op. cit., p. 23.
[144] Schlesinger, op. cit., p. 802.
[145] Ibid., p. 802.

Haste was essential in reaching a decision on how best to respond to Khrushchev's challenge. The missiles were expected to be operational within 10 days. As Schlesinger wrote, "The deadline defined the strategy," and the strategy was inevitably reduced to keeping the management of the crisis in American hands, without the immediate involvement of the United Nations, for example, or the Western Allies.[146]

The executive committee deliberated intensely and continuously for the next 5 days. It examined the problem from every conceivable perspective: From the extremes of doing nothing and launching a full-scale invasion, to the intermediate alternative positions of applying varying forms of diplomatic pressures on Castro and Khrushchev, a naval blockade, and a "surgical strike" on the missile bases. Positions shifted variously in the course of debate. The President evinced a preference for the blockade. The Attorney General, mindful of the serious moral implications, opposed a military solution as a first step. By Thursday, October 18, the balance of decision favored the blockade; the final decision was taken on Saturday afternoon, October 20, to impose the blockade, or a quarantine as it was called, to avoid the serious international implications of the blockade. In a straw vote, 11 favored the blockade, 6 the strike.[147]

As the first step on the American side in this negotiation by action, the blockade concept had many arguments in its favor: It provided a middle course between inaction and combat; it avoided war, preserved flexibility and gave Khrushchev time to reconsider his actions; it could be carried out within the framework of treaty arrangements with Latin America; it could be an instrument for applying steadily increasing pressures on the Soviet Union; it avoided the shock of a surprise attack that would hurt the United States abroad and could provoke a precipitous Soviet response; it provided a way for a Soviet retreat with dignity and without an unacceptable loss of prestige if it worked and retained the option of military action if it failed. "In short," Schlesinger explained, "the blockade, by enabling us to proceed one step at a time, gave us control over the future."[148]

(b) *The initial U.S. negotiating position: Kennedy's speech of October 22*

(1) *On the nature of the Soviet threat*

The President's speech setting forth the U.S. negotiating position was drafted over the weekend by Sorensen, and after further discussion, much review and editing by the President and the Executive Committee, it was approved and ready for delivery on Monday evening, October 22.[149] Amid rumors of impending crisis (by this time secrecy was beginning to break down), and against a background of the continuing hasty buildup of Soviet missiles in Cuba, expanding American surveillance, and preparations for military action, the President addressed the Nation at 7 o'clock. In a speech lasting 18 minutes, he laid before the American people the full dimension of the Soviet threat in Cuba. In building his case for negotiations, the President disclosed the following information:

---

[146] Ibid., p. 803.
[147] Ibid., p. 808. For other detailed accounts of the decision process, see, Kennedy, op. cit., pp. 31–50; Sorensen, op. cit., pp. 682–88; and Hilsman, op. cit., pp. 194–196, 198–206.
[148] Schlesinger, op. cit., p. 806.
[149] Sorensen, op. cit., pp. 693–702.

—The United States had "unmistakable evidence" that within the past few weeks the Soviet Union was preparing "a series of offensive missile sites" in Cuba;

—The purpose of the bases "can be none other than to provide a nuclear strike capability against the Western Hemisphere";

—Several of the missile sites included medium-range ballistic missiles capable of carrying a nuclear warhead for more than 1,000 nautical miles and striking Washington, D.C., the Panama Canal, Cape Canaveral, Mexico City, or any other city in the southeastern part of the United States, in Central America, or in the Caribbean area;

—Additional sites not yet completed appeared to be designed for intermediate-range ballistic missiles capable of traveling twice that distance—"and thus capable of striking most of the major cities in the Western Hemisphere, ranging as far north as Hudson Bay, Canada, and as far south as Lima, Peru";

—Jet bombers capable of carrying nuclear weapons were "now being uncrated and assembled" in Cuba, while the necessary air bases were being prepared;

—This "urgent transformation" of Cuba into an "important strategic base" by the presence of these "large, long-range, and clearly offensive weapons of sudden mass destruction" constituted an "explicit threat to the peace and security of all the Americas in flagrant and deliberate defiance of the Rio Pact of 1947, the traditions of this Nation and hemisphere, the joint resolution of the 87th Congress, the Charter of the United Nations, and my own public warnings to the Soviets on September 4 and 13";

—This action contradicted "repeated assurances" of Soviet spokesmen, including those given personally by Gromyko, both publicly and privately delivered, that the arms buildup in Cuba would retain its original defensive character and that the Soviet Union had neither the need nor desire to station strategic missiles on the territory of any other nation;

—"Neither the United States of America nor the world community of nations can tolerate deliberate deception and offensive threats on the part of any nation, large or small";

—Nuclear weapons were "so destructive" and missiles "so swift" that "any substantially increased possibility of their use or any sudden change in their deployment may well be regarded as a definite threat to peace";

—The United States and the Soviet Union, recognizing this fact, deployed strategic nuclear weapons "with great care, never upsetting the precarious status quo which insured that these weapons would not be used in the absence of some vital challenge";

—The "secret, swift, extraordinary buildup of Communist missiles in an area well known to have a special and historical relationship to the United States and the nations of the Western Hemisphere, in violation of Soviet assurances and in defiance of American and hemispheric policy—this sudden, clandestine decision to station strategic weapons for the first time outside of Soviet soil—is a deliberately provocative and unjustified change in the status quo which cannot be accepted by this country if our courage and our commitments are ever to be trusted again, by either friend or foe"; and finally

—"Our unswerving objective, therefore, must be to prevent the use of these missiles against this or any other country and to secure their withdrawal or elimination from the Western Hemisphere."

(2) *Proposals for resolving the crisis*

The President then explained the following seven initial steps that he directed to be taken which constituted the essence of his negotiating position:

(1) "To halt this offensive buildup, a strict quarantine on all offensive military equipment under shipment to Cuba" was established;

(2) Continued and increased close surveillance of Cuba and its military buildup was ordered and should these "offensive military preparations continue, thus increasing the threat to the hemisphere, further action will be justified";

(3) Any nuclear missile launched from Cuba against any nation in the Western Hemisphere would be regarded "as an attack by the Soviet Union on the United States requiring a full retaliatory response upon the Soviet Union";

(4) American military forces at Guantanamo were reinforced;

(5) The consultative organ of the Organization of American States (OAS) was being immediately called to consider the threat to the hemisphere security and invoke the Rio Treaty to support "all necessary actions";

(6) The Security Council of the United Nations was being convoked without delay "to take action against this latest Soviet threat to world peace" and to consider the American resolution calling for "prompt dismantling and withdrawal of all offensive weapons in Cuba" under United Nations supervision before the quarantine would be lifted; and

(7) A request to Khrushchev "to halt and eliminate this clandestine, reckless and provocative threat to world peace and to stable relations" between the United States and the Soviet Union.

The President went on to make the following additional points:

—He urged the Soviet Union to abandon "this course of world domination" and join in an effort to end the arms race;

—He noted that the United States had "no wish to go to war with the Soviet Union" but desired to live in peace; and he warned that,

—"Any hostile move anywhere in the world against the safety and freedom of peoples to whom we are committed including, in particular, the brave people of West Berlin will be met by whatever action is needed."

The President concluded with an appeal to the Cuban people reassuring them of American regard for their freedom. He warned the American people of the "difficult and dangerous effort on which we have set out," not knowing where the course would lead and what sacrifices it would require. There would be "months in which many threats and denunciations will keep us aware of our dangers," he said, and added: "But the greatest danger of all would be to do nothing." [150]

[150] Text of Broadcast. Documents on American Foreign Relations. 1962. Published for the Council on Foreign Relations. New York. Harper & Row, 1963, pp. 374–380.

(c) Soviet counteractions: Khrushchev's rejection

On the same day President Kennedy sent a long letter to Khrushchev with a copy of his speech appealing for rationality and restraint. The President emphasized that in their discussions and exchanges on Berlin and other international questions, he was "most concerned" about the possibility that the Soviet Government "would not correctly understand the will and determination of the United States in any given situation," since, as he said, "I have not assumed that you or any other sane man would, in this nuclear age, deliberately plunge the world into war which it is crystal clear no country could win and which could only result in catastrophic consequences to the whole world, including the aggressor." [151]

In a reply received on Tuesday the 23d, Khrushchev accused the President of threatening him and the Soviet Union with a blockade and declared that the Soviet Union would not observe it. "The actions of the U.S.A. with regard to Cuba," he said, "are outright banditry or, if you like, the folly of degenerate imperialism." Khrushchev accused the United States of pushing mankind "to the abyss of a world missile-nuclear war," and stated that captains of Soviet vessels bound for Cuba would be instructed not to obey the orders of American naval forces. And then he issued this warning: If any efforts were made to interfere with Soviet ships, "we would then be forced for our part to take the measures which we deem necessary and adequate in order to protect our rights. For this we have all that is necessary." [152] A Soviet Government statement was issued on the same day defining Soviet policy.[153]

(d) Critical days of negotiations: Confrontation and interaction

(1) Positions in conflict: On a collision course

The positions of the adversaries were thus clearly drawn. For the next few days, President Kennedy, who maintained tight control over the management of the crisis particularly in the confrontation of vessels along the quarantine line and in conducting reconnaissance flights over Cuba, pursued four general lines of action. To avoid a Soviet "spasm reaction" and allow a pause in the Soviet response, he ordered the quarantine to take effect on Wednesday, October 24.[154] (Later, he shortened the quarantine line, again to give the Soviets pause to think.) He pressed for and received the support of the OAS (before issuing the quarantine proclamation) and his NATO Allies. Through Ambassador Stevenson, he laid the American case before the Security Council of the United Nations, providing photographic evidence as dramatic proof of Soviet deception. At the same time he stepped up surveillance over Cuba and pushed forward American preparations for a military invasion to knock out the missiles should the initial phase, that of the quarantine, fail. Kennedy's main problem was one of cautious haste, to persuade or pressure Khrushchev into removing the missiles before they became operational. Once they

[151] Kennedy, op. cit., pp. 79–80.
[152] Ibid., p. 80.
[153] For an analysis of this statement, see, Dinerstein, Herbert S. The Making of a Missile Crisis: October 1962. Baltimore, Johns Hopkins University Press, 1976, pp. 217–219, and app. 2, pp. 263–267.
[154] Hilsman, op. cit., p. 213.

were operational, his only recourse, it was generally agreed among his advisers, would be military action with all the fearful consequences that might follow.

On his part Khrushchev, his deception having once been exposed, adopted delaying tactics in order to complete the construction of the missile sites, still hoping to present the United States with a fait accompli. He accepted with alacrity a proposal by British pacifist Bertrand Russell, highly critical of the United States, for a summit conference to end the crisis; it was rejected by Kennedy.[155]

In the United Nations, Khrushchev attempted to undermine the American position by accepting a formula proposed by Acting Secretary General U Thant that would momentarily ease the crisis by suspending both the shipment of arms and the quarantine during direct negotiations. But this proposal was unacceptable to the United States because it did not address the principal issue; namely, the removal of the offensive weapons from Cuba.[156] He also tried to intimidate the United States by issuing a threat through a visiting American business executive, William Knox, president of Westinghouse International. Khrushchev warned that if the United States stopped Soviet ships, Soviet submarines (6 had joined the vessels heading for Cuba) would be forced to sink a U.S. ship and that would bring on World War III.[157] And finally Khrushchev accelerated the last minute missile buildup in Cuba, the completion of which was crucial for the success of his plan. Photographs from low-flying Navy reconnaissance missions, buzzing the missile sites themselves, disclosed on Wednesday, the 24th, that work on the sites continued full speed and for the first time indicated the presence of Soviet ground forces with tactical nuclear weapons. Within 4 days all MRBM's would be operational.[158] Within a month or so all IRBM's would be operational.[159]

In brief, the Soviet Union and the United States were on a collision course; decisions for action were reduced to the principals in Moscow and Washington; the possibilities for a settlement were to be first tested along the quarantine line in what took on the form of negotiations by action.

(2) Negotiations by action along the quarantine line

If there were to be a serious initial conflict (as in the historical parallel of reprovisioning Fort Sumter that immediately brought on the Civil War), it was expected to come along the quarantine line, the point of contact for American enforcement and Soviet acquiesence or resistance. Kennedy approached the problem of enforcement with the greatest circumspection. He allowed the widest berth in order to give himself plenty of room and the greatest flexibility for maneuver and the Soviets sufficient time to meditate on the consequences of their next move. He wanted a hedge against a spasmodic Soviet response or a response that would be irreversible.[160] Realizing the enormity of the risks, he maintained the tightest control over the entire proceed-

---

[155] Survey of International Affairs, 1962, pp. 63–64.
[156] Hilsman, op. cit., p. 214.
[157] Ibid.
[158] Ibid., pp. 214–215, 227.
[159] Sorensen, op. cit., p. 711.
[160] Schlesinger, op. cit., p. 818.

ings, and in his "disable, don't sink" order he stressed the necessity of discretion and certainty before applying force.[161]

There would be no shooting, and Soviet ships were to be kept in view but none boarded until he issued instructions.[162] Kennedy and his closest advisers were convinced that neither side wanted war over Cuba, but they understood the possibility, that either could take measures for reasons of "security" or "pride" or "face" that would require a similar response from the other side and for the same reasons that in turn could bring on a counterresponse and eventually escalate into war.[163]

The moment of greatest peril occurred not long after the quarantine went into effect on Wednesday October 24 at 10 a.m. On the previous evening, Tuesday October 23, Robert Kennedy had conferred with Dobrynin at which time he asked if the Soviet ships were going on to Cuba. An "extremely concerned" Dobrynin, as Kennedy described him, replied that these were their instructions, and he knew of no changes.[164]

Meanwhile, on Wednesday the 24th a convoy of Soviet ships approached within 500 miles of the quarantine line. At 10 a.m. the *Gagarin* and the *Komiles* were within a few miles of it; a Soviet submarine had positioned itself between them. The aircraft carrier *Essex*, supported by helicopters and carrying antisubmarine equipment, was ordered to signal the submarine to surface and identify itself. If it refused, depth charges with a small explosive would be used to force it to surface. According to Robert Kennedy, "these few minutes were the time of gravest concern for the President." [165]

The showdown, the time of final decision, had come.

But this crisis within a crisis dissolved, at least momentarily, when CIA Director McCone reported at 10:25 a.m. that some of the ships stopped dead in the water. Later, the Office of Naval Intelligence reported that 20 Soviet ships closest to the line had stopped, were dead in the water or had turned around. Immediately, the President ordered that these ships were not to be interfered with and that every opportunity should be given for them to turn around.[166] By Thursday and Friday, the 25th and 26th, 16 of the ships, including 5 with large hatches suspected of carrying missile equipment, had turned around and were heading back toward the Soviet Union, accompanied by American planes.[167]

In subsequent encounters at sea, ships continued to be carefully screened. On Thursday, October 25, the Soviet oil tanker *Bucharest* was allowed to pass because there was little likelihood that it was carrying missiles or other armaments covered under the quarantine order.[168]

---

[161] The proclamation stressed that "force shall not be used except in case of failure or refusal to comply with directions * * * after reasonable efforts have been made to communicate them to the vessel or craft, or in case of self-defense. In any case force shall be used only to the extent necessary." (Sorensen, op. cit., p. 708.) See also Hilsman, op. cit., p. 213.
[162] Ibid., p. 215.
[163] Kennedy, op. cit., p. 62.
[164] Ibid., p. 66.
[165] Ibid., p. 69.
[166] Ibid., pp. 71–72.
[167] Sorensen, op. cit., pp. 710–711. The sources are inconsistent on the actual number of ships. Sorensen mentioned 16 of the 18 ships. Kennedy 20, and Hilsman 12.
[168] Kennedy, op. cit., p. 73.

Similarly, an East German passenger ship, carrying 1,500 passengers, was permitted to continue on its voyage to Cuba.[169] The only ship actually boarded and inspected was the *Marcula*, on Friday, October 26. This vessel was an American built Liberty ship, Panamanian owned, registered from Lebanon, and bound for Cuba under a Soviet charter. Found to be carrying only trucks and truck parts by an unarmed boarding party, the freighter was permitted to pass through.[170]

Management of these encounters at sea were a significant element in the larger on-going negotiations during the crisis. By ordering the return of the ships, Khrushchev had clearly indicated his desire to avoid a collision, keep the crisis contained, and permit negotiations to go forward on another level. It also served the purposes of his delaying tactics. In explaining the Soviet side quite at variance with the American view, Khrushchev wrote:

Our ships, with the remainder of our deliveries to Cuba, headed straight through an armada of the American Navy, but the Americans didn't try to stop our ships or even check them. We kept in mind that as long as the United States limited itself to threatening gestures and didn't actually touch us, we could afford to pretend to ignore the harassment. After all, the United States had no moral or legal quarrel with us.[171]

(e) Denouement: Agreement and resolution of the crisis

(1) Fomin-Scali unofficial negotiations, Friday afternoon and evening, October 26

(a) Peaking of the crisis.—Direct bilateral negotiations between Kennedy and Khrushchev reached a climatic turn on the evening of Friday, October 26. They were preceded, however, by the unofficial Fomin-Scali meeting in which Khrushchev used the informal channel of the news media to probe the American negotiating position.

Since Monday, October 22, there had been almost daily communications between the two leaders. On Thursday, October 25, the President responded to Khrushchev's sharply critical letter on the quarantine received on the 23d, again emphasizing what were by then familiar U.S. terms for resolving the crisis.[172] By Friday October 26, time was growing short and tensions began to peak as the sense of crisis mounted and as the small circle of Kennedy advisers awaited Khrushchev's response to the letter of the 25th. Preparations were going forward for the American military invasion and occupation of Cuba. Simultaneously, work on making the Soviet missile sites operational was continuing full speed. A White House announcement on these activities concluded that the Russians were trying to achieve "full operational capability as soon as possible." As Hilsman, a principal at this point in the crisis, observed, "no one on the American side could forget the consequences once all 40 launching pads were operational."[173]

And as President Kennedy told his advisers at a meeting on Friday morning:

We are going to have to face the fact that, if we do invade, by the time we get to these sites, after a very bloody fight, they will be pointed at us. And we must further accept the possibility that when military hostilities first begin, those missiles will be fired.[174]

---

[169] Ibid., p. 77.
[170] Ibid., p. 82 and Sorensen, op. cit., p. 710.
[171] Khrushchev, op. cit., p. 496.
[172] Kennedy, op. cit., pp. 79–81.
[173] Hilsman, op. cit., p. 216.
[174] Kennedy, op. cit., p. 85. See also, Schlesinger, op. cit., pp. 824–825.

(b) *Meeting at the Occidental Restaurant.*—Against this background of rising tensions and stress, John Scali, the State Department correspondent for the American Broadcasting Co., known to be trusted as an accurate and reliable reporter by the highest level of the U.S. Government, received an urgent telephone call at 1:35 on Friday afternoon from Aleksander Fomin, a counselor at the Soviet Embassy, asking for an immediate meeting. On previous occasions Scali had lunched with Fomin but never on such short notice and under such alarming circumstances. For Scali the sense of urgency was important but of greatest importance was the fact that Fomin was known to be the senior Soviet intelligence officer in the United States with his own direct communication lines to the Soviet leadership.[175]

The meeting took place at the Occidental Restaurant. The usually stolid, phlegmatic Fomin now haggard and alarmed said to Scali. "War seems about to break out. Something must be done to save the situation." Scali replied that the Soviet leadership should have thought of that before sending the missiles to Cuba. "There might be a way out," Fomin said after a moment of silence, and then he made a proposal in the form of questions that contained the following elements:

(1) The Soviets would promise to remove the missiles under United Nations inspection.

(2) Khrushchev would promise never to introduce such offensive weapons into Cuba again.

(3) In return, President Kennedy would promise publicly not to invade Cuba.

Fomin added that if Ambassador Stevenson pursued this approach in the United Nations, where U Thant was attempting to mediate the crisis, Soviet Ambassador V. A. Zorin would be interested.[176]

Scali did not know how the administration would respond to these proposals, but Fomin begged him to find out immediately from his friends in the State Department. Writing down his home telephone number and instructing Scali to call him night or day, Fomin declared: "If I'm not at the Embassy, call me here. This is of vital importance." [177]

Scali took Khrushchev's proposal immediately to the State Department where after discussion with the Executive Committee, Secretary Rusk authorized Scali to tell Fomin that the administration saw "real possibilities" for a negotiation. But the Soviet authorities had to understand, he said, that time was short—no more than 48 hours.[178]

(c) *Meeting at the Statler Hilton's coffee shop.*—At 7:30 in the evening, Scali met again with Fomin, this time at the Statler Hilton's coffee shop, and there over coffee passed along the administration's response. Fomin, apparently skeptical as to whether this response represented official views of the U.S. Government, several times asked if the information came from high administration sources. Scali replied that it came from very high sources.[179]

Satisfied on this point, Fomin introduced a new element in the Khrushchev proposal: Since inspection of Cuban bases was to take place, why shouldn't a similar inspection be made of American bases

[175] Hilsman, op. cit., p. 217.
[176] Ibid., and Schlesinger, op. cit., pp. 825–826.
[177] Ibid., p. 826.
[178] Ibid. and Hilsman, op. cit., p. 218.
[179] Ibid.

in Florida, the staging area of a possible invasion of Cuba? Scali countered that this was a new element in the negotiations on which he had no information as to how the administration might react. Speaking as a reporter, however, he explained that this new element would raise, in Hilsman's words, a "terrible complication." The situations were not symmetrical, he said, since no American missiles were directed at Cuba, and he believed that President Kennedy would reject any such proposal. Scali reemphasized the matter of urgency impressed upon him by Rusk—"time is very urgent," Rusk had said. Haggling over the new proposal would consume valuable time and consequent delays might bring on a disaster for Cuba, the Soviet Union and the world.[180]

At this Fomin thanked Scali, repeated his assurance that the information would be relayed to the very highest levels in the Kremlin and simultaneously to Zorin at the United Nations, and departed in such obvious haste that he threw down a $5 bill for a 30-cent check.[181]

(2) Khrushchev's letter of concession, evening of October 26

During the evening of October 26, Khrushchev's response to the President's letter of the 25th arrived in the form of a four-part cable. Contrary to press reports at the time, this letter, still classified, was not hysterical and incoherent but rather, as Robert Kennedy described it, "very long and emotional," and "the emotion was directed at the death, destruction, and anarchy that nuclear war would bring to his people and all mankind. That, he said again and again and in many different ways, must be avoided." [182]

In the letter Khrushchev made this proposal, as Kennedy paraphrased it: "No more weapons to Cuba and those within Cuba withdrawn or destroyed, and you reciprocate by withdrawing your blockade and also agree not to invade Cuba." [183]

At a meeting held late at night, the letter was examined and reexamined by the President's inner circle of crisis managers. For it was, as Sorensen noted, "a bit vague." [184] Finally, it was turned over to the State Department for study and a report on the following day.[185] Robert Kennedy, who had "a slight feeling of optimism," felt that the letter for all its rhetoric "had the beginnings perhaps of some accommodation, some agreement." This feeling was strengthened by subsequent reports of the Fomin-Scali meetings.[186]

After careful study, the State Department, taking into consideration the Soviet-American pledge to U Thant to avoid confrontation along the quarantine line, the unofficial proposals to Scali, and Khrushchev's letter, judged—with some qualifications—that from all the evidence, Khrushchev was sincerely seeking a way out of the crisis.[187]

Thus by the end of the week, the Soviet negotiating position was reduced to three essential points: A promise to remove the missiles under United Nations inspection, a promise never to reintroduce such offensive weapons, in return for an American promise to lift the quarantine and not to invade Cuba.

---

[180] Ibid., pp. 218–219.
[181] Ibid., p. 219.
[182] Kennedy, op. cit., p. 86.
[183] Ibid., p. 89.
[184] Sorensen, op. cit., p. 712.
[185] Kennedy, op. cit., p. 90.
[186] Ibid.
[187] Hilsman, op. cit., p. 220.

(3) Khrushchev's apparent retraction, Saturday morning, October 27

(a) A precipitous downturn in the crisis.—Hopes were running high as the Executive Committee convened at 10 o'clock on Saturday morning, October 27, to draft a reply to Khrushchev's letters. But such hopes were soon dimmed by a series of events that propelled the crisis to its most critical point.

At 10:17 details of a new note by Khrushchev, then being broadcast over Radio Moscow that radically altered his previous negotiating position, were coming in over the news ticker. His offer now was for a mutual trade-off: The Soviet Union would remove its missiles from Cuba and pledge not to invade Turkey, if the United States would remove its missiles from Turkey and pledge not to invade Cuba.[188]

A report was also received that a single Soviet ship had detached itself from others rendezvousing outside the quarantine line and was heading for Cuba. Fear arose among the President's advisers that the Soviets were about to test American determination in a confrontation at sea.[189]

Far graver news quickly followed. The SAM network of antiaircraft missiles had become operational. Proof had come with a report that a U-2 plane had been shot down and its pilot killed during a reconnaissance flight over Cuba. (Adding to the gravity, a U-2 plane had accidently strayed into Soviet territory while on a routine air-sampling mission from an Alaskan base, causing Soviet fighters to scramble.)

Robert Kennedy called the loss of the U-2 over Cuba the beginning of "the most difficult 24 hours of the missile crisis." [190] Hilsman called it the "blackest hour" of the crisis.[191] The crisis had now clearly entered its military phase, for it had been determined that when once the SAM sites became operational and could thus prevent U.S. reconnaissance flights, air strikes against them would become mandatory. The President expressed the problem succinctly. "How can we send any more U-2 pilots into this area tomorrow unless we take out all of the SAM sites? We are now in an entirely new ball game." [192] The latest reconnaissance photographs not only showed a continued speed-up of construction on the missile sites but also the rapid construction of permanent and expensive installations of nuclear warhead storage bunkers and troop barracks.[193] Khrushchev's letter, it will be recalled, had already informed the President that all the missiles had been delivered [194] to Cuba. Khrushchev later recalled, "We had delivered almost everything by the time the crisis reached the boiling point." [195] Thus, American choices were being radically reduced to a single military option.

There was almost unanimous agreement among the President's close advisers to destroy the missile site early the next morning, that is, Sunday, with an attack by bombers and fighters. But the President, anxious to give the Soviets time to reflect upon the folly of their

[188] Kennedy, op. cit., p. 94 and Hilsman, op. cit., p. 220.
[189] Ibid.
[190] Kennedy, op. cit., p. 94.
[191] Hilsman, op. cit., p. 220.
[192] Kennedy, op. cit., p. 98.
[193] Sorensen, op. cit., p. 713.
[194] Kennedy, op. cit., p. 88.
[195] Khrushchev, op. cit., p. 495.

course and hesitant to set into motion a sequence of events that could easily slip out of control, bring on a nuclear war, and end with total destruction, decided to delay before attacking and give diplomacy another chance. As Robert Kennedy recalled: "We won't attack tomorrow, the President said. We shall try again." [196]

(b) *Complicating issue of the Turkish missile bases.*—The issue of Turkish missile bases complicated negotiations in the Cuban crisis. The President was angry that his directive earlier in the year ordering the dismantling of these obsolete bases was not followed through and that the bases had now become, in Robert Kennedy's words, "hostages of the Soviet Union." [197]

But negotiating this issue in the Cuban context was unacceptable. Offensive Soviet missiles in Cuba was the central issue, not obsolete U.S. missiles in Turkey. And the immediate threat was the rapid and continuing construction of these missile bases in Cuba. No negotiations could take place while that buildup continued. A statement to this effect, and suggesting as well that future negotiations on the Turkish bases offered no problem, was drafted as a response to the Soviet proposal and released as a public statement. [198]

(c) *Resumption of the Fomin-Scali negotiations.*—At this point, having chosen the path of diplomacy, the crucial problem facing the President was to get the negotiations back on track, back where they were the night before—and quickly. On Saturday afternoon, Secretary Rusk called in Scali and suggested that he contact Fomin to find out what happened. [199] Concern had been expressed that the military may have taken over in Moscow which could explain the reversal of policy. [200]

The two unofficial negotiators met at 4:15 in a deserted banquet hall off the mezzanine of the Statler Hotel. A puzzled and unhappy Fomin tried to explain away the reversal of Khrushchev's negotiating position as a case of bad communications; namely, that the Saturday morning cable had been drafted before his report on the favorable American reaction had been received in Moscow. [201] A disbelieving Scali exploded, calling the unofficial exchange a "stinking double cross." He reemphasized the urgency of time and the President's determination to get the missiles out of Cuba. With respect to the proposal on the Turkish missile bases he declared that as a reporter well informed on official U.S. policy this proposal was, in Hilsman's account of the meeting, "completely, totally, and perpetually unacceptable." Negotiations on this problem, he said, had to take place in the framework of disarmament, not injected into the Cuban crisis. [202]

At this juncture the two unofficial negotiators parted: Fomin assured Scali that a clarifying reply from Moscow would be forthcoming; Scali repeated his warning about the urgency of time. Scali reported the outcome of this second encounter with Fomin directly

---

[196] Ibid., p. 101. With respect to the problem of escalation, the President told his advisers: "It isn't the first step that concerns me, but both sides escalating to the fourth and fifth step—and we don't go to the sixth because there is no one around to do so. We must remind ourselves we are embarking on a very hazardous course." (p. 98.)

[197] Ibid., p. 95.

[198] Hilsman, op. cit., p. 222.

[199] Ibid.

[200] Schlesinger, op. cit., p. 828.

[201] That Fomin had a plausible argument with respect to bureaucratic complications in drafting a response to an earlier communication without knowledge of Khrushchev's personal letter of Friday was explained in Schlesinger, p. 829.

[202] Hilsman, op. cit., pp. 222–223.

and personally to the State Department and to the executive committee at the White House.[203]

(4) *Kennedy's response to Khrushchev, Saturday evening, October 27*

(a) *Accepting the letter of concession, ignoring the statement of reversal.*—Later in the afternoon, the executive committee met again in the Cabinet Room of the White House, this time to consider the State Department's draft reply to Khrushchev's latest letter. The scene was tense. Sharp disagreements arose over the draft among the President's advisers. By this time they were very tired, irritable, some already near exhaustion. As Robert Kennedy recalled: "All were weighted down with concern and worry." [204]

Controversy centered on the State Department draft that had addressed only the argument set forth in Khrushchev's letter: It rejected his trade-off proposal and maintained that the missiles could not be removed from Turkey. Robert Kennedy disagreed both with the content and tone of the draft. Supported by Sorensen, he suggested that the latest letter of reversal be ignored—Schlesinger referred to this as "a thought of breathtaking simplicity and ingenuity"—and a response be directed only to the Friday letter of concession as refined by the Fomin-Scali negotiations with respect to the removal of the missiles and United Nations inspection and verification in return for a U.S. noninvasion pledge.[205]

At a point of breakdown in the discussion—"we almost seemed unable to communicate with one another," Robert Kennedy noted—the President suggested, with a note of exasperation, that since the Attorney General and Sorensen felt so strongly about the shortcomings of the State Department draft, then they should withdraw and come up with an alternative. This was done and within 45 minutes they prepared a draft and presented it to the President and the Executive Committee. After some alterations and refinement the draft was typed and signed.[206]

In brief, the President's letter of the 27th accepted the vaguely stated Khrushchev proposal of Friday the 26th and also, without directly referring to it, the formula conveyed in the Fomin-Scali unofficial negotiations. The response was carefully drawn and made the following essential points:

1. You would agree to remove these weapons systems from Cuba under appropriate United Nations observation and supervision; and undertake, with suitable safeguards, to halt the further introduction of such weapons systems into Cuba.

2. We, on our part, would agree—upon the establishment of adequate arrangements through the United Nations to insure the carrying out and continuation of these commitments—(a) to remove promptly the quarantine measures now in effect, and (b) to give assurances against an invasion of Cuba.

The President only alluded to Khrushchev's second letter, expressing a desire to reduce tensions and halt the arms race and a willingness to confer on a détente affecting NATO and the Warsaw Pact. But "the first ingredient," he emphasized, was "the cessation of work on missile sites in Cuba and measures to render such weapons inoperable, under effective international guarantees." [207]

[203] Ibid., p. 223.
[204] Kennedy, op. cit., p. 102.
[205] Ibid., pp. 102–103 and Schlesinger, op. cit., p. 828.
[206] Sorensen, op. cit., pp. 714–715 and Kennedy, op. cit., p. 103.
[207] Ibid., pp. 102–104.

The President, in the interests of speed and psychological impact, released the letter publicly as it was being transmitted to Moscow shortly after 8 p.m.[208]

(b) *Robert Kennedy's meeting with Dobrynin.*—As the letter to Khrushchev was being prepared for transmission, the President sat in the Oval Office with the Attorney General and reflected on the unfolding crisis. He talked about the miscalculations that lead to war; the importance of giving the Soviets every conceivable way out of the crisis and to a peaceful settlement that would neither diminish their national security nor humiliate them publicly; the awful consequences of a nuclear war, especially for the children and young people of the world who had yet to play a role in the destiny of their countries; the great tragedy of error and its consequences for the world, especially the young. Troubled by these possible consequences of error, the President decided that Robert Kennedy should see Ambassador Dobrynin and personally convey to him his great concern.[209]

Dobrynin and Kennedy met in the Attorney General's office at 7:45 p.m. Kennedy reviewed the American perception of the crisis, explaining particularly the effect of the Soviet SAM missiles shooting down U.S. reconnaissance planes, as in the case of the U-2, and the "very grave" consequences of an escalation of the conflict. Recalling Soviet deception in establishing the bases while privately and publicly proclaiming that this would never be done, Kennedy said bluntly that the United States "had to have a commitment by tomorrow that those bases would be removed." This was not "an ultimatum" but "a statement of fact." Kennedy wanted it understood that "if they did not remove those bases, we would remove them." The President had "great respect" for the Soviet Union and the courage of its people, but should the Soviet Union feel it necessary "to take retaliatory action," before that was over, "there would be not only dead Americans but dead Russians as well."

What offer was the United States making? Dobrynin asked. Whereupon, Kennedy explained the contents of the President's letter, indicating that no trade-off on the Cuban-Turkish bases could be made. But he noted that the President "had been anxious to remove those missiles from Turkey and Italy for a long period of time"; that he had "ordered their removal some time ago," and that "it was our judgment that within a short time after the crisis was over, those missiles would be gone." The President wanted peace, Kennedy said, and desired to move along the path of diplomacy and negotiations to resolve the problems of Europe, Southeast Asia, and arms control. But progress could only be made after the current crisis "was behind us."

Kennedy terminated the meeting with a warning that, "Time was running out. We had only a few hours—we needed an answer immediately from the Soviet Union * * * we must have it the next day."

Kennedy returned to the White House. Neither he nor the President was optimistic about the outcome. Preparations were underway for an invasion. But the President had not abandoned hope; such hope as there was rested with Khrushchev reversing his course within the next few hours. "It was a hope, not an expectation," Robert Kennedy re-

[208] Sorensen, op. cit., p. 714.
[209] Kennedy, op. cit., pp. 105–106.

called. "The expectation was a military confrontation by Tuesday and possibly tomorrow * * * ." [210]

(5) Resolution of the crisis, Sunday morning, October 28

The crisis was quickly resolved. Just before 9 o'clock on Sunday morning, October 28, Khrushchev's reply to the President's latest letter was broadcast over Radio Moscow. By the fifth sentence, it was clear that he had indeed conceded. Construction of the missile sites would stop; the weapons "which you described as offensive" would be crated and returned to the Soviet Union; negotiations to tie up the loose ends would begin at the United Nations. Looking to the future, Khrushchev said: "We should like to continue the exchange of views on the prohibition of atomic and thermonuclear weapons, general disarmament, and other problems relating to the relaxation of international tension." In brief, a statement of intention to negotiate. [211]

A White House statement was quickly drafted confirming the agreement and broadcast over Voice of America. A more complete reply to Khrushchev's letter was then prepared and released for publication and broadcast. [212]

The crisis was all over, and, as Schlesinger observed, "barely in time." If Khrushchev's response had not come that Sunday and if work had continued on the missile bases, the United States, as Schlesinger concluded, "would have had no real choice but to take action against Cuba the next week." What lay beyond this initial military action no one could say with certainty. But the President, who Schlesinger believed, "saw more penetratingly into the mists and terrors of the future than anyone else," said a few weeks later: "If we had invaded Cuba * * * I am sure the Soviets would have acted. They would have to, just as we would have to. I think there are certain compulsions on any major power." [213]

4. RESULTS AND SIGNIFICANCE OF THE MISSILE CRISIS

(a) As a negotiating experience

(1) Total diplomacy

As a negotiating experience, the missile crisis was an exercise in total diplomacy.

Five basic channels of communications exist for communications between the Soviet and United States Governments: By formal letter between heads of governments using embassy facilities; alternative sets of Soviet channels (for example, the KGB network) that bypass their embassy in Washington and are probably handled in special ways in Moscow; views exchanged formally and officially by notes or letters between officials of lesser stature than the heads of government; informal but still official exchanges, as in the case of oral exchanges between the ambassador and an official in the White House or State

---

[210] Ibid., pp. 107–109.

[211] Schlesinger, op. cit., p. 830 and Hilsman, op. cit., p. 224.

[212] Ibid.

[213] Schlesinger, op. cit., p. 830. In an essay on "History and Diplomacy as Viewed by a Historian," Dr. Raymond J. Sontag, the distinguished American diplomatic historian, well described the sequence of decisions that often leads to war. He wrote: "* * * the diplomatist knows from experience that the decision for war is unlikely to come out of a clear sky; it is far more likely to be the last of a series of decisions, none of which is intended to precipitate war, each of which makes war more difficult to avoid, until at the end there remains no alternative except war. And negative as well as positive decisions can be links in the series." (In, Kertesz and Fitzsimons, op. cit., pp. 113–114.)

Department; and, finally, unofficial channels where a special Soviet officer with a nominal title as a working level official or Tass correspondent with exceptional connections might be used to advance a policy line, communicate a threat, try out a proposal or test a reaction in advance to avoid a premature commitment.[214]

In the missile crisis, all of these channels were used.[215] Formal exchanges took place at the summit level between President Kennedy and Chairman Khrushchev. These were the most important, the most decisive. Less formal exchanges, less important but significant nonetheless, took place between Attorney General Kennedy and Ambassador Dobrynin. Several unofficial conversations took place, hints dropped by Tass correspondents at the United Nations, and conversations with semiofficial Soviet citizens, such as Georgi Bolshakov. The most important of the unofficial type were the negotiations between Fomin and Scali.

International and national institutions also played a significant political and diplomatic role in negotiating a resolution of this crisis. The United Nations became the center for internationalizing the crisis: Ambassador Stevenson's dramatic revelation of Soviet deception had an instant and electrifying effect on mobilizing international support (Moscow, for example, was denied the use of important African bases by its clients); Acting Secretary General U Thant proved to be a catalyst for reconciliation and an important agent for keeping the peace; and the United Nations itself was assigned a principal role in the Khrushchev-Kennedy bilateral agreement to resolve the crisis. Actions by the OAS were also an essential international ingredient in the negotiating process. And direct and continuing consultation with NATO added a substantial element of support to the administration's negotiating position.

On the national level, the Congress played a key role through the passage of supporting resolutions, authorizations for the use of additional military forces, and other formal legislative actions in mobilizing support of the Nation behind the administration. By such actions the Congress conveyed vital signals of intent to Moscow and accordingly provided an essential input into the resolution of the crisis. And the media on both sides were used to publicize each other's negotiating positions and garner national and international support as the negotiating process moved along. Finally, the military establishments were mobilized and their power orchestrated within the negotiating process during the management of the crisis. Raw power was ultimately the deciding factor in determining the outcome of this negotiating experience.

(2) Negotiations by action

(a) *Miscalculation on both sides.*—As a negotiating experience, the missile crisis was a unique illustration of what Ambassador Davies called, negotiations by action. Khrushchev made the first move by sending the missiles to Cuba. This was a miscalculation on both sides. Khrushchev miscalculated on two counts: The gravity of this action for U.S. vital national interests; and the magnitude of the U.S. response. The Kennedy administration also miscalculated as the result

[214] Hilsman, op. cit., pp. 216–217.
[215] Ibid.

of an intelligence failure. No one thought the Soviets would install such missiles in Cuba. The U.S. Intelligence Board made this official judgment on September 19, and only CIA Director McCone (who was on his honeymoon) believed, and then only fleetingly, that the Russians might be so emboldened as to do it.[216]

(b) *Negotiating along the quarantine line.*—In this negotiations by action the U.S. countermove was to establish a quarantine line around Cuba and screen the inflow of shipping. The line established a critical point of contact for testing the will and resolve of both sides. President Kennedy took a very cautious approach and adopted a course of graduated response beginning at the lowest level of provocation. He wanted to give Khrushchev plenty of time to reflect on the consequences of breaking through the line. Accordingly, he redrew the line closer to Cuba, as the crisis proceeded, and initiated a policy of selective enforcement. There would be a careful screening of incoming traffic but no stopping or boarding of Soviet ships without his approval. Delicate naval maneuvers were devised in a mode of ascending pressures.

It was now Khrushchev's move. He faced a new set of conditions: He had to decide whether or not to test the American will. He decided against it and withdrew the approaching Soviet ships. Some ships returned to the Soviet Union; others were deployed in rendezvous well outside the quarantine line.

Negotiations by action along the quarantine line proved to be successful. The effect was to avert a serious confrontation at sea and divert attention momentarily to Cuba itself.

(c) *Negotiations by action in Cuba.*—Compelling the Soviets to remove their missiles from Cuba also took on many of the characteristics of a negotiation by action. Khrushchev's initial move was to virtually complete delivery of all the missiles, thus creating the problem for the United States. (In an apparent error of priorities or because of some unforeseen problem, work on the missile sites and SAM installations proceeded simultaneously, allowing the United States to observe progress from its U-2 flights. Such observations and the concrete evidence of deception gained from them would have been impossible had the first priority been given to completing the SAM sites. With this protective screen, the Soviets could have completed the missile launching pads and thus presented the United States with a fait accompli.)[217]

In a series of countermoves, the President took specific actions: He dispatched the reconnaissance flights, alerted the missile forces, and prepared for air strikes against the SAM sites as a first contingency and then, if necessary, a military invasion of Cuba. Such moves left Khrushchev with a single choice, between war or peace. But at the last minute Kennedy, moving from the level of negotiations by action to that of negotiations by the written word, gave Khrushchev a chance to reverse course and, in the words of his conceding letter, to loosen the "knot of war" and "take measures to untie that knot."[218]

---

[216] Schlesinger, op. cit., p. 798. In recalling a conversation with the President as the crisis unfolded, Schlesinger wrote: "It was strange, he said, how no one in the intelligence community had anticipated the Soviet attempt to transform Cuba into a nuclear base; everyone had assumed that the Russians would not be so stupid as to offer us this pretext for intervention." (p. 811.) See also. Hilsman, op. cit., pp. 172 and 197.

[217] For a discussion of this matter. see, Hilsman, op. cit., pp. 182-183. For Khrushchev's explanation of the Soviet side, see, Khrushchev, op. cit., p. 495.

[218] Kennedy, op. cit., pp. 89-90.

(3) Negotiations through unofficial channels

Most extraordinary in the diplomacy of the missile crisis was the resort to negotiations through informal, unofficial channels. The Fomin-Scali negotiating encounters have no parallel in the history of Soviet-American relations, certainly with respect to the gravity of the negotiating environment. Viewed chronologically, their first encounter at the Occidental Restaurant on Friday afternoon, October 26 marked the first break in the crisis. Though unofficial in the strictist diplomatic sense, it nonetheless had the full authority of Chairman Khrushchev and the Kennedy administration.

But the risks were high.

Here again, as in Stalin's initiation of the Berlin blockade negotiations, Khrushchev resorted to the media as the initial channel of communications and negotiations, at best a dangerously tenuous connection subject to untold human error and external vagaries however successful the outcome. The crisis was fast reaching the "boiling point," as Khrushchev termed it. Time was of the essence, indeed a principal controlling factor in determining the final outcome. And yet the possibilities for miscalculation as the result, for example, of communications failures among others were infinite—witness the Khrushchev reversal letter. Thus, as in the analogous case of the Berlin blockade, the burden of war and peace in the nuclear age would seem to have been far too great to rely upon informal unofficial encounters in a restaurant, hotel coffee shop or hotel lobby.

(4) On secrecy and public disclosure

Absolute secrecy was another unique feature of the negotiations in the missile crisis. The principal actors on the American side tried as best they could to continue their official and private lives as normally as possible so as not to arouse public suspicion. Secrecy was imperative for the Americans from the time of discovery late Monday, October 15 to the President's speech of disclosure a week later on Monday, October 22. Over the weekend, secrecy began to break down, and the President was compelled to intervene personally to halt a New York Times story apparently disclosing essential elements of the impending crisis on grounds that publication might confront him with a Soviet ultimatum before he could get his own plans into effect.[219] During the week of negotiations, secrecy was maintained as the President's advisers planned both a negotiating and a confrontation strategy.

At the same time the administration used the technique of public disclosure to garner support for its negotiating position and to place the other side on the defensive and in the worst possible light. This was evident in the President's speech of October 22, Ambassador Stevenson's dramatic utterances and disclosures at the United Nations, and the immediate but selective publication of significant official statements and documents.

Soviet secrecy and disclosure followed along the same general lines, but in pursuit of Soviet purposes. For Khrushchev, secrecy was vital if he was to successfully present the President with a fait accompli in Cuba. And once negotiations got underway, secrecy was equally vital for both internal and external reasons as Khrushchev sought a way out of this dilemma. Like their counterparts in Washington, Khrushchev and his close associates also tried to put on a calm face and affect a public behavior of serenity and business-as-usual during the crisis.[220] At the same time the Soviet press and other media were used in full vigor to support the Soviet negotiating position and discredit that of the United States, for example, by the publication of extensive commentaries and analyses as well as official documents.[221]

Thus the diplomacy of the missile crisis represents a classic case of secrecy in negotiations and the selective use of public disclosures in the negotiating process.

(5) President Kennedy as a negotiator

(a) *Some qualities of a successful negotiator.*—In managing the confrontation and conducting the negotiations in the missile crisis, President Kennedy demonstrated qualities that have long been regarded as essential for a successful negotiator: Wisdom to grasp the essentials of national interests from the perspective of both sides; a stern sense of resolution combined with flexibility; strong nerves and a moral toughness; an inner calmness and control over the details of the situation; the consultative capacity to draw upon available talent; a desire to reach an agreement; an understanding of the correlation between power and the negotiating process; a determination not to humiliate the adversary and drive him into a spasmodic response; and the necessity of saving the defeated adversary's sense of dignity by not gloating in victory and thus preparing the ground work for building a better relationship.

(b) *An appraisal.*—President Kennedy grasped both the essence and the full dimension of the problem to be negotiated and measured accurately the ratio of vital national security interests committed on both sides. Fundamental in his thinking was the belief that Soviet missiles in Cuba constituted a direct threat to the vital national security interests of the United States (vital in its true meaning as a direct threat to the Nation's security and political existence); it was not vital, however, to the security interests of the Soviet Union.[222]

Recognizing this difference in perceptions of the threat, the President was most careful not to humiliate the Soviet Union, not to disgrace Khrushchev, not to make him escalate responses to an irreversible point because Soviet national interests or security required it. Most of all he wanted to avoid pushing Khrushchev into a spasmodic response. President Kennedy put it succinctly: "We don't want to push him to a precipitous action—give him time to consider. I don't want to put him in a corner from which he cannot escape." [223] Thus he managed the strategy of confrontation and negotiations in the crisis

[220] Khrushchev recalled: "I remember a period of 6 or 7 days when the danger was particularly acute. Seeking to take the heat off the situation somehow, I suggested to the other members of the government: 'Comrades, let's go to the Bolshoi Theater this evening. Our own people as well as foreign eyes will notice, and perhaps it will calm them down. They'll say to themselves, "If Khrushchev and our other leaders are able to go to the opera at a time like this, then at least tonight we can sleep peacefully."' We were trying to disguise our own anxiety, which was intense." (Khrushchev, op. cit., p. 497.)
[221] For an analysis of the Soviet press, see Dinerstein, op. cit., pp. 195–229 and appendix 1 and 2.
[222] Kennedy, op. cit., p. 126.
[223] Ibid., p. 77. This approach was strongly urged upon the President through Schlesinger by Averell Harriman. "We must give him an out," Harriman said. "If we do this shrewdly, we can downgrade the tough group in the Soviet Union which persuaded him to do this. But if we deny him an out, then we will escalate this business into a nuclear war." (Schlesinger, op. cit., p. 821.) For a favorable appraisal of the President's handling of the crisis by Harriman, see Harriman, Russia and America, pp. 201–203.)

with disciplined restraint, flexibility and wisdom. At the same time the President understood the role of power and the correlation of power with changing requirements in the negotiating process.

The President also understood the Soviet obsession with security, and he demonstrated this in two ways: At least momentarily by avoiding a direct challenge, as would have been the case in boarding the Soviet ships along the quarantine line; and in the final resolution of the crisis by settling on a formula for inspection by air that had the virtue of avoiding direct onsite American verification. That he rightly understood the Soviet mentality and sensitivity on this matter of security was later revealed by Khrushchev who recalled:

> Our ships, with the remainder of our deliveries to Cuba, headed straight through an armada of the American Navy, but the Americans didn't try to stop our ships or even check them. We kept in mind that as long as the United States limited itself to threatening gestures and didn't actually touch us, we could afford to pretend to ignore the harassment.

> *   *   *   *   *   *

> I won't deny that we were obliged to make some big concessions in the interests of peace. We even consented to the inspection of our ships—but only from the air. We never let the Americans actually set foot on our decks, though we did let them satisfy themselves that we were really removing our missiles.[224]

That President Kennedy maintained direct and absolute control over the most detailed execution of the strategy of confrontation and negotiation was another distinctive characteristic of this encounter. He personally ordered the reconnaissance flights, for example, and managed in the finest detail the program of graduated pressures along the quarantine line. Burned by the debacle at the Bay of Pigs, the President was not disposed again to let such vital matters get out of his control and create situations that might not be retrieveable through negotiations.

And finally, the President maintained a disciplined restraint and calmness not only during the heat of the crisis but also in the hour of victory. The supporting staff which shared this moment of glory and personal satisfaction was sternly warned against any verbal posturing that would degrade the Soviet Union, injure its pride or discredit its leader. Kennedy, concerned about any potential backlash, preferred to begin building the relationship on a basis of trust and on an understanding of the limits and equilibrium of power. As he said later: "Every setback has the seeds of its own reprisal, if the country is powerful enough." [225]

[224] Khrushchev, op. cit., pp. 496 and 499. The first quotation, at variance with the American view, related to the approach of Soviet ships to the quarantine line early in the crisis; the second related to the final agreement that required inspection and verification.

For a commentary on the connection between the Soviet inclination to conceal weakness and President Kennedy's admission of the missiles in Cuba, see Dinerstein, op. cit., p. 223. Dinerstein wrote: "It had been Soviet practice since the state was first established to conceal from its own people and from foreigners any evidence of weakness. Most Soviet security measures were directed to that end; Soviet opposition to international inspection in an arms control program derived from the fear that inspection would reveal weakness." The Soviets never protested the U-2 flights over the Soviet Union because of their demonstrated inability to stop them. When one was shot down (Gary Powers), they gave it maximum publicity because, as Dinerstein wrote, "now Khrushchev was displaying strength to his domestic and foreign opponents rather than revealing weakness." Thus he concluded, with respect to the missile crisis and Soviet behavior: "Very possibly the Soviet leaders projected their attitudes on to Kennedy and were therefore taken unawares when he publicly confirmed a dramatic shift in power away from the United States."

[225] Schlesinger, op. cit., p. 841.

(c) *A judgment at the time: Prime Minister Macmillan.*—Viewed in the context of a negotiation, the President's conduct revealed a high order of skill and understanding. British Prime Minister Macmillan (with whom Kennedy kept in the closest contact during the crisis) recorded in his diary on November 2, 1962 that the President had conducted this affair with "great skill, energy, resourcefulness and courage." According to Macmillan, "He answered the Communists with their own weapons—for they always use several and even divergent means to secure their ends." He played a "firm military game throughout—acting quickly and being ready to act as soon as mobilised." He played "the diplomatic card excellently" with respect to conferring with the European Allies. And he "played the United Nations admirably", exposing the Soviet "fatal mistake of bare-faced lying." Macmillan concluded: "Altogether the President did wonderfully well. * * *" [226]

(6) *Khrushchev as a negotiator*

(a) *An American appraisal: Soviets handled crisis with "wisdom and restraint".*—Hilsman's appraisal of Khrushchev's role as a negotiator in this crisis seemed close to the mark. "Let it * * * be said that the decision to withdraw required courage on the Soviet side and that although putting the missiles into Cuba was threatening and irresponsible, the Soviets," he wrote, "handled the ensuing crisis with wisdom and restraint." [227]

For Khrushchev there were three personal crises within this larger crisis. They were the critical points at which his decision would determine the American reaction. In all three he responded, as Hilsman said, "with wisdom and restraint."

In the negotiations by action along the quarantine line, Khrushchev withdrew Soviet ships, thus avoiding a showdown at sea with the U.S. Navy. At the negotiating front in Washington, he made the first break toward a negotiated settlement by directing Fomin to contact Scali on the afternoon of the 26th and by writing the long letter of concession to the President in the evening. And finally he reaffirmed his initial decision by reversing a subsequent statement of unacceptable terms in his letter to the President on the 28th. By the 28th. it must be remembered, all the MRBM's were operational; [228] the protective screen of the SAM network was in whole or in part also operational, having already shot down one U–2; the IRBM's would have been operational by December. Despite these initial advantages (though he was robbed of the element of surprise), Khrushchev clearly weighed those advantages against the cost of a likely American military response and possibly war. Realistically, he took the path of negotiations to resolve the crisis.

(b) *Khrushchev's control over the confrontation and negotiations.*—Like President Kennedy, Chairman Khrushchev kept a tight hold on the evolving confrontation and negotiations from the Soviet side. As

---

[226] Macmillan, Harold. At the End of the Day, 1961–1963. New York, Harper & Row. 1973, p. 219. Schlesinger, a participant in managing the crisis, saw in the President a "combination of toughness and restraint, of will, nerve and wisdom, so brilliantly controlled, so matchlessly calibrated, that dazzled the world." (Schlesinger, op. cit., p. 841.)
[227] Hilsman, op. cit., p. 227.
[228] Ibid., p. 227.

noted above, the idea of missiles in Cuba germinated in his mind, but the decision to actually install them and accordingly accept the risk of war was made with the concurrence of the collective leadership.[229]

Once the crisis got rolling, Khrushchev kept things under control. He dictated the messages and conducted the negotiations for the Soviet side.[230] He spent "one of the most dangerous nights" at the Council of Ministers office in the Kremlin, sleeping on a couch in his office with his clothes on.[231] "I was ready," he said, "for alarming news to come any moment, and I wanted to be ready to react immediately." [232]

Khrushchev "vividly" remembered those days after the President "issued an ultimatum." The exchange of correspondence he remembered "especially well" because he initiated it and "was at the center of the action on our end of the correspondence." And he added: "I take complete responsibility for the fact that the President and I entered into direct contact at the most crucial and dangerous stage of the crisis." [233]

(c) *Khrushchev's judgment on the negotiated settlement: "A triumph of common sense."*—At this point in his narrative Khrushchev went on to explain his version of the confrontation and negotiation which differed radically from that of the American. In brief, he placed the burden of responsibility on the President for backing down, emphasizing fears of a military takeover in Washington and overemphasizing the importance of the President's noninvasion pledge. Khrushchev concluded his analysis with the following commentary which underscored the main point that the negotiated settlement was "a triumph of commonsense":

In our negotiations with the Americans during the crisis, they had, on the whole, been open and candid with us, especially Robert Kennedy. The Americans knew that if Russian blood were shed in Cuba, American blood would surely be shed in Germany. The American Government was anxious to avoid such a development. It had been, to say the least, an interesting and challenging situation. The two most powerful nations of the world had been squared off against each other, each with its finger on the button. You'd have thought that war was inevitable. But both showed that if the desire to avoid war is strong enough, even the most pressing dispute can be solved by compromise. And a compromise over Cuba was indeed found. The episode ended in a triumph of commonsense. I'll always remember the late President with deep respect because, in the final analysis, he showed himself to be sober-minded and determined to avoid war. He didn't let himself become frightened, nor did he become reckless. He didn't overestimate America's might, and he left himself a way out of the crisis. He showed real wisdom and statesmanship when he turned his back on right-wing forces in the United States who were trying to goad him into taking military action against Cuba. It was a great victory for us, though, that we had been able to extract from

---

[229] On the decisionmaking process Khrushchev wrote: "I should mention that our side's policy was, from the outset, worked out in the collective leadership. It wasn't until after two or three lengthy discussions of the matter that we had decided it was worth the risk to install missiles on Cuba in the first place. It had been my feeling that the initial, as well as the subsequent, decisions should not be forced down anyone's throat. I had made sure to give the collective leadership time for the problem to crystallize in everyone's mind. I had wanted my comrades to accept and support the decision with a clear conscience and a full understanding of what the consequences of putting the missiles on Cuba might be—namely, war with the United States. Every step we had taken had been carefully considered by the collective." (Khrushchev, op. cit., p. 499.)

[230] Ibid., p. 497.

[231] Khrushchev explained: "I didn't want to be like that Western minister who was caught literally with his pants down by the Suez events of 1956 and had to run around in his shorts until the emergency was over." (p. 497.)

[232] Ibid.

[233] Ibid.

Kennedy a promise that neither America nor any of her allies would invade Cuba.[234]

(7) *Enhanced role of the Ambassador*

(a) *Soviet Ambassador Dobrynin, a key communications link.*— Though this crisis was managed from the center, still some ambassadors, notably Dobrynin and Ormsby Gore in Washington, played important roles in the management of the confrontation and negotiations. Memoirs by American principals, particularly those of Robert Kennedy, revealed the prominent part played by Soviet Ambassador Dobrynin. During the period of deception, he conveyed his government's assurances to leading American officials that there were no missiles in Cuba, though Soviet sources have since denied that he had knowledge of the missiles and assert that he, like Kennedy, had been misled by Khrushchev.[235] When the crisis got underway, he was very much in the center of things as the key communications link between Moscow and Washington. Dobrynin's meeting with the Attorney General, literally at the last moment on Saturday evening, October 27, may have been a deciding factor in Khrushchev's reversal, though Dobrynin's version of the encounter (as reported by Khrushchev) differed radically from the Kennedy account.[236]

(b) *British Ambassador Ormsby Gore, friend of the Kennedys.*— British Ambassador David Ormsby Gore was also featured prominently in the management of the crisis. Having the advantage of being a close friend of the President, he played a key role in reporting back to a most appreciative Prime Minister.[237]

In addition to reporting back extensively and from the closest inner circle of the White House, Ormsby Gore made a significant contribution in the unfolding negotiation by action when he suggested to the President that the quarantine line be drawn closer to Cuba so as to give the Soviet leadership time for reflection. The President, agreeing immediately, called Secretary of Defense McNamara, and over emotional protests from the Navy, issued the appropriate order. "This

[234] Ibid., p. 500. In his "Last Testament," Khrushchev made these comments on Kennedy: "Kennedy was also someone we could trust. When he gave us public assurances that the United States would not organize an invasion of Cuba, either on its own or through its allies, we trusted him. We accepted the concession he was making and made a concession of our own by withdrawing our nuclear weapons from Cuba." Khrushchev also praised the President for his realism in handling the crisis. (Khrushchev, Last Testament, pp. 513–514.) For Khrushchev's retrospective views of Kennedy at the Vienna Conference, see pp. 497–498. He was impressed by Kennedy's grasp of international problems, his understanding of the policy of peaceful coexistence, and confidence in discussions.

[235] Kennedy, op. cit., pp. 65–66. In an extensive article on Dobrynin by Anthony Austin published in The New York Times on June 4, 1979 (p. A6) it was pointed out that, according to "well-informed Soviet sources in Washington," when Dobrynin had misled Robert Kennedy in regard to the missiles, "he was not lying but had been misled himself." These Soviet sources say that Kennedy kept after the Ambassador on the subject sometimes visiting him as late as 2 or 3 a.m. "Thereupon, they recount," according to Austin, "Mr. Dobrynin sent a message to Nikita S. Khrushchev * * * saying that the American Government seemed to be skeptical in regard to his assurance. There being no answer, according to this account, Mr. Dobrynin assured Mr. Kennedy a second time." The Austin story continues: "What happened next, the Soviet sources recount, was that Secretary of State Dean Rusk called Ambassador Dobrynin in and said, 'Anatoly, look here!' and showed him aerial photographs of the offensive missiles in place. 'That,' a Soviet source said, 'was when the Ambassador found out that the missiles were there. Yes, Khrushchev should not have acted as he did. An Ambassador who is thought to be lying has his credibility destroyed.'" Kennedy continued, nonetheless, to use Dobrynin as the principal Soviet channel for negotiating the crisis, and according to Austin, "the pattern was set" for the unusually close relationship that Dobrynin has had with the State Department and White House even to this day.

[236] Khrushchev, op. cit., pp. 497–498.

[237] In the Prime Minister's favorable appraisal of the President's role in the crisis, he noted that the President was "well-served" by "our British representatives, Gore and Dean." (Macmillan, At the End of the Day, p. 219.)

decision was of vital importance in postponing the moment of irreversible action," wrote Schlesinger.[238]

(8) Staff support: Excellence of the executive committee

A final unique characteristic of this negotiating encounter was the staff support provided by the executive committee. As this study has shown thus far, negotiations in Soviet-American relations have taken many forms; they have not been confined just to formal exchanges over a conference table. But a persistent characteristic running through this experience that has often determined successful outcomes has been the quality of staff support given the principals and the ability of the principals to select the most reasonable and appropriate options.

The executive committee was by all measure an exceptional group of planners and advisers, representing a collection of uncommonly talented men with such special virtues as wisdom and vision, independence and boldness of thought; they were especially gifted with insight into human behavior and a capacity to act. Deliberations were carried on with complete equality; rank had no privileges. Accounts of their deliberations reflect a determined and honest effort to give the President viable options in managing the confrontation and conducting the negotiations. In commenting upon the President's satisfaction with the performance of this committee, Schlesinger observed: "The executive committee had proved a brilliant instrument of consideration and coordination." [239]

Singled out and credited with a high performance by his peers on the executive committee was Robert Kennedy. Mindful of the Japanese "sneak attack" on Pearl Harbor and the moral opprobrium it generated, he injected a moral quality into the deliberations by vigorously resisting airstrikes at the missile installations as the first option.[240] He also provided the correct answer to the dilemma created by Khrushchev's letter of reversal. In general, he gave the group a coherent framework for discussion and proved to be a catalyst to searching inquiry by his constant questioning. As Schlesinger wrote: The President was "particularly proud of his brother, always balanced, never rattled, his eye fixed on the ultimate as well as on the immediate." [241]

[238] Schlesinger, op. cit., p. 818.
[239] Schlesinger, op. cit., p. 832. Schleseinger went on: "McNamara, as usual, had been superb. Lewellyn Thompson [a specialist in Russian affairs, a professional diplomat who was to become Ambassador to the Soviet Union] had provided wise counsel; Edwin Martin had managed the Latin American side with tact and efficiency. If the President was disappointed in others, he was not, I think, especially surprised. As a whole, the government could hardly have performed better."
Except for General Maxwell Taylor, the President was "distressed", in the words of the Attorney General, by the predilection of the military representatives "to give so little consideration to the implications of steps they suggested." The President was "disturbed by this inability to look beyond the limited military field." Later when talking about this matter, he said, in Robert Kennedy's words, "we had to remember that they were trained to fight and to wage war—that was their life. Perhaps we would feel even more concerned if they were always opposed to using arms or military means—for if they would not be willing, who would be? But this experience pointed out for us all the importance of civilian direction and control and the importance of raising probing questions to military recommendations." (Kennedy, op. cit., p. 119.)
[240] During the early deliberations when an air strike was felt by most to be the only course, Kennedy passed a note to the President: "I now know how Tojo felt when he was planning Pearl Harbor." (Ibid., p. 31.)
[241] Schlesinger, op. cit., p. 832. Sorensen wrote: "* * * the best performer in this respect was the Attorney General—not because of any particular idea he advanced, not because he presided (no one did), but because of his constant prodding, questioning, eliciting arguments and alternatives and keeping the discussions concrete and moving ahead, a difficult task as different participants came in and out." (Sorensen, op. cit., p. 679.)

(b) Impact on Soviet-American relations: The beginning of détente

The implications of the missile crisis were far-reaching, for the crisis impacted on vital areas of international relations: The Sino-Soviet dispute quickened; NATO allies raised basic questions about U.S. leadership in Europe; and fundamental changes were to begin in Soviet-American relations.

Resolution of the missile crisis generated forces that were to bring on détente. Perhaps this was of transcending importance among its implications. When on October 26, Khrushchev, then the realist and pragmatist and no longer the revolutionary ideologue, communicated his intention of withdrawing the missiles, he denied himself, at least for the near future, the option of nuclear blackmail which had been a central feature of his foreign policy since 1957, and accordingly accepted the only alternative choice of seeking an accommodation with the United States. The Cuban experience had demonstrated to Khrushchev the validity of Kennedy's argument at Vienna for respecting the equilibrium of power and avoiding precipitous changes in it.[242]

Decisions were made in the aftermath to redress the balance of strategic power that had compelled the Soviet Union to back down—never again, the Soviet leadership said—but decisions were also made to establish a détente in Soviet-American relations. The Nuclear Test Ban Treaty in the coming year was the first concrete step in this direction.

Whether the missile crisis was a pivot or a turning point in East-West relations would seem to remain an open question, depending upon the choice of timeframes and perception of the meaning of détente.[243] But with the perspective of nearly two decades, the evidence seems to suggest at this juncture at least a preference on both sides to continue the search for accommodation through negotiations but within a mutually acceptable balance of strategic power. As a negotiating encounter, the missile crisis may, therefore, be judged at some future time as one of the most important negotiations in the history of Soviet-American relations.

C. The Nuclear Test Ban Treaty, 1963: Concluding Negotiations To Control Nuclear Testing

1. TEST BAN NEGOTIATIONS IN PERSPECTIVE

(a) Prolonged stalemate in Geneva

That the missile crisis was to fundamentally alter the course of Soviet-American relations was soon demonstrated by the conclusion of the Nuclear Test Ban Treaty in the summer of 1963. It was also demonstrated by other subsequent arrangements, such as the establishment of the so-called hotline of instant communications between Washington and Moscow. In general, these ameliorating measures were intended to lower the level of tension, facilitate the management

---

[242] Schlesinger, op. cit., p. 891.
[243] Schlesinger wrote: "But the 13 days gave the world—even the Soviet Union—a sense of American determination and responsibility in the use of power which, sustained, might indeed become a turning point in the history of relations between east and west." (p. 841). Hilsman also discussed the question of whether the missile was a turning point in world history (p. 228).

of future crises, and clear the way for greater accommodation. Negotiations to control nuclear testing had stalemated in Geneva. The missile crisis compelled a reordering of Soviet priorities that broke the prolonged stalemate.

(b) A brief survey of negotiations, 1958–62

Negotiations to ban nuclear testing began in the summer of 1958 amid growing international concern for the danger to human life from radioactive fallout and at a time of unilateral moratoria on nuclear testing.[244]

These negotiations were to continue along an uneven course for the next 4 years, perhaps the most difficult years of the cold war, moving, as Ambassador Arthur H. Dean, the head of the U.S. arms control delegation in Geneva, said, "through a tangle of proposals for both comprehensive and partial test bans." [245] The test ban was considered separately; at times it was enmeshed in discussions on general disarmament. Progress had been achieved. Agreement was reached on a preamble, 17 articles and two annexes of a draft treaty for a comprehensive test ban including one article recognizing the principle of international inspection. But deteriorating East-West relations after the collapse of the May 1960 summit arrested further progress.[246]

The incoming Kennedy administration placed renewed emphasis on a comprehensive test ban treaty, and amid a complex of contending views within the national security community and within the administration itself, it judged the treaty to be advantageous to the Nation.[246a] Thus, despite misgivings in some quarters on the home front and an unpromising international environment, the U.S. delegation began in 1961, with the President's full support, what Ambassador Dean noted,

were to be 2 years of hard, unrelenting, intensive, interesting, and challenging work. Consulting often with our own and British scientists, we missed no opportunity to discuss the test ban with Soviet representatives, on and off the record, whether at Geneva, at the United Nations, or in private diplomatic conversations which went on continuously. In spite of a solid wall of Soviet negatives, we kept on trying to adjust our proposals as science and political developments made changes possible. We were convinced of the importance of our goal, and we knew that after careful and persistent preparation, agreement with the Soviet Union could come suddenly and without warning, as had been the case with the Austrian State Treaty of 1955.[247]

At the Geneva meeting in the spring of 1961, Soviet disinterest in a test ban was quickly made known. Apparently pressured by Soviet

[244] For a detailed discussion of the negotiations, see, Jacobson, Harold Karan and Eric Stein. Diplomats, Scientists, and Politicians: The United States and the Nuclear Test Ban Negotiations. Ann Arbor, Mich., University of Michigan Press, 1966, 538 pages; see also, Schlesinger, op. cit., pp. 448–505. This narrative draws heavily on Dean, Arthur H., Test Ban and Disarmament: The Path of Negotiations. Published for the Council on Foreign Relations. New York, Harper & Row, 1966, 154 pages. For the most recent study on the behavioral aspects of the test ban negotiations, see, Jonsson, Christer. Soviet Bargaining Behavior: The Nuclear Test Ban Case, New York, Columbia University Press, 1979, 266 pages. A commentary on Professor Christer's book stated: "Jonsson's exhaustive researches show how, contrary to Western assumptions about an established, unchanging Soviet negotiating stance, Soviet conduct in the test ban negotiations changed significantly over time. These changes coincided with major turning points in East-West relations and shifts in the balance of power between protreaty and antitreaty factions within the Soviet Union. While the test ban issue was of vital importance to the development of the Sino-Soviet dispute, the changes in Soviet negotiating behavior cannot readily be explained in terms of changes in China's influence. This thorough case study indicates that neither external nor domestic factors alone, but rather the complex interplay between the two, can account for Soviet bargaining behavior." Jonsson is an Associate Professor of Political Science at the University of Lund, Sweden.
[245] Ibid. p. 87.
[246] Ibid.
[246a] Ibid., p. 88.
[247] Ibid.. pp. 88–89.

generals and scientists to resume testing in the hope of developing more compact and efficient warheads, they repudiated earlier agreements and demanded a "troika" concept that reduced inspection to self-inspection and, as Schlesinger noted, "thus to absurdity." [248] "Without discouragement or evidence of setback," as Dean put it, the U.S. delegation on April 18, 1961, presented its first complete draft of a comprehensive test ban treaty in all environments. Most Soviet objections that had any validity were met in this draft. The Soviet response was, however, negative, but the U.S. delegation, as Dean wrote, "continued to explore and discuss the test ban in every way we could and to make further proposals." [249]

The reason for the negative Soviet response became clear when on August 30, 1961, at the height of the Berlin crisis, the Soviets announced their intention to break the moratorium and test a supermegaton nuclear device in the atmosphere. The text of the Soviet statement and the rapid followup of the tests confirmed earlier suspicions of American negotiators that the Soviets had misused the arms control talks as a screen for test preparations. [250]

Notwithstanding this setback, the administration remained firm in its commitment. The President and British Prime Minister Macmillan jointly called on the Soviet Union to end further atmospheric testing, accept a treaty barring such tests without any international controls, and return to the conference table to work out a comprehensive treaty. Khrushchev categorically refused; the tests continued into the fall. [251] (In a defensive reaction, the United States, after Khrushchev rejected another offer to negotiate a test ban treaty, resumed testing in the atmosphere in April 1962.) [252]

By mid-1962, Dean was convinced that the Soviet Union would not accept any proposals involving onsite inspections of unidentifiable underground seismic events by foreigners, "no matter how carefully regulated and safeguarded." [253] Accordingly, the U.S. delegation proposed consideration of a partial test ban treaty excluding underground tests, the one environment in which the United States regarded inspections as essential. On August 27, 1962, Dean, as chairman of the U.S. delegation at Geneva, tabled two draft treaties, one a partial ban and the other a comprehensive ban. He explained U.S. willingness to sign a partial test ban treaty in the three environments (outer space, the atmosphere, and under water) without inspection or a comprehensive treaty in all four environments, including on land, with carefully worked out inspection of other unidentified underground seismic events. [254]

Both drafts aroused considerable informal interest among the Soviet representatives at Geneva and at the United Nations before the missile crisis erupted. Officially, however, the Soviets denounced the proposal and countered with one providing for a moratorium on underground testing not prohibited by the partial test ban treaty. [255]

[248] Schlesinger, op. cit., pp. 453–454.
[249] Dean, op. cit., p. 89.
[250] Ibid., p. 90.
[251] Ibid.
[252] Schlesinger, op. cit., p. 497
[253] Dean, op. cit., p. 90.
[254] Ibid., pp. 90–91
[255] Ibid.

The stalemate persisted until immediately after the missile crisis.

(c) Arthur H. Dean: Observations on Soviet negotiating behavior

(1) Dean, a qualified diplomatic observer

Ambassador Dean carried the main burden of negotiating a test ban treaty with the Soviets from January 1961 to December 1962. (He had extensive previous experience in negotiating with the Communists, having taken part in negotiations in Korea during 1953–54 and at the territorial sea conferences in 1959 and 1960.) [256] The final treaty, negotiated by Harriman in July 1963, was based on Dean's draft of August 1962; both were very similar.[257]

Dean was present unofficially at the formal signing of the treaty in Moscow on August 5, 1963, thanks, as he said, "to a courteous and never-to-be-forgotten telephoned invitation" from President Kennedy, who remarked at the time, "After all, it is your treaty." [258]

For nearly 2 years Dean negotiated with his Soviet counterparts in situations ranging from formal conferences to the most informal, intimate settings. He viewed Soviet negotiating behavior at close range and on a subject of great importance, nuclear arms control. Fortunately, for the purposes of this study, Dean recorded many observations in his memoirs.

(2) Soviet style in diplomacy and negotiations: Expectation of hostility and inflexibility in bargaining

"Diplomatic style is a kind of national signature," wrote Dean, "reflecting not only official policies but also characteristics of the society from which the diplomat comes and the outlook in which he has been bred." This style influenced the reactions of a particular diplomat and the procedures he was likely to follow. "Knowing intimately the diplomatic style of one's adversary * * * can be a real negotiating advantage," he concluded.[259]

Dean observed two prominent characteristics in the Soviet style of diplomacy and negotiations: "A dogmatic expectation of hostility" from the outside world, and "an iron determination" to carry out Moscow-formulated programs and policies without variation by diplomats in the field.[260]

The expectation of hostility, rooted in ideology and reinforced by training and experience, permeated "every aspect of official Soviet diplomatic behavior." Accordingly, Western proposals on arms control were examined meticulously to discover their "real, nefarious purpose." Ideological warfare was an expected common behavior on both sides in negotiations. Consequently, the official stance of the Soviet negotiator at the conference table was "rigid, often rude or at least barely polite, secretive, formal, very general, and given to diatribes and not dialog as the safest way of dealing with almost any question." As Dean listened to innumerable such official statements, it seemed to him that

[256] U.S. Congress. Senate. Committee on Foreign Relations. Nuclear Test Ban Treaty. Hearings. 88th Cong., 1st sess., Washington, D.C., U.S. Government Printing Office, 1963. p. 814. (Hereafter cited as, Senate Foreign Relations Committee, Hearings on Nuclear Test Ban Treaty, 1963.)
[257] Ibid. Inserted in Dean's testimony was a copy of the August draft showing the similarities with the negotiated treaty.
[258] Dean, op. cit., p. 92.
[259] Ibid., p. 34.
[260] Ibid.

in form and substance "they concealed a curious mixture of feelings of arrogance and fear." [261]

Both Soviet policy and the conduct of the diplomat charged with carrying it out were marked by a distinctive inflexibility of diplomatic style. Adherence to fixed positions and deprivation of discretionary powers imposed on Soviet negotiators a special requirement when faced with new proposals from the other side to conduct "stalling" and "long talking" tactics while awaiting new instructions. The result, as others have indicated, could be a slowing down of the proceedings for weeks and months.[262]

Western negotiators have become accustomed and impervious to this "gritty official Soviet style," Dean noted, but he doubted that in dealing with the difficult and complex subject of disarmament in a world where none of the major political conflicts had been settled a more flexible and unpolemical style would have guaranteed any better results. Under any circumstances, he said, given the vast differences in purposes, negotiation was "bound to be a difficult and tedious process." [263]

(3) Soviet tactics in diplomacy and negotiations

(a) *Disbelief in getting something for nothing.*—Dean perceived a pattern of negotiating tactics in his exposure to Soviet negotiators, and one that seemed to impress him most was Soviet disbelief in getting something for nothing. Like a skilled chess player, he said, a Soviet diplomat "does not expect his opposite number to give up something for nothing, not even a pawn." Unexplained unilateral concessions by Western negotiators with the expectation of stimulating reciprocal concessions only aroused "suspicion and concern."

Nor was compromise—the notion of splitting the difference—an operable principle of negotiations. To Soviet negotiators such behavior was a sign of weakness in his adversary and a signal to hold fast to his own negotiating position.[264]

(b) *The "twisting technique."*—Soviet diplomats, Dean recorded, would also "take advantage of any indiscretion or mistake and will stretch or cut statements" to fit their political purposes. On one occasion during a visit to Moscow in February 1959, Prime Minister Macmillan was purported to have made a seemingly casual remark to Khrushchev that Western insistence on on-site inspection in the proposed nuclear test ban treaty was intended to pacify American public opinion and that a fixed inspection quota of any symbolic number would be accepted. Soviet negotiators immediately seized on the low number of three as the number and proceeded without regard to available scientific data on which the U.S. position was based.[265]

Khrushchev resorted to the same "twisting technique" in misusing information from conversations between Dean and Soviet negotiator V. V. Kuznetsov. Dean explained that the Soviets seized upon a nonexistent American proposal of an annual quota of two or three on-site inspections of unidentified events in a nonseismic area as a basis for

[261] Ibid.
[262] Ibid., p. 35.
[263] Ibid.
[264] Ibid., p. 43. Dean proceeded to quote Mosely's observations on Soviet rejection of compromise, recommending that his writings on Soviet negotiating behavior "should be the vade mecum of Western diplomats. * * *"
[265] Ibid., pp. 43–44.

an overall agreement, though, as Dean wrote, "they knew perfectly well it was not." "One must be prepared to resist this technique," Dean warned, "no matter how long it may take or how often it may occur." [266]

(c) *The question of time.*—Manipulation of time to wear down an adversary was another Soviet negotiating tactic. Dean recalled the immediate postwar period and the revelation to Western diplomats that their Soviet counterparts had often had quite a different conception of time. They could sit through meetings, talking endlessly and repetitiously, hoping to wear down an adversary, win concessions through sheer fatigue and boredom on the other side, or reach an agreement for agreement's sake that would paper over deep differences. But Dean observed that an agreement without consensus and clear definition could be worse than no agreement at all, and he cautioned:

Overeagerness only plays into Communist hands. It pays to listen, to be precise, determined, and willing to spend a lot of time, without any sign of being impatient, angry, or annoyed. One cannot negotiate successfully with Soviet representatives against a fixed deadline.[267]

In disarmament negotiations Dean was exposed to this cunctator tactic, and he observed how it served Soviet obstructionist purposes. Since obstruction and not agreement suited Soviet purposes during much of the disarmament negotiations, time proved to be a useful negotiating ally. Soviet obstructionism was designed to prolong negotiations, exhaust or provoke the adversary, arouse a critical public opinion in his country sufficiently strong to pressure the negotiator for concessions to insure a "successful" conference. Dean cited the example of the cochairmen meetings at Geneva when Deputy Foreign Minister Kuznetsov would, as Dean noted, "occasionally discuss very pleasantly some point of Communist theory at great length, regardless of its relevance to the matter at hand." [268]

(d) *"Agreement in principle."*—Reaching "agreement in principle" was another Soviet negotiating device Dean warned against as a "pitfall." A case in point would be agreement on disarmament first with details such as inspection among others coming later. "Time and again," Dean observed, "Soviet negotiators will press for a general agreement, often on a principle, such as being for 'peace,' to which it is very difficult to object, and will charge bad faith when this is refused." Knowing Western impatience, they have sought to make agreement seem very close by emphasizing the ease with which it could be recorded in general terms. "By pushing in this way," Dean explained, "they hope for an agreement of such vagueness that they will be able to interpret it in their own way and act to their own advantage while professing to observe the agreement"—as in the case of the Yalta and Potsdam agreements.[269]

Dean explained further that Westerners were trained to pay attention to facts and concrete details; that they reasoned from the particular to the general and then established agreement on this basis as an assurance against a breakdown. In contrast, Soviet diplomats were less concerned with agreements as legal instruments, stressing not the factual basis but seeking an advantageous political position. Some-

---

[266] Ibid. The Khrushchev episode is described on pp. 40–42.
[267] Ibid., pp. 44–45.
[268] Ibid.
[269] Ibid. pp. 45–46.

times, however, Soviet interest required a detailed hard-headed agreement. But Dean cautioned:

We must not allow ourselves to be taken in, especially in matters of disarmament and arms control, where we need extremely specific and detailed agreements and verification controls if we are not to imperil our security. Any idea of agreeing to general propositions as an encouragement to compromise on crucial matters of detail would be folly.[270]

Moreover, differences exist over interpretations of the term "in principle." To Americans and the English, Dean noted, such an agreement was based on the practical steps which the diplomat believed should be carried out in the course of time—not so much in detail as in broad outline. In the Soviet and continental view it did not mean an agreement which could and would be carried out eventually. Rather it represented a common point of view at which the two still divergent views might ultimately converge if it suited either side. Dean explained that there was no commitment to proceed.[271]

(e) *The "waiving" argument.*—Related to the "agreement in principle" tactic was often the follow-on approach, if the former were successful, of the "waiving" argument. By not pursuing a matter of detail or a specific point when the general agreement "in principle" was made, the Soviet negotiator would claim that the other side "waived" it for all time. Dean explained further in the context of negotiations on the Joint Statement of Agreed Principles for Disarmament Negotiations in which the American negotiators took precautionary measures against Soviet resort to this tactic:

It is a favorite device of Soviet diplomats to press the adversary to set aside some aspect of a question in the interests of getting agreement and of moving ahead and then, when the other party brings up the matter later, to claim that by agreeing to set it aside originally the other party had agreed to waive it entirely. We were familiar with this approach and determined to make it crystal clear that nothing had been "waived." [272]

(4) Soviet obsession with secrecy; possible U.S. mitigating response

(a) *Roots of Soviet opposition to onsite verification.*—In addition to explaining Soviet style and tactics in diplomacy and negotiations, Dean searched for the roots of Soviet opposition to what has been for Americans the vital concept of onsite verification in arms control agreements and found them to be in the Soviet obsession with secrecy—in brief, an obsession rooted in fear, a fear of discovery and exposure to hostile outside forces.[273]

In seeking to fathom Soviet reasoning behind this obsession in hopes of divining a possible American mitigating response, Dean acknowledged the conventional wisdom that attributed this obsession to "historical distrust of the foreigner, to a suspicious 'peasant mentality,' to the memories of foreign invasions, and even to the 19th-century controversy between those Russians who wanted to Europeanize the country and those who insisted on the special mission of Slavic Rus-

---

[270] Ibid., p. 46. For further warnings against "agreements in principle," see p. 68 in which Dean cautions that, "they can be nothing but a trap." "If the exact details in a matter so vital as disarmament are not worked out ahead of time," he cautioned further, "suspicion, distrust, and endless wrangling and misunderstanding will result, with increasing tension, setbacks, and accusations of bad faith as their companions."
[271] Ibid., p. 46.
[272] Ibid., pp. 46–47 and 32–33.
[273] Ibid., pp. 54–55.

sia"—the struggle between the Westernizers and the Slavophiles and the messianic notion of the "Third Rome." [273a] He did not deny the impact of these elements upon current Soviet thinking, but he was convinced, after having negotiated with the Russians for so long, that this obsession or fixation had somewhat different roots.[274]

Dean viewed the problem as being on a "parallel track," one involving policy, the other attitudes. With respect to the first track, certain rational considerations reinforced the importance of secrecy, such as the benefits from maintaining strict military secrecy. Combined with this "good" was the often expressed fear of what the West wanted in stage I of disarmament: to verify the location of Soviet missile-launching sites and then mount a preemptive attack instead of proceeding to stages II and III. Though excessive secrecy could boomerang to the Soviet disadvantage, as in the case of the "missile gap" that stimulated a U.S. overreaction in response, still the Soviets clearly have regarded secrecy as a military asset.[275]

But more was involved than safeguarding military secrecy, Dean believed, or else a policy change could be expected with the development of photographic and satellite reconnaissance that would deny absolute secrecy. He called this second of the "parallel track" one of attitudes, and explained:

There is, first of all, an apparently bottomless suspicion which springs from the dogmatic Communist assumption of hostility from the outside world. This attitude is combined with a belief in the inherent superiority of the "socialist" system, seasoned by a considerable lack of knowledge of the reality of what they call the capitalist or imperialist world. The dogma of unending struggle, together with an internal system which requires keeping total control of the Soviet population, leads to the extreme and protective emphasis on national sovereignty which permeates Soviet concepts of international law and many aspects of Soviet foreign policy.[276]

Also, being aware of the gap between the premises of the system on the one hand and the performance and accomplishments on the other, Soviet officials have wanted to hide this gap from "hostile and prying eyes" of foreign inspectors. "It is an attitude," Dean continued, "that suffuses the whole Soviet system and extends to all aspects of life which might expose to a foreigner, weakness, popular discontent, or contradictions between reality and official propaganda." In brief, the Soviets have sought to maintain the principle of "a single loyalty and a single truth" among its people; intrusion of foreign inspectors representing an international agency and bound to see more than weapons and factories, would become as "dangerous" as any other outsider.[277]

Dean perceived compartmentalized knowledge as another element in fortifying Soviet attitudes toward secrecy in addition to the assumption of hostility and the necessity of preserving a single loyalty. Restrictions on information permeated the entire system. Soviet citizens were not informed, and even high-ranking officials gained access to information only on a "need-to-know basis." In such a restrictive

[273a] Ibid., pp. 54–55.
[274] Ibid., p. 55.
[275] Ibid.
[276] Ibid., pp. 55–56.
[277] Ibid., p. 56.

system, an independent foreign inspector, Dean concluded, "cannot find a natural place and would meet hostility, not cooperation." [278]

In sum, the roots of Soviet opposition to onsite verification, as Dean perceived it, lay in traditional antiforeignism and other widely acknowledged elements bred into the Russian historical past; but they lay also in a rational need for military secrecy and in attitudes inbred into the Soviet system, nourished by ideological indoctrination and controlled by a rigidly structured political apparatus, that assumed hostility from the outside and the necessity of preserving "a single loyalty and a single truth."

(b) *Possible mitigating U.S. response.*—Dean addressed the question what the United States could do to allay Soviet fears of security and to change Soviet attitudes from hostility to accepting a workable arms control agreement. He stated categorically: "Unfortunately, there is no dramatic, simple answer either for policy or for attitudes." [279]

Dean acknowledged that attempting to change national attitudes was a "tricky business" with no guarantee that a particular approach might not have an unexpected and undesired effect. But he proposed that "the most promising approach, obviously a long-range one," might be "a search for ways to make Soviet leaders more at ease with representatives of other cultures and societies and more aware of what those societies are in actuality rather than in Soviet mythology." Exchanges of key persons, expansion of trade relations, and the extension of scientific cooperation and of information could contribute to transforming Soviet attitudes. But Dean cautioned that past experiences revealed there was no certainty whether such exchanges "will result in greater sensitivity or greater hostility." Moreover, they offered no certain promise of "really reducing the dimensions of the problem." Dean continued:

In the final analysis, there is little that the United States can do directly to influence attitudes in the Soviet Union on such matters as loyalty to outworn dogma, world outlook, and the resort to secrecy, so long as Moscow's basic approach is what it is. As Soviet leaders do not cease to tell us, and as we have found out from experience, "peaceful coexistence" does not apply on the ideological front or to wars of "national liberation." [280]

Nor did Dean hold out much promise of influencing Soviet policy on disarmament and arms control, causing it to move closer to an accord. Efforts at increased friendliness did not insure a shift to increased harmony in policy. He pointed to the positive effects of the missile crisis, hardly intended initially to generate friendship, in creating the atmosphere for concluding the partial Nuclear Test Ban Treaty. Yet Dean acknowledged that by proposing national instruments of verification in August 1962, at Geneva, the United States had removed a major obstacle to Soviet agreement. In seeking to

---

[278] Ibid., p. 57. Dean pointed out, for example, the restriction of information from the Soviet side during disarmament negotiations. While this revealed limitations on basic research on disarmament in the Soviet Union, or at least nothing comparable to the objective effort being conducted in the United States and Great Britain, it also revealed the Soviet penchant for secrecy. "Our working papers and our statements in the verbatim records were available and did go to Moscow," Dean noted. "Unfortunately for the possibility of careful true dialog, there was no willingness on the part of the Soviet Government to share freely with the world the results of its research on the scientific basis for its policies." (p. 23.)
[279] Ibid., p. 57.
[280] Ibid., p. 58.

explain what really changed Soviet policy, as a way of underscoring the limitations on U.S. actions, Dean observed:

> On balance, it seems to me that, although we did take a number of steps at Geneva which made it possible to seize the opportunity to work out the test-ban agreement, these were only peripherally relevant to the hardheaded calculations that must have gone on in the Kremlin. The Soviet calculations must have dealt at least with the rift with China, reunification and possible nuclear arming of Germany, leadership of the world Communist movement, developments in the "third world," domestic pressures for a reallocation of resources, military-industrial demands, and the general strategy the Soviet Government wanted to adopt toward the United States.[281]

Hence, Dean's belief in the low probability of the United States influencing Soviet attitudes and policy.

But Dean had this positive word of advice to American negotiators who had to deal with the Russians:

> From all these considerations it follows that our best chance of influencing the direction of Soviet policy lies in being true to ourselves, forming our policy according to our own needs and those of the free world, explaining our goals patiently to Soviet representatives, and honestly refraining from actions which contradict the explanations. We must also take care to maintain the position of power without which the Soviet leaders would have no interest in talking about disarmament with us at all.[282]

(5) On the value of informal meetings

Possibilities of influencing individual Soviet negotiators and engaging in civilized diplomatic dialog were enhanced, judging from Dean's experience, by the practice of having informal meetings. Dean placed great value on such meetings because, in the informal setting, the Soviet negotiator was less inclined to engage in polemics and display the excesses in bad behavior that have characterized so many formal conferences. The results could be productive and satisfying.

In Geneva, Dean, as cochairman of the disarmament negotiations, initiated the practice of having informal meetings with his Soviet counterpart. That Dean preferred such informal gatherings over the rigidly structured formal meetings was evident from his appraisal of both:

> In formal sessions attended by large delegations and sometimes also by the press, he [the Soviet negotiator] presents what has come to be the traditional stern face of Soviet diplomacy, with polemics and denunciation his main tools and a scoring of propaganda points his main objective; but in private, off-the-record meetings—such as the daily ones of the cochairmen at Geneva—he can be cordial and much more reasonable. On such occasions it was possible for my Soviet opposite number and myself to talk dispassionately and intelligently about a number of controversial topics, to explore each other's meanings and interpretations, and to get down to detailed drafting. These private working sessions were a welcome relief from the time-consuming, repetitious, and by then rather banal, long-winded, and stereotyped exchanges at the official sessions. In short, experience suggests that the Soviet Government assigns different functions to the two different types of meetings where the audiences differ.
>
> We welcomed the tone of these informal discussions, although we also realized that pleasant conversations and real communication are not necessarily synonymous. We had no direct way of knowing what influence these sessions might have on Soviet policy and thinking, but proceeded on the assumption that any opportunity for the calm, uninterrupted explanation of our position on a con-

---

[281] Ibid., p. 58.
[282] Ibid., p. 58.

tinuing basis was better than none. We also wanted to hear the Soviet point of view in a setting free of polemics.[263]

(6) Staffing and negotiating teams

Soviet negotiators may have had their shortcomings in style and tactics, but clearly at least the upper echelons were talented and skillful diplomats. Dean wrote approvingly of the Soviet practice of maintaining a large number of the same negotiators at the disarmament talks over a period of years. Continuity and depth in expertise were thus maintained over the long haul.[284] This practice has continued into the 1970's, a fact that has distinguished the Soviet negotiating team from that of the American.

Such was not the case on the American side, at least when Dean entered the Kennedy administration in 1961. The personnel situation, he recalled, was not especially promising. The number of State Department officers working in the arms control field had steadily decreased, while the subject offered little allure for military officers who viewed it as hampering to their career advancement and a detriment to the building of a service reputation. "As a result," Dean noted critically, "we had neither adequate staff for research and policy formulation nor seasoned negotiating teams." [285] In the years ahead measures were taken to rectify many of the initial shortcomings on the U.S. side.

(7) Requirements for Western negotiators

Inherent in Dean's observations above on negotiating with the Russians were prescriptions for Western negotiators. Elsewhere he was most explicit, as in the following comprehensive statement of negotiating principles:

Patience, persistence, calm toughness of mind, a nature impervious to insults, a constantly creative and resourceful mind, and unwillingness to be discouraged are all essential characteristics for the Western negotiator. He should have calculated, well-thought-out, and creatively formulated positions; an alertness to negotiate the possible without sacrificing essentials; and then a determination to sit it out as long as necessary. But if science advances or other concrete conditions change, then we should be prepared to adapt our positions accordingly. It does not pay to present proposals designed solely or mainly for the purpose of putting the other side "on the spot," for such a design is readily discernible and therefore usually boomerangs.[286]

[263] Ibid., pp. 35–36. Dean gave the following assessment of the three Soviet cochairmen with whom he negotiated at Geneva. It is instructive not only for the insights it gives in conference procedures with Russian negotiators but also Dean's favorable appraisal of the quality of these top-ranking Soviet diplomats:

"The three Soviet cochairmen with whom I held such meetings were all well-trained, capable, hard-working professionals, devoted Communists, able to take for granted their principles and the general lines of Soviet policy without having to use up all the time talking about them. Of the three, the highly placed Ambassador Zorin was the only one who was willing to agree to changes—including drafting changes of some substance—without having to refer to Moscow ahead of time, and the only one who seemed willing to initiate changes himself. In this, he showed himself a very careful draftsman and analyst. Strict and formal in manner and seemingly not particularly affable by nature, he was always businesslike, courteous, and thoroughly informed, although he gave the impression, at least, that he regarded a matter of substance and the placing of a comma as equal in importance. Semyon K. Tsarapkin, who was not a member or candidate member of the Communist Party Central Committee, as were the others, was very courteous and pleasant, highly intelligent, but ultracautious. V. V. Kuznetsov, the Soviet First Deputy Foreign Minister, who had once studied at the Carnegie Institute of Technology and worked for the Ford Motor Company in Detroit, and was William C. Foster's opposite number at the Conference on Surprise Attack at Geneva in 1958, was outwardly the most affable and agreeable of the three, the one whose courteous personality and fluent English were most likely to appeal to Westerners on casual acquaintance. Actually he was a very tough-minded man in a working situation and, though always quite agreeable, was apparently not interested in initiating substantive changes or making any substantive effort to accommodate the Soviet point of view to that of others." (pp. 37–38)

[284] Ibid., pp. 8–9.
[285] Ibid., p. 8.
[286] Ibid., p. 47

Dean went on to stress the importance of honesty in negotiating with the Russians, quoting Nicolson's commandment on its positive value. "The devious Oriental diplomat, so elegantly described by Harold Nicolson in his book on diplomacy, has no place on an American delegation," Dean asserted.[287] He emphasized a principle that guided him in years of negotiations; namely, that American negotiators "are on firmer ground if we make clear to all that we advance only those honest proposals which we can ourselves live with and carry out wholeheartedly if they are adopted." [288]

Dean, a practicing lawyer, made no value judgments on what professions produced the best negotiators, but he had misgivings about the scientist as a negotiator. Dean observed that from his years of experience in discussing nuclear weapons and their control, the Western scientist—"with his emphasis on the universality of truth and the free exchange of scientific data"—often did not concern himself "with Soviet political objectives or the arts and wiles of Soviet or Communist negotiating tactics." In Dean's view, he sometimes did not "sufficiently grasp the fact that his Soviet counterpart has a directed role to play in a politically determined and far-reaching strategy." [289] Dean explained further:

> Eager to "get the job done," often unaware or scornful of the political implications of technical Soviet proposals, confident, on occasion, that the scientific mind can solve the political and constitutional problems which have long fazed nonscientists, the Western scientist sometimes accepts at face value Soviet proposals which he cannot really judge on his own and the political significance of which he does not fully grasp.[289a]

(8) Importance of continuing negotiations

Dean well understood Soviet purposes both political and strategic; he fully grasped the differing approaches to disarmament between East and West; but most of all he knew from firsthand experience both the value and necessity of continuing negotiations. Five years of test ban negotiations, he said, could be reduced to these simple terms. The Soviet Union had a double purpose; namely, to convince the world it wanted a test ban and to fend off all proposals for verification that went beyond purely national means. The West consistently sought to meet Soviet objections to the satisfaction of its security and within the limits that the progress of science made possible.[290]

Still, Dean did not despair of negotiating with the Russians, and despite difficulties and setbacks, he urged that the negotiating process always go forward.[291]

He perceived disarmament matters as political in content but technical in form. "They are," he said, "an integral part of the totality

[287] Ibid., p. 48.
[288] Ibid., p. 47.
[289] Ibid., p. 15.
[289a] Dean quoted Sir Eric Asby, the Master of Clare College. Cambridge. as observing that the Western scientist was united to other scientists not only by common beliefs in the branch of science in which both were specialists, "but by a willingness to accept on trust the common beliefs of other scientists in fields outside [his] own expert knowledge." (Ibid., p. 15.)
[290] Ibid., pp. 92–93.
[291] This attitude was firm policy in the Kennedy administration as shown by the President's persistence in pursuing the test ban negotiations despite the discouraging response he got from Khrushchev at the Vienna meeting in June 1961. In August, he asked Dean to return to Geneva for one more try, as he said, "with our hopes and prayers, and I believe with the hopes and prayers of all mankind." The President asked Dean, in Sorensen's words. "to outsit. outtalk and outlast the Russian negotiators (in what Dean had once privately called 'the bladder technique' of diplomacy) until he could find out for certain whether any glimmer of progress was possible." (Sorensen, op. cit., pp. 617–618.)

of U.S. relations with the Soviet Union and the Communist world," and should be handled accordingly by representatives trained in international affairs and "acutely aware" of the implications of Soviet and Chinese history, ideology, strategy, and tactics. "Work and negotiation on disarmament must go forward," he cautioned, "whether the political matters have been settled or not, but our proposals and positions must be arrived at and followed up within the total political and military context." [292]

Dean laid down the following principle with respect to the importance of a commitment to negotiations as a continuing process:

> The main points to be made are that negotiations with a state basically hostile to us in its ideology can serve a useful and necessary purpose, and that it is worthwhile to pursue such negotiations—intelligently, steadily, and unemotionally—without regard to the political climate of the day. In some ways, useful negotiations among nations are like good health in individuals: the result of a number of factors other than good cheer. [293]

2. IMPROVING POLITICAL CLIMATE AFTER THE MISSILE CRISIS

(a) Favorable trends and negative countertrends

In the aftermath of the missile crisis the climate of Soviet-American relations improved remarkably. If 1962 was the year of confrontation, then 1963 was the year of détente. [294] Soviet involvement in Cuba was radically reduced with the withdrawal of Soviet missiles, bombers, and troops. The Berlin issue, for so long a critical testing ground of intentions and challenge in the cold war, was temporarily shelved. Easing of Soviet pressure on Berlin and Cuba were coupled with public statements by Soviet leaders expressing their desire for resolving outstanding problems with the West.

An exchange of correspondence between Khrushchev and Kennedy in December 1962 created some hope that progress might be made on the test ban issue with respect to the problem of verification, but informal negotiations in New York and at subsequent meetings of the Eighteen Nation Disarmament Committee failed to reduce the gap of disagreement over the number of allowable inspections between the maximum Soviet figure of 2 or 3 per year to the absolute U.S. figure of 8 to 10, or at least 7. Thus as The United States in World Affairs for 1963 put it, "the prospect of a test ban appeared to have been indefinitely hung up on this seemingly trivial difference over numbers." [295]

(b) Kennedy's American University address, June 10, 1963: An overture to negotiate

Despite the deadlock on nuclear testing, the interplay of other forces in the spring of 1963 contributed to an improving climate in

[292] Dean, op. cit., p. 14.
[293] Ibid., p. 10. Throughout his book Ambassador Dean reiterated this point, as for example, "Working on disarmament, necessary as it is, can seem at times as fruitless as trying to punch holes in water. Weeks and months may go by with all proposals meeting not the slightest positive response from the Soviet side. But, given the modern condition in which major war would mean a world-wide disaster, it is vitally important to make the continuing effort to reach acceptable agreements even when political obstacles make continued negotiations discouraging. The mere process of talking, exploring, and questioning may in itself have certain positive results." (p. 6.)
[294] Watt, D. C. Survey of International Affairs, 1963. Isued under the auspices of the Royal Institute of International Affairs. London. Oxford University Press, 1977, p. 3.
[295] Stebbins, Richard P. The United States in World Affairs, 1963. Published for the Council on Foreign Relations. New York, Harper & Row, 1964, p. 68.

East-West relations. Khrushchev had established a firm position at home, thus strengthening his base for dealing with the United States on new directions. Sino-Soviet relations were deteriorating still further, giving a moderating impulse to Russia's relations with the United States. Concrete negotiations for improving relations were also underway. Soviet and American scientific representatives renewed and extended their agreements on certain cooperative efforts in the peaceful uses of atomic energy and the peaceful uses of outer space. The Soviets finally responded favorably to the proposal to establish the so-called "hotline" connecting Moscow and Washington. After a series of technical discussions, an actual agreement was signed on June 20 to establish such a communications line, thus reducing the danger of either side misreading the intentions of the other in a future crisis.[296]

Against this background of an improving relationship, President Kennedy gave a major address at American University on June 10 in which he revealed Khrushchev's acceptance of the earlier Kennedy-Macmillan proposal to resume a new series of negotiations on a comprehensive test ban. The President added to the solemnity of the occasion and underscored the determination of his purpose by disclosing that the United States would conduct no further nuclear tests in the atmosphere unless others did so.[297]

The American University address, entitled, "Toward a Strategy of Peace," was in brief a call to reexamine the premises of the Cold War and to take steps to establish Soviet-American relations on a more realistic and genuine basis of peaceful coexistence. In its "modesty, clarity and perception," observed Schlesinger, the speech "repudiated the self-righteous cold war rhetoric of a succession of Secretaries of State." [298] As the President said:

Today, should total war ever break out again—no matter how—our two countries would become the primary targets. It is an ironical but accurate fact that the two strongest powers are the two in the most danger of devastation. All we have built, all we have worked for, would be destroyed in the first 24 hours. And even in the cold war, which brings burdens and dangers to so many countries—including this Nation's closest allies—our two countries bear the heaviest burdens. For we are both devoting massive sums of money to weapons that could be better devoted to combating ignorance, poverty, and disease. We are both caught up in a vicious and dangerous cycle in which suspicion on one side breeds suspicion on the other and new weapons beget counterweapons.

In short, both the United States and its allies and the Soviet Union and its allies, have a mutually deep interest in a just and genuine peace and in halting the arms race. Agreements to this end are in the interests of the Soviet Union as well as ours, and even the most hostile nations can be relied upon to accept and keep those treaty obligations, and only those treaty obligations, which are in their own interest.

So let us not be blind to our differences, but let us also direct attention to our common interests and to the means by which those differences can be resolved. And if we cannot end now our differences, at least we can help make the world safe for diversity. For in the final analysis our most basic common link is that we all inhabit this planet. We all breathe the same air. We all cherish our children's future. And we are all mortal.[299]

[296] Ibid., pp. 70–71.
[297] For the text of the President's speech, see, Senate Foreign Relations Committee, Hearings on Nuclear Test Ban Treaty, 1963, pp. 1001–1005.
[298] Schlesinger, op. cit., p. 909.
[299] Senate Foreign Relations Committee, Hearings on Nuclear Test Ban Treaty, 1963, p. 1003.

(c) Khrushchev's response in East Berlin, July 2, 1963

Khrushchev, who later in conversation with Harriman was to remark that Kennedy's address at American University was "the best speech by any President since Roosevelt," [300] at first gave a mixed but predominantly favorable response. His definitive reply came in an address in East Berlin that was aimed at countering the favorable effects of the President's recent visit to West Berlin. While Khrushchev did not directly alter his position on onsite inspection, he gave a positive response to Kennedy's overture. (Kennedy's speech was given widespread circulation in the Soviet Union aided by the decision to end jamming of Western radio broadcasts.) Khrushchev expressed his willingness to conclude an agreement banning nuclear tests in the atmosphere, outer space, and underwater—which did not require inspection—while awaiting an agreement on the more difficult matter of underground tests. [301]

"The conclusion of such an agreement," Khrushchev told his audience, "undoubtedly, will also help to improve the international climate, ease tension and, hence, may facilitate mutually acceptable solutions of other international problems as well." [302]

But, Khrushchev added a possible "catch"; namely, that the test ban agreement be followed by the conclusion of a NATO-Warsaw Pact nonaggression treaty, though he did not make this agreement a condition to the conclusion of a test ban. [303]

3. NEGOTIATIONS AT MOSCOW, JULY 1963

(a) U.S. preparations for negotiations

(1) Harriman, the principal U.S. negotiator

To underscore the importance of the negotiations at Moscow and to increase the prospects for success, President Kennedy named Under Secretary of State Averell Harriman to head the U.S. delegation. With Prime Minister Macmillan's support, the President also arranged to have the U.S. delegation take the lead in the negotiations. Aware that Lord Hailsham, the chief British negotiator, wanted to act as mediator between the Russians and Americans, the President preferred to have Harriman in the driver's seat; as Sorensen noted, "The President had more confidence in Harriman, a shrewd, no-nonsense bargainer and a former Ambassador to Moscow." [304]

That Harriman had great prestige as a negotiator within both the White House (but not necessarily the State Department, according to Schlesinger) and the Soviet Government was evident from Schlesinger's appraisal. The White House aide spoke of Harriman's "almost unsurpassed Russian experience" and noted that "from the viewpoint not only of ability and qualification but of persuading the Russians we meant business, he was the ideal choice." "As soon as I heard that Harriman was going," said a Soviet Embassy staffman to Schlesinger, "I knew you were serious." In the following spring, Khrushchev was to say to William Benton, "Harriman is a responsible man." [305]

---

[300] Sorensen, op. cit., p. 733.
[301] United States in World Affairs, 1963, p. 71.
[302] Excerpt from Chairman Khrushchev's speech, July 2, 1963, in East Berlin, in, Senate Foreign Relations Committee, Hearings on Nuclear Test Ban Treaty, 1963, p. 1001.
[303] United States in World Affairs, pp. 71–72.
[304] Sorensen, op. cit., p. 734.
[305] Schlesinger, op. cit., p. 903.

(2) High quality of American support staff

Support staff for Harriman in Moscow and the President in Washington was of a very high quality. Sorensen referred to Harriman's negotiating aides as constituting a "first-rate team"; [306] Schlesinger described the staff as "small and brilliant." [307]

Harriman regarded himself as being "extremely fortunate" in the high quality of his supporting staff. Success in negotiations required a team with certain characteristics, he said. The members had to be "capable, well-informed men." Equally important, their individual judgments should carry weight in their department or agency in Washington. "And our team certainly did," he noted.

Carl Kaysen, Deputy Special Assistant to the President for National Security Affairs, was "highly regarded" by the President and McGeorge Bundy, the President's aide. John T. McNaughton was General Counsel of the Defense Department, and his judgment was "highly respected" by Secretary McNamara. Adrian W. Fisher, Deputy Director of the Arms Control and Disarmament Agency (ACDA) had worked "long and intimately" with William R. Foster, the Director. William Tyler, Assistant Secretary for Europe, "stood well" in the State Department. And Franklin A. Long of ACDA had the "confidence of the scientists in and out of government."

Summing up this aggregation of talent, expertise and influence, Harriman wrote:

> This well-balanced team was able to deal with the unforseen difficulties that arose in the negotiations. My colleagues had the imagination, initiative, and knowledge to propose compromises which protected our own interests and yet overcame the Soviet objections. Their recommendations carried weight and led to quick decisions in Washington.[308]

In Washington, the President made arrangements with six leading officials outside the White House staff (Rusk, Ball, McNamara, McCorie, Thompson, and Foster) to assist him. They read all the cables from Moscow on a hand-delivered "for-your-eyes-only" basis and conferred with the President each evening during the negotiations and discussed with him the details of the on-going conference.[309] Moreover, Dean, then out of government and in private practice, was kept advised of the proceedings in Moscow, and he gave his approval of the changes made in his draft of August 27, 1962.[310] A uniformed military adviser was not on Harriman's staff, and in the Senate hearings on the treaty Secretary Rusk was pressed hard to explain this shortcoming.[311]

(3) Kennedy in control of negotiations

In a series of meetings with the negotiating team before its departure, the President conveyed his ideas with respect to the importance of the Moscow meeting and the procedures to be followed in negotiations. He felt that this was the last chance to halt the diffusion of nuclear tests and prevent the posioning of the atmosphere. The delegation was to keep in daily contact with him, and it was directed to exercise extreme precaution to prevent premature "leaks" that might jeopard-

[306] Sorensen, op. cit., p. 734.
[307] Schlesinger, op. cit., p. 905.
[308] Harriman, America and Russia in a Changing World, pp. 91–92.
[309] Sorensen, op. cit., p. 734–735.
[310] Senate Foreign Relations Committee, Hearings on Nuclear Test Ban Treaty, 1963, p. 825.
[311] Ibid., pp. 42–43.

ize the negotiations. Hence the tight restrictions on daily cables from Moscow.[312]

From Washington. Kennedy maintained the tighest control over the negotiations in Moscow. As noted above, he conferred daily with his special team of advisers in Washington. All communications to the negotiating team in Moscow had to be cleared through him. Frequently, he changed and completely rewrote daily instructions prepared in the State Department. According to Sorensen, the President "confidently granted considerable leeway to the initiative of his negotiators, and they in turn demonstrated considerable skill in representing his interest. But he made certain that overall direction remained in his hands." [313]

(b) The negotiations from Harriman's perspective

(1) On the value of setting a target date for negotiations

Harriman approached the Moscow conference with a conviction that the negotiations could be concluded in 2 weeks. As he told the press upon arriving in Moscow, President Kennedy wanted a treaty, and he believed that Chairman Khrushchev also wanted one. "If we will meet each other with sincerity," he said, "we can reach an agreement rapidly and we ought to be out of here in two weeks." [314]

Though Harriman felt he was being overoptimistic (the press, he guessed, thought "I was crazy"), but he believed, nonetheless, that it was tactically wise to set a target date in order to put pressure on the Soviets. As it turned out, the negotiations, described by Harriman as "long and intensive", lasted exactly 2 weeks.[315]

(2) Opening meeting with Khrushchev

(a) Khrushchev on the necessity of nuclear arms control.—On July 15, Harriman, Hailsham and some advisers had their first meeting with Khrushchev in the Kremlin lasting over 3 hours. Getting right down to business, Khrushchev told the Western negotiators: "Since we have decided to have a test ban let us sign now and fill in the details later." Harriman agreed and handed him a blank sheet of paper remarking, "Fine, you sign first." [316]

"This was typical of my experience with Khrushchev," Harriman noted. "He was in dead earnest, but often had a light way of saying things—sometimes in order to get your reaction." Harriman interpreted the Chairman's jocular suggestion to mean that his mind was made up and that he was going to make every effort to conclude an agreement.[317]

Khrushchev launched into a serious commentary on the importance of nuclear arms control. People were awaiting results of the conference, he said, not only because of concern for the burden of military expenditures but for life itself. And he continued: "The accumulation of armaments has throughout history led to war and destruction of human beings, including those who accumulated the arms. * * * Today both the robbers and those robbed are in equal positions, since both will be annihilated in nuclear war." [318]

[312] Sorensen, op. cit., p. 734.
[313] Ibid., p. 735.
[314] Harriman, America and Russia in a Changing World, p. 92.
[315] Ibid.
[316] Ibid., p. 93.
[317] Ibid.
[318] Ibid., p. 93.

(*b*) *Khrushchev: No onsite inspection.*—To save time, Khrushchev told the Western negotiators outright that the Soviet Government would not agree to any onsite inspection—not even the two or three it had earlier proposed. It would, however, agree to the black boxes (that is, the locked and tamper-proof seismographic sensors to be situated in a number of places in each country to record seismic disturbances). Onsite inspection, he said, was "outmoded" and thus there was no point in arguing about it. If they would not agree to a comprehensive test ban without inspection, Khrushchev continued, he was ready to agree to a ban limited to three environments; namely, in the atmosphere, outer space, and under water, excluding underground.[319]

Hailsham and Harriman tried to persuade Khrushchev to permit their scientists to consult with Soviet scientists on ways to differentiate between underground nuclear explosions and natural earthquakes. But Khrushchev would have none of it; there was no use talking about on-site inspection, he said; it was a form of disguised espionage. When Harriman tried to assure Khrushchev that the West had no such objective in mind, Khrushchev replied: "You remind me of a cat saying that he would only eat mice and not the bacon lying in the room." Khrushchev would not trust such a cat, "as it would undoubtedly snatch the bacon when no one was in the room." Since only three environments were involved, Khrushchev saw no need for discussions among the scientists. Hailsham tried to argue with Khrushchev about inspection, but the Soviet Chairman brushed him aside, saying, "I know what cats are like." [320]

(*c*) *Tabling test ban drafts.*—After further intense discussions on linkage of the Soviet-proposed NATO-Warsaw Pact nonaggression Pact (opposed by West) and the idea of a nonproliferation treaty (opposed by the Soviets), Khrushchev presented a Soviet draft of a test ban for the three environments.[321]

Harriman and Hailsham tabled the Anglo-American draft, that is, the draft of August 27, 1962, for the partial test ban. It was agreed that they would confer with Foreign Minister Gromyko on the next day and attempt to reconcile their differences. In the event conflicting points could not be reconciled, Khrushchev suggested that they confer with him personally.

But this was not necessary since agreement was reached with Gromyko. In the course of the negotiations it was clear to Harriman that Gromyko was in close touch with Khrushchev. Whenever an impasse was reached with respect to the Soviet position, the next day Gromyko would be back with a compromise position. Neither side at the negotiating level had the authority to agree to compromises without approval from the top. According to Harriman, Washington gave prompt consideration to their recommendations—in fact owing to time differences replies were received overnight. Such speedy action, Harriman felt, was to no small extent due to the President's personal interest in obtaining constructive results from the negotiations.[322]

[319] Ibid., p. 93–94.
[320] Ibid., p. 94.
[321] Ibid., and Schlesinger, op. cit., p. 906.
[322] Harriman, America and Russia in a Changing World, pp. 94–95.

(3) Points at issue in the negotiations

(a) *U.S. draft as basis for negotiations.*—The opening talks with Chairman Khrushchev cleared away a number of issues. The hard bargaining began on the following day at Spiridonovka House with Gromyko representing the Soviet side and Harriman taking the lead for the Anglo-American. For a few days the Western negotiators attempted to engage the Soviets in negotiations on a comprehensive treaty, as had been the initial negotiating strategy discussed in the earlier planning stage. They also attempted to get the seismologists on both sides together, but the Soviets responded negatively saying that their people were out of town or otherwise engaged. Efforts to achieve a comprehensive treaty were dropped, and by mutual agreement discussions were based on the U.S. draft of a partial test ban of August 27, 1962. Even after accepting the U.S. draft, the Soviet negotiators pushed hard for the title of their draft, "Treaty Banning Nuclear Weapon Tests." With great reluctance they finally agreed to the more cumbersome but more accurate U.S. title, "Treaty Banning Nuclear Weapon Tests in the Atmosphere, in Outer Space, and Under Water." [323]

(b) *Foggy language in the preamble.*—Difficulties arose over several issues and one of lesser importance was the foggy language in the preamble that seemed to ban the use of nuclear weapons even in self-defense. Harriman knew this was contrary to U.S. policy and would create problems with the Congress. He demanded that the wording be changed; the Russians acceded to a revision. [324]

(c) *Conflict over the withdrawal clause.*—From the very beginning of the negotiations, the withdrawal clause created the greatest difficulty. The U.S. side proposed that a signatory could withdraw on reasonable notice if testing occurred in violation of the treaty and if it were judged to jeopardize its security. [325] Khrushchev had argued, and Gromyko echoed his points in the exchanges, that a nation always had the sovereign right to withdraw from a treaty which no longer served its interests, and to admit to the Harriman formulation in an explicit withdrawal clause would imply a diminution of this right in other treaties. [326]

Harriman insisted that the United States honored its treaty commitments and that the treaty being negotiated had to provide for withdrawal when specific events in the nuclear field threatened its security. Harriman had in mind the probability that Communist China would not sign the treaty and later might become a nuclear power requiring testing. Besides, Harriman knew that the Senate would not ratify the treaty without a reasonable withdrawal clause. Harriman told Gromyko bluntly that "this was a 'must' for us." [327]

Gromyko still refused to concede on this point and accused Harriman of demanding one-sided concessions. "I stood firm," Harriman recalled, "and for a while it looked as if we had reached an impasse." [328] Harriman flatly told Gromyko that without this clause there would be no treaty. [329] Hailsham was so upset by Harriman's

---

[323] Schlesinger, op. cit., p. 906 and Jacobson and Stein, op. cit., p. 455.
[324] Schlesinger, op. cit., pp. 907–908.
[325] Ibid., p. 95.
[326] Schlesinger, op. cit., p. 907.
[327] Harriman, America and Russia in a Changing World, p. 95.
[328] Ibid.
[329] Schlesinger, op. cit., p. 907.

stiff-necked intransigence that he informed Macmillan that his conduct was jeopardizing the negotiations and asked that he intercede
with the President.[330]

Finally, Gromyko came up with a reformulation of a substitute
withdrawal clause that included the phrase, "exercising its national
sovereignty * * *" and not limiting the reason for withdrawal. "We
accepted the phrase," Harriman wrote, "but insisted and later got
agreement on language satisfactory to us limiting the reasons for withdrawal to events in the field of the treaty." [331]

Apparently, agreement was reached after intercession by Khrushchev. Harriman had talked informally with the Chairman on Sunday, July 21, at the Soviet-American track meet. Khrushchev had
attended the meet unexpectedly with Hungarian Prime Minister Janos
Kadar, and asked that Harriman join him in the official box. Harriman
talked with Khrushchev about a number of things. At one point, during a lull in the competition, he asked Harriman, "How are you getting
along with Gromyko?" Harriman replied, "I get about as much out of
Gromyko as you can squeeze out of a stone." Khrushchev asked, "What
are your difficulties?" To which Harriman replied, "Our major difficulty is about withdrawal." Khrushchev quickly shied away, saying
"I don't want to hear about it—I made a diplomatic blunder—I never
should have brought the subject up!" But Harriman added, "I hope
anyway that you instruct Gromyko to be cooperative." [332]

(d) *Khrushchev's concession on proposal for a NATO-Warsaw Pact
nonaggression treaty*.—In Harriman's view, "perhaps the greatest
difficulty" in the negotiations was to persuade Khrushchev to abandon
his position on linking a NATO-Warsaw Pact nonaggression treaty
with the test ban agreement.[333]

Harriman had made clear to Khrushchev in their conversation opening the conference that the nonaggression pact would require extensive consultations with allies and hence might delay the test ban treaty
for a long time. Harriman also said that such a pact would not be possible without assurances that interference with access to West Berlin
would be considered aggression—a sensitive point that clearly irritated
Khrushchev. Harriman assured Khrushchev that the United States
would consult with its allies on the proposed pact.[334]

Apparently, in the formal negotiations the Soviet negotiators
pushed, though not too hard, for the nonaggression pact, but the Western delegations made it clear that they had no authority to negotiate
such a treaty. Eventually, the issue was disposed of by inserting a
statement in the conference communique stating that the matter was
discussed and that the three delegations agreed to inform their respective allies concerning the talks and to consult with them about continuing discussions, the purpose being to reach an agreement satisfactory to all.[335]

(e) *U.S. concession on testing for peaceful purposes*.—"Of course,
there were concessions we had to make," Harriman recalled. "We broke
some crockery in Washington," he noted, "by eliminating the exception
we had proposed permitting atmosphere explosions for 'Plowshare' ";

[330] Harriman, America and Russia in a Changing World. p. 95.
[331] Ibid., pp. 95–96.
[332] Ibid., p. 96.
[333] Ibid., p. 96.
[334] Schlesinger, op. cit., p. 906.
[335] Jacobson and Stein, op. cit., p. 455.

that is, the use of nuclear explosions for peaceful purposes, such as excavating canals and harbors.[336]

Before departing for Moscow, the U.S. negotiating team had conferred with authorities on the subject. At the time Dr. Jerome Wiesner, Scientific Adviser to the President and a professor at the Massachusetts Institute of Technology, had been "most helpful," Harriman noted, "in pointing out that the Plowshare projects were remote and should not stand in the way of a test ban treaty." [337]

Notwithstanding the concession, Harriman observed that a negotiating record had been established in Moscow that could open the way for future discussions with the Soviets on any modification to deal with a Plowshare type of project. Harriman had discussed the matter with Khrushchev and was assured that if nuclear excavation became practicable, there would be no difficulty in reaching an agreement. The Russians themselves were contemplating mountain-moving projects.[338]

(f) *Problem of treaty accession.*—A major problem arose in the negotiations over the manner of acceding to the treaty. The issue was how to permit accession by states not recognized by other states without conferring on them recognition—for example, the United States did not recognize East Germany; the Soviet Union did not recognize Spain. An outright U.S. proposal for an explicit statement that accession did not mean recognition by the other signatories was rejected by the Soviets who were then seeking improvement in East Germany's international status.[339]

The issue was finally resolved when Fisher and McNaughton, both lawyers, devised a unique and flexible procedure of multiple depositories. Each signatory was free to sign the treaty in all or in one of the three capitals, and the government signing in any one would be fully bound by the treaty.[340]

The Russians, satisfied that this would take care of East Germany, were still not fully satisfied because there were certain governments, such as the Chinese Nationalists on Taiwan, that they never admitted even existed. After working on the problem for hours, it was finally decided by oral agreement that if any one were asked about its view toward an unrecognized signatory, it was free to express its attitude.[341]

With this last remaining issue out of the way, the treaty was ready for initialing on the afternoon of July 25, 1963. After getting the President's approval on this last complex agreement on accession by telephone, arrangements were made with an anxious Gromyko to initial the treaty which took place that evening.[342]

(4) An encounter with the Soviet people

In the afternoon following the initialing of the treaty, Harriman conferred with Khrushchev in his office where they took up the matter of the accession to the treaty of independent-minded France and Communist China. Khrushchev, who was both sensitive and adamant on the issue with respect to China, was not inclined to discuss the problem

[336] Harriman, America and Russia in a Changing World, p. 96.
[337] Ibid., pp. 96–97.
[338] Ibid.
[339] Schlesinger, op. cit., p. 907.
[340] Harriman, America and Russia in a Changing World, p. 97.
[341] Ibid.
[342] Ibid., pp. 97–98.

of another socialist country with a capitalist. Subsequent probing by Harriman failed to get any positive response.[343]

In due course, Khrushchev invited Harriman to walk with him to the dinner he was giving for the Anglo-American negotiating team. They walked to the Great Palace from Khrushchev's office through the Kremlin, once a gloomy fortress in Stalin's day but under Khrushchev's, a public park. On the way, they ran into a large crowd in front of the Palace of Congresses. Khrushchev stopped, pinched a little girl on the cheek, patted another on the head, and said to the crowd, "this is Gospodin Garriman," meaning Mr. Harriman, in Russian. "He has just signed a test ban agreement," Khrushchev continued. "I am going to take him to dinner. Do you think he deserves his dinner?" The crowd responded with a cheer.[344]

On returning to the United States, Harriman went directly to Hyannis Port. The President told him very simply, "Well, this is a good job." [345]

4. THE MOSCOW TREATY: FINAL ACTION

Initialed on July 25, the partial nuclear test ban treaty—referred to as the Moscow Treaty—was formally signed again in Moscow on August 5, by Foreign Minister Gromyko, Secretary of State Rusk, and British Foreign Secretary Lord Home. The treaty was sent to the Senate for its advice and consent to ratification on August 8. Hearings were held before the Senate Foreign Relations Committee in August. The Senate Preparedness Investigating Subcommittee also held hearings throughout this period. On September 3, the Foreign Relations Committee filed its report recommending ratification by a vote of 16 to 1. On September 24, the Senate by a vote of 80 to 19 gave its advice and consent to ratification. On October 7, the President signed the Moscow Treaty completing U.S. ratification procedures. Soviet ratification procedures were concluded on September 25 with the unanimous vote of approval by the Presidium of the Supreme Soviet. The treaty formally entered into effect at 1 p.m. on October 11, 1963.[346]

Briefly, there were two principal obligations under the treaty. The signatories undertook: (1) To refrain from nuclear testing in the atmosphere, outer space, and underwater, and (2) to refrain from causing, encouraging, or participating in such tests by others. The treaty was open to "all states" for signature; any amendment would have to be approved by a majority of the parties; and any party could withdraw on 3 months' notice should it decide that extraordinary events, relating to the subject matter of the treaty, "jeopardized the supreme interests of its country." [347]

5. RESULTS AND SIGNIFICANCE OF THE NUCLEAR TEST BAN TREATY

(a) As a negotiating encounter

(1) Genuine bargaining

What seemed to make the test ban negotiations a distinctive encounter was the element of genuine bargaining. Khrushchev estab-

---

[343] Ibid. and Schlesinger, op. cit., p. 908.
[344] Harriman, America, and Russia in a Changing World, pp. 98–99.
[345] Schlesinger. op. cit., p. 909.
[346] Jacobson and Stein. op. cit., pp. 456–464.
[347] For the text of the treaty and other appropriate documents, see Senate Foreign Relations Committee, Hearings on Nuclear Test Ban Treaty, 1963, pp. 2–8.

lished the frame of reference for the negotiations when he insisted upon a partial and not comprehensive test ban, hence avoiding the sticky problem of agreement on outside verification. The Western negotiators conceded to this reality. And for the next 2 weeks, the scene at Spiridonovka House was one of give-and-take in an ongoing bargaining process, each side making concessions, divining new formulations of statements unacceptable to the other side, but remaining inflexibly obstinate on certain matters of principle and interests. Such negotiating behavior on both sides seemed to reflect a certain normality, nothing worthy of special emphasis ordinarily, but in the Soviet-American context, this was something remarkable.

(2) *Skillful and tough negotiators*

Revelations in the sources, though limited, did not alter the popular image of Gromyko as a tough-minded, cheerless but skillful negotiator for the Soviet side. Harriman's response to Khrushchev when asked how he was getting along with Gromyko that, "I get about as much out of Gromyko as you can squeeze out of a stone," was most revealing. It suggested a Gromyko whose reputation as a tough negotiator remained unsullied.[348]

Harriman was applauded from all sides. As a statesman, he had won the respect and admiration of Khrushchev. A member of the British delegation later called him, "the great man of the meeting." [349]

Harriman could be charming and understanding, but also stubborn and tough. At one point in the discussions, he demonstrated a rigidity in the face of an unacceptable Soviet demand that even provoked the chief British delegate, as the talks approached certain breakdown, to seek Macmillan's intercession with the President. (It proved unnecessary since the differences were resolved and the treaty was successfully negotiated.) But Harriman who had negotiated many times before with the Russians, as this study records, knew precisely what he was doing and said on his return. "I am always right when I know I am right. Sometimes I only guess I am right, and then I may be wrong. This time I knew I was right." [350]

Perhaps Schlesinger best summed up Harriman's strength as a negotiator when he noted that in these "long and difficult" discussions, Harriman, who dominated on the Western side, was "evidently at his best—correct, forceful, his restraint masking a capacity for toughness and even anger." [351]

(3) *Control of negotiations at the top*

One unique characteristic of this negotiating encounter was the element of total control at the top. On the Soviet side, Khrushchev not only set the terms and tone of the conference during his opening meeting with the Western negotiators prior to actual negotiations, but also, as Harriman suggested, he was close by for consultation with Gromyko and the resolution of any problems that might arise. Such tight controls over negotiators have been characteristic for the Soviet side.

But during the Moscow conference, Harriman was also kept under the tightest rein. As noted above, President Kennedy kept all communi-

[348] Harriman, America and Russia in a Changing World. p. 96.
[349] Schlesinger, op. cit., p. 907.
[350] Ibid., pp. 907–908.
[351] Ibid., p. 907.

cations from his Moscow negotiators within his circle of six advisers; he edited and even rewrote instructions to Harriman; and he kept in close touch with his negotiators by telephone on a daily basis. Schlesinger's account of the closing of the negotiations (p. 908) clearly indicated the tight procedures of control, instruction, and approval.[352]

On the American side, the staff was exceptional not only those who supported the negotiators in Moscow but also those assisting the President in Washington. Implied criticism was made, however, of the failure to have transcripts of the conference. Verbatim records of the negotiations were not made, only memoranda of conversations.[353]

(4) Importance of external factors on treaty's success

Finally, the convergence of many external factors contributed to the success of this negotiating encounter. After all, the test ban negotiations had been going on since 1958, but 5 years were to pass before conditions were right for its conclusion. What made this possible was a coalescence of national interests in which both sides had advantages to gain and benefits to accrue from the treaty. Skeptical Americans could get some assurance from the fact that it was a self-enforcing treaty in which violations, an issue of great concern on the American side given the Soviet treaty record, would be detectable. But the key factor was that the treaty served the common interest of both powers.[354]

The October missile crisis was a contributing factor to success. Its outcome had a cooling effect on Khrushchev's seemingly uncontrollable impulse to demonstrate by threat and "missile diplomacy" Soviet superiority and what he construed to be the shift in the balance of forces to the Soviet advantage. It had also compelled him as a consequence to accept the realistic choice of a more genuine peaceful coexistence. Americans, too, having looked into the abyss had now even greater incentive to reach an accommodation with Moscow, as President Kennedy's American University speech had attested.

The Chinese factor also entered into the calculus of forces and clarified for Khrushchev the necessity of accommodation with the

---

[352] In explaining Harriman's position at the negotiations during the Senate hearings, Secretary Rusk said: "I should say that the negotiating positions on a day-to-day basis that came up during the Moscow talks were almost wholly on matters of phraseology. They were political and legal in character and did not really relate to the underlying security issues. the security policy, which were incorporated in the original instructions." Rusk concurred in Senator Gore's statement that "Secretary Harriman went to Moscow, not to make policy, but to negotiate in an attempt to secure agreement in consequence of a policy that had previously, as I say. been determined in precise terms." (Senate Foreign Relations Committee, Hearings on Nuclear Test Ban Treaty, 1963, p. 65.)

[353] Ibid., p. 62.

[354] At the hearings Secretary Rusk explained the official American view: "I think, sir, that although the record of the Soviet Union in the postwar period in keeping major political agreements has not been good, and that record is fully familiar to these committees of the Senate, there nevertheless are agreements which are worth entering into if they rest upon the actual interests of the parties, if both sides feel that they are in their own respective interests, and if there are proper protections in the event the treaty is not kept. * * *

"I think this may come to be the case in this nuclear business. I think that both sides here have a genuine common interest in avoiding a nuclear war, and I think it just may be that this is striking home deeply enough so that even this limited first step would reflect that genuine common interest to both sides.

"And I would think if that were so there is advantage to both in trying to move it, if possible." (Senate Foreign Relations Committee, Hearings on Nuclear Test Ban Treaty, 1963, p. 36.)

Ambassador Dean observed with respect to Soviet trustworthiness in keeping the treaty given its record of violations: "Certainly, the drafters and proponents of the test-ban treaty were well aware of the Soviet record. We were, however, of the opinion then that the record also showed that where the Soviet Union had reached the calculation that a certain agreement was in its national interest, it kept it much as any other nation would in similar circumstances. We had reached the conclusion that the partial test-ban treaty was, in the estimation of the Soviet rulers of the time, in the Soviet national interest. For that reason we thought it likely that the Soviet Union would keep the treaty, especially if it were to be followed by a further détente." (Dean, op. cit., p. 101.)

West. The test ban negotiations were conducted against a background of rapidly deteriorating Sino-Soviet relations; they seemed to have reached a point of no return. A Sino-Soviet conference of party leaders meeting in Moscow during June and July broke up in an open, bitter dispute. The Chinese aired their catalog of ideological grievances against the Russians, adding to the list their condemnation of the test ban as something of a "last straw" in Soviet capitulation to "Western imperialism." The Soviets on their part denounced China, published a bill of indictment against its leaders, and charged, with reference to their attack on the test ban that they were prepared to sacrifice hundreds of millions of lives in a nuclear war.[355]

The experience of the test ban treaty thus underscored the principle stressed by so many American negotiators; namely the value of continuing the negotiating process, however unpromising the political environment, in the expectation that at some point (as in the case of the Austrian State Treaty) conditions both internal and external might create a coalescence of interests upon which an acceptable agreement could be based.[356]

(b) *Impact on Soviet-American relations and international relations*

The partial nuclear test ban treaty was as Secretary of State Rusk told the Senate Foreign Relations Committee a "limited first step" in the control of nuclear weapons. And limited it was. While over 100 governments signed the treaty, others such as France and China did not. Tests could still be conducted underground. The trend toward building nuclear arsenals continued.

"How great a turning point in world history the summer of 1963 may ultimately come to represent," observed The United States in World Affairs cautiously, "will be for later generations to assess." Contemporaries, it continued, could only declare that "it opened up the possibility of far-reaching changes in national attitudes and alinements and could conceivably mark the beginning of a genuine abatement in the danger of nuclear catastrophe." [357]

Perhaps President Kennedy best described the treaty's importance when he said in his message to the Senate that the treaty represented "the first concrete result of 18 years of effort by the United States to impose limits on the nuclear arms race." And the President added, "There is hope that it may lead to further measures to arrest and control the dangerous competition for increasingly destructive weapons." [358]

That the treaty provided some impetus to a détente in East-West relations and had a positive impact on Soviet-American relations and world affairs generally was evident by such measures as the "hot" line agreement, international agreement against orbiting nuclear weapons in outer space, the proposal for joint exploration of the moon, agreement on cooperation in space and agreement on legal principles governing space activities. In assessing the treaty and its impact, Sorensen expressed a cautious mixture of optimism and skepticism

[355] Survey of International Affairs, 1963, pp. 49–51.
[356] For a discussion and analysis of the internal Soviet aspects with respect to the test ban negotiations, see Jonsson, op. cit., pt. 4, pp. 133–208.
[357] United States in World Affairs, 1963, p. 25.
[358] Senate Foreign Relations Committee, Hearings on Nuclear Test Ban Treaty, 1963, p. 2.

when he wrote, "The breathing spell (brought on by the missile crisis) had become a pause, the pause was becoming a détente and no one could foresee what further changes lay ahead." [359]

In a retrospective glance it would seem not too much to say that the test ban treaty with all its limitations has achieved the primary purposes of its negotiators, and accordingly has had a fundamental impact on international relations; that it has furthered the principle of arms control upon which other discussions and agreements have been based; and that it has continued to inspire the hope, as expressed by President Kennedy, that it might lead to further measures of control over the dangerous competition for increasingly destructive nuclear weapons.

---

[359] Sorensen, op. cit., p. 745.

V. KHRUSHCHEV'S LEGACY OF PEACEFUL COEXISTENCE

That Khrushchev had revolutionized Soviet foreign policy and radicalized still further the Soviet style of negotiations during the decade he was in power, there seems to be little doubt. But to his credit in the test ban negotiations he added a variation of reason, civility, and diplomatic traditionalism to Soviet negotiating behavior.

In the large, Khrushchev had redirected the Soviet worldview from the inward continentalism of Stalin to the outward thrust of globalism into the Third World that has so characterized Soviet foreign policy since the mid-1950's. Khrushchev globalized Soviet foreign policy and expanded the diplomatic service, supported by an impressive intellectual infrastructure of institutes, to serve his outreaching policies. Under the misnomer of peaceful coexistence he had threatened and bullied the West in a series of grave challenges across the political frontier of the cold war until the showdown in the Cuban missile crisis compelled him to reassess his approach to the West on a more realistic appraisal of the balance of power and to reorder his priorities accordingly.

Thereafter, peaceful coexistence became a more meaningful definition of Soviet relations with the West, as shown by the conclusion of the partial nuclear test ban treaty and by the resort to the more traditional forms of diplomacy that became more characteristic of Soviet negotiating behavior. A much chastened Khrushchev, who in 1961 could threaten that only six H-bombs would be sufficient to annihilate the British Isles and nine others take care of France, could remark on a visit to Denmark in June 1964, "For centuries people have worked hard to plan and build such beautiful cities as Copenhagen, Moscow, Prague, Warsaw, Paris, London, and many others. Do people really think that anyone could be permitted to wipe all this out in a fraction of a minute?" [1] He could rebuke his Chinese adversaries in July 1963, saying that "only madmen" could hope to destroy capitalism by nuclear war; "a million workers would be destroyed for each capitalist. * * * There are people who see things differently. Let them. History will teach them." [2] And at the signing of the Soviet-East Germany Treaty of Friendship and Cooperation a year later he could depart from his prepared text for a moment and make the simple direct statement that "nuclear war is stupid, stupid, stupid. If you reach for the push-button you reach for suicide." [3]

---

[1] The Washington Post, June 17, 1964, p. A12, and July 12, 1961, p. A17; also, Facts on File, 1961, p. 278.
[2] Quoted in, Schlesinger, op. cit., p. 905.
[3] The New York Times, June 13, 1964, p. 1. Running through principal public statements by Khrushchev and others in the Soviet Government on the question of war and peace since the end of the missile crisis was the persistent theme on the irrationality of nuclear war. Such statements seemed to have been directed at both the Chinese as an act of self-justification for withdrawing the missiles and avoiding war, and at the United States as an indication of peaceful intent, at least for the time being.

Khrushchev had indeed come a long way toward staking a claim to statesmanship. In an introduction to the translation of "Khrushchev Remembers," Edward Crankshaw, a British scholar of Soviet affairs and biographer of Khrushchev, observed, "What was saddening was that he had in his makeup so many of the attributes of a great statesman." But "violence and lawlessness" was "his natural air"—particularly with respect to foreign policy. Yet in a final assessment Crankshaw wrote what has amounted to Khrushchev's legacy to the successor Brezhnev's regime, the legacy of peaceful coexistence:

It was one of Khrushchev's greatest achievements that with all his intermittent saber rattling, his threats, his deceptions, his displays of violence, he nevertheless broke out of the Stalinist mold and made it possible for the Western world to hope that a measure of coexistence more complete than he himself was yet ready to conceive might one day be realized.[4]

It was a peaceful coexistence, however, rooted solidly in the hard realities of military power and in an ideological commitment to the principle of "continuous struggle" against the West. For in the twilight of Khrushchev's reign the decisions were apparently made that were to bear fruit in the dramatic buildup of Soviet strategic missile forces in the late 1960's and early 1970's. As Soviet Deputy Foreign Minister Kuznetsov warned veteran U.S. diplomat John McCloy in his Connecticut home upon giving assurances that the missiles and bombers were removed from Cuba, "You Americans will never be able to do this to us again." [5]

---

[4] Crankshaw's introduction to Khrushchev Remembers, p. xix.

[5] Bohlen, op. cit., pp. 495–496. For a variation of the quote, see, Newhouse, John, Cold Dawn : The Story of SALT. New York, Holt, Rinehart and Winston, 1973, p. 68. The annotation in this source reads, "Never will we be caught like this again."

CHAPTER IX—SOLIDIFYING PEACEFUL COEXISTENCE WITH BREZHNEV, 1965–79

Part I—Building on the Khrushchev Years: International Context, Diplomatic Establishment, and Characteristics

You Americans will never be able to do this to us again.
> —*Kuznetsov to John J. McCloy on the removal of Soviet offensive weapons from Cuba, October 1962.*

Taken as a whole * * * the Soviet diplomatic machine is a powerful and formidable instrument.
> —*Sir William Hayter, 1970.*

I. CHANGING CONTEXT OF SOVIET DIPLOMACY

A. Structural Changes in International Relations

1. GLOBALIZING NATIONALISM; REGENERATION OF THE NATION-STATE

Nationalism, the driving force behind the decline of Western colonialism and its old imperial order in the postwar era, seemed to reach a new and higher stage in the 1960's and 1970's. This new phase of traditional nationalism became truly globalized; it impacted particularly upon the newly independent nations of the Third World and upon those in the Communist world that sought, in what has been termed "polycentrism", greater autonomy from the center. In the West, it was manifested by a political reaction to American predominance within the European alliance system.

This neonationalism constituted a countertrend to the internationalism once fostered by the League of Nations in an earlier generation and more recently by the United Nations, and to the universalism of world communism. It has imposed itself upon the emerging new international system with increasingly greater force. The upshot of this development is that the principle of the nation-state, called by William P. Bundy, editor of Foreign Affairs and formerly a State Department official, "the main engine of organized human action" in the 20th Century, has been reaffirmed and its reality as a power factor in world politics revitalized.[1]

The effects of this rising spirit of nationalism with its revitalization of the nation-state concept have been many and varied. It has meant the proliferation of new states, many often not much beyond the most primitive stage of development, having competing values, interests, and goals among themselves and at variance with those of the great powers. New problems and issues were thus placed on the international agenda. World communism has been fractured into

---

[1] Bundy. William P. Elements of Power. Foreign Affairs. v. 56, October 1977 : 1.

multiple parts, primarily by the disruptive force of nationalism, reducing its claims of universalism to something of an illusion. Regionalism in international politics has become a unique organizational form in this new distribution of power as nations perceived the value of what Bundy called "group power." [2]

Thus, the structure of power relations has in the last decade become far more complicated; it has become multipolar with distinct centers of power. In contrast to the relatively simple bipolar world of the cold war days, individual nations, as Bundy observed, "are far less under the sway of others, more able to throw their own weight around, and groups of nations, regional or economic, stand together as new centers of power." [3] The overall effect of this changing international structure has been to magnify the tasks of diplomacy and to increase the burdens of negotiations.

2. INTERDEPENDENCE, SCIENCE AND TECHNOLOGY, AND THE TRANSFORMATION OF DIPLOMACY

Paradoxically, another powerful force in the changing structure of international relations that has magnified the role of diplomacy and negotiations is interdependence. The essence of this concept is collective action; it is a plea for a new internationalism that arises from a growing awareness of mankind sharing a common destiny; it rejects strictly nationalist solutions for the practical, realistic reason that there is no other way. Its message is that of John Donne's, "No man is an island."

Problems of the international economy, the environment, food distribution, limited materials, access to ocean resources, and the management of outer space have become increasingly perceived as common problems requiring common solutions in the national interests of all. The emergence of the resource-rich Third World and the impact of its political activism, using its newly acquired economic leverage against the industrial nations of the world as an instrument of power (for example, oil), has quickened this awareness of interdependence. Though the Soviet Union has viewed interdependence from its own distinctive conflictual world outlook, it has, nonetheless, been sensitive to its own interests, notably in its efforts to reach agreement with the United States on control of the strategic arms race. [4]

Another aspect of the changing structure of international affairs in the age of interdependence is the emergence of science and technology as vital components of diplomacy. [5] Rapid scientific and technological

[2] Ibid., p. 18.
[3] Ibid., p. 1. For the Soviet view of multipolarity, see. Wessell. Nils H. Soviet Views of Multipolarity and the Emerging Balance of Power. Orbis, vol. 22, Winter, 1979 : 785–813.
[4] For a commentary on the Soviet and Western views of interdependence, see, U.S. Congress. House. Committee on International Relations. The Soviet Union and the Third World : A Watershed in Great Power Policy? Prepared by Joseph G. Whelan. Senior Specialist in International Affairs, and William B. Ingle, Research Assistant, of the Congressional Research Service's Senior Specia'ists Division, The Library of Congress. 95th Congress, 1st session. Washington, U.S. Government Printing Office, 1977. p. 167–171.
[5] For a comprehensive examination of this problem, see U.S. Congress. House. Committee on International Relations. Science, Technology, and American Diplomacy: An extended Study of the Interactions of Science and Technology with United States Foreign Policy. Prepared by the Congressional Research Service of the Library of Congress under the direction of Dr. Franklin P. Huddle, Senior Specialist in Science and Technology, with Mr. Warren R. Johnston as associate project director. Washington, U.S. Government Printing Office, 1977, 3 vols.

change, often at an exponential rate, has had a profound impact upon the world scene, complicating still further the tasks of diplomacy and magnifying the problems of management and control over the international environment. Advances in weapons technology, to name only one, have far outstripped the skill of the negotiators in their attempts to control modern armaments, to bring some rationality and stability to the strategic balance, and thus hopefully to increase the chances for peace.

The effects of these recent changes in the structure of international relations, besides adding to the complexity and burden of diplomacy's tasks, have been far reaching. The number of principals in the negotiating process have increased, and a decided trend toward multilateral diplomacy in the United Nations has evolved.[6] Emphasis has been progressively placed on the role of functional diplomacy. The scale and variety of issues to be negotiated have also increased along with the element of uncertainty. For as Professor Gilbert R. Winham, a specialist on international negotiations, has observed with respect to the impact of science and technology, "in many areas we are simply unaware of the implications of modern technology on human life."[7]

The negotiating process has, moreover, become more bureaucratized as the need for technical expertise (as, for example, specialists on weapons systems in the SALT negotiations or space scientists in negotiations on outer space) has resulted in enlarged staffs and as the issues have become more complex and the negotiating process more politicized blurring the boundaries between domestic and foreign affairs. Accordingly, a new value has been placed on the art of management.[8] As Winham noted, "In past eras it was fashionable to describe negotiation as art, and art it continues to be, but it is now more akin to the art of management as practiced in large bureaucracies than to the art of guile and concealment as practiced by Cardinal Mazarin."[9]

All of this suggests, finally, that the world is entering a new era where the demands upon negotiations have increased, perhaps even exponentially. Winham summed up this recent transformation of modern diplomacy in these words:

Today, governments need more control over forces in the international environment than they can manage independently; conflictual acts like military hostilities, imperial relationships, or alliance building cannot establish the control they once might have. On the other hand, there is not sufficient consensus in world politics to turn over the most pressing of the world's problems to international organizations. We are entering an era in which international negotiation appears to be the predominant mode of relations between states, and conditions in the international system are likely to maintain this mode for some time to come.[10]

3. DÉTENTE; SOVIET INVOLVEMENT IN THE THIRD WORLD; AMERICAN WITHDRAWAL FROM GLOBALISM

The third structural change in international relations has a combination of three elements: the formalization of détente as the guiding principle in Soviet-American relations; Soviet involvement in the

[6] Winham, Gilbert R. Negotiation as a Management Process. World Politics. v. 30, October 1977 : 90.
[7] Ibid., p. 92.
[8] Ibid., pp. 90–91.
[9] Ibid., p. 89.
[10] Ibid., p. 111.

Third World; and the uncertainty of an American response to the requirements of a changing geopolitical world.

True, détente had been initiated by Khrushchev, but Brezhnev built upon that base, expanding its scope and formalizing the concept as a settled policy in the so-called peace program adopted at the 24th Congress of the CPSU in April 1971. As the principal actors in an evolving multipolar world, the Soviet Union and the United States alone have had the military capability of destroying civilization in an all-out nuclear war. By 1970, a broad strategic parity had been recognized in the Soviet-American military balance; in 1972, this balance was formalized in the SALT I agreements. Such a truce between the nuclear superpowers had a visibly restraining effect upon their rivalry and had similarly a calming effect on the larger international scene. Direct, confrontational Soviet challenges in the Khrushchev manner, as in the cases of Berlin and the Cuban missile crisis, were avoided in an apparent effort to maintain stability in the relationship.

But the Soviet propensity for amassing military power, a permanent feature of the system, and its determination to project that power globally, particularly into the vulnerable Third World (as in the cases of Angola and the Horn of Africa), revealed to Americans, who have been disinclined to see the built-in limitations and restraints in Soviet imperial thrusts, the ambiguous nature of détente and the unchanging purposes of Soviet foreign policy.[11] The rivalry may have been visibly calmed in some quarters but in others the Soviet struggle for expanding its political influence in the world, never really forsworn as an ideological imperative, has continued apace. Uncertainty has marked the American response to this changing geopolitical reality.

An equally important element in this changing structure of international relations has been the deglobalization of American foreign policy. In the post-Vietnam era U.S. policy was adjusted to the Nation's restrictive (some would say neoisolationist) impulses of the time. The Nixon doctrine was a response to the call for withdrawal from excessive globalism. This mood—the so-called "Vietnam syndrome", meaning, "never again" will there be military involvement abroad—persisted through the Ford administration; it was clearly manifested in congressional resistance to an administration policy of intervention in Angola. It has continued into the successor Carter

---

[11] Professor Robert Legvold of Tufts University expanded on the factor of restraints on Soviet foreign activities in the Third World. With respect to their limitations in the Horn of Africa, he wrote: "* * * the capacity to influence, even to control, events guarantees neither control after the event nor control over the larger patterns of change. By and large the Soviet Union is, as we are, the beneficiary or victim of the processes of change, not their source. Nothing in the evolution of Soviet power is altering that." (The Nature of Soviet Power. Foreign Affairs, vol. 56, October 1977:60.) For a commentary on factors working for and against the Soviet Union in the Third World, see, House International Relations Committee Study, The Soviet Union and the Third World. pp. 144–155.

Taking a more critical view of Soviet policy, Dr. Helmut Sonnenfeldt, adviser to Secretary of State Kissinger and presently a professor at Johns Hopkins University's School of Advanced International Studies, wrote: "But neither negotiations nor the military programs of the outside world seem likely to divert the Soviet Union from its determination to the other military superpower in the world. The impulse to amass military power seems pervasive among the Soviet ruling elite regardless of generation. Some political dynamics seem to favor it, and the Soviet economic system seems unalterably geared to it." (Russia, America, and Détente. Foreign Affairs, vol. 56, January 1978:284.)

For other observations by Sonnenfeldt on the Soviet "imperial" thrust into the Third World, see, House International Relations Committee Study, The Soviet Union and the Third World, p. 139.

administration, as evidenced by American reluctance to counter directly Soviet involvement in the Horn of Africa. Still responding to the impulses of antiglobalism, the administration attempted to adjust to this new political reality, tailoring its commitments abroad, restricting severely the extent of its overseas commitments, and seeking an accommodation with the Soviets to stabilize still further the strategic balance in a SALT II agreement.

Yet a countertrend to withdrawal, inaction, and uncertainty appears to be in the making. It has been generated by the recent setback in Iran which has meant the temporary loss of this oil rich dependency to the West; the growing threat to American and West European vital interests in Saudi Arabian oil with the stepping up of the Soviet-supported war in Yemen; the perceived loss of American prestige in other parts of the world; and the apparent diminution of its world position. The administration is now criticized for weakness and indecision, both of which appear to have been partly born out of a response to the prevailing national mood of withdrawal. Pressures for a forceful response to these new geopolitical challenges appear to be building. The United States seems to be approaching a time of choice. Some observers perceive an emerging American public opinion that has put the "Vietnam syndrome" behind them and is now prepared to support a forward policy of global engagement in the national interest.[12]

---

[12] Joseph J. Sisco, career diplomat, a top-ranking Middle East specialist in the Nixon and Ford administrations, and now president of American University, recently observed that "the perception of the United States in the world today is that we have become paralyzed as a result of the Vietnam syndrome." But, he has found that the public mood has been changing more rapidly than policymakers have realized. "I am absolutely convinced," he remarked in a Time magazine symposium on the Middle East crisis, "that the Vietnam syndrome is not broadly shared in the United States, that the American people went through a psychological trauma at the gas station in 1974, and they are damned tired of appearing to be pushed around. I believe the American people have largely put Vietnam behind them: they know what we are talking about when we speak of the Persian Gulf and the Arabian Peninsula being a vital interest." (Searching for the Right Response: A Panel of Experts Tries to Redefine U.S. Policy for the Crescent of Crisis. Time, vol. 113, Mar. 12, 1979 : 29.)

Highly qualified news analysts have recently expressed the same theme that the so-called "Vietnam syndrome" was behind the American people and that they were now prepared to take a larger role in international politics, particularly in the Middle East, the vital source of American and West European oil supplies. Howard K. Smith expressed this view in an ABC–TV News commentary on Mar. 9, 1979, and George F. Wills made the same point on the public affairs discussion panel, "Agronsky and Company" on the following evening over CBS–TV. The rationale behind this expressed view was the growing awareness of the involvement of American vital interests. A key to the changing attitude was evident in the fact that a majority of the panelists on the Agronsky program, all opinion leaders, supported the President's action of dispatching the carrier Constellation and other naval forces to the Persian Gulf along with other administration actions to strengthen North Yemen in its war against the Soviet and Cuban backed South Yemen invaders.

According to a press report of a White House meeting of the Special Coordinating Committee dealing with contingency planning in the emerging Yemen-Saudia Arabian problem, the tone and substance of comments of the meeting, attended by President Carter and Vice President Mondale, suggest that President Carter was determined to prevent South Yemen from scoring a military victory over North Yemen, a neighbor and close ally of Saudi Arabia. "There is a feeling that Carter is drawing the line to stop the Russians and Cubans in North Yemen," noted a congressional source apprised of the White House meeting on the crisis. "He seems to think the progress from Angola through Ethiopia has to be stopped here." (Hoagland, Jim and Dan Morgan. United States Speeds Arms for North Yemen. The Washington Post, Mar. 7, 1979, pp. A1 and A16.)

In an article exploring what was perceived to be a shift in U.S. foreign policy in light of its action in Yemen, Richard Burt of the New York Times noted that White House aides described this response as "only part of a broad, new security policy toward the wider region." One White House aide said that "our actions in Yemen and the Middle East process are intimately linked. Both form part of a wider policy of salvaging American influence in the area after Iran." Burt also noted the significance of the fact that the U.S. action in Yemen had "met with general approval at home." (Burt, Richard. Intervention in Yemen Signals Foreign Policy Shift. The New York Times, Mar. 18, 1979, p. E3.)

B. Major Trends in Soviet-American Relations

1. Movement Toward Détente

Within this changing structure of international affairs Soviet-American relations have moved along a steady course leading to a détente. For, despite many fluctuations in the relationship, with periodic heating and cooling, a retrospective glance of 14 years suggests an improving rather than a deteriorating relationship, but a relationship, nonetheless, filled with many disturbing elements.

By and large Soviet foreign policy in the Brezhnev era has been marked by a decided conservatism, reflecting very much the principal characteristic of this colorless, phlegmatic leadership. The excesses of Khrushchev's adventurism, his bombastic claims of Soviet superiority, and his humiliation of many world leaders were tactics abjured for an approach that has been best summed up by the oft-used Soviet term, "businesslike." Caution rather than confrontation has been the hallmark of this gerontocracy's approach to foreign policy; and ideology has reinforced a pragmatic realism to achieve priority foreign policy goals.

Thus, Moscow, the main supplier and supporter of the Vietnamese Communists, never ceased to bitterly attack the United States for its role in the Vietnam war. But in the weeks prior to President Richard M. Nixon's visit to Moscow in May 1972 to conclude the SALT I agreements, it tolerated with only a low key public protest the U.S. bombing of Haiphong Harbor that had damaged four Soviet ships. SALT I, a top Soviet priority, took precedence over loyalty to its fraternal ally.

U.S. involvement in Vietnam appeared to be kept on a separate track and accordingly had no spoiling effect on the larger Soviet relationship with the United States. Such common goals as the Non-Proliferation Treaty, for example, could be pursued without detriment; SALT I negotiations could go forward. Confrontation with the United States was also avoided in the second Arab-Israeli war of 1967 by the timely resort to the communications "hot" line in order to clarify Soviet-American intentions and dampen the crisis. Reasonable confidence in the relationship was restored at the subsequent meeting in Glassboro between Prime Minister Alexei Kosygin and President Lyndon B. Johnson. Even the Soviet bloc invasion of Czechoslovakia in August 1968, spurred by deep feelings of Soviet insecurity, was contained within bounds, and relations with the West were resumed along an orderly and constructive path after a decent interval of time. And finally the resolution of the Berlin problem, along with the recognition of the boundaries between East and West Europe set forth in the Soviet-West German treaty, brought about a stability in Europe hitherto not enjoyed in the turbulent postwar days of Stalin and later Khrushchev.

At least in its relations with the United States and Western Europe the Brezhnev regime appeared to seek stability and ultimately a détente.

2. A COUNTERTREND: SOVIET MILITARY BUILDUP AND EXPANSION INTO THE THIRD WORLD

But Soviet behavior, viewed within a larger strategic and geopolitical frame of reference, could hardly be termed benign. Clearly, the leadership meant it when Kuznetsov told McCloy as the Soviet missiles were being withdrawn from Cuba in the fall of 1962, "You Americans will never be able to do this to us again." [13]

Decisions were made in the aftermath of the Cuban crisis that bore fruit in the form of the alarming Soviet strategic buildup late in the 1960's and 1970's. Almost by stealth the Soviet leadership, without the bombast of Khrushchev but with the seriousness of a great power determined to amass superior military power, improved its strategic position by undertaking an impressive buildup in strategic nuclear weaponry, by constructing a navy having the initial capabilites of a global outreach, and finally by reinforcing their European position with a formidable military buildup of conventional and nuclear forces. So remarkable has the Soviet military buildup become that a rough strategic parity was achieved with the United States in the 1970's.

Equally remarkable (and disturbing to American policymakers) was the global projection of Soviet power. Expanding and refining Khrushchev's policy of moving from continentalism to globalism, Brezhnev rationalized Soviet activity in the Third World, placing economic development on a much sounder and more efficient basis than had been the case under his predecessor.

Programs of military assistance were also linked to Soviet policy in the Third World. Combined with the expansion and improvements in the Soviet Navy, Brezhnev's Third World policy enabled the Russians to further their global purposes. [14]

This Third World policy has been directed toward targets of opportunity rather than being focused within some specific design and motivated by deep-rooted ideological commitments and by the dynamics of power; it has had successes and failures. A turning point in Brezhnev's approach to the Third World came with Soviet military involvement in the Angolan crisis. This successful adventure, undertaken in defiance of Secretary of State Henry Kissinger's warning to Brezhnev that such intervention contradicated the rubrics of détente and that détente could not stand another Angola, was followed by another success with Soviet military intervention in the Horn of Africa. What was remarkable about both of these enterprises was that they proved Soviet capabilities for long-range military intervention in the Third World.

Thus, the combination of the Soviet military buildup and the projection of Soviet power into the Third World suggests the precarious nature of détente in the Soviet-American relationship. It was against this background and along these ambiguous lines of policy and action that this relationship has evolved.

---

[13] Bohlen. op. cit.. pp. 495–496.
[14] House International Relations Committee, The Soviet Union and the Third World, pp. 30–39 and 83–141.

II. THE SOVIET DIPLOMATIC ESTABLISHMENT

A. SOVIET SECRECY, SECURITY, AND THE PROBLEM OF LIMITED INFORMATION

The extensive but rationalized globalization of Soviet foreign policy in the Brezhnev era, especially in the Third World, and the parallel development of détente with the West, notably with the United States, undoubtedly placed a heavy burden on the Soviet diplomatic establishment. Unfortunately, studies on the diplomatic establishment, such as those done in the past by Uldricks, Aspaturian, Slusser, Triska, and Finley from the early period through the Khrushchev era and cited in this work, have yet to be done in any systematic way for the Brezhnev era.

The Soviet penchant for excessive concern for secrecy and security has made such studies difficult for scholars. Data is not easy to come by. Secrecy, for example, still surrounds the work of the Soviet institutions for training diplomats, such as, the International Relations Institute and the Higher Diplomatic School. Little has, apparently, changed since Kaznacheev had reported in the early 1960's that the internal affairs and activities of the I.R.I. "are treated as a state secret," and even more so with respect to the Higher Diplomatic School.[1] And though the Russians have been allowed to visit the American Foreign Service Institute, repeated requests for return visits to their training institutions for diplomats have been turned down.[2]

Illustrative of the secrecy currently surrounding such matters in Soviet diplomacy and the limitations on information about the Soviet system was the published report on the appointment of Deputy Foreign Minister Kuznetsov as First Vice President, or more exactly, First Deputy Chairman of the Presidium of the U.S.S.R. Supreme Soviet. The first sign that this veteran diplomat and party stalwart would be appointed to that post came with his appointment on October 3 as an alternate or candidate member of the Politburo. Diplomats in Moscow were surprised. A later remark by one Western diplomatic official underscored the problem of assessing what goes on within the Soviet system when he said: "If we can deduce 1 percent of what's going on inside the Politburo, we're doing well."[3]

Accordingly, much of what can be said about the Soviet diplomatic establishment in the Brezhnev era must of necessity be inferred from certain institutional developments and certain realities in foreign policy; from impressions by persons who have had contact with Soviet diplomats and their institutions or by scholars, such as Meissner, who have studied them from afar; and from brief commentaries by Soviet diplomats and scholars themselves. At best, the evidence, as Dr.

---

[1] Clark, Eric. Corps Diplomatique. London, Allen Lane, 1973, p. 224.
[2] Ibid.
[3] Whitney, Craig R. 76-Year-Old Kuznetsov Named Deputy to Brezhnev, The New York Times, Oct. 8, 1977, p. 3.

Thomas W. Wolfe, Senior Staff Member of the Rand Corp., said of policy leverage of the Soviet military in foreign and defense policy decisionmaking, can only be "patchy." [4]

And as Dr. Vladimir Petrov, Professor of International Relations at George Washington's Sino-Soviet Institute, wrote in a comprehensive and penetrating article on the formation of Soviet foreign policy:

> The process of foreign policy formation in the Soviet Union has been one of the most difficult subjects to study. No books or articles have been written about it in Russia; for the lack of reliable basic information, Western studies have also been wanting. Intelligence analysts have probably pieced together enough to reconstruct a plausible picture, but intelligence analysts rarely write for publication. [5]

B. EXTENSION OF THE KHRUSHCHEV YEARS

Few if any institutional changes have probably occurred in the Brezhnev years to alter fundamentally the character and course of the Soviet diplomatic establishment. The political and organizational essentials have remained untouched, and with some exceptions, as in the elevation of Gromyko to the Politburo, developments in the diplomatic establishment have by and large probably been an extension of those initiated under Khrushchev.

Hence, political control from the center has remained a constant feature. And while the Foreign Ministry may have gained somewhat in influence and prestige by Gromyko's promotion to one of the highest party posts, still the control at the center has remained firm and unaltered. Conceivably, the tasks of the establishment have magnified with the expansion of Soviet overseas, activity, especially in the Third World.[6] By the same token, the work of the supporting institutes has also undoubtedly grown, and in some instances has become more sophisticated with expanding Soviet foreign policy commitments and activities abroad.

Espionage has continued to be an essential feature within the Soviet diplomatic establishment. As Clark has observed, "At a Soviet mission, up to 70 percent of the 'diplomats' may in fact be spies * * *," for the Communist countries "espionage is an integral part of 'total diplomacy'." [7]

Though still interested in military information, much of the Soviet espionage effort has been directed at obtaining scientific and technological secrets. A measure of this activity was evident in 1971 when the British expelled 90 Russian officials and named 15 others not allowed

---

[4] U.S. Congress. Committee on International Relations. Subcommittee on Europe and the Middle East. The Soviet Union: Internal Dynamics of Foreign Policy, Present and Future. Hearings. 95th Congress, 1st session, Washington, D.C., U.S. Government Printing Office, 1978, p. 119.

[5] Petrov, Vladimir. Formation of Soviet Foreign Policy. Orbis, vol. 27. Fall 1973; 819. In explaining the reasons for Soviet secretiveness with respect to the mechanics of their foreign policy operations, Petrov said that there "are many, the most obvious being that there is nothing to be gained from revealing something that does not have to be revealed." Another principal reason, he noted, "is that in contravention of the Soviet Constitution, it is the Central Committee of the Communist Party of the Soviet Union (CC CPSU), and not the Council of Ministers, which determines the general direction of foreign affairs, and the CC's Politburo which devises specific policies and the ways and means of implementing them." The point here is that the Council of Ministers is the formal institution for the conduct of foreign policy but the reality of power and authority rests within the Politburo and its Central Committee. Secrecy, rooted in a profound concern for security, is the first principle in the operations of the latter.

[6] See, House International Relations Study, The Soviet Union and the Third World, pp. 30–39, 83–141.

[7] Clark, op. cit., pp. 184 and 192.

to return on charges of clandestine activity, the majority of which appeared to be in the areas of industrial, scientific, and weapons technology.[8]

A most recent case of such scientific and technological espionage involved the sale of highly classified secret information on sophisticated electronic equipment for reconnaissance satellites by two Americans to Soviet agents in Mexico City. The compromised information concerned secret U.S. satellite systems used for monitoring Soviet missile testing and verifying compliance with the SALT agreements. One of the Americans was employed at TRW Systems, an aerospace concern in California that worked under contract for the Central Intelligence Agency. Both were convicted of espionage and are now serving prison terms. A random selection of press reports in 1978 indicates that espionage remains an essential part of the activity of Soviet missions abroad.[9]

C. The Soviet Foreign Policy Infrastructure

1. brezhnev's control at the top

Soviet foreign policy is formulated and controlled at the upper echelons of the CPSU. In explaining the foundations of Soviet diplomacy, Zorin reiterated this first principle in Soviet political life when he wrote: "The leadership of the Communist Party determines and has always determined the proper direction and content and the best methods of Soviet diplomacy."[10] Thus, in Meissner's words, the Politburo, the highest body in the party, is "the actual respository of power" in Soviet foreign policy.[11] And the members of this body share not only power but also a common world outlook, the primary ingredient of which is a vital concern for the security of the Soviet state."[12]

As General Secretary, Brezhnev exercises the most influence upon basic foreign policy decisions within the Politburo. His predominance has been illustrated in recent years by his signing of a series of important treaties, notably the SALT I agreements, and by his assumption of the position of President after Podgorny's removal in 1977.

---

[8] Ibid., p. 188.

[9] Lindsey, Robert. Soviet Spies Data on Satellites Intended for Monitoring Arms Pact. The New York Times, Apr. 29, 1979, pp. 1 and 13. In May 1978, 2 Soviet employees of the United Nations were arrested on espionage charges; a third claimed diplomatic immunity. (The New York Times, May 21, 1978, p. 1.). In early 1978, the Canadian Government ordered 11 Soviet diplomats and other personnel home on espionage charges. (The New York Times, June 15, 1978, p. A3.) According to FBI Director William H. Webster, about 1,900 Soviet-bloc spies operated in the United States, and Chicago was among their key targets. The specific areas of interest, he said, were microelectronics, lasers, computers, nuclear energy, and aerospace technology. (The Washington Post, Oct. 20, 1978, p. A4.) In August, the International Labor Organization announced that it had fired a Soviet official who was identified as a KGB agent. (The Washington Post, Aug. 5, 1978, p. A10.)

[10] Zorin, Valerian A. Role of the Ministry of Foreign Affairs of tne U.S.S.R. In, Senate, Committee on Government Operations, International Negotiations, The Soviet Approach to Negotiation, p. 86.

[11] Meissner, op. cit., p. 50.

[12] Wolfe categorizes those elements that the Soviet policymaking elite share in common. The first, for example, is the belief of both the political leaders and military professionals that "the Soviet Union must look out for its own security, along with a reluctance to trust others to take care of it for them." The second is the belief that "the Soviet Union cannot feel secure until her neighbors are no longer capable of posing any real military or political threats to her." The common thread running through these shared attitudes, and there are eight, is concern for Soviet security. (House International Relations Committee, Hearings, The Soviet Union: Internal Dynamics of Foreign Policy, Present and Future, pp. 119–124.)

The Politburo has its own departments handling foreign affairs (and also foreign Communist Party affairs) that are more powerful than the Foreign Ministry; thus this institution and the General Secretary can be essentially independent from the Foreign Ministry and self-sustaining as in the case of concluding the final negotiations for SALT I.[13] In some instances draft agreements on arms limitations and draft decisions on new military programs are prepared for the Politburo by officials in the party's Secretariat with the participation of Brezhnev's assistants.[14]

That the military have an important input in the decisionmaking process on matters relating to foreign policy and defense is described below in the case of SALT. Indicative of this continuing important role was the presence of Marshal Nikolai V. Ogarkov, Chief of the Soviet General Staff and former participant in the SALT negotiations, at Brezhnev's side during the Vladivostok summit with President Gerald Ford and at Gromyko's side during his talks with Secretary of State Cyrus R. Vance on SALT II in April 1978.[15]

It has also been presumed that Y. V. Andropov, head of the KGB, member of the Politburo, and close associate of Brezhnev's who has a background in foreign policy and has military rank, has some influence on the formulation of foreign and security policy.[16] A principal component of Andropov's power are the vast resources of information at his command as intelligence chief.

But the essential point here is that Brezhnev by virtue of his transcending position of authority and power within the Politburo holds the commanding heights of decisionmaking and control in Soviet foreign policy.

2. THE FOREIGN MINISTRY UNDER BREZHNEV

(a) Organization of the Foreign Ministry [17]

The Soviet Foreign Ministry, the formal institution through which Brezhnev exercises his power over Soviet foreign policy, draws its organizational strength from two sources: its close connection with competent party organs, and the specialized knowledge that is concentrated in it. Over the years the activities of the Ministry have grown commensurately with the expanding global interests of the Soviet Union. The breadth of these activities is evident from the fact that in 1977 the Soviet Union maintained diplomatic relations with 113 states. The Soviets, as in the case of the Americans, usually have, moreover, the largest staffs in their missions abroad. Such characteristics of Soviet diplomatic missions as the KGB presence, the increased role of economists and specialists in science and technology along with military advisers, as described above as being relevant to the Khru-

---

[13] Petrov, op. cit., pp. 821–830.
[14] Glagolev, op. cit., p. 771.
[15] The New York Times, Apr. 21, 1978, p. A3. For Wolfe's view on the military input into the decisionmaking process, see, House International Relations Committee, Hearings. The Soviet Union: Internal Dynamics of Foreign Policy, Present and Future, pp. 116–119.
[16] Ibid. p. 26.
[17] Hayter gave this description of the physical setting of the Soviet Foreign Ministry: "The Ministry of Foreign Affairs is housed in an ornate skyscraper, like a vast yellow wedding cake. Its vulgarly carpeted, brightly lit corridors, those at any rate penetrable by foreigners, are curiously empty, silent and lifeless; no one hurries by with a bundle of files, no open door lets out the rattle of typewriters, no visitors gesticulate and complain." (Diplomacy of Great Powers, p. 23.)

shchev era, are durable and unchanging. Given the expansion of Soviet activities abroad under Brezhnev, particularly into the Third World, there would seem to be little doubt that the role of such specialists has been magnified considerably.[18]

Organizationally, the Foreign Ministry is structured into five major departments: the Foreign Minister, the First Deputy Foreign Minister, the Deputy Foreign Ministers, members of the Collegium and ministerial advisers; the General Secretariat; the operative diplomatic departments; the operative nondiplomatic departments; and the administrative and economic departments.[19] The operative diplomatic departments are divided into territorial departments (e.g., the First European Department) and functional departments (e.g., International Organization). The administrative and economic departments include: the General Administrative Department; the Monetary and Financial Department; and Administrative Service for the Diplomatic Corps.[20]

A unique feature of the Soviet Foreign Ministry is the Collegium. Comprised of senior diplomats, deputy directors, and a panel of advisers, this advisory group which confers daily is responsible for short-term foreign policy decisions falling within the Ministry's purview and for handling administrative problems.[21] Though the Collegium has some influence, its impact, according to Clark, "is probably not great." [22]

(b) *The Ministry's leadership*

Gromyko heads the Foreign Ministry. As such, he functions as the principal executive officer in the realm of foreign policy, conducting negotiations, receiving foreign diplomatic representatives at official talks, signing agreements, and, in general, supervising the work of Soviet diplomatic representatives and consuls abroad. He is assisted by nine deputy foreign ministers.[23]

Gromyko's appointment to the Politburo during the plenary session of the Central Committee in April 1973 has given him direct access to the Soviet decision-making process at the highest level. It is assumed that he also belongs to the Politburo's Foreign Policy Commission.[24] The appointment of Kuznetsov, a veteran diplomat, First Deputy Foreign Minister, and party member, as candidate member of the Politburo and first vice president in 1977 has no doubt added to the prestige of the Foreign Ministry and to its influence within the Soviet political system.

(c) *World outlook of the Foreign Ministry*

The Foreign Ministry shares with others in the Soviet elite a common world outlook, as Wolfe would say, on the necessity for insuring

---

[18] For a discussion of overseas missions, see Clark, op. cit., pp. 63 and 224–233. For the organization of the Foreign Ministry, see, Meissner, Foreign Ministry and Foreign Service of the U.S.S.R., pp. 49 and 62. See p. 64 for a discussion of missions abroad.
[19] Ibid., p. 55.
[20] Ibid., p. 59.
[21] Ibid., p. 56. There are now 9 or 10 members, including, A. P. Bondarenko, head of the Third European Department, and O. N. Khlestov, head of the Treaty Law Department who is also concerned with MBFR negotiations in Vienna.
[22] Clark, op. cit., p. 223.
[23] Meissner, Foreign Ministry and Foreign Service of U.S.S.R., pp. 55–56.
[24] Ibid., p. 50.

the security of the Soviet state; it also shares a common ideological heritage. As Zorin explained:

The theoretical foundation of Soviet diplomatic activity is a Marxist-Leninist understanding of the international situation, of the laws of social development, of the laws of class struggle, and of the correlation of internal and and international social forces, which takes account of the specific national and historical features of each country, group of countries, and continents. It is impossible to develop diplomatic activity correctly without a Marxist-Leninist evaluation of the international situation, without an understanding of the laws of social development and concrete knowledge of the situation in a particular country, and without taking into account the historical and national characteristics of a country. And it must be added that a Marxist-Leninist evaluation of international events and the formulation of a line of diplomatic struggle on this basis is a powerful element in Soviet diplomacy. As a rule, the success of the diplomatic activity of the Soviet Union is determined above all by a correct Marxist-Leninist analysis of the situation and of the correlation of forces, and on the contrary, underestimation and imperfect knowledge of the objective laws and of all the changes which are taking place in a country or in several interrelated countries are fraught with miscalculations and mistakes in diplomacy.[25]

(d) On dealing with the Foreign Ministry

Dealing with the Foreign Ministry, however, can often be for Westerners a thankless and useless task. Doubtless not much has changed since the early 1960's, given the unchanging nature of bureaucracies—and the Soviet Union, according to Hayter, has the "world's greatest bureaucracy"—when Hayter wrote from his own experiences as British Ambassador to the U.S.S.R.:

Dealing with the Soviet Ministry of Foreign Affairs may be compared to dealing with an old-fashioned penny-in-the-slot machine. You put in the penny—your question—and in the end, probably, you will get something out; perhaps not what you wanted, an acid drop when you hoped for chocolate, but something; and you can sometimes expedite the process by shaking the machine. It is, however, useless to *talk* to it.[26]

Not much had changed during Jacob D. Beam's tenure as U.S. Ambassador in the early 1970's. Formal contacts with the Foreign Ministry, he recalled, "had settled back into a rather unproductive routine." The Soviet habit of asking in advance about the subject matter being proposed for discussion "did not encourage the idea of dropping in for an informal exchange of views." Whenever Foreign Ministry officials were in a bad mood, they would open the talk with an argument or a complaint. Once in exasperation Beam told one Soviet contact that, "I had gained a clearer and more rational understanding of Soviet foreign policy in my talks with Polish Foreign Minister Rapacki than I had been able to do in Moscow."[27] "It is completely futile to talk to them," Beam recalled, in discussing his experience with the Soviet Foreign Ministry; "it's a waste of time."[28]

Nonetheless, an expanding network of contacts made it possible to gather some information on Soviet foreign policy. It was potentially possible to make lateral contacts with other foreign embassies in Moscow—"tempting", Beam said—but this was a risky business, as his predecessor Ambassador Thompson had cautioned. Crossing wires with the Foreign Ministry could invite provocations.[29]

[25] Zorin, op. cit., p. 85.
[26] Hayter, Diplomacy of the Great Powers. p. 24.
[27] Beam, Jacob D. Multiple Exposure: An American Ambassador's Unique Perspective on East-West Issues. New York, W. W. Norton, 1978, p. 228.
[28] Interview with Jacob D. Beam, May 23, 1979.
[29] Beam, op. cit., p. 229.

Contacts were legitimately enlarged, however, with the efforts by party elements to assert a greater interest in foreign relations. This was also the case in the development of what Beam called a kind of subministry with the expansion of periodic international meetings of scientists and politicians, such as the Pugwash and Dartmouth Conferences. On the American side, participants were private citizens who consulted interested branches of the U.S. Government, and in Beam's case kept him "fully informed" when meetings were held in Moscow. On the Soviet side, all representatives were in effect state officials and thus, as Beam noted, spoke with "an authoritative voice." [30]

Thus, despite the frustrations in dealing with the Foreign Ministry, there were other ways and means of expanding contacts and gathering information—in brief, to fulfill some important aspects of an ambassador's mission.

3. INTELLECTUAL RESOURCES FOR FOREIGN POLICY

(a) The training of Soviet diplomats

The Education and Training Department of the Foreign Ministry is responsible for training candidates for the Soviet Foreign Service and for the further advanced training of diplomats. It also supervises the Higher Diplomatic School, the Moscow State Institute for International Relations and advanced courses in language.[31]

The primary responsibility for training Soviet diplomats rests with the Institute for International Relations. The Institute also trains foreign trade specialists and foreign correspondents. The Higher Diplomatic School is designed chiefly for the advanced training of diplomats and undertakes the task of upgrading their professionalism and regional specialization through intensive study. It is also responsible for training the upper-echelon staff of the Foreign Service. The Soviets do not focus on producing an all-around diplomat—a generalist, in American parlance. Rather they stress specialization in specific languages, cultural regions and groups of countries from the very beginning of study.

The program at the Institute for International Relations is rigorous. The course of study begins upon completion of secondary school and lasts 5 years. Students are weeded out in an elimination process supervised by the party. The Institute is divided into three faculties: World history, international law, and world economics. Ideological training and knowledge of military affairs supplement courses in diplomatic history, international law and practical work in diplomacy. In a 6-year course of study, candidates take what amounts to a 6-week internship in the central office and then spend another 6 months as attachés at a mission abroad. The course requires a thesis to satisfy the requirements for a certificate of completion. It is also possible for a candidate to receive an academic degree or doctorate on the basis of an independent research project.

Students who have completed courses of study at other institutes such as the First Moscow State Pedagogical Institute for Foreign Languages and the Institute for World Economy and International Relations (IMEMO) are also admitted to the Foreign Service.[32]

---

[30] Ibid., p. 230.
[31] Meissner, Foreign Ministry and Foreign Service of U.S.S.R., p. 58.
[32] Ibid., pp. 62–63.

(b) Zorin's standards for a Soviet diplomat

Standards in the Soviet Foreign Service are no less rigorous than those in the training of candidates, if Zorin's criteria are to be taken at face value. The party has always considered it essential, he wrote in his work, "The Bases of Diplomatic Service," that the Foreign Ministry be staffed with "politically mature people, answerable for each one of their steps." The "slightest mistake," he warned, "has an effect on very important phases" of Soviet foreign affairs. The utterance of an "awkward expression" at some reception or other, for example, could come to light in the foreign press and "sometimes cause serious harm" to the prestige and foreign policy of the Soviet Union.[33]

"Efficiency, accuracy and precision in work and an attention to detail," Zorin continued, should characterize the work of the Foreign Ministry. For in diplomacy "there are no minor details, since often out of a petty fact there grow great events." Sometimes "an insignificant fact" can suggest the beginning of a change in a nation's policy, and this possibility obliged the Ministry staff "to be very attentive even to the small facts of international life, the policy of states, and to the behavior of envoys and other diplomatic workers of these states," particularly those among the major powers. Thus, "each word of a diplomat must be well considered. Any thoughtless step might play a negative role."

In contacts with foreigners, Zorin urged firmness and self-control, and in exercising "rational initiative in diplomatic work" he cautioned that it was essential "that this initiative be coordinated with centralization in the work of the diplomatic cadres as a whole"—in a word, initiative could not conflict with the principle of "a firm centralization" of authority in the Ministry.[34]

Clearly, Zorin expected a great deal from the Soviet diplomat—maturity, perfection, wisdom, efficiency, accuracy, and above all, institutional and party loyalty.

(c) The "fourth generation" of Soviet diplomats

The end product of this rigorous academic training and insistence upon high professional standards is what Meissner called "the fourth generation of Soviet diplomats"—a talented, well-trained elite, knowledgeable about the outside world, and representative of an intelligentsia that is more amenable to easing international tensions and to internal reforms than others in the Soviet bureaucracy and intelligentsia.[35]

According to Meissner, the Soviet diplomatic corps represented "an integrating element" within the ruling bureaucratic elite, because of their political and sociological position. They were "well represented" in the party's Central Committee, he emphasized. But, it was "precisely" this fourth generation, Meissner continued, in a retrospective look at the development of the Soviet Foreign Service since the Bolshevik Revolution, that was "more worldly than most party and state functionaries as a result of its professional training and its privileged position with respect to contacts with foreign influences." Moreover, this generation has recruited its members to a great extent from the

[33] Zorin, op. cit., p. 87.
[34] Ibid., pp. 87–88.
[35] Meissner, Foreign Ministry and Foreign Service of U.S.S.R., p. 63.

scientific and cultural intelligentsia, which Meissner contended, "is much more open to internal reforms and a relaxation of tensions with the outside world than the country's bureaucracy and the economic and technical intelligentsia." [36]

In brief, what Meissner was suggesting is that this new generation of Soviet diplomats is distinctive and unique, something exceptional within the Soviet system.

(d) Role of the institutes

(1) Khrushchev's legacy to his successors

Perhaps the most significant long-term legacy that Khrushchev had left to his successors was the broadening intellectualization of the Soviet foreign policy establishment. Brezhnev built upon this legacy, improving the quality and raising the standards particularly of Soviet area studies in the institutes. "Raising Soviet foreign policy research 'to the world standards'," wrote Dr. Oded Eran, an American trained Israeli specialist in Soviet affairs, "has indeed been the guiding line of the policies of the Brezhnev regime." [37] This was a "genuine goal" in the Brezhnev era, but as in the past motivation for improvement has been strictly utilitarian: scholarship in the service of the party and the state government. As Eran concluded: "There is no reason to doubt the sincerity of the Brezhnev regime in resuming the drive for improvement of the standards of social sciences in general, and area-studies in particular, but this should not be confused with an attempt at depoliticization." [38]

In what is a remarkable capsulization of what took place in this post-Stalin period, Petrov wrote:

The departure from the simplistic Stalinist *Weltanschauung* and the enormous complexities of Soviet external relations have placed a premium on competence and professionalism in the party and governmental bodies concerned with the day-by-day conduct of foreign affairs. Greater knowledge of the world combined with a somewhat reduced requirement for total conformity (and conformity itself much less definable than in the past) and the emergence on the scene of a generation only vaguely remembering the Stalinist era, helped to create an atmosphere in which clashes of opinion in closed discussions became fully legitimate. While positions of power remained in the hands of the old-timers, the upward mobility even in the party *apparat* gave a degree of influence to the less dogmatic—although still fiercely patriotic—new breed of experts involved in policy formulation.[39]

(2) Importance of the institutes

The foreign policy institutes, notably the USA Institute, the Institute for World Economy and International Relations and those dealing with specialized areas of the Third World, as depositories of this "new breed of experts", have continued to play an important and expanding role in the Soviet foreign policy establishment. As Petrov wrote with respect to the influx of knowledge and comprehension of the outside world into this establishment, "perhaps more significant in the long run" than the traditional intelligence gathering and diplo-

[36] Ibid.
[37] Eran, op. cit., p. 271.
[38] Ibid.
[39] Petrov, op. cit., p. 841.

matic reporting "is the role played by research institutes of the Academy of Sciences, a role vastly increased in the last decade." [40]

The importance of the institutes derives largely from the fact that neither the Foreign Ministry nor the departments of the Central Committee dealing with foreign affairs conduct systematic foreign area studies. Only limited research is done at the level of the country desks and regional offices. Thus, as Petrov explained,

every time a new problem arises or an old one demands additional information and insight, officials frantically search for specialists in their midst or look for outside expertise. This expertise, as a rule, is now provided by scholars working in specialized research institutes under the jurisdiction of the Section of Social Sciences of the Academy of Sciences, which is headed by the Academy's vice president, Academician Fedoseyev, a de facto CC CPSU representative. [41]

(3) The USA Institute

Illustrative of the contributions that the institutes make to foreign policy is the work of the USA Institute. Americanologists can be found in the Institute of General History, the Institute for World Economy and International Relations, in the Academy of Social Sciences, and in the General Staff organizations. But the USA Institute is the "principal" institute in American studies, and as such keeps track of work done in the others. The institute enjoys a privileged position among its counterparts. Its importance can be measured by the fact that it operates on a substantial budget; maintains control over the leading monthly or quarterly journal in the field; usually has more hard currency for the purchase of books and periodicals, computers, or Xeroxing machines from abroad; has primary claim to quotas for foreign travel; and has more generous funds to subsidize traveling scholars. Such "principal" institutes also play a major role in organizing international conferences in Moscow and in determining the composition of Soviet delegations going abroad to conferences. [42]

(4) On originating studies

At all times the institutes are at the disposal of the Central Committee *apparat*, notwithstanding their formally approved research plans. "Emergency studies" can be launched on request from the Secretary of the Central Committee or from the International Department and Department of Liaison with the Workers' and Communist Parties, known as "The Department," of the Central Committee. Some institutes are also commissioned to prepare periodic situation reports on chronic crises, as in the Middle East. On occasion an official in the Foreign or Defense Ministry on close terms with an institute director or deputy director may request an emergency study. Finally, institutes may themselves originate studies on their own, and, as Petrov explained,

then circulate them among the officials concerned in an attempt to advance a new approach to a critical problem or influence policy. Since institute directors are men of stature and influence, with access to policymakers, such studies represent an important input in the cumbersome decisionmaking process. [43]

---

[40] Ibid.
[41] Ibid. Petrov went on to describe the structural organization of the Social Science Section, noting particularly those that deal with foreign affairs.
[42] Ibid., pp. 842–843.
[43] Ibid., p. 843.

D. EVALUATIONS OF THE SOVIET DIPLOMATIC ESTABLISHMENT

1. FROM THE SOVIET PERSPECTIVE

(a) *High quality of Soviet diplomats*

The Soviets perceive the quality of their diplomatic establishment as being very high. In what is more a paean to their virtues and perfection as representatives of the Soviet Union than a realistic appraisal of their ability as fallible human beings, L. Fyodorov wrote in his work, "The Diplomat and the Consul," that Soviet diplomats are "politically aware, spiritually pure and morally steadfast." According to Fyodorov, the basic characteristics of Soviet diplomats are,

adherence to high principles, party activity, internationalism and humanity. The ethical basis of their personal life is revealed by their devotion to communism, a love of their homeland and other Socialist states, dutiful work for the sake of society, human relationships and a mutual respect for all peoples, honour and justice, moral purity, simplicity and humbleness in personal and public life, intolerance of national and rational enmity, and an uncompromising attitude toward the enemies of communism, matters of world peace, and fraternal solidarity with the workers of all countries and all races.[44]

Other Soviet observers, a former official, members of the diplomatic corps, and institute scholars—"patchy" evidence at best—have given more sober assessments, but, nonetheless, the overall self-perception is favorable. In a "letter" to Brezhnev, Boris Rabbot, a former high-ranking Soviet official, spoke of Foreign Minister Gromyko as being one of "the only politically literate persons left in your immediate entourage." [45] Ambassador Dobrynin, who was educated as an engineer at the Aviation Institute in Moscow and came from the humble background of a father who was a plumber and a mother who, he said, had more of the peasant virtues, recently compared unfavorably the diplomats of his generation (he is 60 years old) with those of the 1970's. "You look around and of Soviet diplomats my age, 70 percent are engineers," he said. "The new ones, ah, they are all trained in the foreign service, they're very polished. I don't think I'm polished even now." [46]

Members of the younger generation of Soviet diplomats and scholars, like Dobrynin, perceive the present diplomatic establishment as being far more sophisticated than the older one. Soviet diplomats are regarded as being intensely trained in languages and area studies, knowledgeable in the diplomatic craft, in international relations as an academic as well as a practical discipline, and in the country and cultural region where they will be assigned. Some strictly political appointees are made, much in the American manner, but such appointees are not seen as lowering the generally high level of the service.

Thus, in the Soviet perception they are producing a new breed of diplomatists with which the Americans will have to negotiate, a view subscribed to by some East European diplomats. This new generation now approaches the conference table with far greater confidence and

---

[44] Quoted in, Clark, op. cit., p. 225.
[45] Rabbot, Boris. A letter to Brezhnev. The New York Times magazine, Nov. 6, 1977: 59.
[46] Dewitt, Karen. Anatoly Dobrynin, the Genial America-Watcher. The Washington Star, Oct. 30, 1978, p. C-2.

skill, and, equally important, without the feeling of inferiority that had been characteristic of the past. This attitude (in which Garthoff would concur) rests on the achievement of superpower status by the Soviet Union, its essential strategic equivalence with the United States, and an awareness of a high level of professionalism in their diplomatic service.

Similarly, the institutes that specialize in foreign policy rank high in the Soviet perception of their diplomatic establishment. The importance of these institutes is threefold: They act as a gathering center for publications and ideas from abroad (data, for example, on American public opinion towards SALT II); they make an important contribution to the foreign policy process as providers of fresh ideas, new syntheses, background studies, analyses of critical problems, and new information; in brief, they create the framework for policy formulation; they have, in addition, a direct connection with the party apparatus and access to political decisionmakers by virtue of their research products and the dual role of their leadership as members of both the academic and political establishment. Admittedly, institute researchers approach their analyses from a unique ideological perspective; but as problem-solvers, seeking solutions to concrete problems, they perceive themselves as searching for realistic solutions (as Petrov also suggested on debate among "insiders"), a practice that they contend brings their analyses closer to objectivity.[47] Ideology may be minimized for the sake of a more pragmatic approach. In this respect ideology per se must be carefully distinguished from propaganda. Accordingly, research analysts may analyze a problem from a certain ideological perspective with its values, but in their view they avoid propaganda as a polluting and spoiling element.

(b) Prestige of the Soviet diplomatic service

One key to Soviet perceptions of their diplomatic establishment is the prestige with which it is held in Soviet society. Briefly, the Soviet diplomat ranks high in the "pecking order" of Soviet society, though perhaps at a somewhat lesser order of magnitude than an academician such as a professor. It is a position of prestige; it is so regarded in the eyes of the intelligentsia and the Soviet people: and the young people aspire to it. Prospects for travel, exposure to other cultures, extensive professional training—all provide incentives for the young to enter the corps.

Service in the United States, a most prestigious post, apparently brings even greater esteem to the diplomat.[48] Dobrynin's longevity as Ambassador to the United States (since March 1962) and his role in conducting high-level negotiations with five administrations has inspired persistent rumors that he would be moving on to a high-ranking post within the Foreign Ministry, possibly even as Gromyko's successor. Doubts have been recently expressed, however, that this might not come about because a "duumvirate" of two first Deputy Ministers has been established in the hierarchy of nine Deputy Foreign Ministers. Even so, one of the "duumvirate" is G. M. Kornienko a profes-

[47] Petrov, op. cit., p. 848.
[48] Dobrynin recalled how upon returning to his home in Moscow his 85-year-old father, seemingly with paternal pride, would bring in the old men of the neighborhood and tell the Ambassador how to do his job and what to tell the Americans. Dobrynin, the diplomat, said that on such occasions he would respond. "Yes. father, I will think it over." (Dewitt, op. cit., p. C-2.)

sional diplomat and arms control specialist with specialized knowledge of and extensive service in the United States. He has also attended all the important bilaterial negotiations with the United States in recent years. Dobrynin has been a candidate member of the Central Committee from 1966 to 1971 and a full member since 1971.[49]

Finally a measure of the prestige of the Soviet diplomat can be taken by the respectable number of up to about a dozen seats that may be allocated at each election to the Central Committee from the Foreign Ministry but most importantly by Gromyko's ascendancy to the powerful Politburo in 1973.[50]

2. FROM THE PERSPECTIVE OF AMERICAN DIPLOMATS, NEGOTIATORS, AND OTHERS FOREIGN POLICY SPECIALISTS

(a) Gromyko et al.

Assessments of the Soviet diplomatic establishment from the American perspective based on limited evidence suggests a mixture of views. Foreign Minister Gromyko has been highly regarded. Going back to his first encounter with the Americans (in this case Secretary Hull) Gromyko has generally seemed to be judged as an able professional diplomat who has carried out his country's foreign policy loyally and effectively.[51] On a visit to Moscow in April 1978 Secretary of State Cyrus R. Vance perhaps expressed what may have been a commonly held view when in "a personal word of respect for Minister Gromyko," he said at his departure from the Moscow airport: "As a thoroughly professional practitioner of the diplomatic trade he has few peers in the modern world. He represents his country's interests with great skill, high intelligence, and a spirit tempered in decades of experience." [52]

Kuznetsov has also been highly regarded by those who have encountered him in the diplomatic arena. Prior to his appointment in October 1977 as First Vice President, Kuznetsov had been a Deputy Foreign Minister for 22 years and one of Moscow's prime negotiators. For his versatility as a diplomat and the diversity of his assignments he was called, a "global troubleshooter." Diplomats who dealt with Kuznetsov at difficult times in the past have said that he is a master of mixing outward cordiality with unyielding toughness in negotiations. "Businesslike," "cordial," "accomplished," and "skilled" are among the words they used to describe him. In his long diplomatic career

---

[49] Duevel. Christian. Moscow Appoints "duumvirate" of First Deputy Ministers of Foreign Affairs, RFE/RL. Radio Liberty Research, RL 1/78, Jan. 1, 1978, 5 p. V. F. Maltsev, a party official-turned diplomat, is the other member of the "duumvirate."

[50] Ibid., p. 4.

[51] Hull recorded in his memoirs, "When I saw Molotov at Moscow in October I spoke in warm praise of Gromyko, saying that he was proving himself very capable. In numerous conversations in 1943 and 1944 Gromyko, who soon became Ambassador to the United States, impressed me most favorably by his practical judgment and efficiency." (Hull. Memoirs, p. 1253.) In 1946, a senior American official (unnamed) who had close dealings with Gromyko said: "An extremely quick-witted and able dialectician, a highly skilled negotiator, always courteous but firm—almost as if he had deliberately schooled himself out of human foibles." (Keeper of the Kremlin's Secrets. The Guardian Weekly (Manchester), Mar. 18, 1979, p. 9.)

[52] Gwertzman, Bernard. "Reporter's Notebook: In Russia. Some Nuances of U.S. Diplomacy." The New York Times, April 24, 1978, p. A-4. The Guardian concluded its appraisal of Gromyko: "Mr. Gromyko's task has always been to reconcile the national interests of the Soviet Union as a nation, with the goal of world revolution to which the Kremlin is committed. There has never been any evidence that he draws up great geopolitical master plans. There are plenty of indications that he is a man who knows how to seize an opening and an opportunity for Russian interests. To the Soviet Union's leaders, he has proved himself reliable, safe, loyal, and persevering." (The Guardian Weekly, Mar. 18, 1979, p. 9.)

Kuznetsov led three Soviet delegations to the United Nations General Assembly where Western reporters regarded him as being pleasant and accessible even after the toughest "anti-imperialist" speeches.[53]

Ambassador Johnson, who had negotiated with Kuznetsov at the 1954 Geneval Conference on Indochina and with Vladimir S. Semonov at the SALT negotiations, noted that he was quite a different person from Semonov. "One could deal with him," the Ambassador said. Kuznetsov had been scheduled to head the talks at SALT I in 1969, but Semonov got the assignment. "Things could have gone better if Kuznetsov was there," Johnson observed, inferring a note of high respect for this veteran Soviet negotiator.[54]

(For Johnson's critical appraisal of Semonov as a diplomat and negotiator, see below under SALT I negotiations.)

(b) On the Soviet diplomatic service

(1) Views on Soviet negotiating staffs

Professor Uldricks, who has devoted much of his scholarly career in the study of the Soviet diplomatic service during its early years, recently observed, "It is my general impression that current Soviet diplomats are, indeed, more skillful and sophisticated than their predecessors, but that opinion is not based on any systematic research." [55] In general, this judgment seems to be borne out by the observations noted below by Americans who have encountered Soviet diplomats across the negotiating table. There seems little doubt that in such important negotiations as SALT the Soviets field an impressive team of diplomats and specialists.

Illustrative of the quality of Soviet diplomatic negotiators in less vital areas is the case of international conferences on outer space. According to Mrs. Eilene Galloway, an international authority on space law and a longtime U.S. delegate at international conferences with the Russians on space matters, the Soviet delegation has been invariably "highly qualified." It has, she said, "great expertise." Particularly significant to her is the Soviet practice of maintaining continuity in staffing. Unlike the Americans who frequently change their delegates, the Soviets generally staff their delegations with the same people so that over the years they develop a great depth of knowledge and expertise. The effect is to create a sort of institutional memory within the staff as negotiations are carried on over the years. (The same has also been said of the Russian SALT negotiating team.) [56]

Dr. Helmut Sonnenfeldt, a participant in high-level conferences with the Soviets as Kissinger's adviser on Soviet affairs, observed that Soviet negotiating staffs, that is, their senior people, were well-informed; they seemed to have "copious briefing papers." In general, Sonnenfeldt credited the Russians with having "a pretty strong staff and support system" for their negotiating teams.[57]

(2) Reservations on diplomats in the field

Little information is available on the more routine aspects of Soviet diplomatic activity during the Brezhnev era. While senior diplomats

53 Whitney, Craig R. Cordial Stand-In for President Brezhnev: Vasily Vasilyevich Kuznetsov. The New York Times, Oct. 10, 1977, p. 14.
54 Whelan Notebook No. 6, Oct. 14, 1977, p. 50.
55 Uldricks to Whelan, Apr. 26, 1979.
56 Interview with Mrs. Eilene Galloway, Oct. 7, 1977.
57 Interview with Helmut Sonnenfeldt, Brookings Institution, June 7, 1979.

like Dobrynin along with negotiating staffs as in the case of SALT have been given high marks in various published assessments, the most that can be said, judging from the high quality of their training, is that in general the Soviet diplomats of today are indeed more skillful and sophisticated than those of the earlier generation.

Yet criticisms have been raised particularly with respect to the detrimental influence of ideology upon their work. As Hayter noted, ideology is the "strongest" obstacle in developing a mutal understanding between Soviet Russia and the West, and its influence is most apparent in the distorted Soviet outlook on the world, a view that colors diplomatic reporting in the field.[58]

"You have to remember," said one Western diplomat, that Soviet diplomats are "all very heavily indoctrinated" before they leave Moscow. "I think it highly unlikely," he concluded, "that they can report with any degree of what we call objectivity." "What they see," it has been said, "is what their Marxist training tells them they ought to see," and thus report accordingly.[59]

The question also arises as to whether the Soviet diplomat in the field, whatever the worth of the information he has collected, would send home honest reports rather than what the regime wanted. Many Western diplomats doubt whether this is possible: "To send back reports that do not fit what people at home want to believe would be an act of courage bordering on the suicidal," one observed. "I doubt if many would risk it. And if they did, how long would they last?"[60]

Another disincentive to honest reporting, according to Clark, is the knowledge that the role of the Foreign Ministry is not one of great importance in the overall formulation of policy. Even if the diplomat's reports were found "acceptable" by the Ministry, it is not likely that they would influence events or policies because the power lies elsewhere.[61]

Candor about Soviet shortcomings, particularly in public, is not a virtue of the Soviet diplomat. Regarded, in Clark's words, as always "rigid, slow-moving and terrified of deviating from detailed instructions," the Soviet diplomat would never concede that anything was wrong with or in Russia. An insight into this timidity, placid conformity and lack of candor in the Soviet diplomat that has been induced by the rigidity and totality of control from Moscow was the response of a Soviet delegate to the United Nations who admitted privately at a social gathering that "every country, including mine, has weaknesses." Asked why he didn't say this publicly: "How could I?"—was his meaningful reply.[62]

---

[58] Hayter, Russia and the World, p. 120.
[59] Clark, op. cit., p. 229.
[60] Ibid.
[61] Ibid.
[62] Ibid., p. 257. Distrust of the West is another deep-rooted and abiding characteristic that even Soviet diplomats with long exposure to the West find difficult to overcome. When Arkady N. Shevchenko, a high-ranking Soviet diplomat at the United Nations, defected, Kathleen Teltsch reported that to Westerners at the United Nations "Mr. Shevchenko was a typical Soviet official, by which they said they meant that he seemed to have a built-in distrust of all things Western." (The New York Times, April 11, 1978, p. 12.) That conformity is a first principle in the conduct of the Soviet diplomat was indicated by Roetter's comment, "As for the Soviet Union, a smooth, impersonal, almost faceless professional uniformity is the order of the day. Among the blandly efficient diplomatic technicians of the Zorin-Zarubin-Malik-Gromyko vintage, one is not likely to discover even the smallest personal idiosyncrasy, not even a goatee beard such as Mr. Maisky, the wartime ambassador in London, used to sport." (Roetter, op. cit., p. 53.)

The veteran British diplomat Humphrey Trevelyan seemed to give a balanced portrayal of the problems facing the Soviet diplomat when he wrote:

Soviet ambassadors are * * * among the most professional, very competent and well-disciplined, though severely restricted in initiative by the Soviet system which keeps its ambassadors tightly on the leash, and hampered by the necessity of appraising the battles of Westminster or the emotions of the Middle East in marxist terms. A good Soviet ambassador can however make a considerable impact in a non-communist country, if he does not overdo his support of the local communists and fellow-travellers.[63]

Ambassador Beam made essentially the same evaluation of Soviet diplomats. He rated them high professionally: they were "very well trained.", he said, but "in their limited, restricted way." Skilled in languages, especially in English, "very able" in memory and in commanding masses of well collated material, "good" at staff work and "competent negotiators", they were held in a "tremendously tight rein" by Moscow with "no discretion at all" in carrying on the business of diplomacy. This reduced their effectiveness. Indoctrinated in the Soviet outlook, but not blinded by an unreasoned addiction to ideology—"ideology is just dry bread"—as practitioners of diplomacy "they carry out their mission which is based on their interpretation of Marxism and Leninism as of that time." With respect to influence, upper echelon diplomats with connections into the Politburo such as Gromyko and with the Central Committee as Dobrynin do have influence and input as "staff experts" into the foreign policy process; but, Beam noted, the Soviet diplomat in the field has none whatever.[64]

(c) *The Foreign Policy Institutes: USA Institute*

(1) *On the journal*

The USA and Canada Institute, among others in the foreign policy area, make available to Soviet decisionmakers an important body of knowledge and well-trained cadres of foreign policy specialists.

The USA Institute publishes a monthly journal called, "USA: Economics, Politics, Ideology." A selected and cursory review of this journal over recent years suggests that contributors present evaluations of American society and policy that seem to be based on a realistic assessment of American problems and provide Soviet readers with reasonably accurate information about the United States. In general, the journal portrays accurately specific events and aspects of American life and their direct impact on American institutions. But the natural Soviet inclination to relate everything within a Marxist-Leninist framework creates significant distortions in such areas of foreign policy as the cold war, activities in the Third World, and perceptions of the world in Soviet terms of the correlation of forces and the "two-camp" (capitalist v. Communist) view. Studies by the institute on Congress, notably those by Dr. Vladimir A. Savelyev, suggest that the

[63] Trevelyan. Humphrey. Diplomatic Channels. London, Macmillan. 1973. p. 21. Whether or not Dobrynin has reported accurately back to Moscow would seem to be open to question. William F. Hyland, a senior staff member of the National Security Council during the SALT I negotiations and an active negotiator of this agreement, recalled that in his many discussions with Dobrynin, the Ambassador neither took notes nor relied on an interpreter in even the most delicate and detailed discussions. "You just hope he hasn't missed the nuances, but you're never really certain what he reports." said Hyland. (Time Nov. 21, 1977: 28.) For Dobrynin's reports during the Cuban missile crisis, quite at odds with the reality. see Khrushchev Remembers, pp. 497–498.
[64] Interview with Jacob D. Beam, May 23, 1979.

Soviets now view Congress as an important factor in the foreign policy process and thus must be taken into account in appraisals of U.S. foreign policy.

(2) Observations on the staff

Appraisals of the staff of the institute have been favorable. Ambassador Beam noted that the institute's members "enjoyed prestige and authority and provided a refreshing change from the stilted pronouncements of the Foreign Ministry bureaucrats." [65] Staffed with very able historians and scholars, he believed that the institute does contribute to the foreign policy process, at least in providing information, background and atmosphere. The products of such institutes as the USA and Canada are reasonably objective—as Beam said, "They're not going to give the store away or deviate too much. They are fairly objective, in economics particularly." In general, he believed that their work, as that of the Academy of Sciences, has a positive influence. It is significant to note that the Ambassador assisted the USA Institute in building its library of Americana (Arbatov, its director, had none in the beginning) and during his tenure exchanged published materials with its staff.[66]

Professor Jonsson of Lund University in Sweden had visited the institute, and his talks with staff confirmed his view that here was a serious academic-research institution with serious-minded specialists. In addition, he felt that there was a search for reasonable objectivity by its staff.[67]

Such appraisals are corroborated by other observations that collectively suggest the image of: foreign policy specialists well-trained in American studies and dedicated to high quality research; able scholars very knowledgeable in American sources and inclined to set ideology aside in search for more pragmatic approaches to problems; young intellectuals exhibiting a real grasp of American foreign policy problems, as in SALT II, and of its institutions, notably the foreign policy role of Congress in the post-Vietnam era, and a realistic understanding of public opinion in the American political process. In brief, members of the institute, representative of the leading Soviet Americanologists, would seem to epitomize the "new breed" of the young Soviet intelligentsia about which Meissner and Petrov have written.[68]

---

[65] Beam, op. cit., p. 231.
[66] Interview with Jacob D. Beam, May 23, 1979.
[67] Interview with Dr. Christer Johnson, Mar. 1, 1978.
[68] Some measure of the high quality of the institute's staff can be taken from the fact that among the young intelligentsia the competition to specialize in American studies is very keen. According to Dimitri K. Simes, Soviet specialist at Georgetown University's Center for Strategic and International Studies and one of this "new breed" in the Soviet institutes who had emigrated to this country a few years ago, there was an intense competition at Moscow University to get into American studies in the general area of contemporary history. He stressed the importance of the fact that only the best came out of this competition. (Interview with Dimitri K. Simes. Jan. 30, 1978.)

In a concluding assessment of the Soviet foreign policy infrastructure under the Brezhnev regime, Eran noted that Brezhnev had encouraged "functional differentiation between individual institutes, in addition to the progressively growing differentiation along regional lines"; he has also allowed the community of international relations specialists "to grow to vast proportions." Moreover, Brezhnev allowed the introduction of new specializations. As Eran explained, "Strategic studies, methodology and the study of the experience of the scientific technical revolution in the West, have all become new responsibilities of the institutes during this period. Both the Khrushchev and the Brezhnev regimes have demonstrated a genuine interest in the improvement of quality of the academic research services, operating on the assumption that only good and respectable scholarship could serve the regime properly. Both regimes continued to regard the community of *Mezhdunarodniki*, particularly the segment operating inside the U.S.S.R. Academy of Sciences, as an important and functional service elite." Both the elite and the institutions have been richly rewarded. (Eran, op. cit., p. 276.)

3. ON BALANCE

To sum up, the Soviet diplomatic establishment, as perceived by the Soviets and the Americans, contrasts sharply in some respects but converge in others. There seems little doubt that the Soviet diplomat of today is well trained, that he represents a "new breed" in the Soviet intelligentsia, that he is a great improvement over the diplomat of earlier generations, and that he enjoys a position of prestige in Soviet society. Prominent Soviet diplomats and negotiating staffs such as that in SALT have won respect in the West as skilled professionals. The USA and Canada Institute is staffed with able scholars who apparently strive for reasonable objectivity in their analyses of the United States, notwithstanding their unique ideological perspective.

Yet, the Soviet diplomatic service remains hobbled in the pursuit of its professional tasks by the detrimental effects of ideology and by the negative characteristics associated with the problem of conducting diplomacy in a totalitarian system.

On balance, much progress and improvement have been made in the Soviet diplomatic establishment but serious deficiencies remain that fundamentally affect the creation of a stable relationship with the United States.

E. INFLUENCE OF THE DIPLOMATIC ESTABLISHMENT ON THE FOREIGN POLICY PROCESS

1. POLITBURO'S RELIANCE ON EXPERT ADVICE

As Petrov infers in his article on the formation of Soviet foreign policy, it would be extraordinarily difficult to try to measure accurately the influence of the diplomatic establishment on the Soviet foreign policy process, meaning here the Foreign Ministry and the foreign policy institutes such as the USA Institute. But inferences, at the very least, can be made from certain realities, and the most important is that the Politburo is open to outside influence.

The Politburo, as noted above, is the repository of all power and authority in the Soviet state. It is the alpha and omega of the system. It has within its Central Committee apparatus its own built-in organizations dealing with foreign policy.[69] At best influence can only be inferred by the extent of access various institutions and individuals have to it. For the Politburo is not a free agent in the foreign policy process; it is subject to pressures, including those from the intellectual community.[70]

The extraordinary complexities of international relations and the immensity of the problems facing the Soviet Union place an increasing premium on competence and professionalism. The Soviet leadership, as practical politicians and administrators with state interests and self-interests at heart and in mind, have been compelled to rely on expert advice, much of it from within the Government, some from outside the formal structure.[71] Pragmatism, the basic principle gov-

---

[69] Petrov, op. cit., pp. 824–827.
[70] Ibid., p. 846.
[71] Ibid., p. 830.

erning this approach, rules debates on policy among the "insiders," a practice that broadens the access of potential influence of the foreign policy elite from the outside.[72]

Thus the point to be made here is simply that the Politburo, for all its awesome power and authority, its own resources for independent action and its claims to total control, is subject to pressures, and by practical necessity and self-interest it is compelled to rely on advice from experts beyond its narrowly constricted institutional walls.

2. INFLUENCE OF THE FOREIGN MINISTRY

(a) *Sources of influence*

The influence of the Foreign Ministry in the foreign policy decision-making process derives from three sources: its control over specialized information flowing into the Government; its close association with party organs; and its institutional role as depository of knowledge in the foreign policy area. Because of these sources of power, as Meissner observed, the Ministry has been able to exert "considerable" influence over foreign policy from its very inception.[73]

(b) *Party connections*

A significant factor in magnifying the Foreign Ministry's influence was the elevation of Gromyko to the Politburo in April 1973. From this position of supreme political authority Gromyko has been able to participate directly in the decisionmaking process, though his actual political base of power remains a question. Only Molotov held such a high party position in addition to being Foreign Minister.[74] It is also assumed that Gromyko belongs to the Politburo's Foreign Policy Commission, along with Brezhnev, Kosygin, Suslov, and Podgorny before his removal.[75]

Helmut Sonnenfeldt, a close observer of the Soviet diplomatic scene from his perspective in the National Security Council and the State Department during the Nixon-Ford administrations, cited Gromyko's seat on the Politburo as a significant source of influence. With "enormous experience" going back 40 years, he has an unrivaled "institutional memory" in the high councils of the Soviet party and government. Thus, Sonnenfeldt believed that Gromyko probably has got "considerable impact," not meaning that he would always get his

---

[72] On this very important point, Petrov explained with respect to the diversity of the Soviet elite: "These are substantial differences, especially for a society that only a quarter of a century ago was rigidly conformist in its political outlook. They are not readily visible to the readers of Soviet publications, which are still strictly controlled by the party ideologues. But while the written word is addressed to the uninformed masses and outsiders, what circulates for official use only and what the insiders say in their meetings behind closed doors is often totally devoid of propagandistic overtones. Debates, as a rule, concentrate on specific issues, and those who attempt to argue the case solely on the basis of what Marx or Lenin, or even the latest party congress resolution, had to say are regarded by their more sophisticated colleagues as dogmatic fools who have no place in deciding important issues." (Pp. 848.)

[73] Meissner, op. cit., p. 49.

[74] Hayter wrote: "The Minister is generally himself more a civil servant than a politician in our sense. Molotov was an exception to this, and so was the short-lived Shepilov: the others. Chicherin. Litvinov. Vyshinsky. Gromyko. have all been men of little or no political standing internally, experts acting under orders from the holders of real power." (Diplomacy of the Great Powers, p. 23.) Apparently. Gromyko's political base remains narrow. According to The Guardian Weekly, "Gromyko the diplomat is familiar enough. As a politician, he is an unknown quantity. He has never had time to build himself a solid support within the Soviet Communist Party. In spite of his seniority, his experience, and his evident closeness to the Soviet leader, Mr. Brezhnev, few suppose that Mr. Gromyko is a candidate for the successor, or indeed that he will turn out to be one of the kingmakers." (The Guardian Weekly, Mar. 18, 1979, p. 9.)

[75] Meissner, op. cit., pp. 49–50.

way, but he "has impact." Moreover, he felt that Gromyko relied "a good bit on his subordinates in the Foreign Ministry," suggesting the existence of an important and influential connection particularly for the Ministry. In addition, Sonnenfeldt cited individual figures in the diplomatic corps, such as Dobrynin and some other Soviet ambassadors, who also have an "impact on Soviet foreign policy." [76]

Other influential and close party linkages enhancing Ministry-party cooperation and thus enlarging the potential areas of the Ministry's influence is that existing between the heads of the Ministry and the personal secretariat of General Secretary Brezhnev. Two of Brezhnev's aides. Alekansdrov-Agentov and Blatov, both former diplomats, belong to Brezhnev's personal secretariat.[77]

The influence of the Foreign Ministry can also be measured by the fact that a total of 24 members of the Foreign Service were elected to important high-level party organizations by the 25th Party Congress in 1976; namely, the Central Committee and the General Auditing Commission. Fifteen of those elected (5.2 percent) are full members of the Central Committee. [78]

(c) Dobrynin's role in SALT negotiations

The influence of Ambassador Dobrynin will be apparent in the discussion below on SALT I negotiations. (See, for example, p. 457.) Briefly, he carried on close and prolonged negotiations in Washington and Moscow with Kissinger in the strictest secrecy on some of the most crucial parts of the agreements. He also played a significant role as a participant in the negotiations during the conclusion of SALT I in Moscow during May 1972.

Recent press accounts on SALT II reveal that once again Dobrynin is playing the role of principal negotitator for the Soviets. Access to the Secretary of State is frequent and continuous, and to the President, on especially important occasions, only a matter of lifting the phone. Neither Ambassador Beam nor his successor Malcolm Toon enjoyed such confidence from their government or such unobstructed access to the Kremlin. In many respects both seemed to have been relegated to the sidelines.[79]

By the time of the signing of SALT II at Vienna, Dobrynin had, according to one observer, "capped his career with a role in the strategic-arms accord that establishes him as virtually the indispensable contact man in Soviet-American relations." [80] After 2 years of sometimes intensive negotiations with Dobrynin, Secretary of State Vance has had "unstinting" praise of his skills in negotiations. "He is very bright," Vance said. "He is imaginative and he is well plugged in. He has a great deal of experience and knowledge of the United States

---

[76] Interview with Helmut Sonnenfeldt, Brookings Institution, June 7, 1979.
[77] Ibid., p. 52.
[78] Ibid.
[79] Perhaps a clue to a measure of Dobrynin's influence is the degree of intimacy established in his relationship with Kissinger as National Security adviser and Secretary of State (discussed below) and with Zbigniew Brzezinski, President Carter's National Security adviser. According to a recent report commenting on Brzezinski's busy day, his only break in a day goes from 6:45 a.m. to 8 or 9 p.m. is for lunch. "Sometimes Soviet Ambassador Anatoli Dobrynin, the only ambassador so favored, comes by for a noontime sandwich," the report stated. "The two doff their coats and eat at a small round table in Brzezinski's office." (Time, June 12, 1978 : 18.)
[80] Austin, Anthony. Ambassador Dobrynin, Key Man in Arms Talks, Long Esteemed as Bridge to Kremlin. The New York Times, June 4, 1979, p. A6.

and how it works, and he has a good sense of what is acceptable in Moscow." With respect to negotiating SALT II, the Secretary noted:

In our talks he played a very significant role as the key strategic-arms negotiator for the Soviet Union. If we came up against a roadblock, instead of saying, "Well, that's it," he would say, "Can we find a way around it?" I would say the same thing, and then we would try to find a way.

Described as a real professional who could convey the image of an "unforced, affable, cultured" and a "very natural man," Dobrynin has also added to his diplomatic virtues an ability to display a great deal of political finesse in carrying out his representational functions. As one American source commented:

Very political, in the way he began to move quietly around Washington, finding out whom to see, what committee of Congress to cultivate, where to look for the real lever of decisionmaking, how to make himself needed. And, most important, his standing at home seemed aces high.

American officials who have known him socially over the years and have negotiated with him on everything from bird migration to Berlin, the Middle East and SALT have been hard pressed to determine whether down deep Dobrynin is a "dove" or a "hawk." Admittedly, he could be shrewd to the point of craftiness, sometimes could "gull the innocent by putting a rosy hue on things Soviet," and place Americans on the defensive with his polite style of "put down" when defending the shortcomings of his own country. But some Americans who have negotiated with him are convinced that he is a force for détente and for closer Soviet-American collaboration and that deep in his heart he is for modernizing and rationalizing the Soviet system. Others more cautious in their appraisals point out that he did very well in the cold war days; that he defended the invasion of Czechoslovakia; and that he can be derisive about Soviet dissidents.

One American who dealt with him in the past made this judgment, stressing his professionalism as a diplomat:

A member of the Central Committee of the Soviet Communist Party and his country's foremost Americanist, Mr. Dobrynin is a superb channel of communications between Washington and Moscow and a formidable defender of the Soviet Government's interests, whatever they may be. "Is he for détente? He is for it because that is his assignment. If his assignment were different, he could be extremely tough and harsh."

Another expressed Dobrynin's role in somewhat different and more benign terms:

He simply has to have some sensitivity to the flow of things and events in Moscow and Washington and a shrewd sense of how to position himself in both capitals so he's with the flow and it doesn't run over him. And, even more, it's that special feel he has for "translating" from the Russian into American and from the American into Russian, and doing it in such a way that the objective is achieved without the desired effects of anger and resentment.

In speaking of Dobrynin's access to and influence with U.S. administrations over the past 17 years—in brief, his ability to carry out his role as ambassador—Beam remarked, "He has a very charmed life." In Beam's estimate, Dobrynin is "very able, no question about it," and he does have influence in the Soviet foreign polocy establishment.[81] But, as it will be shown below, Beam's experience as U.S. Ambassador in Moscow was more like existing in a diplomatic wasteland, notwith-

[81] Interview with Jacob D. Beam, May 23, 1979.

standing the prestige of the office and the excitement of official demands, compared to Dobrynin's in Washington. In this respect there is no "essential equivalency." It might be added parenthetically that Beam has had a distinguished career as a professional diplomat, having held such top-ranking posts in the Communist world as Ambassador to Poland, Czechoslovakia and the Soviet Union during the critical years 1957–73.

(d) Defense Ministry as a competitor

A serious rival in the competition for influence in the foreign policy decisionmaking process is the Defense Ministry. The discussion of SALT I below points out the predominating military presence on the negotiating staff at Geneva and also indicates that one of the principal negotiators for the Soviet side at the Moscow summit was a top-ranking representative of Russia's military-industrial complex.

Close observers of the Soviet decisionmaking process with respect to foreign policy and national security matters have emphasized the preeminence of the military side at the expense of civilians in the Foreign Ministry. In a study on the role of the military in the decisionmaking process on arms control negotiations based on first-hand experience, Igor S. Glagolev, former Chief of the Disarmament Section of the Institute of World Economy and International Relations and a resident of the United States since 1976, concluded:

> On the whole one can say that the entire decisionmaking process with respect to the Soviet position on SALT negotiations is structured in such a fashion as to give preponderant expression to the interests and objectives of the military-industrial complex, which are limited only by the economic and scientific-technological capabilities of the USSR.[82]

Unlike the United States, the Soviets do not have a civilian institution similar to the U.S. Arms Control and Disarmament Agency (ACDA), nor does the civilian head of the Soviet SALT delegation have a role comparable in influence to that of his American counterpart. According to Glagolev, Semonov has himself said that the Foreign Ministry has no decisive voice in the formulation of the Soviet position on arms limitation. Its function is in fact limited to selecting those formulas for possible agreement that will not interfere with "the realization of Soviet military programs." As Glagolev concluded. "The Foreign Ministry collaborates with the Military Establishment."[83]

Speaking in more general terms on this matter, Wolfe concluded that given the Defense Ministry's monopoly on expert advice: "In the absence of overriding objections on technical or economic grounds, * * * the system has seemed to have a bias in defense policy decisions toward the preferences of the military professionals and their close allies in the defense-industrial ministries."[84] Wolfe went on to explain the emerging influence of the institutes in the Academy of Science as a potential source of "outside" advice; nonetheless, he concluded that "more as a consequence of the way the Soviet policymaking mechanism is structured than through an internal elite struggle to enlarge its in-

[82] Glagolev, Igor S. The Soviet Decision-Making Process in Arms-Control Negotiations. Orbis. v. 21. Winter 1978 : 771–772.

[83] Ibid., p. 771.

[84] U.S. Congress. House. Committee on International Relations. Subcommittee on Europe and the Middle East. The Soviet Union : Internal Dynamics of Washington, D.C., U.S. Government Printing Office. 1978. p. 117.

fluence, the military leadership today enjoys a substantial amount of policy leverage." [85]

3. INFLUENCE OF THE INSTITUTES

(a) *Solicited advice from the Academy of Sciences*

The institutes of the Academy of Sciences concerned with foreign policy and national security matters are playing an increasingly larger role as "outside" expert advisers to the party leadership. Senior scientists of the Academy have been invited to high policy councils as consultants in their areas of expertise, not as lobbyists for the scientific community or self-appointed political activists for their own view, but rather to provide individual professional advice. More recently some members of the scientific community may have acquired a broader advisory role. In recent years the practice of bringing in scientific experts as consultants or sometimes staff members in the Central Committee apparatus has also been reportedly on the increase.[86]

Soviet scientists and the technical institutes also play a support role for Soviet negotiators in the field of foreign trade.[87]

Sonnenfeldt acknowledged that it was hard to judge the specific impact that the institutes have on the foreign policy process. Staffs of the institutes, he said, tend to be rather reluctant in describing the degree to which they believe they have influence on the top Soviet policymakers. But it was Sonnenfeldt's impression that "the senior people of those institutes do have a good bit of contact in the Central Committee and in the upper reaches of the Soviet decisionmaking machinery." The institutes, notably the USA Institute and others such as those dealing with Africa and Asia, "do provide a kind of intellectual framework within which the operators function." It was Sonnenfeldt's view that there was now "a fair amount of traffic back and forth between the institutes and the Foreign Ministry and the Central Committee department that deals with these questions." Though "very hard to measure specific influence on a given decision," Sonnenfeldt nonetheless emphasized that "they fertilize the Soviet policymaking process." [88]

(b) *On the Institute of World Economy and International Relations and the Institute of the USA and Canada*

A seminal source of potential influence in the Academy is through its Institute of World Economy and International Relations under N. N. Inozemtsey and the USA and Canada Institute headed by G. A. Arbatov. Both institutes produce studies in the field of foreign policy, defense and arms control. The USA Institute has become a "spokes-

---

[85] Ibid., pp. 118–119.
[86] Wolfe's Statement. House International Relations Committee. Hearings, Internal Dynamics of Soviet Foreign Policy. 1978. p. 112.
[87] Welt, Leo. You Want to Sell in Russia? The Washington Post (Outlook). May 27, 1979. p. C.4 Welt, a long time trade expert working as a middleman between the American businessman and the Soviet Ministry of Foreign Trade, wrote: "Sensing a Soviet bonanza, some American firms lost their perspective. Ill-prepared businessmen journeyed to Moscow, mesmerized by the hugh potential Russian market. Some tried to get deals at any price and lost their shirts. Many times the Soviet negotiators knew the product specifications and market conditions better than the Americans across the table. Soviet scientists and technical institutes had prepared them well, and their trading expertise was exemplified by the Russian grain deals."
[88] Interview with Helmut Sonnenfeldt, Brookings Institution. June 7. 1979.

man for détente" and its Americanists advocates of a relaxation of tensions as opposed to a more aggressive political line.[88a] In a judicious summary statement on the influence of these institutes, Wolfe said:

The largely unknown factor is how much weight the work of these institutes may have in the actual framing of Soviet foreign and military policy. Since neither of the institutes ostensibly is authorized or asked to analyze Soviet strategic, economic and other problems, their inputs to policymaking presumably lie mainly in how they interpret developments abroad—which may differ somewhat from the interpretations provided by the regular Soviet intelligence organizations. Some outside observers feel that institute researchers probably have had a substantial impact on policymaking by providing an alternative transmission belt for information between the United States and the Soviet Union; others have the impression that the interaction between institute researchers and official policymakers has not been very close. It is generally thought, on the other hand, that the directors of the two institutes may have considerably more influence than their research staffs by virtue of their Party standing, and in the case of Arbatov in particular —reputed access to Brezhnev's ear.[89]

(c) Role of Arbatov

Arbatov maintains an international presence, and in the United States he is regarded as an important Soviet spokesman on Soviet-American relations. With some dissenting opinion, sources generally emphasize his close and influential relationship with Brezhnev as an adviser and stress his views on détente and other foreign policy questions that have in some instances provided a refreshing variation in the internal discourse on policy.[90]

According to Ambassador Beam, assessments on the Brezhnev connection were, apparently, true. Moreover, Arbatov was known to have

---

[88a] For a commentary on the positive role of the USA Institute in furthering the policy of détente, see Schwartz, Morton. Soviet Perceptions of the United States, Berkeley, University of California Press. 1978, chapter 6. Schwartz concluded : "The point to be made is that the USA Institute has developed an institutional interest in—and become a lobby for—the policy of détente" (p. 162). And further: "Thus whether out of interest or conviction—or, more probably, a combination of the two—Soviet Amerikanisty endorse a comparatively realistic assessment of the United States. Their relatively pragmatic analysis tends to weaken the hold of traditional ideological imagery, and at the same time to reduce apprehension regarding the intentions of American policy makers" (p. 163). Schwartz referred to the USA Institute as the "spokesman for détente" and noted that its Americanists "appear convinced that a policy of international relaxation presents Moscow with opportunities which a more aggressive political line would preclude." Such an approach helped achieve a number of other policy objectives, for example, "increased trade with the West, reduction of the pace and burden of the arms race, a more stable international environment in which greater attention to domestic problems is feasible", and "it has a generally positive impact on American politics and policies." Schwartz continued : "Thus while a hard line, in given circumstances, may offer certain benefits, institute spokesmen in Soviet policy circles are likely to urge caution. Any premature or imprudent action which might jeopardize Soviet-American relations would, in their view, risk the loss of significant advantages. Given the logic of their assessments, the Amerikanisty are most likely to be found among the Kremlin's counselors of restraint" (pp. 145–146). For a summary of contrasting views on the implications of the improvement of Soviet research on the United States for Soviet policy and perceptions, see pp. 2–4.

[89] Wolfe's Statement, House International Relations Committee, Hearings. Internal Dynamics of Soviet Foreign Policy, 1978, pp. 113–114. Both Inozemtsev and Arbatov are candidate members of the Central Committee, which, according to Wolfe, "gives them positions of moderate but scarcely high prestige in terms of the Party hierarchy."

[90] Ibid., pp. 124–126. In an "exclusive interview" with Arbatov, Jonathan Power of The Observer of London began : "Variously described as a senior adviser to Brezhnev, the Soviet leader, and as Moscow's No. One American-watcher, the precise influence of Georgiy Arbatov is a question of some debate." According to Power. "Some see him, alongside Mr. Anatoliy Dobrynin, Soviet ambassador in Washington, as no more than the key source of information on America for the Politburo. Others see him as a policymaker half way between Mr. Zbigniew Brzezinski. Mr. Carter's national security adviser, and Mr. Marshall Shulman. Mr. Vance's adviser on Soviet affairs—he sees Mr. Brezhnev privately three or four times a year and Mr. Gromyko, the foreign minister. more regularly. perhaps monthly." Powers continued : "For others he is the source of 'disinformation.' the sophisticated propaganda voice that brings Western journalists and parliamentarians in gentle tones that belie the true nature of the harsh self-interest of Soviet power." (The Observer, Nov. 12, 1978, pp 15–17.)

connections with the General Staff. With respect to Arbatov's value as an intermediary with the Soviet ruling elite, Beam wrote:

Arbatov has frequently been very rough in dealing with the United States in his speeches and articles, but we found him a valuable intermediary in that he had the prestige and qualifications to engage in serious discussions which he doubtless reported up the line.[91]

The importance of both Arbatov and Inozemtsev is apparent by their presence on the Soviet parliamentary delegation that conferred on foreign policy problems with U.S. Senators and Representatives in Washington in January 1978 and during April 1979 in Moscow.[92]

A further indication of Arbatov's preeminent role in matters of Soviet-American relations was his offer in May 1979 to come to the United States with his Soviet colleagues to explain the Soviet case for SALT II, if asked by appropriate Americans.[93]

The offer was not long in coming. On May 16, Arbatov appeared with Marshall Shulman, the Secretary of State's Special Adviser on Soviet Affairs, on the nationally acclaimed MacNeil/Lehrer Report over the Public Broadcasting Service where they discussed various aspects of SALT II in what appeared to be a benign and friendly exchange under sometimes sharp questioning. Arbatov's visit was expanded to a month-long tour of the United States, taking him through the Southeastern States under the sponsorship of the Southern Center for International Studies. That the Soviet leadership would give such a critical assignment to Arbatov is a tribute to their confidence in him as probably the most knowledgeable Soviet analyst of the American scene.[94]

Arbatov's position of potential influence, therefore, seems to derive from three factors: His control over resources of information and knowledge on the United States; his close advisory relationship with Brezhnev and his identification with his policy of détente; and his dual function as head of the USA Institute and candidate member of the Central Committee.

(d) Soviet perception of the USA Institute's influence

In many respects the Soviet perception of the influence of the USA Institute in the foreign policy process coincides with American assessments, particularly with respect to the importance of the close connection between Arbatov and Brezhnev. Difficult as it may be to pinpoint specific operational contributions, it is believed that larger studies and other products, such as contributions to position papers for negotiators, prepared at the Institute enable ideas to percolate up through the party apparatus to the political decisionmakers. Conceivably, background studies on such foreign policy problems as those arising from

[91] Beam, op. cit., p. 231. In discussing the difficulties of dealing directly with the Foreign Ministry, Beam said: "It's easier to deal with Arbatov and his crew. I think there was more and more authority coming from him because he's an apparatchik of the Central Committee." Through Arbatov, he said, "there is a direct line to the Politburo." (Interview with Jacob D. Beam, May 23, 1979.)

[92] U.S. Congress. Senate. Report to the United States Senate of the Senate Delegation on Parliamentary Exchange with the Soviet Union. 96th Congress, 1st session. Washington, D.C., U.S. Government Printing Office, April 10, 1979, 37 p. (Doc. No. 96–19) The report by the Senators indicates that Senator Sam Nunn (D-Ga.) conferred with members of the USA Institute in a separate meeting on the problem of the military balance in Central Europe (p. 13.) In another separate meeting Senator Nunn and Senator John Glenn (D-Ohio) conferred with a senior specialists in the Institute of Oriental Studies on the military dimension of the China problem. (p. 17.)

[93] The Washington Post. May 8, 1979, p. A3.

[94] Oberdorfer, Don. Moscow Official Is Selling SALT on Tour of America. The Washington Post, May 20, 1979, p. A4.

the emergence of the triangular relationship among the Soviet Union, China, and the United States are the type that could make an important contribution.

In recent months scholars from the Institute made what have appeared to be careful and detailed field studies of American public opinion, notably congressional opinion, on SALT II. There would seem to be little doubt that their findings have been carefully examined by the upper echelons of the Foreign Ministry and the party.

(e) Petrov's evaluation of the impact by scholars and their institutes

Expert advice from scholars and their institutes outside traditional party and government organizations has thus contributed to the foreign policy process. The extent of their influence has been debatable, but this reasoned overall assessment by Petrov puts the issue in historical perspective:

> It is impossible to measure with any degree of accuracy the overall impact scholars and their institutes have on foreign policy formulation in the Soviet Union. They clearly are no match, in their total influence, to the "insiders" in the CC CPSU and the government; bureaucrats in the USSR, as in other countries still have final say. But the lofty position scientists occupy—in social status, income and job security—assures them an important and visibly growing role in Moscow's high councils, a role difficult to envisage a decade or two ago.[95]

4. NEUTRALIZING COUNTERFORCES

(a) A common outlook of the Soviet elite

Implied in the assessments on the importance of Soviet scholars and their institutes as potential sources of positive change through the inflow of new ideas is the assumption, if not hope or possibly expectation, that their "enlightened" contributions to the decisionmaking process will have an ameliorating effect on Soviet foreign policy—make it less adversarial and aggressive, more to the liking and interests of the United States. Two counterforces seem to be at work that could neutralize such hopes and expectations: One is the common outlook of the Soviet elite that resists establishing a complete harmony of interests; the other is the institutional arrangements that can stifle the rise of creative ideas to the top political leadership.

The Soviet elite share a common outlook that binds them to a set of beliefs, the most fundamental of which, as Wolfe said, bear upon maintaining the security of the Soviet State interpreted generally in anti-Western terms.[96] The component parts of this elite was probably best described by Petrov when he wrote:

> A basic fact about this Soviet elite is that it is not homogeneous. Its common denominator is fierce patriotism, a belief in a one-party political system, a view that the Soviet Union leads the worldwide struggle against the fundamentally hostile West and that this hostility is predetermined by the conflict between two drasically different socio-economic systems. The foreign relations elitists further believe that a major war must be prevented; that for its strength and security the Soviet Union depends on its military might; and that in order ultimately to win the struggle it must keep expanding its ties with friendly nations and socio-political forces eroding the cohesiveness of the opposing camp. Above all, they believe that the Soviet system is fundamentally "good" and that in the long run this goodness will be recognized by the majority of mankind.[97]

[95] Petrov, op. cit., p. 844.
[96] Wolfe's Statement, House International Relations Committee. Hearings, Internal Dynamics of Soviet Foreign Policy, 1978, pp. 119–124.
[97] Petrov, op. cit., pp. 846–847.

Notwithstanding the acknowledged diversity that exists within this elite, the values that bind it are fundamental, though, in the long term not necessarily unchangeable; and while under certain conditions this elite could be a vehicle of change, still at this juncture the realities of international life and the contentious nature of Soviet-American relations are not reassuring.

(b) Built-in mechanisms of control

(1) Neutralizing inflow of ideas

Institutional arrangements can also act as a counterforce, neutralizing the inflow of creative ideas from the Soviet intellectual elite on the outside. While acknowledging the potential creativity of the new breed of diplomats and intelligentsia in the foreign policy institutes, there still can be no assurance that new ideas will percolate up to the top political leadership and become established policy. In staffing out policies, new ideas and inputs flow in from many sources but become integrated within the larger framework of policy and ideologized in conformance with the Soviet world view. In this essentially closed system of decisionmaking, the process and the product cannot be otherwise. The institutional arrangements within the Politburo and the Central Committee apparatus make sure of that.[98]

(2) Senate parliamentary visit: Case study of an encounter with the Soviet leadership

It is difficult for new ideas, even old ideas, to penetrate the top echelons of the Soviet system as a parliamentary delegation of 12 U.S. Senators discovered on their visit to the Soviet Union in November 1978. Press reports of the visit suggest that this encounter with a mixture of the party elite and various elements of the intelligentsia from the Foreign Ministry, the foreign policy institutes, and elsewhere was for them a great awakening. In some respects, judging from press accounts, what they witnessed was the Soviet political system operating in microcosm; for with the political leadership firmly in control, the Arbatovs and Inzomentsev's, presuming a disposition to have any serious and open discussion of foreign policy, could only have expressed what was official policy and then do so in a forceful, dogmatic, unyielding way. In such a formal conference setting, indeed a classic negotiating setting, there could be no free-and-easy discussion, no give and take in the American manner to which the Senators were accustomed.

The Americans raised a host of concerns from human rights to Soviet expansion in Africa, from Russia's anti-Israeli policy in the Middle East to conventional arms transfer and delivery of Mig–23's to Cuba. These issues were on the Senator's minds; they were current foreign policy problems; they could adversely affect Senate ratification of the SALT II Treaty that the Soviets want so badly. But, a "furious" Kosygin responded, "I thought you came to talk peace. These things are not important"; he refused to discuss them and proceeded to blame the United States for the tense state of Soviet-American

---

[98] An example of how this integrating process takes place is shown in Petrov's commentary on the functions of the International Department and the Department of Liaison with the Workers' and Communist Parties: "It can be said that, under the overall guidance of Suslov [longtime Politburo member and chief ideologist], the ID/DLWCP, more than any other organization, is responsible for the continuing ideological thrust of Soviet foreign policy, for it puts all the specific policies in the general framework of Marxism-Leninism (as currently interpreted), and assures their consistency and interpretation in Soviet periodicals and the propaganda media." (Petrov, op. cit., p. 825.)

relations. This response moved Senator John A. Durkin, Democrat of New Hampshire, to say, in a variation of a statement made some time ago with respect to Soviet negotiating behavior, "It's like my sister-in-law. What's hers is hers and what's mine is negotiable." [99]

Perhaps more disturbing to the Senators than this display of intransigence and bad temper was the ignorance of the Soviet political leadership with respect to the role of the Senate in the treaty process. When Senator Abraham Ribicoff (D.-Conn.), co-leader of the delegation, told Grigori Romanov, the Leningrad party leader and at 56 the youngest member of the Politburo, that some Democrats in the Senate might vote against a new SALT II Treaty even if their own party chief President Carter favored it, Romanov asked in astonishment, "But can't you discipline them?" For the Senator this incident demonstrated the vast "comprehension gap" that exists between the American reality and the perceptions of the Soviet leaders. As Senator John Glenn (D-Ohio) put it broadly, "They just don't understand the Senate." [100]

Subsequently, wherever the Senators went they tried to impress upon their Soviet hosts the constitutional role of the Senate and the independent nature of its members.[101]

In brief, the American Senators found themselves in the same position as Mosely in 1946 when he had to explain the treaty process to an unnamed Soviet representative at a Council of Foreign Ministers conference in answer to his inquiry as to why Senators Vandenberg and Connally were present. The failure of the present leadership to grasp this vital reality after 33 years suggests the impenetrability of ideas and concepts, new or old, at the top; for judging from what has been written in the USA Institute on the Congress and observing the extensive lobbying activities of Soviet officials and diplomats on Capitol Hill in recent years, such ignorance is not from lack of available expertise and knowledge.[102]

[99] Klose, Kevin. Soviets' Outlook Baffles Senators on Moscow Visit. The Washington Post, November 19, 1978, p. A16. Senator Henry Bellmon Republican of Oklahoma, coleader of the delegation, expressed very well the difficulty of discussions and negotiations in the formal environment with the Soviets when he said that he was "amazed at how closed these people's minds are. It seems that everything they do in the world is for peace, stability, purity, and that we shouldn't even suspect their motives or challenge them."

[100] Ibid.

[101] The delegation noted in their trip report: "Throughout the delegation's discussions with Soviet officials it was apparent that the Soviet side found it difficult if not impossible to grasp the reality that a SALT treaty negotiated in good faith and supported by the United States government could be defeated by the Senate. The Soviet side repeatedly questioned the grounds upon which individual Senators can challenge the judgment of the Executive Branch on various substantive issues addressed by the treaty, and tended to ascribe to those in the United States who opposed SALT. or were skeptical of its benefits to the United States, motives ranging from unfounded distrust of the Soviet Union to a calculated desired [sic] to resume the Cold War." (Report of Senate Delegation Visit to the Soviet Union, 1979, pp. 11–12.)

[102] The Soviets seemed to have become aware of the powers of the Congress in the struggle during 1973–1974 over the Trade Reform Act and the Jackson-Vanik amendment linking trade concessions with liberalized Soviet emigration policies. During this period particularly, as the press said, they "vigorously" lobbied the Congress in support of the bill without the restrictions.

In March 1973, Vladimir S. Alkhimov, then Deputy Minister of Foreign Trade, headed a delegation to the United States whose expressed purpose was to lobby Congress on behalf of the trade bill and against restrictions. The press spoke of the Soviet officials going on a "political offensive" and "lobbying" Capitol Hill. On March 12, Alkhimov attended a luncheon with 13 Representatives for this purpose. (The New York Times, March 13. 1973, p. 48.) Alkhimov, now the Chairman of the Soviet State Bank, was a member of the delegation at the November 1978 meeting.

In May 1974, Boris N. Ponomarev, then an alternate member of the Politburo, headed a Congressional-sponsored delegation that included prominent members of the Soviet media. for the expressed purpose of lobbying the Congress on the trade bill. (The New York Times, May 11, 1974, p. 5, May 24, 1974. p. 7, and The Washington Star-News, May 24, 1974.) Ponomarev headed the Soviet delegation at the November 1978 meeting. He is now a member of the Politburo and the Secretariat of the CC.

(This episode does not, however, vitiate the great importance of the exchange of parliamentary delegations. Rather it points out their value and necessity. For both sides, such meetings are, like any negotiation, a learning process. And mutual exposure at the top can produce mutual benefits. What transpired in less formal settings, as when the individual Senators were entertained in the homes of their hosts, can only be surmised; but this is significant, for as this study shows in less formal one-on-one encounters a genuine dialog can and often does take place.)

5. SUMMING UP

Influence in the foreign policy process can thus be measured by access to the Politburo. Being subject to pressures, it does draw upon internal resources and does seek outside advice, and accordingly creates avenues for influence. The Foreign Ministry has considerable influence, though not in national security-foreign policy matters where the Defense Ministry is preeminent. The institutes dealing with foreign policy do have some access. But counterforces within the system, notably the commonly shared world outlook of the Soviet elite and the institutional arrangements that insure control from the center, can neutralize the inflow of new, and old, ideas and concepts. Exposure of the Senate parliamentary delegation to the system in microcosm suggests the difficulty of inculcating positive influences and inducing creative change.

F. AND THE FUTURE GENERATIONS

1. WESTERNIZERS VS. SLAVOPHILES

Perhaps one of the most important problems facing American foreign policymakers is what direction the future generation of Soviet leaders will take. The problem was posed by Dr. Marshall D. Shulman in the historical context of the 19th Century struggle between the Westernizers versus the Slavophiles, a struggle, that is, between those Russians who envisioned a Russian future modernized economically and integrated into the Western technological and scientific civilization, or one that was isolationist, innerdirected, nationalistic, and orthodox. Shulman, a professor at Columbia University and internationally know specialist on Soviet affairs, is presently Special Adviser to the Secretary of State on Soviet Affairs. In testimony before the House International Relations Committee on October 26, 1977, he set forth the problem of the coming generation:

—The "central drama of Soviet political life is between tendencies toward orthodoxy and toward modernization, contending in every aspect of domestic and foreign policy, sometimes perhaps within the minds of individual Soviet leaders";

—"There can be observed at both ends of the political spectrum—among the dissidents as well as among the Party elite—the modern equivalent of the dual strains in Russian history of the Slavophiles and the Westerners";

—These divisions impact upon two important questions that affect the present and future development of the Soviet Union;

—The first question is, whether the new generation of men now in their forties and early fifties, better educated, more familiar with the outside world, but not a homogenous group, "will tend to move toward nationalism and orthodoxy, or toward Western-style modernization";

—That, "we cannot now predict," but to the extent that they see their interest in a "responsible involvement" in the world economy and world community, "they should not feel from what we do or say that this option is closed to them";

—The second question is, how the new leadership will "deal with some fundamental structural problems in the Soviet economy," notably low productivity and lags in the advanced technological sector, the solutions to which reflect the "impulses toward orthodoxy versus modernization" and "appear to have some correlation with the differences between the generations";

—While not underestimating Soviet capabilities of managing its "problems on a day-to-day basis without any clear-cut solutions to these choices, it may have some relevance for our own policy. choices that the development of economic relations with the advanced industrial societies of the West is bound to have some influence on the directions that will emerge." [103]

In brief, the age-old struggle between the Westernizers versus the Slavophiles still goes on in the Soviet context and will continue into the next generation of young, more educated Soviet elite pulled in opposite directions toward internationalism and nationalistic orthodoxy; this new elite will be faced more acutely with the problem of economic modernization; integration into the world economy and world community could be imperative for modernization; and the United States should not close out this option to the undecided coming new generation of leaders.[104]

2. RELEVANCE TO FOREIGN POLICY

(a) Engagement or isolationism

The relevance to foreign policy of the direction that the next generation takes is apparent from the economic requirements of modernization. A future Soviet Union that looks to the technologically advanced industrial West for remedies to its economic and technological problems would by necessity have to build a political relationship that was congenial to both sides. A Russia of this type, as the decade of the Soviet policy of détente suggests, would have to be a dealing Russia, a negotiating Russia, pursuing a policy of engagement in the world political and economic community.

In contrast, a Russia accenting orthodoxy, autarchy, nationalism, and isolationism would probably be quite different, if the decade of the cold war after World War II can be a useful guide. In this period of acute internal stress and economic reconstruction, Soviet Russia had turned in upon itself and relied on its own resources. Feeding its fears and anxieties for security from a presumed external threat, it became hostile to negotiations and to the normal conduct of diplomacy.

---

[103] House International Relations Committee, Hearings, Internal Dynamics of Soviet Foreign Policy, 1978, pp. 299–300.

[104] In discussing the ascent of a new generation by 1987 when the 36th Party Congress takes place, Hyland noted that the economy is likely to enter a period of severe strain in which "dependence on the west will grow"; that by 1987 "it is virtually impossible that more than two or three of the present top echelon of leaders will survive, and then only as quite elder statesmen"; and that "in short, a new leadership will for the first time face pressures that have been forestalled, deferred or ignored by the present generation." (Hyland, William G. Commentary: SALT and Soviet-American Relations. International Security, vol. 3, Fall 1978 : 161–162.

While neither course can be predicted, as Shulman cautioned, still the emergence of the era of interdependence would seem to encourage more a future of engagement rather than one of isolationism. But, whatever the choice of future directions, neither the United States nor the West can escape its foreign policy implications.

(b) Lasting security concerns

A persistent, invariable element in considerations on the future generation is the seemingly unchanging fundamental characteristic of Soviet concern with national security. The Soviet policymaking elite, as Wolfe observed, share a common outlook on such matters as national security, though some variations on themes have been expressed suggesting the possibility that some marginal long-term changes could take place.[105] But rapid and radical shifts in underlying attitudes on security shared by a majority of the elite were, as Wolfe contended, "indeed unlikely." Accordingly, he noted looking into the future, Soviet policy "will tend to run more or less consistently in its established groove." While acknowledging the impossibility of predicting precise positions the Soviet decisionmakers would adopt on defense and foreign policy issues, Wolfe made this conjecture:

* * * it would seem that they may be prone to act conservatively, avoiding steps which might appear to involve substantial revision of the military posture the USSR has built at great cost, or drastic revision of the doctrine governing its use. In short, most of the changes in the policies and priorities affecting Soviet military power that the leadership may find it operatively convenient to entertain, seem likely to be more at the margin than fundamental.[106]

With respect to the use of expanded Soviet military power by the successor generation in the decade or so ahead—doubtless "an increasingly disturbing question here and abroad," Wolfe said—caution and acceptance of risks depending upon U.S. power and the prevailing military balance would seem to be the expected behavior. As Wolfe predicted:

If one suggests, as we have, that established habits and attitudes are likely to remain quite persistent, then one could expect the Soviet leaders—even the newer generation that takes over when the present gerontocracy fades from the scene—to proceed with caution and to avoid outright military adventures that could evoke a dangerous response from the United States.

On the other hand, Soviet preception of risks would certainly be influenced greatly by the military balance of the day, suggesting the need for the United States and its allies—not to mention, perhaps, a nonally like Communist China—to maintain a military balance in the world adequate to constrain inimical uses of Soviet military power.[107]

---

[105] Wolfe's testimony, House International Relations Committee, hearings, Internal Dynamics of Soviet Foreign Policy, 1978, pp 35–42.

[106] Ibid., pp. 126–127.

[107] Ibid., pp. 127–128. The Carter Administration has also linked the generational problem with the need for imposing restraints on the future expansion of Soviet military power as claimed in SALT II. In a speech on Apr. 5, 1979, delivered in Chicago, Brzezinski maintained that even with a treaty limiting strategic missiles and bombers through 1984, the Soviet Union and the United States would continue to compete for global influence. Noting that the present Soviet leadership would soon pass from the scene, he contended that it was vital that the new Soviet leaders be confronted with constraints on the expansion of military power. "Behind this statement," wrote Richard Burt in his analysis, "is the belief of many Government experts that a younger generation of Soviet leaders is bound to be more self-confident and perhaps more assertive." (Burt, Richard. A New Approach to Selling the Arms Pact. The New York Times, Apr. 6, 1978, p. A11.)

A view suggesting the perception of the younger Soviet generation with respect to the general attitude toward security seemed to reflect a certain ambivalence. On the one hand, there was a feeling of a greater sense of security by virtue of an awareness of Soviet power. On the other, this generation, who were children during the war and reconstruction, have memories of times of great stress and insecurity. Such attitudes are not easily lost. With the passage of time and the continued growth of Soviet power, the historic feeling of insecurity was expected to diminish.

3. POTENTIAL FOR CHANGE WITHIN THE SOVIET SYSTEM

(a) *Rule by gerontocracy and emerging new professional elite*

Scholars studying political succession in the Brezhnev era agree that a gerontocracy rules the Soviet Union and that a new generation of trained technical specialists and professionals is waiting in the wings to assume power. Indeed, some are already well on the way.[108] The average age of the 13-member Politburo is now 68 years and almost 9 months, and the average age of the heads of 59 ministries of the U.S.S.R. (excluding the three recently deceased) is at present 64.[109]

It is also agreed that the trend toward professionalism is broadly on the increase. As noted above, evidence is considerable showing the emergence of a new elite in the foreign policy establishment. According to Prof. Jerry Hough, a specialist in Soviet affairs at Duke University and a student of changes in the Soviet elite,

The possibility of change in the foreign policy realm is * * * quite great, for the inner core of the 14 top foreign policymakers now average 70 years of age and their most natural successors are some 15 to 20 years younger.[110]

A similar professionalization, also noted above, has been observed in other institutions, including the scholarly community. Albert L. Salter, a specialist in Soviet political affairs, wrote that "a high degree of involvement by the academic institutes in the process of foreign policy formulation has been a conspicuous development in the Brezhnev period, one which may well have become a permanent feature of the Soviet political system." [111]

This trend toward professionalization has also taken place within the party where emphasis has been placed on a preference for the technically skilled as well as the politically adept.[112] The effect has undoubtedly been to fortify, perhaps even insure, the continuation of this broad thrust toward professionalism in Soviet society.[113]

---

[108] For general analysis of this problem accompanied by statistics, see, Salter, Albert L. Portrait of an Emerging Soviet Elite Generation. In. Simes, Dmitri K. et. al. Soviet Succession : Leadership in Transition. Published for the Center for Strategic and International Studies. Georgetown University, by Sage Publications, Beverly Hills/London, 1978. Chapter II, pp. 35–40. (The Washington Papers. No. 59, v. 6.)

[109] Brezhnev Group Strengthened in Kremlin Leadership Shifts. RFE–RL. Radio Liberty Research, RL 266/78, Nov. 28, 1978, p. 2.
The extent of the gerontocracy is evident from a survey done by the research staff of Radio Liberty which "shows that the average of the heads of the 59 ministries of the U.S.S.R. (excluding the three recently deceased) is at present 64. The oldest is already in his 81st year, the youngest is 46. Fourteen ministers are over 70 years old and only 12 are younger than 60. Thirty-three ministers are between 60 and 70 years of age. 22 of them between 65 and 70. Ministries as important as those of Defense, Finance, Foreign Affairs, Foreign Trade. and Internal Affairs are headed by men who have passed their 66th birthdays." (The Natural Hazards of a Geronocracy. RFE–RL. Radio Library Research, RL 13/79, Jan. 12, 1979. p. 1.)

[110] Hough Testimony, House International Relations Committee, Hearings, Internal Dynamics of Soviet Foreign Policy, 1978, p. 269. In explaining the character of the elite within the foreign policy establishment, Hough noted that Dobrynin "was actually a teacher of a number of the people now in the Ministry, and in the institutes when he led seminars in the Foreign Policy Institutes in the late forties. . . ." "It strikes me, as far as the policy toward the United States is concerned," he continued, "one has a complex in the Ministry and in the key institutes involved. It seems to me in this complex just below, you have a group with a great many similarities—educated together in the late 1940's or early 1950's—who give the impression of being a real establishment. That establishment impresses me, particularly on policy toward the United States, as being quite influential, and there is a great deal of contact nad conversation and discussion among them." (pp. 283–284.)

[111] Salter, op. cit., pp. 35–36.

[112] Ibid., pp. 34–35.

[113] See especially Salter's recounting of the 43-year-old Gennadiy Bogomyakov's rise to RFSR obkom first secretary on the strength of his specialized knowledge as a professional geologist. Bogomyakov has been an outspoken advocate of Siberian development especially the exploitation of Tyumen gas. According to Salter, " * * * Bogomyakov can serve, for the moment, as a model of the kind of successful member of the younger generation that is beginning to emerge in the central elite and will increasingly be a factor in Soviet decisionmaking in the future." (Ibid., pp. 38–39.)

(b) *Soviet intellectual elite: "Vehicle of change"?*

Emergence of an intellectual elite, such as that in the foreign policy establishment, is one thing; access to power is another; penetration of influence into the ruling Politburo is still another. Unity of the party elite, encouraged by a recruitment and promotion system of self-perpetuation together with powerful forces of conformity within the Soviet system, make political transformations within the system extraordinarily slow and difficult.[114]

In contrast, the emerging intellectual elite is neither homogeneous nor united; but rather, as Petrov observed, the differences within their set of beliefs are "vast and important," and the elite itself is scattered and disorganized within a system that controls all levers of power.[115] It works against considerable odds. Yet in the course of time, Petrov suggested, the Politburo, for reasons of self-interest, the imperatives of governing the state successfully, and having no need to fear for their power, may come to rely increasingly upon this source of expert "outside advice" from the Soviet intellectual elite, thus "giving tacit approval to this strange adversary relationship in an otherwise tightly-organized system." Petrov looked upon this phenomenon as "at least potentially, a vehicle of change in a regime that has been notorious in its ability to resist evolution." "A natural impulse is not to overrate it," Petrov cautiously concluded, "but in the absence of other positive forces on the scene it clearly warrants watching." [116]

---

[114] For a discussion of conformity and homogeneity within the political system, see. Salter, op. cit., pp. 26–31. The intensity of conformity within the Soviet system was illustrated by the case of Mstislav Rostropovich, the renowned Russian conductor. In the Soviet Union, he said, the "Ministry of Culture makes every plan for me. They decide countries and programs I play. Here I am absolutely free. For artists, that is an incredible feeling. At first, I always think I have forgot to ask permission from somebody. It is like a sickness." (The Magnificent Maestro. Time, v. 110, October 24, 1977 : 88.) Rostropovich is currently music director of the National Symphony Orchester in Washington, D.C.
In explaining the role of the Politburo in policymaking, Petrov stressed the slowness of its deliberations and the uniformity of the membership : "The system assures stability and continuity in the foreign affairs of the Soviet state, but it has serious disadvantages. Policy formation is a slow and cumbersome process, making fundamental revisions of old policies difficult. Since the leaders have virtual life tenure, new blood penetrates upper echelons extremely slowly, and the party bureaucracy makes sure that only compatible individuals move up the ladder." (Petrov, op. cit., p. 830.)
[115] Ibid., pp. 847 and 850.
[116] Ibid., p. 850. Views on the evolution of the Soviet system and on the new generation vary. Dr. Andrei Sakharov, the noted Soviet physicist and leading dissident who epitomizes an element in the Soviet intelligentsia that has opted for a life of protest outside the "system," was optimistic about political evolution in the Soviet Union, but in time. He said in an interview: "I think that at present, the activity of independently-minded people, those who are striving for open public discussion, for freedom to express their convictions, and for more information about the state of the country—all this activity is creating the preconditions for such an evolution in the future. In the first place, it is creating the preconditions for a transformation of public consciousness, which has been deformed by decades of terror, of ideological pressure, and ideological monopoly.
"I have no hope of seeing any real changes in the immediate future. In the broad historical perspective, I see that society is alive and is continuing to develop. In the past 40 years, it has indeed undergone a colossal transformation. It is obvious that in the long run, the human spirit will find within itself the strength to transform life and to transform itself in the way that human dignity demands." (Bower, Elizabeth. When Will Mother Russia Wake Up From Her Long Sleep? The Times [London], November 7, 1977, p. 14.)
Shulman cautioned against the type of person that might emerge from this future generation of leadership. Noting the diversity within the emerging elite in their forties and early fifties, Shulman warned that "it would be a mistake * * * to be beguiled by hopes and think that, because people are younger that they are necessarily more flexible. They might be, but there are also some among them who are really quite nationalistic, some among them who may be quite as rigid and inflexible as their elders. * * *" On the other hand, Shulman appeared to be hopeful about the positive effect of cultural exchanges on this emerging elite : "Just the fact that there are now thousands of people in the Soviet Union, many of them in positions of responsibility, who know the outside world better, are less provincial, makes the regime less likely to make reckless mistakes than it would do if it were still operating with the kind of parochialism that characterized the

Taken in the larger context of rising professionalism within the emerging new generation and in the still larger world setting of interdependence, this phenomenon indeed "warrants watching."

G. Summing Up

In sum, notwithstanding the problem of limited sources, it is possible to suggest a number of generalizations. The diplomatic establishment and the Foreign Ministry in the Brezhnev era represent, by and large, an extension of the trends and a magnification of the characteristics associated with the Khrushchev years, particularly the emphasis on training a new foreign policy elite and developing still further the supporting intellectual resources in the institutes.

Evaluation of the establishment, though on the basis of "patchy" evidence at best, suggests a favorable Soviet self-perception, affirmed in most essentials by assessments in the West, but with some serious reservations with respect to the adverse impact of ideology and common shortcomings normally associated with totalitarian regimes.

The influence of this establishment on the foreign policy process is considerable, though the Defense Ministry is preeminent in matters relating to the national security aspects of foreign policy, as in the case of SALT.

Though a new spirit of professionalism has elevated the quality of the foreign policy establishment, notably the training of diplomats and the enhanced and improved role of the institutes, still the influence and impact of new and old ideas and concepts on the leadership, but foreign to it, through the foreign policy establishment can be neutralized by the negative effects of a commonly held world outlook

Stalin period." (Gwertzman. Bernard. How Shulman Views Soviet Motives and Strategies. Interview. The New York Times. Apr. 10, 1978, p. E4.)

U.S. Ambassador to the Soviet Union Malcolm Toon made the following appraisal of changes in policy when asked if he foresaw any significant change in Soviet foreign or domestic policies when the Brezhnev generation of leaders finally gave way to a new generation: "Not with the next generation. The people we think might possibly succeed to power think basically the same way as the current leadership. The important thing to recognize, it seems to me, is that Soviet policies are by and large a function of events, world conditions, and circumstances rather than being linked to any particular personality. When you have a change in personalities at the top that does not necessarily mean that you're going to see a change in policy. Policies will remain more or less the same." (Interview with U.S. Ambassador to Moscow: Reflections on the Soviet Union and Its Goals. Los Angeles Times, Jan. 8, 1979, pp. 18–19.)

Soviet self-perception of the improving quality of the new generation of diplomats suggests that the expansion of knowledge, combined with more intensive and better training opportunities, would tend to make the Soviet diplomat quite a different person, and particularly, would better equip him to compete with his American counterpart. Whether this means the development of an improved relationship may be open to question. On the one hand, the expansion of knowledge would not lead necessarily to an erosion of ideology and thus alter their behavior vis-a-vis the Americans; differences would still be there. But on the other hand, through this enlargement of technical knowledge and exposure to foreign cultures the possibilities of seeking out and becoming aware of more mutually advantageous areas of interest would also be enlarged and accordingly could increase the prospects for better relations. In large measure, this self-perception is not remarkably unlike Garthoff's view with respect to genuine negotiations with the Soviets.

Ambassador Beam is not particularly sanguine about favorable changes in the future, though he does see continued progress in the SALT process. Expectations with respect to some of the younger members in the leadership such as Romanov, the party boss in Leningrad, have not been borne out. The leadership, young and old, according to Beam, are "really hardboiled people." Whether the Arbatovs and those in the younger generation waiting in the wings will alter the direction of Soviet policy, he said, "really depends upon who is going to take over power and be in power." As an instrument of the leadership, he observed, the direction of Soviet foreign policy and the characteristics of the Foreign Ministry as an institution will depend upon who is in control, and on this point, Beam said, "it's very hard to speculate." (Interview with Jacob D. Beam, May 23, 1979.)

of the Soviet elite and by institutional arrangements of party control over the entire process.

The character of the future generation, waiting in the wings to assume power, is being shaped in the Soviet version of the historic Russian struggle between the Westernizers and Slavophiles. The outcome of this contest, to be determined largely by the choice of solutions to serious economic and technological problems, could determine whether Soviet foreign policy will move in the internationalist direction of continued engagement with the West or retreat to a modified form of isolationism, nationalism, and orthodoxy. For this new generation, whatever the choice—and interdependence is on the side of the Westernizers—national security issues are expected to remain a durable and unchanging concern, and the use of expanding Soviet military power exercised with caution and restraint, depending upon the prevailing balance of military power.

Finally, a crucial factor in this generational problem is the declining gerontocracy on the one hand and the rising professionalism among the nation's young elite on the other. Despite powerful forces of institutional conformity, the emergence of this Soviet intelligentsia as "outside" expert advisers, especially the "new breed" of fourth generation diplomats and their associates in the foreign policy institutes, suggests a potential "vehicle of change" within the system.

III. SOME CHARACTERISTICS OF SOVIET DIPLOMACY AND NEGOTIATIONS IN THE BREZHNEV ERA

A. BREZHNEV'S REPORT TO THE 25TH PARTY CONGRESS

1. AFFIRMING THE KHRUSHCHEV LEGACY OF PEACEFUL COEXISTENCE: PARADOX OF GOALS

Perhaps the most comprehensive presentation of the foreign policy context within which the Soviet diplomatic establishment functions is the General Secretary's report to the Party Congress. Brezhnev's report to the 25th Congress on February 24, 1976, served this function for it gave perhaps the most accurate current reading on the Soviet worldview, particularly with respect to the Soviet desire for accommodation with the West through peaceful coexistence and the pursuit of traditional revolutionary goals principally in the Third World. In his report Brezhnev assessed world affairs from the summit of Soviet power and authority; took stock of the Soviet Union's participation in international affairs since the last 24th Congress in 1971; and judged its impact to be global and significant.[1]

Ordinarily, such reports contain the distilled essence of Soviet thinking on foreign policy. New foreign policy goals are often set forth, old ones reaffirmed; successes are magnified, failures minimized, or muted; priorities assigned, expectations proclaimed—and all within an ideological framework that assumes the assured and ultimate victory of communism and the defeat of capitalism.

Generally, the Brezhnev foreign policy report constituted a summary statement of major foreign policy concerns of the Soviet Union as seen from Moscow. Specifically, it recreates the paradox of a Soviet Union simultaneously seeking revolutionary goals, while affirming a policy of détente. Thus in this report Brezhnev reaffirms the Khrushchev legacy of peaceful coexistence.

2. SUPPORT FOR NATIONAL LIBERATION MOVEMENT IN THE THIRD WORLD

Brezhnev's report, requiring more than 5 hours to deliver, focused on two central foreign policy problems, in this order: (1) Soviet support for the national liberation movements in the Third World; and (2) the viability of détente with the West.

Perceiving a further upsurge of the revolutionary spirit in the Third World and a "deepening of the crisis of capitalism"—and thus

---

[1] Brezhnev, Leonid. Report of the CPSU Central Committee and the Party's Immediate Tasks in Domestic and Foreign Policy. Moscow Domestic Service, Feb. 24, 1976. in, Foreign Broadcast Information Service (FBIS). Daily Report, Soviet Union. Proceedings of the 25th CPSU Congress. vols. 1 and 3, No. 38, supp. 16, Feb. 25, 1976, pp. 6-29. This section draws upon, Whelan, Joseph G. Soviet 25th Party Congress: Foreign Policy Aspects of Brezhnev's Report. Issue Brief: IB76020. Washington, The Library of Congress, Congressional Research Service, Mar. 23, 1976, 5 pp. (Major Issues System). Quoted material is taken directly from the issue brief and is not cited in this text.

new opportunities—Brezhnev reaffirmed Soviet policy of support for the national liberation movements. Soviet relations with the liberated or developing countries "have expanded and become more lasting." The political content of "our ties has become richer." Despite difficulties, "profound progressive changes are taking place" within the Third World; "the class struggle is intensifying;" its influence in world affairs has increased "appreciably." The Soviet attitude toward "the complex processes" in the Third World was "clearcut and definite." Brezhnev explained:

The Soviet Union does not meddle in the domestic affairs of other countries and peoples. Respect for the sacred right of each people and each country to select their own road of development is a firm principle of Leninist foreign policy. However, we do not hide our views. In the developing countries, as everywhere, we are on the side of the forces of progress, democracy and national independence, and we treat them as our friends and comrades-in-arms. Our party is rendering and will render support to peoples who are fighting for their freedom. The Soviet Union is not looking for any benefits for itself, is not hunting for concessions, is not trying to gain political supremacy and is not seeking any military bases. We are acting as our revolutionary conscience and our Communist convictions permit us.

Accordingly, the Soviet Union looked favorably upon the Communist victory in Vietnam, Laos, and Cambodia; the continued achievements of socialism in Cuba; and the success of the People's Republic of Angola in its struggle "to defend its independence," receiving in the process the "support of progressive forces throughout the world." Policies of support for the emerging states of the Middle East and Asia and pledges of "solidarity" with the struggle for African national liberation were reaffirmed——

From the rostrum of our Congress we emphasize once again that the Soviet Union fully supports the lawful aspirations of the emerging states, their determination to rid themselves completely of imperialist exploitation and to manage their national resources themselves.

In this area of "radical social changes," Brezhnev continued, socialism has continued to "strengthen and expand." Victories of the national liberation movements have opened up "new horizons" for the countries gaining their independence. The "class struggle" of the working people against oppression, monopolies, and exploitation was "gaining strength." "The revolutionary-democratic, anti-imperialist movement" was assuming "ever larger proportions." Altogether these forces constituted "the development of a worldwide revolutionary process."

3. VIABILITY OF DÉTENTE

Détente with the United States and the West was reaffirmed as a viable and successful policy, though serious differences in the area of military détente persisted and were acknowledged. According to Brezhnev, experience has "confirmed" what he labeled the realism and wisdom of the 1971 peace program which had laid out the course of moving from cold war to peaceful coexistence and set the stage for the conclusion of the SALT I negotiations. The "normalization of the international climate" was "convincing proof" that the attainment of a "lasting peace" was "a fully realizable task."

Among the positive gains of peaceful coexistence were: the "normalization" of relations with Western Europe; recognition of the inviolability of frontiers; improving relations with France, West Germany, and the other countries of Western Europe; success of CSCE (i.e., the Helsinki agreement) in securing the "interests of détente and a stable peace in Europe"; continuing improvement in relations with the United States based upon a series of agreements the most important being, "The Basic Principles of Mutual Relations," "The Agreement on the Prevention of Nuclear War," and the series of strategic arms limitations treaties and agreements; positive developments in relations with Japan, despite "direct foreign instigation" (i.e., China) in preventing a final peace settlement; and finally the enrichment of relations with Canada and the noticeable expansion of those with Latin America in an environment characterized by the "strengthening of their political and economic independence."

4. BARRIER TO DÉTENTE: ARMS RACE

Economic, scientific-technological, and cultural cooperation with the capitalist states increased "significantly," Brezhnev continued, but the main barrier to peace remained; namely, "the struggle to end the arms race and to achieve disarmament."

To achieve this goal—an "urgent" task—the Soviet Union has advocated: "general and complete disarmament" as "our ultimate end"; restrictions on the proliferation of nuclear weapons and the banning and destruction of chemical weapons; agreement on SALT II, a matter "of very great importance" for the developing Soviet-American relations and for "consolidating general peace"; restrictions on building bases in the Indian Ocean; reduction of armed forces and armaments in central Europe (MBFR), the responsibility for the failure of which rested on NATO for trying to "insure for themselves unilateral military advantages"; and a proposal "to conclude a worldwide treaty on the nonuse of force in international relations."

The "main motive" of the proponents of the arms race, Brezhnev argued, was "the so-called Soviet threat." There "is no such thing as a Soviet threat either to the West or to the East. This is a monstrous lie from beginning to end. The Soviet Union has no intention of attacking anyone. The Soviet Union has no need of war. The Soviet Union is not increasing its military budget." Since "opponents of détente and disarmament" possessed "considerable resources" and "imperialism's aggressive activity" continued, "peace-loving forces must, therefore, show a high degree of vigilance." Accordingly, the CPSU "has paid the necessary attention to strengtening the defense capability of our country and the perfection of the armed forces."

5. REVOLUTION AND DÉTENTE: CONCEPTS IN HARMONY

Brezhnev viewed success in international relations with great satisfaction and pledged to continue his policies "with redoubled energy." He neither doubted the superiority nor the historically assured destiny of communism; nor did he doubt the vigorous growth of the revolutionary process as a continuing world reality and its movement in the direction of communism. "The events of the past few years," he said, presumably having in mind "the deepening crisis of capitalism" and growing political disorders within the Third World, confirmed with "new force that capitalism is a society without a future." Counter-revolution and international imperialism (i.e., the forces of democracy, capitalism, and democratic socialism) were forces "doomed to failure" and the "cause of freedom and the cause of progress" (i.e., communism) were "invincible."

Brezhnev also renewed the Soviet ideological commitment to revolution. "New horizons" (new targets of opportunity?) were opening, especially in the Third World. And yet possible contradictions between adherence to the principle of Communist revolution and that of détente were disallowed. "Détente does not in the slightest way abolish, and cannot abolish or change the laws of the class struggle," Brezhnev said, adding, "We do not conceal the fact that we see détente as a way to create more favorable conditions for peaceful Socialist and Communist construction. This merely confirms that socialism and peace are indivisible."

6. FLAWED LOGIC: PERSISTING CONTRADICTION

Brezhnev's judgment on the global significance of Soviet foreign policy suggests a full appreciation of Soviet power and a will to act in its role as an international superpower and arbiter of world events. It reaffirms the commitment to peaceful coexistence, and paradoxically, it suggests also that the Third World remains a prime target of Soviet foreign policy for the 1970's.

But Brezhnev's analysis of the world around him is seriously flawed: It assumes that it is possible to pursue a policy of peaceful accommodation with the United States and the West, while simultaneously adhering to, advocating, and indeed carrying out a policy of revolution and intervention in the Third World. This is a contradiction in policy and use of power that, however much it may be glossed over with casuistic argument, objectively could invite risks of superpower confrontation and possibly even war. Such were the essential ingredients in the Angolan civil war late in 1975: a superpower confrontation was in the making; and only congressional rejection of indirect military involvement, proposed by the administration, prevented a test of policy. Similarly in the Ethiopian-Somalia crisis of 1977–78, the same ingredients for confrontation were there.

The potentiality remains; for the contradiction is still unresolved.

B. BREZHNEV'S STYLE IN DIPLOMACY

1. A "BUSINESSLIKE" APPROACH

The Brezhnev approach to the conduct of diplomacy, indeed to the administration of the Soviet state, was probably best summed up in the term he himself has frequently used; namely, "businesslike." This conservative, obstensibly cautious, "businesslike" style, at least as revealed in public, contrasted sharply with the radical, emotionally charged, risk-taking style of Khrushchev.

Where Khrushchev was flamboyant, bombastic, and abusive, Brezhnev was sober, cautious, restrained, with good manners on display;

where Khrushchev threatened and aggressively pressured his adversaries in public, Brezhnev was tough and firm but under control; where Khrushchev was explosively emotional and unsteady in the course of policy, Brezhnev was cool, rational, orderly, and, as the Soviets would say, "principled"; where Khrushchev's conduct and utterances in public diplomatic settings were those of a man plagued with a deep sense of inferiority and insecurity, Brezhnev's were those of a leader confident and secure in the knowledge that his country was growing in political and military power.

The paradox of these contrasting personalities is that Khrushchev's diplomacy of threat and intimidation, one that sought political, and inevitably, military showdowns, was based on an unfavorable balance of power, though claiming the contrary, while Brezhnev's "businesslike" approach was based on an emerging strategic parity in the military balance. And while Khrushchev's bravado in diplomacy brought on the humiliation of a backdown in Cuba, the sober, low-pressured, indeed beguiling, Brezhnev succeeded through diplomacy, the largesse of military assistance, and the cautious use of military power, where Khrushchev had failed, in projecting Soviet power on a global scale and into key strategic areas of the Third World.

2. BREZHNEV'S ADDRESS TO THE HEADS OF DIPLOMATIC MISSIONS

Much of the flavor of Brezhnev's diplomatic style was evident in his brief address to the heads of diplomatic missions at a Kremlin reception on July 8, 1977. Brezhnev was gracious and generous in his remarks to the ambassadors, emphasizing particularly the great value of their profession as an instrument of peace and pledging through diplomacy and negotiations to strengthen the forces of peace.

Brezhnev did not want to review Soviet policies which, he said, the ambassadors knew quite well and accordingly reported to their home governments. But he expressed his own appreciation for their "important function" of explaining to the Soviet Government the policies of their countries. Bearing in mind their "responsibilities and interests," he wanted to make only one point, and it was that, "only the profound knowledge" of Soviet policy and "only a weighted and unbiased assessment of any concrete proposals or actions by the Soviet Union" make it possible "to arrive at objective conclusions and to find the right path towards the truth."

Furthermore, only the ambassadors and their embassies could accomplish this task, Brezhnev contended, by virtue of their "subtle and accurate perception of the political pulse of the receiving country"; by "their contacts and their information" that "dissipate misunderstandings and misconceptions" that sometimes arise; by their ability to "see to it every day that the intentions of both sides are understood correctly, that the imaginary is not taken for the reality and vice versa." "In a word," Brezhnev continued, "a lot depends on you, ambassadors, in building an atmosphere of friendship or good will, of greater or lesser confidence in the relations between your respective countries and the Soviet Union." In the exercise of their duties Brezhnev pledged the assistance of the Presidium of the Supreme Soviet and the Soviet Government.

Brezhnev went on to stress that international life was "very dynamic" and that the forces of peace and "threats menacing peace" were actively contending. For Brezhnev, "one of the primary objectives of a far-sighted policy and diplomacy of reason is to expand in every way the range of opportunities" for peace and "to reduce the magnitude of the threats." The role of the ambassadors and their embassies was, he said, "great in achieving this objective, too." The same high standards of professionalism, he assured his audience, were also applied to Soviet diplomats.

Brezhnev asked the ambassadors to convey a message to the leadership of their respective countries, and in it he made these pledges: to establish good relations with all countries of the world; to contribute to the solution of any international problem; to work for the removal by peaceful means of any "seat of military danger"; and to seek control over weapons, particularly those of mass destruction.

Finally, Brezhnev pledged that the Soviet Union "will always be an active participant in any negotiation or any international action aimed at developing peaceful cooperation and strengthening the security of peoples." And in conclusion he expressed the Soviets' "firm belief, that realism in politics, and will to détente and progress will ultimately triumph and mankind will be able to step into the 21st century in the conditions of peace stable as never before. And we shall do all in our power to see it come true." [2]

Thus Moscow's diplomatic corps was given assurances that the General Secretary respected their profession; that he did not doubt the value of their representational functions; that only in such an ambassadorial capacity was it possible to create and maintain mutual friendship and confidence; that the Soviet Government would negotiate to develop peaceful cooperation and strengthen security; and that a stable peace could be achieved by "realism in politics" and "will to détente and progress."

3. DIFFERENTIATION AMONG RELATIONSHIPS: THE CZECHOSLOVAK CASE, 1968

(a) Factors affecting differentiation

To this audience of ambassadors representing a broad spectrum of nation-states, Brezhnev was speaking in very general terms. But differentiations have to be made among countries in considering characteristics of Soviet diplomacy and negotiating behavior. Much depends upon the country: its size, power, resources, location, and relevance to Soviet interests; its political relationship with other power centers in the world; and its role in the larger equilibrium of power. This study focuses primarily on the superpower relationship. What pertains to the Soviet negotiating relationship with the United States does not necessarily obtain with respect to other states, say, Yugoslavia which balances precariously beween East and West and

---

[2] Moscow TASS in English. July 8, 1977 (FBIS, Daily Report, Soviet Union, vol. 3. No. 131, July 8, 1977 : R1–R–2.)

whose security ultimately depends upon the presence of NATO power.[2a] Where the relationship is that of client to sponsor, and the location of the country is beyond the direct perimeter of Soviet vital interests, as in the case of Egypt, Soviet behavior is quite different. Sadat could and did expel the Russians, with impunity.

But, such was not the case between the Soviet Union and Czechoslovakia in 1968 where fundamental Soviet security interests were at stake. A negotiated solution was not possible; the Czechoslovaks had no leverage against the Russians with which to effectively seek a negotiated settlement; the solution was imposed by Soviet diktat and military power. Some "negotiations" did take place between the Soviets and the Czechoslovak Communist leaders, and this case is particularly instructive for showing Brezhnev's diplomatic style when

[2a] Soviet treatment of Yugoslavia in a negotiating setting was revealed in the memoirs of former Yugoslav ambassador to the Soviet Union Veljko Micunovic that were published in 1977 ("Moskovske godine, 1956–1958" ["Years in Moscow, 1956–1958"] Liber, Zagreb, 1977, 530 pp.) In an entry for Feb. 16, 1957, Micunovic described his talks with Khrushchev in which he tried to persuade the Soviet leader to reverse Moscow's decision not to assist Yugoslavia economically. It was apparent that the Soviets wanted to punish Tito for his unwillingness to rejoin the Soviet bloc and for his criticism of the Soviet Union. After a sharp exchange between Khrushchev and the Yugoslav diplomat, the latter asked if that was his last word on Soviet aid because a Yugoslav economic delegation, headed by Nikola Mincev, had already been in Moscow for more than a month. Khrushchev replied, Micunovic noted, that "Mincev might just as well return to Belgrade since nothing could be changed." Micunovic said that the Yugoslav delegation had come to Moscow where instead of conducting negotiations "they were simply urged to sign Soviet decisions which had been prepared in advance. We cannot conduct negotiations in such a way, neither now nor on any other occasion." Micunovic went on to reveal how the Soviet leaders used ideological and political arguments when granting or suspending economic aid. (Stankovic, Slobodan. Memoirs of Yugoslavia's Former Ambassador to Moscow—Part II. Radio Free Europe Research. RAD Background Report/9. Yugoslavia, Jan. 20, 1978, pp. 3–4.)

Another insight into the Soviet-Yugoslav relationship was provided at the meeting between Micunovic and Suslov in April 1958 prior to the opening of the Seventh Congress of the League of Communists of Yugoslavia (LCY). The issue at hand was the Yugoslav party program which in essence amounted to a restatement of Yugoslavia's independent stance and resistance to Soviet encroachment. What was at stake in this encounter was not minor issues in contention but rather the entire LCY program. Micunovic had an unsuccessful talk with Khrushchev. His request for a second meeting was turned down, and he was told to see Suslov with whom, Micunovic realized, a meeting of minds was impossible. Micunovic gave this description of the encounter:

"I went to see Suslov with a pile of papers. I found him in his office hidden behind the mounds of papers and books on his desk. As soon as we had greeted each other, Suslov began criticizing our party program very sharply, in a loud voice. Suslov seemed so angry and furious that he was not able to control himself. He did not even offer me a seat; he was also standing at his desk and I facing him, listening to his embittered condemnation of our draft program. He behaved in such a way that this was not a talk at all. I listened to his attacks against Yugoslavia which were expressed in such a way as to suggest that I, or some other Yugoslav, had personally offended Suslov or his family, so that he now was settling accounts with me. After having reached this point, still standing with a sheaf of papers under my arm. I told Suslov that the matter in question was the party program of the Yugoslav rather than of the Soviet communists. I indicated my intention of interrupting my talk with him and leaving. Only then did Suslov offer me a chair and show any readiness to listen to me" (p. 431). (Stankovic, Slobodan. Memoirs of Yugoslavia's Former Ambassador In Moscow—Part III. Radio Free Europe Research. RAD Background Report/40, Yugoslavia, Mar. 1. 1978, pp. 5–6.)

The execution of Imre Nagy, the deposed Communist leader of the Hungarian revolution of 1956, provided still another example of Soviet contempt for Yugoslav sovereignty concerns. On June 7, 1958, the Soviet press announced the execution of Nagy and his colleagues. As Micunovic recorded in his diary, the diplomatic community in Moscow was "shocked and full of indignation." Though the Soviets attempted to give the impression that Nagy's execution was an Hungarian concern, not Russian, "most of the foreign commentators blame the Soviet Union for Nagy's execution." Micunovic noted that according to an agreement signed by the Yugoslav and Hungarian governments. Nagy and his associates were not to be held responsible for things they did up to Nov. 4. 1956. For that reason Nagy voluntarily left the Yugoslav Embassy in Budapest in November 1956. However, as Micunovic noted, "the Soviet Army forcibly seized them and took them to an unknown place. This is how the Russians, together with the Hungarians, violated the first state treaty signed by the new Hungarian government with another state, in this case with Yugoslavia." On June 19. 1958, Khrushchev received Micunovic for a talk. The atmosphere was tense. Micunovic told Khrushchev that Nagy's execution was "an irreparable mistake." Mention of the incident. Micunovic noticed. was "unpleasant to the Soviet leader." The diary entry continued:

"Khrushchev said this is a thing which concerns the Hungarians, rather than the Russians, that he personally approved the execution carried out by the Hungarians, and that he himself would have done the same. He criticized my referring to world public opinion, which is not worthy of a communist; the communists have other, class criteria in judging such things or similar ones." (Ibid., pp. 10–11.)

vital Soviet interests are at stake and the "negotiating" environment is totally one-sided and under Soviet control.

(b) *An insider's view of negotiating the Moscow "protocol"*

Briefly on the night of August 20–21, 1968, Soviet-led Warsaw Pact forces intervened in Czechoslovakia, seized Alexander Dubcek, the reformist Communist leader, and arrested the remaining party Presidium. On August 23, President Ludwig Svoboda went to Moscow with a delegation of representatives from the party and government where he was joined by Dubcek and other leaders who had been arrested.

In recalling this critical, but predetermined meeting, Zdenek Mlynar, the exiled former secretary of the Czechoslovak Communist Party (CPCZ) Central Committee, said: "What took place was not real negotiations with the two delegations sitting around a table but a series of talks between two or three people." [3]

The Czechoslovak leaders, divided between the reformers and the pro-Soviet "Stalinists" and at that moment isolated from the outside world, still hoped against hope that "the more open and technocratic forces, represented by Kosygin, might prevail over the dogmatic forces, which might be satisfied with the invasion." But that was not to happen. By then the reformers were in a minority and "even they realized that they could not challenge the Soviets lest an armed conflict explode in Czechoslovakia." Their strategy was to save what was possible of the reforms, but this had to be done through a negotiation where all the leverage was on the other side.

Recalling the "negotiations" over the Moscow "protocol", Mlynar said:

> The atmosphere was tense, though formally correct. The Soviets were strict and bureaucratic: They had engaged us in a war of nerves from which they knew that they would emerge victorious, whatever happened. They refused to discuss the invasion or the situation which promoted it, and would only discuss the document which was to govern our future relations. We had prepared a plan but the Russians refused to consider it, saying that we were not in a position to ask for anything. In practice, they asked us to sign a previously prepared statement without even hearing what we had to say: They told us that they were in no hurry and that they could even wait a week or two before we signed. [4]

According to Mlynar, "Brezhnev seemed very sure of himself." He told them that "they should not hope for any outside help, because even the United States regarded as binding the Yalta agreements, which acknowledged Soviet influence over Eastern Europe." Brezhnev was. moreover, confident that the United States "would never intervene in Czechoslovakia or Romania—only with regard to Yugoslavia could there be any doubt." With respect to reactions within the Communist world, Brezhnev told the Czechoslovak leaders, "Tito and the Romanian and Italian Communist parties will protest, but nothing will happen." [5]

After 2 hours of applied pressure in an aggravating war of nerves and with their country now firmly under Soviet military occupation, Dubcek finally signed the "protocol" that in effect legitimized the invasion, established the terms for "normalization," and set into opera-

---

[3] Pietro Sormani interview in Vienna with Zdenek Mlynar, Corriere Della Sera. Aug. 20, 1978, in FBIS, Daily Report, Soviet Union, vol. 2, no. 165, Aug. 24, 1968 : D4–D8.
[4] Ibid., p. D8.
[5] Ibid.

tion a political process in combination with a Soviet military presence, that was to lead to Dubcek's removal and the reversal of reforms under the Soviet-sponsored leader, Gustav Husak.

What heretofore had been implied was now formally proclaimed within weeks after the Moscow meeting; namely, the Brezhnev doctrine of "limited sovereignty"—meaning the presumed Soviet right to intervene when the unity and security of the bloc were threatened.

And, as the Czechoslovak Communist leaders found out, this doctrine is non-negotiable.

C. DIPLOMATIC LIFE IN MOSCOW

1. BOHLEN'S OBSERVATIONS IN 1968

At least partially indicative of Brezhnev's style in diplomacy is the manner in which Western diplomats lived in Moscow. Apparently, some improvements have been made over the previous years, but the major difficulties that make life so uncomfortable and oppressive have remained.

In the immediate background of the Czechoslovak crisis, the situation was generally grim—in fact, a substantial step backward from the advances made in the Khrushchev years. Bohlen made his last trip to the Soviet Union as a Foreign Service officer in July 1969. He drew this blemished portrait of Moscow, a city, he said, without hope:

> Moscow was depressing. The intellectual and cultural atmosphere showed no life except for a few younger artists. The population was apathetic, and certainly the faces on the street were gloomy and unsmiling. The youth, I was informed, were alienated, refraining from political life. They apparently did not even discuss politics among themselves. While in some parts of Moscow, notably on the Kalinsky Prospekt and in the Arbat district, there were some new shops and buildings, in general the physical appearance of Moscow had not altered much. The population was a shade better dressed. There was the same run-down air to many Soviet public buildings.[6]

And of the diplomatic community in Moscow, he wrote:

> I also found Moscow diplomatically sterile. The members of the Politburo practically never appeared in public. Foreign diplomats had little chance of discussing problems with Kremlin leaders. In short, the gains made in the days of Khrushchev, when Soviet leaders appeared at least at informal social affairs, had been wiped out.[7]

2. BEAM ON MARGINAL IMPROVEMENTS

With improvements in East-West relations there was some improvement in the life of diplomats in Moscow, but apparently not very much. Unlike his counter-part in Washington, Beam did not have access to the Soviet leaders—as he said, he had "pactically none." [8] He could not get much higher than Gromyko, though he did have access through distinguished American visitors. In fact, Beam's first contact with Brezhnev (he had been appointed ambassador in January 1969) occurred in April 1972, a month before the first Nixon-Brezhnev summit, when Secretary of Agriculture Earl L. Butz visited Moscow. Such was Beam's access, in contrast to that of Bohlen's and Thompson's during

[6] Bohlen, op. cit., p. 528.
[7] Ibid.
[8] Interview with Jacob D. Beam, May 23, 1979.

the Khrushchev years. Even at official receptions, such as those commemorating national days, not many of the leaders would attend. Only once did Beam remember the attendance of a Politburo member at a reception. "They really didn't socialize as much as the Poles did," Beam recalled. It was really a step back, as Bohlen noted above.[9]

However, communications between junior officers in the U.S. Embassy and their counterparts in the Soviet ministries became, as Beam reported, "increasingly easier even leading to reciprocal hospitality."[10] According to Beam, Ambassador Thompson was the "notable" exception among the few U.S. Ambassadors who seemed to have enjoyed this privilege. Beam's single experience had caused unfortunate consequences for his hosts, two Soviet mathematicians and their wives with whom the Ambassador and his wife "spent a lively social evening with wine and music." Beam's attempt to return their hospitality was met with a polite refusal and a message that they would not even be able to attend the traditional July Fourth reception at the American Embassy.[11]

Thus Beam left Moscow, as others before him, without really making a friend among Soviet officials.[12]

Because of the restriction on access to the political leaders and the unsatisfying relationship with the Foreign Ministry, Beam and his staff (as their predecessors had done before them), were left to analyze published sources such as Pravda in an effort to follow the ebb and flow, the shifts and turns of Soviet foreign policy. Though alternative sources of information were developed, as noted above, it was not possible to engage in a direct dialog with the Soviet leadership as is customary in diplomatic practice.[13]

Even exposure to what Americans would call professional meetings was restricted. In contrast to Washington where Communist diplomats are able to attend public meetings of professional organizations as sources of information, the U.S. Embassy staff in Moscow enjoys no such luxury. At best they have access through visiting scholars and delegations who might be attending meetings in Moscow, but when they leave, the contact ends; there can be no follow-up among Soviet professionals.[14]

Finally, the Ambassador was exposed to continuous surveillance. Nothing has changed in this respect over past practice, including that of bugging. In describing the "ever-present pressures" of duty in the Soviet Union where tours of duty for staff are limited to 2 years, Beam explained:

These [pressures] included indifferent housing, physical surveillance, and constant bugging of conversations by various types of concealed devices. Without revealing any secrets, it can be said that the Embassy and residence were surrounded by an electronic atmosphere of their own. The U.S. Government has been investigating whether such emanations are health hazards.[15]

Notwithstanding these handicaps and the enormous difficulties for an ambassador to function in the customary and normal fashion as understood in the West, still Beam had found life exciting, especially in dealing with multiple and unexpected crises. Nonetheless, the life

---

[9] Ibid.
[10] Beam, op. cit., pp. 231–232.
[11] Ibid., p. 232.
[12] Interview with Jacob D. Beam, May 23. 1979.
[13] Ibid.
[14] Ibid.
[15] Beam, op. cit., p. 227.

of the American diplomat in Moscow, as in the case of the whole foreign diplomatic corps, is a life of pressure and a life in isolation.[16]

3. GENERALIZATIONS BY ERIC CLARK

Eric Clark gave a dreary account of life in Communist countries for Western diplomats in his book on "The World of International Diplomacy," an account not remarkably different from yesteryear though he was writing in 1973. The things that hassled and frustrated Western diplomats before are, apparently, still hassling and frustrating them, notwithstanding the improvement of East-West relations in the Brezhnev era. As he wrote, "Even when relations are comparatively friendly, diplomacy in a Communist country is still hedged with controls, conditions, and frustrations." [17]

The catalog of complaints is long, consistent and familiar: The intensive personal and electronic surveillance that is constant and becomes unnerving; [18] the awareness that Embassy employees (who must be hired through the Soviet Government) report to the KGB, if they are not already KGB agents; [19] the inaccessability of information that is commonplace in the West because of traditional Russian xenophobia and inbred Soviet habits of secrecy; inordinate restrictions on travel; isolation from the people, to the point of stationing men outside embassies "to watch and vet callers—one other way of insuring that the policy of no contact between foreign diplomats and nationals is enforced" [20]—the list could go on.

What is, of course, most striking about even this spotty evidence is the marked difference between the life of the U.S. Ambassador in Moscow compared with that of the Soviet Ambassador in Washington. Sufficient evidence is presented elsewhere in this study to suggest that Dobrynin and his staff enjoy a far more satisfying professional existence, in such ways as extensive access to American officials, the availability of published information, and participation in professional organizations, than their American counterparts in Moscow.

D. SUMMING UP

In many respects the characteristics of Soviet diplomacy and negotiations in the Brezhnev era were an extension of those in the Khrushchev years and a reaffirmation of the Khrushchev legacy to his successors: The emphasis on peaceful coexistence in its most ambivalent meaning; the globalist thrust of Soviet policy; the rapid buildup of strategic forces to the point of parity; the professionalization of the foreign policy establishment. But these characteristics, though rooted in the Khrushchev era, took on the Brezhnev style, distinctive for its caution, conservatism, rationality; yet toughness, determination, and will to act. Aspects of this style are apparent in the case study of negotiations for SALT I.

---

[16] Interview with Jacob D. Beam, May 23, 1979.
[17] Clark, op. cit., p. 210.
[18] Said one diplomat: "You do get edgy. It's not so much not being able to say sensitive things; it's the kind of Big Brother feeling that even your private life is being shared by some faceless Russian." (Ibid., p. 213.) For the American experience during the Moscow summit, see below under SALT I negotiations.
[19] In 1970, the American Embassy alone had 78 Russian employees. Yuri Krotkov, a Soviet defector, who was involved with the KGB, wrote: "* * * every Soviet citizen employed in a foreign embassy—everyone, without exception—is certainly a co-opted member of the K.B.G." (Ibid., p. 215.)
[20] Ibid., p. 714.

CHAPTER X—SOLIDIFYING PEACEFUL COEXISTENCE WITH BREZHNEV, 1965–79

Part II—Concluding Negotiations on SALT I and Commentaries by American Officials on Soviet Negotiating Behavior

> They were alike in the sense that they were both tough, hard, and realistic leaders. Both interlarded their conversation with anecdotes. Khrushchev was often quite vulgar; Brezhnev, however, was just earthy. Whereas Khrushchev had been crass and blustering, Brezhnev was expansive and more courteous. Both had a good sense of humor, but Khrushchev more often seemed to be using his at the expense of others around him. Khrushchev seemed to be quicker in his mental reflexes. In discussions, Brezhnev was hard-hitting, incisive, and always very deliberate, whereas Khrushchev had tended to be more explosive and more impulsive. Both men had tempers, and both were emotional. I was struck by the simple look of pride on Brezhnev's face as he told me that he was about to become a great-grandfather, and that we now had still another generation for which to guarantee peace.
>
> —*President Nixon, 1978.*

IV. A MAJOR NEGOTIATING ENCOUNTER: CONCLUDING NEGOTIATIONS ON SALT I, MAY 1972

A. SALT I Negotiations, 1967–71

1. BRIEF SUMMARY OF THE NEGOTIATIONS

(a) Their importance

SALT I initiated one of the most significant continuous negotiations in the history of Soviet-American relations, perhaps even in modern history. John Newhouse, the historian of SALT I, called Soviet and American attempts to bring strategic weapons under control, "probably the most fascinating, episodic negotiation since the Congress of Vienna . . . likely to go on indefinitely." Newhouse predicted that SALT "could develop a cumulative impact on the world system comparable to that of the Congress of Vienna, whose achievement was to spare Europe any major bloodletting for 100 years."[1]

Dr. Raymond L. Garthoff seemed only slightly less expansive in his appraisal of SALT I. A senior Foreign Service officer in the State Department, an internationally recognized scholar in Soviet military affairs, one of the key negotiators of SALT I, and presently U.S. Ambassador to Bulgaria, Garthoff recalled that SALT "not only deals with a matter of cardinal importance, it also represents the most extensive and intensive Soviet-American negotiation to date, involving professional and political negotiation."[2]

---

[1] Newhouse, op. ct., pp. 1–2.
[2] Garthoff, Raymond L. Negotiating with the Russians: Some Lessons from SALT. International Security, v. 1, Spring 1977: 3. Since Garthoff has published three articles on aspects of the SALT negotiations in three different periodicals, International Security, The Wilson Quarterly, and World Politics, the citations to each after the initial complete one will be made for convenience sake by periodical rather than by the title of the article.

Hence the importance of SALT I as a case study in Soviet, and indeed American, negotiating behavior. "SALT I was rich in experience," wrote Garthoff in a recent article analyzing the negotiations. It revealed the "difficulties in establishing and maintaining sound negotiating objectives and approaches"; it illuminated "other desirable and undesirable negotiating techniques"; and it offered examples and insights as valuable "lessons for future negotiations." [3]

(b) Origins and purposes

The idea of SALT originated not with the arms control bureaucracy but rather with Secretary of Defense McNamara; it had the strong backing of President Lyndon B. Johnson and Secretary of State Rusk.[4] In December 1966, U.S. Ambassador to the Soviet Union Llewellyn E. Thompson was instructed to propose confidentially to the Soviet leadership bilateral talks on strategic arms limitations, notably on the antiballistic missile system (ABM). The primary American purpose was to check the impending Soviet-American race in ABM deployments. McNamara believed that the race would prove ineffective and would, moreover, spark competition in the offensive strategic weapons systems.[5]

The Soviets responded promptly in January 1967. In a cautiously worded reply, they accepted the American offer to negotiate, and to the surprise of some administration officials, proposed that discussions cover offensive missile systems as well as the ABM. Undoubtedly to Moscow's surprise, the United States accepted the Soviet offer. Ironically, 4 years later positions were to be reversed: The Soviets argued for decoupling ABM and offensive missile systems; the United States insisted on linkage.[6]

(c) Delays in negotiations

Soviet agreement in principle expressed in their response of January 1967 did not mean the immediate opening of negotiations. An American proposal in March to send a high level negotiating team to Moscow to begin negotiations was diplomatically deflected, and a long hiatus of over 1 year set in before the Soviets were ready to negotiate. But even then further delays pushed the opening into late 1969.[7]

Delays in the negotiations were caused by a number of factors:

—Soviet insistence upon overcoming their considerable strategic inferiority and reaching numerical parity with the United States in strategic intercontinental missile systems (ICBM's) which was expected in mid-1968;

—The need to establish an international consensus in Moscow on the strategic context and concept underlying a SALT agreement that would limit Soviet ABM defenses to a low level;

—Continuing suspicion of American purposes with important Soviet political and military quarters;

—Tension created by the Middle East war of 1967 and the ensuing threat of a Soviet-American military confrontation in the eastern Mediterranean; the subsequent Glassboro summit in June 1967

---

[3] Ibid., p. 17.
[4] Ibid., p. 3 and Newhouse op. cit., pp. 45–46.
[5] Garthoff, Raymond L. SALT I: An Evaluation, World Politics, vol. 31, October 1978: 2–3.
[6] Garthoff, World Politics, p. 4.
[7] Ibid., pp. 2–3.

gave McNamara a unique opportunity to impress upon "a stolid and somewhat bewildered" Premier Kosygin—in Garthoff's words—the virtues of strategic restraint through negotiations apparently with some effect; [8]

—The Soviet bloc invasion of Czechoslovakia in August 1968 that momentarily revived cold war tensions and temporarily derailed the movement toward a summit—reversal of American policy in Vietnam after the Tet offensive had encouraged the Soviets to signal their readiness to begin negotiations in the summer of 1968, and a summit meeting was set for Leningrad at which time the SALT negotiations were to be launched;

—The uncertainty and caution of the new Nixon administration (born out of mistrust of the Soviets, an apparent initial consciousness of its inexperience, and an awareness that SALT was a Johnson administration initiative) to move into negotiations with the Soviet leaders before making sufficient preparations and an assessment of Soviet aims and American interests; and finally

—The administration's inclination to seek political advantage through linkage to other problems in what was perceived to be a Moscow leadership overanxious for SALT.[9]

(d) Establishing the conceptual foundation of SALT

Even before the Nixon administration had been installed the Soviets signaled their willingness to open negotiations. After a great deal of political skirmishing during which the Soviets rejected linkage of SALT to détente and other political issues, a cautious, unenthusiastic Nixon administration agreed to undertake preliminary SALT discussions in Helsinki in November 1969. The Soviet commitment to SALT was tentative, but after 1 month of preliminary talks, it had become clear that the Soviet leadership had given its firm approval of the SALT process, having judged that the United States was indeed interested in serious negotiations.[10] Formal negotiations by teams from both countries got underway and continued for the next 2½ years at various times in Helsinki, Vienna, and finally on a permanent basis in Geneva.

By the time of the Helsinki preparatory meeting in late 1969, however, the conceptual foundation for SALT had already been established. This foundation was reflected in the SALT I agreements finally concluded in May 1972. In a series of confidential exchanges between Washington and Moscow in 1968 common objectives had been clarified in three vital areas:

—It was agreed implicitly that the main objective of the negotiations would be to achieve and maintain a stable strategic deterrent through limitations on the deployment of strategic offensive and defensive weapons;

—It was agreed implicitly that strategic parity should be accepted and maintained, that a balance through arms limitations should exist giving neither side any military advantage, and that equal security would be assured for both sides; and

---

[8] According to Newhouse, the "Glassboro experience may have moved Kosygin and some of his colleagues to do what Washington thought they had already been doing—looking hard at the problems of stable deterrence." Rusk suggested that Glassboro may have been the beginning of SALT for the Russians. (Newhouse, op. cit., p. 95.)

[9] Garthoff. World Politics, pp. 3–6. See also, Newhouse, op. cit., pp. 130–132, and for details on early skirmishing in the Nixon administration, see chapter 9.

[10] Garthoff. International Security, pp. 4–5.

—It was finally agreed that measures should be taken to reduce the risk of nuclear war, arising from accidents or in any other unintended manner.

In brief, as Garthoff wrote, by the time of Helsinki, "both the United States and the Soviet Union were agreed on the existence of and the need to preserve *parity, mutual deterrence,* and *strategic stability.*" [11]

The task of the negotiators was, therefore, to establish an agreed framework based upon these fundamental principles. The task was enormous, as even a perusal of Newhouse's detailed and thorough history will attest. According to Newhouse, "the major issues are few in number." But, "the trouble is that each conceals lesser, related issues. These, plus the bewildering problems of just defining terms, produce complications"—complications, it might be added, that constitute a mixture of realms complex in themselves, the political and technical, with the former taking precedence in importance.[12]

Basic questions, perceived from different perspectives and generating internal debate, were raised by seeking definitions of such concepts as "strategic," "equal security," and "strategic stability." Further burdening these tasks were, as Garthoff noted, "the added suspicions and desires to hedge in the interests of each side's own security—to say nothing of blatant attempts to gain advantages. * * *" [13]

Verification, so vital a principle to the skeptical Americans and so sensitive a matter to the security-conscious Russians, burdened still further the problem of definitions. In addition, the negative effects of great power rivalry and the deep-rooted suspicion and mistrust that exists naturally among adversaries contributed immensely to the burden of the negotiators and the complexity of their task.[14]

In a word, the negotiators of SALT I clearly had their work cut out for themselves.

(e) *Definition of SALT*

Much has been said here about the problem of definitions in SALT negotiations. But, what can be said about the definition of SALT itself as a negotiating process? Newhouse gave perhaps the most comprehensive and penetrating definition when he wrote of SALT I:

* * * Stripped of its wraps SALT emerges as a colossal multitiered negotiation. At the outer, most obvious tier, it is a negotiation between rival powers. At another level, it is a negotiation between Washington and its chief NATO allies, whose feelings about SALT are mixed; while applauding efforts to stabilize deterrence, they are wary of the political consequences of formal parity and frankly worried that SALT may foreshadow a great-power condominium whose writ would go far beyond the issues at hand. At yet another level—so far, the least consequential—SALT is, in the United States, a negotiation between the executive and the Congress: Key committees and individuals are consulted, but only rarely do they learn enough to have a rounded view of what is happening and why; most important SALT decisions are taken without reference to the Congress.

Finally, and most importantly, SALT is an internal negotiation. It is within the two capitals that the critical bargaining—the struggle to grind out positions—lumbers endlessly, episodically on. The marrow of SALT is found in the contesting views and clashing organizational interests of government agencies.[15]

---

[11] Garthoff, World Politics, p. 3.
[12] Newhouse, op. cit., pp. 13–14 and 34.
[13] Garthoff, World Politics, p. 3.
[14] Newhouse, op. cit., p. 14
[15] Ibid., pp. 31–32.

2. SOME CHARACTERISTICS OF THE NEGOTIATIONS

(a) *Organization and procedures*

(1) *Plenary sessions*

The organizational aspects of SALT I negotiations, at least on the negotiating front, evolved along lines initially established by the American side. Before the opening of the Helsinki talks the Soviet representatives made discreet inquiries into American plans with respect to the general composition and size of the delegation. In effect, the Russians followed the American lead.[16]

Negotiations were in general carried on at four levels: in plenary and informal meetings on the negotiating front in Helsinki, Vienna, and Geneva; often in back channel parallel negotiations between Soviet Ambassador Dobrynin and National Security Adviser Kissinger in Washington and with Brezhnev in Moscow; and finally at the summit with Nixon and Brezhnev in Moscow.

During 1969–73, Ambassador Gerard C. Smith, Director of the Arms Control and Disarmament Agency (ACDA), headed the U.S. negotiating team of up to 100 people, including advisers, interpreters, administrative staff, and Marine guards.[17] Formal plenary sessions were held for several hours twice weekly, usually with about 10 persons attending on each side, for the first year or so. Thereafter, such formal meetings for the record gave way to mini-plenary sessions and other informal meetings.[18]

The plenary sessions took place alternately in the Soviet and American Embassies. The negotiating procedure at the plenary sessions was formal and rigid with little time for actual discussions. The host for the day would welcome his opposite number and invite him to make a presentation. The meetings were thus dry affairs dominated by Smith and his Soviet counterpart Deputy Foreign Minister Vladimir S. Semenov who in turn read prepared statements cleared in Washington and Moscow respectively. After each formal plenary session, the delegates would split up into small groups for a tea break and informal discussions. Such informal private gatherings encouraged a type of candor not possible in the formal session. According to Garthoff, they provided "moderately useful opportunities for clarification and argumentation."[19]

The format of the plenary sessions, established during Smith's tenure as chief of the U.S. delegation, was carried on by his successors, U. Alexis Johnson, a veteran State Department diplomat and seasoned negotiator (1973–76) and Paul C. Warnke, a lawyer, former Defense Department official and Director of ACDA (1977–78).[20]

---

[16] Garthoff, International Security, p. 4.

[17] Ambassador Smith has in preparation a book to be published by Doubleday based on his negotiating experiences entitled, "SALT: The First Strategic Arms Negotiations."

[18] Garthoff, Raymond L. Negotiating SALT. The Wilson Quarterly, vol. 1, Autumn 1977 :76–77.

[19] Ibid., pp. 76–77 and Newhouse, op. cit., pp. 211–212.

[20] Ibid., p. 76. At a symposium on Soviet negotiating behavior held at the Sino-Soviet Institute of George Washington University on October 4, 1977, Ambassador Johnson, by that time retired from the State Department, described in detail the procedures followed at Geneva during his tenure. Plenary sessions were held twice weekly. All members of the delegations attended, meaning presumably the principals and their close advisers. A formal statement would be made by each side, written, carefully prepared and exchanged with the delegations. At such meetings, there was no repartee at the table; Semenov was unhappy about any repartee. There were no exchanges. After the formal presentation,

(Continued)

(2) "Mini-Plenaries," informal meetings and working groups

In the course of time, a strong tendency developed to shift the bulk of the negotiating business from the rigidly formal plenary sessions to small informal meetings, "mini-plenaries" and working groups. As Newhouse observed, "Both delegations were keen to turn over various issues to those delegates and staff experts best able to deal with them." [21]

Only a few senior members participated in the "mini-plenaries," and their tasks usually focused on specific problems in the treaty such as restrictions on the number and location of radars permitted in an ABM system. Discussions were usually exploratory, and as Garthoff recalled, "seldom evoked an authoritative official response or change of position from either side." [22]

Important informal probings and exchanges often took place over long luncheons and dinners preceding private meetings of the principals. Such intimate social gatherings (some relationships were on a first-name basis) proved to be a real asset in negotiations. "They were useful" Garthoff noted, "in scouting out possibilities, in underlining particular proposals or rejections, and in shading degrees of advocacy or opposition without changing formal positions." [23]

Eventually such informal meetings became a principal channel for negotiating many of the most difficult provisions in the SALT I agreement. At these meetings, they resolved such issues as radar controls, ABM levels, the key provisions in Article I of SALT I in which limits were placed on ABM systems and corollary restrictions on other radar systems that could be upgraded for ABM use.[24] Ambassador Johnson recalled that in the SALT II negotiations, much of the hard work was done at this subcommittee level, where, he said, speaking figuratively, "the blood would flow." [25]

Garthoff and Nikolai S. Kishilov, his opposite number as senior adviser on the Soviet delegation, played important roles in these in-

(Continued)

the negotiators would then take a break for coffee. No liquor was served at Johnson's insistence, apparently to some Soviet displeasure. But, as Johnson advised, a negotiator needs a clear head and cautioned that liquor was not a good mixture for negotiations. The delegations would break up into groups according to their opposite numbers, pairing off, scientific types, the military and foreign policy specialists, etc., and discuss issues in informal conversation. Johnson would meet with Semenov in a private room and there carry on a discussion. On such occasions, the hyper-cautious Semenov would read from carefully prepared notes, a practice not followed by Johnson who gently needled his negotiating adversary. In the course of reading his notes, Semenov might ask Johnson if he got all the nuances of his presentation. Johnson would ask to be shown the nuances. Semenov would resist and respond, "If you study the paper, you will see the nuances." By this time, Johnson said, he would be "climbing the walls." Semenov would proceed through his notes, point for point.

Johnson also noted that in the event that either side had an important proposal to put forward at a meeting, it would be done first in a private meeting before the plenary session. Having the advantage of time to study the matter, they could then speak more knowledgeably at the sessions. Both sides followed this practice to stress the importance of a particular proposal. (Whelan, Joseph G. Notebook No. 6, Oct. 4, 1977, pp. 46-48.)

For descriptions of the procedures followed in SALT II, see Pincus, Walter, Behind the Scenes at SALT: Long Complex Sessions. The Washington Post, Dec. 6, 1977, p. A13. and Facing the Russians: It's More Chess Than Poker, Say SALT Insiders. Time, vol. 112, Aug. 14, 1978: 10-11.

[21] Newhouse, op. cit., p. 212.
[22] Garthoff, Wilson Quarterly, p. 78.
[23] Ibid. Ambassador Johnson also recalled the occasional social contacts in which the delegations would entertain each other. In Geneva, he said, the U.S. delegation used to take the Russians on a boat ride; the Russians usually entertained by having meals. "Always too much to eat," he said, adding, "There is no moderation in the Russians." Johnson would also entertain Semenov at lunch, and on every occasion, he recalled, there would be his notes from which he faithfully read. (Whelan, Notebook, No. 6, Oct. 4, 1977, p. 47.)
[24] Garthoff, Wilson Quarterly, p. 79.
[25] Whelan, Notebook No. 6, Oct. 4, 1977, p. 38.

formal talks. Though not formally delegates, they were, nonetheless, principal front-channel negotiators. Called "point men" and "lightning rods" of the talks—Semenov referred to them as "the wizards" (nonparticipating Americans were less complimentary)—they met frequently to work out linguistic problems since each was fluent in the other's language. They explored new issues or proposals enabling each side to have an impression of the other's initial position or attitude or to test new approaches in an effort to move old unresolved problems off dead center. Very often, in meetings with one or two delegates, they attempted to remove or narrow differences on a single point.[26] Garthoff found such informal meetings "highly useful" and personally "the most fascinating part of the work." [27]

In the summer of 1971, more formal working groups were established to address ad hoc technical problems and, on a regular basis, to prepare joint drafts of agreements. Points of disagreement were bracketed showing alternative approaches, a practice also employed by Johnson and Warnke.

As a result of these prolonged and intimate negotiations, a "transnational" or "transdelegation" partnership of interest developed in cases where unanimity did not exist within the delegations. For example, Paul Nitze, the Defense Department delegate, strongly advocated controls on radar while U.S. military representatives were not inclined to press the issue. Nitze's exchanges with Soviet Academician Alexander Shchukin led to Soviet acceptance of some significant restraints on radars.[28]

(3) "Back Channel" negotiations

(a) Garthoff's criticism.—A crucial, perhaps even vital, part of the SALT I negotiating process was the resort to secret "back channel" negotiations by President Nixon with the Soviet leaders and also by Kissinger with Dobrynin and Brezhnev.[29]

Without the knowledge of the U.S. SALT delegation, President Nixon, in January 1971, opened secret "back channel" negotiations with Prime Minister Kosygin. This correspondence was supplemented by a series of secret meetings between Dobrynin and Kissinger. In the course of these exchanges and meetings, agreement was reached on seeking a separate ABM treaty as well as certain but not clearly defined interim measures to restrict offensive strategic weapons rather than continuing to negotiate a single comprehensive treaty. Neither Ambassador Smith nor Secretary of State William P. Rogers were aware of these "back channel" efforts until May 19, 1971, one day before the official announcement of an agreement was made. The President hailed the agreement as "a major step in breaking the stalemate on nuclear arms talks" which he said "have been deadlocked for over a year." [30] So tight was the secrecy surrounding these negotiations that the American SALT negotiators had heard earlier in May that some

---

[26] Newhouse, op. cit., p. 213.
[27] Garthoff, Wilson Quarterly, pp. 78–79.
[28] Ibid., p. 79. Garthoff noted: "To my knowledge, there were no instances on either side of disloyalty to a delegation or its instructed position. But there were issues on which some delegates and advisers sought earnestly to persuade members of the other delegation, while their compatriots did not"
[29] For details of these "back channel" negotiations, see, Garthoff, Wilson Quarterly, pp. 80–81. Garthoff, International Security pp. 8–10, and Newhouse, op. cit., pp. 44, 203–204, 214–217, 221 and 229.
[30] For the partial text of the announcement, see Newhouse, op. cit., p. 217.

special talks were under way, not from American sources but rather from members of the Soviet delegation.[31]

In the spring of 1972, the "back channel" was opened again, involving this time a secret trip to Moscow by Kissinger accompanied by Dobrynin. Semenov was recalled to Moscow for the meeting, but the U.S. SALT delegation and even U.S. Ambassador to the Soviet Union Jacob D. Beam were unaware of the secret negotiations until they had been completed. This new round of "back channel" talks produced high level endorsement for the ABM agreement that had been worked out in April by the SALT delegations and an interim agreement on offensive arms to include SLBM's (Submarine-Launched Ballistic Missiles). A number of other issues were left for the Nixon-Brezhnev summit scheduled for May 1972.[32]

Garthoff has been critical of negotiating in the "back channel." Reflecting the view of a State Department insider who was at once a professional diplomat, an active negotiator, and Soviet specialist, he observed that the "back channel" mode suited the Kissinger style of personal involvement in diplomacy which in many cases, he acknowledged, Kissinger had served "brilliantly." But in other cases, Garthoff noted, Kissinger, whose power base was in the White House and National Security Council, "failed to recognize the role that professional diplomacy and diplomats could play and even came to resent, and perhaps be jealous of the professionals who were effective." Thus, Garthoff observed, Kissinger "curtailed the role of the professionals and in the process spread himself too thin." [33]

The result, Garthoff contended, was mistakes.

Garthoff cited the mistakes that he believed Kissinger had made by "going it alone" and failing to get "needed advice." As a consequence, he concluded, "U.S. interests suffered." In 1971, for example, Kissinger had agreed that it was not necessary to include submarine missile fleets in the interim agreement on strategic offensive weapons, thus allowing both sides to strengthen their SLBM forces. The agreement was to be in effect for 5 years. But, as Garthoff noted, "the United States, unlike the Russians would not benefit." Why? "Evidently Kissinger was unaware that a follow-on navy ballistic missile submarine design was not yet ready," Garthoff observed, "and U.S. submarine-building facilities were committed to work on other types of submarines." Hence, the Soviets could continue on their rapid submarine buildup unimpeded by any restrictions.[34]

[31] Garthoff, Wilson Quarterly, p 80.

[32] Ibid., pp. 80–81

[33] Garthoff continued: "From his early success in mastering issues that came before the Verification Panel, Kissinger developed a conviction that he did not need the Government bureaucracy. A small personal staff, he felt, could skim the cream off the ponderous intragency staff studies that he ordered to keep the bureaucracy occupied. In this way, he thought, he could learn all he needed to know about a subject." The Verification Panel had been established early in the negotiations in Washington to deal with the verification or "policing" aspect of strategic arms control. "Henry Kissinger, in his role as assistant to the President for National Security Affairs," Garthoff noted, "rapidly converted the panel into the sole senior-level American group dealing with SALT, aside from the White House's National Security Council." The Panel which Kissinger chaired included the Deputy Secretaries of State and Defense, Chairman of the Joint Chiefs of Staff, the Director of ACDA, the Director of CIA, and a few others including Attorney General John Mitchell (Garthoff, Wilson Quarterly, pp. 80–81.)

[34] Ibid., p. 81. Garthoff cited other examples of alleged mistakes in International Security, pp. 8–10. In elaborating in the SLBM issue, he wrote:
"Most importantly, the Soviet side, after raising the question was told that SLBM launchers could either be or *not be* included. They promptly opted *not to* limit SLBM's, having but recently begun a major buildup of them after having been well behind the United States. To Dr. Kissinger's chagrin, when this question was posed as the U.S

(*b*) *Sonnenfeldt's rebuttal.*—Dr. Helmut Sonnenfeldt, Kissenger's advisor on Soviet affairs in the National Security Council, a participant in the SALT I negotiations, and later Counselor in the State Department, took sharp exception to Garthoff's criticism on the use of the "back channel." He placed his case largely on constitutional grounds. In dealing with the Soviets and indeed with other governments, Sonnenfeldt contended, there has to be a variety of channels. And he explained: [35]

> * * * it is really quite absurd to suggest that the President of the United States, given his constitutional position, is somehow not entitled to deal in his own channels with other heads of government, or that the Secretary of State on behalf of the President of the United States is not entitled to deal with the heads of states or foreign ministers or designated officials of other governments. And particularly on sensitive issues, I think inevitably there will be several levels of discourse and bargaining and communication that exist, and sometimes the contents of what passes cannot be made widely available, because until it comes to fruition the matters may be extremely delicate. Prestige may be involved. Very delicate matters may be involved. Now obviously, you want to try to keep front and back channels, the different modes of communication, in some kind of harmony. But I think it is really absurd to argue that every official is entitled to know about every communication that passes between heads of government. It has never been the case, and it will never be the case; it is a matter that has to be handled with great care.

Sonnenfeldt went on to say that criticism of using the "back channel" implies some suggestion that "the back channel is sloppy"; that "because of the back channel mistakes get made and unclarities creep into the negotiating process"; and that whatever the flaws of SALT I, "they were the result of the use of the back channel or hurried forms of negotiations." Sonnenfeldt took exception to these charges, noting that this judgment would not "stand up to scrutiny over time when all the documentation is made available."

Still, Sonnenfeldt did not deny the hazards in "back channel" communications. "There were hazards when Churchill and Roosevelt communicated with each other, in terms of operational issues and in terms of those people who were responsible for laboring on the day-to-day work," he said. "There are hazards; but it's a hazardous business." Nevertheless, it was an invalid criticism to "suggest that a head of state or senior officials, or a relatively small group of senior officials should be debarred from communicating in special ways with their counterparts."

(*c*) *On balance.*—Thus, while the "back channel" technique no doubt has served a useful purpose in reaching agreement on important issues—and both Garthoff and Newhouse have acknowledged this—and while such negotiations are among the constitutional prerogatives of the American President (not to speak of other national leaders)—Wilson had his Colonel House, Roosevelt his Harry Hopkins, and

---

Government prepared its negotiating positions in the summer of 1971, all agencies strongly wished to include limitations on SLBM's, particularly in view of the fact that in any event the United States would not te in a position to embark on a renewed SLBM program over the period of the interim limitations. In Moscow in April 1972. Dr. Kissinger was eventually able to get Soviet agreement to include SLBM's only by agreeing on numbers much in excess of what either we or the Soviets then had—and in fact at the maximum level the United States then estimated the Soviet Union might build. No real restraint was provided for the short term of the Interim Agreement. Even that occurred only after the Delegation had to spend a very great deal of negotiating capital for nearly a year in impressing the Soviets that the United States really *would* insist on SLBM inclusion—contrary to what they had taken to be an authoritative position in the spring of 1971." (Ibid., p. 9.)

[35] Interview with Helmut Sonnenfeldt, Brookings Institution, June 7, 1979.

Kennedy, McGeorge Bundy—still this device and particularly this penchant for secrecy, as Garthoff has noted, could have the effect of closing off important, perhaps even vital, sources of information for reaching a decision at a crucial point in negotiations. The technique also might complicate perhaps unnecessarily the tasks of the American delegation negotiating in the main arena and no doubt could cause some embarrassment in negotiating at a decided disadvantage with the better informed Russian delegation, as in SALT I.

On balance, the benefits of exercising this executive prerogative in reaching agreement through the "back channel" would have to be weighed against potential disadvantages, particularly the risk of an imperfect agreement. Sonnenfeldt, himself, seemed to suggest the remedy when he acknowledged the importance of keeping "front and back channels, the different modes of communication, in some kind of harmony." [36]

(4) *Other procedural aspects: Records and interpreters.*—What has been said above and will be noted below on Soviet negotiating style suggest certain procedural aspects of the SALT negotiations, particularly with respect to initiating proposals and the differing approaches to negotiations.

In light of the shortcomings noted in previous U.S. negotiating practice, it is instructive to emphasize in the case of SALT I, the availability of expertise on the sizable U.S. delegation, in the White House, State, and Defense Departments; the interaction within the delegation; and the concern for maintaining official records.

Time spent in preparation for the sessions far exceeded that devoted to formal negotiations. Senior American delegates usually met 5 days a week for two or three sessions lasting several hours each to review the issues and discuss draft presentations and negotiating strategies, presumably based upon extensively prepared positions papers. After the negotiating session, they would repair to their secured quarters to discuss the highlights. Cables were thereafter prepared and sent to Washington, and informal talks, for which there was presumably no verbatim record, were recorded in the form of memoranda of conversation (Memcons). Some 500 were prepared in the course of 2½ years of SALT I. [37]

Concern for the written record by both sides was apparent in the fact that the records of the plenary sessions for phase II of the negotiations, lasting 120 days, were said to have amounted to more than 100,-000 words, consisting mostly of prepared statements by Smith and Semenov. [38]

Interpreters were also available on the American delegation. Hence, reliance upon communicating transactions in negotiations through the

---

[36] For Kissinger's explanation with respect to the final agreement on submarines in SALT I, see. News Conference Remarks by Presidential Assistant Kissinger and ACDA Director Smith: Strategic Arms Limitation Agreements, May 26. 1972. U.S. Arms Control and Disarmament Agency. Documents on Disarmament, 1972. Washington, D.C., U.S. Government Printing Office, May 1974. pp. 208–209 and 215–216. (Publication 69). Sources on SALT I reveal no explanation by Kissinger for the "back channel" negotiations which he seemed to accept as a normal and acceptable way of breaking a deadlock among negotiators at the lower level. In brief, this episode is a classic example of the adversarial relationship that has often arisen between the White House and the State Department over matters of foreign policy.

[37] Garthoff. Wilson Quarterly, pp. 77–78. Walter Pincus noted that during the informal meetings at the SALT II negotiations no records were kept. Presumably. Memcons were used. (The Washington Post. Dec. 6, 1977, p. A13.)

[38] Newhouse, op. cit., pp. 183 and 190.

mind and from the perspective of an American was assured. Garthoff, like Bohlen, had the unique advantage of being able to converse with his Russian counterparts in their language. But it is significant that at the Brezhnev-Kissinger "minisummit" in the spring of 1972, Kissinger began his practice of relying only on Soviet interpreters, the purpose being to prevent possible leakage of information to other American officials. President Nixon adopted the same practice at summit meetings dealing with SALT, but later the practice was abandoned by his successor, President Gerald R. Ford.[39]

(b) Soviet negotiators and staff

(1) Vladimir S. Semenov, chief of the U.S.S.R. delegation

The Soviet delegation, roughly similar in size (up to 100 people) and somewhat in composition to the American, except for greater emphasis on the military presence, was headed by Vladimir S. Semenov, a seasoned negotiator, though not specifically with the United States or on the subject of arms control.[40] Semenov has been Deputy Foreign Minister since 1955. A German scholar, he was a political commissar for Soviet forces in Berlin at the end of World War II and a senior Soviet political adviser in Berlin at the time of the 1948 blockade. At that time he acquired the reputation as the key man in attempting to drive the Allies out of Berlin. As High Commissioner of East Germany in May 1953, he had authorized the military suppression of the East Berlin uprising. In the late 1960's, he had written favorably about peaceful coexistence but in conjunction with the buildup of Soviet power and influence. He has generally been regarded as an advocate of arms control.[41]

Drawing upon 3 years experience in negotiating with Semenov, Ambassador Johnson gave some penetrating insights into his character and style as a negotiator. According to Johnson, Semenov was a timid man and a cautious, careful negotiator, "even more careful than the usual Soviet negotiator." So apprehensive was he about deviating from instructions during negotiations that he spoke of official matters from notes in both informal and even in social meetings with Johnson. A serious-mind man he engaged in no repartee at the plenary sessions. Conscious of the predominance of the military role in arms control negotiations, he was particularly respectful of the military on the Soviet delegation and always deferred to the delegation as a whole when new lines and approaches emerged in negotiations, even in such minor matters as a recess. He displayed also a particular hypersensitivity about disclosing any military secrets and revealed the civilian's ill-at-ease in the presence of military authority. Johnson attributed Semenov's timidity and excessive caution to the consequences of the Berlin uprising that had led to his recall to Moscow and the meting out of the severest punishment to some of his subordinates. That this experience had had its effect on Semenov was evident by his disclosure of taking a sleeping pill every night since he was in Berlin.[42]

Yet Semenov had shown signs of resilience. On one occasion at Geneva Johnson explained his belief that ideological incompatibility lay

---

[39] Garthoff, Wilson Quarterly, footnote on p. 80.
[40] Ibid., p. 77.
[41] Newhouse, op. cit., pp. 52–53.
[42] Whelan, Notebook, No. 6, Oct. 4, 1977, pp. 46–50.

at the roots of the nuclear rivalry and the threatening postures of the United States and the Soviet Union. Drawing the analogy of the Soviet-American hostility with the historic hostility between Islam and Christianity and its eventual dissolution, he observed that eventually the Soviet Union and the United States would become mutually tolerant and learn to live and let live. At such time of mutual toleration, Johnson continued, the outstanding problems between them would fall into place and then be reasonably solvable. Semenov never challenged Johnson's thesis but responded, "Give us time. Things will work out in time." Some Russians, Johnson confided, felt differently.[43]

(2) The Soviet delegation and the military presence

(a) *Comparable to U.S. delegation with exceptions.*—The Soviet delegation was similar in size to that of the United States numbering up to 100 people. However, it has had greater continuity over the years, having far fewer changes than the American. Both staffs were similar in composition except that the Soviets had greater representation from the military and military-industrial complex with no representation equivalent to ACDA.[44]

Included in the Soviet delegation were two senior scientists from the scientific-technological-military production field: Academician Alexander N. Shchukin, a radar specialist and renowned scientist then in his seventies and respected as an "elder statesman" in the military applications of science and technology; and Peter S. Pleshakov, initially Deputy Minister and later Minister of Radio Industry. Both were reserve general officers in the Engineering-Technical Service.[45]

(b) *Military predominance.*—The military were predominant in the Soviet delegation. Never before had officers of such senior rank participated so directly in arms control negotiations. During the first three rounds of SALT I from late 1969 to the end of 1970, Col. Gen. (now Army General) Nikolai V. Ogarkov, then First Deputy Chief of the General Staff of the U.S.S.R. Armed Forces and later a member of the CPSU's Central Committee, was the second ranking delegate. Nonetheless, though second he was in reality, as Newhouse noted, "clearly the most important figure on the Soviet delegation, even though Semenov was the nominal leader." [46] The seriousness of the Soviet commitment to SALT and the delicacy of the negotiations were underscored by the fact that the Soviet leadership allowed so senior an officer to devote 8 months in a 14-month period in negotiations abroad, in addition to the time spent in Moscow preparing for the talks.

Col. Gen. (of the Engineering-Technical Services) Nikolai N. Alekseev was also a member of the delegation in the first two rounds of the negotiations in 1969 and 1970. Both officers were succeeded by Lt. Gen. Konstantin A. Trusov, a senior General Staff officer with a background of overseeing advanced weapons development, and Lt. Gen. (now Colonel General) Ivan I. Beletsky.[47] In Moscow, Ogarkov, as First Deputy Chief of the General Staff, continued to have a strong influence on the Soviet position in SALT.[48]

---

[43] Ibid., p. 35.
[44] Garthoff, Wilson Quarterly, pp. 76–77.
[45] Garthoff Raymond L. SALT and the Soviet Military. Problems of Communism, vol. 24. January–February 1975 : pp. 28–29.
[46] Newhouse, op. cit., p. 212.
[47] Garthoff, Problems of Communism, p. 28.
[48] Newhouse, op. cit., p. 53.

The Soviet military presence was strengthened still further by the direct participation of other Soviet officers, some of general-officer or flag rank, as advisors or experts. The military representatives on the Soviet delegation were highly qualified specialists in such principal areas under discussion as strategic missiles, ABM's, submarines and antisubmarine warfare (ASW), and strategic bombers. All of these specialists worked under senior officers of the General Staff who were responsible for advanced weapon development and procurement.[49]

That the military role was preeminent if not decisive at SALT negotiations was evident by the fact that Semenov and other Foreign Ministry civilian representatives did not have access to classified information on Soviet weapons systems.[50] Accordingly, the civilian negotiators had what Newhouse termed a "lamentable ignorance" about the numbers, location, and characteristics of their own weapons systems.[51] On one occasion Semenov revealed his ignorance of the elementary fact that Soviet ICBM's were much larger than those of the United States when he confused the smaller U.S. Minuteman silos with those of the much larger Soviet SS-9's. Ogarkov put him straight, and later in the same round of negotiations he took the U.S. delegate aside and confided that there was no reason why the Americans should disclose knowledge of Russian military matters to the civilian members of the Soviet delegation. Such data, he cautioned, was strictly the affair of the military.[52]

Perhaps Ambassador Johnson best expressed this preeminent role of the Soviet military when he observed that "the generals were always looking over Semenov's shoulders" and that civilian deference to them on military matters was de rigeur.[53] As Garthoff put it, the generals probably had the last word on military matters discussed in SALT negotiations.[54]

The predominance of the military prescence in SALT was also clear, though indirect, by the control maintained over military matters in the supporting institutes through former military officers. For example, the small arms limitation section in the USA Institute was part of the Institute's Department of Military Policy headed by Maj. Gen. Lieutenant M. Milshteyn who represented the interests of the military establishment. The Commission on Scientific Problems of Disarmament of the Academy of Sciences of the U.S.S.R. Presidium was headed by a specialist on the production of nuclear weapons, V. Yemelyanov, who also represented the interests of the military-industrial complex.[55]

Evidence of the military's role in SALT was further apparent during the Moscow and Vladivostok summit meetings in 1974. Senior Soviet military representatives participated directly in the negotia-

[49] Garthoff, Problems of Communism, p. 28.
[50] Igor S. Glagolev, former Chief of the Disarmament Section of the Institute of World Economy and International Relations from 1961 to 1964 and a resident of the United States since 1976, wrote : "* * * specialists in the civilian scientific institutes and the Ministry of Foreign affairs—precisely those persons who specialize in international agreements on arms limitation and the prevention of wars, in contrast to the personnel of the military-industrial complex who specialize in the expansion of armaments and the conduct of wars—usually are not given access to secret data on existing Soviet arms and weapons programs." (Glagolev, Igor S. The Soviet Decision-Making Process in Arms-Control Negotiations. Orbis. Vol. 21, winter 1978 : 769–770.)
[51] Newhouse, op. cit., pp. 141–142.
[52] Ibid., p. 56.
[53] Whelan, Notebook No. 6, Oct. 4, 1977, p. 48.
[54] Garthoff, Wilson Quarterly, p. 84. This was true on the American side when proposals impinged on existing or planned Pentagon programs ; but the arms control representatives had greater influence on proposals affecting most severely Soviet programs.
[55] Glagolev, op. cit., p. 770.

tions and were closely consulted by Brezhnev. No American military representatives attended these summit meetings.[56]

(c) *Coordination, decisionmaking, and control at the top.*—Steps were taken early in 1968 to coordinate the work of the Ministry of Defense and Ministry of Foreign Affairs in matters dealing with SALT. Also participating in this effort were the political and technical institutes of the Academy of Sciences and representatives of the military-industrial production ministries. The participation of top-level elements in the Soviet system in arms control matters, in addition to the Ministries of Defense and Foreign Affairs, was apparent in concluding the SALT I negotiations in May 1972. At this summit meeting Deputy Prime Minister Leonid V. Smirov played an important role in the final negotiation of the Interim Agreement limiting offensive strategic weapons.

Smirnov was chairman of the Military-Industrial Commission (VPK). Its task was to handle the coordination between the Defense Ministry, ministries involved with military production, and the Academy of Sciences institutes engaged in military research and development. Dmitri F. Ustinov, party secretary and candidate member of the Politburo (now Defense Minister and Politburo member), was the overseer of this section.[57]

The highest ranking Soviet organizational unit dealing with military and defense issues is the Supreme Defense Council. Its membership is made up of the top ranking political and military leaders with Brezhnev as Chairman. Meetings of this Council were sometimes attended by members of the Defense Ministry and General Staff officers, Smirnov and other members of his organization, Foreign Minister Gromyko and specialists from the Academy of Sciences. On a number of occasions the Council has dealt with SALT issues.[58]

The apex of authority in the Soviet system is the Politburo of the CPSU's Central Committee. Brezhnev holds the ranking position as General Secretary. All the principal actions and decisions on SALT have been determined by the Politburo. Included in this body are other political leaders who are not usually concerned with defense or foreign affairs. In unusual circumstances, as during the 5 days of negotiations on SALT I at the Moscow summit in May 1972, the Politburo which meets normally only once a week met at least four times. In 1973, Marshal Andrei A. Grechko, head of the Soviet Defense Ministry, along with Gromyko and KGB Chief Yuri Andropov, were added to the Politburo. Previously, Grechko had attended its meetings only on invitation.[59]

That the Soviet military have played an important, perhaps even formidable, role in the SALT process was evident in this concluding comment by Garthoff in his analysis of the Soviet military's participation in SALT negotiations:

Soviet military participation in SALT planning and decisionmaking, and in the actual negotiations, has been active and vigorous at all levels. The effect of this active role has probably been to exert a conservative and cautious influence

[56] Garthoff, Problems of Communism, p. 29.
[57] Garthoff, Problems of Communism, p. 29.
[58] Ibid.
[59] Ibid.

on Soviet positions, but it has not precluded reaching a number of significant agreements.[60]

(3) Role of Ambassador Dobrynin

Though not formally a member of the Soviet SALT delegation, Ambassador Dobrynin was, nonetheless, a principal in the negotiations. He took on the arduous task of being Moscow's spokesman and negotiator for SALT I in Washington. As such he became the principal negotiator with Kissinger in the "back channel" both in Washington and Moscow, and among his representational functions as Ambassador was to lobby the Congress strenuously on behalf of SALT I. In these efforts Dobrynin was aided by Yuri M. Vorontsov, Minister-Counsellor at the Embassy, described by Newhouse as a "gifted diplomat" and an activist in arms control matters since 1958 who professed a strong bias in favor of SALT.[61] According to Newhouse, the Dobrynin-Vorontsov team in Washington "has functions that may be as important, if not more so, than those of the Soviet SALT delegation." [62] Not surprisingly they were seen as competitors, even rivals, for influence by Semenov's SALT delegation.[63]

Newhouse recorded in detail Dobrynin's secret negotiations with Kissinger in the "back channel" that broke the deadlock in the SALT negotiations and brought a successful resolution of the ABM issue in May 1971 by linking it with control of strategic offensive weapons. As he said, their efforts had moved SALT "onto negotiable ground." [64] However, the role of the ambassador rather than the substance of the negotiations is what makes Dobrynin's part significant for the purposes of this study. Perhaps no ambassador in recent times, considering the low state to which the profession has been reduced, had been invested with such an important responsibility by his government. To this extent, Dobrynin's role in SALT I was, for an ambassador, highly unusual and by any objective measurement effective.[65]

To Harry Brandon, the longtime Washington-based chief American correspondent for the Sunday Times of London and specialist on international affairs, Dobrynin was a superlative diplomat. In a brief characterization of the Soviet ambassador, he gave this favorable overall assessment:

Dobrynin is a master of the diplomatic trade, one of the best practitioners in it that I have come across in 25 years of international reporting. Thanks to his gift of establishing personal relationships and the apparent confidence he enjoys

[60] Ibid., p. 29. Glagolev concluded : "On the whole, one can say that the entire decision-making process with respect to the Soviet position on SALT negotiations is structured in such a fashion as to give preponderant expression to the interests and objectives of the military-industrial complex, which are limited only by the economic and scientific-technological capabilities of the U.S.S.R." (Glagolev, op. cit., pp. 771–772.)
[61] Newhouse, op. cit., pp. 7 and 32. According to Vorontsov, the SALT negotiation "is the most important thing we have to do together. It's closer to the essence of what we both regard as our security. Thus, it cannot be compared to negotiations which, like Berlin, involve other countries. SALT resists comparison with other negotiations" (p. 58.)
[62] Ibid., p. 53.
[63] Ibid., pp. 53 and 216.
[64] Ibid., pp. 217–218.
[65] Newhouse gave this graphic account suggesting the flavor and character of Dobrynin's negotiation with Kissinger :
"The back-channel bargaining had been arduous, especially so, perhaps, for Dobrynin. He told Kissinger at one point that the back-up letter, as it's called, was the only document he knew of that had been worked on by the whole Soviet Government. And, at one point, Kissinger told him that Russians had been easier to deal with when the United States bought Alaska. To which Dobrynin replied that those Russians had not been obliged to contend with Henry Kissinger. Dobrynin also voiced the hope, presumably at some particularly tiresome moment, that Kissinger might one day be an ambassador in a foreign capital far from his source of power." (Ibid., p. 218.)

with the Politburo, he has created for himself a position in Washington that
has made him virtually irreplaceable, or at least made him so during the crucial
period of the preparation for the Moscow summit. He is tall, almost towering,
and his appearance—soft, sensitive, high forehead and gold-rimmed spectacles—
combines with a shy charm that makes him seem more a romantic musician than
an experienced participant in the roughhouse of superpower diplomacy. Those
who have done business with him, however, easy as he is to talk to, consider
him a tough bargainer, always in command of whatever business is at hand. He
has a fetching smile, a pleasant sense of humor and an inborn civility, but he can
also become tough and steely in difficult negotiations; yet he rarely loses his
composure and always remains a gentleman. Like all Soviet officials, of course,
he is subject to the limitations of the Soviet system, yet some can stretch those
limitations and give themselves a little more elbow room under their instructions
and Dobrynin probably has done so at times. He once explained to me his guidelines for an ambassador in this way: "To have the courage to tell the facts as
they are, and report to his superiors as true and fair a picture as possible; to
provide them, when necessary, with honest proposals for action, and to warn
them, again courageously if need be, what reactions they must expect to follow
certain decisions." The role he was able to play in promoting a policy of easing
tensions between the United States and the Soviet Union, despite the many zigs
and zags, seems to have suited him temperamentally and intellectually.

And of the close relationship between Dobrynin and Kissinger that
proved to be so important in the successful conclusion of the SALT I
negotiations, Brandon drew this intimate but realistic portrait:

Dobrynin, quickly recognizing the uneven balance of power between Kissinger
and Secretary of State William P. Rogers and seeing where the center of power
really was, lavished attention, as ought any shrewd diplomat in Washington who
had the opportunity, on Kissinger. He established easy access to him and soon
found out that for quick action, this was the place to call. Dobrynin, as
ambassadors go, saw perhaps more of him than most, and soon earned in
Kissinger a kind of fond respect. Here were two men who could display an
extraordinary amount of charm and wit, but also vie in toughness with each
other. Kissinger even had him home for negotiations—and few have seen the
Kissinger household from the inside—but only after an electronic sanitizing
squad had made certain that the Russians had not bugged the house in advance.[66]

Indicative of Brezhnev's pleasure with Dobrynin's diplomatic efforts in carrying out on his behalf the sensitive "back channel" negotiations on SALT I was the recognition given by his promotion from
candidate member in the Central Committee to full membership at
the 24th Party Congress in April 1971.

(c) Aspects of Soviets negotiating behavior

(1) Seriousness of the negotiations

When asked to comment on the Soviet style and characteristics of
negotiations, Ambassador Johnson replied, "You must compare it
to the matter of how a porcupine makes love: very, very carefully.
Soviet negotiators negotiate very, very carefully."[67]

For American negotiators, SALT I was a lesson not only in the
need for caution in negotiating with the Russians, but more than that,
it was an education in the Soviet approach to negotiations in the traditional manner. SALT was a serious, deadly business, and that is the
way the Soviets came to the negotiating table.[68]

[66] Brandon, Henry. The Retreat of American Power. New York, Doubleday, 1973, pp.
276–277.
[67] Whelan, Notebook No. 6. Oct. 4,1977, p. 46.
[68] In a briefing at CIA in the spring of 1957 prior to assuming a new post in Manila,
Bohlen gave his estimate of the Soviet attitude toward arms control: "The Soviets are
very serious about disarmament. I don't think it's a propaganda stunt. Obviously, being
what they are, they would like to make a deal that would be advantageous to them and
disadvantageous to us, but I think they have not paid out the full string yet of what they
would do in the way of concessions. Why? The real reason is that they genuinely believe
that an uncontrolled arms race is almost certain to end up in war, sooner or later.'
(Bohlen, op. cit., p. 448.)

In marked contrast to earlier negotiating experiences recorded in this study, SALT I was distinguished by an absence of those characteristics that had become generally accepted as uniquely Soviet: the abusive, shin-kicking treatment of the adversary; extraneous ideologizing ad nauseam; propaganda hectoring that often turned negotiations into a public arena for scoring points from onlookers abroad; and irrelevant political discussion that unnecessarily and often intentionally prolonged negotiations and lessened prospects for agreement. The Russians were tough negotiators at SALT, as Garthoff, Johnson and others have attested.[69] But they were tough with a difference: they wanted to negotiate; they wanted an agreement.

Thus SALT I marked a break in the pattern of expected Soviet negotiating behavior: They had turned away from the "Brest-Litovsk" style of their Bolshevik past and returned to the traditional bargaining behavior historically characteristic of great powers who seriously negotiated on matters of vital national interests. How long this break will last and the extent to which it affects other areas of negotiations must remain an open question.

(2) Differing approaches: The general versus the specific

The Soviets and the American approached SALT from two markedly different negotiating concepts: the Soviets from the general; the Americans from the specific. This conflict in approaches made negotiations even more difficult than ordinarily would have been the case.[70]

The Soviets wanted a general politically meaningful accord. They sought "agreement in principle" prior to agreement on specifics. Their approach was directed at a general American acceptance of a rough parity already achieved and a more general restraint in the military buildup while emphasizing political détente.[71]

In contrast, the American approach was pragmatic. It began with specifics. It offered a fairly complete, complex, and detailed package proposal. It focused on concrete, militarily meaningful measures for arms control. It stressed specific measures reflecting "fine tuning" adjustments in the military balance in order to enhance strategic stability and mutual deterrence.[72]

Recalling his on SALT experiences, Ambassador Johnson explained the differing approaches simply: the Soviets liked broad, general statements of political purpose; the Americans liked detailed contracts. The Soviets, for example, resisted the American predilection for definitions. Since the Americans stressed capabilities rather than intentions, definitions were important. Accordingly, the negotiators at Geneva spent the better part of 2 years seeking definitions. What is a Backfire bomber? What is throw-weight? What constitutes an ICBM?[73] Taking a leaf from the American book, the Russians tried unsuccessfully to establish the definition of "a strategic" weapon as one capable of striking the homeland of the other side. Acceptance of this principle would have meant that the U.S. tactical aircraft in Europe were "strategic," but that the Soviet medium-range missiles and bombers targeted on Western Europe were not.[74]

[69] Garthoff, Wilson Quarterly, p. 85, and Whelan, Notebook No. 6, Oct. 4, 1977, p. 54.
[70] Garthoff, International Security, p. 6.
[71] Ibid., pp. 5–6.
[72] Ibid., and Garthoff, Wilson Quarterly, pp. 81–82.
[73] Whelan Notebook No. 6, Oct. 4, 1977, pp. 41–42.
[74] Garthoff, Wilson Quarterly, p. 82.

The Soviet approach offered greater flexibility. It gave them the advantage of nailing down specifics after getting an American commitment to a general line.[75] On the other hand, specificity and precision had its value by establishing in clear terms what was essentially a contractual relationship. The Soviet approach favored those who perceived SALT in more political terms, requiring certain ambiguities; the American approach favored those who perceived SALT as a technical exercise in arms control.[76] The purpose here, however, is not to place a value on one over the other, but rather to record the contrasting approaches that have made the negotiations of SALT I very difficult.

(3) On taking the initiative

In the SALT I negotiations, as in other negotiating encounters, the United States generally took the initiative in making proposals. Whether this tactic was advantageous was a matter of dispute among American negotiators. Garthoff believed it was an advantage because it gave the Americans the opportunity to stake out the negotiating ground first. It also made it possible for negotiations to move along more quickly since the Americans who had far greater latitude in negotiations generally were more flexible and efficient in establishing an agreed negotiating position. It might take months for an agreement to be worked out in Moscow.[77] The binding Soviet bureaucracy coupled with the inflexibility of Soviet negotiators who were obliged to adhere strictly to Moscow's rigid instructions worked against their taking initiatives.

On the other hand the negotiator ran the risk of negotiating with himself in taking the initiative. Ambassador Johnson noted that Soviet inflexibility placed a special burden on the United States which he found "very bothersome." He explained. Each time the Soviets would reject an American proposal the American negotiators would revise it in order to make the proposal more acceptable and then resubmit it. The Soviets may reject the revision in which case the Americans would confer on further revisions. And so forth. The danger Johnson noted, was that American negotiators, if not careful, would in time be negotiating with themselves. A negotiator needs some room for maneuver, he noted; this is part of the negotiating process. But the negotiator had to know where to draw the line limiting his concessions to the other side.[78]

(4) Secrecy, suspicion, control

SALT I reflected the bargaining characteristics of traditional diplomatic negotiations. Both sides meant business; each made proposals, defended and justified positions from its own perspective and with its own rationale; linkage never deflected the negotiators from their primary purpose; namely, control of nuclear weapons.[79] But the negotia-

---

[75] Ibid., p. 82.
[76] Bell, Robert G. and Mark M. Lowenthal. SALT II: Major Issues. Congressional Research Service, the Library of Congress. Washington, Dec. 15, 1978, pp. 16–20. (78–249–F) Multilith.
[77] Garthoff, Wilson Quarterly, p. 82.
[78] Whelan, Notebook No. 6. Oct. 4. 1977, pp. 53–54.
[79] As noted above, Newhouse explained unsuccessful U.S. efforts to link SALT to other issues early in the Nixon administration. In the post-SALT I negotiations, Ambassador Johnson stated that linkage and trade-offs in this manner never really emerged at Geneva. Negotiations never got off into other issues, he said, and consequently a tradition developed of not taking on other issues. Still, Johnson noted, SALT was not something in isolation; there was an unspoken interrelationship with other matters. (Whelan, Notebook No. 6, Oct. 4. 1977, p. 44.)

tions revealed distinctive characteristics and for the Russians the most distinctive was their penchant for secrecy.

Secrecy was agreed to by both sides and by and large confidentiality was strictly observed. Leaks did occur on the American side, some by Kissinger himself, but presumably for the positive purpose of preparing American public opinion for acceptance of the final agreement.[80]

Clearly, the Soviets felt comfortable under this blanket of secrecy for it comported more to their own negotiating style, as evident by Ogarkov's expressed displeasure with American revelations to the Soviet civilian delegates of what was to the Soviets classified military information (though gathered by the U.S. side). A most remarkable manifestation of this penchant toward secrecy was Soviet insistence on not disclosing information on the number and specific types of their own nuclear weaponry but rather negotiating on American intelligence estimates of them—estimates which the Soviets never confirmed. Hence, the Backfire bomber, the subject of sharp disagreement as to its long-range capabilities in SALT II negotiations, is an American and NATO designation, not a Soviet one; and the figures on comparing nuclear launching systems and other military data have been American, not Soviet.

More than any other negotiation SALT I went to the nerve center of the Russian's historic sensitivity for their security, a reality carefully explained by Newhouse. Reminiscent of observations by Ambassador Bedell Smith and others, Newhouse wrote:

Russian attitudes toward SALT are conditioned partly by history. Accumulated humiliations affect the Russian view of the world and the judgment of how much military power the state requires. Suspicion is fed by the anxieties of people whose land, lacking frontiers, has been overrun countless times. The Russian word for security, *bezopasnost*, conveys both a broader and more acute meaning than the English equivalent. It means lack of danger, total safety. Russians are haunted by China and Germany. America is an adversary thrown up by ideology and the realities of power. The German phoenix, if it touches the Russian viscera, is no longer an objective menace. China is both a visceral anxiety and a perceived menace.[81]

Soviet negotiators were, therefore, suspicious from the start of possible American fishing expeditions for intelligence information, a traditional negotiating ploy, particularly before they discovered that the U.S. side was rather forthright in presenting and relying on American intelligence information about Soviet military weapons and forces.

Another element in this Soviet attitude stemmed from an elementary tactic in negotiations. Since, in their own eyes, they were in a weaker strategic military position, they were hesitant to disclose their strategic worries by being the first to propose limitations on specific weaponry.[82]

Another issue that revealed Soviet sensitivity to security matters was on-site inspections. Though once not categorically ruled out by Dobrynin just before the start of SALT I talks in Helsinki, it was in

[80] Garthoff, Wilson Quarterly, p. 81, and Newhouse, op. cit., pp. 224–225.
[81] Newhouse, op. cit., pp. 56–57.
[82] Garthoff, Wilson Quarterly, ff, p. 82.

fact categorically ruled out by Semenov at Helsinki. As Newhouse explained,

The Soviets strenuously oppose on-site inspection, partly because it is intrusive; partly because of an understandable aversion to parading their technological inferiority vis-a-vis the United States; partly because they suspect Americans of seeking targeting information not otherwise available or of just wanting to pry, and perhaps partly because of a concern that to disclose one thing could mean disclosing other things they prefer to keep secret.[83]

Eventually agreement was reached on verification based on national technical means; that is, by reconnaissance satellites. A vital concern for security, rooted in the historical past and fortified by an ideology at once aggressive and defensive, has been a major determining factor in Soviet negotiating behavior, particularly in SALT.

A final Soviet negotiating characteristic was one that has become traditional through years of practice. The Soviet leaders held very tight control over their negotiators. As noted above, Semenov was cautious, timid, and extraordinarily careful to stay within the bounds of his rigidly imposed instructions. On the American side, the White House, through the President, Kissinger's National Security Council, and the Verification Panel also maintained tight control over American negotiators. But the American delegation had far greater flexibility in pursuing their instructions and much more independence than their Soviet counterpart.[84]

B. CONCLUDING SALT I: THE BREZHNEV-NIXON SUMMIT MEETING IN MOSCOW, MAY 1972

1. THE CONTEXT: GENERAL PRESUMMIT DEVELOPMENTS

(a) A Kaleidoscope of interacting events

General developments in the 10 months prior to the Brezhnev-Nixon summit in May 1972 reflected a kaleidoscope of interacting diplomatic, political, and military decisions and actions.

The White House announcement on July 15, 1971, that President Nixon would visit China before May 1972—the visit began on February 21—was generally interpreted as an administration effort to pressure Moscow into making favorable diplomatic responses in this emerging complex triangular relationship.

As if to revive the momentum of détente and satisfy Western conditions for final approval of the much sought after Soviet-West German Treaty, the Soviets rapidly reached agreement on the Berlin issue in August 1971, finally settling the question of Western access to the city and once and for all establishing West Berlin's legal status.

Announcement of the Brezhnev-Nixon summit on October 12, 1971, to take place in the following May added credence to the view of observers who perceived the upcoming China visit as an additional pressure on the Soviets to be amenable in SALT negotiations.[85]

The sudden North Vietnam attack across the demilitarized zone (DMZ) on March 30, 1972, that triggered the administration's de-

[83] Newhouse. op. cit., pp. 179–180.
[84] Garthoff, Wilson Quarterly, p. 84, and Whelan, Notebook No. 6, Oct. 4, 1977, pp. 46–50. Johnson felt that he was never handicapped and also that he was better informed than Semenov.
[85] Newhouse, op. cit., pp. 234–236.

cision in mid-April to bomb Hanoi and Haiphong in retaliation placed renewed strains on the preparation for the summit when four Soviet ships were hit in Haiphong Harbor. The incident proved to be a test of how badly Brezhnev wanted the summit meeting.

Such was the complex background against which negotiations for SALT I were concluded.

(b) Status of SALT negotiations

After the breakthrough on May 20, 1971, SALT negotiations continued on but again became deadlocked. The U.S. negotiating position remained in a holding pattern, presumably to allow time for the China ploy to have its expected impact on Moscow. Under these circumstances some progress had, nonetheless, been achieved in Vienna. The delegations had begun to draft language for a joint text on both the defensive and offensive agreements. Many minor issues had been settled and brackets were left around the unsolved major problems.[86]

Still to be determined under the May 20 arrangement were the level of ABM defense to be permited on two sites and the choice of offensive weapons to be included in the interim freeze. Discussion of these matters continued up to the Moscow summit.

By early 1972, the Soviet Union and the United States had reached a broad agreement on three issues: (1) each side would be limited to two ABM sites, one for its national capital and the other for the protection of an ICBM launcher site; (2) the interim freeze would include ICBM's on both sides; but (3) it would not include bombers and so-called forward-based systems (FBS), in which the United States had the advantage. The crucial question was whether the freeze would also extend to SLBM's.[87] This deadlock was broken late in April in secret "back channel" negotiations between Kissinger and Brezhnev in Moscow with Soviet agreement in principle to include SLBM's in the offensive agreement.[88] As a result of this meeting, Kissinger reported enthusiastically to the President: "If the summit meeting takes place, you will be able to sign the most important arms control agreement ever concluded." [89] Final details were, however, left to be worked out in Moscow between the President and Brezhnev.

2. REACHING AGREEMENT AT MOSCOW, MAY 1972

(a) Negotiating teams and issues to be resolved

The President and his party arrived in Moscow on Monday, May 22, to what he termed "a very cool reception." [90] Clearly, the Russians were still smarting over the bombing of Hanoi and Haiphong. On Tuesday afternoon, May 23, the President and Brezhnev discussed SALT for more than 2 hours; they met again in the evening and continued their discussions for another 3 hours, mostly about SALT. At this juncture they turned the matter over to their advisers but kept in close

---

[86] Ibid., p. 236.
[87] Stebbins, Richard P. and Elaine P. Adam. American Foreign Relations 1972: A Documentary Record. A Council on Foreign Relations Book. New York, New York University Press, 1972, pp. 88–89. (Continuing the Series Documents on American Foreign Relations.)
[88] Newhouse, op. cit., p. 244: Kalb, Marvin and Bernard, Kissinger, Boston. Little, Brown, 1974, p. 294; and for Kissinger's summary of the SALT negotiations, see, Kissinger–Smith News Conference, May 26, 1972 and Kissinger's Congressional Briefing, June 15, 1972, in, ACDA Documents, 1972, pp. 207–217 and pp. 295–309.
[89] Nixon, Richard M. RN: The Memoirs of Richard Nixon. New York, Grossett & Dunlap, 1978, p. 592.
[90] Nixon, op. cit., p. 609.

touch. Kissinger briefed the President at every stage; presumably the Soviet negotiators reported directly to the General Secretary.[91]

On the American negotiating team, besides Kissinger, were Helmut Sonnenfeldt, his adviser on Soviet affairs, and William F. Hyland, another member of the NSC staff who worked with Sonnenfeldt on Soviet and European affairs. A third staff member took notes of the discussions.[92]

The Soviets had an impressive negotiating team: Foreign Minister Gromyko, Ambassador Dobrynin and Leonid V. Smirnov. Andrei Aleksandrov, very able and knowledgeable in foreign policy, was also at Brezhnev's side as his adviser on Soviet-American affairs.[92a] Smirnov, a surprise to the Americans—"he came right out of the blue," as one American put it—was a Deputy Premier, a member of the Central Committee, and Chairman of the Military-Industrial Commission. Smirnov's main job was to direct the manufacture of Soviet missile systems and other modern weapons. In this capacity, as Newhouse noted, he "quite clearly exercised a good deal of influence on the Soviet SALT position." [93]

On the Soviet side, only one major issue remained unresolved; namely, to reach agreement on SLBM replacement. On the American side, there were two additional major issues: Mobile land-based missiles and missile size. The United States sought a ban on mobile missiles and wanted to have more restrictive and precise language on missile size than had been agreed to by the SALT negotiators in Helsinki.[94]

(b) Dilemma of the ABM radars

Both sides still had to resolve the dilemma of the radars for the ABM systems permitted under the draft treaty. This issue of apparently lesser magnitude was resolved when on the first day the principals agreed to set an arbitrary line separating heavy from light radars. Ultimately, they agreed to establish a ceiling of 2 heavy and 18 light radars around an ICBM field in each country and 6 modern ABM radar complexes within 90 miles of their capitals. The security implications in this issue arose from fear that either side might claim they were building a radar complex for space tracking when actually it was building a new and clandestine ABM site.[95]

(c) Restricting mobile ICBM's

The problem of mobile ICBM's mounted on heavy trucks or railroad cars arose from fears that verification by reconnaissance satellites could be circumvented, thus subverting the purposes of the draft agreement. At that time neither side had mobile ICBM's.

On Tuesday night Brezhnev and Nixon discussed this admittedly complex problem at great length. Brezhnev would not agree to an outright ban on mobile ICBM's as part of the interim agreement in keeping with the position already taken by Soviet negotiators at Helsinki. Nixon favored such a restriction. Finally, the President indicated that the United States would set forth its own understanding of the ban

[91] Newhouse, op. cit., pp. 250–251.
[92] Ibid., p. 251.
[92a] Nixon, op. cit., p 611.
[93] Newhouse, op. cit., p. 251.
[94] Ibid.
[95] Kalb, op. cit., p. 319.

in a separate declaration that would be submitted to the Congress and warned that Soviet deployment of mobile ICBM's would be grounds for abrogating the ABM treaty and the interim agreement. (American negotiators in Helsinki had said essentially the same thing.) Brezhnev responded that he understood and agreed to the President's statement. Kissinger had assumed that Brezhnev was under pressure from hard-liners who objected to such sweeping Soviet commitments not to build strategic arms.[96]

(d) On the matter of missile size

According to Newhouse, the Americans "fared little better in dealing with missile size." This issue contained two "persistent difficulties"; namely, silo modifications and the "famous" sublimit on very large missiles.[97]

The Russians agreed that in the restriction on "significantly increasing" silo dimensions such an increase would not exceed 10 to 15 percent. "They were not conceding much," Newhouse observed, noting that a "missile of far greater power than any other could be placed in SS–9 silos increased by 15 percent." [98]

With respect to the sublimit on very large missiles, Newhouse indicated that the language worked out in Helsinki "probably assures adequate protection against any increase in the number of missiles in the SS–9 class." But, he cautioned that it was, nonetheless, "a bit vague and incomplete, lacking, for example, a definition of what constitutes a 'heavy' missile." "The Soviets were determined to keep it that way," Newhouse noted, "And they did." On balance, however, Newhouse stated that any violation of the spirit of this language, let alone the latter, "would probably oblige the United States to withdraw from the agreements. Moscow understands that." [99]

(e) The crucial issue: Replacement of SLBM's

(1) Long, arduous negotiating sessions

After Tuesday night, Nixon and Brezhnev turned to Vietnam and other matters, leaving the final contentious SLBM replacement issue to Kissinger, Smirnov, Gromyko and the other negotiators. The sessions that followed were long and arduous. The negotiators met in an extended session on Wednesday; they met again that night and worked until 4 on Thursday morning; they resumed their talks Thursday evening, following attendance at a performance of Swan Lake at the Bolshoi, and continued discussions at this penultimate session into Friday, finally breaking up at 3 a.m.[100]

At this late moment the crucial issue of SLBM replacement was still unresolved. Newhouse, who explained in detail this highly complex problem, summed up the state of negotiations this way:

> * * * the dispute hung on two points: the number of SLBM's the Soviets actually had, and the number of old missiles they would be obliged to retire in order to reach the agreed totals of 62 submarines and 950 tubes. The Americans were clear and hard, saying in effect: We've agreed that you will have more boats and more missiles, but not for free. You must earn each new SLBM by retiring an old missile.[101]

---

[96] Ibid., pp. 319–320 and Newhouse, op. cit., p. 251.
[97] Ibid., p. 251.
[98] Ibid., pp. 251–252.
[99] Ibid., p. 252.
[100] Ibid., p. 252.
[101] Ibid., p. 253.

(2) The President's final offer

After much consideration, the President instructed Kissinger to make a final offer to the Soviet negotiators. By its terms, close to the final agreement as it turned out, the Soviets could have an absolute ceiling of 62 modern missile-launching submarines and 950 launchers. The United States would accept 44 submarines and 710 launchers. The President insisted, however, that if the Russians wanted to reach that ceiling, they would have to "trade in" or retire approximately 240 old missiles of the SS–7, SS–8 and H–class submarine variety.[102] Should the Soviet's reject this offer, the President was prepared to return home without a SALT agreement.

The rationale underlying this final proposal was the desire to try to arrest the ongoing Soviet ICBM and submarine building programs before the strategic balance had swung decisively to the Soviet side. The Soviets had underway crash programs for these strategic systems while the United States had not added a single ICBM to its arsenal in years and had only just begun to contemplate an advanced submarine called *Trident*. The President was not in a strong bargaining position.[103]

(3) Kissinger-Gromyko final negotiations

After the ballet on Thursday night, Kissinger and Gromyko resumed their negotiations in the Soviet Foreign Ministry. The Soviets were set on completing the negotiations on the agreement for signing on Friday. This was the presummit arrangement worked out with Dobrynin. Kissinger took the line that SALT was too important for haste and expressed the belief that more time should be taken for negotiations if needed. However, Gromyko insisted on a Friday deadline for signing, and while puzzling to Kissinger, it did give him a negotiating advantage.[104]

After reviewing their negotiating positions, Kissinger and Gromyko agreeably resolved the problem of defining what constituted a submarine "under construction"—it was simply, Kissinger mused, when the parts were riveted to the hull. Unresolved was the central question of the number of allowable submarines. At 1 a.m. Friday morning Kissinger presented the President's revised final offer. For 2 or more hours Gromyko and Kissinger debated its merits. Soon it became clear that Gromyko neither could nor would make the final decision. That was Brezhnev's task. By 3 a.m. both negotiators realized that they had reached the limits of their mandates. Kissinger left Gromyko with the clear impression that even though the President wanted a SALT agreement this was his final offer.[105]

(4) Final approval and signing

Late Friday morning, Brezhnev conferred with the Politburo, presumably to discuss the President's proposal. Apparently with little debate the Politburo gave its approval. Meanwhile, Nixon and Kis-

---

[102] Kalb, op. cit., p. 322.
[103] Ibid., p. 322. As Kissinger explained at a press conference after the signing of the agreements, "the question to ask in assessing the freeze is not what situation it perpetuates, but what situation it prevents. The question is where we would be without the freeze. And if you project the existing building programs of the Soviet Union into the future, as against the absence of building programs over the period of the freeze in either of the categories that are being frozen, you will get a more correct clue to why we believe that there is a good agreement and why we believe that it has made a significant contribution to arresting the arms race." (Kissinger News Conference, May 26, 1976, ACDA documents, 1972, p. 209.)
[104] Kalb, op. cit., pp. 322–323.
[105] Ibid, p. 323.

singer were meeting in the President's apartment in the Kremlin and preparing to accept a setback on SALT. A call came from Gromyko at 11 a.m. requesting a meeting in St. Catherine's Hall at 11:30 a.m. Gromyko opened the meeting with a strong suggestion that the deadlock had now been broken and that Brezhnev was prepared to accept the President's final offer with a few minor changes. At a few minutes past 1 p.m. these changes were negotiated and confirmed by the principals on both sides. After some last-minute hectic comings-and-goings, to be described below, the agreements were signed at 11:07 p.m. that same Friday evening.[106]

3. SOME CHARACTERISTICS OF THE MOSCOW SUMMIT MEETING

(a) Organization and procedures

(1) Intensive preparations

Preparations for the Moscow summit meeting have been described as "intensive" and "laborious."[107] For the negotiators, armed with 11 thick briefing books covering subjects from grain trade to trade-in of missiles, the summit represented the culmination of years of arduous, complex negotiations.[108] Judging from the number and titles of the briefing books, the President was well-prepared. In a paneled study next to his bedroom in the Kremlin he had what Safire called his "home-work in neatly organized briefcase." Briefcase A contained the Issues Book: volume I, Soviet Leaders; Europe; volume II, Vietnam; volume III, Middle East; volume IV, SALT; volume V, Basic Issues. In briefcase B, volume I was labeled Bilateral Agreements; volume II, Dr. K. Conversations in Moscow; volume III, Background Reading; volume IV, Soviet Policies and Objectives; volume V, State Department books on Austria, the Soviet Union, Iran, Poland and all the countries on the current trip.[109]

Much of the responsibility for the last minute preparations for the summit fell upon Kissinger. Discussions with Dobrynin in Washington on substantive matters and agenda were extended to Moscow during a secret visit in April where, among other diplomatic tasks, Kissinger worked out further details with Brezhnev and Gromyko. In addition to the sensitive subject of Vietnam, Kissinger and Brezhnev discussed a wide range of subjects—from Berlin to trade. As Marvin and Bernard Kalb noted in their diplomatic biography of Kissinger, "They were determined to lay the groundwork for a successful summit, at which a number of substantive agreements could be signed."[110] According to the President, Kissinger arranged "the entire agenda," except the most sensitive elements of SALT that required direct negotiations between the leaders.[111]

On the last day of the visit Kissinger conferred with Gromyko for 6 hours, working almost exclusively on summit preparations. Last minute details on agreements on health research, environmental problems and "incidents at sea" had to be settled, for this summit was to deal with many subjects and conclude many agreements though

[106] Ibid., pp. 324–327.
[107] Kalb, op. cit., p. 313, and Safire, William. Before the Fall: An Inside View of the Pre-Watergate White House. Garden City, N.Y., Doubleday, 1975, p. 437.
[108] Kalb, op. cit., p. 313.
[109] Safire, op. cit., p. 453.
[110] Ibid., p. 294.
[111] Nixon, op. cit., p. 592.

SALT I was to be the centerpiece. Logistical arrangements had to be made for the press and the housing of staff.[112] And before leaving Moscow, Brezhnev himself proudly showed Kissinger the Presidential quarters in the Kremlin, a detail that revealed to Kissinger the Russian national characteristic of inferiority, in contrast to the superiority complex of the Chinese, but inspired a warning verified in the summit negotiations that "feelings of inferiority can lead to bluster and to arrogance."[113]

(2) Organizational matters

Negotiations at the Moscow summit were essentially bilevel: Smith, Semenov and their respective staffs were on tap in Helsinki, ready to put in diplomatic language and into formal instruments of agreement the political decisions reached in Moscow; the President, the General Secretary and their respective negotiating staffs—some called the Americans, the U.S. "Moscow delegation"—were in Moscow, trying to resolve the remaining outstanding issues. When agreement was finally reached, the negotiators in Moscow took the expeditious and practical step of sending the same instructions to both teams in Helsinki for the sake of accuracy and time. As Kissinger told the press conference in which he described the negotiations and the final conclusion of the agreements,

Then the problem was to get the agreement drafted, and I think it was the first time in the history of Soviet-American relations that joint instructions were sent to two delegations, so that no misunderstandings could occur, and where we were kept informed by the Soviet side about meetings going on in the Soviet delegation in order to speed up the drafting process.

Then the delegation flew here in the American delegation's plane and arrived about 9 o'clock with the treaty draft in their hands, because the decisions that were made at 1 still had to be put into treaty language.

All we did this morning was to arrive at the general framework. The delegations then had to put it into language that will be put before you soon.

So a tremendous amount of work was done by the delegation, and it showed how rapidly things could move in diplomacy when both sides want to move.[114]

By all accounts both negotiating teams were staffed with able negotiators and knowledgeable backup staff. The equanimity of the American staff was tested, however, by a rivalry that surfaced between Smith and Kissinger in the last days of the summit. The dispute over who would brief the press was resolved by each sharing the burden.[115]

---

[112] Kalb, op. cit., p. 295.

[113] William Safire, a White House aide at the time, recalled Kissinger's comments on his return from Moscow in which he contrasted the ways in which the Russians and Chinese had prepared for their Nixon visits. Brezhnev had proudly shown Kissinger the Presidential quarters, something the Chinese would never do, according to Kissinger, since the Chinese have always felt culturally superior, the Russians culturally inferior. Brezhnev had also shown Kissinger the antique urns on pedestals along the corridors of Nixon's Kremlin apartment. "Only one was uncovered, beautifully polished—all the rest were covered with shrouds to keep off the dust," Safire noted. Brezhnev told Kissinger: "We will take off the shrouds 2 hours before President Nixon gets here." Kissinger was amused by this solicitation. "It reminded me of my grandmother," he told his White House colleagues. "The house had to be cleaned spic and span on Thursday, and everything covered up so it would be right for Friday night", the beginning of the Jewish Sabbath. Kissinger laughed again and then became serious. "But never forget," he said in what was to Safire an unforgettable statement (one that was verified in the Moscow negotiations), "that feelings of inferiority can lead to bluster and to arrogance." (Safire, op. cit., p. 439)

[114] Kissinger Press Conference, May 26, 1972, ACDA Documents, 1972, p. 225.

[115] Safire wrote of the Kissinger-Smith relationship: "Kissinger had treated Smith with contempt, more as a front man than a negotiator." After describing the "back channel" negotiations between Kissinger and Dobrynin for over a year he noted, "Kissinger saw no need to give the U.S. negotiator, Smith, more than what Henry decided he needed to know." "Not surprisingly," Safire continued, "Smith and Kissinger came to cordially despise each other." (Safire, op. cit., p. 449.) The Kalbs noted that Kissinger and Smith had argued for "25 embarrassing minutes" about who would do the briefing. "Finally, these negotiators," they continued, "who had cracked the secret of SALT, cracked the secret of ego. They agreed to share the limelight." (Kalb, op. cit., pp. 324–325.)

The Soviets had the procedural advantage of being at their home base. Brezhnev had at his fingertips not not only the powerful Politburo to consult (which he did at least four times) and pass on his negotiating positions as appeared to be the case, but also the immediate logistical and staff support of the Foreign Ministry and other vital elements in the Soviet party and government structure.

In contrast, the President's staff whose administrative center was in the Hotel Rossiya had to keep in touch with Washington via transAtlantic communications, making it extraordinarily difficult to consult with backup staff in the White House, the Joint Chiefs of Staff, Members of the U.S. Senate would have to pass on the agreements, and other Government officials. Kissinger's staff in the White House had the task of preventing the erosion of support for SALT within the Government. Hence the need for continuing communications as negotiating positions changed. Adding to the difficulties was the 7-hour time difference between Moscow and Washington which had the effect, along with the requirements of the negotiators, of setting a "frantic pace", in Newhouse's words, for those staffmen in Washington who had to work virtually around the clock.[116]

The problem of distance was magnified in the final stage of the negotiations. On the Soviet side, Smirnov had a technician's grasp of the complex technical issues but Kissinger and his negotiating staff were, as Newhouse noted, "political animals." Kissinger's technicians—Philip Odeen, Col. Jack Merritt, and Barry Carter—were in Washington, and as Newhouse wrote,

A steady stream of cables and phone calls passed between them and the Kissinger team in Moscow. Some of the calls were made on open lines from the Kremlin. Since the conversations dealt with Soviet submarines and SLBM's, the American negotiators felt that they could not be revealing anything the Russians didn't already know. Hyland, in fact, took a Washington call from Carter at the Bolshoi Theater in the middle of the first act.[117]

Kissinger now had the problem that Dobrynin had pointed out to him a year earlier as being his fate as the Soviet Ambassador in Washington; namely, of trying to negotiate at a distance of several thousand miles from his power base.[118] Clearly this geographic reality added immeasurably to the tasks of the American negotiators.

(3) Summit records and the use of a Soviet interpreter

(a) Summit records.—No complete transcripts were made of the plenary sessions at the Moscow summit. Secretary of State Rogers and Kissinger believed that the main documents submitted to the Congress on the proceedings were a sufficient record (that is, the ABM Treaty, Interim Agreement, Protocol and memoranda of interpretations and common understandings), and they declared that no secret understandings were made.[119]

---

[116] Newhouse, op. cit., p. 253.
[117] Ibid., p. 252.
[118] Ibid., pp. 252–253.
[119] Rogers told the Senate Foreign Relations Committee: "I would like to have Ambassador Smith answer that [Senator Cooper had asked for "the negotiators' papers and instructions * * * the full papers, the complete record," as had been the practice in submitting treaties to the Senate in the past], but let me before he does say that we very carefully considered everything that may be thought of as an agreement or understanding of any significance and everything that is agreed to of any significance we think has been fully reflected in the treaty, in the agreed understandings that are included in this document. In the interim agreement and protocol. Nevertheless, everything

(Continued)

Kissinger had a notetaker from his NSC staff during his negotiations with Gromyko and Smirnov.[120]

Whether or not the President had a record of his discussions with Brezhnev cannot be determined. He used a Soviet interpreter and thus presumably did not have the benefit of a written record as had been the case with Bohlen. Bohlen's practice after interpreting for President Roosevelt, as at Yalta and Teheran, was to prepare a report of each session on the basis of his notes used in interpreting.

However, President Nixon kept a diary, though fearful of bugging—"The Soviets were curiously unsubtle in this regard," he said— he refrained from dictating any entries while in Moscow. However, he took extensive notes during the trip and made several long dictations from them the week after he returned home.[121] The President's memoirs include direct diary entries and presumably his narrative is based upon other documentation and perhaps even other diary entries not produced. There is, therefore, a written record of the proceedings as seen by the President, though not in great detail, but most importantly, as seen through the eyes and filtered through the mind of a Soviet interpreter.

(b) *Using a Soviet interpreter.*—The President did not use the State Department's interpreter—"an excellent one," according to U.S. Ambassador in Moscow Jacob D. Beam—but rather relied on a Russian, Viktor Sukhodrev, Brezhnev's interpreter and assistant. Nixon has been criticized for doing this. Ambassador Beam and others have noted that it was done because the President and Kissinger were fearful of leaks from the American delegation. Sukhodrev was "skillful and had style," reflected Beam (Brandon referred to him as "the charming and adroit Russian who can put on an American as well as an English accent"), but "unfortunately the U.S. side had to rely on the Soviet record of the top leaders' talks." [122]

Ambassador Smith faulted the President and Kissinger on the same count. The normal way to develop an approximately verbatim record of a summit-type conference, he said, was through the interpreter's notes—as in the case of Bohlen. "It can only be regretted," he continued, "if former President Nixon's past Moscow summit practice of not using American interpreters has foreclosed the existence of a faithful record of such a uniquely valuable exchange between the heads of rival nuclear states." This "extraordinary practice" of relying on Soviet interpreters, he surmised, was based on the calculation of no

(Continued)
that has been agreed to has been submitted to the Congress for its consideration and perusal. I don't believe there is anything else that is of any consequence.
"Now, there was not any complete transcript maintained of the plenary sessions: so I think the Congress has everything that reflects in any way on what the treaty and agreements involve." (U.S. Congress. Senate. Committee on Foreign Relations. Strategic Arms Limitation Agreements. Hearings. 92d Congress, 2d session. Washington, D.C., U.S. Government Printing Office, 1972, p. 26) Rogers repeated essentially the same statement on page 44.
Kissinger made essentially the same statement at a White House briefing on June 15, 1972 for the Congress: "There are no secret understandings. We have submitted to the Congress the list of all the significant agreements and interpretive statements, and so forth. What we have not done is to go through the record to see whether Ambassador Smith might have said something that they interpreted in a certain way, and this is why we put on the qualification 'significant', because otherwise we would have to submit the entire record.
"According to the best of our judgment, there are no secret understandings, and all the significant interpretive statements have been submitted to the Congress." (p. 412.)
[120] Newhouse, op. cit., p. 251.
[121] Nixon, op. cit., pp. 618–619.
[122] Beam, Jacob D. Multiple Exposure: An American Ambassador's Unique Perspective on East-West Issues. New York, W. W. Norton, 1978, p. 274. For Garthoff's criticism, see Wilson Quarterly, ff. on p. 80.

risk of leaks to U.S. newsmen or of disclosures to American officials
who in the judgment of the White House had no need to know. "Such
a record would have been an invaluable factor for continuity for the
former President's successors on whom will fall the burden of carrying
on the strategic dialogue," Smith concluded.[123]

Conceivably, the value of an accurate record could go beyond Smith's
criticism with respect to the continuity factor and even to the more
crucial point of what was actually agreed in a private exchange between the principals. Examination of the statements of unilateral interpretation and common understanding will show that some were extracted directly and verbatim from conference proceedings.[124] Though
none were apparently based on the Brezhnev-Nixon discussions, still
the possibility could exist that commitments were made in these conversations the accuracy of which would have been exceedingly important for the record. This was after all the very summit of decisionmaking. That such a possibility is not too farfetched was evident from
Kissinger's comments at the congressional briefing on June 15. When
asked about any secret understandings, Kissinger replied:

> There are no secret understandings. We have submitted to the Congress the list
> of all the significant agreements and interpretive statements, and so forth. What
> we have not done is to go through the record to see whether Ambassador Smith
> might have said something that they interpreted in a certain way, and this is
> why we put on the qualification "significant," because otherwise we would have
> to submit the entire record.
>
> According to the best of our judgment, there are no secret understandings,
> and all the significant interpretative statements have been submitted to the
> Congress.[125]

This explanation may have been true in negotiations by Ambassador
Smith, but could the same be said of the President whose remarks and
those of Brezhnev and other Soviet leaders were transmitted through
a Soviet interpreter, assuming that the Russians had provided a complete transcript based on their interpreter's notes? Developments in the
social science field of psycho-linguistics and cross-cultural relationships indicate that words can mean different things to different peoples
and that serious misunderstandings can result. Thus, the possibility of
error is very real when relying solely on an interpreter from the other
side.[126]

[123] Smith, Gerard. SALT Thoughts. Journal of International Affairs, Spring 1975: 15 (ms copy).
[124] House Foreign Affairs Committee, Hearings, Agreement on Strategic Offensive Weapons., 1972, pp. 143–147.
[125] Senate Foreign Relations Committee, Hearings, Strategic Arms Limitation Agreements, 1972, p. 412.
[126] Sherwood commented on this problem of communicating with the Russians, noting particularly the difficulty of getting a common interpretation of what a "friendly" government in Poland meant. Sherwood wrote: "In all of these discussions of Poland [at Yalta], Hopkins repeated many times that it was the desire of his government that the Polish Government should be friendly to the Soviet Union, and Stalin agreed that this was all that he demanded. But, here again, as Roosevelt had said to Churchill, 'The Russians do not use words for the same purposes that we do'; and there was apparently no way of translating the word 'friendly' from one language to the other so that it would end up meaning the same thing." (Sherwood, op. cit., p. 908.)
Dr. Lorand Szalay of the Institute of Comparative Social and Cultural Studies, Bethesda, Md., has done pioneering work on this problem of psycholinguistics and cross-cultural relationships. One of his major efforts had focused on Korean-American inter-relationships.
Hayter gave the following explanation on what constitutes a good interpreter: "Interpreting is a difficult art. Having done a little in an amateur way myself, I know how hard it is to keep out one's own personality, opinions and knowledge, how tempting it is to correct the errors, disentangle the confusions and soften the asperities of one's interpretee. But a good interpreter should be like a pane of clear glass, through which everything flows undisturbed, including errors, confusions, and asperities. He must help his hearer to get as accurate a picture as possible of the man for whom he is interpreting. Negotiating through an interpreter of this kind can even be advantageous, particularly in the pauses for reflexion that it allows (simultaneous interpretation is useless and even dangerous in detailed negotiation, though invaluable for the set speech)." (Hayter, Diplomacy of the Great Powers, p. 69.)

The President himself, sensitive to this criticism, stated that there had been concern expressed that he should have used a State Department translator. But he gave this explanation for relying only on Sukhodrev: "* * * I knew that Sukhodrev was a superb linguist who spoke English as well as he did Russian, and I felt that Brezhnev would speak more freely if only one other person was present." [127]

On the other hand, according to Brandon, Brezhnev, to the surprise of the President, had insisted that only Sukhodrev be present at their private conversations. "Brezhnev was obviously distrustful of an American interpreter," he wrote, "and refused to accept one." Thus, as Beam had also observed, "Mr. Nixon had to rely on the minutes dictated by a Russian." [128]

(4) Concern for bugging

The President's concern for the "curiously unsubtle" Soviet practice of bugging was also shared by others in the U.S. delegation. "A member of my staff reported having casually told his secretary that he would like an apple," Nixon recalled, "and 10 minutes later a maid came in and put a bowl of apples on the table." [129]

In taking precautions against this practice, Nixon refrained from dictating entries into his diary and made notes for later dictation at home.[130] At Summit III in 1974, he recalled how he and Kissinger "went outside and walked up and down in the open courtyard" so that they might "be able to talk freely." [131]

Members of the U.S. delegation took various precautions against bugging, as in the case of a meeting in the Intourist Hotel where, according to Safire, the purposely generated noise level of the staff, for example, turning up the volume on the television and radio, was so loud that bugging was surely prevented but it was also impossible for them to hear their conversation.[132] On the occasion of a briefing by Kissinger on SALT progress at a Moscow nightclub, reporters present just assumed that the place was bugged.[133]

Yet the Soviets could joke about this practice. During the crucial nocturnal negotiation between Kissinger and Gromyko early on Friday, May 26, Kissinger wondered aloud whether he should speak closer to the orange or the apple in a bowl on the table, implying that he assumed one or the other probably contained a miniature microphone. Gromyko looked up at the ceiling where a sculpture of a woman richly endowed with a large bosom looked down on them. Pointing to one of her breasts, he confided michievously, "No; I believe it is in there." [134]

---

[127] Nixon, op. cit., p. 610. Safire made the following comment on this matter: "To the State Department's dismay, Nixon choose the top Soviet interpreter, Viktor Sukhodrev, to do the running translation, rather than an American translator. This in itself was evidence of trust (besides, Nixon admitted, Sukhodrev is the best in the business today) and the brilliant interpreter's performance supplemented Nixon's own hard work—obviously, nobody told Sukhodrev not to do his dramatic best." (Safire, op. cit., p. 455.)

[128] Brandon, op. cit., p. 290.

[129] Nixon, op. cit., p. 619.

[130] Ibid.

[131] Ibid., p. 1035.

[132] Safire, op. cit., p. 457.

[133] "In this surrealistic setting," the Kalbs wrote, "Kissinger explained the complicated arithmetic of SALT. It was 1 a.m., Saturday, May 27, the start of his 49th birthday, and Kissinger showed no signs of strain. Everyone assumed the nightclub was bugged, and no one could shake the spooky feeling that, as Kissinger spoke, Gromyko was listening from a command post in the Kremlin, just down the block, shaking his head in disbelief at the vision of Kissinger revealing secrets of Soviet security in a Russian nightclub." (Kalb, op. cit., p. 328.)

[134] Ibid., p. 323 and Brandon, op. cit., p. 290.

The humor notwithstanding the Soviet practice of bugging added one more precaution that Americans had to bear in mind when negotiating with the Russians.

(b) Soviet negotiators and their style

(1) Nixon's views on Brezhnev, the man and negotiator

(a) On Brezhnev's human qualities.—The Moscow summit was the President's first encounter with Brezhnev, though the General Secretary, a lesser political luminary at the time, was present, but silent, at the famous Khrushchev-Nixon kitchen debate of 1959. Nixon's memoirs strongly suggest that Brezhnev made every effort to display his human qualities, perhaps as a corrective to the negative image of a brutal and crude dictator that had haunted him since the 1968 invasion of Czechoslovakia, and perhaps also as a means of projecting a more positive image in keeping with the emerging spirit of détente.[135]

Briefly, the President found Brezhnev to be a warm and friendly man with an appealing sense of humor; an emotional man, especially, as he said, "about death in war" and, moreover, easily moved to tears as in his response to the President's address over Soviet television and his reference to the heroine Tanya of beleaguered wartime Leningrad; a backslapper, as Nixon observed, in the style of Lyndon Johnson with the instincts of "a skilled actor or a born politician"; a man who could be called a toucher in his compulsive inclination to grab arms, shake hands, embrace and in numerous other ways make physical contact with those around him. He was like an American politician, as the President described his encounter with the American public on his 1973 visit, "working the crowd at a county fair." To the President, Kosygin was "a very cool customer with very little outward warmth," an aristocrat by Communist terms; Podgorny was "more like a Midwestern Senator"; but Brezhnev was "like a big Irish labor boss, or perhaps an analogy to Mayor Daley [of Chicago] would be more in order with no affront intended to either."

Such human qualities of Brezhnev the man seemed to become more apparent to the President as their relationship deepened and became much closer with each summit meeting.[136]

---

[135] Brandon described Brezhnev's sensitivity to "the terrible things people say about me" and his desire to erase the negative image that many had of him. He went to such extremes, Brandon noted, of shaving down his bushy eyebrows because they gave him a somewhat sinister look and made him an easy target for cartoonists. He had also become more attentive to clothes, wearing during his earlier meetings with Kissinger a light blue jacket and flamboyant tie. For the President he preferred to wear "the sober-suited look of the trade-union boss in his Sunday best." (Brandon, op. cit., p. 289.)

[136] Nixon made many references to Brezhnev's humor. In discussing work habits, Brezhnev said he did not use a dictaphone. The President recalled that Churchill had told him that he much preferred to dictate to a pretty young woman. "Brezhnev and the others agreed," the President noted, "and Brezhnev jokingly added, 'Besides a secretary is particularly useful when you wake up at night and want to write down a note.' They all laughed uproariously." (Nixon, op. cit., pp. 612–613.) Referring to Brezhnev as being "very warm and friendly," Nixon recalled their riding in the car out to his dacha, and noted : "he put his hand on my knee and said he hoped we had developed a good personal relationship." (p. 620). In describing Brezhnev during Summit II at Washington in 1973, the President wrote : "At public functions Brezhnev's demeanor remained ebullient. He obviously enjoyed the attention he was receiving, and, like a skilled actor or a born politician, he knew how to hold center stage." (p. 879). While taking a boatride during Summit III in Moscow during 1974, Nixon recalled how Brezhnev pointed out Yalta and Bear Mountain and other points of interests. "He became very emotional ;" the President recorded in his diary, "he said that he wanted this summit to be one that would be remembered as were the other great events that had taken place, obviously referring, but without saying so, to Yalta." He put his arm around the President and said, "We must do something of vast historical importance. We want every Russian and every American to be friends that talk to each other as you and I are talking to each other here on this boat." (p. 1032)

At this first summit meeting the President properly assessed Brezhnev's overall strength and in his appraisal touched on other characteristics that assured his primacy in the Soviet political firmament. Not only was he younger than the other two contenders—presumably Kosygin and Podgorny—but, as the President observed, "he has a strong, deep voice—a great deal of animal magnetism and drive which comes through whenever you meet him." Sometimes Brezhnev talked "too much and is not too precise," but, according to Nixon, "he always comes through forcefully, and he has a very great shrewdness." [137]

(b) *As a negotiator.*—From the very beginning the President appeared to have developed a healthy respect for Brezhnev as a negotiator. Elaborating on the General Secretary's shrewdness, he noted that in negotiations Brezhnev "also has the ability to move off of a point in the event that he is not winning it." Nixon further noted that Brezhnev's "gestures were extremely expressive. He stands up and walks around, a device he often used during the course of our meetings." Once Brezhnev had told Kissinger, "Every time I stand up I make another concession." [138]

The President contrasted his own unemotional approach to negotiations with that of Brezhnev's. "He must * * * have been affected by the fact that my own conduct was, by comparison, totally controlled," he wrote. Though some would say this was a mistake, the President was "inclined to think it may have impressed him more than if I had been more outwardly emotional in responding to his various charges," presumably with respect to the bombing of North Vietnam.[139]

Safire gave this description of the Brezhnev-Nixon negotiating relationship as they faced off in Moscow:

Through that first day, in private sessions and semipublic dinners, all eyes were on the interplay between Brezhnev and Nixon. Ordinarily, Nixon would let Brezhnev take the lead, responding to rather than leading the conversation. The Soviet leader, who walks with a stately, carefully controlled pace, lets himself become animated when seated. With his right hand, he conducted conversations, cigarette between index and middle finger, elbow on the table, using his hand to shape arguments and indicate nuances. Nixon, who walks stiffly, was relaxed when seated, steepling or folding his hands. Brezhnev champed at the bit while his interpreter was putting his words into English: Nixon though 6 years younger than his counterpart, was infinitely more experienced in communicating across a language gulf, and spoke slowly, using a simple construction and plain words wherever possible, nodding during the translation for emphasis and as if he understood.

In such circumstances, facial expressions are important: both Nixon and Brezhnev, with pronounced and expressive eyebrows, used them to advantage. Brezhnev was adept at an eyes-widened, "so that's it!" expression, briskly nodding and projecting an air of welcome discovery, and Nixon was excellent at an expression on his face that says, "Is that so?" reminiscent of the photo of General Eisenhower when informed that General MacArthur had been fired. Both men knew all about the way to play to photographers, and constantly upstaged each other in their ostentatious deference.[140]

(c) *Brezhnev's toughness and shock tactics: On Vietnam at Summit I.*—The President approached summit negotiations in a spirit of cold realism. As Kissinger observed, "The President has always approached

[137] Ibid., p. 620.
[138] Ibid., p. 620. Ambassador Beam gave the following estimate of Brezhnev as a negotiator: "My impression of Brezhnev, after seeing him in action in these and other meetings, was that he was rational, moderate, in acknowledged authority, but not very quick in debate." (Beam, op. cit., p. 274.)
[139] Nixon, op. cit., p. 620.
[140] Safire, op. cit., pp. 446–447.

these meetings * * * from a totally unsentimental point of view, and he has not had the illusion that he could charm leaders, who have been brought up on their belief of a superior understanding of objective factors, by his personality." [141]

As a realist he risked cancellation of the first summit by ordering the bombing of Hanoi and the mining of Haiphong Harbor. He wanted the summit but calculated correctly that Brezhnev wanted it more. Despite Brezhnev's expansive emotionalism, he had a much more balanced temperament than Khrushchev who, as Brandon said, "undoubtedly would have volleyed his shoes against the wall in anger and canceled the summit." [142] For the Russian leader this retaliatory action was a severe humiliation, though, from the administration's view, it was justified on grounds of an extraordinary Soviet military buildup in support of the DRV's offensive across the DMZ. And Brezhnev had to swallow hard to go through with the summit, even to the point of sacking Pyotr Y. Shelest, the Ukrainian party leader, who clearly felt otherwise. (In a retrospective thought, Kissinger said that Brezhnev was a "really big man" for accepting this humiliation and going through with the summit meeting.) [143]

But neither Brezhnev nor the other Soviet leaders were going to let the President get way with the Vietnam retaliation. Brandon observed that Brezhnev "exudes a dynamic bargaining technique in business discussions." [144] He outdid himself at a 3-hour meeting with Nixon in the presence of Podgorny and Kosygin at his dacha on Wednesday evening May 24.

Everyone was "in a good humor" when they returned to the dacha from a boat ride on the Moskva River, but for the next 3 hours as the two negotiating teams sat facing each other, the Soviet leaders, in the President's words, "pounded me bitterly and emotionally about Vietnam." [145]

The meeting began on a note of acrimony and steadily became worse. "Barbaric!" was Brezhnev's characterization of the mining of Haiphong Harbor. Such phrases as "just like the Nazis" flew around the room, and, as Safire wrote, "before long there was yelling, table-pounding, and threats about what could happen if Soviet ships and sailors were injured by bombs or mines." [146]

The President gave this graphic portrayal of the exchange:

I momentarily thought of Dr. Jekyll and Mr. Hyde when Brezhnev, who had just been laughing and slapping me on the back, started shouting angrily that instead of honestly working to end the war, I was trying to use the Chinese as a means of bringing pressure on the Soviets to intervene with the North Vietnamese.

---

[141] Kalb, op. cit., p. 334. This characteristic of realism was amply displayed at the 1st plenary session with Brezhnev, Kosygin, Podgorny, Gromyko, and Dobrynin. "I decided to establish the straight-forward tone I planned to adopt during the entire summit," he noted. "I would like to say something that my Soviet friends may be too polite to say," he began. "I know that my reputation is one of being a very hard-line, cold-war-oriented, anticommunist." Kosygin responded dryly, "I had heard this sometime back." "It is true that I have a strong belief in our system," the President continued, "but at the same time I respect those who believe just as strongly in their own systems. There must be room in this world for 2 great nations with different systems to live together and work together. We cannot do this, however, by mushy sentimentality or by glossing over differences which exist." "All the heads nodded on the other side of the table," the President recalled, "but I guessed that in fact they would have much preferred a continuation of the mushy sentimentality that had characterized so much of our approach to the Soviets in the past." (Nixon, op. cit., p. 611.)
[142] Brandon, op. cit., p. 289.
[143] Kalb, op. cit., p. 313.
[144] Ibid., p. 289.
[145] Nixon, op. cit., p. 613.
[146] Safire, op. cit., p. 448.

He said that they wondered whether on May 8 I had acted out of thoughtless irritation, because they had no doubt that if I really wanted peace I could get a settlement without any outside assistance. "It's surely doubtful that all of the American people are unanimously supporting the war in Vietnam," he continued. "Certainly I doubt that families of those who were killed or maimed or who remain crippled support the war."

When Brezhnev finally seemed to run out of steam, Kosygin took up the cudgel. He said, "Mr. President, I believe you overestimate the possibility in the present circumstances of resolving problems in Vietnam from a position of strength. There may come a critical moment for the North Vietnamese when they will not refuse to let in forces of other countries to act on their side."

This was going too far. For the first time I spoke. "That threat doesn't frighten us a bit," I said, "but go ahead and make it."

"Don't think you are right in thinking what we say is a threat and what you say is not a threat," Kosygin replied coldly. He said, "This is an *analysis* of what may happen, and that is much more serious than a threat."

Kosygin seemed to gather force as he concentrated his scorn on President Thieu, to whom he referred as "a mercenary President so-called." When I continued to show no reaction to this tirade Kosygin's composure began to break. "You still need to retain the so-called President in South Vietnam, someone *you* call the President, who had not been chosen by anyone?" he asked.

"Who chose the President of *North* Vietnam?" I asked him.

"The entire people," he replied.

"Go ahead," I said.

When Kosygin concluded, Podgorny came to bat. His tone was more cordial, but his words were just as tough. While Podgorny and Kosygin were taking their turns at trying to hammer me down, Brezhnev got up and paced the floor.

After about 20 minutes, Podgorny suddenly stopped and Brezhnev said a few more words. Then there was silence in the room. By this time it was almost 11 o'clock. I felt that before I could let this conversation end, I had to let them know exactly where I stood.[147]

The President explained at length the reason for his decision to retaliate, taken, as he said, in "cold objectivity." He pointed out the withdrawal of over 500,000 men from Vietnam; the restraint shown in the face of the DRV's "massive buildup," not wishing to adversely affect the summit; the death of 30,000 South Vietnamese civilians, men, women, and children, killed by the North Vietnamese using Soviet equipment; his belief that the Soviet leaders did not want this to happen and underscoring the common goal of not trying "to impose a settlement or a government on anybody." "They listened intently to what I said," the President noted, "but none of them made an attempt to respond."[148]

At that, the meeting broke up, and the group went upstairs to attend a lavish dinner. Having made their point, expected no doubt to have a broader impact on the President's negotiating behavior as the discussions on SALT proceeded, Brezhnev and his associates suddenly changed their demeanor. In brief, back to Dr. Jekyll. The atmosphere at the dinner was described as being "jovial." The President made his usual joke about not giving Kissinger too many drinks because he had to go back and negotiate with Gromyko. "They seemed vastly amused by this," the President recalled, "and they proceeded in a comic charade to pretend to ply him with vodka and Cognac. There was much laughing and joking and storytelling—as if the acrimonious session downstairs had never happened."[149]

[147] Nixon, op. cit., pp. 613-614.
[148] Ibid.
[149] Ibid., and Safire, op. cit., p. 448. Safire gave other details of the exchange over Vietnam. At one point after a "particularly savage blast," the President coolly asked, "Are you threatening here?" This was a ploy Nixon had learned from Khrushchev. After being translated, there was a silence, and the meeting went on in a more restrained atmosphere for a few moments, and "then back to the one-sided onslaught."

Brezhnev continued this reversal of behavioral gears in the next to the last meeting with the President, and the President responded in kind. Nixon went to his office for what was to be a half-hour courtesy call, but they ended up spending 2 hours talking about Vietnam. "Unlike at our meeting at the dacha, however, he was calm and serious," the President recalled.[150]

After some initial skirmishing, Brezhnev remarked, "Would you like to have one of our highest Soviet officials go to the Democratic Republic of Vietnam in the interest of peace?"

The President responded that such a visit might make "a major contribution to ending the war," and he pledged to suspend the bombing during the period the Soviet official was in Hanoi.

As the President was leaving, they paused at the door, and in a conciliatory tone he reiterated his commitment "that privately or publicly I will take no steps directed against the interests of the Soviet Union." But he cautioned the General Secretary that he should rely on what he said in the private channel and "not on what anyone else tells you." "There are not only certain forces in the world, but also representatives of the press," he concluded reassuringly, "who are not interested in better relations between us." [151]

(d) *Brezhnev's toughness and shock tactics: At San Clemente during Summit II.*—Brezhnev resorted to the same "shock tactic" during the Summit II meeting in Washington during 1973. On the itinerary was a visit to San Clemente. There, Brezhnev stayed in the President's home. After a reception and poolside cocktail party attended by many Hollywood celebrities, the President had a small dinner party for Brezhnev. Since the dining room accommodated only 10 people, the dinner was kept deliberately informal, "so that he could feel at home," the President said, referring to his Soviet guest.

At the dinner the President made an elaborate toast to Brezhnev's health, that of the other guests, "but even more so to Mrs. Brezhnev, to your children and our children and all the children of the world who, we trust, will have a happier and more peaceful future because of what we have done."

When the toast was translated, Brezhnev's eyes "filled with tears." "He impulsively got out of his chair and walked toward me," the President recalled. "I rose and walked toward him. He threw his arms around me with a real bear hug and then proposed an eloquent toast to Pat and our children and all the children of the world."

After dinner, the President and Brezhnev exchange personal gifts at which time Brezhnev made an emotion-filled comment on the simplicity of his gift (a scarf for Mrs. Nixon woven by artisans in his home village) and on the affection and friendship of the Soviet people for the Americans and, as the President noted, "which Mrs. Brezhnev and I have for you and President Nixon." Again as he spoke tears came to his eyes.

The hour was growing late; Brezhnev was tired; and the President walked him to the door of Tricia Nixon's room where they said goodnight. The President decided to turn in early, and while reading in bed around 10:30 p.m., there was a knock on the door from a Secret Service agent with a message from Kissinger. The Russians wanted to

[150] Nixon, op. cit., p. 617.
[151] Ibid.

talk. When Kissinger came in, the President asked what this was all about.

"He says he wants to talk," Kissinger replied.

"Is he restless or is this a ploy of some kind?" the President asked.

"Who ever knows with them?" Kissinger answered skeptically with a shrug.

The President and Kissinger went to the study where Brezhnev, Gromyko, and Dobrynin joined them.

"I could not sleep, Mr. President," Brezhnev said with a broad smile.

"It will give us a good opportunity to talk without any distractions," responded the President as he settled in his easy chair.

The President gave this account of the subsequent exchange:

> For the next three hours we had a session that in emotional intensity almost rivaled the one on Vietnam at the dacha during Summit I. This time the subject was the Middle East, with Brezhnev trying to browbeat me into imposing on Israel a settlement based on Arab terms. He kept hammering at what he described as the need for the two of us to agree, even if only privately, on a set of "principles" to govern a Middle East settlement. As examples of such principles, he cited the withdrawal of Israeli troops from all the occupied territories, the recognition of national boundaries, the free passage of ships through the Suez Canal, and international guarantees of the settlement.
>
> I pointed out that there was no way that I could agree to any such "principles" without prejudicing Israel's rights. I insisted that the important thing was to get talks started between the Arabs and the Israelis, and I argued that if we laid down controversial principles beforehand, both parties would refuse to talk—in which case the principles would have defeated their purpose.
>
> Brezhnev was blunt and adamant. He said that without at least an informal agreement on such principles he would be leaving this summit empty handed. He even hinted that without such an agreement on principles he could not guarantee that war would not resume.
>
> At one point he made a show of looking at his watch and furrowing his brow. "Perhaps I am tiring you out," he said. "But we must reach an understanding."
>
> As firmly as he kept demanding that we agree on such principles—in effect, that we jointly impose a settlement that would heavily favor the Arabs—I refused, reiterating that the important thing was to get talks started between the parties themselves.[152]

To Nixon, this "testy midnight session" was a reminder of the "unchanging and unrelenting Communist motivations beneath the diplomatic veener of détente." Brezhnev's "shock tactics at the ostensibly impromptu meeting in my study" was a calculated risk, the President wrote; but he would not "rise to the meager bait," and noted that the firmness shown that night reinforced the seriousness of his message to the Soviets when he ordered a military alert 4 months later during the Yom Kippur War.

For the purposes of this study, however, the episode at San Clemente was another example of a distinctive feature of Brezhnev's negotiating behavior; namely, the "shock tactic"—to soften up the adversary putting him off balance with displays of kindness and good-fellowship to be followed by the delivery of a hard offensive thrust intended to put him on the defensive and hence more amenable to concession.[153]

(e) *Brezhnev and Khrushchev compared.*—At Summit II in 1973, the President had an opportunity to know Brezhnev better and thus

---

[152] Nixon, op. cit., pp. 883–885.

[153] Brezhnev resorted to the same tactic again during summit III in 1974. The President recorded in his diary after the first day of formal sessions that dealt with a nuclear test ban: "During this session, Brezhnev was very tough, just like at the dacha in 1972 on Vietnam. He rewrote the script here, and none of us were prepared because it had been their idea in March, which they had explored with Kissinger, to have a threshold test ban." (Ibid., p. 1028.)

was better able to take his measure as a leader and man. In 1972, he had spent 42 hours with him; in 1973, 35 hours. From these personal contacts the President believed that he had gained "important insights." [154]

During Summit II Nixon found the General Secretary "more interesting and impressive" than during their first meeting. Away from the constraints of the Kremlin, he said, Brezhnev was able "to indulge the more human and political sides of his personality." On the occasion of a signing ceremony when Brezhnev's "antics made him the center of attention," the President jokingly said, "He's the best politician in the room!" Brezhnev seemed to accept the statement "as the highest possible praise." Acting as his "straight man" on these occasions, the President found it difficult "to balance politeness against dignity." Brezhnev showed the "typically Russian combination of great discipline at times with total lack of it at others." The President cited the devious manner in which the General Secretary would obediently take a cigarette from his case that had a built-in timer set at one hour and was designed to cut down on his chain-smoking, but then a few moments later take another from his jacket pocket from a regular pack. [155] Thus he satisfied both impulses: discipline and indulgence.

At Summit I, the President had made some mental comparisons between Brezhnev and Khrushchev. During Summit II, he had the chance to observe and analyze the difference in much more depth and detail. The President wrote:

They were alike in the sense that they were both tough, hard, and realistic leaders. Both interlarded their conversation with anecdotes. Khrushchev was often quite vulgar; Brezhnev, however, was just earthy. Whereas Khrushchev had been crass and blustering, Brezhnev was expansive and more courteous. Both had a good sense of humor, but Khrushchev more often seemed to be using his at the expense of others around him. Khrushchev seemed to be quicker in his mental reflexes. In discussions, Brezhnev was hard-hitting, incisive, and always very deliberate, whereas Khrushchev had tended to be more explosive and more impulsive. Both men had tempers, and both were emotional. I was struck by the simple look of pride on Brezhnev's face as he told me that he was about to become a great-grandfather, and that we now had still another generation for which to guarantee peace. [156]

Nixon perceived the difference between the two leaders in terms of power relationships existing at the time of their tenure and the correlation of power with their conduct as negotiators. Referring to 1959 when he had observed Khrushchev with President Eisenhower in the same White House office, Nixon wrote:

Khrushchev had known that he was speaking from a position of weakness and had felt that it was therefore necessary to take a very aggressive and boastful line. Since then the power balance had evened out, particularly as the gap in the decisive area of nuclear development and capability had been closed. Brezhnev could afford to speak more quietly. In 1973, the United States overall still held the stronger hand, but Brezhnev could laugh and clown and vary his stern moods with warmth, based on the confidence that comes from holding very good cards. [157]

(f) *On Soviet negotiating techniques.*—By and large, Soviet negotiating behavior was only inferred in Nixon's memoirs from the particular diplomatic episode he happened to be discussing. In only two

---

[154] Ibid., p. 886.
[155] Ibid., pp. 886–887.
[156] Ibid.
[157] Ibid., p. 879.

instances did he specifically refer to Soviet negotiating technique. With respect to the time limit on SALT I, the President wrote:

It is a technique of Communist negotiators to introduce some ideal but impractical change in an area where the details have already been agreed upon. When we were wrangling over specific provisions of the SALT proposal, which both sides had agreed would last for five years, Brezhnev suddenly asked, "Why not make it for ten years? Why only five?" Kissinger calmly pointed out that the Soviets themselves had originally wanted the agreement to last for only eighteen months.

"I would consider this interim agreement a great achievement for us and all the world," I said. "I want to reach a permanent agreement, but my time is limited—less than five years. After then, I am out—swimming in the Pacific. Maybe even before."

"Don't go out before that, Mr. President," Brezhnev said.[158]

The other instance concerned matter of surprise, which Nixon described as follows:

Surprise is another favorite technique of Communist negotiators. After the ceremony on Wednesday afternoon when we signed an agreement on cooperation in space exploration, Brezhnev and I walked out of the room together. He began talking about the dinner planned for us at one of the government dachas outside Moscow that evening. As we neared the end of the corridor, he took my arm and said, "Why don't we go to the country right now so you can see it in the daylight?" He propelled me into an elevator that took us down to the ground floor where one of his limousines was parked.

We climbed into the limousine and were on our way while the Secret Service and the others rushed around trying to find cars and drivers to follow us. The middle lane of all the main streets in Moscow is reserved solely for party officials, and we drove along at a very fast clip.

As soon as we arrived at the dacha, Brezhnev suggested that we go for a boat ride on the Moskva River. This was exactly what Khrushchev had done thirteen years before. But times had changed: he led us not to a motorboat but to a small hydrofoil bobbing gently in the water. The pilot was skilled, and we had a smooth ride. Brezhnev kept pointing to the speedometer, which showed us traveling at ninety kilometers an hour.[159]

What surprise awaited the President other than this hasty and unscheduled drive to Brezhnev's dacha and the fast boat ride in the impressive hydrofoil was, of course, the bruising encounter with the Soviet leadership over Vietnam.

(g) *On the skill, ability, and self-confidence of the Soviet leaders.*—Nixon came away from his first visit to Moscow with a very healthy respect for the ability, skill and self-confidence of the Soviet leaders. He rejected the thesis of Robert Conquest, the British specialist on Soviet affairs, that the Soviet leaders were "intellectually third-rate." To Nixon, this estimate was "simply off the mark." Americans "constantly misjudge the Russians," he said in his diary, "because we judge them by their manners, and so forth, and we do not look beyond to see what kind of character and strength they really have." [160]

It took a "great deal of toughness" and a "great deal of political ability," the President observed, for anyone to get to the top of the Soviet hierarchy and stay there. "All three leaders [Brezhnev, Kosygin, and Podgorny] have this in spades," the President concluded, "and Brezhnev in particular." "His Russian may not be as elegant, and his manners not as fine, as that of some of his sophisticated European and Asian colleagues," the President continued, "but like an American labor leader, he has what it takes, and we can make no

[158] Ibid., p. 612.
[159] Ibid.
[160] Ibid., p. 619.

greater mistake than to rate him either as a fool or simply an unintelligent brute." [161]

The President perceived a fondness in the Soviet leaders for good clothes and fine things; he also detected a diminution of the inferiority complex that existed in the Khrushchev period. "They do not have to brag about everything in Russia being better than anything anywhere else in the world," he said. "But they still crave to be respected as equals, and on this point, I think we made a good impression." [162]

Clearly, Summit I was for the President not only a negotiating encounter of a new and extraordinary kind but also a mind-opening learning experience on the quality, character, and ability of Brezhnev and his associates. In the course of time, the President and Brezhnev were to develop a very close relationship based upon mutual respect as individuals and as men of power. It was a "demonstratively warm" relationship filled with paradox, as Ambassador Beam explained:

There is little doubt that Brezhnev felt a close personal attachment to Nixon and was probably more at ease with him than with Communists like Tito and Ceaucescu or other leaders whom he could not come to accept as equals. The re'ationship was a paradoxical one. Basically, Brezhnev respected power, which Nixon possessed during his first term; Brezhnev liked the channel of access which Nixon and Kissinger reserved for him in their exclusive method of transacting business. It obviated bothersome distractions: except for occasional outbursts over Soviet human rights violations, Congress generally approved détente; the troublesome State Department, which always seemed to know too much about Soviet affairs, was bypassed by Nixon and Kissinger.

Two examples of paradox come to mind. The Soviets recognized Nixon as a determined anticommunist foe but believed that, like Brezhnev, he was committed to détente for the rewards it could produce domestically and internationally. The Soviets also knew that Nixon was unpredictable and would not hesitate to use force, as he did in Cambodia in May 1970 and when he ordered the bombing of North Vietnam in May 1972 and again at Christmas of the same year. Consequently, the Soviets treated his warnings with great seriousness.

The personal relationship between Nixon and Brezhnev, which survived some tough talking was demonstratively warm. Even after Brezhnev belatedly became alerted to Nixon's troubles over Watergate, he treated the President with high respect. It appears that Brezhnev's courtesy continued through the last trip to Moscow in the summer of 1974, which Nixon planned for the main purpose of boosting his failing prestige. [163]

(2) Commentaries on other Soviet negotiators and on Soviet negotiating style

(a) *Smirnov, Gromyko, Dobrynin, and Aleksandrov.*—Smirnov came as a surprise to the American negotiators. They had never seen him before and had not expected to see him at the Moscow summit, but he did most of the talking for the Soviet side in hammering out a settlement with the American negotiating team. [164] In the evening after

[161] Ibid.
[163] Ibid. Hyland also had considerable respect for Brezhnev, more for his political shrewdness than his native intelligence. Hyland recalled how he listened with fascination as Brezhnev recounted minute details of a negotiation held three years earlier, and without referring to notes. Brezhnev also had an asset not shared by all of his colleagues: "He can be frank without getting acrimonious," according to Hyland. Brezhnev also demonstrated human qualities in such instances as teasing Hyland during meetings, often pretending to steal Hyland's briefcase, full of top-secret papers. Hyland's ability to size up the Soviet negotiators seemed implied in Time's comment that he "has logged more hours negotiating with Soviet leaders during the past decade than any other American."
With respect to Nixon's style, Hyland said that the President was a tough and able bargainer. He would discuss one or two issues, establish the general guidelines of U.S. policy, then leave, turning the matter over to subordinates to handle the details. And on President Ford: "Ford was good on SALT, and more willing to go into details than Nixon." (Time, Nov. 21. 1977 : 28.)
[163] Beam, op. cit., pp. 292–293.
[164] Newhouse, op. cit., p. 251.

Nixon's tough encounter on Vietnam and before the SALT talks actually began, Brezhnev told a worried Kissinger who apparently neither liked surprises in a negotiating environment nor liked to deal with the unfamiliar and untested: "We have assigned Smirnov to conclude SALT. He's never met a foreigner before." Described as a hardline Deputy Prime Minister in charge of Soviet arms production and close to Kosygin, he was an unknown quality to the Americans.[165] According to Newhouse, Smirnov was "a tough and skilled negotiator," but being a specialist in developing missile systems, operating from a solid base in the party, government, and Russia's military-industrial complex, and untutored in the folkways of diplomacy, he "showed little sensitivity to the political stakes in the enterprise." Gromyko often intervened in the negotiations to prevent a stalemate.[166] In assessing Smirnov's role at the SALT negotiations, Garthoff noted that he played "an important direct part" in negotiating the interim agreement on limiting strategic offensive weapons.[167]

As for Gromyko and Dobrynin, the sources revealed that both diplomats were deeply engaged in the negotiating process and that their performances attracted no unusual comment would seem to arise from the generally high estimate of their professionalism as diplomats and negotiators. Hyland, for example, acclaimed Gromyko's agility as a negotiator. In contrast to the more phlegmatic Brezhnev, he was a "clever tactician with great aplomb" who could change positions in midsentence without giving an explanation.[167a]

Aleksandrov played a significant role as Brezhnev's adviser on American affairs and was at the General Secretary's side during his key talks with the President.[168] During the negotiations Brezhnev rarely seemed to depend on the expertise of the Foreign Ministry but rather leaned on this spare, bespectacled diplomat and linguist who has been described as "a Soviet Kissinger."[169] Aleksandrov's role, though formidable, appeared to be more as an adviser to Brezhnev than as a negotiator.

In all, the Soviets fielded a formidable team of negotiators. Knowledgeable in the intricacies of SALT, with a toughness that comes from survival and advancement in a highly competitive political system, clear on their negotiating objectives, and determined in their negotiating techniques in achieving them, they provided a crucial test to the President and his men. How well each side would do would depend not only on their power base but also on their distinctive skills as negotiators.

(b) *Newhouse on Soviet and American negotiating characteristics.*— In a comprehensive summary statement generalizing on the SALT negotiating experience from its beginning in Helsinki to its conclusion in SALT I in Moscow, Newhouse suggested some critical characteristics of both American and Soviet negotiating behavior: Impatience, inconsistency, and negotiating against a deadline for the former; sus-

[165] Safire, op. cit., p. 449.
[166] Newhouse, op. cit., p. 252.
[167] Garthoff, Problems of Communism, p. 29.
[167a] Time, November 21, 1977 : 28.
[168] Nixon, op. cit., p. 611.
[169] Kalb, op. cit., p. 317.

picion and hardening defensism in the face of unconventional tactics for the latter. Newhouse wrote:

Negotiating with the Russians requires patience and consistency. In the early rounds of SALT, the Americans often showed neither. After an initial period of studied caution, they did a great deal more talking than listening. In effect, America did the running, too often at the expense of consistency. Washington knew from experience in other negotiations that only by holding to the core of a position would useful agreement emerge. This was the case with the Austrian settlement, with the recent Berlin negotiations, and with other arms-control agreements. But in Vienna and Helsinki, American proposals were sometimes thrown up like pasteboard figures, withdrawn at the first sign of resistance, and replaced by other equally perishable offers.

In fairness, the seemingly chaotic and inconstant character of the talks arises in part from their complexity. Unlike most arms-control negotiations, a basic SALT proposal can have many combinations and permutations; each variant may have merit. The difficulty is that Russian suspicions of entrapment are aroused by this kind of versatility. Americans may understand what they are doing, but Moscow does not. The Soviet leadership normally reacts to unconventional tactics by hardening its own position.

Negotiating against a deadline is always risky. But by arranging to sign a SALT agreement in Moscow, that is what Nixon elected to do. In effect, he placed himself in what French diplomats call the worst of positions: *demandeur*. It is hard for the other side to react to a self-anointed *demandeur* other than to exploit him. Yet, as it turned out, nobody seems to have been exploited. Brezhnev wanted, and apparently felt that he needed, the agreements as much as Nixon.[170]

4. FINAL ACTION ON THE SALT I AGREEMENT

SALT I, signed in Moscow on May 26 contained two major agreements; namely, a treaty limiting the deployment of ABM's, and an executive agreement termed, "interim agreement," placing limits on offensive strategic weapons. Also included among the instruments in the transaction were a protocol and various memoranda of interpretations and understandings.

Very briefly, under the terms of the ABM Treaty, the Soviet Union and the United States were limited to one ABM each the defense of their capitals and one additional site each for the defense of an ICBM field. The interim agreement limited the number of offensive weapons to those already under construction or deployed when the agreement was signed. Limitations were also placed on the number of missile-carrying submarines that could be constructed. Moreover, the Soviet Union could field about 300 of its new, large SS-9 missiles in silos occupied by older models. The total number of the larger type could not, however, be increased. Both sides could construct new SLBM's of the Polaris and Poseidon type if they compensated by dismantling an equal number of land-based ICBM launchers or older submarine launchers. The number of submarines could increase, therefore, but not the total number of warheads.

Under this arrangement the Soviets were left with more land- and sea-based missiles in their arsenal. On the other hand, the United States, because of its development of MIRV's (multiple independent re-entry vehicles), would have more than three times the Soviet number of deliverable warheads. The Soviets had not yet tested a multiple warhead weapons system, though they were permitted to do so under the treaty.

---

[170] Newhouse, op. cit., p. 270.

Monitoring of the agreements was to be undertaken by national technical means, that is, by reconnaissance satellites. Each side also pledged not to interfere with the other side's gathering of technical data, and promised further not to try and conceal their missile deployments or tests.[171]

Hearings were held by the Senate Foreign Relations Committee in June and July 1972 and by the House Foreign Affairs Committee (on the interim agreement only) in July and August. (Hearings were also held by the Senate and House Armed Services Committees on technical matters and implications of the agreements.) The ABM Treaty was unanimously approved by the Senate Foreign Relations Committee and endorsed by the vote of 88 to 2 in the Senate on August 3, 1972.[172] The resolution approving the interim agreement was adopted by the Senate vote of 88 to 2 on September 14, and by a House vote of 307 to 4 on September 25, 1972.[173]

Shortly thereafter, on September 29, 1972, the Soviet Union completed its ratification procedures. On September 30, President Nixon ratified the ABM Treaty and signed the Joint Congressional Resolution authorizing approval of the Interim Agreement and Protocol. The two accords entered into force simultaneously on October 3, 1972, with the exchange of ratification and notification of U.S. acceptance of the Interim Agreement and Protocol.[174]

5. RESULTS AND SIGNIFICANCE OF SALT I

(a) *As a negotiating encounter*

(1) *Soviet willingness to negotiate seriously*

Newhouse described the first Brezhnev-Nixon summit meeting as having "flair" and "panache." But most importantly as a negotiating encounter, it succeeded. As he wrote, the summit "reversed the form of earlier summit conferences by ending happily. * * *"[175] The reason for this success lay in the fact that, as Kissinger noted, the negotiated agreement satisfied the best interests as perceived by both sides.[176]

In sorting out certain aspects of this negotiating encounter, one element has seemed to stand out in high relief; namely, the Soviet willingness to negotiate seriously. As Bohlen wrote some years ago, "The Soviets are very serious about disarmament."[177] And so they

[171] Summarized in The Congressional Quarterly, June 3, 1972:3, and Documents on American Foreign Relations, 1972, pp. 89–90 and 95–97. For full texts of the agreements, see Documents on American Foreign Relations, 1972, pp. 90–95 and 97–101; ACDA Documents, 1972, pp. 197–207 (contains other relevant material). Senate Foreign Relations Committee, Hearings, Strategic Arms Limitation Agreements, 1972, contains further documentation. See also U.S. Congress. House. Committee on Foreign Affairs. Agreement on Limitations of Strategic Offensive Weapons. Hearings, 92d Congress, 2d session. Washington, D.C., U.S. Government Printing Office, 1972, 155 pp.
[172] Documents on American Foreign Relations, 1972, pp. 101–104.
[173] Ibid.
[174] Ibid., p. 104.
[175] Newhouse, op. cit., p. 249.
[176] At a press conference on May 26, 1972, Kissinger stated that it "is foolish or short-sighted to approach the negotiations from the point of view of gaining a unilateral advantage. Neither nation will possibly put its security and its survival at the hazard of its opponent and no agreement that brings disadvantage to either side can possibly last and can possibly bring about anything other than a new circle of insecurity. Therefore, the temptation that is ever present when agreements of this kind are analyzed as to who won is exceptionally inappropriate." From the very beginning, Kissinger went on, "We have approached these negotiations * * * with the attitude that a wise proposal is one that is conceived by each side to be in the mutual interest and we believe that if this agreement does what we hope it will, that the future will record that both sides won." (ACDA documents, 1972, p. 208.)
[177] Bohlen, op. cit., pp. 447–448.

were in this negotiating encounter. Perhaps, Garthoff best summed up this changing reality in the Soviet approach to negotiations when he concluded:

Today there is a greater Soviet readiness to look for possible agreements on a broad range of issues. Compromise is no longer a taboo for Soviet negotiators. In part, this reflects increased Soviet sophistication. It also reflects growing self-confidence. To this extent, the growth of Soviet strength to a level of near equality with the United States has produced not greater intransigence but a more businesslike approach. Agreements on mutually advantageous strategic arms limitations are not easy to reach—but they are attainable.[178]

With respect to Soviet negotiating behavior, the SALT I experience revealed a significant distinction: The emergence of elements of traditionalism in negotiations at the SALT delegation level, in contrast to a continuation of the crude "shock tactics" at the highest political level reminiscent of the past.

As Garthoff suggested, a type of traditionalism has seemed to set in the actual negotiating process at the SALT delegation level. In brief, the professionalism of the European diplomatic tradition may be in the process of breaking through the outer crust of Sovietism. That this could occur would seem to derive from the seriousness of the subject matter being negotiated—namely, survival, the most vital of national interests; the achievement of near parity in the Soviet-American strategic balance; the complexity of the negotiations that has required outside technical expertise, thus broadening the perspective of the negotiators from narrowly restricted political considerations; the growing professionalism and sophistication of the Soviet diplomatic establishment; and the objective desire on both sides to reach an agreement on some form of control over nuclear weapons.

As a counterpoint to the apparent professionalism at the delegation level, the SALT I experience revealed a contrasting resort to "shock tactics" in negotiations at the highest political level not remarkably different from that of Stalin or Khrushchev. The conduct of the Soviet leadership, particularly that of Brezhnev, during the first meeting with the President could be explained by the feeling of outrage and humiliation at the bombing of North Vietnam, but the tactic itself, repeated by Brezhnev at San Clemente in Summit II and at Moscow during summit III, revealed that excessive toughness and "rough-and-tumble" in-fighting remain a fixed element in the negotiating behavior of the Soviet leadership.

Thus, the professional diplomats and negotiators in such negotiating encounters as SALT may be taking on the patina of traditionalism with their display of rationality, good manners, and professionalism in their craft, but this would not seem to be the case where it counts most, in negotiating with the political leaders at the top.

(2) Summitry, Nixon and Kissinger as negotiators; and the SALT process

Whatever the arguments for or against summitry, it had proven its usefulness in this instance, for two reasons: it enabled Brezhnev and Nixon to resolve the outstanding four or five issues that had deadlocked the SALT negotiators in Geneva; and it set into motion the SALT process, the importance of which lay in the fact that SALT has been

---

[178] Garthoff, Wilson Quarterly. p. 85.

considered primarily a political matter and only secondarily a technical one.[179]

As noted above, the Moscow summit was well organized; preparations were intense and thorough; and the staffs on both sides were experienced and knowledgeable negotiators. Reliance on a Soviet interpreter at the crucial Brezhnev-Nixon meetings was, as explained above, a lapse in sound judgment since it opened up the possibility of error in verbal exchanges between the two leaders and thus in the record of the conference proceedings. What the President received were Brezhnev's thoughts, ideas and words filtered through a Soviet mind and not that of an American. The difference is fundamental.

The complexity of the negotiations—Kissinger referred to their "enormous technical complexity"—added to the burdens of the negotiators.[180]

The convenience of having the seasoned SALT negotiators at Helsinki made it possible for the negotiators in Moscow to establish the political framework of agreement and pass on their decisions to Helsinki for formulation into language suitable for a treaty and international agreement.

The burden of negotiations on the American side fell upon the President and Kissinger, both of whom appeared to have demonstrated considerable negotiating ability. According to Ambassador Beam, "the President was impressive in his meetings with the Soviets—forceful, concise, and in control of the subject matter." [181]

And with respect to Kissinger, Beam wrote:

While Kissinger was highly respected by the Soviets, they identified in him some of the characteristics they most feared in the Germans. He was never petty in negotiations, but won his points with ruthlessness and skill. Taking his dealings with the Soviets in isolation, I find little to fault him for. He is known to have had a rather low opinion of his Soviet counterparts, with the exception of Ambassador Dobrynin * * * A question mark in the Soviets' mind was the degree of influence Kissinger had on Nixon, whom they regarded as unpredictable but in whom they had a certain implicit trust because his political stake in détente matched that of Brezhnev.[183]

William Safire, a White House insider who was present at Moscow, gave this account of the Nixon-Kissinger negotiating style:

In negotiating technique, Nixon and Kissinger put on a formidable display, like a two-man interrogation team where one man holds a truncheon and the other offers a cigarette.

Nixon's way was to appear rigid, sit tight for a long time, and then go for a "bold new approach" that can be considerably different from his original position.

[179] Newhouse, op. cit., p. 34.
[180] Kissinger press conference, May 26, 1972. ACDA documents. 1972, p. 207. Newhouse has numerous references to the complexity of the negotiations, and sources on SALT negotiations conveniently refer to Newhouse s work when discussing technical details. The negotiations at Moscow on the matter of SLBM's and missile-carrying submarines were so complicated that Newhouse wrote after his explanation of the proceedings : "(As confusing as all this may seem it was only slightly less so to the experts themselves. After the White House party returned to Washington, several meetings of the verification panel were spent largely in trying to establish exactly what had been agreed to on SLBM s and what precisely it all meant.)" (Newhouse, op. cit., p. 254.)
[181] Beam, op. cit., p. 276. With regard to the Nixon-Kissinger relationship, the Ambassador wrote : "In all meetings, whether in Washington or Moscow, where I have seen Nixon and Kissinger together, the latter invariably yielded, not only in manner but also with respect to having the final say. Some former White House insiders make the same point in recent writings, that Nixon was generally dominant in initiating and determining policy. Whether or not this was really the case, the public impact of the administration's decisions owed much to Kissinger's skill in interpretation and explanation." (p. 276.) The latter point was particularly the case in SALT I where Kissinger had briefed the press extensively in Moscow and had a major Congressional briefing at the White House upon returning to Washington.
[183] Ibid., pp. 265–266.

Kissinger, on the contrary, was willing to invest heavily—in money and, if necessary, in lives—to achieve bargaining credibility, that is, an understanding by his adversary that a Kissinger proposal has about five degrees of leeway in it and no more. "Have the other guy punch pillows," Henry explained to me, "never confront, but never yield." A proposal put forth by Kissinger on behalf of Nixon, then, was not to be lightly discounted or the counter-offer to be too far away if the adversary had any inclination to make a deal; then, if the imaginative stroke was needed, Nixon would supply it or Kissinger would attribute it to him. There was an added complexity: sometimes Kissinger played the tough guy, sometimes Nixon did, so the bid they presented could not always be analyzed in terms of the next steps. "I have the reputation of being a hard-line anti-Communist," Nixon stressed at one of his first Kremlin meetings, and he had made certain that Kissinger had pointed that out to the Russians in the preliminary negotiations. When Nixon pronounced that statement, Alexi Kosygin, who was created to exemplify the adjective "dour," cracked his first thin smile of the summit and replied, "We know, we know."

Nixon's greatest negotiating strength came from the fact, which he went out of his way to reiterate, that his roots were on the political right; that the traditional, conservative suspicion of a Yalta-style "secret agreement" was out of the question with Nixon at the negotiating table.[183]

Informality was a keynote of the summit, a characteristic that was especially pleasing to the President because it created optimal conditions for negotiations.[184]

Observers generally credited the conclusion of SALT I at the Moscow summit with setting into motion the SALT process, a dialog between the superpowers that in the long term was hopefully expected to bring about greater control over nuclear armaments. Garthoff put it simply: "SALT I launched and provided a basis for continuing negotiations on strategic arms limitation and measures to enhance strategic stability."[185] This was also the President's firm conviction. In referring to the "nit-picking" criticism that Summit III had not been as successful as the other two, the President confided in his diary:

The main thing is that the process went forward, and this is in itself an achievement. Peace is never going to be achieved once and for all—it must be constantly worked on. That's why these continuing summits between major powers must go forward, even though we don't have great announcements to make after each one.[186]

(3) Problem of hasty negotiations

Criticism has been leveled at the SALT I summit negotiators for the haste with which the agreements were finally concluded. Garthoff, who was a principal actor in this final scene of SALT I, attributed flaws in the interim agreement to the "haphazard and hurried last-

---

[183] Safire, op. cit., pp. 442–443. Safire is now a columnist for the New York Times.

[184] The President made the following entry into his diary after Summit III in 1974: "I am inclined to think that in arranging the next summit, it's the informal meetings which provide the greatest opportunity for progress. I think the formal ones—the plenary sessions—produce the least, because everybody's talking for the record and making a record." The President continued: "Brezhnev has been much forthcoming when we meet informally in the car or elsewhere than when we are sitting down in a formal group with others present. The larger the group, the less free the conversation is. This is something that is true in all forms of society, but it is particularly true in the Soviet Union and in the Communists states." (Nixon, op. cit., p. 1037.)

[185] Garthoff, World Politics, p. 18. For references and excerpts on the importance of the dialog, see footnote 3 on page 10.

[186] Nixon, op. cit., p. 1037. Ambassador Johnson made essentially the same point with respect to the great value of the continuing dialog between the Soviet Union and the United States. Many exchanges had occurred at all levels, he said, and in the process "something rubs off: there is a greater mutual understanding." "But," he cautioned, "don't expect a definitive agreement, one to bring on the millennium. The differences between both sides are more fundamental and there can be no single panacea for their outstanding and continuing problems." As the dialogue goes on, he said, "it is important to see it as a process rather than an end in itself. You can't put this genie back in the bottle in any easy manner." (Whelan, Notebook No. 6, Oct. 4, 1977, p. 44.)

minute high-level negotiations by President Nixon and Dr. Kissinger" during the "frantic" 5 days in May that culminated in its signature.[187]

Newhouse wrote that the summit ended happily, but "in a kind of vertiginous confusion reminiscent as much as anything else of the Keystone Cops." [188] In his account of the confusion and haste during final days of the negotiations Newhouse interspersed his narrative with such comments as, "The pace was hectic" and "The pace was frantic." [189] On the day of the signing, he wrote, "the day had been long and had provided surprise, suspense, drama, confusion, pith, and moment. It was not over yet." [190]

Newhouse recorded the details of the last minute efforts by the negotiators in Helsinki to draft the protocol and to get themselves and the completed documents to Moscow as soon as possible for signature. He also recorded the many mistakes that were made in the drafting.[191] So hasty was the final drafting that not even the figures were accurate. Nonetheless, all four copies of the agreements (two in Russian; two in English) were signed at the concluding ceremony containing major errors, and scarcely anyone knew about it. On the following day, after the errors were corrected and a polished and final draft was completed, the leaders repeated the signing ceremony but in total secrecy.[192]

A factor in this error-filled conclusion of SALT I was the decision to negotiate against a deadline, and the Administration has been criticized for it. In hearings before the House Foreign Affairs Committee, Chairman Thomas E. Morgan, asked for comment on the charges made in the Senate that because of the self-imposed deadline the United States made "major concessions * * * which gravely increased the disadvantages to us in the final agreements." Ambassador Smith denied that a deadline had entered into the proceedings: insisted that "The discussions in Moscow were not conducted in a rushed fashion;" and expressed the belief that the negotiations did not result "in any concessions because of time pressure." [193]

(4) Problem of unilateral statements

The administration has also been criticized for introducing the practice of placing in the conference record unilateral statements of interpretations on issues unresolved in the negotiations. Included in the total package of SALT I agreements presented to the Congress were statements pertaining to land-mobile ICBM launchers, concealment of facilities, ABM radars and testing, and the replacement of "light" by "heavy" ICBM's. In explaining the rationale behind this practice, Kissinger told a Congressional briefing on June 15, 1972:

Finally, there are a number of interpretative statements which were provided to the Congress along with the agreements. These interpretations are in several forms: Agreed statements initiated by the delegations, agreed interpretations or common understandings which were not set down formally and initialed, unilateral interpretations to make our position clear in instances where we could not get total agreement.

[187] Garthoff, World Politics, p. 13.
[188] Newhouse, op. cit., p. 249.
[189] Ibid., pp. 249 and 253.
[190] Ibid., p. 258.
[191] Ibid., pp. 256–257.
[192] Ibid., p. 258, and Kalb, op. cit., pp. 326–327.
[193] House Foreign Affairs Committee, Hearings, Agreement on Limitation of Strategic Offensive Weapons, 1972, p. 11.

In any negotiations of this complexity, there will inevitably be details upon which the parties cannot agree. We made certain unilateral statements in order to insure that our positions on these details was included in the negotiating record and understood by the other side.

The agreed interpretations and common understandings for the most part deal with detailed technical aspects of limitations on ABM systems and offensive weapons. For example, it was agreed that the size of missile silos could not be significantly increased and that "significantly" meant not more than 10 to 15 percent.

In the more important unilateral declarations we made clear to the Soviets that the introduction of land mobile ICBM's would be inconsistent with the agreement. Since the publication of the various unilateral interpretative statements, suggestions have been heard that the language of the treaty and agreement in fact hide deep-seated disagreements. But it must be recognized that in any limited agreements, which are between old time adversaries, there are bound to be certain gaps.

In this case the gaps relate not so much to the terms themselves, but rather to what it was impossible to include. The interpretations do not vitiate these agreements, but they expand and add to the agreements.[194]

Thus, the interpretive statements were acknowledged to be not part of the "letter" of the SALT I agreement, but in presenting the complete documentation to Congress, they were characterized as "safeguards" insuring that American interests were not prejudiced.[195]

American lawmakers were troubled by the ambiguity of such unilateral statements and especially by their implications. Particularly troubling was the statement pertaining to the conversion of "light" land-based ICBM launchers to "heavy" ICMB launchers. The crucial question was definition; that is, what constituted a "heavy" ICBM launcher as opposed to a "light" one? The Soviets did not accept the American interpretation and went ahead with replacements that violated the unilateral American understanding but not the specific provisions of the Interim Agreement. The question then arose as to whether the Russians were really violating the agreement, if not the "letter", then the "spirit."[196]

Despite this experience a general consensus has emerged justifying the introduction of unilateral statements that distinguishes between the possible and the impossible. Such declarations are not expected to restrain one side from taking actions that the other side had failed to have incorporated as a prohibition in the text of the negotiated agreement. But it is agreed that they could serve a useful purpose, as in some instances in SALT I, when both sides agree that a particular pledge is mutually acceptable though not appropriate in the text of the agreement.[197]

(5) Secrecy and excessive Soviet concern for security

Excessive Soviet concern for security was clearly manifested at the Moscow summit by their obsession with secrecy. As the conference moved along, even the President became worried, as Safire put it, "that the habit of secrecy would stay with us all after the necessity for some credit-taking had begun."[198] That the administration had not been entirely unsympathetic with the Soviet inclination for secrecy was

[194] Senate Foreign Relations Committee. Hearings, Strategic Arms Limitation Agreements, 1972. pp. 399–400.
[195] The matter of unilateral statements is discussed in, Bell, Robert C. and Mark M. Lowenthal. SALT II: Major Issues. Congressional Research Service, Library of Congress, Washington, Dec. 15, 1978, pp. 16–26. (78–249–F)
[196] Ibid., p. 26–29.
[197] Ibid., p. 26.
[198] Safire, op. cit., p. 453.

revealed in its preference for secret back channel talks between Kissinger and Dobrynin, and particularly the Kissinger presummit visit to Moscow to see Brezhnev. Such a veil of secrecy enshrouded this negotiating visit that even the U.S. Ambassador in Moscow was kept in the dark about Kissinger's presence until the last day.[199]

A most revealing example of the deeply engrained Soviet habit of secrecy was their refusal to submit figures on their arsenal of strategic weapons for negotiating purposes but rather depended on the American intelligence estimates. General Ogarkov, it will be recalled, was outraged by the American disclosure of these estimates to Soviet civilian negotiators. His reaction was apparently mild compared to that of Smirnov when he met Kissinger for the first time (and any foreigner for that matter) during a critical moment in the SALT negotiations at the Moscow summit.

To the assembled negotiators meeting at 2:30 a.m., Kissinger proceeded to coolly describe the characteristics of Soviet weapons. He recalled afterward that it "was like telling J. Edgar Hoover about his most sensitive procedures—Smirnov practically had an apoplectic fit." In brief, Smirnov lost his temper, and unfortunately, the flavor of his remarks were also lost in translation. "He didn't contest anything I said," Kissinger later remarked, "only my right to say it." As Kissinger continued to described Soviet weaponry to Smirnov's outrage, Gromyko stepped in and asked for a 15-minute break. Gromyko cooled off the Soviet arms specialist—or, as Safire noted, "they agreed that the tactic of outrage was not working"—and got down to serious business at 3:30 in the morning.[200]

Ambassador Beam called the Soviet refusal to supply their figures "almost unbelievable, but nevertheless true." "We believe these estimates to be fairly accurate." Beam noted, referring to American estimates, "but as a general rule the Soviets refuse to confirm the information we have obtained through our own devices."[201] Thus, the integrity of Soviet figures on nuclear arms and delivery systems has remained protected and secure.

Tight Soviet secrecy during SALT negotiations had also worked to their advantage. According to Beam, Americans dissipated a great deal of energy in bureaucratic negotiations since the Pentagon, the White House, CIA, the State Department, and Congress have a legitimate, indeed overriding, vested interest in arms control. Leaks have occurred during the ensuing infighting within the agencies in their effort to win public approval of a particular point with the result that the Soviets have often had a preview of a new U.S. negotiating position.[202]

[199] Kalb, op. cit., p. 295.
[200] Safire. op. cit., p. 451.
[201] Beam, op. cit., p. 277.
[202] Newhouse explained the background of what was termed the "July 23d leak" and "the Beecher leak". for William Beecher of The New York Times. According to Newhouse, this was "the most sensational of the various SALT leaks." July 23 was the day on which the U.S. delegation was beginning its presentation of the new U.S. position to the Russians. "The Beecher article performed the same service." Newhouse wrote. "laying out the essentials and even revealing one of the American fallback positions." According to one official closely involved in the proceedings, "It could not have come at a worse time. To parade the U.S. position in a newspaper even before we'd been able to show it to the Russians was a major disservice to the SALT talks. If I knew who it was, he'd have a half-hour to clean out his desk and leave the government." After extensive investigations by various government agencies. Newhouse wrote, "the daring culprit is still unknown. Nor can anyone, even now, establish his motives." Some believed it was to sabotage the talks; others said it was an attempt by some high official to freeze the U.S. position and discourage any fallback by going public. (Newhouse, op. cit., pp. 224-225.)

Sometimes agreement could not be reached within the U.S. Government, and accordingly varied options on particular points would be put forward. "When the Soviets understand them," declared Beam, "they naturally choose the most favorable." Accordingly, he concluded, "Only rarely do they feel compelled to put forward a viable initiative on their own." [203]

More subtle was the observation made by Ambassador Smith with respect to future U.S. planning and the advantages to a closed society in SALT negotiations. In exploring the problem of the negotiator from an open society in dealing with a negotiator from a closed one, he pointed out that the characteristics of American weapons and their costs were ventilated in the proceedings of Congress, in the press, and other public sources. "Rather clear courses for American weaponry for years ahead" were thus projected, "and the Soviets can shape their programs accordingly." American intelligence sources have assessed quite well the current state of Soviet strategic deployments, new construction, and the state of development of new delivery systems; but because of the Soviet penchant for secrecy, *de rigeur* in their closed society, "the future remains murky." The advantage to the Soviets is clearly evident when considering that before a single keel was laid, as Smith said, "the Soviets knew the programed size of the Trident program, its general characteristics and the rate and timing of planned commissioning of the submarines." That a similar Soviet program would have come to American attention, he acknowledged, "is questionable." "It is in knowledge of the others future forces that there is the least equivalence in the Soviet-American balance," he noted, and then he explained its relevance to negotiations:

This more than any other factor accounts for the difficulty in negotiating strategic arms limitations. The U.S.S.R. is negotiating in the context of a known U.S. future force structure and thus has a clear criterion for judging how much to concede in the negotiations. The U.S. in good part is "in the dark" in this respect.[204]

Thus, secrecy has not been without its benefits for the Soviet negotiators.

(b) *Impact of SALT I on Soviet-American relations and on the international scene*

(1) *Emergence of détente*

As a negotiating encounter in a more strictly technical sense, SALT I was highly significant; but its greatest significance lay in the far-reaching impact that it had on Soviet-American relations and on the international scene. To the President, the SALT agreements "marked the first step toward arms control in the thermonuclear age." And those agreements, together with the others concluded at Moscow, notably the code of good behavior set forth in the document on "Basic Principles of Mutual Relations," constituted, as the President said, "the first stage of détente." He defined détente as an effort "to involve Soviet interests in ways that would increase their stake in international stability and the status quo." [205]

SALT I accomplished two things: It established a framework of negotiations for controlling nuclear weapons—the objective, to pre-

[203] Beam, op. cit., pp. 277–278.
[204] Smith, op. cit., pp. 19–20.
[205] Nixon, op. cit., p. 618.

serve international stability and an equilibrium of power based on mutual acceptance of the principle of mutual assured destruction; it also initiated what Newhouse called, "a serious process, as well as a continuing one," namely; the SALT process. To him, writing in 1973. the record of SALT I of seven rounds of talks and the Kissinger-Dobrynin conversations on the margin "is neither reassuring nor disappointing; it is inconclusive." A modest interim agreement had been achieved at the Moscow summit. From the beginning both sides engaged in a frank, nonpolemical dialog on weapons most vital to their national interest. But as Newhouse concluded, optimistically: "That itself is a watershed. Certainly, it is not to be taken lightly or for granted." [206]

Thereafter Soviet-American relations formally entered into the era of détente, for the essence of SALT, as Newhouse contended, was political not technical—"Politics * * * lies at its heart"—and thus SALT meant mutual accommodation on a political basis.[207] Expectations were high and the rhetoric excessive on both sides. The concentric circle of vital mutual interests had narrowed as negotiations were resumed on SALT II.

(2) Soviet counterpressures in the Third World

But the arms race. though appreciably restrained by SALT I. has continued apace in other allowable areas. The conflictual relationship. though somewhat contained for a time within the SALT process, has extended beyond its boundaries. The soothing euphoria that SALT had momentarily generated in the relationship gave way to suspicion, distrust, and contention as opportunities arose in the Third World, notably in Angola, inviting the attention and intervention of Moscow. Amid claims that the National Liberation Movement was an inextricable part of the inevitable historical process as they perceived it and that Soviet involvement on its behalf was not incompatible with détente, the Soviet leadership has attempted to pursue two incompatibly opposite policies; namely, détente as incorporated in the SALT process. and military, economic, and political support for revolutionary activists in the Third World. The effect has been to create new centers of international conflict beyond the continent of Europe in the Third World and to compel the United States to reevaluate the extent of its global involvement that had been diminishing in the post-Vietnam era.

(3) Durability of the SALT process

Notwithstanding these external pressures and the ambiguity of Soviet policy, the SALT process has continued to function, and though the structural framework established on May 26, 1972, has sometimes seemed fragile and vulnerable, nonetheless, negotiations for SALT II have continued to go forward. After 7 years of negotiations. the SALT II treaty was finally signed on June 18, 1979.

[206] Newhouse, op. cit., p. 269.
[207] Ibid., pp. 5, 34, 262, and 272. "Technical issues." he said, "are used on all sides to shore up political and strategic biases." (p. 5.)

V. COMMENTARIES BY AMERICAN STATESMEN, DIPLOMATS AND NEGOTIATORS ON SOVIET NEGOTIATING BEHAVIOR

A. General and Specific Observations

1. summary of ambassador johnson's comments

Data presented in this chapter suggest in an unsystematic way certain characteristics of Soviet negotiating behavior. Particularly instructive were the observations made by Ambassador Johnson, among which were:

— The tradition of focusing specifically on SALT and not linking other external matters with it in a system of tradeoffs; [1]

— The importance of drafting agreements carefully in the belief that the Soviets will act on the letter of the agreement but not necessarily in its spirit; [2]

— The great care with which the Soviets negotiate, observing particularly strict adherence to instructions and in the case of SALT, deferring to the predominant influence of the military; [3]

— The tendency to let the other side take the initiative and to reject as unacceptable counterproposals through a series of exchanges with nothing coming from the Soviet side until the other side risks negotiating with itself; [4]

— The need for confidentiality in serious negotiations such as SALT, and the risk of inviting Soviet displeasure, as the Carter administration had done in early 1977, by going public on a new negotiating position, as the administration had done with respect to reducing the number of allowable strategic weapons as agreed to at Vladivostok; [5] and,

— The Soviet inclination toward broad, general, politically oriented statements in contrast to the detailed contractual approach of the Americans.[6]

2. affirmation from ikle

(a) *Precision in drafting language*

Dr. Fred C. Ikle, Director of ACDA and specialist on negotiations, affirmed and elaborated on some of the points made by Johnson. In

---

[1] Whelan, Notebook No. 6, Oct. 4, 1977. p. 49.
[2] Ibid., p. 53. See also, Interview with U. Alexis Johnson. From a Veteran Diplomat: How to Deal With the Russians. U.S. News & World Report, Apr. 4, 1977: 25–26. Johnson said: "But one thing on which I am very, very firm is the need to get everything down on paper—and get it down exactly * * * To do this is very difficult and time consuming. Nothing should be left to unilateral statements, nor to expressions of hope that the other side will or will not do something or other." Recalling SALT I, Johnson said that the Russians have "gone right up to the edge, but they've observed the letter thus far. That's why it is very important to get everything spelled out in exact detail."
[3] Whelan, Notebook No. 6, Oct. 4, 1977, p. 49.
[4] Ibid., pp. 50–51.
[5] Ibid., pp. 51–52.
[6] Ibid., pp. 41–42.

testimony before the Senate Foreign Relations Committee on January 14, 1977, he underscored the importance of precision in drafting language for an agreement. He reported as "good news" that "substantial progress" had been made in 1976 "in drafting treaty language, article by article, to flesh out the Vladivostok Accord." "Without such a detailed and specific text," he said, "we could not know what we have agreed on, and this would leave room for evasion and foster future disputes. Our negotiators deserve much credit for having worked out these essentials." According to Ikle, it is "always an uphill struggle to obtain Soviet consent to treaty language that is sufficiently specific." [7]

(b) Danger of self-negotiation

Ikle also emphasized the danger of self-negotiation, as Johnson had warned. During the 5-month period between the fall of 1975 and early spring 1976, the U.S. negotiators had made five different proposals to solve the cruise missle/Backfire issue, but the Soviets remained adamant in their opposition. As Ikle explained:

Yet the Soviet Union failed to make any effort to come up with counter-proposals of its own which could help to resolve these issues. In retrospect, perhaps we took too many initiatives, giving our adversaries the impression that they could wait us out. Had the Soviet Union shown only some of this flexibility, an agreement might long since have been completed. We must keep in mind that the SALT process cannot function without a disposition to reasonable compromise on both sides. [8]

(c) Litvinov's old "bazaar tactic"

Continuing, Ikle stressed the importance of compromise in any successful negotiation—"the important point is that it must be a balanced compromise." He recalled the "most notorious attempt" by the Soviets to obtain a one sided advantage in SALT. Early in the negotiations the Russians had claimed that they should have a larger number of strategic forces to compensate for the U.S. nuclear systems deployed at forward bases overseas. The issue was ultimately resolved in the Vladivostok agreement. This agreement, Ikle said, established the principle of equal numbers of strategic offensive weapons. And he then explained the relevance of this experience to the cruise missile/Backfire issue as illustrating a Soviet negotiating tactic (employed long ago by Litvinov), the age-old "bazaar tactic" of making exorbitant demands initially and expecting concessions from the other side as a price to be paid for withdrawing the original demands. Ikle explained:

* * * it is important to recall this earlier history because we continue to hear suggestions that the United States must in some sense pay the Soviets off for dropping these demands by accepting Soviet terms for resolving the cruise missile and Backfire issues.

This notion would establish the curious principle that by making unwarranted claims, and then dropping them, one becomes entitled to other concessions. The United States should, of course, continue to be willing to accept balanced limitations on weapons that are in the grey area between clearly tactical and clearly strategic systems. [9]

[7] U.S. Congress. Senate. Committee on Foreign Relations and the Subcommittee on Arms Control, Oceans and International Environment. United States/Soviet Strategic Options. Hearings. 95th Cong., 1st sess. Washington. D.C.. U.S. Government Printing Office, 1977. p. 7.
[8] Ibid., p. 8.
[9] Ibid., p. 8.

3. NITZE AND LODAL ON SOVIET NEGOTIATING INTENTIONS: SHYSTERS OR HARD BARGAINERS?

In the course of the hearings on Soviet-American strategic options, Mr. Paul H. Nitze, former Deputy Secretary of Defense and member of the U.S. SALT delegation, was asked to address the question of Soviet intentions. Nitze responded by referring to an editorial in the Wall Street Journal as "the best thing" he had seen on the subject. The article reviewed the defense that the previous administration had made of the Soviet position on the question of ABM test ranges. The writer, Nitze said,

* * * came to the conclusion that the best interpretation of their position on this was that they handled the negotiations like shysters. This, I think, was crystal clear. The ABM agreement says that in addition to the ABM components that they can have in a circle around Moscow and in one missile defense field, they can have a limited number of ABM components at test ranges for the purposes of tests at existing test ranges and at additionally agreed test ranges. I think that is the language.

Then we tried to get an agreement from them as to exactly what those existing test ranges were. We drafted a statement saying our ABM test ranges were at Kwajalein and at White Sands. We understood theirs was at Shari Shagan.

They did not disagree but said they would prefer to put in a parallel statement. In that statement they said that they agreed that national technical means of verification are adequate to determine where existing test ranges are, et cetera. Then, much later, they claimed, that all along Kamchatka had'been an additional existing test range on their side. Subsequently I understand they have claimed all test ranges, whether they be tank test ranges or anything else, can be ABM test ranges; therefore, they could have 15 ABM's on any one of an indefinite number of test ranges.

We told them the way we interpreted the treaty language. They didn't tell us they had a different interpretation. They then claimed that the language of their unilateral statement does not specifically say that they had only one ABM test range at Shari Shagan.

If that isn't negotiating like a shyster, I don't know what is. Maybe Jan would like to come to their defense.[10]

Jan M. Lodal, executive vice president of American Management Systems, an authority on arms control and panelist at the hearing, claimed unfamiliarity with the latest exchange about the test ranges, but he expressed the belief that "we did learn in the SALT I process that it is important to tie down the language very precisely in these agreements."

"Sometimes you can't do it," Nitze interjected.

Lodal understood this, but noted that in some cases "we reached good agreements with the Soviets afterward on some of these issues, with compromises on both sides." And he took issue with Nitze on Soviet negotiating intentions. "I wouldn't say they negotiated like shysters," he said. "I say they negotiated hard and tough. We have to realize they are going to continue to negotiate that way."[11]

---

[10] Ibid., pp. 101–102.
[11] Ibid., p. 102. Nitze conveyed to President Carter his skepticism of Soviet negotiating intentions. The President had urged Nitze to join his negotiating team and help work out a treaty that would be good for the United States and one "the Russians would think is fair." That disturbed Nitze who insisted, and told the President so, that "The Russians do not understand what we mean by fairness." (Sidey, Hugh. The White-Haired Hawk. Time, Feb. 26, 1979: 17.)

B. Ambassador Smith's "Do's and Don'ts" in Negotiating With the Soviets

1. LUSTING FOR THE SUMMIT, AND THE "HOME COURT" ADVANTAGE

Early in the Carter administration when resumption of SALT II negotiations was about to begin and even more drastic proposals on arms control than those considered by previous administrations were being projected, Ambassador Smith, at that time Chairman of the Trilateral Commission, laid out a series of 10 principles, "do's and don'ts", as he said, to guide the new President in the next round of talks. The first principle was, "Don't lust for the summit." [12]

Linking SALT I negotiations with a summit meeting in Moscow affected (presumably adversely) "the timing and perhaps the substance of SALT I," Smith asserted. From the beginning President Nixon set his sights on a summit with SALT I as its centerpiece. When plans for a 1971 meeting fell through, the Soviets "had little incentive to reach early agreement." As Smith explained, "Time was working in their favor." Accordingly, they exploited this negotiating advantage and proceeded to add launchers to their strategic forces that were to be limited by agreement. In Smith's view the agreement reached in 1972 could have been concluded a year earlier. [13]

Adding to the problem was what might be called the "home court" advantage given the Soviets by meeting in Moscow. Negotiating complex technical matters, Smith continued, can be a "hairy business." In Moscow, Kissinger telegraphed him in Helsinki that he never knew from hour to hour with whom he would meet or what topic would be discussed. In this respect, Smith went on, "The Soviets have a way of bending local arrangements to their advantage." To illustrate the point Smith quoted the following "ironic guidelines" entitled, "The Last 20 Minutes of the Negotiations Are the Most Important," that were jotted down by an American delegate returning from the signing ceremony:

First, arrange for the negotiations to be conducted at several levels. Try to pocket the optimum for your side arising at any one of the levels. Subtechniques include (a) general statements at top subsequently withdrawn at a lower level, (b) introduction without prior notice of added starters at an intermediate level to swing the situation in your favor. At political meeting, introduce "expert" prepared to use his special knowledge to your advantage under circumstances where those on the other side are not in a position to contradict him. * * * Use your interpreters for both. Have no typewriters or Xerox machines available when needed. Give other side as minimum secure communications facilities as possible. [14]

Smith was not proposing that the President follow this advice, but he did caution that if the next round of negotiations does take place in the capital of either country, then it should be in Washington.

2. AVOID "TWO-CHANNEL" NEGOTIATIONS

In his second principle, Smith cautioned against "two-channel" negotiations, or as Garthoff called it, "back channel" negotiations—one, of delegates at the negotiating table; the other, of officials at the White House and in the Kremlin. [15]

[12] Smith, Gerard C. Negotiating with the Soviets. The New York Times Magazine, Feb. 27, 1979: 18.
[13] Ibid.
[14] Ibid.
[15] Ibid.

The ABM agreement was reached in 1972, as Smith explained, at the very low negotiating level in the first channel; agreement on the interim freeze of new offensive missiles was in large part reached in the second. Negotiations in the first channel were a "careful process" in which a "comprehensive record of exchanges through formal communications" was made. Those in the second, involving Nixon, Kissinger, Dobrynin and the Soviet leadership, were informal, usually with no records available for the SALT delegates, at least the American. "As a result," Smith complained, "our delegates were sometimes left in the dark as to what was going on." [16]

Smith argued that the best results would be achieved by using a single negotiating channel under the direction of the President. For a kind of Gresham's law applied in a plural approach to negotiations: "It becomes increasingly difficult to resolve issues at a lower level." [17]

3. "DON'T EXPECT QUICK RESULTS"

Since SALT is a "slow and painstaking process," Smith proclaimed as his third principle of negotiations, "Don't expect quick results." [18] The reasons for the slowness of the process were attributed to inbred Soviet habits of secrecy and Soviet bureaucratic delays, and to the carefully designed negotiating procedures that require time.

Soviet delegates, at least the civilians, had only limited information on their own weapons systems. This caused delays. Moreover, no machinery for coordinating policy among Soviet agencies existed, except for the Politburo. Smith cited as a consequence an observation that is traditional in Soviet negotiating behavior: "Not surprisingly, the Soviets seemed better at reacting to American initiatives than to taking their own." [19]

Adding to the slowness of the proceedings were such things as the "very short rein" kept on the delegates by both sides, requiring a great deal of communications with the home base, and the physical arrangements of meeting at the Embassies of both countries. Preparation of statements for plenary sessions also required hundreds of man-hours. In explaining this time-consuming procedure, Smith wrote:

More than 20 high-level officials worked on each statement, which was usually the product of five or six drafts. After Semyonov and I orally delivered these statements in plenary meetings, they were exchanged in order to insure accurate translation of the English and Russian texts. It took American interpreters four to eight hours to produce a final translation that, we were confident, reflected all important shades of meaning. In addition to these formal statements, full reports of all informal exchanges, usually involving about 12 people on each side, were forwarded to Washington. [20]

Notwithstanding the unavoidable problems inherent in dealing with the Soviet bureaucracy and the slow procedural pace of negotiations, Smith insisted that, "this is the process best designed to produce solid arms controls." [21] For in his judgment the ABM treaty "has worked well;" the interim freeze will have served its purpose in restraining, as agreed, the number of missile launchers; and its extension was foreshadowed by the Vladivostok accord of 1974. [22]

---

[16] Ibid.
[17] Ibid.
[18] Ibid.
[19] Ibid.
[20] Ibid.
[21] Ibid.
[22] Ibid.

4. ON TABLING UNEQUAL PROPOSALS AND UNCERTAIN POSITIONS

Smith set down as his fourth principle: "Don't waste time on obviously inequitable propositions." He cited the example of the United States pressing for an unequal ABM agreement favoring its side, only to end with an agreement on two sites for each side. "The time expended on this was better used by the other side," he said.[23]

Nor did Smith think it wise to table uncertain positions. It was a "useful technique," he said, when at the preliminary SALT round at Helsinki in 1969, the United States presented a set of "illustrative elements" to stimulate dialog. "They were examples," he said "not offers." But after negotiations got underway, the American side tabled a number of what appeared to be proposals but were actually "approaches" giving the President an option of repudiating them if prudent. "A number of alternate ABM limitations were tabled," he explained, "thus giving the Soviets a plausible claim that a choice had been offered." When their choice conflicted with U.S. policy, "confusion and delay resulted." Thus Smith cautioned: "Negotiations are not seminars; we should table only those positions we have decided to support."[24]

As if in afterthought, Smith also expressed the belief that while much of the above time-consuming routine was necessary, little was to be gained by oral presentations of statements in plenary session. If eliminated, the negotiating process could be speeded up.[25]

5. UNDERSTAND THE DIFFERENT NEGOTIATING STYLES

Smith's fifth principle was simply to understand the difference between Soviet and American negotiating styles. What may seem polemical to Americans, he said, may only reflect a difference in style. Emphasizing a point made by other negotiators, Smith explained further the Soviet inclination toward general proposals with political meaning (fill in the "fine print" later, they would say), in contrast to the American which stresses the specific and the technical. For the Soviets, arms control has seemed primarily to be "a matter of international policies having technical aspects," while for the Americans, though appreciating its high political significance, it was seen "more as a search for solutions to the complex technical problems of establishing force levels and weapons characteristics by international agreement."[26]

The American emphasis on detail, especially in matters of verification where its distrust has been born out of sad experience, has in the past tended to fortify a negotiating approach that stresses "loophole closing." But not all loopholes can be closed, Smith noted, particularly in situations prejudicial to the interests of sovereign negotiating powers and where verification may not be possible. Verification of SALT I, he said, was simple, but in "future negotiations, we may face choices between leaving some conceivable loopholes open or abandoning the whole negotiation." "Future agreements may be harder to verify infallibly," he averred, but that "does not necessarily mean that they would be prejudicial to our interests."[27]

---

[23] Ibid.
[24] Ibid., pp. 18–19.
[25] Ibid.
[26] Ibid., p. 19.
[27] Ibid.

6. TACTICAL NEGOTIATING ADVANTAGES OF THE CLOSED SOCIETY

"Realize that the Soviets enjoy a tactical negotiating advantage because of the closed nature of their society"—such was Smith's sixth principle.[28]

Smith reiterated a point made in the above section on SALT I with respect to the advantages of a closed society over the open in a negotiating encounter. From open sources the Soviets know the number of American strategic weapons in place or to be deployed; they also know "a good deal" about their designs. In contrast, American intelligence findings are far from infallible and do not reveal full information on future deployment plans. "They know precisely how many American missiles are to have multiple warheads," Smith cited as an example; "we can only estimate the scope of their MIRV progress." [29]

Still, Smith was confident that SALT I compensated in part for this asymmetry. It was "no small accomplishment," he asserted, that because of the interim freeze, "our knowledge of what their aggregate missile force numbers would be in 1977 approached their knowledge of ours." With respect to appraising possible future agreements, Smith cautioned that "Moscow's superior command of information tends to be neutralized by arms-control agreements as they are carried out." He also stressed that Soviet commitments "not to interfere with—or conceal weapons systems from—national means of verification increase the reliability of the information obtained by these means." [30]

7. DON'T OVERREACT TO LEAKS; AVOID OVEROPTIMISTIC STATEMENTS AND "POOR-MOUTHING" U.S. DEFENSE POSTURE

As the seventh guiding principle in negotiating with the Soviets, Smith urged: "Don't overreact to the inevitable leaks." [31]

Rather accurate projections of American negotiating moves had been made available to the Soviets through leaks to the American press. Smith attributed White House exclusion of SALT officials from needed information (and the cost "is still hard to assess") to the "inability of Washington agency officials to keep their mouths shut." Smith contended that the importance of the leaks was exaggerated, and that the leakers "had nothing more sinister in mind than to manipulate the press to advance negotiating positions they favored or to retard those they opposed." [32]

The Soviets accrued a "more serious negotiating advantage." Smith contended, whenever the White House put out optimistic predictions on SALT prospects. "Generating expectations of agreements," he explained, "does not add to bargaining power for your side." [33]

Finally, Smith cautioned about underrating and "poor-mouthing" the U.S. military posture vis-a-vis the Soviet Union in order to get Congressional approval of Defense Department appropriations. This administration practice was hurtful to the American image abroad,

[28] Ibid.
[29] Ibid.
[30] Ibid.
[31] Ibid.
[32] Ibid., p. 26.
[33] Ibid.

and, therefore, was presumably detrimental to negotiators in dealing with the Soviets.[34]

8. NONINTERFERENCE WITH NEGOTIATING PROCESS

For his eighth principle, Smith urged: "Don't interfere with the negotiating process once it has begun." [35]

Leading officials should intervene in a negotiating process, according to Smith, only in extremes, when collapse of the whole entire negotiation is the "clear alternative." Even in such cases, Smith cautioned, "the negotiating process should be much more carefully handled than was the case during the high-level phases of SALT I." [36]

Smith acknowledged that deadlines were useful in some international negotiations, but not necessarily in SALT. In criticism of negotiations at the summit, he urged that "the overt role of heads of government should be limited to public ratification of what, under their direction, has already been done by their agents." [37]

9. PATIENCE WITH ELUSIVE RESULTS

"Don't worry if, at first, results seem to elude you," Smith said in laying down his ninth principle. "Prolonged SALT negotiations are not necessarily a bad thing." [38]

Smith went on to emphasize the educating function of SALT negotiations for both sides. For the first time, he said, certain Soviet civilian officials entered deeply into such arcane subjects as nuclear arms doctrine and planning. And officials on both sides have spent years exchanging views on strategic arms and methods of their control. Thus, Smith declared:

Behind the specific value of SALT agreements is the great worth of the process itself. The strategic relationship has already been altered for the better as a result of the negotiations thus far, and more negotiations can only be of further benefit.[39]

10. SALT AS AN IRREVERSIBLE PROCESS

In citing the tenth principle, Smith made a special plea for the continuation of SALT negotiations: "Above all, do everything possible to turn the beginning made in SALT I into an irreversible process." [40]

Smith proceeded to argue on behalf of the process, giving particular emphasis to these points: That arms control has become a "respectable part of national security policy;" that authorities in the Defense Department have come to recognize it as "a fact of military life;" and that both the Soviet Union and the United States "must see it in their security interest to keep the first agreements and build on them." [41]

11. IMPORTANCE OF SMITH'S PRINCIPLES

What makes Smith's prescription for negotiations especially instructive is that they represent the views of a diplomat with years of

---

[34] Ibid.
[35] Ibid.
[36] Ibid.
[37] Ibid.
[38] Ibid.
[39] Ibid.
[40] Ibid.
[41] Ibid.

practical experience negotiating with the Russians on a subject of vital interest to both sides, nuclear arms control, and without the intrusion of other extrinsic issues. By and large this experience had been a successful one and the subject matter of the negotiations of vital importance, so that his advice is colored more by a sense of positive realism than by negativism and frustration, which has so often been the case with other negotiators. If Smith downgrades the value of summitry and "back channel" negotiations, by no means incontestable, still they reflect the preferences of a man negotiating "on the firing line," so to speak, whose views are derived from experience and not theory and accordingly deserve attention.[42]

C. AMBASSADOR BEAM ON SOVIET NEGOTIATORS: THEIR COMPETENCE AND TECHNIQUES

1. THEIR COMPETENCE

With years of experience as a practitioner observing the conduct of Soviet diplomacy in Moscow and elsewhere in Eastern Europe, Ambassador Beam credited Soviet diplomats and negotiators with a high degree of professionalism, though measured within the narrower framework of the Soviet political system. Able and competent and trained according to the requirements of the Soviet system, they come to the negotiating table well prepared to engage the other side in debate, armed with an abundance of documentation and information to buttress their arguments and press their case.[43]

2. CONTROL FROM THE CENTER

Control from the center is firm and unrelenting. Beam likened the Soviet negotiator to a soldier who was bound by strict orders and had to abide by those orders without deviation unless commanded otherwise by his superior. The Soviet negotiator has "no discretion at all," Beam said; they are held "in tight rein, tremendously tight rein." Policy is decided in the Politburo and Secretariat of the Central Committee; it comes down through the Foreign Ministry, and "they follow it, completely, unswerving." Hence, "there is practically no give, no chance really for discussion."

3. SOME CHARACTERISTICS OF SOVIET NEGOTIATORS

(a) An aggressive sense of realism

An aggressive sense of realism seems to be the most visible characteristic of the Soviet negotiator. Asked if Soviet diplomats were hardheaded, realistic, tough negotiators, Beam responded in a firm, "Yes." He had found them "competent negotiators" but "always unpleasant, mostly unpleasant." They "antagonize you right away when they start out; they try to put you on the defensive right away."

Soviet negotiators do not compromise willingly, according to Beam—as he said, "not unless they have to and then with authority; they may have been given fallback positions but very rarely; they usually had to go back and get new instructions."

---

[42] For a commentary on the American approach to negotiating with Communists, see, Ikle, Fred Charles. American Shortcomings in Negotiating with Communist Powers, in, Senate, Committee on Government Operations, International Negotiations, 1970, 17 pp.
[43] This entire section is based on an interview with Ambassador Beam on May 23, 1979.

Guided as they are by a sense of realism, Soviet negotiators find ideology to be no barrier. As Beam said, for them "ideology is just dry bread"; but, nonetheless, "they carry out their mission which is based on their interpretation of Marxism and Leninism as of that time."

(b) Avoiding the initiative

A distinctive Soviet negotiating characteristic that Beam observed from his experience is the inclination to let the other side take the initiative. This tactic invites the danger of self-negotiation, as Johnson warned; it also permits the Soviets to select the most desirable proposal from many options.

By and large, the thinking and designing of proposals along with taking the initiative come from the American side—"much too much," according to Beam. To illustrate his point on the origination of ideas and negotiating concepts, he cited the Soviet proposal for an Asian security treaty where, having "nothing constructive" themselves to offer, they tried to draw out the United States and get its views.

(c) Convergence of diplomatic styles

To Beam, Soviet behavior in negotiations is radically different from that of the West. Asked if he foresaw the Soviets conforming to the traditional negotiating behavior as practiced in the West, a convergence of diplomatic and negotiating styles, he responded, "in the proprieties, yes," but, he cautioned, "it's dealing with different people, a different style."

4. ON THE VALUE OF BEAM'S COMMENTARY

Beam's commentary has a special value. It is not just because of his position as an ambassador. Rather it is because his diplomatic career, spanning the period from cold war to détente, has been almost entirely in the Communist world or associated with East-West negotiations—a "multiple exposure," so to speak. Thus he brings to his views insights born out of more than just experience as a practicing professional diplomat; but insights as well of a person immersed in the milieu of a unique environment with the "feel" for the nuances of life and policy under communism and with a perspective of three decades. An added value comes from the fact that Beam's negotiating experience was wide ranging, from the routine day-to-day tasks of directing a diplomatic mission to negotiating at the upper echelons of power.

D. GARTHOFF'S LESSONS ON NEGOTIATING WITH THE SOVIETS

1. ESSENTIAL PRECEPTS AND CHANGING SOVIET APPROACH TO NEGOTIATIONS

Garthoff is perhaps the most published of any participant in the SALT I negotiations. Drawing from his many years of expertise as an active negotiator, adviser, and specialist on Soviet affairs, he has analyzed the achievements and failures of SALT I.[44] But more importantly for the purposes of this study he listed the following lessons on negotiating with the Soviets as he himself learned them firsthand during his SALT experiences: [45]

---

[44] Garthoff, World Politics. pp. 17–25.
[45] Garthoff, International Security, pp. 22–24.

(a) Firm leadership and support

I would stress above all the need in negotiating with the Russians for firm leadership, direction and support for the negotiation from the President down.

(b) Clear and consistent negotiating objectives

Negotiating objectives must be clear and consistent. Bargaining room and bargaing chips have a place, but as means and not as part of the objective; it is necessary to keep leeway for compromise without a constant reshuffling of goals. It is much more difficult for us, given the nature of the American political process, to reach internal agreement even within a small group in an Administration on negotiating objectives, and to hold to them during the course of negotiation. A negotiation is bound by the nature of the process to require changes from initial *proposals* and even *positions*, and there may well be differing views on such matters. But if the very objectives of a negotiation are unclear or unagreed on a side, and bureaucratic struggle over them continues, the center of gravity will tend to shift to the *internal* "negotiation" at the expense of the one with the other side. This has been a recurrent problem in American negotiations with the Soviet Union.

(c) Negotiating tactics and techniques

The problem of establishing, and maintaining, clear negotiating objectives also becomes mixed with the question of negotiating tactics and techniques, and has a tendency to interfere with the ability to design and implement a negotiating strategy toward the other side. Many criticisms of American negotiating behavior in dealing with the Russians have concerned matters which were really determined by intra-American divergences leading to inconsistent negotiating positions and less satisfactory outcomes.

(d) Integrity of negotiating channels

Integrity of the negotiating channel must be preserved. There may be times when highest level intervention is needed to assist the negotiation, but the temptation to skip back and forth between secret back-channels and the ostensible forums as in SALT I, or to use the latter as a facade as occurred in large measure in SALT II through 1976, must be resisted.

(e) Unnecessary constraints and burdens

Unnecessary constraints or burdens on negotiation should be avoided. Excessive propaganda is one risk, though not an American propensity. Demands that may obscure the possibility of real negotiation should be eschewed. Artificial time pressures unilaterally imposed must be avoided, as with summit deadlines. Premature commitment to a specific outcome should also be avoided, while keeping true to the fundamental negotiating objectives.

(f) Publicity and confidentiality

Sufficient information on a negotiation to sustain public and congressional understanding and support is essential, but this should be coupled with sufficient confidentiality to permit the negotiating process.

(g) Taking the initiative

While the Soviet Union continues to have the advantage of greater unity in the establishment of negotiating objectives and positions, it also has greater sluggishness. We should not shy away from the initiative.

Soviet negotiators today, as compared to their counterparts twenty or thirty years ago, generally have a greater sophistication about the West and its political processes, and greater flexibility. "Compromise" is no longer taboo, and there is greater leeway for exploratory probing. But Soviet negotiators continue to have little discretion.

(h) Bargaining room and calculated ambiguity

Initial negotiating positions and proposals should provide sufficient "bargaining room"; not so much as to mislead on a possible outcome, but not so little as not to allow tradeoffs and compromise. Calculated ambiguity on "quantities" (literally and figuratively) may be useful, but not on essential qualities of the objectives. Precise tactical matters such as the timing of advancing proposals must be judged in each case.

(i) *Patience and firmness*

Patience and firmness are necessary virtues in negotiation, but unproductive, indiscriminate or unduly protracted obstinacy is not. Controlled flexibility is necessary. (If both sides stake out ample bargaining room and then are infinitely patient and resolutely firm, there will be no real negotiation and no agreement.) It is, in short, necessary to be able to discriminate between patience and obstinacy, firmness and flexibility, and to know when and how to use each.

(j) *Informal probing*

Carefully controlled use of informal probes and testing of possible compromises by trusted and experienced negotiators prior to formal changes of position can be invaluable.

(k) *Relevance of external developments*

Finally * * * the relationship of the negotiation to relevant developments beyond the negotiation itself is important, and can affect greatly negotiating strategy, but should not unduly affect tactics, and a negotiation should not be overburdened with more than it can bear.

(l) *Shared objectives and success*

The most important intrinsic element in determining success of negotiation is the extent of shared or congruent—they need *not* be identical—objectives and interests.

(m) *Changing Soviet approach to negotiations*

The Soviet approach to and conduct of negotiations has always depended mainly on their aims with respect to a given negotiation. Agreements can be reached when the Soviets see value in agreements; they cannot be reached when the Soviets do not want them. What has changed is that in recent years there is greater readiness to scout out possible agreements on a wider range of subjects. This change in part reflects greater Soviet sophistication and awareness of the world outside their own still sheltered sphere. In part it also reflects a greater feeling of self-confidence, and the changed "relation of forces" in the world. In this respect, greater equality between the power of the Soviet Union and the United States in recent years has led not to greater intransigence and overbearing Soviet behavior, as many feared, but generally to more responsible and business-like negotiation. Moscow feels less need for defensive posturing and overcompensation for weaknesses.[46]

2. A SUMMING UP

The lessons to be learned in negotiating with the Russians are thus disarming in their simplicity and illuminating in their commonsense. In sum, a successful negotiation with the Russians requires: having leadership, direction and support from the top on down; establishing clear and consistent negotiating objectives; designing skillful negotiating tactics and techniques to achieve the desired goals; maintaining the integrity of the negotiating channels; avoiding unnecessary constraints or burdens; keeping the proper balance between publicity and confidentiality; taking the initiative; staking out sufficient bargaining room but avoiding loss of objectives in calculated ambiguity; being patient and firm but not to the point of obstinancy and inflexibility; engaging in informal probing of the adversary's negotiating position in search for areas of common interest; and resisting the intrusion of irrelevant external developments, burdensome linkages with other problems, summit deadlines and other artificial time pressures connected with domestic political concerns.

---

[46] Garthoff concluded his article in the Wilson Quarterly (p. 85.) : "The lesson in all this is that negotiating with the Russians requires firm leadership, direction, and support from the President on down. Objectives must be clear and consistent. The integrity of the principal negotiating channel—the two SALT delegations—must be preserved despite the powerful temptation to skip between secret back-channels and official forums. The attraction of summit deadlines and other artificial time pressures linked to domestic political concerns must be vigorously resisted ; they simply give additional leverage to Moscow."

Success depends finally on shared but not identical objectives and interests.

And the last word: success is possible in negotiating with the sophisticated Russians of today, self-confident in their power and proven in their ability, so long as a negotiated agreement has value.

E. SONNENFELDT'S VIEWS ON SOVIET DIPLOMACY AND NEGOTIATIONS [47]

1. QUALITY OF THE SOVIET DIPLOMAT

Based on his experience with Soviet diplomats, Sonnenfeldt judged them to be "quite professional" and "knowledgeable about the areas in which they work or specialize." Not having access to their political reports, he could not assess them on this important function. Still, he observed: "I don't imagine that they show all of the prejudices we wouldn't share, in fact wouldn't consider professional. But on the other hand I think they are quite capable of making some astute judgments." Sonnenfeldt had heard them do so in conversation, adding that many of those he had dealt with have acquired "quite a sophisticated understanding of the countries in which they serve."

One of the past problems the Soviets have had to cope with, according to Sonnenfeldt, was the "high degree of compartmentalization of information." To some extent that has been modified, though it remains a "big problem" for them. Gromyko's elevation to the Politburo has probably brought about some improvement, so that at least he, and presumably some of his immediate staff, have access to the broad range of information and access also to the top-level people in the Politburo. Because of this limitation, Soviet diplomats tend to be "less well-informed about a range of issues and also about matters concerning their own country" than would be the case with Western diplomats.

With respect to the training of Soviet diplomats. Sonnenfeldt emphasized what has been noted elsewhere in this study: their skill in languages (which he felt was "sometimes exaggerated"); their knowledge of the technicalities of diplomacy through international law; their training in area studies at the various institutes. In contrast to the generalist approach of the Americans, the Soviets tend toward specialization, notably for service within the Foreign Ministry and the other ministries dealing with foreign affairs. In general, Sonnenfeldt believed that Soviet diplomats probably have "quite as solid and intensive a training" and more specialized than would be the case in other countries.

2. SOVIET PERCEPTIONS OF NEGOTIATIONS

The Soviets have a broad conception of what constitutes negotiations. They are "generally serious" about it, according to Sonnenfeldt. But they resort to extraneous elements and extra-negotiating techniques beyond the negotiating table to get support for their position. For them negotiations do not necessarily mean only "sitting down and haggling over language at the bargaining table," but rather it means "maneuvering for position, and achieving certain adjustments by one means or another, including the threat of force, or agitation, or bribery, or inducements, or any number of things."

[47] Unless otherwise indicated. this section is based on an interview with Sonnenfeldt on June 7, 1979.

Traditionally, the Soviets have not been as much concerned about concluding an agreement in negotiations as in using the process "to promote their own interests." American often feel uneasy if a negotiation does not conclude with a "success"; that is, a completed document, signed, sealed and delivered. Not so the Russians, according to Sonnenfeldt. They have often been prepared "to engage in endless talk and negotiations without conclusion and still attempt to promote their interests through that process and the surrounding activities and noises."

The Soviets, therefore, value negotiations. In the last 20 to 25 years, Sonnenfeldt pointed out, they have seen "virtue" in conducting negotiations on a whole range of issues "where they think they can protect and advance their interests"—on arms control, political matters, and in economic areas. Sonnenfeldt did not think that,

they want agreements at any price. Far from it. They always have a very steep price. In any case they see virtue in negotiations and have long since overcome whatever inhibitions they once had about signing agreements or completing agreements with class adversaries.

Sonnenfeldt concluded: "So I think they have to be treated as serious negotiators."

3 ASPECTS OF SOVIET NEGOTIATING BEHAVIOR

Sonnenfeldt seemed to respect the Soviets as negotiators, but he himself did not hold to the belief that they were "infallible supernegotiators who get their way in every case through tenacity or trickery or shrewdness or knowing more about the subject than their counterparts." According to Sonnenfeldt, "there is a kind of mystic that the Soviets outbargain everybody. I don't think that is true."

As negotiators, the Russians are "tenacious." Usually, they begin a negotiation, Sonnenfeldt recalled, by taking a very firm position and putting the burden of compromise on the other side, though they try to "put a reasonable face" on their position. They say, in effect, "this is our position; of course, we are willing to hear yours, and so on." But, as Sonnenfeldt said, "they do tend to convey the impression that they have a really firm position." From all the negotiations that Sonnenfeldt had been involved in, it was clear that the initial Soviet position was, indeed, "not the final position and that there is give, certainly within limits, and that when they want an agreement they have come to understand that it requires compromise." The extent of compromise, however, depends upon the negotiating skill of the other side on what might be called "the objective surrounding circumstances" and "on how much incentive the Soviets have to come to terms or think they have to come to terms."

"But they yield points rather grudgingly," Sonnenfeldt continued. In yielding, they resort to a tactic of dramatizing their concession. They use "their own readiness to compromise on a particular point to extract a greater compromise from the other side in return. They try to make you awfully grateful for what they have done."

Frequently, Soviet negotiators will yield on a point that should not have been held for so long a time. But, once they start adjusting, Sonnenfeldt said, "they always seem to be in a great hurry to wrap things up." There are risks in this tactic, as Sonnenfeldt explained:

That is a technique of using concessions to get a greater concession from the other side. One has to be careful not to be caught up in this sort of spiral of euphoria and gratitude and being made by the Soviets to feel as if we are indebted to them."[48]

4. CONVERGING DIPLOMACY STYLES

Changes in Soviet negotiating behavior since the days of the cold war raise a basic question about the possible convergence of diplomatic styles. To Sonnenfeldt, a certain "normal behavior" has been discernible in the conduct of Soviet negotiators, "normal" is the sense that negotiators are,

engaged in a time-honored practice for which there are certain ground rules that have long been established in international custom, and so the Soviets, having started in 1917 by putting themselves outside of the conventional international system, have had to walk back into the international system and adapt themselves to many of the practices.

In brief, the Soviets have accommodated to the stylistic requirements of diplomacy and negotiations in the international relations of today.

But there is a difference; perhaps, it is the "something else" that Nicolson referred to when differentiating Soviet diplomacy from that of the West. For Sonnenfeldt, the difference was apparent when comparing the American experience in negotiating with its allies and with the Soviets. In negotiating with the Soviets, he said,

you do not ever have the sense of the degree of comity, commonality of approach; there is always a strong residue, and more than a residue, of antagonism so that you recognize that by and large negotiations with the Soviets are adversary proceedings. That is not to say that negotiations with friends are not adversary proceedings also when you have conflicting interests on economic matters and things of that sort, but you do not have the sense with the Soviets of that overarching belief in common values, and that I think is different.

Sonnenfeldt did not deny that the Americans and Russians hold certain things in common not shared by other nations. It is "control of this vast machinery of destruction" and "the fear of war and concern about the responsibility of preventing horrible wars" that perhaps unites us with the Russians even more than with our closest friends, because "we have looked into the abyss together." Sonnenfeldt acknowledged that to some extent this was the case when sitting down with the Russians in arms control negotiations or at the summit level and talk about crisis problems or problems of the world order. "You cannot help but have the sense that here are representatives of two countries sitting who do in many ways have the peace of the world and the future of mankind in their hands."

But, Sonnenfeldt cautioned against exaggerating the degree of commonality that this shared relationship produces, because the relationship "is still with all of that an adversary relationship." Sometimes this problem of responsibility for the peace of the world acquires what Sonnenfeldt said was "the characteristic of a tough game of chicken, of who can be pushed the furthest given the fear of cataclysmic war."

---

[*] The tenacity of Soviet negotiators was also noted by Hyland: "Avoiding the fray was a good tactic" noted Hyland, in describing President Nixon's practice of establishing the guidelines of policy and then leave the hard negotiating to the subordinates, as "it is extremely frustrating negotiating with the Soviets because they insisted on winning every minor point. There is endless haggling and bitterness. The atmosphere gets very tense over the nitpicking. The Soviets sometimes win the small point but lose the significant one. Still, it's a hell of a problem to turn them around. You can only trust them to pursue their own interests with great dedication any way they can." (Time, Nov. 21, 1977; p. 28.)

Leo Welt observed the same tenacity, taken to such an extreme as to sacrifice large potential gains for minor victories: "At the very end of the bargaining, the Soviet negotiators will always press for the last discount. They may get the discount and save $50,000 but lose $1 million in good will. The American company gets the deal, but its executives go away feeling that they've been put through the wringer." (Washington Post, May 27, 1979, p. C4.)

Thus, while acknowledging that there was something to the notion of "a commonsense of responsibility," this ought not "be carried too far," for in Sonnenfeldt's view, it did not outweigh "the many aspects of the relationship which are also present at the negotiating table, which remain highly antagonistic, and which involve quite different values and quite different outlooks on the world."

In brief, what Sonnenfeldt seemed to suggest is that Soviet and American diplomatic styles in diplomacy and negotiations may converge into a mutual respect for Western diplomatic customs and traditions, but the deeper substance of policy, power and interests act as barriers to complete convergence.

5. THE GENERATIONAL PROBLEM AND THE FUTURE

"Caution" would be the best word to describe Sonnenfeldt's attitude toward the generational problem and its implications for future Soviet foreign policy. Only a residue of the first generation prewar and wartime diplomats remain; a new postwar generation is taking over. Exposure of this "new breed," as Meissner and Petrov termed this new generation, to various international institutions, such as the United Nations and to a host of embassies in a manner typical of the international system generally, has had an impact upon them. Accordingly, as Sonnenfeldt said, "they do many of the things that other diplomats do and in a sense one can say that they have joined the traditional processes of international diplomacy."

But, Sonnenfeldt cautioned that the work of diplomacy, whether it be in the Foreign Ministry, foreign embassies, or with staffs and delegations in international organizations, represents "just one facet of Soviet foreign policy—or any country's foreign policy." In the Soviet case, there are two additional components of diplomacy that affect their attitudes and behavior: The power component, that is, "their drive for power and influence in the world, much of which is based on their military power"; and the "continuing heritage of their ideology, their outlook on the world." Thus Sonnenfeldt cautioned:

One ought not to be too categorical; one ought to be somewhat careful in not drawing too far-reaching conclusions from the fact that a Soviet diplomat, a Soviet professional diplomat, can seemingly speak the same language and be engaged in the same tasks as other countries' diplomats. That is just one facet of the conduct of international affairs by the Soviet Union. You have to put the other things in the scale.

Notwithstanding these particular components that tend to make Soviet diplomats a special case in the world of diplomacy, Sonnenfeldt acknowledged that powerful forces were pulling the Soviet Union, its decisionmakers, its diplomats, and Soviet foreign policy in the direction of greater involvement in the existing international system. In this world of interdependence—Sonnenfeldt preferred the term, "interrelatedness"—the Soviets have become "conscious by reality", indeed, "forced by reality" to become involved. They see benefits to be gained in areas of economics and in the regimes of the oceans and the skies. Accordingly, "there has grown up in the Soviet Union a rather greater and more widespread reliance on the external world than was initially the case, particularly under Stalin."

Thus, forces are pulling the Soviets in two directions, and presumably the inward pulling force is strengthened by the Soviet awareness of their own self-isolation. "They still have an enormous sense of particularity about themselves," Sonnenfeldt said; and "they are fundamentally very isolated, in some respects self-isolated." "They have no real friends in the world," he continued; "they have temporary friends; they have prudential friends." In some ways they are "the most unloved government." While differentiating the great respect of the world for the Russian people, Sonnenfeldt noted, "they are the most unloved regime in the world * * * they are friendless by and large, and perhaps from their own standpoint, most seriously unloved in what used to be their own camp." Sonnenfeldt added, parenthetically, that this did not necessarily mean that the United States was "adored and loved by everyone."

The pull into the world is there, Sonnenfeldt reiterated; but it is also true that here lies the challenge for the U.S. policy and that of the outside world; namely,

to make this process of Soviet involvement in the world a process of getting the Soviets in return for that involvement, or as part of that involvement, to accept the disciplines of it and the constraints of it; and to make them recognize that if on the one hand they want the benefits, but on the other hand they regard themselves as relatively free to throw their weight around, that those two modes of conduct are not compatible.

6. GUIDE FOR NEGOTIATORS

With respect to guidelines for Americans negotiating with the Soviets, Sonnenfeldt offered these suggestions:

—Be patient;
—Be knowledgeable in the subject matter being negotiated, not only in a narrow sense but in its relationship to the broader scheme of things;
—Be ready to go outside the negotiating table and bring external pressures to bear on the negotiations—in the arms control and SALT negotiations, for example, the military balance, actual and prospective, was "an extremely important factor in the negotiations" and "keep the interconnections in mind which we sometimes tend not to do";
—Be "very meticulous" in negotiations without being overlegalistic, a fault that "sometimes gets in our way";
—Involve responsible senior negotiators also in the policymaking process, notwithstanding the value of sometimes not having the negotiator aware of his fallback positions;
—Be careful not to treat negotiations "so special that we lose sight of some of the general rules of negotiations," and the "relationships between nations," for dealing with the Soviets "is a special situation that stems from the particular type of people that the Soviets are, the type of people that we are, and undoubtedly their psychological and ideological baggage has a lot to do with it"; and, finally,
—Be careful not to "become overly entranced with broad prescriptions and with pat theories about how the Soviets negotiate," for "some recurring patterns" do obviously exist that are important for American negotiators to understand. But,

there is also a strong personal element that should not be forgotten that plays into the negotiating process in its formal sense. And then above all I think the important thing to remember is that negotiation, in the strict sense of the term, diplomatic exchange, bargaining, the effort to achieve agreements, to achieve documents constituting agreement, is only a portion of the broad process of negotiation that goes on all the time."

F. ON THE VALUE OF THESE COMMENTARIES

Such are the observations on Soviet diplomacy and negotiating behavior by Johnson, Smith, Beam, Garthoff, and Sonnenfeldt. What adds credence to their commentaries, notwithstanding the distinctive coloration unavoidable in personal judgments, is that they are all historical figures. They are participants in the process of making American diplomatic history at a very crucial juncture in world affairs. And as such their commentaries give to this study a tone and spirit of historical authenticity.

"Leo Welt had some perceptive observations on his negotiations with the Soviets in the area of foreign trade and economics. He wrote: "The Russians are tough, skillful traders. This is not a business for amateurs and do-gooders." In noting the difficulties of being an independent operator negotiating without the support of large recognizable corporations and the ability to rally public opinion, he said: "In any event, no blushing violet would last long in this business." Welt also emphasized the intensity of the Soviet economic negotiator whose negotiating position is supported by the Soviet state because trade is monopolized by the State and such characteristics as their sole responsibility "for buying and selling", the sanctity of contracts, "filling them with time limits and penalty clauses," and that "no planned decision is made on whim." Welt continued: "Every Soviet purchase is carefully planned to aid the fulfillment of the five-year plan production targets. It is a waste of time to try to persuade planning and trade officials to buy something that doesn't fit the five-year plan." Finally, Welt offered this comprehensive statement of advice: "One who does business with the Soviet Union must be prepared to negotiate for hours on end in bare, comfortless rooms, to camp for days in spartan Moscow hotels, always careful to remain above the suspicion of either the CIA or the KGB. The American businessman must be authorized by his company to make major decisions without consulting the home office. But most important, he must be prepared to close his briefcase and walk away from a hundred-million-dollar deal after weeks of intense bargaining if he cannot reach a fair deal. If one is weak, his Soviet counterpart will sense this and will fight for a business advantage. It is sad that the American and Soviet systems are so polarized that they must do business under such rigid conditions. You spend years with these Russians, negotiating, visiting factories, even showing them facilities in the United States, but it is never possible to become more than 'friends' in quotation marks. The system does not allow more." (The Washington Post, May 27, 1979, p. C4.)

VI. FACING THE 1980'S: A NEW ERA OF DIPLOMACY AND NEGOTIATIONS

The decade and a half of solidifying peaceful coexistence under Brezhnev occurred within the context of a changing structure of international relations. This change was brought on largely by a globalizing nationalism and regeneration of the nation-state; the emergence of interdependence and science and technology as transforming forces in diplomacy; and a complex of interacting forces in Soviet-American relations; namely, detente, the expansion of Soviet strategic power to the point of "equivalency" and thrust into the Third World, and the American retreat from globalism.

Building on the Khrushchev years, Brezhnev improved and strengthened the infrastructure of Soviet diplomacy, increased its avenues of access to influence within the political leadership, and stimulated discussion in the West on the generational problem of "Whither Russia." Brezhnev affirmed the foreign policy principles of his predecessor but changed the style of leadership to a less threatening but nonetheless beguiling "businesslike" approach. Negotiations for SALT I, completed against a background of emerging detente, created a process that in the long term may be compared to the impact of the Congress of Vienna on the peace of 19th Century Europe.

Thus in facing the 1980's, the Russians and the Americans seem to be entering a new era of international relations where negotiations and diplomacy could take on a new meaning and become a new force.

(511)

CHAPTER XI—PERMANENCY AND CHANGE IN THE SOVIET APPROACH TO DIPLOMACY AND NEGOTIATIONS; IMPLICATIONS FOR U.S. FOREIGN POLICY

> We are entering an era in which international negotiation appears to be the predominant mode of relations between states, and conditions in the international system are likely to maintain this mode for some time to come.
>
> —*Gilbert R. Windham, 1977.*

> Today there is a greater Soviet readiness to look for possible agreements on a broad range of issues. Compromise is no longer a taboo for Soviet negotiators. In part, this reflects increased Soviet sophistication. It also reflects growing self-confidence. To this extent, the growth of Soviet strength to a level of near equality with the United States has produced not greater intransigence but a more businesslike approach. Agreements on mutually advantageous strategic arms limitations are not easy to reach—but they are attainable.
>
> —*Raymond L. Garthoff, Autumn 1977.*

> One must negotiate, negotiate, and always negotiate.
>
> —*Talleyrand.*

I. CHANGING STRUCTURE OF INTERNATIONAL RELATIONS

A. Some Elements of Change

1. IN HISTORICAL PERSPECTIVE

The first point to be made in concluding this study is the radical transformation of international relations and its effect on creating a new era of diplomacy and negotiations. With the eye of a diplomatic historian Professor Sontag well described this transformation when he wrote in the late 1950's:

Diplomacy has changed so greatly since the beginning of the twentieth century that the diplomatic historian is driven to wonder whether his subject has any relevance to the contemporary world. Then and now—let us set them against each other. Then Europe was the center of diplomatic action; now the diplomat's mind must compass the globe. Then he need take account of a few powers, all with settled traditions of policy. Now he must try to estimate the direction of policy in states with no settled traditions, like Indonesia, while even in older states like Italy and Germany tradition is not a safe guide. Then the diplomat was, for the most part, concerned with narrowly political subjects; now he must study and report on many and diverse subjects. Then information was easy to come by; now, over much of the earth's surface, heroic efforts are made to conceal essential facts and figures. Then there was intimacy and confidence within the group concerned with diplomacy in any country; now discussion is carefully kept within the scope of the lowest security clearance in the room. Then diplomacy was a leisurely business—Bismarck buried in the country for months on end, Salisbury deep in chemical experiments at Hatfield House. Grey feeding his beloved ducks. Today incessant activity is the mark of the statesman. "I spent 350 of my 562 days as Secretary of State at international conferences," boasts Governor Byrnes. Secretary Dulles' air mileage surely exceeded that of any traveling salesman.[1]

---

[1] Sontag, op. cit., p. 109.

2. FROM BIPOLARITY TO MULTIPOLARITY AND INTERDEPENDENCE

Further changes, perhaps equally as far reaching, have occurred during the near two decades since Sontag recorded these historical observations.[2] As noted elsewhere in this study, the bipolar world of the postwar years, then dominated by the Soviet Union and the United States, has become multipolar. Though commanding center stage by virtue of their possession of awesome nuclear arsenals, still the practical use of that power, along with other factors, have diminished the political effect of their preeminence as superpowers. The devolution of power within the competing East-West blocs; the rise of the Third World in a tide of nationalism that has regenerated the concept of the nation-state and globalized its impact; the emerging reality of an interdependent world that has become, perhaps, as sharply divided North-South as it is East-West; and the impact of science and technology on world affairs that has created new problems for mankind while solving old ones—all have contributed to changing the structure of international relations. In many respects, therefore, the world of diplomacy today, extending Sontag's theme, is very different from the days of Witte and Theodore Roosevelt, of Churchill, Stalin and Roosevelt, and even of Kennedy and Khrushchev. Indeed, a new international system seems to be emerging, creating a new context for U.S. diplomacy.

B. EFFECTS OF INTERNATIONAL CHANGES ON WORLD OF DIPLOMACY

1. INCREASED BURDENS AND OPPORTUNITIES FOR NEGOTIATORS

The effects of these structural changes on the world of diplomacy have been to increase the burdens, and the opportunities, for diplomatists and negotiators. John Stremlau, an international affairs specialist with the Rockefeller Foundation, observed this change over the last 5 years and commented early in January 1979: "Internationally, I'm impressed by the explosion of diplomacy. There has been a decline in the salience or use of force. This has become the age of negotiation." [3] An American commentator concluded: "Diplomacy as once known is at an end." To which Eric Clark responded in his study on diplomacy: "Yet if the diplomat is dead, the last person to realize it is the diplomat himself. His profession has been one of the growth industries of this century." [4]

Roetter observed in his study of diplomacy: "Instead of a craft practiced by a select few, diplomacy has become an expanding mass industry. There is more of it than ever before." [5] And Winham con-

[2] For a general discussion of the international scene at the end of the 1970's. see, On Power, Foreign Affairs, vol. 56, October 1977 : 1–111. The articles by Bundy and Legvold have already been cited. Other articles appearing under this general title are : Hoffman, Stanley, "The Uses of American Power"; Ralf Dahrendorf, "International Power: A European Perspective"; and John C. Campbell, "Oil Power in the Middle East."

[3] Cattani, Richard J. New Methods for Solving Disputes, The Christian Science Monitor, Jan. 16, 1979, p. 12.

[4] Clark, op. cit., p. 1. Clark continued : "The 15 heads of mission who represented their countries in one capital, London, in 1914 had become 114 by 1971. They were surrounded by other diplomats, from lowly third secretaries to counsellors and ministers ; by the late 1960's the number of foreign diplomats and their wives in London entitled to varying degrees of diplomatic privileges and immunity totaled over 3,300, more than double the number in 1945. The privileged few had not disappeared. It had simply become the privileged many."

[5] Roetter, op. cit., p. 12.

cluded his thoughtful study on the expanding complexity and multi-plicity of diplomacy and negotiations today: "We are entering an era in which international negotiation appears to be the predominant mode of relations between states, and conditions in the international system are likely to maintain this mode for some time to come." [6]

In this complex interdependent world of expanding new power centers and flourishing regional arrangements of increasingly intersecting and parallel interests, it seems apparent that the instrumentalities of diplomacy and the mechanism of negotiations are taking on a new order of importance. In the cold war days, diplomacy was debased and limited by the negative interaction of challenge and response between the two major adversaries and their blocs of allies. The political world was divided, and the lines of interests seldom if ever met. Today it is different: Great burdens have been placed on diplomacy and negotiations. Neither the Soviet Union nor the United States have full and unimpeded sway in seeking their own interests and purposes. Issues must be negotiated as with the United States in the case of the Panama Canal Treaty, and with the Soviet Union even within its own backyard of Eastern Europe, except when Soviet security is clearly threatened. The multiplicity and complexity of problems in the world today have magnified the role of diplomacy and given it a new status. In many ways the world seems headed in the direction of an international system that has truly global dimensions and increasingly intersecting interests. Diplomacy and negotiations seem destined to be one of the principal instrumentalities for bringing some order out of this environment.

2. ENHANCED ROLE OF DIPLOMATS

In this emerging era of negotiations it seems evident that the role of the ambassador and diplomat in general will become more meaningful, depending upon the country of posting, his personality and political influence, and the gravity of the issues to be resolved. The ambassador's tasks have already been magnified by the expanding requirements of international diplomacy. This study has shown the unique roles played by such ambassadors as Harriman, Bohlen, Thompson, Malik, Jessup, Dobrynin, and Ormsby-Gore. Beam, it should be noted, was the principal American negotiator with the Chinese during 1958–61 when he was Ambassador in Warsaw. This was the only "official" link between Peking and Washington.

A Soviet diplomat speculated that notwithstanding the erosion of the ambassador's tasks by modern communications and the other factors reducing his role, he still felt that the personal presence of the ambassador was most significant in the representation of his country's interests. It was important to have personal evaluations from the field based on firsthand experience, knowledge, and relationships with the leaders of the host country. Thus, he was not prepared to foreclose on the future of this profession.

---

[6] Winham, op. cit., p. 111. Arthur Lall, formerly Ambassador to the United Nations, Head of the Indian Delegation, and Professor at Columbia University, began his book on international negotiation: "The procedures and forums for modern international negotiation are numerous and varied. They are increasing in complexity year by year, and their forms and functions are evolving in adaptation to the changing needs of a rapidly expanding community of nations." (Lall, Arthur. Modern International Negotiation: Principles and Practice. New York, Columbia University Press, 1966, p. 1.)

In a final statement in his study of diplomacy that seems to accurately sum up what the future holds for the diplomat, and notably the ambassador at the top of this profession, Roetter offered this evaluation:

Indeed, internationalism and interdependence are in the air. The development of the thermonuclear weapons and the demands of trade and economics make it impossible to tackle the problems of our age in terms of over five-score independent sovereign nation states. The United Nations, the Common Market, the Atlantic Alliance and the untidy collection of international agencies are all evidence of this trend, but the exact pattern of international relations—if we avoid nuclear war—is not yet clear. Certainly the people who are helping to evolve the pattern, and who will eventually have to make it work, are our diplomats.

It can hardly be called an errand boy's job.[7]

---

[7] Roetter, op. cit., p. 248. For a penetrating and somewhat sardonic commentary on the diplomat and diplomacy from the perspective of an American practitioner, see, Kennan's, "History and Diplomacy as Viewed by a Diplomatist," in, Kertesz and Fitzsimons, op. cit., ch. 7. "The diplomatist," he wrote, "believes deeply in the importance and necessity of his menial function. He harbors the desperate, instinctive conviction that if he were not there to perform it, things would be much worse. And he cherishes this conviction with double intensity, because he is so lonely in it. * * * The professional diplomatist is, after all, only a species of physician. He has, like all physicians, a shabby and irritating group of patients: violent, headstrong, frivolous, unreasonable. He will go on treating them as long as he is permitted to, saving them from such of their follies as he can, patching up the damages done by those follies from which he could not save them. He will do this because it is his professional nature to do it, and because he probably loves those shabby patients in his heart even while he despairs of them. But do not ask him to enthuse about them, to idealize them, or to expect them to change. Whether he approaches them from the vantage point of a diplomatic chancery abroad or from the standpoint of a late and poorly baptized historian, the difficulty is the same. He has seen them too much. He knows them too well." (p. 108).

II. PERMANENT ASPECTS OF SOVIET DIPLOMACY AND NEGOTIATIONS

A. IMPERATIVES OF SECURITY

1. ROOTED IN HISTORY, DOCTRINE, AND REALITY

If anything seems permanent in the Soviet approach to diplomacy and negotiations (other than the enduring impact of geography, economics, and the Russian historical experience), it is an abiding concern for security. The principal theme that stands out in high relief in this study is this obsession with security. Ambassadors Kennan, Smith, and Beam explained the historical roots of this national characteristic by the centuries long Tartar conquest; the reality of Russia, an imperial entity created from other nations and contiguous territories; the vulnerability of the open plains, the deep-rooted xenophobia and feelings of inferiority in the extreme—all of which nourished a sense of insecurity that could only find satisfaction in the building of large military forces. Periodic military invasions, as in the Napoleonic War, World War I, Allied intervention during 1918–21, and World War II deepened this fear which in the Soviet period had become encased in the doctrine of the "capitalist encirclement." The prevailing fear of war in the nuclear age has magnified still further this concern for security.

In a recently published Adelphi Paper: No. 150, Sonnenfeldt and Hyland described the character of the Soviet obsession with security as it evolved since the Bolshevik revolution in a series of expanding concentric circles from the continentalism of Stalin to the globalism of Khrushchev and Brezhnev. The Bolshevik regime was born insecure and remained so for many years within a hostile world and among a people whose total loyalty they could not claim. The requirements for security magnified with each outward thrust of Soviet power, thrusts that compelled a defensive response from the West.[1]

In this circular fashion the Soviet obsession with security has fed upon itself: It has been nourished by the Soviets' own fears. Even when "equal security" was recognized as a central principle in Soviet-American relations, these fears have not subsided but rather have magnified in the interacting cycle of escalation that in turn has induced the other side to seek redress.[2]

---

[1] Sonnenfeldt, Helmut and William G. Hyland. Soviet Perspectives on Security. Adelphi Papers: 150. London, International Institute for Strategic Studies, 1979, 24 pp.

[2] Lester Pearson gave the following compact description of escalation in the nuclear arms race: "All history shows that security—or peace—cannot for long be guaranteed merely by superiority in arms. The attempt to do so inevitably provokes countermeasures on the part of those against whom you arm, which in turn makes an even greater effort on your part necessary. The vicious circle of fear and arms, insecurity and more arms begins, and the ending cannot be a happy one even when it is not disastrous." (Pearson, Lester B. Diplomacy in the Nuclear Age. Westport, Conn., Greewood Press, 1959, p. 65.)

To the Soviets, security means total safety, a lack of danger, or as
Dimitri K. Simes of Georgetown University's Center for Strategic and
International Studies explained: "* * * The Soviets, like the Czars
before them tend to interpret security as an adequate shield against
all conceivable scenarios." The main ambition of those in charge of
determining Soviet defense policy "is to make the Soviet Union safe
from foreign threats, real and imaginary, to the extent that all rivals
are left without many teeth with which to defend their vital interests." [3] Thus, Nitze rejected the idea that the Soviets only want to be
"equal": "To them a bigger advantage is a bigger advantage." [4] And
as Simes concluded: "As long as this absolutist definition of security
prevails in the Soviet political circles, it will be a major obstacle to
any meaningful arms control and, indeed, genuine reconciliation with
the United States." [5]

That the spiralling arms race induces an enduring sense of threat
and danger and magnifies the Soviet obsession with security, there
seems to be little doubt; for as Warnke said, "arms control negotiations do go to the basic fabric of national security." [6] Other elements
reinforce this attitude. The dispute with the Chinese has regenerated
the old fear of a two-front war, adding immeasurably to Soviet concerns for their security.[7] The isolation of the Soviet Union from the
genuine comity of nations feeds upon these ancient fears. As an observer of the Soviets at close range in negotiating SALT II, Warnke,
like Sonnenfeldt, said that the Soviets are really friendless. Time
and again, he said, the sense of loneliness had shown through: They
have no real allies; partnerships are forced and unreliable; they are
powerful, but friendless. On every horizon, Warnke noted, the Soviets
see some threat.[8]

2. LIKELIHOOD OF CHANGE

Will the Russians ever feel secure? A Soviet diplomat felt that
change would come about in time within the younger generation. This
feeling of insecurity and inferiority will diminish with an awareness
of Russia's growing power and strength. Memories of World War II
and reconstruction linger on; the insecurity that these experiences
brought to the mind of a child are not easily lost. But with the passage
of time and the continued growth of Soviet power this historic feeling of insecurity will diminish.

[3] U.S. Congress. Senate. Committee on Foreign Relations. Perceptions: Relations Between the United States and the Soviet Union. Washington, D.C., U.S. Government
Printing Office, 1979, p. 94. (Italics added.)
[4] Time, Feb. 26, 1979: p. 17.
[5] Senate Foreign Relations Committee, Perceptions Between the United States and
the Soviet Union, p. 94.
[6] The Christian Science Monitor, Nov. 25, 1977, p. 1.
[7] Samuel Pisar, a long-time specialist in Soviet affairs, explained the Soviet "paranoid
preoccupation with security" and citing the case of China as an additional source of fears,
wrote: "Today, that population is subject to the added fear of a growing threat from China.
I recall how, at the high-level Soviet-American meeting in Kiev in July 1971, our eminent
Soviet hosts, including Georgi Arbatov, the Kremlin's foremost adviser on American affairs,
could hardly contain their consternation when the news broke that Kissinger had just
completed a secret mission to Peking." (Pisar, Samuel. Let's Put Détente Back on the Rails.
The New York Times Magazine, Sept. 25, 1977: 112.) Even a cursory review of Soviet
materials on China reveals just how deep Soviet anxieties are over this dispute and how
it stimulates deep-rooted concerns for security in the Soviet far east. In the Soviet view,
the Chinese have replaced the Japanese as a threat on this front. In the early 1920's the
Japanese had invaded the Soviet far eastern provinces, and in the 1930's an undeclared
war broke out between both countries. Soviet concerns, therefore, are not illusory, but are
rooted in their history.
[8] Time, Jan. 29, 1979: 17.

Ambassador Beam was not so sanguine, even given the growth of Soviet power. "None of them trust each other," he said; the problem is "really endemic," going back to the days of the Tartar conquest.[9]

To Gen. Samuel Wilson, former head of the Defense Intelligence Agency and a specialist in Soviet affairs who had extensive tours of duty in Moscow, the Soviets will never feel comfortable until they have a ratio in strength of 7 or 8:1. "They might relax," he said, "if it were 15:1."[10]

Sonnenfeldt suggested the possibility of an easing of Soviet security fears should it ever forgo the amassing of military power and join into the international system on terms of an acceptable balance of power. (This concept is discussed on p. 541.)

Thus the Soviets cannot escape their history. It seems to have left a lasting imprint upon the psyche of the nation and established an enduring pattern of thought and action that defines the outer limits of their national interests in terms of an exaggerated sense of absolute security.[11] Cognizant of their own economic, political, and military vulnerability and seeking solutions to their problems and satisfaction for their fears through the further amassing of military power, the Soviets seem caught in an interacting cycle of challenge and response in their relationship with the United States, the driving force of which is a quest for an unachievable absolute security. This obsession with security is, therefore, an enduring historic reality; it has become bureaucratized and its durability reinforced by national policy and Soviet doctrine: To a large extent it is for the Soviets a self-inflicting wound.[11a]

B. IMPERATIVES OF IDEOLOGY

1. QUEST FOR LEGITIMACY

The imperatives of ideology provide another component of permanency in the Soviet approach to diplomacy and negotiations. Ideology, it is true, is on the decline, but more as a specific operational principle in managing the state than as a philosophic principle providing the underpinning, the raison d'etre, of the regime and the larger design of the world and the direction it is going.

In large measure ideology gives the Soviets what they seem to crave most, next to security, and that is legitimacy. In essence the Soviet Union is a revolutionary state and its ideology a revolutionary

---

[9] Interview with Jacob Beam. May 23, 1979.

[10] Address by Gen. Samuel Wilson, Whithall Pavilion, Library of Congress, Nov. 15, 1978.

[11] National characteristics, once deeply embedded in a nation, have an enduring quality. It is an instruction for Americans of the 1970's to read Alexis de Toqueville's book, "Democracy in America" and in many respects see in his penetrating observations a mirror of themselves. This book, considered a classic of its kind, was published in 1840, based on De Toqueville's travels in the young American Republic.

[11a] For a vivid account of the travails of an American historian attempting to do research in Soviet library facilities, see, Byrnes, Robert F. Moscow Revisited: Summer 1978. Survey, vol. 23, Autumn 1977–1978: 1–18, Dr. Byrnes is the Distinguished Professor of History at Indiana University. Director of the University's Russian and East European Institute, and a noted specialist on Soviet affairs. His account places in high relief Soviet restrictions on access to information—in this case harmless historical data ; Soviet restrictions on relationships between their scholars and visiting foreign scholars, even in this case of an American scholar visiting and doing research under an official exchange with the Academy of Sciences ; and, finally, the gross inequity between the treatment accorded Soviet scholars in the United States whose libraries and research facilities are available on an unrestricted basis and that accorded to Americans in the Soviet Union whose purposes are suspect and freedom of research restricted accordingly. In brief, here is a classic account showing Russian distrust of the foreigner, the Russian obsession with security—even in protecting their historical past, and the inefficiency and frustrations perpetuated by a binding bureaucratic control.

ideology. It has broken the natural line of European historical development where legitimacy in its 19th century meaning lingers on as a significant principle and seeks to establish a new legitimacy on the revolutionary principles of Marxism-Leninism. Its claims of a symbiotic relationship with the national liberation movements of the Third World and its revolutionary message to its leaders fortify the belief in mankind's redemption through socialism. This is the messianism of the new Russia carried on from the old but in a changed form. As Simes put it: "The centuries-old Russian messianism serves as a convenient substitute for Communist internationalism." [12] The Soviet elite cannot deny this belief for in so doing they will deny their own self-proclaimed criterion for legitimacy.

2. IDEOLOGY AS MOTIVE POWER

In a more practical sense ideology provides two other essential Soviet needs: The larger design of the world's destiny and the motive power for achieving its larger foreign policy goals. Soviet ideology is a philosophy of history, parallel, but in a worldly and secular sense, to St. Augustine's "City of God." However imperfect its prescriptions and flawed its goals and purposes, the Soviet believer holds to its truths and these truths sketch out a larger design of the world's future destiny which is communism. This ideology, an acknowledged "good" as an assured truth, gives elan, a sense of purpose, a sense of meaning to the Soviet believer and provides the inner dynamic to achieve its goals.

Thus, as this study shows, Khrushchev could not agree to Kennedy's preception of a world balance of power and his prescription for a mutual recognition of it. This would be the surrendering of a vital principle based on the assumption that the world, far from being static, was moving in the direction of socialism. The explosion of the national liberation movement in the Third World was his evidence.

For the same reason, Brezhnev has insisted, as noted above, that there can be no détente in ideology, meaning that the "struggle" goes on along an historically predestined course, and in this struggle the Soviet Union must support the national liberation movements or forfeit its "sacred" cause, its birthright.

In this sense, therefore, ideology insures an incompatibility of purposes in East-West relations. For the Soviets it is a vital and enduring concept. As Simes wrote: "The Soviet elite is not in a position to renounce the sacred international liberationist mission that the U.S.S.R. claims is its destiny." [13] And for the United States and the West, it is a central issue in contention. The contest has been joined in the Third World where ideology and conflicting power interests meet.

Thus, as instruments of the Soviet state and an integral part of its superstructure, diplomacy and negotiations inevitably reflect the purposes of its ideology. In turn, ideology, which gives the decisionmaker a tool of analysis in foreign policy, reinforces the uniqueness of the Soviet approach to diplomacy and negotiations, endowing it with preserving elements that insure its permanence.

---

[12] Senate Foreign Relations Committee, Perceptions in Relations Between the United States and the Soviet Union, pp. 93–94.
[13] Ibid., p. 93.

C. Imperatives of the Political System

1. INSTITUTIONAL PERMANENCY

The imperatives of the political system provide still another component of permanency in the Soviet approach to diplomacy and negotiations. It is now 62 years since the Bolshevik revolution. The political system has survived civil war, internal chaos in its aftermath, the debilitating Great Purge, a devastating World War II and demanding reconstruction, the stresses of the cold war, the burden of globalism, and the internal and external challenges of détente. The party maintains its monopoly of power and authority; the institutions, however flawed from the democratic perspective, remain intact; dissidents on the periphery have been silenced.

Soviet success, despite known economic weaknesses and serious shortcomings in technology, has been affirmed, if not by demonstrable internal realities, then by its recognition as a superpower, so that Brezhnev can rightly claim that virtually no major world problem can be resolved without Soviet participation.

In brief, the party is in control, the institutions in place: Their permanency, at least in the near future and perhaps even in the more distant future, seem assured.

2. EFFECTS UPON THE FOREIGN POLICY STRUCTURE AND ESTABLISHMENT

(a) Predetermined existence

Encased in this larger static, highly bureaucratized political and institutional structure, the foreign policy establishment has virtually a predetermined existence. Foreign policy is made in the upper reaches of the Politburo and controlled by the party apparatus either directly or by the dual party/government role of officials in the foreign affairs area. The Foreign Ministry and the diplomats are an appendage of the political system, an instrument for implementation. Whatever changes occur, for better or worse, must ultimately be directed from within this firmly set institutional framework.

Since foreign policy is an unchanging prerogative of Soviet decisionmakers at the top, Soviet diplomacy and negotiating style, its instrumentalities, will invariably reflect the requirements of that policy. As this study shows, except for the basic characteristics cited below, there is no single comprehensive Soviet style in diplomacy and negotiations, but rather a behavior that is generally adapted to the specific needs of the times: Hostility in the era of the Nazi-Soviet pact and the cold war, a diplomacy of weakness; calculated conciliation during the Grand Alliance and the Khrushchev-Brezhnev era of peaceful coexistence, a diplomacy of strength.

(b) Enduring characteristics in diplomacy and negotiations

Nonetheless, as this study also shows, certain characteristics in the Soviet approach to diplomacy and negotiations are common to all eras. The following suggest some of the more basic and tractable characteristics:

—*Respect for power.*—As Simes said, "The Russians have a traditional respect for power." [13a] Power is the alpha and omega in

[13a] Senate Foreign Relations Committee, Perceptions on Relations Between the United States and Soviet Union, p. 94.

the Soviet conduct of diplomacy and negotiations. The vital center is a determination of what they call, "the correlation of forces," meaning not just military power, but the total aggregate of power: Military, political, economic, and social. Paramount, however, is the amassing of military power. Since 1956, the Soviets have claimed that the balance of forces have tilted in their favor and against the West. This calculation is based on the erroneous assumption that a symbiotic relationship exists between world communism and the socialist-oriented regimes in the Third World.

Implied in this respect for power, applicable at all levels of negotiations, is recognition of its leverage as a central element in any negotiations. Also implied is Soviet disdain for weakness and uncertainty. (Recall Khrushchev's critical appraisal of President Eisenhower.)[14]

—*Appreciation of Realism.*—A corollary to respect for power is the high value placed upon realism. Sentimentality plays no role in Soviet negotiations, except as a calculated ploy as in the case of the Nixon-Brezhnev encounter at San Clemente when a tearful Brezhnev could within an hour become a hard-hitting negotiator on the offensive against his adversary. The Soviets pride themselves on their realism, and they respect it in others. Observers have noted that President Nixon's hard realism in negotiating with the Soviet leaders had been a positive factor in his ability to establish a rapport with them and to achieve some successes in negotiations. (Recall the background of the May 1972 summit, the bombing of the DRV and his visit to China; both were interpreted as provocations to the Soviets, having occurred immediately prior to his Moscow visit.)

Associated with this characteristic of realism is Soviet determination to achieve their national interests as a principal negotiating target. Thus for Stalin at Yalta, the question of Poland's future was for all practical purposes nonnegotiable; Kennedy's perception of the balance of power was for Khrushchev similarly nonnegotiable; and in the extreme, Dubcek's effort to put a "human face on socialism" in Czechoslovakia was for Brezhnev nonnegotiable—all impinged on vital Soviet national security interests,

[14] The Russian respect for power and its correlation with diplomacy was well expressed by Nicolson in his study on the Congress of Vienna. "Better the French as enemies than the Russians as friends," was an expression that won swift acceptance at the Congress. Nicolson wrote: "The Russian generals and diplomatists * * * having convinced themselves that Russian arms alone had liberated Europe from an odious tyranny, being intoxicated by the military prestige which Russia had unexpectedly acquired, began on every occasion and in every country to indulge in self-assertiveness and intrigue. 'Well, so far as that goes,' boasted a Russian general when discussing the impending Congress, 'one does not need to worry about negotiations when one has 600,000 men under arms'." (Nicolson, Harold. The Congress of Vienna. New York, Harcourt Brace, 1946, p. 187, quoted in Newhouse, op. cit., p. 57.)

The relationship of leverage to power in dealing with the Russians was very persuasively illustrated by Dr. Marshall I. Goldman, an American specialist on Soviet economics, who had been a Fulbright lecturer at Moscow State University in 1977. Goldman skillfully used leverage when his wife, a research specialist in Chinese affairs at Harvard University, had been persistently denied an interview with a specialist at the Academy of Sciences during her 2-week stay in Moscow. Finally after being put off many times (the last excuse the Soviets gave was that the specialist had gone on vacation and would not be back until after she departed), Goldman took action: "I pointed out to his secretary that Soviet Sinologists frequently seek interviews at Harvard's East Asian Center, where my wife is a research associate, and that they have always been warmly received. 'If my wife is not received by your institute on Monday, she will do her best to insure that in the future, Harvard's Center will not welcome your specialists.' " There was a pause: "Just a moment." Another pause, and then, "Fine. She can come at 9 o'clock on Monday." (Goldman, Marshall I. Winning and Losing at Soviet "Football." Teaching in Moscow—III. The New York Times, Jan. 27, 1973, p. A25.)

523

—*Value of total diplomacy.*—Khrushchev demonstrated the Soviet habit of bringing all conceivable instrumentalities to bear in negotiations. He epitomized the idea that negotiations are a continuing political process that go beyond the strict confines of the negotiating table. Hence, he resorted to such external devices as propaganda, threats, public demonstrations, and dramatic space launchings—all, for the political purpose of advancing his position, intimidating his adversary and putting him on the defensive. In the same manner, Brezhnev and other Soviet officials have resorted to many of the same devices, but at a far lower key of dissonance. The Soviet propaganda machine is never silenced and is always geared to ongoing or upcoming negotiations. (Recall the recent visit of the delegation of Senators to Moscow and the diatribe by Kosygin.)

—*Toughness.*—A common threat running through this study is Soviet toughness in negotiations. Whatever the period of the negotiations, whether it was Roosevelt negotiating with Stalin, Kennedy with Khrushchev, or Nixon with Brezhnev, the Soviets have invariably demonstrated that they are remarkably tough negotiators. This characteristic has also been abundantly displayed at the lower level of negotiations. The durability of this characteristic is evident by the recent comment of a senior European diplomat with respect to the Yugoslav temptation to concede as much as possible on the nonvital areas in negotiations with the Soviets: "But the Russians are tough negotiators. They take what you give them—and then they demand more." [15]

—*"You can't bank goodwill."*—Linked to realism and toughness is the belief among American negotiators that with the Russians, "You can't bank goodwill." American negotiators had used this expression consistently in recalling their wartime experiences. The expression implies the importance of the "quid pro quo" in dealing with the Soviets. But this is a durable characteristic, as recently demonstrated in the American effort to build a new embassy in Moscow. Against the background of the ongoing SALT II negotiations—the negotiations began in May 1972—and the Vienna summit in June 1979, the United States had been negotiating with the Soviet Union to get an agreement that would allow

---

[15] Dobbs, Michael. Tito-Brezhnev Talks Focus Attention on Yugoslav Future. The Washington Post, May 17, 1979, A21. Recall that Ambassador Standley said essentially the same thing to Secretary Hull upon his departure for the Moscow Conference in October 1943: "Watch for their self-interest. And take care of our own. They're mighty skillful negotiators, with all the trumps. * * * They don't ever give anything away, Mr. Secretary, not even for something." (Standley and Ageton, op. cit., p. 500.)

Soviet toughness and resort to abusive tactics were recently demonstrated at a "stormy private luncheon" at the Madison Hotel in Washington, where Soviet Foreign Trade Minister Nikolai S. Patolichev met with American industrialists and high-ranking government officials. At the luncheon Senator Ribicoff remarked that congressional action to grant MFN to the Soviet Union was unlikely without Soviet action to ease restrictions on Jewish emigration. The press report continued: "Raising his voice and his fist and sometimes pointing his finger, Patolichev mounted what a witness called a 'Khrushchev-like' response. At one point he claimed that only 1 percent of Soviet Jews wish to emigrate and at another point declared that 'all you are concerned about is Jews.'" He charged that "provocateurs" were trying to spoil Soviet-American relations by raising the emigration issue and insisted that the Soviet Union did not need American business: "We don't want your trade—we can live without it." A participant at the luncheon interpreted Patolichev's denunciation "as a relatively standard Russian means of showing displeasure through shock tactics." "It was unusual from our point of view," he said, "but not so unusual from the Russian point of view." Nonetheless, the incident, according to the report, "cast a pall over the meeting of Americans and Russians leading to further pessimism about the chances of trade advances." The luncheon was given by the executive board of the U.S.-U.S.S.R. Trade and Economic Council in honor of Patolichev. (Oberdorfer, Don. Soviet Trade Minister Denounces U.S. Policy. The Washington Post, June 15 ,1977, p. A26.)

each side to build a new embassy and other facilities in the other side's capital. Each was to move in simultaneously. In an apparent good will gesture, the United States had long ago approved the building of the Soviet Embassy in Washington. No such approval came from the Soviet side. The Soviets were "clamoring" to move in; neither a contract had been drawn nor a spade of dirt turned in Moscow by early May. The Washington Post of May 4, 1979, carried an editorial entitled, "Mr. Good Guy," explaining the futility of expecting reciprocation for acts motivated by good will.[16] On June 30, the Soviet Union and the United States ended the dispute with the signing of a contract for a new American Embassy complex in Moscow. Construction on the new Embassy is scheduled to begin in early October and the new Moscow complex was expected to be completed in late 1983. The Soviets can now move into their new Washington complex. During the delay in negotiations U.S. authorities held up the Soviet move.[17]

—*Control from the Center and the Binding Bureaucracy.*—It is axiomatic that Soviet negotiators still function on a very tight rein, far more so than the Americans. Such behavior inevitably creates delays and frustrations, calling on great reserves of patience and other virtues from the other side. Suggestive in many of the encounters examined in this study is the negative role played by the binding Soviet bureaucracy, the effect of which is to cause delays, build up frustrations, and encourage initiatives from the other side. Such initiatives carry the risk of self-negotiations, but they also can give the advantage of staking out an area of one's choosing for negotiations. The extreme case showing the value of initiatives was that of General Eaker when near the end of the war he arbitrarily established the bombing line in southeastern Europe after the failure of a Soviet response to his request. This action relieved the Soviets of a decision that would have had to be made through the bureaucracy on up to even Stalin. They did not complain about the General's arbitrary action.

Other characteristics have been pointed out in the course of this study, but those cited above seem to be the most durable. Many are normal with any country (or for that matter, any individual) in any negotiating environment; others are distinctively Soviet. What is important to discern in judging the permanency of such characteristics is the time-frame. For to the Soviets, diplomacy and negotiations are really political instruments; they are weapons to achieve political goals; and in times of weakness when "defensive diplomacy" is the chosen course of diplomacy, as in the cold war, the more disruptive, unpleasant characteristics are put on display: Deception, the tactics of

---

[16] The Washington Post concluded its editorial: "It is a painful spectacle and, especially if the United States does not play it right from this point onward, it will make many Americans ask if the Carter administration is negotiating on SALT any more effectively than it has on the embassies. The Russians have behaved like Russians, turning American impatience and good will to their own advantage, exploiting every comma, frustrating and tiring their negotiating partners. But have the Americans behaved like * * * Americans? The Carter administration's decision to let the Russians start building first looks pathetic in retrospect. If the administration were to be equally 'reasonable' now and to heed Soviet pleas to allow the new premises to be occupied, it would have only itself to blame for the inevitable adverse effect on its efforts to get approval for other deals it makes with the Russians." (Mr. Nice Guy. Editorial. The Washington Post, May 4, 1979, p. A20.)
[17] The Washington Post, July 1, 1979, p. A6.

abuse, outright distortions, arrogance, incivility—all of the negative characteristics described above by those negotiators who faced the Russians in the cold war and that had so debased the profession of diplomacy. In the present era, dating since the Cuban missile crisis and the conclusion of the Nuclear Test Ban Treaty, Soviet behavior has been modified and indeed moderated, so that except for periodic displays of coarseness and bad behavior, as by Brezhnev and other Soviet leaders, the general trend is toward traditionalism in the wider European sense of the term. Caution ought to be exercised, therefore, in analyzing Soviet negotiating behavior, making sure of the correct correlation of behavior with the periods when the encounters took place.[17a]

[17a] For a recent analysis of Soviet negotiating behavior in economic and commercial bargaining, see, U.S. Central Intelliegnce Agency. National Foreign Assessment Center. Soviet Strategy and Tactics in Economic and Commercial Negotiations with the United States. A Research Paper. Washington, June 1979. 11 pp. (ER79–10276). Reproduced in the appendix.

III. CHANGING ASPECTS OF SOVIET DIPLOMACY AND NEGOTIATIONS

A. INSTITUTIONAL CHANGES

The imperatives of security, ideology, and the political system endow Soviet diplomacy and negotiating behavior with a certain institutional permanency. But within these institutions significant changes are taking place that could modify, not necessarily the outer authoritarian structure of the party and state, but rather the inner direction of Soviet policy and possibly even the future development of the Soviet Union itself.

The foreign policy establishment, as this study shows, has been transformed in the Khrushchev-Brezhnev era. It has become intellectualized, though in a restricted Soviet sense. A new breed of diplomat is being produced, recruited from a new generation of a young questioning elite whose professionalism is highly respected. Gromyko's position on the Politburo has opened up an avenue of direct access to the elite power brokers heretofore never available. The prestige of the establishment has increased accordingly.

Supporting institutes in the Academy of Sciences, notably the USA and Canada Institute and the Institute of World Economy and International Relations, provide on a continuing basis a meaningful contribution to the foreign policy process, giving the Soviet decisionmaker wider options of choice than those provided by the normal inflow of information. These products, as well as the positions of influence held by such officials as Arbatov and Inozemtsev, broaden the avenue of access to influence.

Perhaps most important of all, the Politburo is no longer a closed association of self-sufficient corporate leaders. Responding to the demands of managing a modern industrial state of enormous complexity, to the human desire for success, to the unique moral imperatives of Marxist-Leninist ideology, and to the deeper compulsions to hold on to power, the leadership has opened up avenues of access to the experts and professionals from the academies and the institutes. Elements of a new constituency whose power is knowledge and expertise have taken shape outside the strict formal confines of the party. Within the party itself as well as in the Government, the criterion has been shifting from one of strict political professionalism to the professionalism of the specialist in science, technology, and in the running of a complex national economy. A new generation of trained specialists whose mentality is geared to the management of a modern industrial state is waiting in the wings; in some areas the transition has already begun.

Thus, the formal institutions of the Soviet state may seem stolid and static, but important institutional changes are taking place within them that could have an important impact on Soviet foreign policy.

B. Decline of Ideology

Along with these institutional changes there has been a decline of ideology, not in its larger cosmic application but rather in the day-to-day management of the state and as a device for solving concrete problems. Scholars agree with Ambassador Beam's judgment that "ideology is just dry bread." [1]

To Adam Ulam, a specialist in Soviet affairs at Harvard University, "as a guide to actual policies, ideology takes a back seat. * * *" [2] And Prof. Arthur Lall suggested the following general principle with respect to ideology and negotiations:

At the negotiating table, or in informal negotiations or exchanges, the ideological beliefs of a country tend to have little influence on its demands and attitudes regarding matters of substance. Its assessment of its own best advantage in terms of material gain or military power, and the general protection and promotion of its other vital interests, will predominantly determine its conduct. [3]

Pragmatism, therefore, predominates Soviet decisionmaking; ideology, except in certain instances noted above, is a wasting, expendable commodity.

C. Effects of Institutional Changes and Decline of Ideology

1. ON SOVIET DIPLOMACY AND NEGOTIATING BEHAVIOR

The effects of these institutional changes and the decline of ideology, aided by changing power realities, are twofold: (1) to modify and moderate the style of Soviet diplomacy and negotiating behavior; and (2) to pull the Soviet Union more decisively into participating in the emerging international order.

With respect to the first point, there seems little doubt that Soviet diplomacy and negotiating behavior have been modified and moderated substantially in the late Khrushchev and Brezhnev eras. Soviet diplomacy is no longer carried out in the tyrannically paranoid style of Stalin or in the buccaneering style of early Khrushchev. Except for isolated, periodic displays of the old "Brest-Litovsk style" by Brezhnev and other senior Soviet officials, the general tenor of Soviet negotiating is one of European traditionalism, flavored, however, with unique Soviet ingredients. Perhaps Garthoff best summed up this change when he concluded:

Today there is a greater Soviet readiness to look for possible agreements on a broad range of issues. Compromise is no longer a taboo for Soviet negotiators. In part, this reflects increased Soviet sophistication. It also reflects growing self-confidence. To this extent, the growth of Soviet strength to a level of near equality with the United States has produced not greater intransigence but a more businesslike approach. Agreements on mutually advantageous strategic arms limitations are not easy to reach—but they are attainable. [4]

What accounts for this changing approach is the shift in the correlation of forces and the Soviet thrust toward strategic parity with the

---

[1] Interview with Jacob D. Beam, May 23, 1979.
[2] Senate Foreign Relations Committee, Perceptions in Relations Between the United States and the Soviet Union, p. 132.
[3] Lall. op. cit., p. 287.
[4] Garthoff, Wilson Quarterly, p. 85. Professor Richard Pipes, an historian specializing in the Soviet Union at Harvard University, wrote: "Whenever they happen to be interested in a settlement, Communist diplomats act in a traditional manner, efficiently and undeterred by difficulties." (Quoted in, Jonsson, op. cit., p. 77.)

United States. Perhaps for the first time in Soviet history, its leaders are negotiating from "a position of strength"—a term coined by Secretary Acheson during the cold war and viscerally loathed by the Soviets even to this day. A defensive diplomacy of weakness with all its unpleasant and disruptive manifestations has given way to a diplomacy of strength and confidence. And stripped of its outer layer of an outdated and selectively irrelevant ideology, Soviet diplomacy reflects the most basic of all considerations in foreign policy, power. This explains the reversion to the old-fashioned traditionalism of European diplomacy, a traditionalism that was fundamentally based on and nourished by a balance of power.

It is, therefore, possible to agree with Christer Jonsson with respect to Soviet negotiating behavior when he wrote: "The unavoidable conclusion emerging from our study is that it does not seem very meaningful to speak of any one unique, invariable Soviet negotiating behavior." [5] For there are many styles and forms of Soviet diplomacy and negotiating behavior; they are adapted to the times; and as instruments of the party that style reflects the preferences of the leadership; and their preferences are based upon considerations of power and the correlation of forces.

What seems most significant about the change in Soviet diplomacy and negotiating behavior is, however, the possibility of its permanence, at least in the near future. Power is the principal criterion in Soviet diplomacy. The existence of strategic equality and the creation of a mutually acceptable balance of power would seem to argue for a continuation of this traditionalism.

2. PULL TOWARD THE EMERGING INTERNATIONAL SYSTEM

The second effect of the institutional changes and the decline of ideology, at least indirectly, is the pull of the Soviet Union more decisively into participation in the emerging international order. The movement from continentalism to globalism under Khrushchev was the primary force in revitalizing, creating, and expanding the Soviet Union's foreign policy institutes and improving the entire diplomatic establishment. In response to this basic policy shift, this vast Soviet infrastructure for diplomacy has established the intellectual basis and nourished the ideas for carrying out the Soviet global policy.

Other factors have also drawn the Soviet Union into the emerging international system:

—The realities of the nuclear age that have required not only agreement on transcending bilateral strategic issues with the United States but also addressing the multilateral problem of nuclear proliferation around the world;

—The emerging era of interdependence that makes Soviet involvement an imperative since size and military power are no longer the sole criteria for influence in this era of science and technology but rather the role of resources in a world in short supply and the interdependency of nations in matters of technology and economic development; and, finally,

[5] Ibid.

—The emergence of a complex multipolar political world, stimulated by the regeneration of the nation-states in the Third World and the evolution of varying centers of power in response to a new distribution of world power which, along with other elements, has produced a new era of diplomacy and negotiations.

Satisfaction of national interests, whatever the social structure of the state, requires global involvement, especially for a nation with the size and power of the Soviet Union. This is the historical imperative of the modern age. Thus, Sonnenfeldt could conclude:

* * * the Soviet Union can never return to the isolation cell to which Stalin condemned it to make his brand of socialism in one country a reality at home and a virtual impossibility abroad. That isolation is now past history, though there is probably little the Soviets can do for years to come to make themselves "beautiful Russians" around the world. By the same token, the costs and risks of using power for political ends, and the impediments to doing so, are amply present in the world at large. And the world at large, in all its variety, increasingly stretches its influence into domains hitherto controlled by the Soviet rulers.[6]

D. WESTERNIZERS VERSUS SLAVOPHILES

Considerations on the permanent and changing aspects of the Soviet approach to diplomacy and negotiations occurring within the larger changing structure of international relations lead inevitably to speculation on the future; and that in turn brings up the Shulman thesis with respect to the problem of the Westernizers versus the Slavophiles.

Some experienced observers of the Soviet scene—literally—offer no great hope of change to the better in the next generation of leaders. Asked in January 1979 if he foresaw any significant change in Soviet foreign or domestic policy when the current generation gives way to the next, U.S. Ambassador to the Soviet Union, Malcolm Toon said:

Not with the next generation. The people we think might possibly succeed to power think basically the same way as the current leadership. The important thing to recognize, it seems to me, is that Soviet policies are by and large a function of events, world conditions and circumstances rather than being linked to any particular personality. When you have a change in the personalities at the top that does not necessarily mean that you're going to see a change in policy. Policies will remain more or less the same.[7]

Others are more sanguine. Dr. Cyril E. Black, a noted American specialist on Soviet affairs and director of the Center of International Studies at Princeton University, linked the upcoming new generation with harmonious relations with the West. He explained:

Closely related to this transformation of ideology has been a generational change that has affected all aspects of Soviet society. The men and women rising to positions of influence in the 1970's are more confident than their parents in the legitimacy of the Soviet system, more concerned with material welfare, and better equipped in terms of education and knowledge of the outside world to assert their values. While reaffirming the high priority assigned in the past to the economic and social development of Soviet society, the new generation has a much more pragmatic sense of what is involved in societal transformation and a greater recognition that progress toward this goal calls for harmonious relations with the West.[8]

---

[6] Sonnenfeldt, Russia, America and Détente, p. 291.

[7] Interview with U.S. Ambassador to Moscow: Reflections on the Soviet Union and Its Goals. Los Angeles Times, Jan. 8, 1979, pp. 18–19. Ambassador Beam was also skeptical about the successor leadership, but he felt it was hard to speculate on the course of future policy until one knew who was going to be in power. (Interview with Jacob D. Beam. May 23, 1979.)

[8] Senate Foreign Relations Committee, Perceptions in Relations Between the United States and the Soviet Union, p. 103.

Black made this projection of what he perceived to be the direction of Russia's future:

Change in Soviet society flows essentially from the generational evolution of values on the part of the great majority of politically active citizens who are party members and non-party supporters of the system, and the trend in this realm is toward greater freedom of criticism and debate, a more pragmatic approach to policy, and recognition that cooperative relations with the West are in the Soviet interest. While temporary reversions to dogmatism and nationalism may occur, especially if foreign threats are perceived to Soviet security, the long-term trend toward a gradually increasing pluralism is likely to prevail.[9]

Dr. Simes is similarly persuaded that the next generation is quite different from the old—and he can speak from personal experience as a member of that young Soviet generation of intelligentsia who was given the option to emigrate to America only a few years ago. The new successor generation, he said, may be strikingly different from the old: They had not suffered from or during World War II; for them this is only an experience in history books, not a reality. They know the reality of Soviet power as they are now experiencing it. But they take a more pragmatic, power-oriented look at international relations; they are less ideological in approach. They see the United States more as a rival superpower than in the ideological dimension. Convinced that it was possible to work with this power-oriented generation, Simes, like Shulman, suggested a policy course that would offer the new generation the possibilities of integration into the international system.[10]

As the decade of the 1970's draws to a close, the Soviet Union seems to be approaching a very important time, perhaps a critical time, in its history. Despite the permanency of its institutions, important changes are occurring within that could have a significant impact upon the direction of its future. The older generation of leaders and their associates in the party will soon be leaving the scene, handing over the reins of power to a generation much younger, more sophisticated, more imbued with the values of this postindustrial age of science and technology. However the issue of the Westernizers versus the Slavophiles is ultimately resolved, and the tilt now seems to be in favor of the former, it must for the moment remain an open question; but its meaning for the future is clear. That these generational changes in this era of transition will have great implications for U.S. foreign policy, there seems to be little doubt.

---

[9] Ibid., p. 106.
[10] Horn of Africa: Lessons for an African Policy and for U.S.–U.S.S.R. Relations. Seminar. Georgetown University, Center for Strategic and International Studies, Apr. 12, 1978.

IV. IMPLICATIONS FOR U.S. FOREIGN POLICY

A. Diplomacy and Negotiations: Instruments of Accommodation and Stability

1. NEW OPPORTUNITIES; NEW BURDENS

There are two major implications suggested in this study for U.S. foreign policy in its relations with the Soviet Union: One is that diplomacy and negotiations provide the instrumentalities for accommodation in the Soviet-American relationship; the other is that the balance-of-power factor provides the theoretical mechanism for establishing a viable relationship between the two adversaries in the future, thus giving greater assurance of peace in the world, provided that the potentialities of confrontation and crisis in the Third World can be avoided.

Diplomacy and negotiations as instruments of accommodation and stability present new opportunities and impose new burdens for U.S. foreign policy. This possibility arises from the belief that the world is entering an era of renewal for diplomacy and negotiations, and from the growing tendency in Soviet diplomacy and negotiating behavior to revert to forms, and perhaps even the norms, of traditional diplomatic behavior as understood in the Western diplomatic tradition.

Diplomacy and negotiations offer the possibility of bringing the Soviet Union into an acceptable international system, a development that could have a moderating influence on Soviet policy. The imperatives of international relations in the modern era, sketched out above, act as a magnetic force pulling the Soviets into this system. As Legvold wrote, the Soviet Union has a "growing stake in what for it has long been a repugnant international order."[1] The most compelling of these forces is the necessity of avoiding a nuclear war.[2]

A factor only slightly less compelling for bringing the Soviets into the international system is the opportunity provided by peaceful coexistence or détente. Peaceful coexistence does not mean the dissolution of the Soviet-American rivalry, for this contest goes on, stimulated by the dynamic forces of power and ideology. But there is a difference between this era and that of the cold war, and it is that

---

[1] Legvold, op. cit., p. 68. Legvold noted the changing complexity of the international order, citing such changes as the "filled power vacuums in Europe and Asia, the fractured monolith of socialism and most of all the shadow of nuclear war"—all of which "have transformed the context in which we contemplate Soviet ambition." Citing the growing Soviet stake in the international order, he concluded: "The paradox stems not only from the Soviet Union's commitment to economic cooperation with the West and the utility it sees in, say, a stable law of the seas, but also from the disruptions it cannot afford to sponsor if it counts on Western forbearance in the face of its growing global role."

[2] On this point Lester Pearson wrote: "A sane and enlightened diplomacy * * * will always realize that in today's nuclear world where man now has the power of eliminating himself, national interests cannot any longer be separated from humanity itself. Indeed, by far the greatest national interest is, and must remain, the prevention of a war which would destroy humanity." (Pearson, op. cit., p. 33.)

peaceful coexistence, as Legvold concluded, "introduces the new prospect of managing, not merely maintaining" the rivalry through diplomacy. The task of managing this rivalry, no one doubts, will remain extraordinarily difficult.[3]

For Americans, a major consideration for the future would seem to be how they perceive the emerging global system and how they view their role and that of the Soviet Union within it. Some with a mindset of the cold war era, not appreciating the constraints on Soviet power in the Third World and the new potentialities for advantage that the Soviets might want to seek within a new global system, might contend that the international system has not changed. Others might hold that a new system is emerging, but that it is taking on the values and preferences of the West without making allowances for those of the Soviet Union and the Third World who as outsiders must join the system on the West's terms. Still others hold that a new international system is, indeed, developing based on the imperatives of interdependence that requires to an extent much greater than ever before a diplomacy of common purpose.[4]

On the assumption that this last perception is correct, and many signs point in that direction (e.g., necessity of avoiding nuclear war and of coping with the problem of energy), then Americans would have to address the question, as Legvold suggested, of how the Soviets

[3] Legvold continued: "It is an historic opportunity but one with almost insuperable internal tensions. For, on the one hand, we in our rivalry are challenged to collaborate consciously and explicitly in order to moderate the contest; on the other hand, we in our collaboration must cope with the permanent reality of the contest, a reality constantly underscored by global instabilities and constantly heightened by the evolution of the Soviet Union's military power. The delicate task of designing and perhaps even codifying the 'rules of the game,' if that is what we set out to do in the Moscow agreements of 1972, is continually interrupted by moments of chaos when in Chile, Angola, Indochina or perhaps Yugoslavia our conflicting interests are reemphasized." (Legvold, op. cit., p. 69.)

[4] On the matter of interdependence, Legvold wrote: "If one starts with interdependence, that complex network of involvements dominating so many of the stakes in international politics, including the structure of the international economic order, the Soviet Union's influence remains marginal. It will not do to dismiss this state of affairs as the Soviet Union's choice, as a game it prefers not to play, and may be the better off thereby. For clearly the Soviet Union *has* chosen to play and would like to play more, were the rules more within its control. Increasingly it has a stake in interdependence but little leverage over the governing institutions and rules." Legvold commented later on: "* * * in an interdependent world, self-sufficiency is inefficiency, increasingly so in the Soviet Union, and the Soviet leadership knows it." (Legvold, op. cit., pp. 57-58.)

Schwartz also underscored the importance of advancing the principle of interdependence within the larger context of détente and the necessity of reinforcing the tendency toward moderation particularly after the departure of Brezhnev by stressing the benefits of détente to the Soviet Union. Schwartz urged that "special attention" should be focused on what the Soviets have increasingly called questions of "pan-human" or "global" scale. Inozemtsev, the Director of the Institute for World Economy and International Relations, has in particular been stressing the existence of common problems confronting all nations of whatever social system, problems deriving, as he described it *"from contradictions in the development of the human race as a whole."* Among these problems he focused on two: the prevention of a new world war which is "the prime task of all mankind, on it depends 'the preservation of human society,'" and environmental questions—depletion of resources, pollution of the environment, population growth—"problems of the greatest import from the point of view of future prospects," he wrote. Schwartz quoted another Soviet source, as an example of moderate elements within the Soviet foreign policy infrastructure, that said, "the emergence of progressively new problems on a global scale" required "joint efforts by all states," and that "peaceful competition not only does not rule out but on the contrary presupposes the widescale development of mutually advantageous cooperation among states." (Schwartz, op. cit., pp. 168-169.)

A confirming Soviet view on solutions to global problems was made by V. Zagladin and I. Frolov in the May 1979 issue of Kommunist. In this most authoritative party journal the authors critically examined solutions to world problems on the principle of interdependence as projected by Western scientists, political scientists and futurists. They rejected such ideas as convergence and stated as an "unquestionable fact" that "the transition to a communist civilization * * * will save human civilization in general, and that progress on the path to socialism and communism is, precisely a prerequisite for new great successes in science and technology. * * *" Nonetheless, they conceded that "problems of a global nature require for their solution efforts on a global scale." And while the victory of socialism in the world would create "the best conditions for this," still, "the Marxist-Leninists are convinced of the fact that now as well, while two opposite social systems exist, factual possibilities exist for making serious progress in resolving global problems through the development of international cooperation." (Zagladin, V. and I. Frolov, Global Problems and Mankind's Future. Kommunist, No. 7: May 1979:92-105, translated in. U.S. Joint Publications Research Service, JPRS 73780, June 28, 1979:119-120.)

can be brought into this system, ever mindful that progress in moderating Soviet behavior in diplomacy has thus far seemed to have come about by and large as a result of American initiatives (e.g., beginning the SALT process). The Soviet leadership, inherently conservative and resistant to change, has responded slowly and often reluctantly to such initiatives and changes. To this extent, Americans, who are by instinct innovators and who live within a system that places a premium on progress, change, and new ideas, would seem to have an advantage and perhaps even a special obligation as a superpower.

Not long ago Kennan, in an effort to start building a new consensus on the American attitude toward the Soviet Union, contended that owing to the changes in the world and within the Soviet Union, Americans, notably the foreign policy elite, would have to rethink the premises of their old positions and bring them up-to-date with current realities.[5]

Perhaps it is the global imperatives, along with changes taking place within the Soviet Union itself, that are compelling such reevaluations. In such cases these reevaluations would seem to place a special burden on American diplomacy, as Legvold observed, to formulate new ground rules, some new "rules of the game," for the conduct of diplomacy in a new era.[6] The Soviet leadership already acknowledges the necessity of giving the overall competition stability and predictability, and Soviet foreign policy specialists are now discussing the importance of developing "rules of the game." [7]

The second element in providing new opportunities for and imposing new burdens on U.S. foreign policy is the growing tendency in Soviet diplomacy and negotiating behavior toward taking on the traditionalism of European diplomacy. Some time ago Bohlen gave some thought to the time when the style of Soviet diplomacy might change. He once declared, in speculating about the possibilities of improvement in future Soviet-American relations, that "the only hope, and this is a

---

[5] In an address before the Council of Foreign Relations, Kennan said: "What I am thinking of * * * is a certain process of reeducation in the realities of Soviet power and leadership—a common effort on the part of all of us who have been prominently involved in this debate—a process in which we would check our existing views at the door, together with our hats, and would listen and ask questions and try to get a new view of the facts before we drew conclusions. I suspect that in an experience of this nature, designed not to promote the clash of old views but to make possible the common development of new, more realistic and more up-to-date ones, we would come closer than in any other way to the composing of our differences." In reference to the coming new generation of Soviet leaders, he wrote: "Nothing could be more unfortunate, surely, than that a new and inexperienced team of leaders should come into power in the Soviet Union confronting what appear to be a blank wall of hostility and rejection at the American end—a situation in the face of which they would see no choice but to look for alternatives other than those of good relations with the United States. This is no time to foreclose other people's options, and particularly not the options of people new to the experience of power and obliged to define new lines of policy that may represent commitments for many years to come." (Kennan, George F. A Plea by Mr. X 30 Years Later: George F. Kennan Urges a New Vision of Russia as We Near SALT Crossroads. The Washington Post Outlook, December 11, 1977, pp. D1 and D5.)

[6] Legvold concluded his article on the nature of Soviet power: "The dialectical quality of détente, with its competitive/cooperative essence, makes it hard to revive the search for 'rules,' for a more explicit modus vivendi, for a moderation of means in lieu of agreement over ends. But the search is ultimately the only hope we have of restoring coherence to the quest for a restructured Soviet-American relationship. It includes new and untried standards of behavior like those suggested by Marshall Shulman some years ago—one, the principle of 'noninterference by force in processes of internal change,' the other, the 'right of free access,' permitting nations to 'compete, not for the control of territory, but for the establishment of mutually beneficial and nonexploitative relations, and thereby for political influence.' These are the decisive 'rules of the game,' for it is they that will tell us how much either side really trusts a moderated contest and wants its advantages." (Legvold, op. cit., p. 71.)

[7] Legvold, Robert. The Super Rivals: Conflict in the Third World. Foreign Affairs, vol. 57, Spring 1979: p. 776.

fairly thin one, is that at some point the Soviet Union will begin to act like a country instead of a cause." But he cautioned:

Illusion has no place in any negotiations with the Soviet Union. We should always seek to find the areas where the two countries' interests coincide. Even in areas where interests do not coincide, skillful diplomacy can sometimes produce manageable arrangements of benefit to both.[8]

Certainly, as this study suggests, the Soviet Union is beginning "to act like a country instead of a cause." This is especially true in the SALT negotiations, and perhaps even in relations with other advanced industrial countries such as those in Western Europe where it seems to be adhering to the norms of traditionalism. But the crucial test of this apparent change, as will be explained below, is in Soviet policy toward the Third World. For Soviet aspirations and activities in the Third World, as in the cases of Angola, the Horn of Africa, and now Afghanistan, suggest a country exploiting instability for its own political purposes rather than one seeking to establish a harmony of interests that would insure both regional and world peace.

Thus new opportunities have opened up and new burdens have been placed upon U.S. foreign policy as the Soviet Union and the United States enter the 1980's. How well both countries measure up to their new responsibilities in "managing" their rivalry and thus maintaining world peace is, to borrow a phrase from Khrushchev, "the question of questions."

2. ON THE VALUE OF DIPLOMACY AND NEGOTIATIONS IN SOVIET-AMERICAN RELATIONS

(a) In historical perspective

If diplomacy and negotiations are expected to play a new and commanding role in Soviet-American relations, it is proper to give some thought to their development in the historical perspective of Russian-American relations, particularly in the evolving SALT process, and to consider whether or not Soviet diplomacy is really diplomacy.

Diplomacy and negotiations, as Nicolson and other scholars and practitioners suggest, are positive values whose strength and moral worth lie in their ability to maintain peace among nations and stability in their relationships. To Sir Robert Peel, diplomacy was the "great engine" of civilization, and so it has been since its formal beginning in ancient Greece and in its slow and often painful evolution through the development of Western civilization. Diplomacy is at once a symptom of the struggle for power among sovereign nations and the mechanism for maintaining order and peace so that the progress of man to a higher level of civilization can continue. If peace is to be preserved and orderly relations maintained, as Morgenthau said, sovereign nations "must try to persuade, negotiate, and exert pressure upon each other. That is to say, they must engage in, cultivate, and rely upon diplomatic procedures."[9]

Hence the instruction,
—of Talleyrand, "One must negotiate, negotiate, and always negotiate";[10]

---

[8] Bohlen, op. cit., pp. 540–541.
[9] Morgenthau, op. cit., p. 532.
[10] Kertesz, op. cit., p. 133.

—of Eisenhower at the Geneva summit of 1955, "War has failed. The only way to save the world is through diplomacy"; [11]

—of Dulles at one of the most difficult times in the early Khrushchev era, "There *is* a place for negotiation. * * * negotiation is one of the major tools of diplomacy" and it would be "the height of folly to renounce the use of this tool"; [12]

—of Kohler at a similarly difficult period in 1958, " * * * negotiations are often valuable and sometimes essential. We must negotiate constantly, using every means and channel that gives promise of constructive results"; [13]

—of Kennedy, apparently, during the Berlin crisis, "we have nothing to fear from negotiations * * * and nothing to gain by refusing to take part in them"; [14] and

—of Bohlen on negotiating with the Soviets during the early Khrushchev years, "the United States should never refuse any offer for serious talks." [15]

Diplomacy and negotiations have always had a special value for Americans. They have encompassed the national experience from the earliest days of the Republic, as a means of averting war and settling disputes with its English and Spanish neighbors and with other nations on the larger international stage since the turn of the century; as a mechanism for national territorial expansion as in the Louisiana Purchase, the Transcontinental Treaty, and the Alaska Cession; and for maintaining the lifeblood of the Nation by establishing harmonious commercial relationships with the nations of the world. Diplomacy and negotiations are thus firmly placed in the Nation's historical tradition.

In U.S. relations with the Soviet Union diplomacy and negotiations take on an even more special value because they provide the only device for bringing rationality into the management of a relationship that is fraught with great complexities and high risks. Consider a relationship in the 1980's without diplomacy and negotiations and the consequent risks to the Nation's security of a Soviet Russia as it was in Stalin's postwar era: A total breakdown in communications; a debasement of diplomacy; and a resort to "negotiations by semaphore" in the manner of that ending the Berlin blockade as the only means for resolving grave disputes.

(b) Diplomacy and the SALT process

(1) SALT: A distinction between the treaty and the process

In the nuclear age, diplomacy and negotiations take on a new meaning, and, indeed, a new imperative for both the United States and the Soviet Union. For they provide the vital mechanism for survival.

Before exploring this facet of diplomacy, it is important to digress for a moment and make clear that there is a distinction between the SALT treaty and the SALT process.

Many supporters of arms control, notably of SALT I and II, among specialists and practitioners in international relations, tend to base

[11] Eisenhower, Mandate for Change, p. 518.
[12] Dulles, op. cit., p. 159.
[13] Kohler, op. cit., p. 910.
[14] Sorensen, op. cit., p. 516.
[15] Bohlen, op. cit., p. 391.

their case more strictly on the political side of SALT. They tend to stress the political value of the perpetuation of the SALT process as a negotiating mechanism, rather than on what Kennan called, "military mathematics," that is, "the mathematics of possible mutual destruction in an age of explosively burgeoning weapons technology." [16]

Critics of SALT II do not necessarily abjure the SALT process but value it as a mechanism for negotiations. They may dispute the treaty and even reject it, but not the process. Indeed, Nitze, a stalwart critic of SALT II, was a negotiator on the SALT I American delegation.[17]

Critics tend to base their opposition on the more strictly technical weapons side of arms control. They contend, for example, that the treaty freezes the United States into a position of nuclear inferiority and that the Nation is already in peril. Some critics are especially concerned about the new Soviet "heavy" missiles which, augmented by an effective civil defense, may give them a "war-winning" capability. Accordingly, believing that nuclear war is "thinkable," they contend that in a few years the Soviets could destroy virtually all land-based U.S. missiles in a single strike. They are, moreover, uneasy about the problem of verification.[18]

Still other critics of SALT II contend that the treaty will stimulate the arms race with each side using loopholes to build new and more lethal weapons. There is, however, apparently no reason to believe that they dispute the validity of the SALT process as a valuable negotiating mechanism.[19]

On the other hand, some critics reject outright not only the treaty but also the SALT process and even détente itself. They perceive them as injurious to U.S. security interests, providing a false sense of security while the balance of strategic and military forces is changing decisively against the United States.

Supporters of the SALT II treaty and the SALT process dispute the arguments made by critics on this issue.

This commentary is, therefore, not intended to make a brief for any side on the SALT II issue. It merely suggests the importance of the negotiating process, that is, the importance of diplomacy and negotiations which is the central point of this study.

(2) On the value of the SALT negotiating process; a contrasting view

The emergence of the new era of negotiations, coinciding with the tendency in Soviet diplomacy to revert to traditionalism, opens up new prospects in Soviet-American relations. Perhaps the convergence of these international realities and their intersection with the potentiality of nuclear war in the modern age was best described by Canada's foremost diplomatist Lester Pearson when he wrote in his book on, "Diplomacy in the Nuclear Age":

There never was a time in history when, for this supreme purpose [the prevention of a war which would destroy humanity] negotiation, through all the varied mechanisms of diplomacy, was more important, more difficult, and, at

---

[16] Kennan. George F. A plea by Mr. X 30 Years Later. The Washington Post (Outlook). Dec. 11, 1977, p. D5.
[17] For a commentary on Nitze's views on strategic matters, see, Zelnick, C. Robert. Paul Nitze: The Nemesis of SALT II. The Washington Post (Outlook), June 24, 1979, p. G1.
[18] The various points of view are summarized in, Harwood. Richard. SALT: Straight Answers for Confused Citizens. The Washington Post (Outlook), June 10, 1979, p. D1.
[19] Ibid.

times, more frustrating. Negotiation, it should be remembered, means more than prepared monologues delivered at international Congresses, or pronouncements at press conferences, or ex cathedra statements designed to frighten adversaries or impress reluctant allies.

Today, when the alternative to peace may be nuclear suicide, it is more important than ever to keep the channels of diplomacy open. Moreover, we should not be content merely to take advantage of any opportunities for negotiation that may arise. We should create such opportunities by a positive and dynamic diplomacy.[20]

Negotiations on arms control, notably the SALT process, go to the heart of the Soviet-American relationship. As Warnke said, they "go to the basic fabric of national security"; in the words of Arbatov during a recent broadcast to the American television audience, SALT "really is the most important part of our relationship * * * [it is] talk about war and peace and survival." [21]

As Bohlen remarked some years ago with respect to the Soviet view of disarmament, they are "very serious about disarmament" because "they genuinely believe that an uncontrolled arms race is almost certain to end up in war, sooner or later." [22] And more recently at a meeting with a Senate delegation in the autumn of 1978, Brezhnev said, "Carter and I know we both have a couple dozen minutes when satellites will tell us missiles are coming" in case of war. "There will be no more United States. But we will still get it in the neck." [23]

Accordingly, Ambassador Beam looks upon rejection of SALT II as a "political disaster, a tremendous political setback"—but not a disaster from the standpoint that it would mean an end to discussions and negotiations. The Soviets value negotiations, he said, "they never want to lose contact." [24]

Arbatov perceived "very bad results for both sides" should the SALT II treaty be rejected. Rejection was not just rejecting another important treaty, he said, "it is somehow cutting up the whole process of dialog between two countries" in which much labor and intellectual efforts have been invested. To cut off this dialog "at such a serious moment of development in science and technology, in armaments technology, in international relations, would be a very serious thing." In such an eventuality, he felt sure that "our people will come simply to a conclusion that it is impossible to have serious business with Americans." Adding to the other disappointments as in the trade agreement, the Soviet people will conclude, he said, that "you are simply impossible partners." [25]

The most authoritative official Soviet statement correlating Senate amendments (which would require renegotiation) with possible rejection of the treaty and termination of the SALT process was made on June 25 when Gromyko stated in a Moscow press conference:

I tell you frankly, it is impossible to resume negotiations. It will be the end of negotiations * * * the end * * *. No matter what amendments would be made,

---

[20] Pearson, op. cit., pp. 33–34.
[21] The Christian Science Monitor, Nov. 25, 1977, p. 1, and, ABC News, Issues and Answers, Arbatov, May 27, 1979, p. 14. Vorontsov, an arms control specialist at the Soviet Embassy in Washington during negotiations on SALT I, said, the SALT negotiations "is the most important thing we have to do together. It's closer to the essence of what we both regard as our security. Thus it cannot be compared to negotiations which, like Berlin, involve other countries. SALT resists comparison with other negotiations." (Newhouse, op. cit., p. 58.)
[22] Bohlen, op. cit., p. 448.
[23] The Washington Post, June 10, 1979, p. A1.
[24] Interview with Jacob D. Beam, May 23, 1979.
[25] ABC News, Issues and Answers, May 27, 1979, p. 10.

it would be impossible on the basis of these amendments to open negotiations * * * a fantastic situation.[26]

That possible rejection of the SALT II treaty should evoke such a vigorous Soviet reaction stems largely from the fact that the SALT process has, in large measure, become the centerpiece of the Soviet-American relationship. As an essentially conservative undertaking, it attempts, as Prof. Joseph J. Kruzel of Duke University wrote, "to stabilize the strategic nuclear balance, not to do away with it. SALT is concerned with managing the arms race, not ending it."[27] Or as Winham observed, SALT I "did not reduce arms appreciably, but it did permit Soviet and American planners to exercise greater control over the environment in which they project defense needs."[28] And as Richard Harwood, managing editor of the Washington Post, concluded a recent pro/con article on SALT II: "But it does establish the principle that at some point enough is enough. And it provides the link for future parleys at which future negotiators may decide that enough is really too much and that it is time to rid ourselves of some of these weapons."[29]

Processes such as SALT that are designed to reduce variety and uncertainty through negotiations and thus increase international stability are not new in international relations. As Nicolson said, the chief aim of diplomacy is the search for international stability, and governments have long sought to reduce uncertainty about intentions and capabilities of their adversaries through negotiated agreements. "What is different" today, observed Winham, "is that the complexities of the present age are greater, due largely to technical change, and as a result environmental control is a more urgent task than before." National leaders are uncertain about the future, and as Newhouse cautioned, "it is the unknown, not the known, that fosters instability."[30]

Specialists in national defense and foreign policy are, however, by no means agreed on the value of the SALT process, indeed, on the value of diplomacy itself when it involves the Soviet Union. Some would deny that stability is at all achievable in negotiations with Moscow. And they dispute, sometimes vigorously, the underlying assumption that the SALT process and the search for stability represent shared values.[31]

One view sees a national strategic unity in the simultaneous Soviet pursuit of détente and the SALT process in the West and its broadly

[26] The Washington Post, June 26, 1979, p. A1.
[27] Senate Foreign Relations Committee, Perceptions in Relations Between the United States and the Soviet Union, p. 356.
[28] Winham, op. cit., p. 94.
[29] Harwood, Richard. SALT: Straight Answers for Confused Citizens, The Washington Post (Outlook), June 10, 1979, p. D4.
[30] Winham, op. cit., p. 95.
[31] William Greider, editor of the Washington Post's Outlook and specialist in defense matters, questioned the value of the SALT process in an article entitled, "The Assured Madness of Arms 'Control'," published in the Outlook section of July 1, 1979 (pp. C1 and C4). Greider wrote: "I have been urged to find reassurance in the 'SALT process,' as it is called in this town (there is something ludicrous in the name alone, if you think about it). I am familiar with the arms control theology but I do not find the results reassuring. If one puts aside theories and hopes and examines only the concrete results, the SALT process looks quite dangerous to me, dangerous because it convinces unattentive citizens that somebody is doing something to control the nukes." Greider continued: "I don't see much control." He recorded the degree of the arms buildup since the early 1970s and noted what was expected by 1985, adding: "Wishful optimists may call this 'arms limitation' if they wish, but it should not deceive the rest of us." In conclusion Greider expressed this hope: "Maybe the great debate will change my mind, but I am not convinced these arms treaties have much lasting meaning."

adventurous initiatives in the developing world. In this analysis, the
SALT process assures that the West will be deterred from the use of
nuclear weapons, while the swiftly growing Soviet superiority in conventional arms and its political/military advance on the resources,
populations, markets, and strategic geography of the developing world
will leave the West decisively disadvantaged. To analysts of this persuasion, the SALT process lulls the West into the mistake of assuming
that a balance of nuclear power is the same as a balance of power
overall. This is seen as a prescription for long-term and virtually certain defeat.

Nonetheless, supporters of the SALT process would contend that
the value of the process lies in its ability to give some form, structure,
and substance to the Soviet-American relationship, to inject into it
that very important element of rationality, and to provide the means
for reducing the uncertainties of the future and imposing some control
over an environment that might otherwise get out of control. Through
inevitable linkages, the process affects other areas of the relationship,
and in the long term it could be one of the major forces in determining
the future course of the next Soviet generation.[32]

(3) *Converging Russian-American interests in historical perspective*

The strength of the SALT process lies in the fact that it is fundamentally based on converging Soviet-American vital national interests
and not on any vacuous spirit of trust and confidence. Such convergence of interests in the past came about not so much from a response
to specific internal needs as from a response to the larger imperatives
of historically determined external forces. It is they that have shaped
the course of this relationship in such shared national experiences as:
The American Revolution that found Russia, as a continental power,
taking actions that to some extent served the American interest; the
War of 1812 in which Czar Alexander actively sought mediation between the British and Americans; in the American Civil War when
Russia was the only major European power to support the Northern
cause of national unity (Britain and France actively sought the dissolution of the Republic); and in World Wars I and II when both
countries opposed a common enemy. Realistic appraisals of national
interests, responding to the imperatives of larger historical forces,
determined these policies; not sentimentality or any shallow romanticism. (Recall how Witte disliked Americans and loathed their democratic institutions.) In the same way much larger historical forces in
this modern nuclear age are compelling an accommodation through
negotiations in the relationship, making the need much more immediate, affecting and vital, and its potentialities more enduring.

(4) *Analogy between the SALT process and the Congress of
Vienna*

Thus it seems not to be an exaggeration to draw an historical analogy, as Newhouse had done, between the SALT process and the Con-

---

[32] For a statement addressing the criticisms of Greider among others see. Hyland. William G. SALT or Limbo. The Washington Post. June 21. 1979. p. A19. Hyland argued that
it would be "astounding" if the two rivals were to agree to sweeping limitations on their
primary means of military security. He noted that the agreement was "basically a political
agreement ; to provide a margin of reassurance and thus add an element of stability to the
general relationship."

gress of Vienna that had kept the peace of Europe for a 100 years. Rarely are international problems ever completely solved; rather, based upon an understanding and commitment to the necessity of solutions, they are managed over time in attempts to adjust interests and needs through negotiations. The value of the SALT process, which began over 12 years ago in December 1966, is that it has provided the mechanism for the management of the relationship and the potentiality for control over the strategic environment.

The process also permits the satisfaction of peripheral, but nonetheless significant, interests, through functional diplomacy. As General Wilson believes, it is the larger, long-range and transcending world problems (hunger, overpopulation, pollution, and energy in short supply), spawned in the age of interdependence, that provide the opening for genuine negotiations and possible accommodation in the future.[33] Similarly, a Soviet diplomat has emphasized the value of functionalism in the future of Soviet-American relations. Multiple connections through such instrumentalities as international exchange and trade contribute to creating a climate of mutual trust and accommodation that in the long term could have a positive influence.[34]

The SALT process has thus taken on a value of its own. In reality the process transcends the specific technicalities of the strategic balance; it impacts upon the larger dimension of Soviet-American relations. And thus it provides, what Kennan said decades ago about the value of diplomacy, that "cushion of safety" for mankind.

(c) *Is Soviet diplomacy really diplomacy?*

(1) *Diplomacy, but with a difference*

Given the Soviet commitment to the SALT process, is it then possible to say that Soviet diplomacy is really diplomacy and not, as Nicolson said in 1953, "something else"?[35] Writing in 1959 during the cold war period, Charles Thayer, who could speak with the authority of a professional diplomat with service in Moscow, made an important ethical distinction between Soviet and Western diplomacy. As a method of negotiations, "in many instances a very effective one," he said, "Soviet diplomacy seems to fall within the definition of the diplomatic art if not within the ethical limitations imposed by Western diplomacy."[36]

---

[33] In his address at the Library of Congress on Nov. 15, 1978, General Wilson cited the four problems of hunger, overpopulation, pollution, and energy as being paramount in American concerns. These were the crucial long-range problems that faced the Nation. He noted that it was necessary to move in the direction of cooperating with the Soviet Union in solving these problems and that it was in our interest to do so. Wilson was optimistic on the possibilities of negotiating with the Soviets on these problems mainly because, unlike SALT and MBFR, the costs are far less to the Soviets. He perceives this as a long-term enterprise, not something that can be accomplished quickly. It is something for an agenda in the future that will take time, even a generation, but it was worth trying, he said. Prospects for some success through negotiations were good.

[34] Important also in the long-term nature of the Soviet-American relationship, according to the Soviet view, is what they believe is the American misperception that the Soviet Union is an aggressive predator nation and fail to understand the profound concern that the Soviet people have for the devastation of war. Having gone through World War II, they do not relish the thought of another one in the future.

[35] In his classic lectures on the evolution of diplomacy, Nicolson addressed the matter of "the scientific dialectic of the Marx-Lenin formula" that is the basis for Soviet diplomacy and concluded : "I have not observed as yet that this dialectic has improved international relationships, or that the Soviet diplomatists and commissars have evolved any system of negotiation that might be called a diplomatic system. Their activity in foreign countries or at international conferences is formidable, disturbing, compulsive. I do not for one moment underestimate either its potency or its danger. But it is not diplomacy : it is something else." (Nicolson, Evolution of Diplomatic Method, p. 90.)

[36] Thayer, op. cit., p. 49.

Soviet diplomacy is, as Ambassador Dean said of diplomatic style in general, "a kind of national signature, reflecting not only official policies but also characteristics of the society from which the diplomat comes and the outlook in which he has been bred." [37] The Soviet national signature is "socialist," and, accordingly, they correctly describe Soviet diplomacy as "socialist diplomacy."

Whatever the designation, Soviet diplomacy is no doubt diplomacy, at least in the formal sense of using internationally recognized instrumentalities to achieve Soviet national interests, to moderate differences with other states, and to seek solutions through negotiations. The Soviet commitment to the SALT process suggests a tendency toward a reversion to the norms of traditional European diplomacy with respect to negotiating procedures, behavior, and declared purposes. But Thayer's fine ethical distinction remains valid for this era of peaceful coexistence as it had been for that of the cold war; because in pursuit of revolutionary policies in the Third World, Soviet diplomacy has debased the higher values and purposes that Nicolson claimed for diplomacy. The goal of regional peace and moderate political change based upon a reasonable interpretation of the principle of self-determination is not a Soviet goal. The Soviet revolutionary heritage runs too deep for them to turn away from the opportunities that have been opening in the Third World. For them these are targets of opportunity for the further conquest of power, though in practice there are many constraints on their activities and their past failures have been many.

In this respect Soviet diplomacy, though diplomacy in the formal sense of diplomacy as an art, is, indeed, "something else"; there is a valid ethical distinction; it is a diplomacy with a difference, and that difference is a fundamental, ideological, and political commitment to revolution in the Third World. It is this difference that makes Soviet diplomacy "socialist diplomacy," as the Soviets themselves would be the first to acknowledge, and gives it that essential element of incompatibility with the United States and the other liberal democracies in the world.

(2) Intellectualism in the service of party policy

With this distinction and difference in mind, it is important to understand that the intellectual transformation of the Soviet diplomatic establishment has the value of opening the minds of the Soviet elite to new information, other perspectives, changing realities. This transformation can and does work to the advantage of the West, though not necessarily intended that way, as in the case of the education of the Soviet elite that has clarified their policy options in the nuclear age. But it ought not to be assumed that the circumstances and policy choices will always be to the West's advantage. The same bright and competent diplomatic establishment could encourage a sensible and positive approach to the SALT process, but it could also, and probably does, advocate and provide the intellectual analysis and ideological justification for such dangerous and disruptive adventures as intervention in Angola, southern Africa, and in the strategically important Horn of Africa. The diplomatic establishment is, after all, an arm of the party in the service of the party's policy. As Eran concluded in his assessment of the Soviet foreign policy infrastructure:

---

[37] Dean, op. cit., p. 34.

It is apparent that the same Soviet conception of foreign policy studies which developed in the Communist Academy in the twenties and early thirties, has remained acceptable to the Soviet regime throughout the years, and reached the Twenty-Fifth Congress of the CPSU [in 1976] practically unmodified. The Brezhnev regime has been as interested as its predecessors in scholarly endorsement, as well as in the exploitation of expertise and scholarship for the better reading of the outside world. It continued therefore to regard scholarship as a service to politics.[38]

(d) Judgments on Soviet diplomacy and negotiators

Finally, how is the quality of Soviet diplomacy and the skill of its negotiators to be judged? Much has been noted in this study to justify Sonnenfeldt's skepticism—they are not "infallible supernegotiators"—and that of others such as Ikle and Hayter.

Ikle summed up his study on Soviet negotiations, covering the West's negotiating experience through the cold war to publication in 1964, with this critical judgment:

We can find some common elements in the shortcomings of Soviet negotiators. They often ask for a whole loaf where they could get half a loaf—and wind up with nothing. They fritter away the credibility of their threats and the value of their promises, the two key tools for every diplomat. They cannot find the right dosage of demands and inducements. Curiously, they walk out of negotiations when they should stay in, while at other times they keep on talking in violation of their own deadlines. They insult those whose good will they ought to cultivate, and become self-righteous and rigid where they ought to be ingratiating and inventive. They fight furious battles against an empty phrase or a vague principle, although they are past masters at twisting the meaning of words and at utilizing agreements-in-principle for their own ends.

"In short," Ikle concluded, "the shrewd and skillful negotiating style of the Soviet Government turns out to be a myth." He cautioned Western diplomats, however, not to be "too sanguine about Soviet blunders, for many of these blunders are simply a failure to take advantage of Western vulnerabilities." [39]

And Hayter, writing from the perspective of a practitioner in 1959, gave this perceptive and damaging appraisal of Soviet diplomacy:

All in all, it is important not to overrate Soviet diplomacy. It possesses great advantages; very able personnel, apparently unlimited funds, the capacity to mobilize the entire resources of the nation in its support, the presence in the background of immense military power, organized sympathizers in most countries, a complete freedom from inhibiting scruples. But it has also great handicaps; a certain clumsiness, amounting on occasion to an alienating brutality; an inability to inspire confidence in anyone, the counterpart of its lack of inhibiting scruples; and above all an almost total, perhaps incorrigible, lack of understanding of the real character, motives and feelings of the foreign countries and peoples with whom it has to deal.[40]

3. SUMMING UP

Thus, new opportunities are opening up and new burdens are being placed on U.S. foreign policy in the nuclear age. This development is stimulated by the emergence of an era of negotiations and by peaceful coexistence in East-West relations which offer the possibility of bringing the Soviet Union into the changing international system.

Diplomacy and negotiations have a distinctive value in Soviet-American relations; they offer the mechanism, as they have throughout history, for accommodation, stability, and peace. In the nuclear age they take on a new meaning, a new imperative as a mechanism

[38] Eran, op. cit., p. 273.
[39] Ikle, How Nations Negotiate, p. 234.
[40] Hayter, Diplomacy of the Great Powers, p. 32.

for survival. Herein lies the value of the SALT process because this process is based upon converging national interests, more significant perhaps than at any other time in the history of Russian-American relations. In this respect the analogy between the SALT process and the Congress of Vienna that kept the peace of Europe for 100 years is valid.

Still, in negotiating with the Soviets and conducting diplomacy, Americans are confronted with traditional diplomacy only as it relates to the SALT process; for in other areas of diplomacy, notably in the Third World, it is diplomacy with a difference, a very important ethical and ideological difference. By the same token the intellectualism of the Soviet diplomatic establishment is a mixed blessing because it is an intellectualism in the service of party policy which need not always augur well for the United States and the West. Finally, Soviet diplomacy and Soviet negotiators have many assets but also many serious liabilities that work against their purposes: Both Soviet diplomacy and the skills of Soviet negotiators can be overrated.

B. The Balance of Power Factor and the Future

1. THE POWER FACTOR AND THE THIRD WORLD IN SOVIET-AMERICAN RELATIONS

The second of the two major implications suggested in this study for U.S. foreign policy in its relations with the Soviet Union is that the balance-of-power factor provides the theoretical mechanism for establishing a viable relationship between the two adversaries, thus giving greater assurance of peace in the world. But the assurance of peace is conditioned on the reduction of potentialities for confrontation and crisis in the Third World.

Diplomacy and negotiations are effective instruments in seeking international accommodation and stability, but the central element that determines their effectiveness is the existing balance of power. For the reality of power is the first principle in relations between nations, and diplomacy is but a reflection of that reality. Leverage is the vital element in negotiations, and power the fulcrum upon which it rests.

The Soviets have a traditional respect for power, and the principle upon which Soviet foreign policy is based is a power principle; namely, the correlation of forces, or in Western terms, the balance of power. For them, as Nitze said, with respect to the place of nuclear power within the larger concept of the balance of power, "The nuclear balance is only one element in the overall power balance. But in the Soviet view, it is the fulcrum upon which all other levers of influence—military, economic, or political—rest." [41] Accordingly, the Soviet experience, especially in recent years, has been one of amassing military power, to what ultimate purpose is debatable: To attain superiority, to have simply a tool for carrying out policy, or to satisfy their historic yearning for security? [42]

---

[41] Time, Feb. 26, 1979: p. 17.
[42] For an analysis and commentary on this Soviet predilection for amassing military power and its implications for the United States, see, Sonnenfeldt. Russia, America and Détente. Sonnenfeldt wrote: "But neither negotiations nor the military programs of the outside world seem likely to divert the Soviet Union from its determination to be the other military superpower in the world. The impulse to amass military power seems pervasive among the Soviet ruling elite regardless of generation. Soviet political dynamics seem to favor it, and the Soviet economic system seems unalterably geared to it" (p. 284).

Constraints can be placed upon this amassing of power through diplomacy and negotiations but only within the larger equation of power that creates an inescapable reality that the Soviets must reckon with. The SALT process could represent the search on both sides for a livable power balance from which arises the expectation of some tolerable form of international stability.

But Soviet policy in the Third World by design and effect works against the purposes of international stability through the SALT process. It is a destabilizing element in the Soviet-American relationship. And notwithstanding the intrinsic constraints on Soviet policy in the Third World, and their blemished record of failures is but one illustration, the fact remains that such activity, especially in areas strategically important, indeed vital, for the United States and its allies, is threatening to Western interests and contain the seeds of confrontation and crisis.[43]

In brief, the Soviets want it both ways: Stability in their relations with the United States and its allies in Western Europe, but freedom to pursue their revolutionary goals and power thrusts in the Third World. This contradiction places a heavy burden on "managing" détente; it creates perplexing ambiguities in declared purposes and actual policies that cannot but adversely affect their relationship with the United States.

2. ON THE NECESSITY OF STRENGTH AND PURPOSE

(a) Unending cycle of challenge and response

Americans have never doubted the necessity of strength and purpose in dealing with the Soviets, though uncertainty now prevails with respect to the Third World. Thus the history of the relationship since World War II has been one of an unending cycle of challenge and response with no end in view as weapons technology has outpaced the diplomatists at the negotiating table.

One persistent idea seems to run through this study, and it is this cycle of challenge and response that has been built into the relationship over the years. The Soviet drive for an unachievable absolute security, enlarging as Soviet policy moved from continentalism to globalism, has triggered an American defensive response; which in turn has generated another Soviet upward thrust in military power, provoking a commensurate American response; and so on.

Whether the Soviets will ever really feel secure, thus breaking the cycle, is an open question. Some observers believe that they will never feel secure; others, only if the ratio of strength is overwhelmingly in their favor.

But concern for security is a two-sided coin. Americans, like the Russians, also have deep concerns about their security and recall the pledge made by President Roosevelt in his Pearl Harbor address on December 8, 1941, that "we will not only defend ourselves to the utter-

---

[43] For a commentary on Soviet failures and constraints in the Third World, see, House International Relations Committee, Soviet Union and the Third World, ch. 6, and Legvold, op. cit., pp. 59–67. For a more recent analysis of Soviet-American relations as they are affected by the Third World, see, America and Russia: The Rules of the Game, Foreign Affairs, vol. 57, Spring 1979: 733–795. Under this heading appear three articles: Into the Breach: New Soviet Alliances in the Third World, by Donald Zagoria; The Super Rivals: Conflict in the Third World, by Robert Legvold; and U.S.-Soviet Relations: The Need for a Comprehensive Approach, by Richard J. Barnet.

most, but will make it very certain that this form of treachery shall never again endanger us." This experience and these words have been deeply embedded into the American consciousness. The vulnerability of the United States and the amassing of Soviet strategic power have kept these fears of security very much alive. And for the generation of Americans brought up in the 1960's the Cuban missile crisis, with all it implies for insights into the risks the Soviets will take and the danger to which the United States can be exposed, will remain an enduring memory.

(b) On achieving a balance of power

Conceivably, by maintaining an acceptable balance of power, managed through diplomacy and negotiations such as in the SALT process, at least some form of stability could come to the relationship. Exaggerated anxieties about security on both sides might subside as the relationship, expanding in concentric circles through functional diplomacy, became more interdependent and interrelated. As confidence and trust, based on self-interest and security, grew, and with a Soviet Union more conscious of its stake in the international order and becoming more decisively a part of it, then the massive nuclear arsenals on both sides might be scaled down through negotiations. As Sonnenfeldt explained it: By holding open to the Soviets the possibility of balanced arrangements and benefits that they seek economically and in other respects; by taking reasonable recognition of their security interests; and by making clear to them, through U.S. strength and that of its allies, that security cannot be achieved through the amassing of military power that will only be matched by the West—then, they may come to accept "a real balance of some durability." [44]

In brief, the theoretical mechanism of the balance of power offers perhaps the only realistic expectation of accommodation and stability in the relationship. It is significant that détente itself and the growing acceptance of even a qualified form of traditionalism in diplomacy are essentially a creation of strategic parity.

(c) Total diplomacy

Attainment of this relationship places a heavy burden on the United States to maintain its military strength and to pursue what used to be called "total diplomacy." This is a diplomacy that correctly recognizes

---

[44] Sonnenfeldt gave the following explanation of the roots of Soviet insecurity and a prescription of how the United States might deal with it: "I don't know if we can do a whole lot about this problem, because I think some of these insecurities are deeply engrained. Some of them are the product of the very way the Soviet system was born, as a tiny minority claque taking over a huge country and imposing on it a system for which it wasn't ready and which the vast bulk of the population did not want. It was a conspiratorial party in its very nature, and it set the Soviet Union apart from the rest of the world, and in effect declared some form of permanent conflict on the rest of the world. So they brought this on themselves in many ways. And the outside world—even in periods of great euphoria about the prospects of better cooperation with the Soviet Union—retains a high degree of suspicion of the Soviet Union, precisely because they have over the years shown themselves to be very difficult partners in the international system. So I think the problem is deep-seated, and there is not any pat solution to it. I think it has to be managed, and I think the way to manage it is, on the one hand, to hold open to the Soviets the possibilities of balanced arrangements and various benefits that they seek economically and in other respects and take a reasonable recognition of their security interests; and on the other hand to make clear to them that through our military programs and through our alliances and every other way that we can think of, that security cannot be obtained by constant amassing of military power that will be matched by military power in the outside world, and that somewhere, sometime, the Soviets are going to have to accept a real balance of some durability, and not constantly try to upset it. That is a very long and tough row to hoe: it is very expensive and Americans do not like long, tough rows to hoe. We prefer solutions that come quickly and are sort of final, like Salk vaccine." (Interview with Helmut Sonnenfeldt, June 7, 1979.)

the correlation between military power and foreign policy. As Lester Pearson explained the importance of this relationship: "Military power * * * used wisely and with an understanding of its limitations, is an essential support for policy. But sound policy and astute diplomacy are themselves as much a source of strength as military power. The two are, in fact * * * interrelated and interdependent."[45]

The requirements of total diplomacy are demanding, not only on resources and political wisdom, but on the spirit of the Nation; because it places a special burden on patience, forbearance, determination, and vision in the pursuit of goals not immediately achievable. It has been said that Americans are not psychologically equipped to handle the long haul; thus the vast dimension of this challenge.[46]

(d) Problem of the Third World

Perhaps the most serious immediate problem the Americans face is the management of their differences with the Soviet Union along the peripheral areas of their relationship in the Third World. The Soviets are determined in their commitment and in their course. In contrast, the Americans, still caught up in the "Vietnam syndrome," have seemed to be uncertain and hesitant even about sketching out the possible concentric circles of their interests and preparing for the future.[47]

Only since the Iranian crisis in early 1979 has the United States given serious attention to planning contingencies in the strategically critical Middle East.[48]

---

[45] Pearson, op. cit., p. 77.

[47] Townsend Hoopes wrote : "Our difficulty is that as a nation of short-term pragmatists accustomed to dealing with the future only when it has become the present, we find it hard to regard future trends as serious rea'ities. We have not achieved the capacity to treat as real and urgent—as demanding action today—problems which appear in critical dimension only at some future date. Yet failure to achieve this new habit of mind is likely to prove fatal." (Quoted in Acheson. Present at the Creation. p. 16.)

Recently, the retiring NATO Commander General Alexander Haig said with respect to a question on the sufficiency of a 3 percent more a year increase on NATO members' budgets : "We Westerners are always looking for the millenium. But there is no contract to be made on this subject. Security is an unending struggle, just as life itself is." (The Christian Science Monitor, June 1. 1979, p. 6.)

[47] For a discussion of this problem of U.S. policy in the Third World, see, House International Relations Committee. Soviet Union and the Third World. ch. 6.

[48] See above, p. 393 for some estimates made in March 1979 of a changing attitude in the administration and among the American people with respect to military involvement abroad. On July 1, 1979, it was reported that the administration's principal foreign policy body, the Cabinet-level Policy Review Committee, had adopted policy recommendations at meetings on June 21 and 22 to increase U.S. naval forces around the Persian Gulf. Some leading policymakers were also reportedly hoping that the decisions ultimately coming out of the wide-ranging Middle East review would signal a new willingness by the administration to go beyond the post-Vietnam era mood of noninvolvement and to use military power abroad again if needed to protect U.S. interests. It was also reported that plans were still being worked up in the Defense Department to create a 110,000-man quick-response force that could intervene in the Persian Gulf or elsewhere in the Third World. This "surge deployment" planning had grown out of the Iranian crisis and the concern of the Joint Chiefs of Staff at that time over problems encountered in attempting to move an F15 squadron to Saudi Arabia and an aircraft carrier task force into the Arabian Sea. (Hoagland, Jim. Rise in U.S. Mideast Presence Approved. The Washington Post, July 1, 1979, p. A1.)

Recently, Legvold gave this prescription for an American approach to its Soviet rival in the Third World : (1) open a dialog on the problem of regional stability ; (2) make a "far more strenuous effort" to reduce the risks and moderate the effects of the rivalry by taking the initiative to establish "rules of the game" and "patterns of restraint" on mutual standards of behavior (The Soviet leadership acknowledges this need in the overall competition, and Soviet foreign policy specialists are now discussing the importance of drawing up such rules ; the time may be ripe for serious discussion of the problem) ; (3) discriminate among the different patterns of Soviet behavior and acknowledge Soviet restraint when evident ; (4) address regional problems for their own sake, bearing in mind solutions or partial solutions that place the "healthiest limits on Soviet opportunities", rather than focusing just on Soviet and Cuban actions ; and (5) maintain military power in line with the planned "mobile strike force" being considered in the Defense Department to support policy and introduce the element of risk to the Soviets, but under

Retiring NATO Commander Gen. Alexander Haig explored this problem in a recent commencement address at St. Anselm's College in Manchester, N.H., and gave this prescription:

What we are observing is the maturing consequences of over 15 years of increasing spending on the part of the Soviet leaders for their defense needs [and not a "precipitous change of mood in Moscow"]. I have maintained that this will require a new style of post-Vietnam American leadership. A leadership which not only recognizes that our involvement in Vietnam is over, but abandons the self-mesmerizing, neutralizing impact of that sterile involvement in the conduct of our current international affairs. It is a new kind of leadership which will require the development of a global Western strategy. The strategy which will determine for us, in the process of its development, vital American and Western national interests. It is a strategy which will permit us to determine and to sort out properly those events on the strategic horizon which involve an acceptable loss of vital interest or an acceptable accrual of Eastern power, from those issues which should be left to purely local solution. It is a strategy which should depart from the hyperactive American foreign policy of the post-World War II period in which we Americans saw Soviet duplicity behind every single deleterious effect on the strategic horizon, but which does not recoil from the needs to challenge blatant illegal Soviet interventionism wherever it occurs.

And finally, it is a new style of American leadership, and a fundamental strategy, which seeks a far more intimate consultation with those nations of the free world who share our values, and seeks to share the burdens of the maintenance of these values among those allies.[49]

(e) Mosely's advice: Strength and negotiations

Perhaps the wisdom of Mosely, expressed over a quarter of a century ago, is relevant to the present generation which is seeking to cope with the Soviet problem. His advice was simply to maintain the Nation's strength and at the same time to hold open the course of negotiations to the Soviets. Applied to the present international environment, this approach suggests a posture for the United States and among its allies in the West where the risks for the Soviets to seek critical advantages, whether in the strategic balance or in the Third World, outweigh the possibilities of gain, while at the same time keeping open the option of resolving differences through negotiations. This approach implies also an integrated policy with an appropriate balance between competition and cooperation. In the course of time perhaps the excessive economic burdens demanded by continuing the nuclear arms race, a desire to enter into the international sys-

three conditions—(a) apply force only in a "direct and appropriate recourse," not a "quick fix," (b) regard its use as a "momentary necessity," not a "permanent imperative" until mutual intentions and roles are clarified through negotiations, and (c) "face squarely the dilemma of when, where, and how we ourselves would contemplate using force to influence change." (Legvold, Robert. The Super Rivals: Conflict in the Third World. Foreign Affairs, vol. 57, Spring 1979 : 775–777.)

For another perspective on the American approach to its rival in the Third World, see, Zagoria, Donald. Into the Breach: New Soviet Alliances in the Third World. Foreign Affairs, vol. 57, Spring 1979 : 733–754. Zagoria took a far more critical and darker view of Soviet intentions, activities, and possibilities in the Third World than Legvold. He perceived greater dangers to American interests, and his article reflected a tone of alarm: "But the lack of response today—indeed the lack of comprehension—is just as frightening" (p. 741) ; "This appalling lack of understanding of developments within the Third World and their relation to U.S. security is a national scandal" (p. 751). Among the elements in Zagoria's prescription for a U.S. policy were : a call for a deeper and larger U.S. involvement in the Third World, including development of closer relations with regional organizations and devising security arrangements to protect critical countries as Saudi Arabia assuring them of support in case of external attack ; the "need to adopt a much higher profile in the entire region from Afghanistan to the Horn of Africa" ; support for the creation of a "quick strike force" for intervention in trouble areas in the Third World where U.S. interests were at stake ; a "broad dialog" with the Soviets on "rules of the game" to maintain regional stability and security ; and the use of leverage, as in trade, to influence Soviet conduct in the Third World and move away from perceiving détente as "narrow and unreciprocal."

[49] Haig, Alexander. General Haig in the Post-Vietnam World. The Christian Science Monitor, June 20, 1979, p. 24.

tem and partake of its benefits and advantages, and finally the futility of the search for a decisive political advantage in the volatile and unpredictable Third World, might moderate Soviet ambitions, making them more concerned about limitations and constraints and more conscious of the value of rationality and pragmatism in determining Soviet national interests.[49a]

3. DIPLOMACY, NEGOTIATIONS, AND THE POWER BALANCE

The task of establishing stability through some form of a balance of power is a long, difficult process that would test the mettle of the American people. As part of the historical process, it is an ever continuing process: It does not end at a designated point in time, but rather changes in form and substance as other elements impact upon it.

Diplomacy and negotiations are instrumentalities for bringing about this equilibrium of power. And if they are to fulfill the expected purpose of international stability that Nicolson claimed for them, it will be done within this evolving, ambiguous structure of power, balanced in some measure by the interests and fears of the principal adversaries, the Soviet Union and the United States.[50]

[49a] For a Soviet criticism of the correlation of military power with diplomacy, see, Petrov. V. The Search for a "New" Diplomacy in the USA. International Affairs (Moscow, No. 6. June 1979 : 92–99. Petrov contended that the "heightened U.S. interest in negotiations as an important factor in international politics" attested to "the failure of methods of confrontation and a position of strength, above all with the Soviet Union, and is also an attempt to use it to consolidate American positions in a fast-changing world." He chided "bourgeois political science" for its inability to formulate an all-embracing theory of diplomacy, citing two reasons : (1) "it is unable to furnish a truly scientific basis for the foreign policy of a system doomed by history, which attempts to erect obstacles to social progress and the free and equitable development of all peoples" ; and (2) "it bases its findings on the element of military force, making it the absolute criterion and thus attempts to prove the inevitability of the arms race, war and the threat of war as a permanent institution of human society." Petrov asserted that the American use of military power as a lever for political pressure in negotiations contradicted the policy of "strict adherence to the principles of mutual understanding and trust between states, the non-use or threat of force, and the solution of controversial issues by exclusively peaceful means." In this commentary, flavored more with traditional Soviet propaganda than based on hard, objective analysis, Petrov concluded that the United States "is creating stumbling blocks on the way to achieving mutually acceptable agreements on international problems" in contrast to the Soviet negotiation-oriented policy" that rejected "an approach to negotiating partners solely as adversaries." The Soviet Union, he said, "has every right to expect the same in return" (p. 99).

[50] In a detailed and perceptive commentary on the future of détente in Soviet-American relations. Sonnenfeldt came to the following conclusion : "Thus. given the pervasiveness of United States-Soviet interactions, geographically and functionally. our policies toward the U.S.S.R. are likely to remain the most active and far-flung among our external policies. Certainly, because of the military aspect. they will continue to place the largest single external demand upon our resources and the Federal budget. And however much we may seek to 'de-link' issues in given instances, we will not be able to avoid the essential interrelationship between them. Nor should we. Efforts to regulate military competition by negotiation and agreement will not stand alone as an island in a sea of crises or virulent antagonisms. On the contrary, though it is likely to be limited in impact on military programs, the effectiveness of SALT and other negotiations will depend heavily on the rest of the relationship. Similar points can be made about virtually every major facet of United States-Soviet negotiations. Above all, it is unlikely that the incidence and intensity of crises, whatever our diplomatic skill and other restraints, can long be held to moderate levels unless there is in operation a whole range of constraints and incentives that give each side a stake in restraint.

"What is involved is. of course, a long-term evolution which requires constant attention and effort and which will see many occasions that will defy clear characterization as to whether they represent progress, retrogression, success, failure, or 'irreversibility.' There is no joy in ambiguity, especially for Americans. But that is precisely what will mark our relations with the Soviet Union for a long time to come. We will probably never stop arguing over whether we actually have a détente that, in the President's words, constitutes 'progress toward peace.' That will have to be a judgment of history." (Sonnenfeldt. Russia, America and Détente, pp. 292–293.)

A SELECTED BIBLIOGRAPHY
BOOKS

1. Acheson, Dean A. Present at the creation. New York, W. W. Norton, 1969. 798 pp.
2. Acheson, Dean A. Sketches from life of men I have known. New York, Harper, 1959. 206 pp.
3. Alderman, Sidney S. Negotiating on war crimes prosecutions, 1945. In, Dennett and Johnson, Negotiating with the Russians, 1952. Ch. 3.
4. Aspaturian, Vernon V., ed. Process and power in Soviet foreign policy. Boston, Little, Brown, 1971. Ch. 18.
5. Bailey, Thomas A. America faces Russia: Russian-American relations from early times to our day. Ithaca, N.Y., Cornell University Press, 1950. 375 pp.
6. Beam, Jacob D. Multiple exposure: An American ambassador's unique perspective on East-West issues. New York, W. W. Norton, 1978. 317 pp.
7. Beloff, Max. The foreign policy of Soviet Russia, 1929–1941. London, Oxford University Press, 1947. 2 vols.
8. Basler, Severyn. Andrei Andreevich Gromyko. In, Simmonds, George, ed. Soviet leaders. New York, Thomas Y. Crowell, 1967, pp. 164–171.

    Also has sketches of Kuznetsov and Zorin.

9. Bishop, Donald C. The Roosevelt-Litvinov agreements: The American view. Syracuse, Syracuse University Press, 1965. 297 pp.
10. Bishop, Joseph Bucklin. Theodore Roosevelt and his time. New York, Charles Scribner's, 1920. Vol. 1, 505 pp.
11. Blakeslee, George H. Negotiating to establish the Far Eastern Commission, 1945. In, Dennett and Johnson, Negotiating with the Russians, 1951. Ch. 5.
12. Bohlen, Charles E. Witness to History, 1929–69. New York, W. W. Norton, 1973. 562 pp.
13. Bokhovitinov, N. N. On the present state of American studies in the Soviet Union. In Walker, Robert H. American studies abroad. Westport, Conn., Greenwood Press, 1975, pp. 101–103.
14. Brandon, Henry. The retreat of American power. New York, Doubleday, 1973. 368 pp.
15. Browder, Robert Paul. The origins of Soviet-American diplomacy. Princeton, N.J., Princeton University Press, 1953. 256 pp.
16. Burns, E. L. M., Lt. Gen. A struggle for disarmament: A seat at the table. The Toronto, Clarke, Irwin & Co., 1972. 268 pp.
17. Byrnes, James F. Speaking frankly. Westport, Conn., Greenwood Press, 1947. 324 pp.

17a. Callieres, Francois de. On the manner of negotiating with princes. Translated by A. F. Whyte. Paris, M. Brunet, 1716. Notre Dame, Ind., University of Notre Dame Press, 1963. 145 pp.

18. Churchill, Winston S. The Second World War: Closing the Ring Boston, Houghton Mifflin, 1951. 5, 749 pp.

19. Churchill, Winston S. The Second World War: The Grand Alliance. Boston, Houghton Mifflin, 1950. Vol. 3, 903 pp.

20. Churchill, Winston S. The Second World War: The hinge of fate. Boston, Houghton Mifflin, 1950. Vol. 4, 1,000 pp.

21. Churchill, Winston S. The Second World War: Triumph and tragedy. Boston, Houghton Mifflin, 1953. Vol. 6, 800 pp.

22. Clark, Eric. Diplomat: The world of international diplomacy. New York, Taplinger 1974. 276 pp.

23. Clay, Lucius D. General. Decision in Germany. Garden City. N.Y., Doubleday, 1950. 522 pp.

24. Craig, Gordon. Techniques of negotiation. In, Ivo J. Lederer, ed. Russian foreign policy, essays in historical perspective. New Haven, Conn., Yale University Press. 1962. Ch. 11.

25. Craig, Gordon. Totalitarian approaches to diplomatic negotiations. In, A. O. Sarkissian (ed.). Studies in diplomatic history and historiography in honour of G. P. Gooch. London. Longmans, Green. 1961. Ch. 7.

26. Craig, Gordon A. and Felix Gilbert, eds. The diplomats, 1919–39. Princeton, N.J., Princeton University Press. 1953. 700 pp.

27. Crankshaw, Edward. Khrushchev: a career. New York. Viking. 1966. 311 pp.

28. Dean, Arthur H. Test ban and disarmament: The path of negotiaton. Published for the Council on Foreign relations. New York, Harper & Row. 1966. 153 pp.

29. Deane, John R. Negotiating on military assistance, 1943–45. In, Dennett and Johnson. Negotiating with the Russians, 1951. Ch. 1.

30. Dean, John R., General. The strange alliance: The story of our efforts at wartime co-operation with Russia. New York, Viking Press, 1946. 344 pp.

31. Dennett, Tyler. Roosevelt and Russo-Japanese war. Garden City, N.Y., Doubleday, Page & Co., 1925. Ch. 4 and 5.

32. Dennett, Raymond and Joseph E. Johnson, eds. Negotiating with the Russians. Boston, Mass., World Peace Foundation, 1951. 310 pp.

33. Dinerstein, Herbert S. The making of a missile crisis: October 1962. Baltimore, Johns Hopkins University Press, 1976. 302 pp.

34. Druckman, Daniel. Human factors in international negotiations: social-psychological aspects of international conflict. Beverly Hills, Calif., Sage Publications, 1973. 96 pp.

35. Duchacek, Ivo D. With the collaboration of Kenneth W. Thompson. Conflict and cooperation among nations. New York, Holt, Rinehart and Winston, 1960. 649 pp.

Part II, The Struggle for Power and Order, and Part V, Negotiations.

36. Eden, Anthony, Sir. The memoirs of Anthony Eden: Full circle. Boston, Houghton Mifflin, 1960. 676 pp.

37. Eden, Anthony, Sir. The memoirs of Sir Anthony Eden, Earl of Avon: The reckoning. Boston, Houghton Mifflin, 1965. 716 pp.

38. Eisenhower, Dwight D. Mandate for change. Garden City, N.Y., Doubleday, 1963. Vol. 1, 650 pp.

39. Eisenhower, Dwight D. The White House years: Waging peace, 1956–61. Garden City, N.Y., Doubleday, 1965. Vol. 2. 741 pp.

40. Emmerson, John K. The Japanese Threat: A life in the U.S. Foreign Service. New York, Holt, Rinehart & Winston, 1978. 465 pp.

41. Eran, Oded. Mezhdunarodniki: An assessment of professional expertise in the making of Soviet foreign policy. Tel Aviv, Israel, Turtledove Publishing, 1979. 331 pp.

42. Ethridge, Mark and C. E. Black. Negotiating on the Balkans, 1945–47. In, Dennett and Johnson, Negotiating with the Russians, 1951. Ch. 7.

43. Farnsworth, Beatrice. William C. Bullitt and the Soviet Union. Bloomington, Ind., Indiana University Press, 1967. 244 pp.

44. Feis, Herbert. Between war and peace: The Potsdam conference. Princeton, N.J., Princeton University Press, 1960. 367 pp.

45. Feis, Herbert. Churchill-Roosevelt-Stalin: The war they waged and the peace they sought. Princeton, Princeton University Press, 1957. 692 pp.

46. Fischer, Louis. The Soviets in world affairs: A history of the relations between the Soviet Union and the rest of the world, 1917–29. Princeton, N.J., Princeton University Press, 1951. 2 vols.

47. Fisher, Roger, Basic negotiating strategy. New York, Harper & Row, 1969. 194 pp.

48. Gerson, Louis L. John Foster Dulles. New York, Cooper Square Publishers, 1967. 372 pp.
   (Series: The American Secretaries of State and Their Diplomacy.)

49. Gromyko, A. A. Through Russian eyes: President Kennedy's 1,036 days. Washington, International Library, 1973. 239 pp.

50. Haas, Michael. International systems: a behavioral approach. New York, Chandler Publishing, 1974. 433 pp.

51. Harriman, W. Averell. America and Russian in a changing world. Garden City, N.Y., Doubleday, 1971. 218 pp.

52. Harriman, W. Averell and Elie Abel. Special envoy to Churchill and Stalin, 1941–46. New York, Random House, 1975. 595 pp.

53. Hayter, William, Sir. The diplomacy of the Great Powers. New York, Macmillan, 1961. 74 pp.

54. Hayter, William, Sir. The Kremlin and the embassy. New York, Macmillan, 1966. 160 pp.

55. Hayter, William, Sir. Russia and the world: A study of Soviet foreign policy. London, Secker & Warburg, 1970. 133 pp.

56. Hazard, John N. Negotiating under Lend-Lease, 1942–45. In, Dennett and Johnson, Negotiating with the Russians, 1951. Ch. 2.

57. Hilger, Gustav and Alfred G. Meyer. The Incompatible allies: A memoir-history of German-Soviet relations, 1918–41. New York, Macmillan, 1953. 350 pp.

58. Hilsman, Roger. To move a nation: The politics of foreign policy in the administration of John F. Kennedy. Garden City, Doubleday, 1967. 602 pp.

59. Hingley, Ronald. The Russian mind. New York, Charles Scribner's, 1977. 307 pp.

60. Hoopes, Townsend. The devil and John Foster Dulles. Boston, Little, Brown, 1973. 562 pp.

61. Hull, Cordell. Memoirs. New York, Macmillan, 1948. 2 vols.

62. Ikle, Fred Charles. How nations negotiate. New York Harper & Row, 1964. 274 pp.

   See bibliographic note for extensive citations on sources for diplomacy and negotiations.

63. Jacobson, Harold Karan and Eric Stein. Diplomats, scientists, and politicians: the United States and the nuclear test ban negotiations. Ann Arbor, Mich., University of Michigan Press, 1966. 538 pp.

64. Johnson, Lyndon Baines. The vantage point: perspectives of the Presidency, 1963–69. New York, Holt, Rinehart, 1971. 636 pp.

65. Jones, Robert Huhn. The Roads to Russia: United States Lend-Lease to the Soviet Union. Norman, Okla., University of Oklahoma Press, 1967. 326 pp.

66. Jonsson, Christer. Soviet bargaining behavior: the nuclear test ban case. New York, Columbia University Press, 1979. 266 pp.

67. Kalb, Marvin and Bernard. Kissinger. Boston, Little, Brown, 1974. 577 pp.

68. Kaznacheev, Aleksandr. Inside a Soviet embassy: experiences of a Russian diplomat in Burma. Philadelphia, Lippincott, 1962. 250 pp.

69. Kennan, George F. History and diplomacy as viewed by a diplomatist. In, Kertesz and Fitzsimons, Diplomacy in a changing world. Ch. 7.

70. Kennan, George F. Memoirs, 1925–50. Boston, Little, Brown, 1967. Vol. 1, 583 pp.

71. Kennan, George F. Memoirs, 1950–63. Boston, Little, Brown, 1972. Vol. 2, 368 pp.

72. Kennan, George F. Russia and the West under Lenin and Stalin. Boston, Little, Brown, 1960. 411 pp.

73. Kennan, George F. Soviet foreign policy, 1917–41. Princeton, N.J., Van Nostrand, 1960. 192 pp.

74. Kennan Institute for Advanced Russian Studies. The U.S.S.R. and the sources of Soviet policy. A seminar sponsored by the Council on Foreign Relations and the Kennan Institute for Advanced Russian Studies, The Wilson Center, Smithsonian Institution. Washington, 1978. 124 pp. (Occasional Paper 34.)

75. Kennedy, Robert F. Thirteen days: a memoir of the Cuban missile crisis. New York, W. W. Norton, 1969. 224 pp.

76. Kertesz, Stephen D. American and Soviet negotiating behavior. In, Kertesz and Fitzsimons. Diplomacy in a changing world, 1959. Ch. 10.

77. Kertesz, Stephen D. and M. A. Fitzsimons. Diplomacy in a changing world. South Bend, Ind., University of Notre Dame Press, 1959. 407 p.

An anthology on diplomacy with essays by some leading American scholars (e.g., Morgenthau, Halle, Fox, Wright, and Campbell.)

78. Khrushchev, Nikita S. Khrushchev remembers. With an introduction, commentary and notes by Edward Crankshaw, translated and edited by Strobe Talbott. Boston, Little, Brown, 1970. 639 pp.

79. Khrushchev, Nikita S. Khrushchev remembers: the last testament. Translated and edited by Strobe Talbott, with Forward by Edward Crankshaw, and an Introduction by Jerrold L. Schecter. Boston, Little, Brown, 1974. 602 pp.

79a. Kohler, Foy D. SALT II: How not to negotiate with the Russians. Monographs in international affairs. Advanced International Studies Institute in association with the University of Miami, Coral Gables, Fla., 1979. 34 pp.

80. Korostovetz, Ivan I. Pre-war diplomacy: the Russo-Japanese problem. Diary of Korostovetz. London, British Periodicals Ltd., 1920. 160 pp.

81. Lall, Arthur. Modern international negotiation: principles and practice. New York, Columbia University Press, 1966. 404 pp.

82. Lall, Arthur S. Negotiating disarmament: the eighteen nation disarmament conference, the first two years, 1962–64. Ithaca, N.Y., Cornell University, 1964. 83 pp.

83. Leahy, William D., Fleet Admiral. I was there. New York, McGraw-Hill, 1950. 527 pp.

84. Leites, Nathan C. The operational code of the Politburo. Rand Corporation. New York, McGraw-Hill, 1951. 95 pp.

85. Leites, Nathan C. A study of Bolshevism. Glencoe, Ill., Free Press, 1953. 639 pp.

86. Macmillan, Harold. At the end of the day, 1961–63. New York, Harper & Row, 1973. 572 pp.

87. Macmillan, Harold. Tides of fortune, 1945–55. New York, Harper & Row, 1969. 729 pp.

88. McClellan, David S. Dean Acheson: the State Department years. New York, Dodd, Mead, 1976. 466 pp.

89. Maisky, Ivan. Memoires of a Soviet ambassador: the war, 1939–43. New York, Charles Scribner's, 1967. 408 pp.

90. Mikesell, Raymond F. Negotiating at Bretton Woods, 1944. In, Dennett and Johnson, eds. Negotiating with the Russians, 1951. Ch. 4.

91. Morgenthau, Hans J. Politics among nations: the struggle for power and peace. 5th ed. New York, Knopf, 1973. 617 pp.

92. Mosely, Philip E. The Kremlin and world politics: studies in Soviet policy and action. New York, Vintage, 1960. 557 pp.

93. Mosely, Philip E. The new challenge of the Kremlin. In, Kertesz and Fitzsimons, Diplomacy in a changing world. Ch. 10.

94. Mosely, Philip E. Some Soviet techniques of negotiation. In, Dennett and Johnson, Negotiating with the Russians, 1951. Ch. 10.

95. Murphy, Robert D. Diplomat among warriors. Garden City, N.Y., Doubleday, 1964. 470 pp.

96. Newhouse, John. Cold dawn: the story of SALT. New York, Holt, Rinehart and Winston, 1973. 368 pp.

97. Nicolson, Harold. Diplomacy. New York, Harcourt, Brace, 1939. 264 pp.

98. Nicolson, Harold. The evolution of diplomatic method. London. Constable, 1954. 93 pp.

99. Nixon, Richard M. RN: The memoirs of Richard Nixon. New York, Grosset & Dunlap, 1978. 1,120 pp.

100. Osborn, Frederick. Negotiating on atomic energy. 1946-47. In, Dennett and Johnson, Negotiating with the Russians, 1951. Ch. 8.

101. Pearson, Lester B. Diplomacy in the nuclear age. Westport, Conn., Greenwood Press, 1959. 114 pp.

102. Penrose, E. F. Negotiating on refugees and displaced persons, 1946. In, Dennett and Johnson, eds. Negotiating with the Russians, 1951. Ch. 6.

103. Ponomaryov, B., A. Gromyko and V. Khvostov. History of Soviet foreign policy, 1917-45. Moscow. Progress Publishers, 1969. 498 pp.

104. Roberts, Henry L. Maxim Litvinov. In, Craig and Gilbert, eds., The diplomats, 1919-39, 1953. Ch. 11.

105. Roetter, Charles. The diplomatic art: an informal history of world diplomacy. Philadelphia. Macrae Smith, 1963. 248 pp.

106. Rosen, Baron. Forty years of diplomacy. London, George Allen & Unwin, 1922. Vol. 1. 315 pp.

107. Safire, William. Before the fall: An inside view of the pre-Watergate White House. Garden City, N.Y., Doubleday, 1975. 704 pp.

108. Satow, Ernest, Sir. A guide to diplomatic practice. Rev. ed. London, Longmans, Green, 1958. 510 pp.

109. Schlesinger, Arthur M., Jr. A thousand days, John F. Kennedy in the White House. Boston, Houghton Mifflin, 1965. 1,087 pp.

109a. Schwartz, Morton. Soviet perceptions of the United States. Berkeley, University of California Press, 1978. 216 pp.

110. Seabury, Paul, ed. Balance of power. San Francisco, Calif., Chandler Publishing, 1965. 219 pp.

A collection of essays and articles giving the views on the balance of power of such world leaders as, Burke, Wilson, Trotsky, Khrushchev and Kennedy.

111. Sherwood, Robert E. Roosevelt and Hopkins: An intimate history. New York, Harper, 1948. 979 pp.

112. Simmons, Ernest J. Negotiating on cultural exchange, 1947. In, Dennett and Johnson, eds., Negotiating with the Russians. 1951. Ch. 9.

113. Slusser, Robert M. The role of the foreign minister. In, Ivo J. Lederer, ed. Russian foreign policy, essays in historical perspective. New Haven, Conn., Yale University Press, 1962. Ch. 7.

114. Smith, Gaddis. Dean Acheson. New York, Cooper Square, 1972. 473. pp. (Series: The American Secretaries of State and Their Diplomacy.)

115. Smith, Jean Edward. The defense of Berlin. Baltimore, Md., The Johns Hopkins Press, 1963. 431 pp.
116. Smith, Walter Bedell. My three years in Moscow. Philadelphia, Lippincott, 1950. 346 pp.
117. Sontag, Raymond J. History and diplomacy as viewed by a historian. In, Kertesz and Fitzsimons, Diplomacy in a changing world, 1959. Ch. 8.
118. Sorensen, Theodore C. Kennedy. New York, Harper & Row, 1965. 783 pp.
119. Standley, William H., Admiral, and Arthur A. Ageton, Rear Admiral. Admiral ambassador to Russia. Chicago, Henry Regnery, 1955. 533 pp.
120. Steibel, Gerald L. How can we negotiate with the Communists? New York, National Strategy Information Center, 1972. 46 pp.
121. Stettinius, Edward R., Jr. Roosevelt and the Russians: The Yalta conference. Garden City, N.Y., Doubleday, 1949. 367 pp.
122. Stuart, Graham H. American diplomatic and consular practice. New York, Appleton-Century-Crofts, 1952. 477 pp.
123. Survey of International Affairs. Issued under the auspices of the Royal Institute of International Affairs. London Oxford University Press.
124. Terchek, Ronald J. The making of the test ban treaty. The Hague, Martinus Nijhoff, 1970. 211 pp.
125. Thayer, Charles W. Diplomat. New York, Harper, 1959. 299 pp.
126. Thornton, Thomas P., ed. The Third World in Soviet perspective: Studies by Soviet writers on the developing areas. Princeton, N.J., Princeton University Press, 1964. 355 pp.
127. Trevelyan, Humphrey. Diplomatic channels. London, Macmillan, 1973. 157 pp.
128. Triska, Jan F. and David D. Finley. Soviet foreign policy. New York, Macmillan, 1968. 518 pp.
129. Truman, Harry S. Memoirs. Garden City, N.Y., Doubleday, 1956. 2 vols.
130. Uldricks, Teddy J. Diplomacy and ideology: The origins of Soviet foreign relations, 1917–30. London/Beverly Hills, Sage Publications, 1979. 229 pp.
131. United States in World Affairs. Published for the Council on Foreign Relations. New York, Harper and Row.
132. Von Laue, Theodore H. Soviet diplomacy: G. V. Chicherin, Peoples Commissar for Foreign Affairs. 1918–20. In, Craig Gordon A. and Felix Gilbert, eds. The diplomats, 1919–39, 1953. Ch. 8.
133. Vucinich, Wayne S. Soviet studies on the Middle East. In, Lederer, Ivo J. and Wayne S. Vucinich, eds. The Soviet Union and the Middle East: The post-World War II era. Stanford, Calif., Hoover Institution Press, 1974. Ch. 9.
134. Witte, Sergius. The memoirs of Count Witte. Translated and edited by Abraham Yarmolinsky. Garden City, N.Y., Doubleday, Page & Co., 1921. 445 pp.
135. Zimmerman, William. Soviet perspectives on international relations, 1956–67. Princeton, Princeton University Press, 1969. 336 pp.

ARTICLES, PAMPHLETS, NEWSPAPERS

136. Adomeit, Hannes. Soviet risk-taking and crisis behaviour: From confrontation to coexistence? Adelphia Papers 101. London, The International Institute for Strategic Studies, 1973, 40 pp.

137. Allen, Henry. The negotiator's art. The Washington Post (Potomac Section), September 21, 1975, pp. 22, 24, 26–28.

138. Austin, Anthony. Ambassador Dobrynin, key man in arms talks, long esteemed as bridge to Kremlin. The New York Times, June 4, 1979, p. A6.

139. Bundy, William P. Elements of power. Foreign affairs, vol. 56, October 1977: 1–26.

140. Campbell, John C. Negotiations with the Soviets: Some lessons of the war period. Foreign affairs, vol. 34, January 1956: 305–319.

141. Canadian Institute of International Affairs. Diplomatic method. International journal, v. 30, winter 1974–75. Whole issue.

  Volume consists of articles on diplomacy published by the Canadian Institute of International Affairs.

142. Davison, W. Philips. News media and international negotiation. Public opinion quarterly, vol. 38, summer 1974:174–191.

143. Dewitt, Karen. Anatoly Dobrynin, the genial America-watcher. The Washington Star, October 30, 1978, p. CC1–2.

144. Druck, Daniel and Robert Mahoney. Processes and consequences of international negotiations. Journal of social issues, vol. 33, winter 1977:60–87.

145. Edmead, Frank. Analysis and prediction in international mediation. UNITAR, 1971. 50 pp. (UNITAR PS No. 2.)

146. Facing the Russians: It's more chess than poker, say SALT insiders. Time, vol. 112, August 14, 1978:10–11.

147. Fairlie, Henry. The subtle arts of diplomacy. (Fairlie at large). The Washington Post, Oct. 1, 1978, p. C8.

148. Farrell, R. Barry. Foreign policy formation in the Communist countries of Eastern Europe. East European quarterly, vol. 1, March 1967:39–74.

149. Garthoff, Raymond L. Negotiating SALT. The Wilson quarterly, vol. 1, autumn 1977:76–85.

150. Garthoff, Raymond L. Negotiating with the Russians: Some lessons from SALT. International security, vol. 1, spring 1977: 3–24.

151. Garthoff, Raymond L. SALT and the Soviet military. Problems of communism, vol. 24, January-February 1975:21–37.

152. Garthoff, Raymond L. SALT I: An evaluation. World politics. vol. 31, October 1978: 1–25.

153. Glagolev, Igor S. The Soviet decisionmaking process in arms-control negotiations. Orbis, vol. 21, winter 1978: 767–776.

154. Grant, Natalie. The Russian section: A window on the Soviet Union. Diplomatic history, vol. 2, winter 1978:107–115.
155. Gwertzman, Bernard. How Shulman views Soviet motives and strategies. Interview. The New York Times, April 10, 1978, p. E4.
156. Hopmann, P. Terrence. Bargaining in arms control negotiations: The Seabeds Denuclearization Treaty. International organization, vol. 28, summer 1974: 313–343.
157. Hopmann, P. Terrence and Timothy King. Interactions and perceptions in the test ban negotiations. International studies quarterly, vol. 20, March 1976: 105–142.
158. Hyland, William G. Commentary: SALT and Soviet-American relations. International security, vol. 3, fall 1978:156–162.
159. Hyland, William G. Dealing with the Russian leaders. Interview. Time, November 21, 1977:28.
160. Ikle, Fred Charles. On negotiating with Communist powers. Foreign service journal, April 1971:21–25, 55.
161. Johnson, U. Alexis. From a veteran diplomat: How to deal with the Russians. An interview. U.S. News & World Report, April 4, 1977:25–26.
162. Keeper of the Kremlin's secrets. (On Gromyko) The Guardian weekly (Manchester), March 18, 1979, p. 9.
163. Kennan, George F. A plea by Mr. X 30 years later: George F. Kennan urges a new vision of Russia as we near SALT crossroads. The Washington Post (Outlook), December 11, 1977, p. D1 and D5.
164. Kupperman, Charles M. The Soviet world view. Policy review, No. 7, winter 1979:45–67.
165. Legvold, Robert. The nature of Soviet power. Foreign affairs, vol. 56, October 1977: 49–71.
166. Legvold, Robert. The super rivals: Conflict in the Third World. Foreign affairs, vol. 57, spring 1979: 755–778.
167. Luce, Clare Boothe. How to deal with the Russians: The basics of negotiation. Air Force magazine, vol. 62, April 1979:30–33.
168. Meissner, Boris. The Foreign Ministry and foreign service of the U.S.S.R. Aussenpolitik, vol. 28, No. 1, 1977: 49–64.
169. Mills, Richard M. One theory in search of reality: The development of United States studies in the Soviet Union. Political science quarterly, vol. 88, 1972:63–79.
170. Negotiation. Journal of conflict resolution, v. 21, Dec. 1977: whole issue.

> Partial contents.—Negotiation as a learning process, by J. Cross.—Negotiation as a psychological process, by B. Spector.—Negotiation as a joint decisionmaking process, by I. Zartman.—A game-theoretic analysis of the Vietnam negotiations: Preferences and strategies 1968–1973, by F. Zagare.—Tactical advantages of opening positioning strategies: Lessons from the seabed arms control talks 1967–1970, by B. Ramberg.—An application of a Richardson process model: Soviet-American interactions in the test ban negotiations 1962–1963, by P. Hopmann and T. Smith.

170a. Petrov, V. The search for a "new" diplomacy in the USA. International affairs (Moscow), no. 6, June 1979: 92–99.

> A Soviet critique of commentaries by American scholars on diplomacy and negotiations.

171. Petrov, Vladimir. Formation of Soviet foreign policy. Orbis, v. 27, fall 1973 : 819–850.
172. Pincus, Walter. Behind the scenes at SALT: long, complex sessions. The Washington Post, December 6, 1977, p. A13.
173. Pisar, Samuel. Let's put détente back on the rails. The New York Times magazine, September 25, 1977 : 31–33.
174. Salter, Albert L. Portrait of an emerging Soviet elite Generation. In, Simes, Dmitri K. et. al. Soviet succession: Leadership in transition. Published for the Center for Strategic and International Studies, Georgetown University, by Sage Publications, Beverly Hills/London, 1978. Ch. 3. (The Washington Papers, No. 59, vol. 6.)
175. Scheidig, Robert E., Major. A comparison of Communist negotiating methods. Military review, December 1974 : 79–89.
176. Searching for the right response: A panel of experts tries to redefine U.S. policy for the crescent of crisis [in the Middle East]. Time, vol. 113, March 12, 1979 : 28–31.

    The panel of experts included: James E. Akins, James A. Bill, Richard M. Helms, Walter Levy, Dmitri K. Simes, Joseph J. Sisco, and Dale R. Tahtinen.

177. Smith, Gerard C. Negotiating with the Soviets. The New York Times magazine, February 27, 1977 : 18–19, 26.
178. Smith, Gerard C. SALT after Vladivostok. Journal of international affairs, vol. 29, spring 1975 :7–18.
179. Sonnenfeldt, Helmut. Linkage: a strategy for tempering Soviet antagonism. NATO review, No. 1, February 1979 : 6–8, 20–28.
180. Sonnenfeldt, Helmut. Russia, America and detente. Foreign affairs, v. 56, January 1978 : 275–294.
181. Sonnenfeldt, Helmut and William G. Hyland. Soviet perspective on security. Adelphi papers: 150. London, International Institute for Strategic Studies, 1979. 24 p.
182. Toon, Malcolm, U.S. Ambassador to Moscow: reflections on the Soviet Union and its goals. Los Angeles Times, January 8, 1979, pp. 18–19.
183. Uldricks, Teddy J. The impact of the Great Purges on the People's Commissariat of Foreign Affairs. Slavic review, vol. 36, June 1977 : 187–204.
184. Uldricks, Teddy J. The Soviet diplomatic corps in the Cicerin [Chicherin] era. Jahbucher fur Geschichte Ost Europas, 23, No. 2, 1975 : 213–224.
185. Weiler, Lawrence D. The arms race, secret negotiations and the Congress. Sponsored by the Stanley Foundation, Muscatine, Iowa, 1976, 40 pp.
186. Welt, Leon. You want to sell in Russia? The Washington Post (Outlook), May 27, 1979, pp. C1 and C4.
187. Wessell, Nils H. Soviet views of multipolarity and the emerging balance of power. Orbis, vol. 22, winter, 1979 : 785–813.
188. Whelan, Joseph G., George Kennan and his influence on American foreign policy. Virginia quarterly review, vol. 35, spring 1959 : 196–220.
189. Whelan, Joseph G. Khrushchev and the balance of world power. The review of politics, vol. 23, April 1960 : 131–152.

190. Whitney, Craig R. Cordial stand-in for President Breshnev: Vasily Vasilyevich Kuznetsov. The New York Times, October 10, 1977, pp. 14.
191. Winham, Gilbert R. Negotiation as a management process. World politics, vol. 30, October 1977:87–114.
192. Winham, Gilbert R. and H. Eugene Bovis. Agreement and breakdown in negotiation: Report on a State Department training simulation. Journal of peace research, vol. 15, 1978:285–303.
193. Wright, C. Ben. Mr. "X" and containment. Slavic review, v. 35, March 1976:1–31. (See Kennan's reply in same issue on pp. 32–36; and Wright's rebuttal in the June 1976 issue, pp. 318–20.)
194. Zagoria, Donald. Into the breach: New Soviet alliances in the Third World. Foreign affairs, vol. 57, spring 1979:733–754.
195. Zartman, I. William, ed. Negotiation. The journal of conflict resolution, vol. 21, December 1977:563–760.

A special issue of 9 articles devoted to negotiations.

196. Zartman. I. William. The political analysis of negotiations: How who gets what and when. World politics, vol. 26, April 1974: 383–399.

A review article.

U.S. GOVERNMENT PUBLICATIONS

197. Bell, Robert G. and Mark M. Lowenthal. SALT II : major issues. Congressional Research Service, the Library of Congress, Washington, December 15, 1978, 137 p. (78–249–F) Multilith.

197a. Duevel, Christian. Moscow appoints "Duumvirate" of First Deputy Ministers of Foreign Affairs. RFE/RL. Radio Liberty Research, RL 1/78, January 1, 1978. 5 pp.

198. Dulles, John Foster. Secretary of State. The role of negotiation. U.S. Department of State Bulletin, Washington, D.C., vol. 38, February 3, 1958 p. 159–168.

199. Foreign Relations of the United States, 1943. Cairo and Teheran conferences. Wash., U.S. Government Printing Office, 1961. 932 pp.

200. Foreign Relations of the United States. The conferences at Malta and Yalta, 1945. Wash., U.S. Government Printing Office, 1955. 1,032 pp.

201. Foreign Relations of the United States, 1949. Eastern Europe and the Soviet Union. Wash., U.S. Government Printing Office, 1976.Vol. 5, 1,011 pp.

202. Foreign Relations of the United States, 1933–1939. The Soviet Union. Wash., U.S. Government Printing Office, 1952. 1,034 pp.

203. Foreign Relations of the United States, 1941. General : the Soviet Union. Wash., U.S. Government Printing Office, 1958. Vol. 1, 1,048 pp.

204. Kohler, Foy D. Deputy Assistant Secretary for European Affairs. Negotiation as an effective instrument of American foreign policy. U.S. Department of State Bulletin, vol. 38, June 2, 1958, pp. 901–910.

205. Soviet Affairs Symposium, 9th Garmisch-Partenkirchen, Ger, 1975. U.S. Army Institute for Advanced Russia and East European Studies. The Soviet Union as a negotiator. 45 pp.

205a. Stankovic, Slobodan. Memoirs of Yugoslavia's former ambassador in Moscow. Munich, Radio Free Europe. Part I, RAD Background Report/252, Dec. 21, 1977, 20 pp.; Part II, RAD Background Report 9, Jan. 20, 1978, 17 pp.; Part III, RAD Background Report/40, Mar. 1, 1978, 11 pp.

> Three reports on the first volume of memoirs by Veljko Micunovic, Yugoslavia's former ambassador in Moscow, 1956–1958 and, for the second time, 1969–1971 and in Washington, 1962–1967. This 530-page work is entitled "Moskovske godine 1956–1958" ("Years in Moscow, 1956–1958") and was published in Zagreb in 1977. The memoirs, a best seller, gave an unflattering account of the Soviet Union, its leaders and the Soviet system. The Soviets protested its publication. The Economist (Dec. 10, 1977) said that the book's main message was : "treat with the Russians if you must, but make no secret deals with them if you want to stay independent."

206. U.S. Arms Control and Disarmament Agency. Documents on Disarmament, 1972. Wash., U.S. Government Printing Office, May 1974. 959 pp.

206a. U.S. Central Intelligence Agency. National Foreign Assessment Center. Soviet strategy and tactics in economic and commercial negotiations with the United States. A research paper. Washington, June 1979. 11 pp. (ER79–10276)

Reproduced in the appendix.

207. U.S. Congress. House. Committee on Foreign Affairs. Agreement on Limitation of Strategic Offensive Weapons. Hearings. 92nd Congress 2nd session. Wash., U.S. Government Printing Office, 1972. 155 pp.

208. U.S. Congress. House. Committee on International Relations. Science, technology, and American diplomacy: an extended study of the interactions of science and technology with United States foreign Policy. Prepared by the Congressional Research Service of the Library of Congress under the direction of Dr. Franklin P. Huddle, Senior Specialist in Science and Technology, with Mr. Warren R. Johnston as associate project director. Wash., U.S. Government Printing Office. 1977. 3 vols.

209. U.S. Congress. House. Committee on International Relations. The Soviet Union and the Third World: A watershed in great power policy? By Dr. Joseph G. Whelan, Senior Specialist in International Affairs, and William B. Inglee, Research Assistant, Senior Specialist Division, Congressional Research Service Library of Congress, 95th Congress, 1st session. Wash., U.S. Government Printing Office, 1977. 186 pp.

210. U.S. Congress. Committee on International Relations. Subcommittee on Europe and the Middle East. The Soviet Union: Internal dynamics of foreign policy, present and future. Hearings. 95th Congress 1st session. Wash., U.S. Government Printing Office. 1978. 333 pp.

211. U.S. Congress. Senate. Committee on Foreign Relations. Nuclear Test Ban Treaty. Hearings. 88th Congress, First Session. Wash. U.S. Government Printing Office, 1963. 1,028 pp.

212. U.S. Congress. Senate. Committee on Foreign Relations. Perceptions: Relations between the United States and the Soviet Union. Wash., U.S. Government Printing Office 1979. 462 pp.

213. U.S. Congress. Senate. Committee on Foreign Relations. Strategic Arms Limitation Agreements. Hearings. 92nd Congress, 2nd session. Wash. U.S. Government Printing Office, 1972. 435 pp.

214. U.S. Congress. Senate. Committee on Government Operations. Subcommittee on National Security and International Operations, International negotiations. Wash., U.S. Government Printing Office, 1969–1972.

A multivolume series with hearings on the subject of negotiations, including translations from Soviet sources on the Soviet approach to negotiations.

215. U.S. Congress. Senate. Committee on Government Operations. Subcommittee on National Security Staffing and Operations. Staffing procedures and problems in the Soviet Union. 88th Congress, 1st session. Wash., U.S. Government Printing Office, 1963. 62 pp.
216. U.S. Congress. Senate. Committee on Government Operations. Subcommittee on National Policy Machinery. National Policy Machinery in the Soviet Union. 85th Congress, 2d session. Wash., U.S. Government Printing Office, 1960. 70 pp. (Report No. 1204)
217. U.S. Congress. Senate. Report to the United States Senate of the Senate delegation on Parliamentary exchange with the Soviet Union. 96th Congress, 1st session. Wash., U.S. Government Printing Office, April 11, 1979. 37 pp.

APPENDIX

SOVIET STRATEGY AND TACTICS IN ECONOMIC AND COMMERCIAL NEGOTIATIONS WITH THE UNITED STATES

(A Research Paper Prepared by the U.S. Central Intelligence Agency, National Foreign Assessment Center, ER–10276, June 1979)

KEY JUDGMENTS

All Soviet negotiating teams prepare extensively for their talks with U.S. Government and industry executives. Their "game plan" is developed from thorough biographic and substantive research and closely resembles a chess strategy. However, the strict instructions within which Soviet negotiators must operate leaves them little authority to make on-the-spot decisions. This constraint also helps explain why they often have difficulty responding to unanticipated U.S. proposals and maneuvers.

The Soviets believe that their approach to negotiations is fundamentally different from the U.S. approach. On the one hand, they assume that the business and achievement-oriented background of most U.S. negotiators causes the U.S. team :

—To regard compromise as both desirable and inevitable.

—To experience deep feelings of frustration and failure when an agreement is not achieved promptly.

On the other hand, the Soviets pride themselves on being great "sitters," who frequently are content to operate at a slow deliberate pace. They believe that this formula serves to frustrate U.S. strategy for a quick agreement and ultimately to induce major concessions.

Soviet negotiating teams for the most part are composed of veteran professionals who have often worked together. This provides the official (state-to-state) as well as commercial delegations with an institutional and substantive memory regarding the details of earlier U.S.–U.S.S.R. negotiations.

The Soviet commercial and official negotiating teams are similar in terms of composition, adherence to internal discipline and protocol, and competence, although there are a number of notable differences :

—The commercial delegations are larger and are supplemented by a constant shuttle of experts and end-user representatives who make one-time appearances.

—There are more frequent incidents of breakdown in team discipline in the commercial negotiations (usually involving a dispute between foreign trade organizations and end-user representatives).

—Some organizations seem to be more competent and have greater clout in the official level negotiations than in the talks with the U.S. private sector.

The Soviet teams have developed a number of unique tactics designed to frustrate and counter opposing delegations. Anchoring many of these tactics is Moscow's fabled "waiting game"—the assumption that time invariably works in its favor. In addition, the negotiating teams have a repertoire of tactics and ploys that includes most of the maneuvers that are standard in international business and government forums.

In the official negotiations, the Soviets usually want the most generally worded agreement possible. Moscow believes that this kind of language provides it with greater flexibility when the accord goes into effect. In contrast, the commercial negotiators seek a highly detailed contract—much more detailed, in fact, than the typical international business agreement.

Preface

Since the early 1970's, negotiations on economic issues have been an integral part of the U.S.S.R.'s dialogue with the West. This briefing aid identifies Soviet attitudes and behavior in negotiations with official as well as private sector representatives. It reflects a consensus—drawn primarily from the experiences of the past 5 years—on the basic patterns of Soviet bargaining strategy and tactics. Features of the U.S.S.R.'s negotiating style that appear to be typically "Soviet" are highlighted. The paper also points out any significant differences in the U.S.S.R.'s approaches to official and private sector negotiations. Finally, while U.S. negotiating behavior is not discussed directly, recommendations for appropriate U.S. strategies and tactics often are implicit in descriptions of the Soviet approach to negotiations.

Negotiations With the Public Sector

Preparing For Negotiations

Soviet negotiating teams prepare extensively for their talks with the United States. Thorough biographic and substantive research provides the raw data for a detailed "game plan" which may be approved by the Council of Ministers and, on occasion, by the Politburo. The result of this advance work closely resembles a chess strategy in its step-by-step program for negotiating success.

The Game Plan

The U.S.S.R.'s detailed advance work results in a "game plan" or set of instructions to the negotiating team. All indications are that a deputy minister is responsible for the collection and coordination of an interministerial package of negotiating materials. These documents are presented to his minister (for example, the Minister of Foreign Trade). For the more important negotiations, the minister is responsible for delivery the following items to the Council of Ministers for its approval: The goals and terms to be negotiated, the list of participants, letters outlining the team chief's authority to negotiate, and all other related data. This plan not only spells out the objectives and bargaining strategy and tactics, but equally important, includes the underlying assumptions about the likely U.S. responses.

Assessing U.S. Team Members

The Soviets try to derive insights into their counterparts' personalities as well as their political connections within the Washington community. Prior to the opening of negotiations, Soviet officials try to determine the U.S. team chief's "marching orders"—his degree of authority, the pressures on him to conclude an agreement promptly, and the extent to which his instructions have been coordinated among executive branch departments. Information obtained by the Embassy and other local representation through regular official contacts in the United States plays a prominent role in the resultant analysis. These sources are supplemented by biographic assessments believed to be prepared by KGB officers and the staffs of the leading foreign affairs research institutes.

Research and Logistics

Specialists in ministries, the party apparatus, and key research institutes examine closely the various issues listed on the proposed agendas. As a result, Soviet negotiating teams almost always have a clear idea of their ultimate goals. To help in this effort, the Soviet delegations also review carefully the histories of previous negotiations with the United States—a task that is facilitated by the rather low rate of turnover among negotiators. It is not unusual for senior Soviet negotiators to have had a decade or more of experience concluding agreements with Western governments.

One area of preparation in which the Soviets do not excel is the planning of schedules and other logistical matters for negotiations in the United States. While Moscow's advance teams have responsibility for arranging appointments and related matters, apparently they have little authority to make decisions. In fact, it is not unusual for the final decisions on schedules to be made only after the team chief has arrived in the United States.

The Soviets apparently perceive no major advantage to either side in the location of the talks. Their more senior negotiators, who have traveled frequently to the West, seem to prefer Moscow as the site—probably because of the greater ease in communications and the access to both materials and administrative-clerical services. On the other hand, the younger delegates with more limited exposure to the West probably prefer to hold the meetings abroad. The actual settings for the negotiations often are a function of the Soviet familiarity with and confidence in the U.S. side. The Soviets are quite sensitive to any unforeseen disruptions in the established arrangements of a negotiation. Their concern for routine and precedent extends even to the location of social events, which usually follow a strict rotation of sites.

THE AGENDA AND OTHER WORKING DOCUMENTS

The agenda is the agreed basis for the negotiations. In almost every instance the Soviets have pressed for a vague or generally worded outline of the proposed discussions. They believe that this kind of agenda permits them great flexibility in determining the scope and direction of the talks.

As a rule, the Soviets will prepare but not present their proposed agenda, preferring instead to respond to the U.S. version.[1] This pattern is a departure from standard international practice where the host country assumes responsibility for drafting the agenda. Once the Soviets have become accustomed to an agenda, they likely will insist on using it without change in subsequent sessions. Since the Soviets feel so comfortable with this routine, they will quickly balk at any attempt to change the system.

TYPES OF SESSIONS

U.S.-U.S.S.R. economic negotiations, like most international talks, are conducted in plenary sessions of the entire delegations, smaller working groups of experts, and private discussions between team leaders. Most work is accomplished at the meetings of experts, who forward any unresolved problems to the private sessions.

The standard format is to open the negotiations with a formal plenary session at which the basic position papers are presented. This is followed by a number of smaller working groups in which the delegates negotiate specific issues. Parallel with these sessions are the private meetings between U.S. and Soviet team leaders to resolve major problem areas. Informal contacts between midlevel members of the delegations also serve as a communications channel—for example, to signal changes in negotiating positions. At the conclusion of a successful negotiation, the two delegations reassemble in plenary session to review and endorse the agreements. While most U.S.-U.S.S.R. negotiations follow the above sequence, there may be deviations from the norm.

CHARACTERISTICS OF THE NEGOTIATING TEAM

Soviet negotiating teams typically are composed of highly professional personnel representing several state ministries and agencies. Most of the delegates have had considerable negotiating experience. The team members are specialists in their fields and, equally important, usually have worked together on previous assignments. This provides the Soviet team with a kind of historical memory bank on substantive issues as well as on the details of earlier U.S.-U.S.S.R. negotiations.

COMPOSITION

For most U.S.-Soviet meetings on economic questions the leadership of the delegation has been entrusted to a deputy minister, and on occasion a minister may assume this responsibility. The Soviets try to appoint as team chief someone of the same rank as the U.S. chief. The subordinate members of the delegation are recruited from the various state ministries and committees. Negotiating teams for trade-related issues, for example, include representatives from the Ministry of Foreign Trade, the State Committee for Foreign Economic Relations (GKES), the State Planning Committee (Gosplan), and elsewhere. The dominant role, however, is invariably assumed by Ministry of Foreign Trade personnel.

---

[1] A number of U.S. negotiators have found it advisable to send Moscow a copy of the proposed agenda (both English and Russian versions) at least a month in advance of the negotiations.

Included in the supporting cast are numerous junior specialists who are young, technically astute, and who provide expertise on particular issues. As a group they are very conservative and bureaucratic, anxious to avoid any public action or decision which might later be held against them. In addition, the delegation includes several older "political hacks" who have endured due largely to strong party ties but who are often weak substantively. Finally, there are the Committee for State Security (KGB) watchdogs who usually masquerade as "advisers" or interpreters. All Soviet negotiators, regardless of their rank, take copious notes throughout the sessions and will use them as reference points later in the negotiations.

TEAM DISCIPLINE AND SENSITIVITIES

Tight discipline is a trademark of Soviet negotiators. The team chief is the sole spokesman for the group in all official meetings. Public dissent by team members usually is avoided, even to the point of defending glaring mistakes committed by the chief. On those rare occasions when team discipline breaks down, the reason may be the impatience of a junior member. A second cause for a lapse in team discipline is sheer fatigue and weariness of the participants.

Soviet negotiators are exceptionally sensitive to the concerns of protocol. They treat each other with the courtesies accorded to age, rank, and experience, and fully expect similar treatment from the U.S. team. They will not easily tolerate a situation in which a young albeit senior U.S. official gives the appearance of lecturing to an older Soviet negotiator. Not only do the Soviets strive for strict internal discipline and protocol, but they also expect to see this behavior practiced by the U.S. delegation. They find it quite difficult to appreciate the easy bantering style frequently adopted by U.S. teams.

THE DELEGATION'S AUTHORITY TO NEGOTIATE

The Soviet delegation negotiates within the framework of a detailed plan and instructions approved previously in Moscow. The delegation's mandate and negotiating strategy usually have been well thought out beforehand, leaving little room for independent judgment. Any problems and questions that arise are handled through regular communications channels between the team chief and his superiors in Moscow. Among the factors that determine whether the team chiefs will be able to respond promptly to unexpected situations are whether the issues cross ministerial boundaries, the chief's political connections, and his personal authority. The chief's authority to negotiate and the flexibility built into his instructions also are partly a function of the political level a which his "game plan" was approved.

On most occasions, the delegation's instructions probably represent a consensus of competing ministries and agencies. In these instances, the authority of the team chief to respond to U.S. proposals may not always be clear, in which case he must consult these ministries for further instructions. When the negotiating team represents a single ministry, however, the team chief has only one "master" to whom he must report. This arrangement greatly facilitates the process of obtaining new instructions.

AN OUTLINE OF SOVIET NEGOTIATING TACTICS

The Soviets use all the standard international negotiating ploys in presenting and arguing for their proposals. A brief selection is presented below. Anchoring many of these tactics is Moscow's fabled "waiting game"—the assumption that time invariably works in its favor.

TACTICS USED IN MAKING PROPOSALS

The Shopping List Ploy. One of the Soviets' favorite tactics is to present a lengthy list of highly exaggerated demands when, in fact, they truly are interested in winning only a few of these points. During the lengthy process of haggling over each item, the Soviets will appear to be making numerous concessions to the United States. However, when only a few items remain—the ones most critical to Soviet interests—the team chief will demand that the U.S. side "even the tally" and make reciprocal concessions.

Padding Proposals With Redundancy. The initial Soviet proposals likely will make the same point in several different sections. In this way, the Soviets can afford to make concessions in one place without really sacrificing an important interest.

Letting the U.S. Side Offer the Initial Proposals. The Soviets assume that the U.S. position is usually a moderate one, and is therefore a good beginning point from which to bargain. In addition, this tactic permits them to determine the approximate scope of the U.S. team's authority to negotiate. The latter point is particularly important when presenting counterproposals following the first round of bargaining.

SELECTED BARGAINING TACTICS

Reluctance to Provide Information to the U.S. Side. As a rule, the Soviets do not respond promptly and completely to U.S. requests for information pertinent to the issues under review.

Preference for Seeking Trade-Offs Between Issues. The Soviet approach to negotiations places a low priority on trying to reach a compromise on each separate issue. Rather they attempt to "horsetrade": give in on Issue A if the U.S. side will yield on Issue B.

Playing the "Foot-Dragger." This classic waiting game is played by Moscow in two ways. The Soviet team chief may let one of his working group experts assume the role of the "heavy," refusing all compromises and considerably delaying the talks. Then, in the later stages, the team chief is able to reenter the bargaining fray in the roles of "objective compromiser" and "benevolent mediator." A second version of foot-dragging calls for the team chief to do the delaying. Indeed, some Soviet senior negotiators are so skilled at this tactic—negotiating for the sake of negotiating—that they have gained reputations as specialists in conducting lengthy but unfruitful negotiations with Western countries.

TACTICS THAT MAY TIP OFF AN UNWILLINGNESS TO CONCLUDE AN AGREEMENT

Bogging down the negotiations in minutiae.

Delaying on handing over information requested by the U.S. team.

Lengthy polemics and tirades against the capitalist system. While some of these monologues clearly are pro forma rituals, others are used deliberately to wear down the U.S. team's resolve or simply as a dilatory technique to avoid negotiating seriously.

UNDERSTANDING OF U.S. POLITICS

Both before and during the negotiations the Soviet delegation probes to determine whether the U.S. team has good political connections (read: White House and Congress). The Soviets also seek out possibilities for influencing the course of the talks by taking advantage of any rivalries and policy disputes between U.S. officials. Soviet negotiators evidence an uneven but improving appreciation of the U.S. political system. Moscow's appreciation of the U.S. political scene is based on several reporting channels, including a network of working- and executive-level contacts within the Washington community. These ties have been built up over the years by Embassy officials, many of whom visit U.S. Government offices on a regular basis. These overt activities, including attendance at Congressional committee sessions, result in a wealth of materials useful in negotiations, such as data on personalities and policy issues.

SENSITIVITY TO PUBLICITY

The Soviets' passion for confidentiality in negotiations with the United States is well known. They become visibly unsettled when, either by plan or accident, the U.S. team brings the Western press into the negotiating picture. While the Soviets are sensitive to the confidentiality of all discussions, they are exceptionally sensitive regarding the private talks between team chiefs on the proposed terms of agreement. As such, the Soviets always insist on limiting the access of the Western press to information about U.S.-U.S.S.R. negotiations. In part, of course, this attitude stems from the secretiveness and strict censorship of their own domestic press. However, it also results from an inadequate understanding of the role of the press in Western industrialized societies.

INTERPRETERS

The Soviet interpreters are an integral part of the negotiating team: they participate fully in the team's planning sessions, take copious notes during the official meetings, and provide their superiors with timely information and insights into the evolving U.S. positions. An indication that Soviet interpreters are more than "technicians" is that several have reappeared in later negotiations as delegation chiefs or working group leaders. As a rule, Moscow's interpreters have been competent and professional. There are no known instances where the interpreters deliberately mistranslated a statement. However, they apparently have some authority to "clean up" the language of their delegation's more earthy parlances—unless the team chief insists on a precise literal translation.

It is standard practice for the host country to provide the interpreters, although each side usually brings its own along. When negotiations are held in Moscow, the Soviets try to use the same interpreters for all negotiations on a particular subject. This ensures continuity and also contributes importantly to the team's "memory bank," thereby giving the Soviet chief an occasional edge over his U.S. counterpart. At times the interpreter has been able to alert his superiors to U.S. deviations from positions taken at earlier meetings. Soviet interpreters also assume the roles of "lobbyist" and "informant" during recesses in the negotiations.

Because many of the Soviet negotiators speak and understand English, they can use the interpreters effectively to set the pace of the sessions. For example they can dispense with the consecutive interpretation [2] when they wish to accelerate the conduct of business. Alternatively, they can rely on the lengthy interpreting process to provide them with additional time to think through their responses to questions from the U.S. side.

LANGUAGE OF DOCUMENTS

In almost every instance, the Soviets' preference has been for a generally worded agreement. They believe that a loosely defined document provides them with greater flexibility when the accord goes into effect. Once the documents have been drafted, the Soviets are highly suspicious of U.S. motives behind any last-minute changes in the accepted wording. At times, the Soviet team chief, sensitive to his position vis-a-vis his superiors, has viewed these changes as an affront to his competence as a negotiator. His displeasure has been even more pronounced if the original accord has been sent to Moscow for preliminary approval.

PERSONAL RELATIONS

Informal "friendship" ties are welcomed between U.S. and U.S.S.R. representatives. However, the Soviets take great care that these relationships not interfere with the task of conducing state-to-state talks. This segregation of business and personal ties is enforced by "watchdog" members of the delegation, presumably KGB personnel. The Soviets are rather formal in the initial stages of negotiations, and remain that way until trust and confidence in their U.S. counterparts have been established. On balance, it appears that a relationship on the professional level—one built on mutual understanding and trust—is far more important to the outcome of negotiations than are the informal, personal relationships.

Regardless of the types of personal ties involved in a given negotiation, continuity in the makeup of the U.S. team remains a matter of great concern to the Soviets. Their penchant for routine and precedent is such that they exhibit unusual discomfort when the U.S. delegation is led by an "unknown quantity"— a frequent occurrence because the turnover rate is considerably higher among U.S. senior negotiators than it is among the Soviets. During the transition from the Ford to the Carter administrations, Soviet officials were visibly anxious about the composition of future negotiating teams.

Social events such as dinners, luncheons, and cocktail hours are viewed as important opportunities to continue negotiations-related business in still another forum. The entire Soviet delegation (including junior and support personnel) swings into action at these social affairs and conducts what amounts to "second level" negotiations—pressing an issue, smoothing "ruffled feathers," sizing up the U.S. team and probing for weaknesses. The Soviets seem to prefer standup buffet affairs because these allow greater opportunities for conducting private conversations among senior officials than do formal sitdown dinners.

---

[2] Some U.S.–U.S.S.R. negotiations permit simultaneous translation while others allow only consecutive translation. For some unexplained reasons, the Soviets are loath to break precedent and allow a negotiation to switch from one method to the other.

NEGOTIATIONS WITH THE PRIVATE SECTOR

FORMAT OF THE NEGOTIATIONS

U.S.-U.S.S.R. commercial negotiations where the U.S. firm is the supplier are almost always held in Moscow. Standard international business practice dictates that the seller discuss sales at the buyer's place of business; it is no different for dealings with the U.S.S.R. The Soviets regard this as an advantage over the foreign company, especially those which lack a Moscow office and are forced to use their hotel rooms as their base of operations. Unlike the state-to-state talks, which involve plenary, working group, and private leadership meetings, the commercial negotiations are conducted largely in sessions in which all the negotiators are present. The duration of the talks ranges from a few days to a few months, and depends only partly on the Soviets' need for a given product.

The format for most commercial negotiation is as follows: first, the size of the order and its technical specifications are discussed; then other contract-related issues are decided, such as warranties and guarantees; and finally, the negotiators hammer out the price and terms of financing. No set pattern governing the pace and duration of the negotiations is apparent. The Soviets' need for a particular product is not always a reliable indicator of how long the talks will last or even if the negotiations will be successful. Some U.S. companies have negotiated contracts within a week, with a minimum of hard bargaining on substantive issues. Other business delegations have had to endure consecutive 12-hour marathon meetings and, after waiting weeks for the concluding session, had to bargain hard right up to the eleventh hour before their departure flight.

The negotiations usually take place on the basis of the U.S.S.R.'s standard contract for each foreign trade organization. Although the Soviets insist that both the organization and content of their draft is firm, in reality almost everything is negotiable. In any event the working documents generally are supplied by the U.S.S.R., but are modified as appropriate during the bargaining sessions. The initial contract negotiated by a U.S. firm takes on special importance in view of the Soviet predilection for routine and precedent; this contract usually becomes the basis for negotiations in all subseqent deals. In fact, some companies have found that they have worked with the same contract so frequently that they no longer consider it to be a Soviet-supplied document.

On rare occasions the Soviets will relax their insistency that their standard contract serve as the basis for the negotiations. These instances can be explained by the urgency of Moscow's need for a particular product and/or by the personalities of the U.S. businessmen.

CHARACTERISTICS OF THE NEGOTIATING TEAM

As a rule, the Soviet commercial and official negotiating teams are similar in terms of composition, discipline, and competence. There are, however, several important differences: the commercial delegations usually are larger and are supplemented by a constant shuttle of experts and end-user representatives who make one-time appearances; there are more frequent incidents of breakdown in team discipline among the commercial negotiators; and finally, the Soviets' sensitivity to their position of relative technological inferiority is more evident at the commercial than at the official level.

COMPOSITION OF THE TEAM

The Soviet delegation may include upwards of 20 people, usually outnumbering the U.S. side by a substantial margin. The core of the team consists of representatives of foreign trade organizations and mid- to senior-level officials from various ministries. During highly technical segments of the negotiations, specialists and end-users make brief appearances to offer opinions and supply needed information. In addition, the ultimate end-users are almost always brought into the sessions when the negotiations are nearing a successful conclusion. At the formal contract signing, this cast of characters may be bolstered by the presence of high-ranking officials who had not appeared at any of the bargaining sessions.

As is the case with the official level talks, there are numerous individuals who, although not involved in the actual bargaining, play important roles in the team's overall strategy. For example, several junior members sit quietly and take prolific notes on the proceedings; occasionally, the team chief calls upon them for expert advice on specific issues. Completing the Soviet roster are a number of "silent extras" whose functions are never clearly defined. Some, of course, are KGB-watchdog types who usually sit through every negotiating session. At times, however, they attend only the first few meetings and, content that nothing "suspicious" is happening, will gradually drop out of sight. The number of Soviets whose functions cannot be explained rises substantially when the talks are held outside of the U.S.S.R. Many of these individuals may simply be "along for the ride."

TEAM DISCIPLINE

Soviet negotiators adhere to a code of strict discipline and observance of protocol. As a group, they give the clear impression of compatibility and solidarity. The team chief alone presents and argues the Soviet position, although periodically he calls upon his subordinates to address particular issues. Because commercial negotiations, however, are carried on in a less-rigid atmosphere than at the official level and involve end-user representatives who may not be professional negotiators, there are many more incidents of a breakdown in team discipline.

A less disruptive type of breakdown in team unity is observed in the technical sessions that mark the early rounds of negotiations. There, team unity is reduced somewhat because of two factors. First, the low- to mid-level specialists who play an important part in these meetings frequently have not collaborated in previous negotiations—even if they work in the same plant. Secondly, the mood at these meetings is quite relaxed ; the two sides sit around a table, with everyone joining in freely to contribute opinions and ask questions.

SENSITIVITY

The Soviets consistently display a deep sensitivity to age, rank, and protocol. Even senior specialists, while not government officials, expect to be accorded a certain respect from the U.S. side. When they perceive that this attitude is lacking, their annoyance is immediate.

THE DELEGATION'S AUTHORITY TO NEGOTIATE

Soviet commercial negotiators have even less authority to make on-the-spot decisions than do the official level negotiators. This appears to be due to two factors : (a) the generally lower rank and political clout of the commercial negotiators, and (b) the issues involved in commercial negotiations—price, quantity, and terms—are the kinds of matters for which detailed instructions can be prepared beforehand. The delegation's lack of authority to make decisions outside a narrow band of responsibility goes far in explaining why the Soviet teams prefer to have routine and precedence govern their negotiations.

The negotiating teams generally know precisely what type of equipment they wish to buy before negotiations begin. Although the foreign trade organizations do their homework in advance, this does not prevent the Soviets from changing their specifications during the course of the negotiations (primarily on some of the larger deals). In many instances, however, the negotiators' instructions are written so tightly that they develop a kind of "tunnel vision" and overlook seemingly attractive proposals from the U.S. supplier.

If the Soviet negotiating team has little authority to deviate from its instructions when in the United States, it has even less leeway when the talks are held in Moscow (as they usually are). No one on the Soviet team, including the team chief, has the authority to make on-the-spot decisions on issues not covered explicitly in his instructions. As a result, the negotiations frequently bog down while the team "consults" with ministry and foreign trade organization officials. The delays can range from a day to several weeks.

RIVALRIES WITHIN THE SOVIET NEGOTIATING TEAM

Despite their best efforts, the Soviets' veneer of team unity can be shattered by interministerial and agency bickering. These incidents often develop when the production ministries lose patience with the alleged "foot-dragging" of the foreign trade organization responsible for negotiating the contract with the U.S. supplier. The foreign trade organizations, in turn, have become highly agitated when they perceive the end-user "going behind its back" to deal directly with the foreign company. During the course of negotiations, more than one U.S. business delegation has been caught in the cross-fire between rival Soviet factions.

COMMUNICATIONS AND ADMINISTRATIVE SUPPORT

When the negotiations are held in Moscow, the Soviet team chief meets at least daily with his superiors to provide an update on the bargaining sessions. There are a number of communications problems between the various state ministries and agencies, however, and at times some major-slip-ups result. Beyond these problems, carelessness and inefficiency characterize the administrative-clerical support given the Soviet team. In fact, this support often is so poor that the Soviets are forced to cancel or postpone meetings with the U.S. delegation.

In Moscow, the chief Soviet negotiator communicates personally with his superiors, most likely at the end of each day's sessions. Depending on the substance of the talks, details of the sessions are quickly passed along to other "interested" parties—such as research institute personnel—who are not involved directly in the negotiations. When in the United States, the Soviet team chief probably reports via Embassy channels, although on a less frequent basis.

Interagency communications and coordination *within* the Soviet bureaucracy appear to be managed in a rather careless manner. At times, this sloppiness is counterproductive to the negotiations. Administrative support for the Soviet team, even in Moscow, is also far below the standards of Western commercial negotiations. The Soviets' "ability" to lose files and documents is legendary, as is their inability to provide timely and efficient typing, xeroxing, and other clerical support.

AN OUTLINE OF NEGOTIATING TACTICS

The USSR's repertoire of negotiating tactics includes many of the maneuvers that are standard in international business forums. In addition, the Soviet Union has developed a number of unique tactics designed to frustrate and counter opposing delegations. These tactics point out the similarities in the Soviet commercial and offical negotiating teams' techniques. The favorites include: (a) the much heralded "waiting game"; (b) alternating "hard" and "soft" lines by changing team chiefs without notice; (c) manipulating the U.S. delegation into intervening in squabbles between the Soviet team and its superiors in Moscow; and (d) threatening to play off one Western competitor against another.

One tactic that is used in almost every negotiation is "the waiting game." According to most experienced observers, "The Soviets play this game better than anyone else in the world." This tactic is based on two assumptions: (a) that the U.S. team has relatively little patience, and (b) in order to avoid returning home emptyhanded, foreign businessmen eventually will agree to terms that they normally would reject. It is not at a'l unusual for the Soviets to hold a 1- or 2-hour initial bargaining session and then keep the U.S. team waiting for days, hoping to pressure them into a "departure time decision." The waiting time is shortened considerably, however, when the U.S. company has a unique product for which the Soviets have an urgent demand. A second popular tactic involves changing the team's leadership without any warning or explanation to the U.S. side. (The Soviets employ this maneuver more frequently in the commercial negotiations than in the official level talks.) Interestingly, the Soviets are just as likely to change their team leader when they move from a hard line to a soft line as vice versa. Another favorite tactic is to get the U.S. team involved in the dialogue between the Soviet negotiators and their superiors in Moscow. Sometimes this is done when the Soviets feel that they will have difficulty selling parts of the proposed contract to their bosses. In these instances, the Soviets "consult" with the United States on how best to "package" their arguments on behalf of the contract. At other times, the Soviet negotiators will solicit U.S. help in resolving a bureaucratic snafu.

One other favorite tactics is to conduct negotiations in Moscow with two or more U.S. (or Western) competitors. This situation permits the Soviets to play off one company against another. In most cases, this tactic is pursued by selectively using information from one negotiation to try to influence the terms under consideration in the other negotiations. In contrast to this subtle approach, the Soviets at times have bluntly informed U.S. companies that unless they concede a particular point(s), the contract would be awarded to a competitor "who just happens to be in Moscow at this very moment."

Besides the four tactics discussed above, there are numerous other ploys which the Soviets will use. Among these maneuvers are the following:

—Accepting in principle the language of a particular clause, but indicating later that "if we could change just a few words" the contract would be even more acceptable to their superiors.

—Agreeing to a multimillion dollar contract, but prior to final approval, quibbling about charges for items worth only a few dollars. The Soviets use this tactic to impress their superiors that "not even the smallest detail has been overlooked in the negotiations."

—Merely "going through the motions" of bargaining. This tactic is used when the Soviets have no genuine intention of concluding an agreement with a firm at a particular time, but may wish to do so at a later date.

THE ROLE OF SOCIAL FUNCTIONS

Social functions play a very minor role when commercial negotiations are conducted in Moscow. (This contrasts sharply with the importance of social events at official negotiations.) The Soviets do sponsor a few dinners and luncheons for their U.S. guests, but usually only for the sake of courtesy. Business is not discussed and rarely are there the excesses of eating or drinking which sometimes occur at state-to-state talks. The one social function which does take place almost without exception occurs at the signing of a contract. Here, the Soviet team puts on a low-key celebration at a ministry office, complete with champagne toasts.

On rare occasions, the Soviets will make a special effort to entertain a visiting businessman. However, these instances seem to be a function of the personality or professional standing of the U.S. individuals involved. As a matter of course, U.S. businessmen entertain more extensively when talks are held at their home offices (or in third countries). The Soviets seem to appreciate these functions, especially when the U.S. team leader invites them to his home for a "typical" American dinner or cookout.

In every respect, the Soviets evidence a more open and informal behavior when conducting business in the United States. Expeditions to area shopping centers, where the Soviets reportedly "clear the shelves," are high on their list of priorities. They also are fond of initiating their own late night parties for their hosts, replete with delicacies "imported" from the Soviet Union.

PERSONAL RELATIONS

Lasting personal relationships between U.S. and Soviet negotiators are very rare. Of considerable importance, however, are the feelings of mutual trust and confidence developed gradually through the experience of doing business together. The Soviets permit very few opportunities for the development of deep ties of friendship with U.S. team members. In a sense, this situation is a consequence of Moscow's basic strategy of "playing a waiting game" with the Western businessman. The unexplained delays and cancellations in bargaining sessions, meager attention to the requests for information, and the paucity of group and individual social functions—indeed, the opposite of the behavior expected by businessmen in international dealings—create an atmosphere in which personal ties are difficult to cultivate.

Those few instances where the Soviets have allowed a personal relationship to develop seem to be the exceptions that prove the rule. Even here, however, these ties were not instrumental in the eventual success of the negotiations. The Soviets do place considerable emphasis on trust and confidence in the Western firm's intention and ability to deliver on its part of the negotiated contract (that is, its past performance record). It is notable, however, that this trust primarily is attached to an institution (the corporation) as distinct from its officers.

SENSITIVITY TO PUBLICITY

In sharp contrast to the official level negotiations, the Soviets are not at all concerned about keeping private the details of their negotiations with Western businesses. In fact, one favorite Soviet tactic for squeezing out better contract terms is to tell one company the details of negotiations with its competitors. By Western business standards, however, Soviet efforts to play off one competitor against the other are rather crude.

DEGREE OF DETAIL PREFERRED IN FINAL AGREEMENT

For the most part, Soviet commercial negotiators seek to include the greatest possible degree of detail in their agreements with the United States. (This is contrary to their preference at the official level negotiations.) However, they try to keep the warranty and guarantee sections very general, so as to allow for a liberal interpretation of any claims they might make on the foreign supplier.

The Soviets demand a much more detailed final agreement than is seen in the typical international business transaction. Many of the latter take place via a purchase order agreement; the entire deal can be concluded quickly by telephone and confirmed by telex. This type of contractual agreement covering only the bare essentials is almost never found in negotiations with the U.S.S.R.

The preferred Soviet wording of the warranty and guarantee selections stands in sharp contrast to the rest of the contract. Here they will battle stubbornly for the most general and open ended wording possible. They hope that this kind of language will cover almost any kind of claim they may wish to make later against the Western manufacturer. The U.S. and U.S.S.R. delegations frequently are at loggerheads on the wording of these sections, however, because of the continued Soviet refusal to grant free access to the foreign company for the necessary on-site inspections of its equipment.

THE SOVIETS AS NEGOTIATORS: A COMPARISON OF SELECTED SOVIET AND WESTERN PRACTICES

Commercial negotiations with the U.S.S.R. represent a very different "game" from the typical international business negotiation. The major differences lie in a number of business practices, attitudes, and assumptions which Western businessmen tend to take for granted. For example, by many Western business standards, Soviet conduct of negotiations often is "sloppy" and "unprofessional." In particular, of all the countries with which U.S. companies do business, the U.S.S.R. may be the most unreliable in terms of responding to correspondence—even when it was Moscow that had initiated the negotiations.[3]

A second quality which sets the Soviets apart is that they are notoriously "tight-lipped" about providing technical and other necessary information to the U.S. team. For example, they are reluctant to release even the minimum amount of data normally required in international negotiations for the preparation of price quotes and equipment specifications. Sometimes the U.S. supplier is not even told where his equipment ultimately will be installed. This secretiveness, which far exceeds international business norms, is due to a combination of the traditional Soviet penchant for statistical secrecy and a lingering suspicion of Western business motives.

Another area in which U.S.-U.S.S.R. negotiations differ from the Western experience is the fact the formal contract negotiations are always required. In Western business dealings, for instance, it is quite common for sales to be concluded via a simple purchase order with, of course, some discussion over possible price discounts. In contrast, Soviet foreign trade organizations insist on formal negotiations in which they literally "nitpick" over every detail. This behavior leads to another unique feature of Soviet negotiations—the time involved. Bargaining sessions can stretch into years before a contract is worked out—and even then the size of the purchase may be only a fraction of what was originally envisaged. This aspect of negotiations may result partly from the nature of the Soviet system: for example, the limited authority of the team chief, and interministerial rivalries. On the other hand, the importance of the "waiting game" in the Soviets' strategy and the assumption that time works in their favor surely must account for some of the lengthy delays.

---

[3] The Soviets seem to have a double standard on the question of acceptable business conduct. For example, they fully expect that the U.S. team will both abide by precedent and exhibit predictable behavior. Yet, the U.S. businessman can depend on erratic and unpredictable behavior from the Soviets. They are often late for appointments, or may simply cancel them without notice. When a meeting does take place as scheduled, rather than seeing Comrade X as expected, the U.S. delegation is likely to see Comrade Y (an unknown) instead.

(NOTE.—The U.S.S.R.'s negotiating practices differ not only from Western standards but also from the practices of its East European allies. Indeed, on many points, Eastern Europe is much closer to the West's negotiating norms than is the U.S.S.R.)

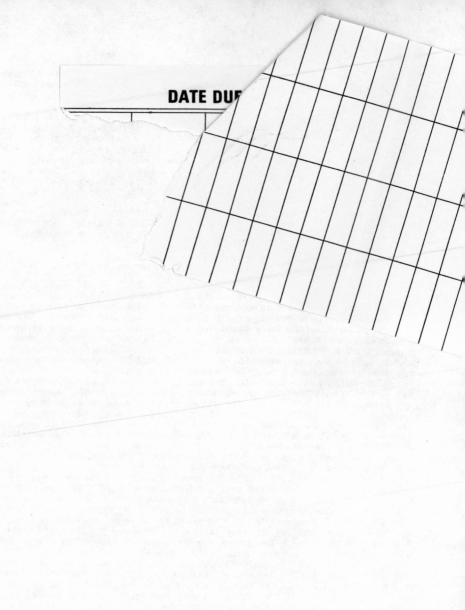